OCCUPATIONAL HEALTH AND SAFETY LAW: TEXT AND MATERIALS

Second Edition

Cavendish
Publishing
Limited

OCCUPATIONAL HEALTH AND SAFETY LAW: TEXT AND MATERIALS

Second Edition

Professor Brenda Barrett MA, PhD, Barrister
Professor of Law, Middlesex University Business School,
Middlesex University

Professor Richard Howells LLB, LLM, PhD
Emeritus Professor of Law, Westminster University

Cavendish
Publishing
Limited

London • Sydney

Second edition first published in Great Britain 2000 by Cavendish Publishing Limited, The Glass House, Wharton Street, London WC1X 9PX, United Kingdom
Telephone: +44 (0)20 7278 8000   Facsimile: +44 (0)20 7171 278 8080
Email: info@cavendishpublishing.com
Website: www.cavendishpublishing.com

Barrett, Brenda
Occupational health and safety law: text and materials – 2nd ed
1 Industrial safety – Law and legislation – Great Britain – Cases
2 Industrial hygiene – Law and legislation – Great Britain – Cases
I Title II Howells, Richard III Cases and materials on occupational health and safety law

344.4'1'0465

ISBN 1 85941 560 1

Printed and bound in Great Britain

ACKNOWLEDGMENTS

The authors would like to thank the European Agency for Safety and Health at Work, the Health and Safety Executive, the *New Law Journal*, the Sheffield Information Centre, HSE and the Institute of Employment Rights for giving permission to reproduce materials in this book.

Every effort has been made to trace all the copyright holders, but if any have been inadvertently overlooked, the publishers will be pleased to make the necessary arrangements at the first opportunity.

PREFACE

The primary purpose of this text is to assist students of occupational health and safety law. It is believed that this book will appeal to both undergraduate and postgraduate students who have an interest in this area. In addition, it may prove to be a useful reference text for practitioners of safety management, though the latter may wish to use it as a preliminary to more detailed study of the particular topic they are researching.

The text draws heavily on legislation and law reports, but some references to other materials are made when this has seemed to the authors to be an appropriate way of developing, explaining or commenting on the legal materials.

The presentation is thematic. Accident prevention and accident compensation are both covered and this in itself suggests two major themes – namely, the respective roles of the criminal and the civil law in encouraging the operation of safe systems at the workplace. Within these themes, the role of the European Union, the UK Parliament and the European and UK courts of law have to be accommodated. The thematic approach dictates that individual extracts from source materials are relatively short, although, within the covers of the book, much of the major relevant law will be found.

The complex nature of the relationships between England, the UK and the European Union have to be kept clearly in view by the lawyer. This text is written from the viewpoint of English lawyers, but the English lawyer cannot, in the 21st century, ignore the impact of the European Union on English law. The authors have tried to indicate whether Acts of Parliament or decided cases are relevant to the whole, or only parts of, the UK.

The law set out in the text is, unless otherwise indicated, the law in force in June 2000. Sometimes the authors have referred to interpretations of laws no longer directly relevant, because there is, in their view, a principle embedded in that law which is still relevant today. On occasions it has seemed pertinent to draw attention to laws which, at the time of going to press, were only in draft.

Note: following a recent review of procedure in civil litigation, the person who initiates litigation is no longer referred to as a 'plaintiff'. The person who sues is now named a 'claimant'. The new terminology is used by the authors when explaining the law but, inevitably, the old terminology has to be retained when citing cases decided before the introduction of the new language.

BNB

RWLH

June 2000

CONTENTS

TABLE OF CASES

TABLE OF STATUTES

Table of Statutes

TABLE OF STATUTORY INSTRUMENTS

TABLE OF EUROPEAN LEGISLATION

Directives

Treaties and Conventions

INTRODUCTION: THE CONCEPT
OF RISK MANAGEMENT

This book sets out the authors' understanding of the law of occupational health and safety in England today, as laid down in legislation and judicial statements. Broadly, the law is likely to be the same in all three jurisdictions that make up the UK, particularly as the three jurisdictions are counted as one for the purposes of membership of the European Union. Unless otherwise stated, the law set out here is that which applies in England; however, Scottish compensation cases, going on appeal to the House of Lords, have made a considerable contribution to the development of English law and have, therefore, been drawn upon fairly extensively.

The message constantly repeated in the following pages is the importance of managing risk by setting up and maintaining safe systems at the workplace. While, naturally, the cases cited are almost exclusively concerned with injury suffered at the workplace, it has been necessary, from time to time, to cite from cases which are not, at first sight, concerned with such injuries, because these cases include important principles of liability. The responsibility for safe systems lies heavily upon organisations, particularly upon employers, but individuals also have their personal responsibilities.

In this chapter, some consideration will be given to the reasons why it is desirable to install and maintain safe systems at the work place. First, it will be noted what the law has to say about safe systems and a broad indication will be given of some of the criteria by which the law and lawyers determine whether a system is sufficiently safe; comparing the criteria of the civil and the criminal law.

The chapter will then touch upon some of the literature in which problems related to the failure to operate safely have been addressed, with some proposals for improving safety. In an introduction to a legal text, the survey of this literature can only be partial and superficial, but even such a small insight into the literature may serve to indicate that the law does not operate in a vacuum.

The chapter will conclude with a summary of the themes that have emerged. These themes will be identifiable in the remainder of the book.

CHARACTERISTICS OF THE LAW

Commitment to safe systems

The British approach is to allow victims of industrial accidents and diseases to sue in the civil courts for compensation. Early recognition that the fear of having to pay compensation was not a sufficient incentive to induce organisations to operate safely led Parliament to legislate standards for the workplace and to provide for inspectors to 'police' the workplace, in order to ensure that the statutory standards were being met. A failure to comply with the legislation leads to penalties, following conviction in the criminal courts.

Some of the very earliest judicial statements about occupational safety law made reference to the need for employers to maintain safe systems. Today, both judges and Parliament repeatedly indicate the need for a systematic approach. This is true in both the civil law, relating to accident compensation, and the criminal law, relating to accident prevention. Two short examples will illustrate this.

Safe systems in case law

In the leading case of *Wilsons and Clyde Coal Company Ltd v English*,[1] Lord Wright described the employer's duty to his employees:

> The obligation is threefold, 'the provision of a competent staff of men, adequate material, and a *proper system* and effective supervision ...'.

This case is often regarded as the foundation of the modern law concerning employers' civil liability to compensate the victims of workplace accidents and diseases. Lord Wright was relying on authorities that went back to the nineteenth century. Today, a worker who claims damages to compensate for personal injury suffered at the workplace may bring an action for the tort of negligence. The success of the action is likely to depend on whether the worker can bring evidence to satisfy the court that the employer failed to provide a safe system of work.

Safe systems in legislation

The principal British statute on occupational health and safety is the Health and Safety at Work Act 1974. The Act imposes its first and, arguably, most important duty upon employers. Section 2(1) of the Act states:

> It shall be the duty of every employer to ensure, so far as is reasonably practicable, the health, safety and welfare at work of all his employees.

---

1   [1938] AC 57, p 78.

Section 2(1) does not attempt to itemise what the employer must do, although s 2(2) does, 'without prejudice to the generality' of s 2(1), give an indication of some of the matters that have to be dealt with. The intention of s 2(1) is to impose upon employers the task of reviewing the totality of their operations, to ensure that, in every aspect, they are as safe as is reasonably practicable. Regulations made under the 1974 Act have spelt this out, particularly the Management of Health and Safety at Work Regulations. These require employers to make an assessment of the risks to which their employees are exposed and then set up systems appropriate for dealing with these risks.

Employers who fail to comply with the duties contained in the Health and Safety at Work Act 1974 and regulations made under it are liable to criminal prosecution.

Safe workplaces are unlikely to be achieved unless those who work there are informed of the need to operate safely, trained to ensure that they know how to operate safely, and monitored to ensure that safe systems are actually being operated. Safe systems depend not only on investing in plant and equipment, but also on investing in people. Safety and human resource management are, therefore, closely related and it is difficult to divorce occupational health and safety law from employment law more generally.

- *The organisation that wishes to avoid civil and criminal liability has considerable reason to endeavour to set up and maintain safe systems.*
- *In setting up systems, employers will need to consider not merely investment in plant and equipment, but also human resource management.*

The penal element in the law

It might be thought that the objective of the criminal law is to punish and that of the civil law is to compensate, but this is not entirely so. The Health and Safety at Work Act 1974, while containing criminal sanctions, gives considerable powers to inspectors to issue improvement and prohibition orders and in practice, inspectors more frequently issue such orders than they institute criminal prosecutions. Broadly, such orders inform the persons (usually employers) on whom they are served that in the inspector's opinion something (as set out in the order) needs to be done to make the workplace healthier or safer. If the order is complied with it is likely that no criminal charges will be made.

Quite apart from this, it has always been a tradition of the British safety inspectorate to provide advice. This is done through publications for the purpose of giving guidance to organisations generally and, also, wherever this is not in conflict with the inspectorate's enforcement role, to organisations individually.

In the broadest sense, however, both the criminal and the civil law impose 'penal' sanctions. The person who is convicted of a criminal offence is likely either to have to pay a fine or to serve a term of imprisonment: the defendant who loses a civil case is likely to have to pay the claimant (victim) a large sum of money to compensate for the injury which has been suffered. The penal element of civil law is masked where compensation is paid by the defendant's insurance company. Punishment is normally considered as related to wrongdoing. Unfortunately, however, in health and safety matters, there is not necessarily a direct co-relationship between wrongdoing and injury suffered. On the one hand, a minor lapse may lead to a major injury and, on the other, good fortune may decree that reprehensible behaviour causes little or no injury.

The criminal law is properly committed to the punishment of wrongdoing; so, it can properly relate the punishment to the behaviour of the accused, rather than to the consequences of the accused's behaviour. Ideally, wrongful behaviour will be identified before injury occurs. Health and safety legislation aims to achieve this, because it decrees that the offence is in failing to observe the standards which safety legislation has prescribed: the offence is committed if the conduct is unlawful, whether or not any personal injury has occurred. Nevertheless, in practice, it may be difficult to persuade a court that a situation is dangerous if, over many years, no injury has occurred. On the other hand, if a relatively minor lapse has caused a major catastrophe, there tends to be an emotive reaction: it is easy to look for a human scapegoat. At the present time, even if catastrophe is attributable to a natural cause, such as exceptionally heavy rainfall, questions are asked as to whether someone ought to have anticipated the situation and taken pre-emptive action, such as prohibiting urban development in the flood plain of a river.

The dilemma of the civil law is greater than that of the criminal law: it has to balance the needs of the victim against justice to the 'wrongdoer'. One classical theory was that in civil law, as in criminal law, only those who were blameworthy should be required to pay compensation. Thus, it was said of civil (tort) liability by JW Salmond, author of a seminal text:

> Pecuniary compensation is not in itself the ultimate object or a sufficient justification of legal liability. It is simply the instrument by which the law fulfils its purpose of penal coercion. When one man does harm to another without any intent to do so and without any negligence, there is, in general, no reason why he should be compelled to make compensation. The damage done is not thereby in any degree diminished. It has been done, and cannot be undone. By compelling compensation the loss is merely shifted from the shoulders of one man to those of another, but it remains equally heavy. Reason demands that a loss shall lie where it falls, unless some good purpose is to be served by changing its incidence; and in general the only purpose so served is that of punishment for wrongful intent or negligence. There is no more reason why I should insure other persons against the harmful results of my own

activities, in the absence of any *mens rea* on my part, than why I should insure them against the inevitable accidents which result to them from the forces of nature independent of human actions altogether.[2]

In practice, it is the exception, rather than the rule, for civil liability to be imposed on a defendant who is without fault. In this respect the common law is unlike either the former workmen's compensation scheme or the current social security system.

Some compensation litigation is founded on an allegation that the defendant has broken a duty imposed by statute. Such a duty may be a strict one; however, it is arguable that Parliament, having identified the risk and the need to avoid it, the defendant who does not honour the statute is clearly a wrongdoer.

The compensation part of this book will be concerned primarily with the common law. It will, however, refer to other compensation schemes from time to time as appropriate.

• *Liability in both the criminal and the civil law is, in the main, fault-related.*

Impact of insurance on legal rules

The philosophy of restricting civil liability to circumstances in which the defendant is what might morally be considered a wrongdoer is not necessarily justifiable when the impact of insurance is taken into account. Arguably there might be merit in making it unlawful for people to insure themselves against the consequences of their wrongdoing. However, if this approach were adopted there would almost certainly be victims of wrongdoing who would go without compensation, for the wrongdoer would most likely be without funds to pay for the harm caused. If insurance is compulsory, then, provided the legal obligation to insure is honoured, victims are assured of compensation once they have made their cases. Once insurance is compulsory the argument for fault liability is weaker. An alternative argument can be made for requiring anyone who engages in a specified activity to be insured against any and every injury occurring in connection with that activity. Since the end of the last century workmen's compensation and social security schemes have operated broadly to this criterion. Thus, the British workmen's compensation scheme, introduced by the Workmen's Compensation Act 1897, required an employer to make payments to (certain) employees who suffered an accidental injury 'arising out of and in the course of employment'. The Act therefore imposed a form of strict liability upon employers to compensate for

---

2   Salmond, WH, *Law of Torts*, 6th edn, 1925, quoted by the present editors in Salmond, WH and Heuston, RFV, *Law of Torts*, 21st edn, 1996, Heuston, RFV and Buckley, RA (eds), London: Sweet & Maxwell, p 21.

the industrial accidents which their employees suffered. Such compensation schemes normally only provide for minimum income maintenance.

Today the Employers' Liability (Compulsory Insurance) Act 1969 requires employers to take out insurance cover to meet civil liability, in order to be able to compensate employees who suffer injury while in the course of their employment.

- *A system of liability insurance raises questions as to whether liability should be stricter.*

The cost of breaking the law

The preceding section suggests that breaking the law is likely to be a costly business and this is indeed the case. The following are some of the costs that may be incurred:

Direct financial penalties

The costs involved in the legal proceedings that may follow industrial injuries may well be heavy. A prosecution in a magistrates' court could, in some instances, result in a fine of £20,000 for a single breach of the law: a prosecution in the Crown Court could result in a fine in the region of £1,000,000. Similarly, a case of serious personal injury could lead to an award of damages of over £1,000,000. The costs of employing lawyers and calling expert evidence may far exceed the sum that the court orders to be paid.

Human resource management

Among other less obvious costs of accidents are factors related to human resource management. An organisation which does not prioritise health and safety is unlikely to have a satisfactory policy for the utilisation of the services of the people who work for it. Industrial injuries are wasteful of expensive labour: accidents cause disruption at the workplace, interfering with the productivity of persons other than the immediate victim. Hazards at the workplace may result in poor labour relations, possibly including withdrawal of labour. An unsafe workplace may not, therefore, be working at optimum productivity: such a workplace may have a higher than necessary labour turnover, involving management costs in recruitment, administration and training.

Poor public image

Most organisations today are very conscious of their public image. Companies wish to be perceived as caring organisations, and environmentally aware. For some cultivating this image may be a conscious part of their marketing strategy, but, even for those who have not invested in developing such an image, the climate of the times is such that they cannot afford to acquire a poor reputation for health and safety and environmental protection. A poor public image may result in a fall in the value of a company's shares on the Stock Exchange; it may cause consumers to refrain from buying its products and it may also deter people from seeking employment with it.

Insurance premiums

While insurance may cushion wrongdoers from the full impact of compensating for workplace injuries, a poor safety record is likely to result in high insurance premiums. Additionally, research shows that the uninsured costs of accidents far exceed the insured costs.

- *Breaking either the criminal or the civil law may be costly to the wrongdoer, even though, in civil law, insurance may cushion the wrongdoer from the full cost of the wrongdoing.*

Distinct roles of the criminal and civil law?

It has been noted that the concept of safe system is found in both the criminal law, which is concerned with accident prevention and the civil law, which is concerned with accident compensation. Prosecutions for operating unsafe systems take place in criminal courts; claims for damages by the victims of workplace injuries are brought in the civil courts. It might be thought, therefore, that there would be a clear separation of the two branches of the law and that each branch would have quite clear and separate objectives. If this were so there would be no relationship between what certain expressions and concepts have come to mean in the criminal courts and what they mean in the civil courts. In practice this is not strictly so because the reports of cases decided in the civil courts may be subsequently cited in the criminal courts and, to a somewhat lesser extent, vice versa.

The civil action for breach of statutory duty has, historically, been a substantial source of cross-fertilisation between the civil and the criminal law. Statutory interpretations made in the civil courts for the purposes of compensation claims have impacted back on the criminal courts determining the meaning of legislation for the purposes of prosecution. There is, however, no reason why judicial interpretation of the common law in compensation cases should not also feed into the development of statutes for the purposes of accident prevention and the following case demonstrates this.

R v SWAN HUNTER SHIPBUILDERS LTD AND TELEMETER INSTALLATIONS LTD [1981] IRLR 403

HMS Glasgow was under construction in Swan Hunter's shipyard when a fire broke out in the ship and eight men were killed. The fire occurred, when welding was being carried out by the employees of contractors engaged by Swan Hunter, because the atmosphere had become oxygen enriched as a result of a leaking oxygen cylinder. The question before the Court of Appeal (Criminal Division) was whether Swan Hunter were in breach of the duties imposed upon them by the Health and Safety at Work Act 1974. Their Lordships had to decide whether the shipbuilders had to take any steps to ensure that the employees of contractors operated safely. The criminal court had no hesitation in adopting a large part of a judgment from an earlier civil case. The following extract is from the judgment of Dunn LJ:

> Mr Potts, for the Crown, submitted that there was nothing revolutionary or novel in the duties imposed by ss 2–3 of the 1974 Act. He pointed out that before 1974 there was a duty on the main contractor to co-ordinate the operations at a place of work, so as to ensure the safety not only of his own employees, but also the employees of subcontractors. He referred us to *McArdle v Andmac Roofing Co and Others* (1967).[3] That was a case involving building works and the plaintiff was employed by one of two sets of subcontractors in roofing. He was injured by reason of the negligence of the other firm of subcontractors. Another company, called Pontin (Contractors) Ltd, although not apparently the main contractors, were in charge of the work and responsible to the building owners for its supervision. It was held that as Pontins were employing subcontractors who worked in proximity with one another, Pontins assumed the duty of co-ordinating the work and were thus under a duty to see that reasonable safety precautions were taken for the other contractors' men on the job.
>
> ...
>
> So, said Mr Potts, as Monkman puts it in the latest edition of his *Employers' Liability,* the duties imposed by the 1974 Act are modelled on the common law duties of care and do not constitute any significant departure from those duties as was suggested ...

– – –

- *While accident prevention laws are enforced in the criminal courts and accident compensation claims are pursued in the civil courts there is, through judicial references to previous cases recorded in the law reports, some cross-fertilisation between the two bodies of law.*

---

3   [1967] 1 All ER 583.

Relevance of foresight

Both the criminal and the civil law accept that absolute safety is not achievable. Both branches of the law are concerned with the containment of foreseeable risks.

Foresight in civil law

It has been noted that there are two ways in which a claimant may found a civil claim for damages caused by a work related injury. The claim may either be that the defendant has broken a statutory duty or that the defendant has been negligent. While claims for breach of statutory duty are subject to very technical rules, that will be considered later (in Chapter 7), it is sufficient to say, at this point, that the very fact that Parliament has laid down a statutory standard is evidence that it is generally accepted that it is foreseeable if this standard is not observed, personal injury will occur.

The tort of negligence has developed from the concept that persons should be liable for conduct which, objectively evaluated, creates a foreseeable risk of injury to others. However, the House of Lords has further diluted the criterion of liability by holding that probability, rather than mere foreseeability, must be considered.

BOLTON AND OTHERS v STONE [1951] 1 AC 850

Lord Porter said at p 857:

> My Lords, in the action and on appeal, the respondent contended that the appellants were negligent or guilty of creating a nuisance in failing to take any sufficient precautions to prevent the escape of cricket balls from the ground and the consequent risk of injury to persons in Beckenham Road. In her submission it was enough that a ball had been driven into the road even once: such an event gave the appellants warning that a ball might be hit into the road, and the appellants knowing this must, as reasonable men also know that an injury was likely to be caused to anyone standing on the road or to a passer by.
>
> ...
>
> But the question remains: Is it enough to make an action negligent to say that its performance may possibly cause injury, or must some greater probability exist of that result ensuing in order to make those responsible for its occurrence guilty of negligence?
>
> ...
>
> Undoubtedly they knew that the hitting of a cricket ball out of the ground was an event which might occur and, therefore, that there was a conceivable possibility that someone would be hit by it. But so extreme an obligation of care cannot be imposed in all cases. If it were, no one could safely drive a motor car since the possibility of an accident could not be overlooked and if it occurred some stranger might well be injured however careful the driver

might be. It is true that the driver desires to do everything possible to avoid an accident, whereas the hitting of a ball out of the ground is an incident in the game and indeed, one which the batsman would wish to bring about; but, in order that the act may be negligent, there must not only be a reasonable possibility of its happening but also of injury being caused.

– – –

Liability for not achieving what is 'reasonably practicable'

In the criminal law, particularly since the enactment of the Health and Safety at Work Act 1974, a defendant is frequently required to do what is reasonably practicable to achieve a safe system.

MAILER v AUSTIN ROVER GROUP PLC [1989] 2 All ER 1087

Lord Goff had to consider the criteria of liability under s 4(2) of the Health and Safety at Work Act 1974 which requires a controller of premises '... to take such measures as it is reasonable for a person in his position to take to ensure, so far as is reasonably practicable ...' that the premises are safe. Section 40 of the 1974 Act provides that once the situation is shown to be unsafe the burden is on the defendant to satisfy the court that it was not reasonably practicable to do more to control the hazard. Lord Goff said at p 1092:

> In other words, the complainant has only to prove that the defendant has failed to ensure (so far as he can reasonably do so, having regard to the extent of his control) that the relevant premises are safe and without risks to health in the sense I have described: the onus then passes to the defendant to prove, if he can, that it was not reasonably practicable for him to eliminate the relevant risk. It is at this stage that reasonable foreseeability becomes relevant, in the sense that there has to be an assessment of the likelihood of the incidence of risk.

What is foreseeable is a matter of fact

What is foreseeable is likely to vary from situation to situation. For example, if contractual arrangements are made stating that a certain system must be followed, this may possibly indicate that this was deemed necessary because to have done the job another way would not be safe. If the evidence is indeed that this was the reason for making the requirement a question arises as to whether the person who imposes this term in the contract is to be freed from liability if the term is broken and an accident occurs. The danger was foreseen and has been, up to a point, provided for. The question which remains, however, is: 'Was it foreseeable that the term of the contract would not be honoured?' If so ought the party who foresaw the initial risk to have foreseen the need to monitor the performance of the contract? This, it will be found, has been an issue in several leading cases.

Foreseeability is related to experience

It may not be foreseeable that if glass ampoules containing anaesthetic are immersed in disinfectant the anaesthetic will be contaminated, but events may prove that this can happen. The fact that an accident has occurred once may make it foreseeable that it will happen again (*Roe v Ministry of Health*,[4] below) and it may even be probable that it will happen (*Bolton and Others v Stone*)![5] Thus standards may be tightened from one generation to the next in the light of experience.

- *Liability is normally liability for foreseeable risks.*

Liability is for causing both accidents and diseases

In discussions about occupational health and safety it is very easy to fall into a sort of shorthand and speak – and perhaps even think – merely of prevention of accidents. It must not be forgotten, however, that it is just as important to prevent persons at work suffering damage to their health as it is to protect them from suffering accidental injury. Both the criminal law and the civil law recognise this. Increasingly the criminal law is concerned with the establishment of systems that protect workers from exposure to circumstances which may over time cause injury to their health. Similarly the civil law provides compensation to those who have contracted industrial diseases; though it is often more difficult to establish the cause of ill-health than to provide the evidence that injury has resulted from an accident.

- *The law is concerned with the prevention of and compensation for ill-health as much as for accidents caused by working conditions.*

SAFETY LITERATURE

For nearly two centuries, Royal Commissions and Select Committees have investigated and reported on various aspects of occupational health and safety. For the last half century safety experts and academics have produced a considerable amount of literature on the subject. A recurrent theme in this literature is the cost of accidents and ill health to the victims, to industry and to society more generally. What follows are a number of extracts from some of the better known or particularly relevant of these publications. The literature is therefore concerned with identifying means by which the total cost of work related injury can be effectively reduced and with finding socially acceptable means of allocating cost when it occurs.

---

4   [1954] 2 QB 66.
5   [1951] AC 850.

Prevention is better than compensation

In 1931 the Chairman of the Uniform Boiler and Pressure Vessel Law Society Inc and sometime Superintendent, Engineering and Loss Control Division, the Travellers Insurance Company, published in the USA a book that was to become a classic, recognised in both the USA and the UK and the foundation on which much subsequent work was based:

INDUSTRIAL ACCIDENT PREVENTION: A SCIENTIFIC APPROACH
by HW Heinrich[6]

'An injury prevented is a benefaction, an injury compensated – an apology.'

The exact origin of this quotation is not exactly clear but it is credited to the largest multiple-line insurance carrier in the country. The term 'compensated' relates to workmen's compensation insurance, but the underlying thought expresses the strongest possible endorsement of accident prevention as it is advocated in this text. This is so because the injury results from the accident.

If further support of need and value should be desired attention is directed to the following quotation:

'The plain fact is that our nation cannot afford the needless loss of skilled workers if we are to produce for prosperity in this country and for peace abroad.'

This statement is quoted from an address by the President of the United States before the National Conference on Industrial Safety ...

...

The implications of accident prevention are far more comprehensive and dramatic than casual thought might indicate. No great imagination is required to conclude that the prosperity and security of the nation, if not indeed of the world, are affected and endangered by its lack. This is not merely to say that the thousands of deaths, the millions of injuries and the loss of billions of dollars caused by occupational accidents in one year alone could not be absorbed without serious disturbance to our national economy. Rather it is to point out that these tragic results are but the reflection of conditions that strike at the very foundation of the American way of life. In addition the effect of accidents, aside from the loss of life, property and dollars, is to restrict seriously both employment and the production of goods and services on which the welfare of the nation is so utterly dependent.

– – –

---

6   McGraw-Hill. Quotation from 4th edn, 1959, pp 3 and 5.

Risk management

In 1970 the British Safety Council took up the theme in the following booklet:

MANAGEMENT INTRODUCTION TO TOTAL LOSS CONTROL
by James Tye[7]

How can we measure the size of the problem?

Before we try to measure the total accident costs, it is wise to have a look at the measuring tools and techniques which have evolved in the last 50 years. But bear in mind that for a long time the only accident statistic which was measured was that of fatalities.

Some 40 years ago an American safety man, Heinrich, found, on studying several thousand accidents that there was a definite ratio of major to serious to minor injuries, and the point that he made over and over again was that the proper way to avoid the serious accidents was to tackle the minor accidents, and indeed if you were able to avoid or cut down the minor accidents inevitably you were able to avoid or reduce the serious accidents and the fatalities.

Eighteen months ago Frank Bird, Safety Director of the Insurance Company of North America, measured 1,700,000 accidents and extended the theory that Heinrich originated.

Frank Bird's study showed the accident ratio of one serious to 10 minor injuries to 30 property damage injuries to 600 near misses. Of course the ratio will vary from industry to industry.

In a light radio assembly industry the ratio of cut fingers to broken backs will be entirely different from coal mining where you will probably have five to 10 times more broken backs. But the principles will remain the same, that the way to avoid serious injuries is to investigate not only the major and minor injuries, not only the property damage accidents, but also the near misses (or what I prefer to call the near hits).

As a further example let us have a look at a brick falling on a building site.

600 times an accident occurs in that the brick falls; 30 times the brick will fall on property or equipment and will cause damage to property.

10 times, the brick will fall on someone and cause a minor injury and once it will either kill or seriously injure someone.

But I do stress, and the point I want to make is, that all 600 times that the brick falls it does so accidentally, and it is only by measuring accidents that you can see the total size of the problem, the property damage as well as the injury ...

– – –

---

7   James Tye, *Management Introduction to Total Loss Control*, British Safety Council publication. Quotation from 1971 reprint, pp 8–9.

Government inquiry into means of improving workplace safety

In 1972, a Select Committee of the House of Commons, known as the Robens Committee, reported:

SAFETY AND HEALTH AT WORK
Report of the Committee 1970–72[8]

Preface

1. We were appointed on 29 May 1970 with the following terms of reference:

   'To review the provision made for the safety and health of persons in the course of their employment (other than transport workers while directly engaged on transport operations and who are covered by other provisions) and to consider whether any changes are needed in:

   (i) the scope or nature of the major relevant enactments; or

   (ii) the nature and extent of voluntary action concerned with these matters, and

   to consider whether any further steps are required to safeguard members of the public from hazards, other than general environmental pollution, arising in connection with activities in industrial and commercial premises and construction sites, and to make recommendations.'

2. The task given to us was indeed a formidable one. Safety and health at work is a vast, diverse and complex field of study. No one can speak authoritatively on all of its facets and aspects, and in presenting this report, we make no large claims. There can be no such thing as a definitive report on this subject. We can only hope to have made a constructive contribution

   ...

The nature of the problem

10. Every year something like 1,000 people are killed at their work in this country. Every year about half a million suffer injuries in varying degrees of severity. 23 million working days are lost annually on account of industrial injury and disease.

11. We shall have something to say in a later chapter about the validity of some of these figures and about the need for caution in drawing conclusions from them. But whatever qualifications and reservations may be made, the orders of magnitude are plain enough. It is unnecessary to dwell on what the bare statistics mean in terms of human tragedy and suffering; nor on the economic cost to the nation in terms of lost production and diverted resources: the rough figures, however imperfect, speak for themselves. For

---

8   (1972) (HMSO) (Cmnd 5034). Quotations from p xiv and p 1.

both humanitarian and economic reasons, no society can accept with complacency that such levels of death, injury, disease and waste must be regarded as the inevitable price of meeting its needs for goods and services.

– – –

Government questions the fault based system of compensation

By 1972, there was sufficient concern about the operation of the common law system of compensation of accident victims for a Royal Commission to be set up under the chairmanship of Lord Pearson to investigate and report on the matter. It reported to Parliament in March 1978.

Although the Commission considered its terms of reference to be less than comprehensive (and its report represented this somewhat piecemeal approach) it is clear that it covered much more than work related accidents and ill-health. Among the facts and figures identified in Chapter 3 of Volume 1 of the three volume report were that, in the 1970s, in the areas within the remit of the Commission 720,000 of the 3,050,000 injuries and 1,300 of the 21,420 accidental deaths which occurred each year were suffered at work. These statistics do not necessarily bear a close relationship to the situation in the 2000s, but they form a useful background.

The work of the Pearson Commission did not lead to any root and branch reform of the system: the most important point to note is that tort was at that time providing only about 25% of the compensation paid to accident victims, whereas the social security system provided over 50%. These proportions are likely to remain broadly the same today. It may also be noted that the figures provided by the Commission in Table 4 were only estimates. It is in fact extremely difficult to establish the amount of money paid out through insurance companies in the private sector, particularly as many claims are settled out of court. It must, however, also be borne in mind that inflation has been such that the annual totals are likely to be very much higher today:

ROYAL COMMISSION ON CIVIL LIABILITY AND COMPENSATION FOR PERSONAL INJURY REPORT
Volume One[9]

Chapter 1 Introduction

Appointment and terms of reference

1. We were appointed on 19 March 1973:

    'to consider to what extent, in what circumstances and by what means compensation should be payable in respect of death or personal injury

---

9   Cmnd 7054-1, 1978, pp 3–4 and 13.

(including antenatal injury) suffered by any person

(a) in the course of employment;

(b) through the use of a motor vehicle or other means of transport;

(c) through the manufacture, supply or use of goods or services;

(d) on premises belonging to or occupied by another; or

(e) otherwise through the act or omission of another where compensation under the present law is recoverable only on proof of fault or under the rules of strict liability,

having regard to the cost and other implications of the arrangements for the recovery of compensation, whether by way of compulsory insurance or otherwise.'

2. When the then Prime Minister (Mr Heath) announced the decision to establish the Royal Commission on 19 December 1972 he said:

'The Government have been considering proposals made from time to time in the past, which are now particularly relevant in the light of the Report of the Robens Committee on Safety and Health at Work and in connection with the recent concern over the thalidomide cases, that there should be an inquiry into the basis of civil liability in the United Kingdom for causing death or personal injury. It is the Government's view that a wide-ranging inquiry is required into the basis on which compensation should be recoverable.'

...

Table 4 Scale of present sources of compensation for injury
United Kingdom, based on data for 1971–76

	Aggregate value of compensation payments (£ million a year)[1]	Approximate number of new beneficiaries Numbers a year
Social Security	421	1,550,000
Tort/delict	202	215,000
Other	204	
Occupational sick pay	125	1,000,000
Occupational pension		54,000
Private insurance[2]	51	200,000
Criminal injuries compensation	17	18,000
Other forms of compensation[3]	6	150,000
All forms of compensation	827	1,700,000[4]

1   At 1 January 1977 prices.

2   Excluding life insurance, for which we can make no reliable estimate.

3   Rent and rate rebates, trade unions, friendly societies and charities.

4   After double counting has been excluded.

Figures estimates by the Commission.

— — —

Academic criticism of the tort system in the 1990s

In the years since the Pearson Report was published some of its recommendations have been followed, but, as indeed the Committee recommended, the tort system remains. As the following extract from a recent radical text indicates, not everyone is satisfied:

THE WRONGS OF TORT
by Joanne Conaghan and Wade Mansell[10]

Contemporary perspectives on accident compensation

There is no doubt that the publication of the Pearson Report and its barely lukewarm reception represented a turning point in the public debate on accident compensation in Great Britain. The Report's relative timidity, combined with the election of a Conservative government in 1979, ensured that throughout most of the 1980s accident compensation was no longer on the agenda. Recent signs however indicate a revival of interest in the questions Pearson appeared to answer so unsatisfactorily. In particular, the principle of fault-based liability has come under renewed scrutiny.

First, in the area of defective products, the UK government has been compelled by an EC Directive (*Products Liability Council Directive No 85/373/EEC*, 25 July 1985) to adopt a form of strict liability (Consumer Protection Act 1987, Part One ...). The fault principle has come under further scrutiny in the context of the recent tragic plight of haemophiliacs and others who contracted AIDS from HIV infected blood (and tissue transfer) supplied by the National Health Service and imported from the United States in the early 1980s. The efforts of those affected to secure satisfactory compensation from the government, who insisted that they were not at fault in the matter, have further highlighted both the inability of the tort system to cope with such a visible tragedy and the piecemeal and reactive nature of the government's response to such tragedies. The willingness of the government to retreat behind the legal technicality of fault and the arbitrary and capricious distribution of entitlements which may result from such a position echoes the tragedy of vaccine damaged children, whose plight caught the public imagination and sympathy in the late 1970s.

...

The technical and distributional problems which medical litigation inevitably generates has led to calls from a number of organisation, including the British Medical Association (BMA), for some kind of no-fault alternative.

– – –

10   Pluto Press, (1993) pp 99–100.

Governmental agency investigates cost of accidents

Over the years, the number of deaths and injuries and the causes of them have changed but the problem of costing them remains. In 1993 the Health and Safety Executive published a report on five case studies. Possibly the most significant outcome of the studies related to the ratio of insured costs to uninsured costs. The situation may be compared with an iceberg: the hidden costs, represented as below the water line, far exceed the insured costs: in some cases more so than others. The following extracts are from the introduction:

THE COSTS OF ACCIDENTS AT WORK
Health and Safety Executive[11]

Introduction

Managers in industry know that accidents cost money. Whether people are injured, plant and machinery damaged or product wasted, organisations lose money.

Large scale losses such as those arising from major fires or explosions, or involving loss of life, are very visible and some have been costed on an individual basis. For example, the *Piper Alpha* explosion involved the loss of 167 lives and is estimated to have cost over £2 billion, including £746 million in direct insurance payouts. BP estimate that the refinery fire at Grangemouth in 1987, in which one person died, cost £50 million in property damage and a further £50 million due to business interruption. Compensation given to people injured at work often involves large sums of money: for example a car worker who suffered repetitive strain injury was recently awarded around £60,000. Less well understood, however, is the nature and extent of loss from accidents of a more routine nature: those accidents which injure but do not kill people, which damage plant and interrupt processes. The costs of these sorts of accident can often be hidden in sick pay, increased insurance premiums or maintenance budgets. Few firms have the mechanisms to identify them separately and fewer still actually identify and examine the costs of accidents systematically.

...

Against this background, in 1989, HSE's Accident Prevention Advisory Unit (APAU) began a series of five case studies with organisations from various sectors of industry. The aim was to develop a methodology to accurately identify the full cost of accidents, to publish the methodology and results and thereby provide an incentive for all organisations to take the management of health and safety more seriously.

APAU has for many years advanced the view that there is no contradiction between health and safety and profitability; a view to which an increasing number of managers in industry subscribe. Those organisations which perform well and have high standards of health and safety are often the most

---

11   Health and Safety Series booklet HS(G)96, 1993, London: HMSO, pp 1–2.

successful, irrespective of size or industry. The common thread running through these organisations is the application of the principles of sound and effective management of health and safety, together with the integration of health and safety into their overall management agenda.

...

The five studies produced results that could be compared with different operational parameters: for example, accidents cost:

- one organisation as much as *37% of its annualised profits*;
- another the equivalent of *8.5% of tender price*;
- a third organisation *5% of its running costs*.

None of the participating organisations suffered major or catastrophic loss during the study periods. Nor were there any fatal injuries, prosecutions or significant civil claims, all of which could have increased the levels of loss well beyond those recorded.

– – –

Distinguishing between hazards and risks

It is necessary to distinguish between 'hazard' and 'risk', though there is a tendency to use these words as if they were synonymous. The Health and Safety Executive has made the distinction by the example shown below:

ESSENTIALS OF HEALTH AND SAFETY AT WORK
Health and Safety Executive[12]

A hazard is anything that can cause harm (for example, chemicals, electricity, working from ladders, etc).

Risk is the chance (big or small) of harm actually being done.

As an example, think about a can of solvent on a shelf. There is a hazard if the solvent is toxic or flammable, but very little risk. The risk increases when it is taken down and poured into a bucket. Harmful vapour is given off and there is a danger of spillage. Things are made much worse if a mop is then used to spread it over the floor for cleaning. The chance of harm, ie the risk, is then high.

– – –

Assessment of risk

Absolute safety is not attainable; even if the danger is apparent, the cost of removing it may be disproportionately high: all that can be hoped for is to keep risks to an acceptable level. The need to distinguish between hazards and risks has been officially addressed:

---

12 1988. Reprinted 4/94 C1000, p 2.

REVIEW OF THE IMPLEMENTATION AND ENFORCEMENT OF EC LAW IN THE UK
Department of Trade and Industry[13]

Scientific evidence

3.9 We are concerned by the virtual lack of scientific evidence, risk assessment or information on compliance costs to influence EC proposals or the UK's negotiating objective. The need for sound scientific input is particularly significant in areas which generate public concern such as health, safety and environmental questions. No one we spoke to wanted to challenge the essential underlying objectives of, say, proper hygiene for food or safety protection for employees although we encountered people, including officials, who misunderstand the Government's policy on deregulation and believe that it means putting business interests before, say, health and safety of the public. Some found it difficult to appreciate that there are often alternative solutions to a particular problem and that provided the objective can be met, the least burdensome approach benefits business, the economy and then the general public.

...

3.10 Other Departments have cited a tendency for EC negotiations on technical matters to proceed without the pooling of technical evidence on risk. Some suggested that we could use well directed research in a positive way to promote national interests in the EC. Certainly we believe that *policies to reduce near market research should be reviewed in order to ensure that Government is properly advised about technical arguments in legislation and does not have to rely on outdated research in promoting the interests of UK business.*

Risk assessment

3.11 Closely linked with sound scientific knowledge is the assessment of risk – the likelihood that a hazard will cause a predictable adverse effect. We found that risk assessment and hazard assessment are often confused in the minds of officials, business and enforcers leading to a tendency towards disproportionate responses in which theory replaces practical experience. The statistics on fatalities from workplace fires, as opposed to domestic fires, do not point to a significant gap in existing safety provisions yet the UK and other Member States have expended costs on negotiation, consultation and implementation of new directives; business have had the prospect of high compliance costs hanging over them and there are potentially longer term enforcement costs. In international negotiations risk assessments may vary between Member States often for good reasons. For example food handling measures necessary in Mediterranean climates will be different to those necessary to achieve the same hygiene standards in colder climates. *More attention should be given to comparative risk assessment* ie what difference will the proposed change

---

13 An Efficiency Scrutiny Report commissioned by the President of the Board of Trade, July 1993, pp 27–28.

make to the risk assessment in each Member State. Where the difference is negligible we believe proposals for change should be resisted ...

– – –

Accidents and diseases

The need to cater within the law for ill-health as well as accidental injury has been of increasing concern in recent years. Indeed the concern that changing working conditions could result in a higher incidence of industrial disease as a result of exposure to toxic substances used in work processes was one of the reasons for setting up the Robens Committee in 1970.

Within the Robens Report, it was noted:

> 18. ... In recent years, widely publicised compensation cases concerning asbestosis and bladder cancer have stimulated public concern about the insidious and potentially deadly nature of the long term risks to which certain groups of workers may be exposed. Of course the use in industry of toxic substances and materials that can in certain circumstances damage the health of those who work with them is by no means new. What is new is the rapid increase in the number of new chemical substances and mixtures being brought into use in industrial and commercial processes, and the greatly increased scale on which they are used ...[14]

In practice, the distinction between injury caused by accident and ill-health caused by disease is not always clear cut. In the early 1980s, one of the present authors ventured that:

> Work related disablement may be broadly divided into four categories, according to the type of disability and the circumstances in which it occurs. First, in the typical accident situation, the worker is involved in an event which causes him immediate disablement – for example he might fall and break a limb. In the second type of situation the worker is exposed for a short time to a hazard which in due course leads to his disability: for example a worker in a medical laboratory might contract an infectious disease as a result of a specimen he handled there. In the third type of case the worker, after long term exposure to hazardous conditions, might contract an illness such as cancer. In the fourth type of case the worker, after long term exposure to a hazard, might develop a physical disability such as deafness. The first and second categories described are similar in that the physical condition is caused by an incident which occurs at a precise moment of time, although it is conceded that in the second example there may be difficulty in identifying exactly when that incident occurred. The third and fourth categories are similar in that, while the disablement manifests itself in a different form in each case, the victim in both

---

14 The Robens Report, *Safety and Health at Work*, p 3.

cases suffers a gradual deterioration in health as the result of long exposure to unsatisfactory conditions ...[15]

The problems identified nearly 20 years ago remain and have indeed become more apparent, though the type of ill health has, to some extent, changed. The major problems of the 1990s include stress, both physical (repetitive strain injury) and mental (caused either by exposure to catastrophe or by long term pressures to increase productivity).

Search for an effective European system

The following extract shows that there is investigation within the European Union to find a way of effectively using the system of insuring against compensation claims to provide incentives to improve health and safety:

EUROPEAN FOUNDATION FOR THE IMPROVEMENT OF LIVING AND WORKING CONDITIONS
News from the Foundation No 42 (1994)

Incentives work toward a safer workplace

Ways to improve the working environment beyond the minimum level set by legislation are the concern of governments and social partners throughout the European Union – and increasingly so. Some consider that even with the large number of European Union directives and regulations seeking to improve health and safety in the workplace, the situation has remained inadequate. As a result, several countries within and outside the Union have been looking at whether economic incentives could provide the catalyst to stimulate a search for higher occupational standards of health and safety. Most likely to achieve this goal appear to be schemes which are based on some form of risk assessment.

...

The Foundation first looked at this issue in 1988, when following from a study of the reporting of occupational accidents and diseases in the EC, it examined ways by which the United States, Canada and other nations were seeking to improve health and safety at work. Phase One of the project produced a catalogue of different economic incentive schemes operating in Member States, North America and Canada. The majority are linked to insurance premiums, with the premium rising according to the company's health and safety record. Thus, the greater the safety record, the lower the premium. The health and safety record is measured using a record of accidents.

The book, *Economic Incentives to Improve the Working Environment, summary and conclusions of an international study*, emerged from Phase Two. It summarises and presents the conclusions of the Foundation's international study.

---

15 Barrett, B, 'Employers' liability for work related ill health' (1981) 10 Industrial LJ 101.

While most incentive programmes are based on insurance schemes, the premium levied could equally be devised as a tax or as contributions to social funds. All the incentive schemes reviewed in the catalogue are intended to be self financing. Scope exists, however, for considerable variation in premiums charged. An excess income could be drawn to provide a budget for health and safety promotion. The schemes could be designed so that companies with the worst record for health and safety funded the rebates or the promotional activities. In 1993, the Foundation established a European forum to exchange views on the issue.

There is unanimous agreement among countries operating incentive schemes that they are beneficial, even essential.

...

While there is clearly great potential to reduce human suffering and economic loss through economic incentive schemes, so too there are risks. The danger with the most common scheme to date, that based on insurance premiums, is that by focusing on accidents, it ignores diseases – some of which may take 30 years to develop – such as occupational cancer. Similarly, in the safety field, research has shown that some companies offer a bonus to individuals for reducing the number of accidents. This reward system can create group pressure not to report accidents.

Also, if incentive schemes for employers are based on accident records, they might be more likely not to report the accidents to insurance companies or the public authorities. This kind of under-reporting would make preventive action more difficult.

Economic incentive schemes cannot be considered in isolation. The implications are potentially extensive for the national social security system, for the enforcement of health and safety law and for the civil law system.

– – –

Innovative Canadian package

The Workers' Compensation Board in Vancouver, British Columbia, Canada has three essential responsibilities when administering the province's Workers' Compensation Act:

1. paying compensation for work-related injuries and illnesses;
2. funding the system through a levy on the employer's payroll;
3. occupational safety and health, including education, inspection and enforcement. Roughly 85% of the workforce is covered by the legislation – some 850,000 employees [1993 figures].

There are 62 rate groupings, established on the basis of industry type. Employers in these groupings are solely responsible for the costs associated with injuries or ill-health arising from their group. In return, they are protected under the act from any law suit brought by workers for compensation. The levy paid out is a percentage of payroll. The Board operates a programme of Experience Rated Assessment through which the levy on any individual employer can be increased or reduced by up to one third. Assessment is calculated for individual companies on the basis of their claims costs in the last two years compared to the average for their industrial group. Visits by inspectors are targeted on high risk operations.

The levy is designed to cover the cost of current year injuries – regardless of when they are paid, current year administration costs and an amount to cover any balance in the group brought forward from the previous year. Any overall reduction in injury costs thus results in a lower assessment for employers in the group. For every 3% variance from the group average, a company is issued a 1% merit or demerit – a direct incentive to improve safety. Occasionally the Board offers other financial inducements.

– – –

THE ECONOMICS OF SAFETY

Economic Impact of Occupational Safety and Health in the Member States of the European Union

A 1998 publication of the European Agency for Safety and Health at Work states at p 7:

> This report on the Economic Impact of Occupational Safety and Health in the Member States of the European Union summarises the second major information project undertaken under the auspices of the Agency since it started work in September 1996. The aim of this project has been to produce an overview of how economic factors are related to the formulation of occupational safety and health policy in the Member States.
>
> The results from this project show that estimating the cost and benefit of OSH measures has become an important issue in most Member States of the European Union and that the attention paid to it is still increasing. At the same time it should also be recognised that most Member States stress the importance of ethical considerations when it comes to the formulation of OSH policy.
>
> *Considerations regarding the costs and benefits of OSH measures*
>
> In some Member States the assessment of the economic impact is one of the standard pieces of information considered in political decision-making. However, the way economic assessment influences decision-making varies from one Member State to another. In general, in seeking consensus with social partners, cost-benefit analyses (CBA) are not the major factor in decision-making. Nonetheless it seems that the clarity provided by economic assessments makes it easier to reach viable compromises. This methodology serves as a quality check in which the efficiency of a measure in considered systematically.
>
> *The Economic Impact of Occupational Safety and Health Policy*
>
> In order to have information available about the effects of measures (such as introducing new or adapting existing regulations) it is in many Member States common to prepare an evaluation before introducing the legislation (ex-ante).

In some Member States such an ex ante impact assessment is done on a routine basis and sometimes it is even mandatory. The scope of the assessment varies from country to country and may also vary with the nature of the measure and the severity of the problem in question. Assessment of other measures such as campaigns etc occurs on a much lesser scale.

Measures can also be assessed afterwards (ex-post). The goal of ex-post assessment can be to test the effectivity and efficiency of the measure. The result of CBA after implementing can be used in adjusting the measures in question. Usually it is legislation that is assessed. Few countries evaluate other types of measures in this way.

In ex-ante and, indeed, in ex-post evaluations the benefits are hard to estimate. One of the problems is that the benefit of prevention may only become apparent after a long time. In general it can be said that due to lack of reliable data and to difficulties in isolating relevant factors it is difficult to produce this kind of evaluation.

– – –

Time to review the system?

It is now more than a quarter of a century since the Health and Safety at Work Act 1974, the principal British safety legislation, was enacted. In that time the European Union has required Members States to implement directives relevant to occupational health and safety. In Britain these have been implemented by Regulations subordinate to the 1974 Act. In addition there have been many economic and social changes. These matters have led to some debate as to whether the British regulatory system requires revision:

ROBENS REVISITED: THE CASE FOR A REVIEW OF OCCUPATIONAL HEALTH AND SAFETY LEGISLATION
AN INTERIM REPORT FROM THE
INSTITUTE OF EMPLOYMENT RIGHTS
by D Walters and P James
June 1998

Over one million employees suffered a work-related injury in the year 1995/96. A further two and a half million workers are estimated to have suffered from illness, which they believed to have been caused or made worse by their work.[15] Despite being preventable, occupational injuries, ill health and fatalities continue to be an unacceptable burden on society. Working conditions are still a source of discomfort and stress for thousands of people at work. The economic cost of occupational accidents, ill-health and fatalities represents a significant drain upon the economy not only in term of the direct economic losses associated with such events but also through the cost to the public exchequer for treatment, rehabilitation and other forms of support for victims.

---

15 See *Health and Safety Statistics 1996/97*, 1997, Health and Safety Commission.

Much the same was said at the outset of the Committee of Inquiry on Safety and Health at Work (the Robens Committee) over 25 years ago. This committee called for fundamental changes in the way that health and safety was regulated in Britain. Its proposals, many of which were incorporated in the Health and Safety at Work [HSW] Act 1974, were seen as providing the basis for the creation of a more effective system of regulation which would result in improved levels of worker protection.

Yet 25 years later occupational injuries, ill health and fatalities continue to represent an unacceptable and largely preventable burden on society. Perhaps it is time to revisit the question of what is the most appropriate and effective system for preventing work-related injuries and ill-health in Britain and also to inquire how such injuries and ill-health might be most effectively ameliorated. To address these issues the Institute of Employment Rights has embarked on a comprehensive review of the system for health and safety in Britain. It is hoped that the result of the review, which will be published in 1999, will stimulate a renewed and informed debate on how occupational health and safety should be regulated in the new millennium.

The aim of this interim report is to present the case for a re-examination of the system for regulating health and safety in the UK in the light of enormous changes that have taken place in the economic, social and political environment over the last 25 years. One starting point for the review is the impact of the HSW Act 1974 and the approach to regulation advocated by Robens whose report formed the basis of the Act. The review will question whether the 1974 Act and the Robens Report really was the radical rethinking of health and safety regulation that it was claimed to be and whether it resulted in a greatly improved sustainable system for health and safety ...

REVITALISING HEALTH AND SAFETY
Health and Safety Commission, Consultation Document
July 1999

1. This year marks the 25th anniversary of the Health and Safety at Work etc Act 1974. John Prescott[17] has commissioned a strategic appraisal which aims to:

   - inject new impetus into the health and safety agenda;
   - identify new approaches to reduce further rates of accidents and ill-health caused by work, especially approaches relevant to small firms;
   - ensure that our approach to health and safety regulation remains relevant for the changing world of work over the next 25 years; and
   - gain maximum benefit from links between OSH and other Government programmes.

17 The Deputy Prime Minister.

The **Health and Safety at Work etc Act 1974** brought a transformation in health and safety policy. Employers previously needed to comply with a confusing array of prescriptive standards. The 1974 Act gave a new emphasis to prevention. It places a duty on all employers to protect workers and the public from the risks presented by their business activity. The Act covers the whole of Great Britain. Health and safety legislation has not been devolved to the Scottish Parliament and Welsh Assembly.

The Act brought fragmented health and safety policy makers and inspectorates together, creating the **Health and Safety Commission and Executive** (HSC/E).

- The Health and Safety Commission advises Ministers on health and safety policy, and has powers to propose new law and standards.

- the Health and Safety Executive advises and assists the Commission. Its main independent responsibilities are to enforce health and safety legislation and investigate accidents.

For certain premises, the responsibilities fall to **local authorities**.

2   The Government considers that the basic framework set by the HSW Act 1974 has stood the test of time. This is a tribute to the effectiveness of the tripartite Health and Safety Commission in securing consensus on sometimes difficult issues. The fatal injury rate for employees has now fallen to a quarter of what it was at the beginning of the 1970s. Yet we cannot be complacent. Fatal injury rates now seem to have reached a plateau. **Each year, some 400 people lose their lives in work-related accidents, over one million people suffer a workplace injury and some two million suffer from ill-health caused by work, resulting in 25,000 people leaving the workforce. We can, and should, do better.**

Better for business

3   Health and safety failures damage businesses and the wider economy. We must set the right framework for further improvements in health and safety performance over the next 25 years. The world of work has already changed dramatically since 1974. Fewer people work in large companies or belong to trade unions. Small businesses and self-employment have flourished. Today's trend is for all but core business activities to be carried out by contractors or commercial partners.

4   The Department of Trade and Industry's Competitiveness White Paper sets out the Government's vision for a knowledge-based economy. Health and safety has much to contribute to this vision. We must demonstrate and promote the business case for a workforce that is 'happy, healthy and here'. And we must pursue new approaches to raising standards that will match new economic structures. In May, the Health and Safety Commission launched a new Strategic Plan for the next three years, which starts this work.

5   The last 25 years have seen much new regulation in the field of health and safety, often driven by European legislation, which has made an important impact, but is now in decline. This appraisal is not about further regulation or new burdens on business. It is about demonstrating the business case for further improvement and finding new ways of working in partnership with others to get the positive message across, that good performance aids, not hinders, business.

Better for people

6   Action to promote the wider well-being of individuals and the wider health and safety agenda must also gain greater recognition and momentum. Risks presented by work are one part of the range of risks faced by people in the home, at leisure and while travelling. Wider health and safety matters, such as public health, transport safety, environmental protection and consumer safety are dealt with by a range of Government institutions. Government must show leadership in working effectively across institutional boundaries if the overall impact of these programmes is to be greater than the sum of their individual parts.

PROPOSALS FOR THE HEALTH AND SAFETY (MISCELLANEOUS MODIFICATION) REGULATIONS 1999 AND THE AMENDMENT OF THE MANAGEMENT OF HEALTH AND SAFETY AT WORK APPROVED CODE OF PRACTICE
Health and Safety Commission, Consultative Document, 1999

Introduction

5.   We are consulting you about our proposal to modify five current sets of health and safety regulations.[18] This is part of the Government's drive to ensure that the UK fully discharges its obligation to implement European Directives. The proposed Modification Regulations are intended to put beyond doubt the adequacy of our implementation of the health and safety Framework Directive (89/391/EEC). The European Commission raised a number of these issues during their examination of how we had transposed the Directive in UK law, as part of their wider review of transposition in all Member States. The Government agreed to consider certain changes to the law to lay to rest any debate on the adequacy of our transposition.

6.   Most of the provisions of the Directive were transposed into law by the Management of Health and Safety at Work Regulations 1992 (the Management Regulations). Hence, the Modifications Regulations primarily relate to detail in the Management Regulations clarifying the position on principles of prevention, arrangements for contacting external services, the appointment of competent persons to advise on health and safety and the

---

18   Management of Health and Safety at Work Regulations 1992. The Health and Safety (First Aid) Regulations 1981. The Offshore Installations and Pipeline Works (First Aid) Regulations 1989. The Mines Miscellaneous Health and Safety Provisions Regulations 1995. The Construction (Health, Safety and Welfare) Regulations 1996.

employer's responsibility in law, including to members of the public. In addition there are proposals to clarify issues on first-aid.

...

Changing Pattern of Employment Programme

41. In 1996 the Commission published a discussion document entitled *The Health and Safety Implications of Changing Patterns of Employment*. The Commission invited comments on whether the existing health and safety legislation provided an adequate framework for the protection of certain atypical groups of workers such as homeworkers, part-time, casual and temporary workers and the self-employed.

42. One of the issues identified was in relation to a worker who is responsible for his or her own tax and national insurance, but works under the direction or control of someone else. Such workers are generally considered to be an 'employee' for health and safety purposes. To clarify the position, the Commission agreed that a standard statement should appear in all relevant HSC AcoPs and guidance to raise awareness of this situation. This AcoP has been revised to incorporate the standard statement in paragraphs 4 and 5 and is also referred to in paragraph 93.

43. The changing patterns consultation exercise also identified areas where clarity is needed to explain employers' duties to those workers who do not fit into the traditional definition of a worker or employee. The AcoP has been revised to make specific reference to those workers, such as the self-employed, mobile workers and homeworkers, to ensure there is no confusion that such workers are protected under health and safety legislation. These workers are covered in the AcoP, mainly under regulation 3, paragraph 18.

44. The final amendment to the AcoP as a result of changing patterns is to address a concern that all employers and self-employed people should co-operate on matters concerning health and safety arrangements where their workers share a workplace and especially where workers do not share the site permanently. The guidance under regulation 9 has been rewritten to cover all people who may be at risk sharing a workplace, including situations where an employer may not be physically present at that workplace ...

– – –

SUMMARY

Both occupational compensation law and occupational health and safety law are concerned with personal injury.

- The term 'personal injury' covers both injury by accident and ill-health caused by disease.
- Personal injury is less likely to occur if safe systems are operated.

- Personal injury includes injury caused by both accident and disease.
- Absolute safety is not attainable.
- Failure to operate safely can be expensive.
- Risks must be distinguished from hazards.
- The main factors which the law has to take into account are:
    (a) the state of scientific knowledge;
    (b) the foreseeability that injury will occur;
    (c) the probability of injury occurring;
    (d) the cost of preventing injury occurring.

These are the themes which will run through the following pages. First the civil and then the criminal law will be reviewed.

PART I

CIVIL LIABILITY

CHAPTER 2

THE BACKGROUND TO THE MODERN CIVIL LAW

I THE ROLE OF CASE LAW

The rules governing accident compensation law have been very largely judge-made. In this respect accident compensation law is in sharp contrast to accident prevention law: in the latter, the behaviour that people are expected to demonstrate to minimise the risk of personal injury has been enacted by Parliament in regulatory legislation. Although, in relation to compensation law, Parliament has, from time to time, legislated to clarify or modify the system developed through the judge-made common law. In respect to accident prevention law, judges have been, and are, frequently required to interpret the language used by Parliament. Nevertheless, judicial interpretation of regulatory legislation has largely been in civil courts when accident victims have brought civil actions for breach of statutory duty.

Judgments, once reported in law reports, are 'on the record' for all time. A judge – particularly a judge sitting in a higher court – may, in a later case, distinguish the earlier decision or even overrule it or Parliament may alter the law. Subsequent developments do not, however, cause the original decision to be removed from the law library and it remains possible for a barrister to refer to the old case and attempt to persuade a court that, in spite of the changes that have occurred, there is still a relevant statement of principle in that case. For example, a case might contain a statement of general principle and then proceed to apply that principle to particular facts. Subsequent case law, or statutes, might rule that the principle did not apply in the particular situation. The statement of principle could nevertheless remain valid. The uncertain status of old case law can make it difficult for those looking for clarity in the common law. Students, or commentators, ignore the old cases at their peril!

It can also happen that a particular judicial decision has a great influence on the law for a time and during that time subsequent case law is developed in the shadow of it. If the case is considered authoritative, but, possibly because of changed social conditions, it has ceased to be appropriate, courts may do everything possible to avoid following it. Judgments which in this way seek to change the common law may well be difficult for the reader to empathise with unless the reason for their complexity is fully understood.

Industrial injury compensation law has a long history and during the course of its development it has had to adapt to quite fundamental changes in society with fairly limited intervention from Parliament. Thus it is not possible to provide a straightforward, definitive, but simple account of the present law.

II PHASES IN THE DEVELOPMENT OF THE LAW

It is convenient to regard the development of this branch of personal injury law as falling into three periods:

(a) 1837–97:   from *Priestley v Fowler* to the Workmen's Compensation Act 1897;

(b) 1897–1948: the era of the Workmen's Compensation Acts;

(c) 1948–2000: the period following the repeal of the Workmen's Compensation Acts.

Some might question this division, for there were, within these broad divisions, important developments which might have been chosen as the landmarks. It might be argued forcefully that so much has happened since the end of the Second World War that this half-century should not be considered as a single period. Be that as it may, these three periods will be adopted here for the purposes of a very brief outline of what lies behind the law as generally understood today.

1837–97

(a) Origins of employer's liability

PRIESTLEY v FOWLER (1837) 3 M & W 1

This was the first reported personal injury case in which any significance was attached to the fact that the victim was a worker and the defendant was an employer. The case has been much criticised and much fault has been found with the somewhat brief judgment of Lord Abinger CB. This criticism is rather unfair, because the problem was less a matter of what Lord Abinger said than the way in which other Victorian judges chose to build on what he said!

The case was heard on appeal by Lord Abinger. The original judgment had been for the victim but, as a result of the appeal, the plaintiff lost his claim for damages. The facts were that the plaintiff was a servant of the defendant butcher, who had required him to go on a journey with certain goods that had been loaded into a van. The declaration on which the appeal was based stated:

> ... it became the defendant's duty to use proper care that the van should be in a proper state of repair and should not be overloaded, and that the plaintiff should be safely and securely carried thereby; nevertheless that the defendant did not use proper care that the van should not be overloaded, or that the plaintiff should be safely and securely carried; in consequence of the neglect of which duties, the van gave way and broke down, and the plaintiff was thrown to the ground, and his thigh fractured.

Lord Abinger gave the following judgment:

> It is admitted that there is no precedent for the present action by a servant against a master. We are therefore to decide the question upon general principles, and in doing so we are at liberty to look at the consequences of a decision the one way or the other.
>
> If the master be liable to the servant in this action, the principle of that liability will be found to carry us to an alarming extent. He who is responsible by his general duty, or by the terms of his contract, for all the consequences of negligence in a matter in which he is the principal, is responsible for the negligence of all his inferior agents. If the owner of the carriage is therefore responsible for the sufficiency of his carriage to his servant, he is responsible for the negligence of his coach maker, or his harness maker, or his coachman. The footman, therefore, who rides behind the carriage, may have an action against his master for a defect in the carriage owing to the negligence of the coach maker, or for a defect in the harness arising from the negligence of the harness maker, or for drunkenness, neglect or want of skill in the coachman; nor is there any reason why the principle should not, if applicable in this class of case extend to many others. The master, for example, would be liable to the servant for the negligence of the chambermaid, for putting him into a damp bed; for that of the upholsterer, for sending in a crazy bedstead, whereby he was made to fall down while asleep and injure himself; for the negligence of the cook, in not properly cleaning the copper vessels used in the kitchen; of the butcher, in supplying the family with meat of a quality injurious to the health; of the builder, for a defect in the foundation of the house, whereby it fell, and injured both the master and the servant by the ruins.
>
> The inconvenience, not to say the absurdity, of these consequences, afford a sufficient argument against the application of this principle to the present case. But, in truth the mere relation of the master and the servant never can imply an obligation on the part of the master to take more care of the servant than he may reasonably be expected to do of himself. He is, no doubt, bound to provide for the safety of his servant in the course of his employment, to the best of the judgment, information and belief. The servant is not bound to risk his safety in the service of his master, and may, if he thinks fit, decline any service in which he reasonably apprehends injury to himself; and in most of the cases in which danger may be incurred, if not in all, he is just as likely to be acquainted with the probability and extent of it as the master. In that sort of employment especially, which is described in the declaration in this case, the plaintiff must have known as well as his master, and probably better, whether the van was sufficient, whether it was overloaded, and whether it was likely to carry him safely. In fact, to allow this sort of action to prevail would be an encouragement to the servant to omit that diligence and caution against the misconduct or negligence of others who serve him, and which diligence and caution, while they protect the master, are a much better security against any injury the servant may sustain by the negligence of others engaged under the same master, than any recourse against his master for damages could possibly afford.

– – –

This short judgment, given in the belief that there were no precedents, touches on a number of the issues which were to be, and still are, to some extent, central to compensation cases. It is therefore worth identifying them.

1 The contractual relationship

The declaration which was the basis of the appeal (under a procedure which has been long since obsolete) described the plaintiff as 'servant' of the defendant; that is, an 'employee'. Lord Abinger questioned whether the contract of employment gave rise to any duty on the employer to 'cause the servant to be safely carried'.

2 General duty

Lord Abinger suggested that independently of the contract there might be a general duty on the employer, but did not develop this proposition. A general duty might be implied in all contracts of a certain type, such as employment contracts. It might, alternatively, be a duty arising independently of the existence of a contract; in modern law such duties arise in the tort of negligence.

3 Vicarious liability

Lord Abinger was alarmed lest the employer be liable for the wrongdoings of a wide variety of persons. The modern rule is that an employer is liable for the wrongdoings employees commit when in the course of their employment. Some of the people in examples given by Lord Abinger were not employees; indeed he suggested that the defendant's liability might arise from the relationship of principal and agent rather than that of employer and employee.

4 Plant and equipment

There are suggestions that the employer's van might not have been sound. Alternatively it might not have been appropriate for the load that had to be carried, or the goods might not have been properly loaded onto the vehicle. The nature and extent of the employer's liability for plant and equipment, and the instruction and supervision of employees in the use of it remain important issues.

5 Personal responsibility of the employer

The judge stated that the employer 'is, no doubt, bound to provide for the safety of his servant in the course of his employment, to the best of the judgment, information, and belief'. This suggests that there may be an obligation on the employer quite apart from vicarious liability.

6   Fault or strict liability?

There is no suggestion of an absolute duty to provide either a safe workplace or safe working arrangements. The propositions about the vicarious liability of the employer assume that such liability would only arise in relation to the 'consequences of the *negligence*' of those named in the examples. The judge's concern on this matter was exactly that the employer might be responsible for the wrongdoings of these people, even though he, the employer, might not personally be at fault. That is the employer might be strictly liable for the wrongdoing of others. This indeed, is the nature of vicarious liability today.

7   The personal responsibility of the employer

This is also addressed in terms of fault (negligence) rather than strict liability. It is said that the master cannot be required to take more care of the servant than he may be expected to take of himself.

8   Personal responsibility of the employee

The judgment imposes a considerable responsibility on the employee personally. It is said that he may decline dangerous work. It also says that he is possibly better placed than the employer to evaluate the dangers (it suggests that this may be because the employee is on the spot, while the employer may be elsewhere). It concludes that the employee has a duty towards the employer, as well as towards himself, to ensure that the task is done safely, so that the employer's interests do not suffer.

(b) Developments after *Priestley v Fowler*

While the themes identified in *Priestley v Fowler* recur throughout the history of this branch of the law, their development in the nineteenth century did not assist the victims of industrial accidents to obtain compensation.

1   Employers' and public liability

The relationship between employer and employee imposed upon the employer responsibilities of a different order from those in relation to other persons:

(a) duty based on contract – the employer's duty to take reasonable care for the safety of the employee was said to be implied in the contract of employment. It was not necessarily implied in other contracts;

(b) common employment – the employer was not vicariously liable for an employee's wrongdoings which caused personal injury to another of his employees: the employer was so liable if the victim was a member of the general public or a worker other than one employed by him.

2 Employee's acceptance of risk

The doctrine of common employment was justified on the basis that the employee had, when entering the contract of employment, accepted the risk of injury by other workers employed by the employer. A further development of the same argument was that, by accepting the work and continuing in the employment in the knowledge that there were risks involved, the employee accepted the risks and could not claim damages from the employer if injury were suffered. The employee could be deemed to have accepted risks that a careful employer might have removed.

3 Employer's duty was to take care

The employer's duty was not a strict one: it was only to exercise reasonable care. However, because of the emphasis placed upon the employee's acceptance of risk there were relatively few occasions on which a court had to decide whether the employer had shown care. Moreover, when technology was primitive and scientific knowledge was limited conditions which would be totally unacceptable today might be regarded as quite normal.

(c) Signs of change

As the nineteenth century entered its final decade there were signs of change:

(i) the notion that the employee accepted risks of which he was aware was reviewed by the House of Lords;

(ii) the concept of civil liability for breach of statutory duty was introduced by the Court of Appeal;

(iii) a form of strict liability for income maintenance was introduced by Parliament.

(i) Knowledge of risk is not necessarily acceptance of it

In the important case of *Joseph Smith (Pauper) v Charles Baker & Sons* (see below) the House of Lords had to consider whether the worker, who was the victim of an industrial accident, was barred from bringing a civil action for damages to compensate him on the ground that he had continued to work for the employer even though he was aware of the risk which was to cause his accident. The issue was whether the employers could raise the employee's acceptance of the risk as a defence. Such a defence was known as *volenti non fit injuria*, loosely translated as 'Assumption of Risk'. A majority of their Lordships found that the mere fact that a worker had knowledge of the risk did not mean that he had accepted it. The principle laid down in this case has never been challenged; later cases have been concerned with whether the victim both knew of *and* accepted the risk.

JOSEPH SMITH (PAUPER) v
CHARLES BAKER & SONS [1891] AC 325

The following extract is taken from the judgment of Lord Halsbury LC, beginning at p 334:

> ... The action was an action in which the plaintiff sued his employers for injuries sustained while in the course of working in their employment. He was employed in working at a drill while two other fellow-workmen were engaged in striking with a hammer at the drill, which he was employed to hold in the proper position. The nature of the employment was one which involved his attention being fixed upon the drill that it might be held in the proper position when receiving alternative strokes from the hammers wielded by his fellow workmen. The place where he was employed was in a cutting, and in his immediate proximity another set of workmen were engaged in working in the cutting and taking stones out of it. For the purpose of this operation a steam crane was used, and occasionally, though not invariably, the stones lifted by the crane were swung over the place where the plaintiff was employed, and on the occasion which gave rise to the action a stone was swung over the plaintiff, and from some cause not explained and not attempted to be explained, the stone slipped from the crane, fell upon the plaintiff, and did him serious injury.
>
> ...
>
> The objection raised, and the only objection raised, to the plaintiff's right to recover was that he had voluntarily undertaken the risk. That is the question, and the only question, which any of the courts, except the county court itself had jurisdiction to deal with. Now, the facts upon which that question depends are given by the plaintiff himself in his evidence. Speaking of the operation of slinging the stones over the heads of the workmen, he said himself that it was not safe, and that whenever he had sufficient warning, or saw it, he got out of the way. The ganger told the workmen employed to get out of the way of the stones which were being slung. The plaintiff said he had been long enough at the work to know that it was dangerous, and another fellow workman in his hearing complained that it was a dangerous practice.
>
> ...
>
> My Lords, I am of opinion that the application of the maxim 'Volenti non fit injuria' is not warranted by these facts. I do not think the plaintiff did consent at all. His attention was fixed upon a drill and while, therefore, he was unable to take precautions himself, a stone was negligently slung over his head without due precautions against its being permitted to fall. My Lords, I emphasise the word 'negligently' here, because with all respect, some of the judgments below appear to me to alternate between the question whether the plaintiff consented to the risk, and the question of whether there was any evidence of negligence to go to the jury, without definitely relying on either proposition.
>
> ...
>
> It appears to me that the proposition upon which the defendants must rely must be a far wider one than is involved in the maxim Volenti non fit injuria. I think they must go to the extent of saying that, wherever a person knows there

is a risk of injury to himself, he debars himself from any right of complaint if an injury should happen to him in doing anything which involves that risk. For this purpose, and in order to test this proposition, we have nothing to do with the relation of employer and employed. The maxim in its application in the law is not so limited; but where it applies, it applies equally to a stranger as to anyone else; and if applicable to the extent that is now insisted on, no person ever ought to have been awarded damages for being run over in London streets; for no one (at all events some years ago before the admirable police regulations of later years) could have crossed London streets without knowing that there was a risk of being run over.

It is, of course, impossible to maintain a proposition so wide as is involved in the example I have just given; and in both *Thomas v Quartermaine* (1887)[1] and in *Yarmouth v France* (1887),[2] it has been taken for granted that mere knowledge of the risk does not necessarily involve consent to the risk. Bowen LJ carefully points out in the earlier case (*Thomas v Quartermaine*) that the maxim is not '*Scienti non fit injuria*', but '*Volenti non fit injuria*'. And Lindley LJ, in quoting Bowen LJ's distinction with approval, adds: 'The question in each case must be, not simply whether the plaintiff knew of the risk, but whether the circumstances are such as necessarily to lead to the conclusion that the whole risk was voluntarily incurred by the plaintiff.' And again, Lindley LJ says: 'If, in any case, it can be shown as a fact that a workman agreed to incur a particular danger, or voluntarily exposed himself to it, and was thereby injured, he cannot hold his master liable. But in the cases mentioned in the Act,[3] a workman who never in fact engaged to incur a particular danger, but who finds himself exposed to it and complains of it, cannot in my opinion, be held, as a matter of law, to have impliedly agreed to incur that danger or to have voluntarily incurred it, because he does not refuse to face it.' Again, Lindley LJ says: 'If nothing more is proved than that the workman saw danger, reported it, but, on being told to go on, went on as before in order to avoid dismissal, a jury may, in my opinion, properly find that he had not agreed to take the risk and had not acted voluntarily in the sense of having taken the risk upon himself.'

I am of the opinion myself, that in order to defeat a plaintiff's right by the application of the maxim relied on, who would otherwise be entitled to recover, the jury ought to be able to affirm that he consented to the particular thing being done which would involve the risk, and consented to take the risk upon himself. It is manifest that if the proposition which I have just enunciated be applied to this case, the maxim could here have no application. So far from consenting, the plaintiff did not even know of the particular operation that was being performed over his head until the injury happened to him and consent, therefore, was out of the question ...

— — —

---

1   18 QBD 685.
2   19 QBD 647.
3   Employers' Liability Act 1880.

(ii) Breach of statutory duty may create civil liability

Nineteenth century regulatory legislation, such as the Factories Acts, which required persons, such as employers, to comply with safety standards, normally provided for criminal sanctions to be imposed on those who failed to meet the required standards. Towards the end of the century the courts decided that those who suffered injury as the result of a failure to comply with standards imposed for their protection might use the statutory provision as the basis on which to found civil liability.

The principle thus allowed has remained part of the law up until this day, though it will in due course be seen that it has not always been accepted without dispute and in every case there may be questions as to whether the principle is applicable in relation to the particular statute relied upon. The principle was very helpful to accident victims at a time when the common law of negligence had yet to be developed. The following case is usually regarded as the origin of the principle:

GROVES v WIMBORNE (LORD) [1898] 2 QB 402

The action was to recover damages for an alleged breach by the defendant of the statutory duty imposed upon him by s 6 of the Factory and Workshop Act 1878, in allowing certain dangerous machinery to be and remain unfenced, causing the worker to suffer personal injury. The worker was a boy employed by the defendant at Dowlais Iron Works. Among the machinery in the works was a steam winch, at which the victim was employed. The winch had revolving cogwheels that, if unfenced, were dangerous to a person working the winch. There was evidence that there had originally been a guard to these cogwheels, but it had been removed and there had been no guard throughout the six months of the victim's employment. The victim's right arm was caught by the cogwheels and was so badly injured that the forearm had to be amputated.

The judge held that an action would not lie for breach of the statutory duty imposed by s 6, but the damages were provisionally assessed at the sum of £150. The judge entered judgment for the defendant and the victim appealed. The following extracts are from the judgment of AL Smith LJ, given in the Court of Appeal, beginning at p 406 of the report:

> In this case the plaintiff sues the defendant, who is the occupier of the Dowlais Iron Works, for breach of a duty to fence certain machinery imposed upon him as such occupier by the Factory and Workshop Act 1878, by reason of which breach of duty the plaintiff sustained personal injuries. The learned judge at the trial gave judgment for the defendant, being of opinion that no action lay for the breach of duty alleged by the plaintiff ... The Act now in question, as I have said was clearly passed in favour of workers employed in factories and workshops and to compel their employers to perform certain statutory duties for their protection and benefit. It is to be observed in the first place that under the provisions of s 82 not a penny of the fine necessarily goes to the person

injured or his family. The provision is only that the whole or any part of it may be applied for the benefit of the injured person or his family, or otherwise, as a secretary of state determines. Again, if proceedings for the fine are taken before magistrates, upon what consideration are they to act in determining the amount of the fine? One matter to be considered clearly would be the character of the neglect to fence. This neglect might be either of a serious or of a venial character. Suppose that it was of the latter character, but a person was unfortunately killed or injured in consequence of it. What fine are the magistrates to impose? Are they to impose a fine of the same amount as if it were a flagrant case of neglect to fence? The first thing one would say that they would have to consider would be whether the offence was of a grave character or otherwise. It may be said that in determining the amount of the fine the character of the injury sustained by the workman would be considered, but I am not sure that is the meaning of the section. It seems to me that the fine is inflicted by way of punishment of the employer for the neglect of the duty imposed by the Act and must be proportionate to the character of the offence. This consideration and the fact that whatever penalty the magistrates inflict does not necessarily go to the injured workman or his family lead me to the conclusion that it cannot have been the intention of the Legislature that the provision which imposes upon the employer a fine as a punishment for neglect of his statutory duty should take away the *prima facie* right of the workman to be fully compensated for injury occasioned to him by that neglect. Another observation which makes the matter still clearer arises from the fact that, having regard to the provisions of s 87, it may not be the employer, presumably a person of means and capable of paying a substantial fine, who would have to pay the fine. Under that section the employer may be exempted from the penalty and the fine may be imposed upon the actual offender, who may be a workman employed at weekly wages; and yet it is said that a fine payable by such a person is the only remedy given by the statute to the injured workman for breach by the occupier of the imperative statutory duty. I cannot read this statute in the manner in which it is sought to be read by the defendant. I think that s 5 does give to the workman a right of action upon the statute for injury caused by a breach of the statutory duty thereby imposed, and that he is not relegated to the provisions for the imposition of a fine on the employer, or it may be a workman, as his sole remedy.

– – –

(iii) Strict liability for income maintenance

In the second half of the nineteenth century the industrial accident victim was entirely dependent on the outcome of common law litigation for compensation. Apart from this there was only charity: there was no State social security system.

Awards made as the result of successful litigation then, as now, took the form of damages. There are normally two elements in awards of damages: there is the general, or unliquidated element and the special damages. The general damages are described as unliquidated because it falls to the court to put a monetary value on the injury. The special damages are to compensate for the more readily quantifiable loss for which the victim can 'bill' the defendant: if the victim has received no wages during a period of sickness, and had no other substitute income (for example, sick pay) this is likely to be a major element in this part of the claim. If the victim has income support during incapacity the defendant's liability will be that much the less, always assuming that there is no mechanism for ensuring that the defendant reimburse the body which has provided income support. It is therefore possible to argue that income support systems are undesirable because they can reduce the cost of the accident to the defendant. Such an argument, however, emphasises the penal role of compensation law while paying insufficient attention to the paramount need to provide for the victim.

The Workmen's Compensation Act 1897 was the first legislative attempt to provide a system of income maintenance at least for certain categories of the victims of industrial injury.

WORKMEN'S COMPENSATION ACT 1897

Chapter 37

An Act to amend the Law with respect to Compensation to Workmen for Accidental Injuries suffered in the course of their Employment (6 August 1897).

Section 1

Liability of employers

(1) If in any employment to which this Act applies personal injury by accident arising out of and in the course of the employment is caused to a workman, his employer shall, subject as herein-after mentioned, be liable to pay compensation in accordance with the First Schedule of this Act.

(2) Provided that–

(a) The employer shall not be liable under this Act in respect of any injury which does not disable the workman for a period of at least two weeks from earning full wages at the work at which he was employed;

(b) When the injury was caused by the personal negligence or wilful act of the employer, or of some person for whose act or default the employer is responsible, nothing in this Act shall affect any civil liability of the employer, but in that case the workman may, at his option, either claim compensation under this Act, or take the same proceedings as were open to him before the commencement of this Act; but the employer shall not be liable to pay compensation for injury to a workman by accident arising out of and in the course of the employment both independently of and also under this Act, and shall not be liable to any proceedings independently of this Act, except in case of such personal negligence or wilful act as aforesaid;

(c) If it is proved that the injury to a workman is attributable to the serious and wilful misconduct of that workman, any compensation claimed in respect of that injury shall be disallowed.

– – –

1897–1948

Within the period covered by the Workmen's Compensation Acts the accident victim had, as the extract above indicates, to elect between a common law action for damages and a claim for income maintenance under these Acts. The original legislation was amended from time to time, and later amendments brought prescribed industrial diseases within the scheme. A prescribed industrial disease being a disease identified as a risk in certain types of employment. In order to make a successful claim, the victim had to have contracted the disease and have worked in a type of employment for which the disease was recognised. The victim did not have to establish that the injury was caused by the fault of the employer in order to qualify for payments, so although payments were relatively small the lower burden of proof on the victim and relatively cheap claims procedures made it more attractive to the victim to claim compensation under the scheme than to sue for damages at common law. In some ways the scheme was more favourable to the worker than the State industrial injuries scheme which succeeded it in 1948, for the worker did not have to contribute to it. On the other hand, there was, for most employers, no requirement to insure against accident claims and so workers could not be confident that the funds would be available to provide payments to which the scheme entitled them.

Towards the end of the period there were important developments in common law liability. There were two especially important developments brought about by House of Lords in appeal cases. These cases remain of significance to industrial accident compensation law:

- *The emergence of principles of liability for negligence*
- *The re-assertion of the employer's personal duty to take care for the safety of employees*

(a) Liability for negligence

In the following case, which, at first sight, has more to do with product liability than with industrial injuries, the majority of the judges hearing the appeal to the House of Lords held that the manufacturer of an article of food, medicine or the like, which is put into circulation in circumstances where the consumer will be unable to discover, by inspection, any defect, is under a legal duty to the consumer to take reasonable care that the article is free from any defect likely to cause injury to the consumer. Two judgments are especially significant, that of Lord Atkin, which contains one of the most quoted statements in English civil law, and that of Lord Macmillan. In the account below Lord Macmillan's judgment (beginning at p 605) is cited first, because it sets out the facts of the case.

DONOGHUE v STEVENSON [1932] AC 562

Lord Macmillan:

> My Lords, the incident which in its legal bearings your Lordships are called upon to consider in this appeal was in itself of a trivial character, though the consequences to the appellant, as she describes them, were serious enough. It appears from the appellant's allegations that, on an evening in August 1928, she and a friend visited a café in Paisley, where her friend ordered for her some ice cream and a bottle of ginger beer. These were supplied by the shopkeeper, who opened the ginger beer bottle and poured some of the contents over the ice cream, which was contained in a tumbler. The appellant drank part of the mixture and her friend then proceeded to pour the remaining contents of the bottle into the tumbler. As she was doing so a decomposed snail floated out with the ginger beer. In consequence of her having drunk part of the contaminated contents of the bottle the appellant alleges that she contracted a serious illness. The bottle is stated to have been of dark opaque glass, so that the condition of the contents could not be ascertained by inspection, and to have been closed with a metal cap, while on the side was a label bearing the name of the respondent, who was the manufacturer of the ginger beer of which the shopkeeper was merely the retailer.

> The allegations of negligence[4] on which the appellant founds her action against the respondent may be shortly summarised. She says that the ginger beer was manufactured by the respondent for sale as an article of drink to members of the public, including herself; that the presence of a decomposing snail in ginger beer renders the ginger beer harmful and dangerous to those consuming it; and that it was the duty of the respondent to exercise his process of manufacture with sufficient care to prevent snails getting into or remaining in the bottles which he filled with ginger beer. The appellant attacks the respondent's system of conducting his business, alleging that he kept his bottles in premises to which snails had access, and that he failed to have his bottles properly inspected for the presence of foreign matter before he filled them.

> ...

> Having regard to the inconclusive state of the authorities in the courts below and to the fact that the important question involved is now before your Lordships for the first time, I think it desirable to consider the matter from the point of view of the principles applicable to this branch of law which are admittedly common to both English and Scottish jurisprudence.

> The law takes no cognisance of carelessness in the abstract. It concerns itself with carelessness only where there is a duty to take care and where failure in that duty has caused damage. In such circumstances carelessness assumes the

---

4   The case concerned the question of whether there would be a legal duty if the facts were as the appellant alleged: it was never established as a matter of evidence whether the snail was in the ginger beer bottle and it got there through the respondent's negligent conduct. Towards the end of the judgment Lord Macmillan alluded to the burden of proof, which remained with the appellant and which she would have to discharge before she could obtain damages.

legal quality of negligence and entails the consequences in law of negligence. What, then, are the circumstances which give rise to this duty to take care? In the daily contacts of social and business life, human beings are thrown into, or place themselves in, an infinite variety of relations with their fellows; and the law can refer only to the standards of the reasonable man in order to determine whether any particular relation gives rise to a duty to take care as between those who stand in that relation to each other. The grounds of action may be as various and manifold as human errancy, and the conception of legal responsibility may develop in adaptation to altering social conditions and standards. The criterion of judgment must adjust and adapt itself to the changing circumstances of life. The categories of negligence are never closed. The cardinal principle of liability is that the party complained of should owe to the party complaining a duty to take care and that the party complaining should be able to prove that he has suffered damage in consequence of a breach of that duty. Where there is room for diversity of view, it is in determining what circumstances will establish such a relationship between the parties as to give rise, on the one side, to a duty to take care, and on the other side, to a right to have care taken.

No account of this case would be adequate if it did not include the following extract from Lord Atkin's judgment, beginning at p 579:

... my own research, such as it is, satisfies me that the principles of the law of Scotland on such a question as the present are identical with those of English law; and I discuss the issue on that footing. The law of both countries appears to be that in order to support an action for damages for negligence the complainant has to show that he has been injured by the breach of a duty owed to him in the circumstances by the defendant to take reasonable care to avoid such injury. In the present case we are not concerned with the breach of the duty; if a duty exists, that would be a question of fact which is sufficiently averred and for present purposes must be assumed. We are solely concerned with the question whether, as a matter of law in the circumstances alleged, the defender owed any duty to the pursuer to take care.

...

The liability for negligence, whether you style it such or treat is as in other systems as a species of *culpa*, is no doubt, based upon a general public sentiment of moral wrongdoing for which the offender must pay. But acts or omissions which any moral code would censure cannot in a practical world be treated so as to give a right to every person injured by them to demand relief. In this way rules of law arise which limit the range of complainants and the extent of their remedy. The rule that you are to love your neighbour becomes, in law, you must not injure your neighbour; and the lawyer's question, Who is my neighbour? receives a restricted reply. You must take reasonable care to avoid acts or omissions which you can reasonably foresee would be likely to injure your neighbour. Who, then, in law is my neighbour? The answer seems to be – persons who are so closely and directly affected by my act that I ought reasonably to have them in contemplation as being so affected when I am directing my mind to the acts or omissions which are called in question.

The effect of this case was to establish a general concept of liability for negligent conduct, a tort of negligence. Shortly afterwards, Lord Wright could say:

> In strict legal analysis, negligence means more than heedless or careless conduct, whether in omission or commission; it properly connotes the complex concept of duty, breach and damage thereby suffered by the person to whom the duty was owing [*Lochgelly Iron and Coal Co v M'Mullan*].[5]

The significance of the case for industrial injury litigation is that employers' liability (within Lord Macmillan's phraseology, a 'category of negligence') was brought within the general concept of negligence liability and so, as the way was opened for the expansion of liability of personal injury generally, industrial injuries were caught up in the general trend. It was also possible to consider other category relationships that might be found at the workplace. For example, the manufacturer's duty could apply equally to the worker using articles and substances in the course of work as to the consumer in the home or the restaurant.

(b) The employer's personal duty to employees

The doctrine of common employment was very inappropriate for work organisations in the twentieth century. If the employer was a corporation it had no personal capacity to do anything: the conduct of the employer's business was entirely dependent on human persons working for the organisation. The Employers' Liability Act 1880 had made slight inroads into the doctrine, but it continued to protect the employer from liability to a very large extent. In the following case the House of Lords avoided the consequences of the doctrine. Their Lordships found a personal duty on the employer, although the negligent conduct causing the accident was that of a qualified miner who was properly appointed as mine manager by an employer who lacked the statutory qualifications personally to operate the mine.

WILSONS AND CLYDE COAL CO LTD v ENGLISH [1938] AC 57

Lord Thankerton said, at p 62:

> The facts may be briefly stated as follows:

> The respondent, on the date in question, was employed underground on the work of repairing an airway leading off the Mine Jigger Brae, one of the main haulage roads. When he was proceeding, at the end of the day shift, between 1.30 pm and 2 pm, to the pit bottom by way of the Mine Jigger Brae, the haulage plant was put in motion and, before he could reach one of the manholes provided he was caught by a rake of hutches and crushed between it

---

5   [1934] AC 1 at p 25.

and the side of the road. The respondent's case was that the time fixed by the appellants for raising the day shift men up the pit was between 1.30 and 2 pm, and that it was a necessary part of a safe system of working that the haulage should be stopped on the main haulage roads during this period, and that this was in accordance with usual and recognised mining practices in Scotland. The appellants denied this averment and stated that there was an alternative road open for the respondent's return to the pit bottom, and that, in any event, he should have informed the man in charge of the haulage machinery, who was within easy call, of his emergence into the Mine Jigger Brae, and should not have proceeded along the Brae until he had ascertained that the haulage had stopped for the shift or arranged that he could safely proceed ...

Lord Wright said, at p 76:

The observations which I go on to make are directed to considering certain recent authorities in the Court of Appeal, which, it seems to me, contain propositions of law which contradict the settled authorities binding on this House in regard to the obligation of an employer towards his employees, to use the modern terminology ...

... In *Rudd's* case (1933),[6] the Court of Appeal ... held that the employers could escape liability by showing that they had appointed competent servants to see that the duty was fulfiled. This House held that, on the contrary, the statutory duty was personal to the employer, in this sense that he was bound to perform it by himself or by his servants. The same principle, in my opinion, applies to those fundamental obligations of a contract of employment which lie outside the doctrine of common employment and for the performance of which employers are absolutely responsible. When I use the word absolutely, I do not mean that employers warrant the adequacy of plant, or the competence of fellow-employees, or the propriety of the system of work. The obligation is fulfilled by the exercise of due care and skill. But it is not fulfilled by entrusting its fulfilment to employees, even though selected with due care and skill. The obligation is threefold – 'the provision of a competent staff of men, adequate material, and a proper system and effective supervision'; I repeat the statement of the duty by Lord M'Laren quoted with approval by Lord Shaw in *Black v Fife Coal Co* (1912)[7] and again approved in the *Lochgelly* (1934)[8] case. The rule has been stated so often that I hesitate to multiply authorities. What the Court of Appeal have said amounts to reducing the three heads of duty to one only – that is, to engage competent employees of the higher grades and then everything else may be left to them. If that is done, the employers, it seems, will be free from further responsibility. Those whom they have engaged, if chosen with due care and skill, may appoint any other employee, may deal with the provision of plant and material, may determine the system of work. However negligently they may act, and however dangerous the results of what they do may be to the workpeople, the employers on this view will be free from

---

6   *Rudd v Elder Dempster & Co* [1933] 1 KB 566.
7   [1912] AC 149, p 173.
8   [1934] AC 1.

liability. The employee will have no remedy against the employer. His only remedy will be against his fellow-employees, which will be difficult to establish and in all probability worthless.

The well established, but illogical, doctrine of common employment is certainly one not to be extended, and indeed has never in its long career been pushed so far as the Court of Appeal sought to push it ...

... I have chosen these few examples to show that the doctrine of common employment which was hinted at in connection with a butcher's cart and has roamed in its application to colliers, seamen, railwaymen, apprentices, chorus girls and, indeed every sphere of activity, has always distinguished between the employer's duty to the employee and the fellow-servant's duty to the employee. The rule is explained on the ground that the employee by his contract of employment agrees with his employer to assume the risk of his fellow-servant's negligence. The principle is stated, with little regard to reality or to modern ideas of economics or industrial conditions, to be that this particular risk is included in the agreed remuneration. The result is stated rather as a dogma to flow logically from the relation of master and servant. Notwithstanding repeated expressions of disapproval, the doctrine has survived, largely because of statutory remedies given to employees to minimise what to modern ideas appears to be its obvious injustice. But it has never been carried to the extremity of excluding all remedy against employers or all duty in the employers so long as they have exercised care in the selection of manager or foremen. It is difficult to see what that duty would mean in the case of an absentee or infant or inexpert employer, or what it would mean in the case of a great modern industrial concern. But in truth the employer's obligation, as it has been defined by this House, is personal to the employer, and one to be performed by the employer *per se* or *per alios*.

...

The extent of the employer's obligation has several times been stated by this House. Thus, in *Wilson v Merry and Cunningham* (1868)[9] Lord Cairns said: 'What the master is, in my opinion, bound to his servant to do, in the event of his not personally superintending and directing the work, is to select proper and competent persons to do so, and to furnish them with adequate materials and resources for the work.' To this must be added a third head – namely, to provide a proper system of working ...

– – –

After 1948

Following the end of the Second World War there were at least four important changes in the legal system which contributed to the encouragement of litigation for personal injuries in general and for injuries suffered at the workplace in particular:

---

9   [1868] LR 1 HL (Sc) 326, p 332.

1   The Law Reform (Contributory Negligence) Act 1945 made it possible for judges to make awards of damages to plaintiffs who had been in part responsible, by reason of their own negligence, for causing their injury: prior to this Act, if the plaintiff were at all negligent no damages could be awarded.

2   The National Insurance (Industrial Injuries) Act 1946 replaced the Workmen's Compensation Scheme with a State system of providing income maintenance for the victims of industrial accidents and prescribed industrial diseases. Employees shared responsibility with employers for contributing to the funding of this scheme. When the State scheme was brought into operation the plaintiff no longer had to choose between claiming income maintenance and suing for common law damages.

3   The Law Reform (Personal Injuries) Act 1948 abolished the doctrine of common employment.

4   A legal aid scheme was introduced to make better provision for assisting those who could not afford the costs of litigation.

In this new climate the tort of negligence and the rules relating to compensation for breach of statutory duty were tested and developed. The body of law that has emerged will be considered in the following chapters.

CHAPTER 3

THE FRAMEWORK OF CIVIL LIABILITY TODAY

It has been noted that from the very first case a number of fundamental issues were discernible as to the framework of civil liability. These issues have retained their importance throughout the long development of liability for personal injuries. They are of relevance to both common law liability and liability for breach of statutory duty. In this chapter consideration will be given to the way in which they impact on compensation law today, under the following headings:

(a) strict or fault liability?
(b) is there a distinction between employers' and public liability?
(c) where are the boundaries of organisational responsibility?
(d) the relevance of insurance.

I STRICT OR FAULT LIABILITY?

In the Report of the Pearson Commission it is stated:

No-fault as a novelty

176 Secondly, we have found a widespread ignorance of the fact that in this country we already have a considerable element of no-fault provisions. Many witnesses urged the introduction of no-fault schemes, either for particular categories of injury or for all injuries, as though this would be a complete novelty. It is true that what was generally envisaged was a scheme which would replace or at least substantially modify, tort, but the advocates of no-fault schemes did not appear to recognise that we have had no-fault provision on quite a considerable scale since the 1897 Workmen's Compensation Act. Now, as well as the contributory benefits of the social security scheme, we have non contributory benefits available to disabled people, the medical benefits of the National Health Service, and local authority social services provision of various kinds.[1]

The Commission used 'no-fault liability' as synonymous with 'strict liability' or even 'absolute liability'. What they were considering was the principle of insurance, albeit state operated. What has to be considered here is the standard or standards imposed by the common law in litigation. This chapter is not concerned with entitlement under the social security system.

---

1   Royal Commission on Civil Liability and Compensation for Personal Injury, Vol 1, p 46.

The fundamental rule of both civil and criminal law is that the party who makes an allegation of wrongdoing (that is, the claimant in civil law and the prosecution in criminal law) has to bring evidence to prove that allegation. The question is: How heavy is the burden of proof which has to be discharged in order to prove the allegation? The burden of proof will depend on the nature of the liability. Broadly, liability, criminal or civil might be:

(a) absolute – That is a person has to ensure that a goal is achieved or a state of affairs maintained and is liable if the stipulated state of affairs did not exist without any room for consideration of why this might be. English law very rarely imposes absolute liability;

(b) strict – That is a case is made out as soon as it is shown that the required standard has not been achieved: the burden of proof then shifts to the alleged wrongdoer to establish a defence by proving the existence of circumstances which satisfy the court that liability should not be imposed;

(c) fault liability – The alleged wrongdoer will not be liable unless the person making the allegation can satisfy the court both that the party concerned has brought about the wrongful state of affairs and that the situation occurred because of the wrongful conduct of that party. In civil law the proscribed behaviour is negligent conduct. Whether the defendant has been negligent is considered objectively: the court is not concerned with the defendant's state of mind – it is only concerned with how reasonable people would evaluate the defendant's conduct.

Common law favours fault liability

In civil law, common law liability for causing personal injury tends to be fault liability. Only two areas of liability are at all relevant, ie, the torts of negligence and battery. There are few industrial injury cases in which the allegation is that the defendant intended to attack the claimant; in practice therefore only the tort of negligence is relevant. The courts have discouraged plaintiffs from seeking to rely on any other tort than negligence where injury is accidentally rather than wilfully inflicted. The matter is well stated by Lord Macmillan at p 170 in the following case.

READ v J LYONS & CO LTD [1947] AC 156

My Lords, nothing could be simpler than the facts in this appeal; nothing more far-reaching than the discussion of fundamental legal principles to which it has given rise. The appellant, while employed as an inspector by the Ministry of Supply at the Elstow Ordnance Factory in Bedfordshire, where the respondents were engaged in the manufacture of high explosive shells for the government, was injured by an explosion in the filling shop. She sued the respondents for damages. In her statement of claim she made no allegation of negligence on the part of the respondents. All that she averred was that the respondents were engaged in the manufacture of high explosive shells in premises occupied by them, that the respondents knew that high explosive shells were dangerous things and that while she was on their premises in the course of her duties a high explosive shell exploded and caused her injury. For aught that appears the explosion may have been a pure accident for which no one was to blame. The trial judge (Cassels J) found for the appellant.

...

In my opinion the appellant's statement of claim discloses no ground of action against the respondents. The action is one of damages for personal injuries. Whatever may have been the law of England in early times I am of the opinion that as the law now stands an allegation of negligence is in general essential to the relevancy of an action of reparation for personal injuries.

...

The appellant in her printed case in this House thus poses the question to be determined: 'Whether the manufacturer of high explosive shells is under strict liability to prevent such shells from exploding and causing harm to persons on the premises where such manufacture is carried on as well as to persons outside such premises.' Two points arise on this statement of the question. In the first place the expression 'strict liability', though borrowed from authority, is ambiguous. If it means the absolute liability of an insurer irrespective of negligence then the answer in my opinion must be in the negative. If it means that an exacting standard of care is incumbent on manufacturers of explosive shells to prevent the occurrence of accidents causing personal injuries I should answer the question in the affirmative, but this will not avail the appellant.

...

The sound view, in my opinion, is that the law in all cases exacts a degree of care commensurate with the risk created. It was suggested that some operations are so intrinsically dangerous that no degree of care however scrupulous can prevent the occurrence of accidents and that those who choose for their own ends to carry on such operations ought to be held to do so at their peril. If this were so, many industries would have a serious liability imposed on them. Should it be thought that this is a reasonable liability to impose in the public interest it is for Parliament so to enact. In my opinion it is not the present law of England.

...

– – –

Vicarious liability

The principle of vicarious liability (described below) which enables an accident victim to sue a wrongdoer's employer provides a major exception to the general rule of 'no liability without fault'. This means a faultless employer can be required to pay for the wrongdoings of an employee.

Statutory criteria

Where civil actions are brought for breach of statutory duty the claimant has to establish that the statutory duty has been broken. The claimant has, therefore, to satisfy the court that the defendant has failed to achieve the standard required by the particular statutory duty. Traditionally many statutory duties have, in criminal law, imposed strict liability. A much litigated statutory provision was s 14(1) of the Factories Act 1961, which provided that:

> Every dangerous part of any machinery, other than prime movers and transmission machinery, shall be securely fenced unless it is in such a position or of such construction as to be as safe to every person employed or working on the premises as it would be if securely fenced.

In criminal law this provision was deemed to impose strict liability on the occupier of the factory to ensure that dangerous machinery was properly guarded. Once the prosecution established that the machinery was both dangerous and unguarded the case against the accused was made out and the accused was guilty unless able to establish an available defence. However the duty was deemed strict, rather than absolute, both because there were limited possibilities of raising a defence and because the courts held that a situation would not be deemed dangerous if the possibility of personal injury was not foreseeable. Strict liability applied also in the civil courts, though in this instance, there was more possibility of the defendant establishing a defence; for example, the claimant might have been contributorily negligent.

Section 14 of the Factories Act was repealed in 1992. However, regulation 11 of the Provision and Use of Workplace Equipment Regulations 1998 imposes on every employer a similar strict duty to ensure the safety of machinery. Like its predecessor s 14 of the 1961 Act this regulation can be relied on in civil litigation.

Today criminal law duties are often expressed as obligations to do what is reasonably practicable to achieve a safe situation. Where such duties can be litigated in the civil courts (the general duties under the Health and Safety at Work Act 1974 cannot be so used) they have traditionally been treated as imposing strict liability subject to the defence that it was not reasonably practicable to do more than the defendant had done to make the situation safe. However there is now some authority that in *criminal law* such duties are absolute subject to the defence of reasonable practicability. That is to say the defendant may have to prove that the hazard was not foreseeable, rather than the prosecution having to establish that it was foreseeable. It is not clear whether the same approach will apply in civil cases. The situation in *criminal law* is addressed in the judgment of Lord Goff in the following case at p 1089:

MAILER v AUSTIN ROVER GROUP PLC [1989] 2 All ER 1087

... The case is concerned with the construction of s 4(2) of the Health and Safety at Work Act 1974 ...

Section 4(2) makes provision, therefore, for the duty of a person who has, to any extent, control of the relevant premises or of the relevant plant or substance. That duty is defined in a passage, three parts of which have been the subject of discussion before your Lordships. These may be segregated as follows (my emphasis):

1   *to take such measures as it is reasonable for a person in his position to take to ensure;*

2   *so far as is reasonably practicable;*

3   *that the relevant premises, plant or substance is or are safe and without risks to health.*

...

I find it convenient to consider first the third expression 'safe and without risks to health'. Counsel for the respondents submitted that, for present purposes, premises should be regarded as 'safe and without risks to health' if they are in such condition as to be unlikely to be the cause of injury, harm or risk to health to persons who are, or who may reasonably be expected to be, in them. This interpretation he derived from certain authorities concerned with the construction of s 14(1) of the Factories Act 1937 (now s 14(1) of the Factories Act 1961), which requires that dangerous parts of machinery shall be securely fenced. In a series of leading cases it has become established that, for the purposes of that subsection, machinery is to be regarded as dangerous if it is a reasonably foreseeable cause of injury to anybody acting in a way in which a human being may be reasonably expected to act in circumstances which may be reasonably expected to occur: see *Hindle v Birtwistle* (1897),[2] *John Summers & Sons Ltd v Frost* (1955)[3] and *Close v Steel Co of Wales Ltd* (1961).[4] Furthermore, in *Allen v Avon Rubber Co Ltd* (1986)[5] the definition of 'dangerous' in the foregoing cases was invoked by the Court of Appeal for the purpose of interpreting the word 'safe' in s 29(1) of the 1961 Act, which provides as follows:

'There shall, so far as if reasonably practicable, be provided and maintained safe means of access to every place at which any person has at any time to work, and every such place shall, so far as is reasonably practicable, be made and kept safe for any persons working there.'

Stocker LJ, with whose judgment the other members of the court agreed, expressed the opinion that, for the purpose of the appeal then before the court and probably in many, if not at all, other cases, this test seemed to be as apt in respect of a place of work as it was to the safety of the machine. Counsel for the respondents, very understandably, invoked *Allen v Avon Rubber Co Ltd* as authority for the proposition which he advanced before your Lordships.

---

2   [1897] 1 QB 192, pp 195–96; [1895–99] All ER Rep 175, p 177, *per* Wills J.
3   [1955] 1 All ER 870, p 882; [1955] AC 740, pp 765–66, *per* Lord Reid.
4   [1961] 2 All ER 953; [1962] AC 367.
5   [1986] ICR 695.

This proposition I am, however, unable to accept. To me, the words 'safe and without risks to health' mean, *prima facie*, what they say, though, no doubt, they have to be related to the use for which the relevant premises are made available. Take the example of premises which, owing to an unknown and indeed unforeseeable defect, are in fact unsafe for such use; or a substance which, unforeseeably possesses a characteristic which likewise renders it unsafe for such use. I do not for my part see how the unforeseeable nature of the defect or of the characteristic can nevertheless mean that the premises or the substance are safe. The duty is to take such measures as it is reasonable for a person in the position of the defendant to take to ensure, so far as is reasonably practicable, that the relevant premises or substance is or are safe. It may be that if the danger in question is not foreseeable, the defendant will not be held to have been in breach of his duty; but, if so, that will not be because, in the examples I have given, the premises or substance are to be regarded as safe, but because the qualified nature of the duty may not give rise to any liability in the particular circumstances. The cases concerned with the fencing of 'dangerous' machinery do not, in my opinion, provide any assistance. It was inevitable that a qualified meaning of the word 'dangerous' would have to be adopted in those cases, otherwise any part of any machinery which happened to cause injury would, if not fenced, give rise to liability. That was obviously not the intention of Parliament, and so the courts interpreted the word 'dangerous' in that context in the manner I have indicated.

...

It follows from the passages which I have quoted that, for the purpose of considering whether the defendant has discharged the onus which rests on him to establish that it was not reasonably practicable for him in the circumstances, to eliminate the relevant risk, there has to be taken into account, inter alia, the likelihood of that risk eventuating. The degree of likelihood is an important element in the equation. It follows that the effect is to bring into play foreseeability in the sense of likelihood of the incidence of the relevant risk, and that the likelihood of such risk eventuating has to be weighed against the means, including cost, necessary to eliminate it.

This is, in my opinion, an important matter to bear in mind when considering the meaning of the first group of words which I have segregated 'to take such measures as it is reasonable for a person in [the defendant's] position to take to ensure ...'. I have come to the conclusion that it is not a function of the word 'reasonable' in this passage to qualify the duty of the defendant with reference to reasonable foreseeability by him of the incidence of risk to safety. This is because the question of reasonable foreseeability, in the sense of likelihood, arises at a later stage, by the introduction of the qualifying words 'so far as is reasonably practicable', words which introduce a qualification to the duty of a strictly limited nature, in respect of which the onus of proof rests on the defendant. It must, in my opinion, be inconsistent with the limited nature of this qualification to read the previous words as qualifying the duty imposed on the defendant with reference to a broad criterion of reasonable foreseeability, because, where liability is imposed subject to the limited qualification 'so far as is reasonably practicable', the element of likelihood of the risk eventuating is taken account of in the balancing exercise involved in deciding whether or not it was reasonably practicable to ensure the safety of the premises for the relevant use ...

– – –

II EMPLOYERS' LIABILITY AND PUBLIC LIABILITY

It is arguable that the contract of employment creates a status relationship between employer (master) and employee (servant) because rights and duties flow automatically from the relationship, in a similar way to that in which marriage creates status rights and duties between husband and wife.

Historically occupational health and safety legislation has tended to impose duties for the protection of employees. In compensation law the employee was, following *Priestley v Fowler* (1837),[6] set apart from other accident victims because the contract of employment was said to contain an implied duty that the employer would take reasonable care for the safety of the employee. On the other hand the doctrine of common employment restricted the employer's liability to employees.

In the present context the term 'public liability' is used to cover liability to all persons other than employees: thus it is wide enough to cover persons such as customers or users of the highway, as well as persons who are working in a capacity other than as the employee of the particular employer. If a narrower approach is taken, and the comparison is between one class of worker and another, then workers may be categorised into those who work under a contract of employment (otherwise known as a contract of service) and those who are self-employed and may, from time to time, have a personal contract for services with a particular organisation (for example, for the maintenance of a piece of equipment). Incidentally, two employing organisations may enter into a contract for services under which one organisation agrees to deploy its employees to carry out a task for the other organisation. In fact when 'self-employed' workers enter into contracts for services they are holding themselves out as business organisations, rather than as individuals.

The idea that the employer has a special relationship with, and special responsibilities in respect of, employees is suited to a model of employment in which the worker is exclusively in the full time employment of one organisation over a long period of time, so that the worker becomes a part of that organisation. It is less well suited to part time or temporary employment. From the viewpoint of the twenty-first century, this model of employment relationships seems outdated, more suitable for the nineteenth century when, following the Industrial Revolution, many workers were employed in factories. Before this period, many workers were what would, in modern

---

6   (1837) 3 M&W 1.

terminology, be regarded as self-employed master craftsmen; and following the reduction of the manufacturing base of the British economy there has, in the last 10 years, been a move towards part time and temporary employment and an encouragement of small businesses under the control of the person who provides the labour on which the business depends. While the distinctions are less significant today, some understanding of history is necessary to appreciate the case law.

Judicial tests

Following the decision in *Yewens v Noakes* (1880)[7] the courts were constantly involved in developing tests by which servants might be identified in order to determine the rights and duties of the parties in dispute. Such disputes would normally, but not necessarily, be between an employer and a worker; they could, however, be between one of the parties to the employment contract and a government agency, such as the Inland Revenue or the Department of Social Security. In *Yewens v Noakes* (1880) Bramwell B stated that:[8]

> A servant is a person subject to the command of his master as to the manner in which he shall do his work.

While Bramwell B used the word 'command' it quickly became recognised that the essence of the relationship was the element of 'control' which the employer exercised, if not over the detailed execution of the work, then at least of the wider context in which the work was carried out. Nevertheless, the control test proved difficult to apply as organisations became larger and individual workers possessed skills which gave them such a high degree of professionalism that their employers might have difficulty in monitoring their execution of the tasks allotted to them.

The limitations of the control test caused the courts to seek alternative tests. Their task was not made easier because they were looking for a single formula which would serve equally for the wide range of situations for which it was needed to identify the employee; including industrial injury cases, regulatory legislation, vicarious liability, social security and liability to income tax. The modern law stems from the following case:

READY MIXED CONCRETE (SOUTH EAST) LTD v MINISTER OF PENSIONS AND NATIONAL INSURANCE [1968] 2 QB 497

This was a test case to determine whether lorry drivers contracted by the company to deliver their concrete had, by virtue of the terms of their contract become self-employed persons, or whether they were employees of the company. Their liability to make contributions under the National Insurance

---

7   [1880] 6 QBD 530.

8   *Ibid*, pp 532–33.

Act 1965 depended on whether they were employees. The written contract between the company and the drivers was long and complicated but central to the contract was that the driver agreed to work for the company as an owner-driver and entered into a contract for the carriage of concrete, and also into a hire purchase contract relating to the lorry in which the concrete was to be carried. McKenna J gave careful consideration to the terms of the contract and decided that the contract was such that the driver was not an employee. For present purposes what is important is the test which he adopted as a yardstick against which to measure the facts of the case. At p 515 he said:

I must now consider what is meant by a contract of service.

A contract of service exists if these three conditions are fulfilled:

(i) The servant agrees that, in consideration of a wage or other remuneration, he will provide his own work and skill in the performance of some service for his master.

(ii) He agrees, expressly or impliedly, that in the performance of that service he will be subject to the other's control in a sufficient degree to make that other master.

(iii) The other provisions of the contract are consistent with its being a contract of service.

I need say little about (i) and (ii).

As to (i) – there must be a wage or other remuneration. Otherwise, there will be no consideration, and without consideration no contract of any kind. The servant must be obliged to provide his own work and skill. Freedom to do a job either by one's own hands or by another's is inconsistent with a contract of service, though a limited or occasional power of delegation may not be: see Atiyah's *Vicarious Liability in the Law of Torts* (1967), pp 59–61 and the cases cited by him.

As to (ii) – Control includes the power of deciding the thing to be done, the way in which it shall be done, the means to be employed in doing it, the time when and the place where it shall be done. All these aspects of control must be considered in deciding whether the right exists in a sufficient degree to make one party the master and the other his servant. The right need not be unrestricted.

'What matters is lawful authority to command, so far as there is scope for it. And there must always be some room for it, if only in incidental or collateral matters' – *Zuijs v Wirth Brothers Proprietary Ltd* (1955).[9]

To find where the right resides one must look first to the express terms of the contract, and if they deal fully with the matter, one may look no further. If the contract does not expressly provide which party shall have the right, the question must be answered in the ordinary way by implication.

---

9   93 CLR 561.

The third and negative condition is for my purpose the important one and I shall try with the help of five examples to explain what I mean by provisions inconsistent with the nature of a contract of service:

(i) A contract obliges one party to build for the other, providing at his own expense the necessary plant and materials. This is not a contract of service, even though the builder may be obliged to use his own labour only and to accept a high degree of control: it is a building contract. It is not a contract to serve another for a wage, but a contract to produce a thing (or a result) for a price.

(ii) A contract obliges one party to carry another's goods, providing at his own expense everything needed for performance. This is not a contract of service, even though the carrier may be obliged to drive the vehicle himself and to accept the other's control over his performance: it is a contract of carriage.

(iii) A contract obliges a labourer to work for a builder, providing some simple tools, and to accept the builder's control. Notwithstanding the obligation to provide the tools, the contract is one of service. That obligation is not inconsistent with the nature of a contract of service. It is not a sufficiently important matter to affect the substance of the contract.

(iv) A contract obliges one party to work for the other, accepting his control, and to provide his own transport. This is still a contract of service. The obligation to provide his own transport does not affect the substance. Transport in this example is incidental to the main purpose of the contract. Transport in the second example was the essential part of the performance.

(v) The same instrument provides that one party shall work for the other subject to the other's control, and also that he shall sell him his land. The first part of the instrument is no less a contract of service because the second part imposes obligations of a different kind: *Amalgamated Engineering Union v Ministry of Pensions and National Insurance* (1963).[10]

Since this case there have been others which, in the main have been measuring the facts of the situation in dispute against the third of the conditions in McKenna's test. The rule broadly is that if the worker has capital equipment which is necessary to the performance of the contractual task then that worker is likely to be deemed to be running a business and have entered into a contract for services rather than a contract of service. Similarly if the worker is not to receive payment when 'resting' between one task and the next the contract is less likely to be a contract of employment, for in a contract of employment (except where the contract is for piecework) the employer usually bears the cost of the periods in which the worker is idle waiting for a task.

---

10 [1963] 1 WLR 441.

Declining importance of distinction

In the last 30 years it has become somewhat less important to distinguish the employees of the employer from other workers for the purposes of determining liability to compensate for industrial injury.

(i) The abolition of the doctrine of common employment

This removed one of the reasons for distinguishing the employee from other categories of accident victims: the disappearance of that doctrine took from the employer a large degree of protection from liability to employees injured while at work.

(ii) The weakening of the category approach

In *Donoghue v Stevenson* (1932)[11] Lord Macmillan had posited that 'The categories of negligence are never closed.' The case added another category (namely, manufacturers and consumers) to the relationships in which a duty of care might exist. This new category was comparable to the existing categories which included master and servant and occupier and visitor. Within this approach the personal duty of the master to the servant was different from the duty of the occupier to visitors and indeed the occupier's duty varied according to whether the visitor were an invitee or a licensee. The content of the duty was deemed to be a matter of law and could not therefore vary according to the evidence in a particular case. The employer's duty was spelt out in *Wilsons and Clyde Coal Co Ltd v English* (1938)[12] and other cases as being a duty to provide, *inter alia*, safe premises, safe plant and equipment and a safe system of work.

In occupiers' liability the invitee was someone whose presence on the premises was of benefit to the occupier: a licensee was someone whose presence the occupier did not invite but did tolerate. The occupier had a greater responsibility for the safety of the invitee than for that of the licensee. A visiting workman would normally be an invitee. At one time, since the occupier's liability was not protected by the doctrine of common employment, the visiting workman might be more likely to obtain compensation for an injury suffered on the occupier's premises than might the employee of the occupier. However, following the decision by the House of Lords in *London Graving Dock Co Ltd v Horton* (1951)[13] the visiting worker was less likely to succeed in a claim against the occupier because in that case their Lordships held that a visiting worker who continued to work knowing there was a hazardous situation would be deemed to have accepted the risk of any injury

---

11 [1932] AC 562.
12 [1938] AC 57.
13 [1951] AC 737.

arising from that hazard (in other words, the distinction between knowledge and acceptance of risk introduced in *Smith v Baker* (1891)[14] in favour of the employee was not extended to the visiting worker). After *Horton* visiting workers would often argue that they had temporarily (that is, *pro hac vice*) become the employees of the occupier of the premises until statute abolished the distinctions between the various categories of visitor:

OCCUPIERS' LIABILITY ACT 1957

Section 1

Preliminary

(1) The rules enacted by the two next following sections shall have effect, in place of the rules of the common law, to regulate the duty which an occupier of premises owes to his visitors in respect of dangers due to the state of the premises or to things done or omitted to be done on them.

...

Section 2

Extent of occupier's duty

(1) An occupier of premises owes the same duty, the 'common duty of care', to all his visitors ...

– – –

The simplification of the legal content of the occupiers' duty, by the abolition of categories of visitor, paved the way for the breakdown of the category system more generally. The matter was addressed by the Court of Appeal in the following case, an appeal by the defendants from a judgment delivered in a circuit court by Parker CJ.

SAVORY v HOLLAND, HANNEN AND CUBITTS (SOUTHERN) LTD [1964] 3 All ER 18

The defendants were contractors engaged to build a factory for another organisation. The contractors engaged sub-contractors (H) to blast rock. H sent the plaintiff, with equipment. The defendants were to supply five men, three of whom would be flagmen to give warning when blasting was to take place, but one of the flagmen was often missing so that the plaintiff had to act as a flagman. When he had to act as flagman, the plaintiff would light the fuse and then climb 12–15 ft up one of the banks of the excavation. One day in November, when the bank was muddy and slippery, the plaintiff, having acted as flagman, slipped and fell as he was going back down the bank and he suffered injury. He brought an action for damages against the defendants, claiming that he had, for the time being, become their servants. Diplock LJ said, at p 21:

---

14 [1891] AC 325.

I agree that this appeal be allowed. Before 1945, when the law of negligence was bedevilled by such unattractive doctrines as contributory negligence being a complete bar to recovery, as common employment and as the rigid rules as to the duties of care owed by occupiers to different categories of persons such as invitee, licensee and the like, there grew up a number of distinctions between the duty which one man owed to another man, based on particular legal categories into which each fell. Since those unattractive doctrines have one by one been abolished in 1945, 1948 and 1957, it seems to me that the law of negligence can now be put in the simple form in which Lord Somervell of Harrow suggested that it should be put in *Cavanagh v Ulster Weaving Co Ltd* (1959):[15] to exercise 'reasonable care in all the circumstances' is the duty which one man owed to another.

It seems to me that, in this case, Lord Parker CJ, founding himself, no doubt, on *O'Reilly v Imperial Chemical Industries Ltd* (1955)[16] which was one of those cited to him, regarded it as essential for the purposes of deciding the case, to determine whether or not the plaintiff occupied the position of a servant *pro hac vice*, whatever that means, *vis à vis* the defendants, because, as was stated by Jenkins LJ in *O'Reilly's* case:

'If there is here no relationship of master and servant ... then it seems to me that the plaintiff's case must necessarily fail. I decline to erect in cases of this kind a new duty which is neither the duty subsisting between invitor and invitee nor the duty arising from the relationship of employer and employee.'

I think that, with great respect, at any rate since the passing of the Occupiers' Liability Act 1957, and since the decision of the House of Lords in *Cavanagh v Ulster Weaving Co Ltd*, that is an incorrect approach to the question of negligence in a case like this. The question for the court is not whether the plaintiff was in the category of servant to the defendants *pro hac vice*. The only question is whether, in all the circumstances, the defendants used reasonable care for the safety of the plaintiff. The doctrine of master and servant *pro hac vice* today seems to me to be relevant only to a question of vicarious liability; it is a mere adjunct of the doctrine of *respondeat superior* for determining whether A is the superior of B. As my Lords have pointed out, Lord Parker CJ, taking the view that he did that, unless there was a master and servant relationship, there was no liability in this case, directed his mind to the question whether there was a master and servant relationship. For the reasons given by my lords, I agree that no such relationship, *pro hac* or any other *vice* was established in this case.

The question therefore arises whether or not a breach of the duty of reasonable care in all the circumstances has been established ... In fact, the allegation of negligence here on the facts comes down to the failure of the defendants' foreman to give some advice to the plaintiff. Warnings have already been given from the House of Lords as to not extending the nursemaid school of negligence. I would certainly not extend it in this case to a duty to advise someone who is the servant of an independent contractor. It being, I think,

---

15 [1959] 2 All ER 745.
16 [1955] 3 All ER 382.

open to this court to determine the matter, I have no hesitation in saying that, in my view, the plaintiff has not made out a case of lack of reasonable care in all the circumstances against the defendant.

– – –

The present position

The position today is that for the purposes of determining an organisation's responsibilities to provide for the safety of workers, the distinction between employees and other workers is less important than formerly, but it remains important:

(a) in determining what factually the defendant organisation has to do to discharge the duty of reasonable care; for example, it may not be necessary to train workers who are not employees;

(b) because statutory provisions may be for the protection of only one category of worker; for example, the employers' duty to insure, as set out in the Employers' Liability (Compulsory Insurance) Act 1969 is only a duty to insure against liability to employees;

(c) because employers are vicariously liable only for the wrongdoings of their own employees.

III THE BOUNDARIES OF ORGANISATIONAL RESPONSIBILITY

Personal liability

It has been noted that an organisation has both personal and vicarious liability. The personal responsibility of the organisation was described in *Wilsons and Clyde Coal Co Ltd v English* (1938) as a duty to take reasonable care to provide a safe system of work. *Wilsons'* case, and others identified detailed aspects of the duty and included the provision of competent staff, safe premises, plant and equipment. *Wilsons'* case made clear that the personal duty of the employer was quite distinct from the vicarious liability of the organisation for wrongdoings of employees.

Vicarious liability

At common law the rule is that the employer is vicariously liable for the wrongdoings (in effect, the torts) of the employee acting in the course of employment. This is sometimes known as *'respondeat superior'*; the employer is not vicariously liable for the torts of individual workers who are either not of the status of employee or are employed by another organisation. The employer will only be liable in relation to injuries caused by such people or organisations if the employer has been to some extent personally at fault.

The problems usually concern whether in relation to vicarious liability the actual wrongdoer was:

(a) the defendant's employee;

(b) acting in the course of the defendant's employment.

In relation to the employers' personal liability, the matter is nowadays generally a question of fact as to whether or not the organisation ought to have made provision for what has occurred. Some of the more interesting cases have been ones in which the argument has been that the organisation was personally at fault either for failing to give sufficient support to employees or for failing to ensure that persons, who were not the employees of that organisation, made a proper contribution to the organisation's system of operation.

(a) The defendants' employee?

The difficulties which the courts have experienced in trying to identify and apply tests for establishing whether a worker is employed under a contract of employment, and therefore has the status of employee, have already been discussed. The related problem of determining which of two organisations is the employer has also been alluded to in *Savory v Holland*. The leading case concerning which of two employers is employer of the particular employee, for the purposes of vicarious liability, is the following.

MERSEY DOCKS AND HARBOUR BOARD v COGGINS AND GRIFFITH (LIVERPOOL) LTD AND ANOTHER [1947] AC 1

A harbour authority let a mobile crane to a firm of stevedores. The authority supplied a driver with the crane. The driver was hired, paid and liable to be dismissed by the authority, but the contract between the authority and the stevedores stipulated that the driver supplied would be deemed to be the servant of the stevedores while carrying out the work under the contract. While carrying out the contract the driver caused personal injury to John McFarlane. It was accepted that the driver was a servant, not a self-employed person, and it was also accepted that the accident was due to his negligence. The only question was which of the two organisations should be held vicariously liable to the victim. The House had to consider an appeal by the general employer from a decision against them by the Court of Appeal. It was not suggested that there was any personal fault on the part of either of the organisations.

The following extracts are taken from the judgment of Viscount Simon, beginning at p 9:

My Lords, in this appeal the Mersey Docks and Harbour Board (hereinafter called the appellant board) against whom a plaintiff named John McFarlane has obtained judgment at Liverpool Assizes for £247 damages with costs on the ground of negligence in the working of a mobile crane belonging to the appellant board, seeks to have the judgment against the appellant board discharged and to have substituted for it a judgment in favour of McFarlane for the same amount against Coggins and Griffith (Liverpool) Ltd, the respondent company, who are master stevedores and who had hired from the appellant board the use of the crane, together with its driver, for the purpose of loading a ship called the *Port Chalmers* lying at the quay at the North Sandon Dock, Liverpool. The question in the case is, therefore, whether Newall, the driver of the crane, is to be regarded, for the purpose of McFarlane's claim, as employed by the appellant board or by the respondent company. Both the trial judge, Croom-Johnson J, and the Court of Appeal (Scott, du Parq and Morton LJJ) held that the appellant board was responsible to the plaintiff for Newall's negligence, but the appellant board contends that Newall was not at the time of the accident and for the purpose of the operation in which he was then engaged a servant of the appellant board but was the servant of the respondent company.

...

What has now to be decided is whether, in applying the doctrine of *respondeat superior*, liability attaches on these facts to the appellant board as the regular employers of Newall, or to the respondent company as the persons who were temporarily making use of the crane which Newall was driving. The appellant board had engaged Newall and it paid his wages: it alone had power to dismiss him. On the other hand, the respondent company had the immediate direction and control of the operations to be executed by the crane driver with his crane, eg, to pick up and move a piece of cargo from shed to ship. The respondent company, however, had no power to direct how the crane driver should work the crane. The manipulation of the controls was a matter for the driver himself. In the present case the accident happened because of the negligent way in which the crane driver worked his crane, and since the respondent company had no control over how he worked it, as distinguished from telling him what he was to do with the crane, it seems to me to follow that Newall's general employers must be liable for this negligence and not the hirers of the apparatus.

...

Even if there were an agreement between the appellant board and the respondent company that in the event of the appellant board being held liable for negligent driving of the crane while it is under hire to the latter, the latter will indemnify the appellant board, this would not in the least affect the right of the plaintiff to recover damages from the appellant board as long as the appellant board is properly to be regarded as the crane driver's employer. It is not disputed that the burden of proof rests on the general or permanent employer – in this case the appellant board – to shift the *prima facie* responsibility for the negligence of servants engaged and paid by such employer so that this burden in a particular case may come to rest on the hirer who for the time being has the advantage of the service rendered. And, in my opinion, this burden is a heavy one and can only be discharged in quite exceptional circumstances.

...

The Court of Appeal in this case, following its own decision in the case of *Nicholas v FJ Sparkes & Son* (1945)[17] applied a test it had formulated, where a vehicle is lent with its driver to a hirer, by propounding the question: 'In the doing of the negligent act was the workman exercising the discretion given him by his general employer, or was he obeying or discharging a specific order of the party for whom, upon his employer's direction, he was using the vehicle ...?' I would prefer to make the test turn on where the authority lies to direct, or to delegate to, the workman, the manner in which the vehicle is driven. It is this authority which determines who is the workman's 'superior'. In the ordinary case, the general employers exercise this authority by delegating to their workman discretion in method of driving, and so the Court of Appeal correctly points out that in this case the driver Newall, 'in doing of the negligent act was exercising his own discretion as driver – a discretion which had been vested in him by his regular employers when he was sent out with the vehicle – and he made a mistake with which the hirers had nothing to do'. If, however, the hirers intervene to give directions as to how to drive which they have no authority to give, and the driver *pro hac vice* complies with them, with the result that a third party is negligently damaged, the hirers may be liable as joint tortfeasors.

– – –

(b) When is the employee at work?

The employer is only vicariously liable for the wrongs which the employee commits when acting in the course of employment. This has led to many cases concerned with whether the employee's wrongdoing is actually in the course of employment. There are two problems which have especially concerned the courts:

(i) does doing something which is wrong, possibly even disobedient, take the employee outside of the employment?

(ii) does the employee remain within the employment when not directly employed in the task to which the contract of employment relates. For example, when travelling to and from the workplace or during a lunch break?

Modern case law has taken a somewhat broad approach to both these questions and tended to find, as a matter of fact, that the employee was in the course of employment.

17 [1945] KB 309.

(i) The disobedient employee

ROSE v PLENTY AND ANOTHER [1972] 1 WLR 141

A milkman was prohibited by his employer from taking children with him on his round in order to help him deliver milk and collect empty bottles. In spite of this prohibition, the milkman paid a child of 13 to help him. The child was injured as a result of the negligent driving of the milkman. The trial judge found that the milkman's employers were not vicariously liable for the milkman's negligence because in doing something he was prohibited to do he had ceased to be within the course of his employment. The majority of the Court of Appeal held that the employer should be vicariously liable. The following extracts are from the judgment of Lord Denning MR, beginning at p 142:

> Mr Plenty was a milk roundsman employed at Bristol by the Co-operative Retail Services Ltd. He started working for them at Easter 1970. There were notices up at the depot making it quite clear that the roundsmen were not allowed to take children on the vehicles. One notice said: 'Children and young persons *must not, in any circumstances, be employed by you* in the performance of your duties.' Both employers and trade union did their utmost to stop it. No doubt Mr Plenty knew it was not allowed. But in spite of all these warnings, the practice still persisted. Boys used to hang about the depot waiting to be taken on and some of the roundsmen used to take them.
>
> Soon after Mr Plenty started work as a milk roundsman a boy, Leslie Rose, who was just over 13, went up to Mr Plenty and asked if he could help him. Mr Plenty agreed to let him do it. The boy described his part in these words:
>
> 'I would jump out of the milk float, grab the milk, whatever had to go into the house, collect the money, if there was any there and bring the bottles back.'
>
> That is what he did. The milk roundsman paid the boy 6 shillings for the weekends and 4 shillings for the weekdays. While the boy was going round some houses the roundsman would go to others. On 21 June 1970, unfortunately, there was an accident. After going to one house, the boy jumped on to the milk float. He sat there with one foot dangling down so as to be able to jump off quickly. But at that time, the milk roundsman, I am afraid, drove carelessly and negligently. He went too close to the kerb. As the milk float went round the corner, the wheel caught the boy's leg. He tried to get his leg away, but he was dragged out of the milk float. His foot was broken with a compound fracture, but it was mended. So it was not very serious.
>
> Afterwards, he, by his father as his next friend, brought an action for damages against the roundsman and against his employers.
>
> ...
>
> In considering whether a prohibited act was within the course of the employment, it depends very much on the purpose for which it is done. If it is done for his employers' business, it is usually done in the course of his employment, even though it is a prohibited act ... In the present case it seems to me that the course of the milk roundsman's employment was to distribute the

milk, collect the money and to bring back the bottles to the van. He got or allowed this young boy to do part of that business which was the employers' business. It seems to me that although prohibited, it was conduct which was within the course of the employment; and on this ground I think the judge was in error. I agree it is a nice point in these cases on which side of the line the case falls; but, as I understand the authorities, this case falls within those in which the prohibition affects only the conduct within the sphere of the employment and did not take the conduct outside the sphere altogether. I would hold that the conduct of the roundsman was within the course of his employment and the masters are liable accordingly, and I would allow the appeal.

– – –

(ii) During working hours?

SMITH v STAGES AND ANOTHER [1989] 1 All ER 834

The case came before the House of Lords. It concerned an accident which occurred when one employee was in his own car, driving another employee home from work. The facts are fully stated in the following extracts from the judgment of Lord Goff, starting at p 835:

> My Lords, Mr Machin and the first defendant, Mr Stages, were employed by the second defendants, Darlington Insulation Co Ltd (the employers). The employers specialise in the insulation of pipes, boilers and power stations. Mr Machin and Mr Stages worked for them as laggers at power stations; they had both worked for the employers in that capacity for many years. In August 1977 they were members of a group of about 20 laggers, employed by the employers, working at Drakelow power station at Burton-on-Trent. At that time Mr Machin appears to have been living in Burton-on-Trent; it is not clear where Mr Stages was living. There was another job to be done at Pembroke power station. Mr Pye, the employers' contract manager, visited the power station at Pembroke to assess the job. It was urgent, and had to be completed by 29 August 1977. So, it was decided to withdraw Mr Machin and Mr Stages from Drakelow to do the job at Pembroke. They went down to Pembroke on Monday, 22 August, travelling in Mr Stages's car. They started work there on Tuesday, 23 August: they worked right through the rest of the week and the following weekend, working long hours, and, by working straight through Sunday and Sunday night, finished the job by 8.30 am on Monday, 29 August, which was the August bank holiday. Shortly after finishing work on the Monday morning, they drove back home in Mr Stages's car. On the way there was a serious accident. Mr Stages's car left the road; it crashed through a brick wall into a field and both men were seriously injured. No other vehicle was involved. Mr Stages, the driver, was plainly at fault. Mr Machin survived the accident, but he died about two years later from lung cancer unconnected with the accident.
>
> In December 1978, before his death, Mr Machin commenced proceedings against Mr Stages for damages for his personal injuries arising out of the accident. In the following March the employers were joined as second

defendants; this was, no doubt, because Mr Stages proved to be uninsured. Mr Machin alleged that the employers were vicariously liable for the negligence of Mr Stages. This allegation raised the crucial question in the case, which was whether, at the time of the accident, Mr Stages was acting in the course of his employment with the employers.

...

The present case can be seen as one of those cases, which have troubled the courts in the past, in which the question has arisen whether an employee, travelling to or from a place of work, is acting in the course of his employment. In order to consider the question in the present case, it is necessary first to examine the facts of the case in a little detail. The full facts are set out in the speech of my noble and learned friend Lord Lowry, on whose account I gratefully rely.

The employers set aside a normal working day (Monday, 22 August) for the two men's journey to Pembroke; they were paid as for an eight-hour day for the journey. In addition, each received the equivalent of their rail fare as travelling expenses. The employers made no direction as to the means by which the men travelled. The two men were however expected to start work at 8 am on Tuesday, 23 August and to finish the job by 8.30 am on Monday, 29 August, which, to their great credit, they did. After that, they were expected to report for work at Drakelow at 8 am on Wednesday, 31 August. While they were working at Pembroke, they were paid for the actual hours worked by them, the usual premium rate being paid for overtime. An allowance was paid for their lodgings in Pembroke. At the end of the job they were also paid eight hours' sleeping time, because they had worked for one day and one night consecutively (on Sunday, 28 August). Although the men were expected to sleep on the next day, Monday, there was no way in which the employers could compel them to sleep on that day. Since Monday was the August bank holiday, they were also paid holiday time for that day. Another working day (Tuesday, 30 August) was made available for the journey back. The two men were again paid as for an eight hour day for the journey; they were also given the same allowance for travelling expenses as on the way out. Once again, it is plain that they could travel by any means they liked; their duty was to report for work at Drakelow on the Wednesday morning.

I now turn to the applicable principles of law. The fundamental principle is that an employee is acting in the course of his employment when he is doing what he is employed to do, to which it is sufficient for present purposes to add, or anything which is reasonably incidental to his employment.

...

As usual, it is comparatively easy to state the principle; but it is more difficult to apply it to the facts of individual cases. Even so, it is important always to keep the principle in mind.

As I have already observed, we are here concerned with a case which may be seen as one of those cases concerned with travelling to or from work. I have used guarded language in so describing it, because (as will appear) I do not consider the present case to fall strictly within that category of case. Even so, it is helpful to use the cases in that category as a starting point. We can begin with the simple proposition that, in ordinary circumstances, when a man is travelling to or from his place of work, he is not acting in the course of his employment. So a bank clerk who commutes to the City of London every day from Sevenoaks is not acting in the course of his employment when he walks across London Bridge from the station to his bank in the City. This is because he is not employed to travel from his home to the bank: he is employed to work at the bank, his place of work, and so his duty is to arrive there in time for his working day. Nice points can arise about the precise time or place at which he may be held to have arrived at work; but these do not trouble us in the present case. Likewise, of course, he is not acting in the course of his employment when he is travelling home after his day's work is over. If, however, a man is obliged by his employer to travel to work by means of transport provided by his employer, he may be held to be acting in the course of his employment when so doing.

These are the normal cases. There are, however, circumstances in which, when a man is travelling to (or from) a place where he is doing a job for his employer, he will be held to be acting in the course of his employment. Some of these are listed by Lord Atkin in *Blee v London and North Eastern Rly Co* (1937).[18] So, if a man is employed to do jobs for his employer at various places during the day, such as a man who goes from door to door canvassing for business, or who distributes goods to customers, or who services equipment like washing machines or dishwashers, he will ordinarily be held to be acting in the course of his employment when travelling from one destination to another, and may also be held to do so when travelling from his home to his first destination and home again after his last. Again, it has been held that, in certain circumstances, a man who is called out from his home at night to deal with an emergency may be acting in the course of his employment when travelling from his home to his place of work to deal with the emergency. ...

...

I turn to Mr Stages's journey back. Another ordinary working day, Tuesday, 30 August, was made available for the journey, with the same pay, to enable him to return to his base in the Midlands to be ready to travel to work on the Wednesday morning. In my opinion, he was employed to make the journey back, just as he was employed to make the journey out to Pembroke. If he had chosen to go to sleep on the Monday morning and afternoon for eight hours or so, and then to drive home on the Monday evening so that he could have Tuesday free (as, indeed, Mr Pye expected him to do), that would not have detracted from the proposition that his journey was in the course of his employment. For this purpose, it was irrelevant that Monday was a bank holiday. Of course, it was wrong for him to succumb to the temptation of driving home on the Monday morning, just after he had completed so long a spell of work, but once again that cannot alter the fact that his journey was made in the course of his employment.

— — —

18 [1937] 4 All ER 270, p 273; [1938] AC 126, pp 131–32.

Relationship between personal and vicarious liability

Vicarious liability is well suited to attach liability to the employer for a road accident caused by the negligent driving of an employee driving the company van in the course of employment. On facts such as this the employer will be made strictly liable; the employee's conduct is negligent, but the employer may well be without fault.

In practice the distinction is not always entirely clear, for the organisation is normally a corporate body and, as such, is physically incapable of setting up a system of work: this can only be done for the corporation by the human beings who manage it or work for it.

If the road accident was caused because the vehicle was badly maintained or because the employee was overtired as a result of working too many hours, it might be less clear whether the employer's liability was personal or vicarious. The facts might be that the vehicle failure was due to poor maintenance work carried out by another employee or the driver was overtired because his work schedule had been badly drawn up by a line manager. In both these circumstances the employer's liability might again be vicarious, because, although the driver was not the actual wrongdoer, the actual wrongdoer was also an employee of the organisation.

If the circumstances were that there was no mechanism within the organisation for ensuring that vehicles were maintained or, as the case might be, for supervising the work load of drivers, then it would, perhaps, not be possible to identify the individual employee who had negligently allowed the situation to occur. In such circumstances the fault would lie in the system operating within the organisation and the fault would lie with the employer personally.

The following two cases demonstrate aspects of the relationship between the vicarious and the personal liability of an organisation. In both cases the organisation was held liable although the evidence did not establish in either case that an employee of the organisation had been at fault. In the first case it was not clear which, if any, person working within the organisation was at fault, and not all persons in the team, which might have contained the wrongdoer, were necessarily employees. In the second case the employee involved had simply been asked to do more than could reasonably be expected from one individual.

In both cases the plaintiff was a member of the public rather than an employee, so the accidents were not industrial accidents, but, nevertheless, the cases have a valuable part to play in illustrating the principles of the organisation's liability for safe systems. Much of the following chapter will be concerned with analysing the concept of safe system in cases concerning personal injury suffered by persons at work.

CASSIDY v MINISTRY OF HEALTH [1951] 2 KB 343

The plaintiff entered hospital for an operation on his hand. After the operation the hand was put in a splint and kept bound up for 14 days. When the bandaging was removed the hand was found to be useless. It was not clear whether the fault lay with the surgeon or the doctors and nurses who had looked after him following the surgery. There were precedents for the view that doctors and consultants were not employees of the hospitals using their services. The following extracts are from the judgment of Denning LJ, delivered in the Court of Appeal, beginning at p 360:

> ... In my opinion authorities who run a hospital, be they local authorities, government boards or any other corporation, are in law under the selfsame duty as the humblest doctor; whenever they accept a patient for treatment, they must use reasonable care and skill to cure him of his ailment. The hospital authorities cannot, of course, do it by themselves: they have no ears to listen through the stethoscope and no hands to hold the surgeon's knife. They must do it by the staff which they employ; and, if their staff are negligent in giving the treatment, they are just as liable for that negligence as is anyone else who employs others to do his duties for him. What possible difference in law, I ask, can there be between hospital authorities who accept a patient for treatment and railway or shipping authorities who accept a passenger for carriage? None whatever. Once they undertake the task, they come under a duty to use care in the doing of it, and that is so whether they do it for reward or not.
>
> It is no answer for them to say that their staff are professional men and women who do not tolerate any interference by their lay masters in the way they do their work. The doctor who treats a patient in the Walton Hospital can say equally with the ship's captain who sails his ship from Liverpool and with the crane driver who works his crane in the docks, 'I take no orders from anybody'. That 'sturdy answer', as Lord Simon described it, only means in each case that he is a skilled man who knows his work and will carry it out in his own way; but it does not mean that the authorities who employ him are not liable for his negligence. See *Mersey Docks and Harbour Board v Coggins and Griffiths (Liverpool) Ltd* (1947).[19] The reason why the employers are liable in such cases is not because they can control the way in which the work is done – they often have not sufficient knowledge to do so – but because they employ the staff and have chosen them for the task and have in their hands the ultimate sanction for good conduct, the power of dismissal.
>
> ...
>
> It has been said, however, by no less an authority than Goddard LJ in *Gold's* (1942)[20] case that the liability for doctors on the permanent staff depends 'on whether there is a contract of service and that must depend on the facts of any particular case'. I venture to take a different view. I think it depends on this:

---

19 [1947] AC 1.
20 [1942] 2 KB 293.

who employs the doctor or surgeon – is it the patient or the hospital authorities? If the patient himself selects and employs the doctor or surgeon as in *Hillyer's* (1909) case,[21] the hospital authorities are, of course, not liable for his negligence, because he is not employed by them. But, where the doctor or surgeon, be he a consultant or not, is employed and paid, not by the patient but by the hospital authorities, I am of opinion that the hospital authorities are liable for his negligence in treating the patient. It does not depend on whether the contract under which he was employed was a contract of service or a contract for services. That is a fine distinction which is sometimes of importance; but not in cases such as the present, where the hospital authorities are themselves under a duty to use care in treating the patient.

...

Turning now to the facts in this case, this is the position: the hospital authorities accepted the plaintiff as a patient for treatment, and it was their duty to treat him with reasonable care. They selected, employed and paid all the surgeons and nurses who looked after him. He had no say in their selection at all. If those surgeons and nurses did not treat him with proper care and skill, then the hospital authorities must answer for it, for it means that they themselves did not perform their duty to him. I decline to enter into the question whether any of the surgeons were employed only under a contract for services, as distinct from a contract of service. The evidence is meagre enough in all conscience on that point. But the liability of the hospital authorities should not, and does not, depend on nice considerations of that sort. The plaintiff knew nothing of the terms on which they employed their staff; all he knew was that he was treated in the hospital by people whom the hospital authorities appointed; and the hospital authorities must be answerable for the way in which he was treated.

This conclusion has an important bearing on the question of evidence. If the plaintiff had to prove that some particular doctor or nurse was negligent, he would not be able to do it. But he was not put to that impossible task: he says, 'I went into the hospital to be cured of two stiff fingers. I have come out with four stiff fingers, and my hand is useless. That should not have happened if due care had been used. Explain it, if you can.'

– – –

CARMARTHENSHIRE COUNTY COUNCIL v LEWIS [1955] AC 549

This was an appeal by employers, the county council, to the House of Lords, against a decision by the Court of Appeal. The respondent was the widow of a lorry driver who lost his life when his vehicle crashed into a telegraph pole, while he was swerving to avoid a small child who ran into the road. The driver was not negligent. It was agreed that the cause of his death was the action of the child, who had ran into the road from the playground of the school operated by the appellants, the local education authority. The child was barely four; he escaped from the school while the teacher (Miss Morgan) was

---

21   [1909] 2 KB 820.

attending to another child, who had fallen and injured himself. The majority of their Lordships were of the view that there was no negligence on the part of the teacher but the council were personally negligent in the system they operated. The following extracts are taken from the judgment of Lord Tucker, starting at p 568:

> My Lords, such an occurrence I think calls for an explanation from the appellants. Not because the facts and circumstances are exclusively within their knowledge – a theory to which I do not subscribe – but because it was an event which should not have happened and which *prima facie* indicates negligence on the part of those in charge of the child just as much as the presence of a motor car on the foot pavement *prima facie* points to negligence on the part of the driver.
>
> How then, did the appellants seek to explain or justify this child's presence in the road?
>
> Their case was that the mistress in charge, Miss Morgan, had left this child and one other unattended by any adult for a few minutes while she went to the toilet before taking them out for a walk in the town and that she had been unexpectedly detained for a few minutes longer attending to another child who had received an injury, and during her absence the two children had got out of the school premises onto the road. The evidence with regard to times and distances showed that the children must have run out almost immediately after Miss Morgan left the room.
>
> At the trial the only question debated, apart from that of the duty owed to the deceased man, seems to have been whether or not Miss Morgan had been guilty of negligence. On this issue Devlin J, although considering the case a borderline one, decided in favour of the respondent. This view was upheld in the Court of Appeal, although Romer LJ clearly indicated that but for the fact that he did not feel justified in interfering with the trial judge's finding he would have held otherwise. If the speeches in this House in the recent case of *Benmax v Austin Motor Co Ltd* (1955)[22] had been available to the Lord Justice he would, I think, undoubtedly have dissented.
>
> My Lords, on this issue I agree with my noble and learned friends, Lords Oaksey and Goddard, that the evidence disclosed no negligence on the part of Miss Morgan. It is easy after the event to think of several things she might have done which would have avoided the accident which resulted from her absence, but the question is whether her failure to take such action in the circumstances which existed amounted to negligence. For myself, I have no hesitation in holding that Miss Morgan was not shown to have been guilty of any negligence and that no responsibility for the death of the deceased man attaches to her.
>
> This does not, however, dispose of the case. The explanation put forward by the appellants entirely fails to explain how or why it was possible for this tiny child to escape from the school premises onto the street. The trial judge drew the inference that the child got out through the unlocked side gate opening

22 [1955] 2 WLR 418.

onto a lane leading into the street. This was the way the child was brought to and taken from school, and I think the judge's inference was the most probable one. No explanation was given as to why the gate was kept unlocked or in such a condition that it was possible for a child of four to push it open and unlatch it. Nor was any other means of exit suggested as likely, except by going through other portions of the school premises not forming part of the nursery school and out of a gate leading directly onto the street.

My Lords, I think the appellants failed altogether to show that the child's presence in the street was not due to any negligence on their part or on that of those for whom they are responsible. It is true that no questions were directed to the appellants' witnesses on this matter, but the respondent should not suffer for the appellants' failure in this respect. If, as is no doubt the fact, it is not possible for every child in the nursery school at every moment of time to be within sight of a mistress in view of the contingencies which must arise from time to time – such as those which occurred in this case – then reasonable precautions must be taken which will be effective to prevent children of this tender age running out onto a busy street. No such precautions were shown to have been taken in this case and on the evidence as it stood at the conclusion of the trial the appellants had, I think, failed to rebut the presumption of negligence arising from the facts disclosed.

While entirely absolving Miss Morgan from the finding of negligence against her, I am none the less of opinion that the appellants do not thereby escape responsibility, and, for these reasons, I would dismiss the appeal.

– – –

IV THE IMPACT OF INSURANCE

The vicarious liability of the employer for the wrongdoings of the employee in the course of employment is a valuable principle for the victim of the employee's wrongdoing. The principle does not relieve the actual wrongdoer from liability should the victim prefer to sue the employee, rather than the employer. However, the employer is more likely to have the funds with which to meet a successful claim. Indeed it was suggested in *Smith v Stages* that the reason the employer, rather than the employee driver, was sued was that the driver was not insured.

Again, in the *Mersey Docks and Harbour Board* case the dispute between the two employers as to which should compensate the victim of the crane driver's negligence was probably related to the arrangement concerning insurance. Possibly the owners of the crane in effect said to the borrowers of it, 'The charge we make to you for hiring the crane is small, but you must take out insurance to cover any accidents'. The normal terms of an insurance contract are that the insurers will only make payments in respect of claims their insured is liable to meet. If therefore this was in fact the situation, there was, possibly, in the outcome, no insurance to cover the accident. The contract required the hirer to accept the risks. If, therefore, the hirer rather than the owner of the crane were the insured, the party who took out the cover was not liable and the party who was liable would not have been insured. The House of Lords found that the organisations could not through their contractual arrangements determine the legal question of who was the employer: they could have agreed that in cases where the (general) employer was vicariously liable for the driver's negligence the other organisation would indemnify the employer.

It has been noted that an organisation may face either employer's liability or public liability. The former Workmen's Compensation Acts did not impose a statutory duty on employers to insure against liabilities arising from that legislation. Wiser employers did take out insurance cover. While an employer is now required by the Employers' Liability (Compulsory Insurance) Act 1969 to have insurance to cover injuries suffered by its employees, there is still no similar obligation to have public liability insurance. The expectation that the employer will have funds to meet liability has tended to encourage litigation against employers.

DAVIE v NEW MERTON BOARD MILLS
AND ANOTHER [1959] AC 604

This was an appeal to the House of Lords by a maintenance fitter, employed by the first defendant, injured while attempting to separate two metal parts by using a drift (that is a tapered bar of metal intended for this purpose) and a hammer. When he struck the drift with the hammer the drift broke and a piece entered the appellant's eye. The victim sued his employers, and at a later stage the manufacturers of the drift were joined as defendants. At the trial it emerged that the fault in the drift had been entirely due to the negligence of the manufacturer. There had been no personal negligence on the part of the employers in purchasing or maintaining the drift. If liability were attached to the employers they would, in effect, have been made vicariously liable for the negligence of the manufacturers of the tool. The House of Lords declined to impose such liability, holding that the employers had discharged their personal duty to take reasonable care by buying from a reputable source a tool whose latent defect they had no means of discovering. The following extract from the judgment of Viscount Simonds, beginning at p 624, indicates the reasoning of their Lordships:

> I turn, then, to Lord Maugham[23] ... As I have tried to show, the contention, as stated in its first form, that the employer is liable for the acts of himself, his servants and agents and, subject to whatever limitations might be thought fit, independent contractors, could not lead to success in this action: for the manufacturer could not by any legitimate use of language be considered the

---

23   In *Wilsons and Clyde Coal Co Ltd v English* [1938] AC 57, pp 87–88.

servant or agent of, or an independent contractor with, the employer who buys his manufactures in the market. It was then sought to reach the same result by a different road. The employer, it was said, was under a duty to take reasonable care to supply his workmen with proper plant and machinery. It was assumed that this included tools such as drifts, and I, too, will, without deciding it, assume it. It was then said that the employer could not escape responsibility by employing a third party, however expert, to do his duty for him. So far, so good. That is what Lord Maugham said and I agree. But then comes the next step – but I would rather call it a jump, and a jump that would unhorse any rider. Therefore, it was said, the employer is responsible for the defect in goods that he buys in the market, if it can be shown that the defect was due to the want of skill or care on the part of anyone who was concerned in its manufacture. But, my Lords, by what use or misuse of language can the manufacturer be said to be a person to whom the employer delegated a duty which it was for him to perform? How can it be said that it was as the delegate or agent of the employer that the manufacturer failed to exhibit due skill and care? It is, to my mind, clear that he cannot and equally clear that Lord Maugham was not contemplating such a case nor using language which was apt to cover it.

...

As I have already said, a large number of authorities were cited to us, many of them relating to the liability of an employer or, more often of an occupier of land, for the default of an independent contractor. It may one day fall to the House to explain and, perhaps, to reconcile these cases. It is not the occasion for that task when the fault lies at the door of one who was not an 'independent contractor', however wide a meaning may be given to those words.

One more thing I must say. It was, at one time suggested – I do not use a more emphatic word, for learned counsel was rightly discreet in his approach – that the House should take into consideration the fact that possibly or even probably the employer would, but the workman would not, be covered by insurance, and for that reason should be the more ready to fasten upon the employer's liability for an accident due neither to his nor to the workman's carelessness. I will only say that this is not a consideration to which your Lordships should give any weight at all in your determination of the rights and obligations of the parties. The legislature has thought fit in some circumstances to impose an absolute obligation upon employers. The Factories Acts and the elaborate regulations made under them testify to the care with which the common law has been altered, adjusted and refined in order to give protection and compensation to the workman. It is not the function of a court of law to fasten upon the fortuitous circumstances of insurance to impose a greater burden on the employer than would otherwise lie upon him.

For these reasons, therefore, which I will sum up by saying that the claim was against reason, contrary to principle, and barely supported by authority, I would dismiss the appeal with costs.

– – –

Ten years after this case, two short Acts of Parliament stipulated that employers must be insured against their liability:

(a) for personal injury to their employees; and

(b) for injuries to their employees which are attributable to any defect in equipment provided by the employer for the purposes of the employer's business.

The first Act in no way extended common law liability: it intended merely to provide funds from which the employer's liability could be met. The second Act in effect reversed the decision in *Davie v New Merton Board Mills* and accordingly extended the employer's liability. However the Act did provide that the employer could seek an indemnity from the wrongdoing manufacturer of the defective equipment:

EMPLOYERS' LIABILITY (COMPULSORY INSURANCE) ACT 1969

Section 1

Insurance against liability for employees

(1) Except as otherwise provided by this Act, every employer carrying on any business in Great Britain shall insure, and maintain insurance, under one or more approved policies with an authorised insurer or insurers against liability for bodily injury or disease sustained by his employees, and arising out of and in the course of their employment in Great Britain in that business, but except in so far as regulations otherwise provide not including injury or disease suffered or contracted outside Great Britain.

EMPLOYER'S LIABILITY (DEFECTIVE EQUIPMENT) ACT 1969

Section 1

Extension of employer's liability

(1) Where after the commencement of this Act–

(a) an employee suffers personal injury in the course of his employment in consequence of a defect in equipment provided by his employer for the purposes of the employer's business; and

(b) the defect is attributable wholly or partly to the fault of a third party (whether identified or not),

the injury shall be deemed to be also attributable to negligence on the part of the employer (whether or not he is liable in respect of the injury apart from this subsection), but without prejudice to the law relating to contributory negligence and to any remedy by way of contribution or in contract or otherwise which is available to the employer in respect of the injury.

...

(3) In this section:

... 'equipment' includes any plant and machinery, vehicle, aircraft and clothing.

– – –

The word 'equipment' has been broadly interpreted in litigation. In *Coltman v Bibby Tankers Ltd* (1988)[24] the House of Lords held that it included a large ship which sank due to defects in design and construction and in *Knowles v Liverpool City Council* (1993)[25] the House held that, as equipment covered every article of whatsoever kind furnished by the employer for the purposes of his business, a flagstone could be equipment.

---

24 [1988] AC 276.
25 [1993] IRLR 588.

CHAPTER 4

LIABILITY FOR PERSONAL INJURY 1: DUTY OF CARE IN THE TORT OF NEGLIGENCE

INTRODUCTORY NOTE

Persons who claim damages because they have suffered injury at work normally base their claims on the tort of negligence. It may be possible to claim there has been a breach of statutory duty, but this is less common now the tort of negligence is so fully developed.

The tort of negligence has since the 1930s been recognised as comprising a complex relationship between duty, breach and damage (*Lochgelly Iron and Coal Co v M'Mullan* (1934) *per* Lord Wright).[1] To win an action based on the tort, the claimant must, according to this analysis, prove:

(a) the defendant owed a duty of care to him/her. This is a matter of law, determined by judicial interpretation of precedents;

(b) the defendant's conduct was in breach of that duty. This is a matter of fact determined by a judge (formerly by a jury) on the evidence;

(c) the defendant's conduct has caused actionable damage to him/her.

Whether the defendant is liable for breach of statutory duty depends on a similar analysis, but, in that case Parliament, rather than the courts, has laid down the persons to whom the duty is owed and has also stipulated the standard of conduct which must be observed. Thus the criteria of liability will be different: in particular many statutory duties impose strict liability. It is possible for a claimant, in the same action, to make claims of both common law negligence and of breach of statutory duty.

Cases normally only find their way into the published series of law reports if they contribute to the development of the law: cases which turn solely on evidence do not create precedents.

The significance of these matters in relation to workplace injuries will be examined in this and the following chapters.

---

1   [1934] AC 1, p 25.

I THE DUTY OF CARE

Impact of *Donoghue v Stevenson*

It has been noted that, in *Donoghue v Stevenson* (1932)[2] Lord Atkin declared:

> You must take reasonable care to avoid acts or omissions which you can reasonably foresee would be likely to injure your neighbour.

Duty and conduct are entwined in Lord Atkin's statement, but it is generally regarded as establishing the criteria for determining whether a duty of care exists. Lord Macmillan's comment in the same case that, 'the categories of negligence are never closed' (p 619) and indeed passages in the speech of Lord Atkin himself, indicate that Lord Atkin's explanation has to be seen in the context of a category approach to neighbour relationships.

While the category approach to the duty issue prevailed, therefore, there were two aspects to the *duty issue* in any particular case:

(a) was a duty owed?

(b) what was the content of the duty?

The importance of these issues is still reflected in the law today.

(a) Was a duty owed?

A hundred years before *Donoghue v Stevenson* it had been recognised that there was a category of liability called 'employer's liability' arising from the contract of employment. Similarly occupiers' liability dates back to the nineteenth century, though the occupier's duty has subsequently been clarified by statute.

When are persons neighbours?

The question whether there were duty relationships other than those recognised as stemming from the contract of employment and the occupancy of premises, was addressed in the following cases.

Liability of contractors to workers

MCARDLE v ANDMAC ROOFING CO AND OTHERS
[1967] 1 All ER 583

The Court of Appeal was required to deal with appeals by three defendants against a High Court decision in an action brought by the workman for damages for personal injuries sustained from a fall through an opening in the roof of a building at Pontin's Holiday Camp at Blackpool, where he was

---

2   [1932] AC 562, p 580.

working. The following extracts are from the judgment of Sellers LJ, starting at p 586:

> In the spring of 1962 considerable work was being undertaken at the Blackpool camp. In particular, as far as this case is concerned, a flat roofed one storey building, which had been a dining hall, was being converted into a billiard hall. On the existing roof were two parallel roof lights just over 100 feet long and eight feet wide, raised from the roof by a side wall or coaming eighteen inches high. The glass in those strips had to be removed and then one strip had to be completely filled in and the other similarly filled in except for some twenty-eight feet at one end which was to be left for some new skylight over some lavatories which were to be constructed below them.
>
> The arrangements made by Pontin for this work were that Pontin were to supply the joists to be placed across the strips at intervals and the 'Stramit' boards which were to be placed on top of the joists to fill in the two strips. These boards were four feet wide and approximately the size to go across, although they had to be fitted or packed. The material was, I apprehend, brought by Pontin somewhere convenient to the site where it was required for the labourers' work. Newton were a small local firm of joiners and shipwrights who had been called on to provide labour to assist in and expedite the erection of some chalets within the camp. Mr Newton was asked to provide men to remove the glass from the two strips and to recover the area (except for the skylights) with the joists and 'Stramit' boards provided by Pontin. This was an oral contract made between Mr Armistead of Pontin and Mr Newton ... and nothing was said about, and no monetary provision was made for, safety precautions in a task which meant making with constant change of size a large cavity in each strip as the work of the removal of the lights took place and leaving cavities until the fitting in was completed and at the conclusion, until the skylights were erected, leaving the cavity twenty-eight feet long at the end of one strip.
>
> Mr Armistead of Pontin directed when and where the work of Newton was to be done, and there is some evidence that he directed the detail or manner in which it was to be done ... The men with their skill were to do the work which Pontin required. That would be the same if they had been employed individually and directly as servants with Mr Newton as foreman. Payment by Pontin was in bulk, instead of individually. It was said in argument, and I think rightly, that the Newton men were as nearly servants for the time being of Pontin, using Pontin's material and laying it as Pontin desired, as could be found short of their being held to be their temporary servants.
>
> ...
>
> The work which Newton's men were doing came under the Building (Safety, Health and Welfare) Regulations 1948, and the employers for that work (whoever they were) were at the time of the accident in breach of regulation 30 and would have been liable if one of the Newton men had fallen and been injured. No provision had been made in the contract of hire of labour for any fence or barrier, either in the cost of labour-time or in the material to be supplied by Pontin. The injured plaintiff was employed by Andmac and any claim by him, therefore, to succeed against Pontin or Newton must be

established under the common law. Before dealing with that it is necessary to turn to the work which Andmac were separately employed to do.

The 'Stramit' boards, when laid had to be covered with felt, bitumen and chippings, according to Pontin's requirements and it was desirable that the boards should be covered without long exposure to the weather. Andmac is a small partnership of Mr Anderson and Mr McNally, who carry on a specialist business as roofing felt layers. They were engaged by Pontin to do their specialised work at the Blackpool camp including the covering of the two strips with felt, bitumen and chippings, and they employed the plaintiff and two other men for the purpose. The work was done on a time and material basis at the request and direction of Mr Armistead of Pontin.

On 28 April 1962, ... the plaintiff was pouring the bitumen from a bucket ... Some time after 12 noon, Newton's men left off laying the 'Stramit' boards when they were still some twelve feet short of the twenty-eight feet mark. They left for a break without telling the plaintiff ... and without leaving any barrier, however temporary or improvised, to protect the large hole which still remained uncovered. This callous indifference to those whom they were leaving behind and this direct cause of the accident do not seem to me to be adequately reflected in the extent of the liability placed on Newton by the judge. The situation called for some, even elementary, care on their part to those who were so closely connected with their work and I find it hard to believe how the men could be so unconcerned. The plaintiff and Mr Roby worked on and the plaintiff, who cannot have appreciated that the work ahead had ceased, walking, it would seem, half backwards while pouring out the bitumen, reached the open edge of the unfinished boarding and overbalanced, carrying the bitumen bucket three quarters full with him, and received appalling injuries.

... As the judge said, this was just the type of accident against which it was necessary to protect the man concentrating on his work. With regard to the defendants' liability respectively, I agree with the judge when he said:

'The real trouble in this case is that each defendant left it to the others to take the necessary precautions and that appeared to extend over the whole field of their relationship. In the result nobody gave the matter any thought, and certainly nobody took any action.'

The responsibility for this would appear to lie, as the judge thought, in the first place on Pontin, who had made no arrangement whatsoever for safety in relation to this dangerous work which was being undertaken at their request. In a practical sense Pontin were conducting and organising the operations and had not, as I see it, parted with overall responsibility to anyone. Under the conditions which changed as the work progressed there arose a continuing duty on all the defendants to take reasonable care that those who might be expected to be in the vicinity of the danger (none more obviously so than the plaintiff) were not confronted with unnecessary risks.

... the facts which I have already stated leave no doubt as to the duty of both Pontin and Newton to take reasonable care for the safety of the plaintiff. Andmac, too, were under a like duty; but they were also clearly in breach of their statutory duty and on appeal accepted this liability. The question therefore is whether reasonable care in all the circumstances was taken by Pontin, their servants or agents, or by Newton, their servants or agents, towards the plaintiff and towards his colleagues working with him, who happily were not injured.

I have already expressed my views of the conduct of Newton's men towards Andmac's men working alongside them. The duty was utterly disregarded. Pontin argued more strenuously against liability, but they were directly concerned with the work in hand and they did nothing to ensure safety and had no reason to think that Newton would take any safety precautions on the contract for labour only which they made with them. It would have been apparent to them, if they had contemplated the position, that danger would arise. Ordinary care required that provision should have been made expressly by them in the particular circumstances of the two small contractors working in such close proximity. I agree with the judge that both Pontin and Newton were liable to the plaintiff under our common law.

...

There remains the question of the apportionments ... Here each member of the court came separately to the view that no distinction should be made between the defendants and that each should be held one-third to blame, and the liability for the damages and the costs of the plaintiff below and in the Court of Appeal should be so apportioned between them.

– – –

The significance of this case in extending the range of workers to whom an organisation may be under a duty to take care cannot be over-estimated. The concept that a contractor might be liable for the safety of employees of sub-contractors has now been built into the criminal law by s 3 of the Health and Safety at Work Act 1974 and it has been noted that *McArdle* was cited in the Court of Appeal Criminal Division when that court had to determine the implications of the duty in criminal law. In the civil law the case establishes that the duty of an employer to provide a safe system of work is not confined to taking care of those who are its own employees.

Liability of manufacturers and suppliers to workers

In the following case, the High Court had to discuss whether the manufacturer of a product might share liability with the employer for industrial disease suffered as a result of exposure of workers to a toxic substance during the course of their employment.

WRIGHT v DUNLOP RUBBER CO LTD AND ANOTHER; CASSIDY v SAME (1971) 11 KIR 311

The workers alleged that they had contracted cancer of the bladder as a result of being exposed, in the 1940s, during the course of their employment, to Nonox S, a chemical containing carcinogenic substances manufactured by the second defendants and sold to the first defendants. By 1949 it had become apparent from medical research that there was an unusual incidence of bladder cancer among men who had worked in Dunlop's Fort Dunlop Works at Speke, and it seemed probable that Nonox S might be the responsible agent. Dunlop were told of these findings and warned that they might have a grave problem of bladder cancer among their workforce. In 1949 Dunlop stopped using Nonox S and ICI (the second defendants) stopped making it and withdrew it from their sales list. It was not until 1966 that these workers were diagnosed as suffering from the disease. The following extracts are from the judgment of O'Connor J, beginning at p 315:

Chapter II: The Case against ICI

The foundation of the plaintiffs' case against ICI is that they should have foreseen at some date before 1 January 1947, that Nonox S might be a cancer hazard to persons employed in the rubber industry. If the plaintiffs can lay this foundation successfully it is not disputed that ICI owed a duty to them to take action; what action and its probable effect I will consider hereafter.

[His Lordship reviewed the evidence and continued:]

The duty of a manufacturer of chemical products can, I think, be simply stated. It is to take reasonable care that the product is safe in use. What is reasonable care will vary from situation to situation, for example, warnings of dangers and proper directions for use may suffice; see the hair dye cases, and the familiar 'highly inflammable', 'keep away from children and dogs', etc on a host of products in daily domestic use. If a manufacturer chooses to use a chemical which he knows to be a dangerous carcinogen in the manufacture of a product and knows or ought to know that the product contains a proportion of the carcinogen, and if he chooses to market the product without giving warning of the presence of the carcinogenic material, then I hold that the law imposes a very high duty indeed upon him to satisfy himself that the product will not prove dangerous when used for the purposes for which it is supplied. The discharge of the duty requires that he should inform himself of the circumstances in which the product will be used, the quantities in which it will be used, and the possibilities of exposure to which men may be subjected. If in the state of knowledge at the time he cannot say positively that the proportion of carcinogen present in the product will be harmless, then I hold that he cannot market it without giving adequate warning of the presence of the carcinogenic material.

...

In the result I find no good reason for modifying the conclusions to which I would have come on the earlier evidence and they now become my conclusions on the whole of the evidence. It follows that I hold that the plaintiffs have proved that ICI are in breach of duty ... and, subject to the plea of limitation are entitled to recover damages from them.

...

Chapter IV: Screening

...

As the facilities expanded and as knowledge of the true extent of the risks sank home, Dr Parkes and the research unit of the Rubber Manufacturers

Employers' Association altered their policy so that, in January 1960 a circular went out recommending that all employees engaged prior to 1949 in a factory which made use of Nonox S should have a urine test not less than once a year and in 1961 in the pamphlet which went out to members, including Speke, the recommendation was that all such employees should have a urine test at least every six months. For some reason which was never explained Speke neither acknowledged receipt of this literature nor did the management at Speke act upon it. The recommendation was not implemented until late in 1965 and thus it was that Cassidy was not screened until October of that year and Wright until February 1966 for the first time.

The plaintiffs allege that, if the recommendation for screening men such as themselves had been implemented in 1960 or 1961, the probability is that the growth of tumours in each of them would have been discovered a good deal earlier than it was.

The plaintiffs allege against both ICI and Dunlop that it was a breach of duty to fail to offer them the opportunity of screening at an earlier date and/or to warn them of the risk to which they had been exposed and advise them of the need to seek medical advice.

...

When I turn to the allegation against Dunlop, the position is quite different. The English law of tort imposes no duty of rescue or succour of the victims of the fault of another or indeed of accidental injury or illness. The relationship of master and servant is a special one giving rise to reciprocal rights and duties; its true foundation, in my judgment is the contract existing between the two parties.

The plaintiffs contend that the duty of the master to take reasonable care for the safety of his servants requires a master who has without negligence on his part exposed his servant to a risk of injury by using materials in the course of his operations to take such action as is reasonable in all the circumstances to secure the well-being of his servant as soon as he has learnt of the risk of injury to which he has been exposed.

[His Lordship referred at some length to the judgment of Lord Herschell in *Smith v Baker* (1891)[3] and then continued:]

Of course I am aware that Lord Herschell cannot have had the sort of facts with which I am concerned in mind, but I think that the earlier passage which I have cited explains what Lord Herschell had in mind when referring to 'unnecessary risk' in the well known passage of his speech, namely, 'a risk to the employed which may or may not result in injury created or enhanced by the negligence of the employer'. I am content to adopt that passage as a correct statement of the law. I have found nothing in the subsequent cases to the contrary and I apply it to the facts of the present case. Dunlop did not create the risk of injury to the plaintiffs by any negligence, as I have found in an earlier chapter, but I am in no doubt that the failure of the management at Speke to implement the recommendation sent to them and received by them to advise all men

3   [1891] AC 325.

employed before 1949 to submit specimens of urine for screening enhanced the risk of injury to the plaintiffs who were at all material times still in the employ of Dunlop.

I am not unmindful of some of the difficulties which result from this conclusion. These were discussed in full in argument; for example, a large number of men must have left the employ of Dunlop between 1949 and 1960. As I have come to the conclusion that the Speke management cannot be blamed for not publishing the availability of screening and cannot be blamed for not giving any warning of the risk up to that date, it follows that no breach of duty could be established by those men who had left their employment at Speke before 1960. On analysis I do not find this a valid criticism; there came a time when the proper discharge of their duty to their servants called for certain action on the part of Dunlop. It did not call for action to those who were no longer their servants.

...

--- --- ---

It is, perhaps, surprising that his Lordship considered that he was breaking new ground in holding that employers would be negligent if they failed to bring to their employees' attention that they had been exposed to dangers which could, in due course, result in illness. This very matter had been addressed by Swanwick J in *Stokes v Guest, Keen and Nettlefold (Bolts and Nuts) Ltd* (1968).[4] While that, then recent, case was of relatively small authority, having been heard at Birmingham Assizes, it nevertheless received quite considerable publicity at the time. The facts were that a widow brought an action against her late husband's employers after he had died of scrotal cancer, contracted as a result of having been constantly sprayed with cutting oils during the 15 years in which he had worked for them as a tool setter. The Factory Inspectorate had issued a leaflet describing the risk and the deceased was the second employee of the defendants to die of this form of cancer. However, the defendants' very experienced medical officer had decided not to give specific warnings of the risk (because he considered the incidence of the disease was too low to warrant frightening workers) and no medical examinations were carried out by the defendants of those long service employees who were most at risk. Swanwick J held that GKN were liable for the negligence of their doctor in failing to issue warnings of the risk and carry out medical examinations.

The decision as to the employer's liability in both the *Dunlop* and the *GKN* cases, while dealing with novel problems are arguably concerned with no more than the factual content of the employer's undoubted duty to exercise reasonable care for the safety of their employees. The decision in the *Dunlop* case that ICI the manufacturer of a substance used at the workplace, owed a duty of care to the workers who might be thereby exposed to risks of injury

---

4   [1968] 1 WLR 1776.

did, however, considerably extend the concept of safe systems of work. After *Donoghue v Stevenson* (1932)[5] it was immediately arguable that the worker might, in a sense, be regarded as a 'consumer', to whom the manufacturer owed a duty of care in relation to products. Additionally, there is, in the decision, an indication that, in order to discharge their duty, the manufacturer may have to work with the employer to identify the uses to which the employer intends to put the substance and then take into account whether this use creates any risk which might not be present in other types of user.

The existence of the manufacturer's duty was not denied in *Davie v New Merton Board Mills* (1959)[6] which was in effect an employee's attempt to make his employer vicariously liable for the negligence of the manufacturer of a *tool*. The Employer's Liability (Defective Equipment) Act 1969, by allowing the employer to seek an indemnity from the manufacturer, also impliedly accepted that the manufacturer did have a duty to the employee. All these authorities, however, relate more to articles than to substances. It must be questionable whether the statute, being concerned with plant and equipment could be deemed to extend to substances (equipment is interpreted as 'includes any plant and machinery, vehicle, aircraft and clothing').

Today, the workers might have preferred to sue ICI as producers under the Consumer Protection Act 1987. Liability under that Act is strict and it is not immediately apparent that ICI would have been able to plead any of the defences provided by the statute.

Finally, the *Dunlop* and *GKN* cases mark an increased awareness, due partly to improved medical knowledge, and partly to changing forms of manufacturing processes, that workers are as much, if not more, at risk of suffering injury from exposure to dangerous substances as they are from exposure to dangerous plant and equipment.

We are all neighbours

It will be apparent that the majority of the cases determining who, apart from the employer, owed a common law duty of care to the worker were heard in the 1960s. The issue of determining relationships giving rise to a duty of care, in law, was really laid to rest by the following case.

HOME OFFICE v DORSET YACHT CO LTD [1970] AC 1004

The case concerned the Home Office's liability for property damage caused by Borstal boys when they escaped from the supervision of Borstal officers. The following brief extracts from the judgment of Lord Reid, beginning at p 1025, serve to clarify the attitude of the House of Lords:

---

5   [1932] AC 562.
6   [1959] AC 604.

My Lords, on 21 September 1962, a party of Borstal trainees were working on Brownsea Island in Pool Harbour under the supervision and control of three Borstal officers. During that night seven of them escaped and went aboard a yacht which they found nearby. They set this yacht in motion and collided with the respondents' yacht which was moored in the vicinity. Then they boarded the respondents' yacht. Much damage was done to this yacht by the collision and some of the subsequent conduct of these trainees. The respondents sued the appellants, the Home Office, for the amount of this damage.

The case comes before your Lordships on a preliminary issue whether the Home Office or these Borstal officers owed any duty of care to the respondents capable of giving rise to a liability in damages. So it must be assumed that the respondents can prove all that they could prove on the pleadings if the case goes to trial. The question, then, is whether on that assumption the Home Office would be liable in damages. It is admitted that the Home Office would be vicariously liable if an action would lie against any of these Borstal officers.

...

In later years there has been a steady trend towards regarding the law of negligence as depending on principle so that, when a new point emerges, one should ask not whether it is covered by authority but whether recognised principles apply to it. *Donoghue v Stevenson* (1932) may be regarded as a milestone and the well known passage in Lord Atkins's speech should, I think, be regarded as a statement of principle. It is not to be treated as if it were a statutory definition. It will require qualification in new circumstances. But I think that the time has come when we can and should say that it ought to apply unless there is some justification or valid explanation for its exclusion.

– – –

Are trespassers neighbours?

The common law did not impose any duty on an occupier to take care for the safety of those who trespassed on to their property. The Occupiers' Liability Act 1957 was concerned only to rationalise the then existing common law duties of the occupier to lawful visitors. It was not until the Occupiers' Liability Act 1984 that a statutory duty was imposed on occupiers of premises to persons other than visitors (which includes, but is not confined to, trespassers). The new statutory duty was only for personal injury suffered by reason of the state of the premises or activities carried on there (s 1(1)).

OCCUPIERS' LIABILITY ACT 1984

Section 1

Duty of occupier to persons other than his visitors

(1) The rules enacted by this section shall have effect, in place of the rules of the common law, to determine–

    (a) whether any duty is owed by a person as occupier of premises to persons other than his visitors in respect of any risk of their suffering injury on the premises by reason of any danger due to the state of the premises or to things done or omitted to be done on them; and

(b) if so, what that duty is.

(2) For the purposes of this section, the persons who are to be treated respectively as an occupier of any premises (which, for those purposes, include any fixed or movable structure) and as his visitors are–

(a) any person who owes, in relation to the premises the duty referred to in s 2 of the Occupiers' Liability Act 1957 (the common duty of care); and

(b) those who are his visitors for the purposes of that duty.

(3) An occupier of premises owes a duty to another (not being his visitor) in respect of any such risk as is referred to in subsection (1) above if:

(a) he is aware of the danger or has reasonable grounds to believe that it exists;

(b) he knows or has reasonable grounds to believe that the other is in the vicinity of the danger concerned or that he may come into the vicinity of the danger (in either case, whether the other has lawful authority for being in that vicinity or not); and

(c) the risk is one against which, in all the circumstances of the case, he may reasonably be expected to offer the other some protection.

(4) Where, by virtue of this section, an occupier of premises owes a duty to another in respect of such a risk, the duty is to take such care as is reasonable in all the circumstances of the case to see that he does not suffer injury on the premises by reason of the danger concerned.

(5) Any duty owed by virtue of this section, in respect of a risk, may, in an appropriate case, be discharged by taking such steps as are reasonable in all the circumstances of the case to give warning of the danger concerned or to discourage persons from incurring the risk.

(6) No duty is owed by virtue of this section to any person in respect of risks willingly accepted as his by that person (the question whether a risk was so accepted to be decided on the same principles as in other cases in which one person owes a duty of care to another).

– – –

The statutory duty created by this Act may be significant to employers in respect of unauthorised entries on to their premises by children or vandals. It should be noted, however, that occupiers will only be liable if they know or have reasonable grounds to believe that the trespasser is in the vicinity; occupiers may, in this instance, discharge their liability by giving warning of the danger, and the trespasser may, whether there is a warning or not, according to the circumstances, be deemed to have accepted the risk of injury. It should also be borne in mind that if persons who have no business with the employer are not discouraged from entering the premises, for example, the general public using them as a short cut, such persons may cease to be trespassers and become lawful visitors.

(b) What is the content of the duty?

Whether a duty is owed is a matter of law for the judge: whether the duty has been broken is a matter of fact. If, as was formerly the case, a jury were involved, the jury would decide whether the duty had been broken.

Before, and for some years following, *Donoghue v Stevenson*, the content of the duty was a matter for the judge and the content varied from one category situation to another. This was especially the case as between employers' liability and the two categories of occupiers' liability.

Employers' liability

The distinction between the content of the employer's duty and that of other categories of duty relationships was emphasised by *Wilsons and Clyde Coal Co Ltd v English* (1938)[7] which, it has been noted, in an earlier chapter, spelt out the employer's personal duty in order to disentangle it from the doctrine of common employment. Subsequent cases built on the framework laid down in that case. Some of these cases might more properly be deemed today to be concerned with whether factually the duty had been broken (for example, *Bux v Slough Metals Ltd* (1974))[8] and they are therefore considered later under breach of duty.

Occupiers' liability to visitors

Until the Occupiers' Liability Act 1957 the duty of the occupier depended on the status of the visitor: thus within occupier's liability, there were several sub-categories of duty. For example, the occupier's liability to an invitee was different from that to a licensee. It was often difficult to determine to which category the visitor belonged. One of the purposes of the 1957 Act was to simplify the common law by removing the *legal* significance of these categories.

This is now covered by the Occupiers' Liability Act 1957. This Act was passed in order to simplify the earlier common law. It made the duty of the occupier to all its lawful visitors a duty of reasonable care in all the circumstances.

OCCUPIERS' LIABILITY ACT 1957

Section 2(1)

> An occupier of premises owes the same duty, the 'common duty of care', to all his visitors, except in so far as he is free to and does extend, restrict, modify or exclude his duty to any visitor or visitors by agreement or otherwise.

7   [1938] AC 57.
8   [1974] 1 All ER 262.

(2) The common duty of care is a duty to take such care as in all the circumstances of the case is reasonable to see that the visitor will be reasonably safe in using the premises for the purposes for which he is invited or permitted by the occupier to be there.

– – –

Section 2(3) to (6) sets out what the occupier has to do to discharge this duty in relation to special categories of visitor. These subsections and cases concerning their interpretation are considered in the next chapter.

The legal duty is reasonable care

The impact of the Occupiers' Liability Act was not only to bring to an end the category approach within occupiers' liability but to cause the courts to reconsider the content of the duty in other categories of liability. If the position were indeed that the duty to exercise reasonable care were a duty to have regard to specified matters which might vary as between categories of relationships, then defendants who failed to carry out all the aspects of all the matters specified for the category in which they found themselves, would have to be found liable, even though, in the particular case it was not necessarily appropriate to have regard to these matters. The House of Lords had to address this problem in the following case.

QUALCAST (WOLVERHAMPTON) LTD v HAYNES [1959] AC 743

The appellant employers were appealing against a judgment which had originally been made against them in the Wolverhampton County Court. The respondent, Haynes, was aged 38, and he had been a moulder all his working life. While the respondent was casting at the moulding boxes the ladle of molten metal which he was holding slipped and some of the metal splashed on to his left foot causing him some injury from which, after a few months, he entirely recovered. The respondent alleged that the appellants had failed to provide spats and/or other protective clothing. The appellants not only denied that they were negligent, but also said that the accident resulted from the negligence of the respondent himself. The county court judge apportioned three-quarters of the blame for causing the accident to the respondent and one-quarter to the appellants. The Court of Appeal affirmed that judgment.

The material facts on which the case turned were contained in the following passage in the judgment in the county court:

> ... I find that there were spats in the stores which could be had for the asking, and that there were also strong boots in the stores which could be had on payment. The plaintiff was not ordered or advised by the defendants to wear protective clothing and I think that was because he was an experienced moulder. The foreman, who gave evidence, Kenneth Charles Bloor, stated that had the plaintiff been a learner he would have advised him about wearing

protective clothing but, as he was an experienced man, he considered that he did not need any warning; he knew and appreciated the risks ...

The judge considered that the worker was so experienced that he needed no warning, and that there was therefore no negligence on the part of the defendants, but held that he was bound by authority to decide that it was the employer's legal duty to warn him.

Their Lordships concluded that it was not part of the common law *duty* of the employers to instruct the worker that he had to wear spats: when the worker was experienced such instruction might not be necessary. The *legal* duty being to exercise reasonable care it was a matter of *fact* whether in the particular circumstances the employer would have failed to exercise reasonable care if no instructions were given. The following extracts are from the judgment of Lord Somervell, beginning at p 757:

My Lords, I also would allow the appeal. In the present case the county court judge, after having found the facts, had to decide whether there was, in relation to this plaintiff, a failure by the defendants to take reasonable care for his safety. It is, I think, clear from the passage cited by my noble and learned friend that he would have found for the defendants but for some principle laid down, as he thought, by the authorities, to which he referred.

I hope it may be worthwhile to make one or two general observations on the effect on the precedent system of the virtual abolition of juries in negligence actions. Whether a duty of reasonable care is owed by A to B is a question of law. In a special relationship such as that of employer to employee the law may go further and define the heads and scope of the duty. There are cases in your Lordships' House which have covered this ground, I would have thought by now, exhaustively (*Wilsons and Clyde Coal Co Ltd v English* (1938), *Latimer v AEC Ltd* (1953),[9] *General Cleaning Contractors Ltd v Christmas* (1953),[10] and there are, of course, others). There would seem to be little, if anything, that can be added to the law. Its application in borderline cases may, of course, still come before appellate tribunals. When negligence cases were tried with juries the judge would direct them as to the law as above. The question whether on the facts in that particular case there was or was not a failure to take reasonable care was a question for the jury. There was not, and could not be, complete uniformity of standard. One jury would attribute to the reasonable man a greater degree of prescience than would another. The jury's decision did not become part of our law citable as a precedent. In those days, it would only be in very exceptional circumstances that a judge's direction would be reported or be citable. So far as the law is concerned they would all be the same. Now that negligence cases are mostly tried without juries, the distinction between the functions of judge and jury is blurred. A judge naturally gives reasons for the conclusion formerly arrived at by a jury without reasons. It may sometimes be difficult to draw the line, but if the reasons given by a judge are to be treated as 'law' and citable, the precedent system will die from a surfeit of authorities.

9   [1953] AC 643.
10   [1953] AC 180.

...

In the present case, and I am not criticising him, the learned county court judge felt himself bound by certain observations in different cases which were not, I think, probably intended by the learned judges to enunciate any new principles or gloss on the familiar standard of reasonable care. It must be a question on the evidence in each case, whether, assuming a duty to provide some safety equipment, there is a duty to advise everyone, whether experienced or inexperienced, as to its use.

...

I have come to the conclusion that the learned judge's first impulse was the right conclusion on the facts as he found them and for the reasons which he gives. I will not elaborate these reasons or someone might cite my observations as part of the law of negligence.

– – –

II EXTENDING THE BASIS OF LIABILITY

Liability under *Donoghue v Stevenson* is essentially liability for causing physical injury by actions. Two important extensions of liability for negligent conduct in the last half century have been the development of liability for negligent misstatement and liability for causing psychiatric injury.

Liability for statements

A new development in the 1960s was the extension of the tort of negligence to cover negligent misstatements. The leading case on this was the decision of the House of Lords in *Hedley Byrne & Co Ltd v Heller & Partners Ltd* (1964).[11] It opened the way for professionals, such as accountants and surveyors, to be made liable for negligent statements made in the course of their work. As far as industrial accidents are concerned the decision of the House of Lords was paralleled by the following case, which concerned the liability of an architect for an accident on a building site.

CLAY v AJ CRUMP & SONS LTD [1964] 1 QB 533

The following extracts are taken from the judgment of Upjohn LJ, starting at p 565:

> On the facts, I only desire to examine a little further the behaviour of the architect on the morning of March 20, 1958 or thereabouts. The owner, Cope, observed Knott [the demolition contractors' foreman] starting to demolish the

---

11 [1964] AC 465.

wall which subsequently fell on the plaintiff and he asked him to stop doing so and said he would ring up the architect, Young. He did so and, according to his (Cope's) recollection, Young said, 'Leave it to me; I will look into it', and so far as Cope was concerned, that was the end of the matter. Young had in his office the second plan, which, of course, would have shown the red line indicating that a bank of five feet was to be left against the walls to be left standing but not against those to be demolished. He admitted that he never even bothered to refresh his mind by looking at it. He spoke to Whitehouse [the demolition contractors' managing director] on the telephone and asked him to leave the wall 'if it was safe to do so'. In his own words, 'In other words I put the onus on to him, perhaps incorrectly, but that is what I did.' Whitehouse apparently relied on Knott, who seems to have been an experienced but not very intelligent foreman, who did not claim to possess any technical knowledge, and so the wall was left standing in a most dangerous state. It seems to me quite remarkable that Young never even referred to the plan in his office; had he done so he would have been bound to ask: 'Have you yet removed the earth against that wall?' The answer to that question on the findings of fact by the judge would have been 'Yes'. Furthermore, on looking at the plan he must have asked 'have the buttressing walls been left?' to which there is no doubt that the answer was 'No'. Later on he visited the site on a number of occasions and never even noticed that the bank had been demolished and that the wall was in fact standing on a precipice of some five to seven feet high.

Thus Young was in a complete and in a literal sense in blind breach of his duty to the owner. He took not one of the steps which it was his bounden duty to take before permitting the wall to remain standing. He cannot, of course, escape that duty by putting the onus on to Whitehouse. Furthermore, he knew that Whitehouse's work was very nearly finished and that the demolition contractors would be vacating the site in a day or two and that some period would elapse before the building contractors came on the site to do the rebuilding work. In fact about six weeks elapsed before they did so and during this time there was a good deal of rain which could get into the foundations and weaken them. During this interregnum, no one else was on the site; the one person really responsible for the safety of the buildings left standing was Young, the architect in charge of the whole operation. If liable at all, he must be gravely to blame. But can the architect or the demolition contractors be made liable at all?

To bring home liability to the defendants, the first matter is to establish some duty to the plaintiff. As to the building contractors, who were the plaintiff's employers, of course, there is no difficulty; it is contractual. The difficult question is whether a liability in tort against the architect and demolition contractors can be established.

...

The clear answer to this question, as given by Lord Atkin in *Donoghue v Stevenson* (1932) in his famous question and answer, is that you owe a duty to 'persons who are so closely and directly affected by my act that I ought reasonably to have them in contemplation as being so affected when I am directing my mind to the acts or omissions which are called in question'.

But, it is plain that this test, though given in relation to a defective bottle, may properly be applied to a much wider range of circumstances. We now know from the recent case of *Hedley Byrne & Co Ltd v Heller & Partners Ltd* (1963)[12] that it may be applied, for example, to the giving of information about the financial standing of another.

I cannot see any logical reason why it should not be applied to this case. This wall was left standing with a very serious, but to the layman latent defect. The question whether the architect and demolition contractors ought to have had the plaintiff in contemplation when the wall was left standing is one of fact and degree. Not everyone who may be injured is necessarily within the class of neighbour; not, for example a felon injured when climbing the wall to effect an illegal entry; nor, possibly a lorry driver bringing loads to the site who, unknown to the architect and demolition contractors, made a habit of walking by the dangerous wall to stretch his legs while smoking a cigarette.

But I would have thought that the plaintiff, one of the employees of the building contractors who would naturally and normally be one of the first to work on the site after the demolition contractors had withdrawn, should properly be described as one of the class of closest neighbours to the architect and demolition contractors. But they say that as the building contractors had the last opportunity of examining the wall, the plaintiff is not within the class of persons whom they should have had in contemplation as being their neighbour.

...

The real truth of the matter, as I think, is that causation is almost entirely a question of fact in each particular case.

...

To that simple question of fact there can, as I think, be only one answer. The principal cause of the accident was (for reasons given earlier) the failure of the architect to perform any of the duties cast upon him. The second cause (in order of importance) was that of the demolition contractor who relied on an entirely unqualified employee and the third (least in importance) was the building contractor, who was not entitled to assume the other two had completely fulfilled their duty. I, therefore, think that the judge rightly assessed the architect, the demolition contractor and the building contractor to be liable in that descending order. I would not disturb his figures of degree of blame, though, personally, I think I should have made the architect's proportion of blame rather higher.

– – –

---

12 [1963] 3 WLR 101.

Liability for psychiatric injury

Development of liability for nervous shock

Liability for causing a person to suffer nervous shock can be traced back to *Dulieu v White & Sons* (1901)[13] The plaintiff was a pregnant barmaid who suffered serious shock when the defendant's horses were negligently driven into the public house where she was working. As a result her child was born prematurely. It is significant that the barmaid suffered a miscarriage: at that time understanding of psychiatric illness was limited. The court held that the barmaid was entitled to damages as the shock suffered was due to fear for her own personal safety.

The case contained two limitations on liability that have been largely maintained: (a) the claimant was in fear of suffering physical injury; and (b) the injury was suffered in the form of shock, that is, the injury was what is today known as post-traumatic stress disorder. Neither of these two limitations are rigidly observed in employment related cases today.

Coming to the aftermath

In *Chadwick v British Railways Board* (1967)[14] damages were awarded in respect of the psychiatric illness suffered by a volunteer as a result of experiences when helping in the rescue operation following a major rail crash. Today it could be said that Mr Chadwick came to the aftermath of the disaster.

The concept of 'the aftermath' stems from *McLoughlin v O'Brian* (1983)[15] In this case a negligent lorry driver was found liable to compensate a mother for the nervous shock she suffered when she was taken to the hospital casualty ward and saw the injuries the road accident had caused to members of her family. The House of Lords held that the illness the mother suffered was a reasonably foreseeable consequence of the negligence of the defendant even though she was not at the scene of the accident and was never herself in danger of suffering physical injury.

The implications of *McLoughlin v O'Brian* were considered by the House of Lords in *Alcock v Chief Constable of South Yorkshire Police* (1992)[16] This case was brought by relatives and loved ones of the victims of the catastrophe at the Hillsborough Football Stadium. Many claims had been settled out of court and, in the event those involved in this litigation were unsuccessful. Some of the claimants had not been present at the stadium and had only viewed events on television. Others who were at the stadium were deemed not to have sufficient ties of love and affection to the victims. The case is important

13 [1901] 2 KB 669.
14 [1967] 1 WLR 912.
15 [1983] AC 410.
16 [1992] 1 AC 310.

here, because their Lordships distinguished between 'primary' and 'secondary' victims. Primary victims were participants. That is, persons present at the catastrophe and at risk of personal injury. Secondary victims were persons, who were either mere bystanders (with no entitlement to compensation) or those who witnessed the suffering of their loved ones, being physically present, either at the time and place of the disaster or seeing their loved ones in the immediate aftermath of the disaster. Their Lordships suggested that rescuers might be classified as 'primary' victims, even if not at risk of personal injury.

Alcock v Chief Constable of South Yorkshire Police has been interpreted restrictively, as the following cases demonstrate.

Claimant was neither at personal risk nor a rescuer

MCFARLANE v EE CALEDONIA [1994] 2 ALL ER 1

The principal judgment of the Court of Appeal was delivered by Stuart-Smith LJ. It is largely concerned with identifying the facts. These may be summarised as follows.

The case concerned the catastrophe on the oil platform *Piper Alpha*, on 6 July 1988, in which 164 persons lost their lives and many more were seriously injured. One of the vessels which went to assist was the *Tharos*. At the time that the emergency arose, the claimant was in bed on board the *Tharos*, but he got up and went out on to the walkway; from this position he witnessed a rescue boat engulfed in a fireball, killing its occupants.He also saw men jumping from the platform to their death. He was at no time nearer than 100 metres to the platform. No one on the *Tharos* suffered any physical injury that night and the vessel itself was undamaged, apart from some blistering of paint. He claimed that, as a result of his experiences that night, he suffered psychiatric injury.

The matter came before Mrs Justice Smith on a preliminary issue as to whether the defendants, who were the owners and operators of the *Piper Alpha*, owed the plaintiff a duty of care to avoid causing him psychiatric injury. She found that the claimant had been a participant in the events; he had been in fear of his life and it was plainly foreseeable that a man of reasonable fortitude might suffer psychiatric injury if exposed to the shock of being in fear of his life; findings which resulted in her giving judgment for the claimant. The defendants appealed against her judgment.

On appeal, Stuart-Smith LJ found that there were three situations in which a person might be a participant when he suffered psychiatric injury: first, where he was in the actual area of danger, but escaped physical injury by chance or good fortune; secondly, where the claimant was not actually in danger but, because of the sudden and unexpected nature of the event he reasonably thought that he was; and, thirdly, where the claimant, who was not originally within the area of danger, came into it later. In the third instance, he could only claim to be owed a duty of care by the defendant who created the danger if he came to the scene as a rescuer. His Lordship then continued, at p 11:

> The plaintiff does not come into either of the first two categories, and Mr Hamilton submits that he does not come into the third. The *Tharos* never was in actual danger ... No one sustained any physical injury and there is no evidence that anyone other than the plaintiff sustained psychiatric injury. In my judgment it cannot be said that the defendants ought reasonably to have foreseen that the plaintiff or other non-essential personnel on board her would suffer such injury ... If indeed the plaintiff had felt himself to be in any danger, he could have taken refuge in or behind the helicopter hanger, which was where non-essential personnel were required to muster. The judge thought it was entirely understandable that the plaintiff and other non-essential personnel should wish to see what was happening on the *Piper Alpha*. I agree with this. What I do not agree with is that someone who was in truth in fear of his life from spread of the fire and falling debris should not take shelter. Only someone who is rooted to the spot through fear would be unable to do so. The plaintiff never suggested that; he accepted that he had moved about quite freely and could have taken shelter had he wished.
>
> ...
>
> I turn then to the matters raised in the respondent's notice.
>
> It is submitted by Mr Wilkinson that the plaintiff was a rescuer and that even if his injury did not result from fear for his own safety he was entitled to recover because it was due to his experiences in rescuing the survivors. In *Chadwick v British Transport Commission* (1967)[17] the plaintiff's deceased husband had gone to the assistance of those involved in the Lewisham train disaster. For 12 hours he gave valuable help at very close quarters to those injured in the carnage. He was entitled to recover damages in respect of the psychoneurotic condition that resulted from his experiences. But the judge held that the plaintiff was not a rescuer even though he was on board the *Tharos* which went to assist in rescue operations. I agree with the judge's conclusions. The plaintiff was never actively involved in the operation beyond helping to move blankets with a view to preparing the heli-hanger to receive casualties and encountering and perhaps assisting two walking injured as they arrived on the *Tharos*.
>
> ...
>
> Secondly, it is submitted that the plaintiff was obliged to witness the catastrophe at close range and that it was of such a horrendous nature that even as a bystander the defendants owed him a duty of care ...
>
> [His Lordship referred to decided cases.]
>
> The whole basis of the decision in *Alcock v Chief Constable of South Yorkshire Police* (1991) is that where the shock is caused by fear of injury to others as opposed to fear of injury to the participant, the test of proximity is not simply

---

17 [1967] 2 All ER 945; [1967] 1 WLR 912.

reasonable foreseeability. There must be a sufficiently close tie of love and affection between the plaintiff and the victim. To extend the duty to those who have no such connection, is to base the test purely on foreseeability.

...

In my judgment both as a matter of principle and policy the court should not extend the duty to those who are mere bystanders or witnesses of horrific events unless there is a sufficient degree of proximity, which requires both nearness in time and place and a close relationship of love and affection between plaintiff and victim.

– – –

Rescuers are not a special case

WHITE v CHIEF CONSTABLE OF SOUTH YORKSHIRE POLICE
[1999] IRLR 110, HL

The Court of Appeal had found for the police officers in this case (under the name of *Frost v Chief Constable of South Yorkshire Police*). On appeal to the House of Lords, their Lordships were divided. The majority considered that no special case could be made for rescuers who were neither at risk of personal injury nor had ties of love and affection with the victims. Their Lordships also upheld the decision in *Chadwick*, although the law report does not make it clear that he had been in personal danger!

The following extracts are from the opinion of Lord Griffiths, one of the dissenting Lords. His reasoning, up to his conclusion about rescuers, is broadly in line with the other members of the House. The extracts begin at p 111:

> In *Alcock v Chief Constable of South Yorkshire Police* [1992] 1 AC 310, claims were brought by those who had suffered psychiatric injury as a result of the Hillsborough disaster. Two of the plaintiffs were spectators in the grounds, but not in the pens, where the disaster occurred, the remainder of the plaintiffs learned of the disaster through radio or television broadcasts. All the plaintiffs lost, or feared they might have lost, a relative or fiancé in the disaster. Thus it will be seen that two of the plaintiffs were witnesses to the disaster, but not in peril themselves, the remainder were not in the ground when the accident occurred. One of the plaintiffs gave some assistance to the injured but the case was not argued on the basis that he should be treated as a rescuer. The two plaintiffs at the ground were treated as bystanders who witnessed the disaster. All the plaintiffs lost their cases because they did not fulfil one or other of the control mechanisms, all of which the present law requires in cases where damages for psychiatric injury are claimed by plaintiffs who were not directly threatened by the accident but learned of it through sight or hearing of it. These control mechanisms are as Lord Hoffmann sets out in his opinion.
>
> '(1) There must be a close tie of love and affection between the plaintiff and the victim.

(2) The plaintiff must have been present at the accident or its immediate aftermath.

(3) The psychiatric injury must have been caused by direct perception of the accident or its immediate aftermath and not by hearing about it from somebody else.'

There is a further requirement in the bystander case and that is that psychiatric injury was reasonably foreseeable as a likely consequence of exposure to the trauma of the accident or its immediate aftermath. The law expects reasonable fortitude and robustness of its citizens and will not impose liability for the exceptional frailty of certain individuals. This is not to be confused with the 'eggshell skull' situation, where, as a result of a breach of duty the damage inflicted proves to be more serious than expected. It is a threshold test of breach of duty: before a defendant will be held in breach of duty to a bystander, he must have exposed them to a situation in which it is reasonably foreseeable that a person of reasonable robustness and fortitude would be likely to suffer psychiatric injury. However, as in the situation we are considering, namely the bystander who is seeing or hearing of the event from a safe distance, the only injury that he could suffer would be psychiatric injury so we can substitute personal injury for psychiatric injury and this will fit more easily with *Page v Smith* [1996] AC 155 to which I now turn.

In *Page v Smith*, the plaintiff was driving his car at 30 miles an hour when the defendant turned right immediately into his path. The consequence was an accident in which both cars suffered considerable damage but the occupants all escaped physical injury. The plaintiff, however, had suffered for 20 years from a condition known as chronic fatigue syndrome, which manifested itself from time to time. The judge held that the shock of the accident re-activated this condition which was now in all probability permanent and that it was unlikely that the plaintiff would be able to return to full-time employment, and he awarded damages of £162,153. The Court of Appeal allowed the defendant's appeal on the ground that psychiatric injury was not a foreseeable consequence of the accident. The House of Lords by a majority held that in circumstances such as a road accident in which a defendant owes a duty of care not to cause personal injury it mattered not whether the injury suffered as a result of the defendant's negligence was physical injury or psychiatric injury and liability would be established without the necessity to prove as an independent part of the cause of action that psychiatric injury, in the absence of physical injury, was foreseeable.

...

Having set out my understanding of the present state of the law I turn to consider the position of the plaintiffs in the appeal. They were all police officers and it is agreed that as such they are to be considered for the purposes of the law as though they were employees of the Chief Constable. The case by the police officers is put in two ways. First, it is said that they are entitled to recover for a breach of the duty owed to them as employees; and, secondly, that at least some of them are entitled to recover as rescuers.

Their case as employees is put thus: they were all at the ground in the course of their duty, as employees. The Chief Constable owed them a duty to take reasonable care not to expose them to unnecessary risk of injury during the course of their employment. The Chief Constable is vicariously liable for the negligence of the police officer who caused the catastrophe by admitting the crowd into the pens. It was the impact of the horror of the situation on the minds of the police officers that caused them psychiatric injury. By the negligent creation of the horrific situation the Chief Constable was in breach of his duty not to expose the police to unnecessary risk of injury and is consequently liable for their injuries.

If this approach is right, it means that the police will be entitled to recover damages, whereas spectators and others on duty in the ground who were exposed to the same horror and risk of psychiatric injury will not be able to do so. I cannot believe that this would be a fair or acceptable state of the law. If anything, one would expect the police to be at a disadvantage. The police are trained to deal with catastrophic incidents and are reasonably well compensated under the terms of their service if they do suffer injury in the course of their duties.

The law of master and servant is not a discrete and separate branch of the law of tort, but is to be considered in relation to actions in tort generally. Here, we are considering the tort of negligence and the nature of the duty of care owed by one who negligently creates a catastrophic situation. In order that there shall be some limits to the consequence of the negligence for which the defendant is to be made liable the law imposes the controls I have discussed in *Alcock*.

In my view, these should apply to all those not directly imperilled or who reasonably believe themselves to be imperilled, irrespective of whether they are employees or not. Accordingly, I would allow the appeals in so far as the police rely upon their status as employees.

I turn last to the special category known as 'rescuers'. If a tortfeasor creates a dangerous situation, he can foresee that others will attempt to rescue the victims, or potential victims of his negligence. It is well settled that if a rescuer suffers physical injury in the rescue attempt he will be entitled to damages from the tortfeasor. If it is foreseeable that the rescuer may suffer personal injury in the form of psychiatric injury rather than physical injury, why should he not recover for that injury? The fear is expressed that if foreseeability of psychiatric injury is sufficient it will open the floodgates to claims, many of the unmeritorious kind, from those who give assistance to any accident. I believe that the courts are well capable of controlling any such flood of claims. Whether or not a person is to be regarded as a rescuer will be a question of fact, to be decided on the particular facts of the case. Trivial or peripheral assistance will not be sufficient; see *McFarlane v EE Caledonia Ltd* [1994] 2 All ER 1.

If the rescuer is in no physical danger, it will only be in exceptional cases that personal injury in the form of psychiatric injury will be foreseeable for the law must take us to be sufficiently robust to give help at accidents that are a daily occurrence, without suffering a psychiatric breakdown. But where the accident is of a particular horrifying kind and the rescuer is involved with the victims in the immediate aftermath it may be reasonably foreseeable that the rescuer will suffer psychiatric injury, as Mr Chadwick did when trying to bring relief and comfort to the victims of the Lewisham train disaster. Mr Chadwick suffered his injury because of the terrible impact on his mind of the suffering he witnessed in his rescue attempt, and not because of any fear for his own safety; see *Chadwick v British Railways Board* [1967] 1 WLR 912. What rescuer ever thinks of his own safety? It seems to me that it would be a very artificial and unnecessary control, to say a rescuer can only recover if he was in fact in physical danger. A danger to which he probably never gave thought, and which in the event might not cause physical injury.

A line has to be drawn in rescue cases between rescue in the sense of immediate help at the scene of the disaster, and treatment of the victims after they are safe. I do not believe that this will be difficult to recognise on the facts of a particular case.

...

... I do not share the view that the public would find it in some way offensive that those who suffered disabling psychiatric illness as a result of their efforts to rescue the victims should receive compensation, but that those who suffered the grief of bereavement should not. Bereavement and grief are a part of the common condition of mankind which we will all endure at some time in our lives. It can be an appalling experience but it is different in kind from psychiatric illness and the law has never recognised it as a head of damage. We are human and we must accept as a part of the price of our humanity the suffering of bereavement for which no sum of money can provide solace or comfort. I think better of my fellow men than to believe that they would, although bereaved, look like dogs in the manger upon those who went to the rescue at Hillsborough.

– – –

No liability to bystanders

In *Robertson and Rough v Forth Bridge Joint Board* (1995)[18] the Court of Session held that an employee was not entitled to damages for psychiatric injury suffered as a result of witnessing a fatal accident in which a fellow employee was killed due to the negligence of the employer. There was no particular tie of love or affection between the plaintiffs and the deceased and the claimants were in no personal danger. This case can be contrasted with two others.

In *Dooley v Cammell Laird & Co* (1951)[19] the High Court granted damages to a crane driver for nervous shock suffered when a defective sling allowed the crane's load to fall into the ship's hold where men were working. This decision is usually explained on the basis that the negligence of other workers caused the driver to believe he had personally caused injury to another.

18   [1995] IRLR 251.
19   [1951] 1 Lloyd's Rep 271.

In *Young v Charles Church (Southern) Ltd and Another* (1997)[20] the claimant had suffered psychiatric illness after seeing his workmate electrocuted close to him when the pole they were moving touched an overhead electric wire. The employers of the two men were both negligent and in breach of the Construction (General Provisions) Regulations, regulation 44. In this case it was held that the claimant was personally at risk; it was chance that it was his colleague, rather than he, who was killed. Therefore, the claimant was entitled to compensation.

Liability for stress caused by work overload

The reluctance of the courts to grant compensation for psychiatric injury caused otherwise than by nervous shock has now been overcome in cases where an employee has suffered a foreseeable mental breakdown as a result of work overload endured over a period of time. The leading cases of *Johnstone v Bloomsbury Health Authority* (1991) and *Walker v Northumberland County Council* (1995) are considered later in this and the next chapter.

III CAN LIABILITY BE AVOIDED?

While the cases before 1970 were concerned with whether the relationship between the plaintiff and defendant had, by operation of law, created a duty of care owed by the defendant to the plaintiff, there remains a question as to whether circumstances, or the expressed intention of the parties, may override the normal legal duty. This question has been considered in at least two cases.

In both of the cases set out below the defendant was the employer of the claimant, so they were traditional cases of employer's liability. The employer's duty is subject to the following limits:

(a) it lasts for the period during which the employee is within the course of that employer's employment; and

(b) it is based on an implied term in the contract of employment.

These were the matters concerning which issues were raised.

(a) Was the employee in the defendant employer's employment?

In the following case, the question was whether, having loaned the employee to another employer, the principal employer had been released from the duty to provide a safe system of work. It will be recalled that *Wilsons & Clyde Coal Co Ltd v English* (1938) had laid down that, *while* the employee was working for the employer, the employer had a non-delegable duty to take reasonable

---

20 (1997) *The Times*, 1 May.

care to provide a safe system of work. Was there an exception to this rule when the employee was loaned to, *and working for*, another employer?

MCDERMID v NASH DREDGING AND RECLAMATION CO LTD
[1987] 1 AC 908

The following are extracts from the judgment of Lord Hailsham, beginning at p 909:

> The plaintiff was employed as a deckhand by a contract in writing dated 18 June 1975 in connection with dredging work on a fjord at Lulea in Sweden. In the first sentence of this contract it was expressly agreed: 'The employee shall safely comply with the lawful directions of the company's representatives ...' It must be noted that the defendants' employers were a subsidiary (it is believed, wholly owned) of a Dutch company Stevin Baggeren BV ('Stevin'). The function of the defendants was to provide and pay the British staff engaged in the operation.

> At the time of the accident, by direction of the defendants, the plaintiff was working on the deck of a tug (the *Ina*) owned by Stevin and under the command of her Dutch skipper (Captain Sas) who was an employee of Stevin. The tug was in fact operated turn and turn about by Captain Sas and a British skipper (Captain Clifford) who was an employee of the defendants. At all material times, however, and by direction of the defendants under clause 1 of the contract of service, the *Ina* and the plaintiff were both under the total operational control of Captain Sas and subject to his orders.

> The accident may be very simply described. The plaintiff's duty, so far as material, was to tie and untie the *Ina* from a dredger to which she was made fast fore and aft by means in each case of a nylon rope attached to a bollard on the dredger by an eye and to the tug by a number of figure of eight loops and two half hitches. At the time of the accident the plaintiff was under orders to untie with a view to the *Ina* going astern. He safely untied the aft rope and stowed it inboard the *Ina*. He then went forward to untie the forward rope from the dredger. His correct drill, had he completed it, would have been to slacken the rope on the *Ina*'s starboard bollards in order to reduce the tension, to allow the deckhand on the dredger (whom he could clearly see) to take the eye of the rope off the dredger's port bollard and then haul the rope in and stow it safely inboard the *Ina*, proceed to the wheelhouse and give it a double knock with his hand, in order to signal to Captain Sas that it was safe to move. In the event, after he had loosened the forward rope from the *Ina*'s bollards, and before the deckhand on the dredger had had time to remove the eye of the rope from the bollard on the dredger, Captain Sas, who was at the wheel of the *Ina*, put the engine hard astern. As a result, the rope snaked round the plaintiff's leg, pulled him into the water and caused him injuries which involved the amputation of his leg and damage, recently (28 April 1986) assessed at £178,450.05 by Staughton J, to whom the case had been remitted for this purpose by the Court of Appeal.

> The plaintiff's claim in the proceedings was based on the allegation, *inter alia*, of a 'non-delegable' duty resting on his employers to take reasonable care to

provide a 'safe system' of work: cf *Wilsons and Clyde Coal Co Ltd v English* (1938). The defendants did not, and could not, dispute the existence of such a duty of care, nor that it was 'non-delegable' in the special sense in which the phrase is used in this connection. This special sense does not involve the proposition that the duty cannot be delegated in the sense that it is incapable of being the subject of delegation, but only that the employer cannot escape liability if the duty has been delegated and then not properly performed. Equally the defendants could not and did not attempt to dispute that it would be a central and crucial feature of any safe system on the instant facts that it would prevent so far as possible the occurrence of such an accident as actually happened, viz injury to the plaintiff as the result of the use of the *Ina*'s engine so as to move the *Ina* before both the ropes were clear of the dredger and stowed safely inboard and the plaintiff was in a position of safety.

...

The 'system' was therefore not being operated and was therefore not being 'provided' at all. It matters not whether one says that there was no 'system' in operation at all or whether one says that the system provided was unsafe or whether one says that the system in fact provided was not in use at the crucial stage. In any event the defendants had delegated their duty to the plaintiff to Captain Sas, the duty had not been performed, and the defendants must pay for the breach of their 'non-delegable' obligation.

Before your Lordships it was strenuously argued that the fact that Captain Sas operated the engine in such dangerous circumstances was the 'casual' or 'collateral' negligence of an employee of an independent contractor, ie Stevin. Since Stevin was itself the holding company of the defendants, the defendants being its wholly owned subsidiary, I find this morally an unattractive proposition. But the fact was that the defendants had delegated their own 'non-delegable' duty to Captain Sas who had charge of the whole operation and his negligence was not 'collateral' or 'casual' but central to the case and in total disregard of the duty owed to the plaintiff to see that the engine was not put in operation at all until it had been ascertained that it was safe to do so. Whether the system as designed by Captain Sas was adequately safe or not, whether it can truthfully be said that there was in any real sense a system at all or whether there was a system not unsafe but not being operated, the defendants had delegated their own 'non-delegable' duty and it had not been performed.

...

In the event this appeal must be dismissed with costs. In my view it is, and always was, unarguable.

– – –

The case leaves unanswered whether employers would be liable if their employee were injured by another organisation's negligence in operation of the safe system which the employer had stipulated. Suppose that an employer lent a crane with an employee to operate it, giving the employee and the hirer instructions that the crane should never be moved, without the driver being given guidance from another person. Would the employer be liable if the crane driver suffered injury because the employee of the hirer failed to warn him, while the crane was being moved, of the proximity of an overhead electric cable? On these facts, the employer would not, as in *McDermid*, be denying the duty of care, but would be claiming that it could not be vicariously liable for the negligent conduct of someone not in its employment.

(b) Can an express term override the implied duty of care?

One of the questions which had to be addressed in the following case was whether the employers' duty to take reasonable care, being an implied duty, could be overridden by an express term of the contract of employment.

JOHNSTONE v BLOOMSBURY HEALTH AUTHORITY
[1991] IRLR 118

The employee claimed that the employers were under a duty to take all reasonable care for his safety and that they were in breach of that duty by requiring him to work intolerable hours. Before the case went to trial, the master granted the employers' application under rules of the High Court to strike out that part of the claim which sought a declaration that the claimant could not lawfully be required to work for more than 72 hours. However, Mr Bennett QC, sitting as a deputy High Court judge, allowed the claimant's appeal. On a further appeal to the Court of Appeal that court, by a majority, held the employers could not lawfully require the claimant hospital doctor to work so much overtime in any week as it was reasonably foreseeable would damage his health, notwithstanding the express terms of his contract. The following extracts are taken from the judgment of Stuart-Smith LJ, beginning at p 120:

> The effect of this [contractual] provision is that the plaintiff is required to work a basic 40 hours a week and the Authority are bound to provide and pay for 40 hours a week. In addition, however, the plaintiff is required to be available, on call, for up to a further 48 hours on average. This means that in some weeks he may have to work considerably more than 88 hours in total, though the average must not exceed this each week taken over a period. It is also worth noting that payment for any hours worked over 40 are somewhat unusually not paid at a higher rate than the basic pay, but at one-third of this rate.

> By paragraph 4 of the statement of claim the plaintiff alleged that the Authority owed him a number of duties as his employer. But the only one relevant to this appeal is paragraph 4(a), which alleged that the Authority were under a duty to take all reasonable care for his safety and well being. Although there has been some ambivalence in the plaintiff's pleadings as to the basis upon which this duty arises, namely, whether in tort or by implication of law into the contract of employment, the distinction is immaterial, since it can be both, see *Matthews v Kuwait Bechtel Corp* (1959).[21]

---

21 [1959] 2 QB 57.

...

In my opinion paragraph 4(b) gave the Authority the power to require the plaintiff to work up to 88 hours per week on average. But that power had to be exercised in the light of the other contractual terms and in particular their duty to take care for his safety.

– – –

The majority of their Lordships being of the view that it remained the employers' duty, regardless of any contractual terms, to provide a safe system of work, the case could go to trial on the question of whether, on the facts, the employers had failed to do so.[22]

---

22 The case was settled out of court; the employers made a payment of £5,600 ((1995) *The Times*, 6 July).

CHAPTER 5

LIABILITY FOR PERSONAL INJURY 2: BREACH OF DUTY

The judge, hearing a claim for common law negligence, listens to the evidence presented by the parties and decides whether the defendant has broken the duty of care owed by the defendant to the claimant. As was pointed out by Lord Somervell in *Qualcast v Haynes* (1959)[1] the findings of fact, which judges make when evaluating evidence, and the rulings which they make as to whether these facts show there has been a lack of reasonable care, do not create precedents. Now that it is clear that in any case the duty is simply to take reasonable care, the determination of whether the claimant is entitled to compensation is normally more concerned with determining the facts than with clarifying the law. Consequently, since 1970, relatively few personal injury cases have reached the law reports. Also, perhaps fewer claims are litigated and more are settled out of court by insurers.

Criteria of liability

The duty in the common law tort of negligence is to 'take reasonable care'. The duty is owed to the foreseeable victim. The duty is broken by a defendant who fails to take reasonable care, by reason of negligent conduct. Again, the criterion is governed by foreseeability. The classic statement of negligent conduct was made by Alderson B in *Blyth v Birmingham Waterworks Co* (1856),[2] a case which much pre-dated the recognition of the separate tort of negligence:

> Negligence is the omission to do something which a reasonable man, guided upon those considerations which ordinarily regulate the conduct of human affairs, would do, or doing something which a prudent and reasonable man would not do.

This statement is not very helpful today. First, the defendant is more likely to be a corporate body than a human person. Secondly, that corporation is likely to be a commercial enterprise, holding itself out as an expert in its field. Such legal persons are expected to have tested their products and employed expertise in setting up their systems. They must also ensure that their systems are maintained and updated in the light of experience.

---

1   [1959] 1 AC 743.
2   (1856) 11 Ex 781.

The following cases indicate the criteria that the courts will take into account when deciding whether conduct has been negligent. Arguably, nearly all of these cases are concerned with the prevention of injury that is foreseeable.

(a) Defendants are expected to learn from experience

A brief reference has already been made to *Stokes v GKN* (1968), a case which illustrated how industry is expected to learn from experience, their own and that of others, so that, while one accident may be unforeseeable and, therefore, excusable, a second may not. This point was well made in the following case.

ROE V MINISTER OF HEALTH [1954] 2 QB 66

The claimants had entered hospital for surgery, for which they were given anaesthetic (nupercaine) by spinal injection. These injections caused them to become paralysed. Subsequent investigation suggested that the anaesthetic had been contaminated because sterilising fluid (phenol) had percolated through fine cracks in the glass ampoules in which the anaesthetic was packed. The following extracts are taken from the judgment of Denning LJ, beginning at p 86:

> Asking myself, therefore, what was the risk involved in careless handling of the ampoules, I answer by saying that there was such a probability of intervening examination as to limit the risk. The only consequence which could reasonably be anticipated was the loss of a quantity of nupercaine but not the paralysis of a patient. The hospital authorities are therefore not liable for it.

> When you stop to think of what happened in the present case, you will realise that it was a most extraordinary chapter of accidents. In some way the ampoules must have received a jolt, perhaps while a nurse was putting them into the jar or while a trolley was being moved along. The jolt cannot have been very severe. It was not severe enough to break any of the ampoules or even to crack them so far as anyone could see. But it was just enough to produce an invisible crack. The crack was of a kind which no one in any experiment has been able to reproduce again. It was too fine to be seen, but it was enough to let in sufficient phenol to corrode the nerves, whilst still leaving enough nupercaine to anaesthetise the patient. And this very exceptional crack occurred not in one ampoule only, but in two ampoules used on the self same day in two successive operations; and none of the other ampoules was damaged at all. This has taught the doctors to be on their guard against invisible cracks. Never again, it is to be hoped, will such a thing happen. After this accident a leading textbook was published in 1951 which contains the significant warning: 'Never place ampoules of local anaesthetic solution in alcohol or spirit. This common practice is probably responsible for some of the cases of permanent paralysis reported after spinal analgesia.' If the hospitals were to continue the practice after this warning, they could not complain if they were found guilty of negligence. But the warning had not been given at

the time of this accident. Indeed, it was the extraordinary accident to these two men which first disclosed the danger. Nowadays it would be negligence not to realise the danger, but it was not then.

– – –

(b) Evaluation of risk

Denning LJ's judgment in *Roe* is interesting not only because it indicates the importance of learning from experience, but because he also recognises that negligence is related to the evaluation of risk. This was also recognised in *Bolton v Stone* (1951)[3] (noted in Chapter 1) where the distinction was made between foreseeability and probability and it was held that it was not necessarily negligent to ignore an eventuality which was possible; but it was negligent to ignore something which might probably occur.

In *Read v J Lyons* (1947)[4] (noted in Chapter 3), Lord Macmillan (at p 172) also related negligent conduct to risk, stating: 'The more dangerous is the act the greater is the care that must be taken in performing it.' Lord Macmillan in that case was considering the use of explosives. He was therefore considering an operation which was 'risky' in two ways: there was both a likelihood of explosion and a likelihood of serious injury occurring. Liability for negligent conduct is concerned with both these aspects of risk. For example, it may be possible to earn high fees for performing a juggling act which involves spinning china saucers on the point of a stick. It is highly probable that the trainee juggler will break many saucers while perfecting the art, but this is unlikely to deter the novice, as old saucers are not costly when compared with the fee that it is possible to earn. The juggler might also be prepared to accept a few minor injuries (such as blisters or small cuts) in the course of learning his art. In other words evaluating whether a risk is acceptable is a cost-benefit exercise.

In deciding whether it is negligent to ignore a risk judges have to take into account both the likelihood of an accident occurring and the severity of the injury which is likely to result. However they also have to consider the cost of avoiding the injury.

(i) Loss of production

LATIMER v AEC LTD [1953] AC 643

The floor of a factory was flooded as a result of an unusually heavy rainstorm and the flood water caused oily waste to be swept from drainage channels and deposited on the factory floor, leaving the floor slippery. Sawdust was put on

---

3   [1951] AC 850.
4   [1947] AC 156.

the floor, but there was insufficient to cover the whole surface. A workman slipped and suffered injury. The House of Lords held that the defendant employers were not negligent in allowing their employees, including the plaintiff, to continue to work while this risk existed. The following extract is from Lord Porter's speech, beginning at p 652:

> My Lords, undoubtedly the respondents did their best to get rid of the effects of the flood, employing such of the day workers as could be spared and obtaining volunteers from them for work in the interval between day and night work and from the night shift at a later period, but in the learned judge's opinion it was not possible for them to take any further steps to make the floor less slippery. I understand his view to have been, however, that, inasmuch as the effect of the storm left the gangway in question, and possibly other portions of the works, somewhat slippery and therefore potentially dangerous, they should have shut down the whole works if necessary, or at any rate such portion as was dangerous.

> My Lords, the difficulty which I feel about this solution is that neither the necessity for such an action nor its effect was ever pleaded, explored or considered until the respondents' counsel was in the course of making his final speech.

> ...

> Upon the issue of common law negligence as now presented the direction which should be given is not in doubt. It is that the duty of the tribunal is to determine what action in the circumstances which have been proved would a reasonably prudent man have taken. The probability of a workman slipping is one matter which must be borne in mind but it must be remembered that no one else did so. Nor does the possibility seem to have occurred to anyone at the time. It is true that after the event Mr Milne, one of the respondents' witnesses, expressed the opinion that he would not have gone on to the floor in the condition in which it was and that it would be too dangerous to do so. But this was after the event, and, though he was the respondents' safety engineer and was present until late that night, it seems never to have occurred to him that there was any danger or that any further steps than those actually taken were possible or required for the safety of the employees. The seriousness of shutting down the works and sending the night shift home and the importance of carrying on the work upon which the factory was engaged are all additional elements for consideration and without adequate information on these matters it is impossible to express any final opinion. Moreover, owing to the course taken at the trial there is no material for enabling one to judge whether a partial closing of the factory was possible or the extent to which the cessation of the respondents' activities would have retarded the whole of the work being carried on. In my view, in these circumstances, the appellant has not established that a reasonably careful employer would have shut down the works or that the respondents ought to have taken the drastic step of closing the factory.

– – –

(ii) Cost of prevention versus cost to victim

PARIS v STEPNEY BOROUGH COUNCIL [1951] AC 367

The appellant motor mechanic had, to the knowledge of the defendant employers, sight in only one eye. He was trying to remove a rusty bolt from a vehicle when a metal chip flew out and injured his good eye. His employers had not provided him with goggles. All their Lordships were of the view that the special risk of serious injury to the particular man, who was already, to the knowledge of the employers, seriously disabled was a factor to be taken into consideration when deciding whether the employers were in breach of the duty which they owed to him personally. The majority of their Lordships found the employers had been negligent in failing to provide goggles. The following extract is taken from the speech of Lord MacDermott, beginning at p 389:

> ... For workman and employer alike such expressions as 'risk', 'danger' and 'safety' would lose much of their everyday meaning if divorced from the results to life and limb. In this sphere they must surely, in the very nature of things, connote consequences as well as causes. If a bricklayer says that the risk is greater at the top of a building he means that a slip there is more likely to bring him death or injury, and if he says that a particular form of scaffolding is dangerous or not safe he means not merely that it may fall, but that those who use it may get hurt. What may happen to those engaged is no less important than how it may happen. It is the consequences that necessitate the precautions in this field. The habitual association of cause and effect in workshop and factory is perhaps nowhere more clearly recognised than in the nature of some of the safeguards in common use. Suitable goggles, for example, must be worn by those employed at grinding machines. The particles that fly upward may strike the cheeks as readily as the eyes, but the eyes are protected and the cheeks are not, because the eyes are delicate organs and the consequences of their being struck are likely to be serious. Again, special precautions to prevent electric leakage are the usual practice in places like wash houses where those working are well 'earthed' and a shock might prove fatal. Instances of this sort could be multiplied, but I think it is enough to say that the employer's duty to take reasonable care for the safety of his workmen is directed – and, I venture to add, obviously directed – to their welfare and, for that reason, if for no other, must be related to both the risk and the degree of the injury. If that is so and if, as was very properly conceded, the duty is that owed to the individual and not to a class, it seems to me to follow that the known circumstances that a particular workman is likely to suffer a graver injury than his fellows from the happening of a given event is one which must be taken into consideration in assessing the nature of the employer's obligation to that workman.

To the above may be added the comment of Lord Oaksey at p 385:

> ... It is a simple and inexpensive precaution to take to supply goggles ...

– – –

(iii) Standards may differ in an emergency

WATT v HERTFORDSHIRE COUNTY COUNCIL [1954] 1 WLR 835

The claimant was employed by the defendants, the local fire authority, as a fireman. An emergency call was received, while the claimant was on duty, that a woman was trapped under a heavy vehicle about 200 or 300 yards away. The officer in charge instructed the claimant's team to go to the accident in a lorry, taking a jack weighing several hundred pounds. The jack was not often required and the vehicle normally used to transport it was not available. The lorry actually used had nothing by which the jack could be lashed in place. It would have taken at least ten minutes to get a suitable lorry from another fire station. During the journey the lorry had to brake and the jack was thrown on to the claimant, seriously injuring his ankle. The Court of Appeal upheld the judgment of the trial judge in favour of the defendants. The short judgment of Denning LJ at p 838 is quoted in full:

> It is well settled that in measuring due care you must balance the risk against the measures necessary to eliminate the risk. To that proposition there ought to be added this: you must balance the risk against the end to be achieved. If this accident had occurred in a commercial enterprise without any emergency there could be no doubt that the servant would succeed. But the commercial end to make profit is very different from the human end to save life or limb. The saving of life or limb justifies taking considerable risk, and I am glad to say, that there have never been wanting in this country men of courage ready to take those risks, notably in the fire service.
>
> In this case the risk involved in sending out the lorry was not so great as to prohibit the attempt to save life. I quite agree that fire engines, ambulances and doctors' cars should not shoot past the traffic lights when they show a red light. That is because the risk is too great to warrant the incurring of the danger. It is always a question of balancing the risk against the end. I agree that this appeal should be dismissed.

– – –

(c) The custom and practice of industry

In deciding whether a risk is unacceptable the judges have regard to the custom and practice within an industry. In *Paris v Stepney Borough Council*, already cited in this chapter, the fact that it was not the practice of the industry to provide goggles to men working under motor vehicles was considered and strongly influenced the dissenting judges. However, as the following extracts from the judgment of Lord Simonds, at p 376, demonstrate, such evidence is not conclusive:

> My Lords, a study of the evidence leaves me in no doubt that an employer could not be held guilty of negligence if he did not generally provide goggles for the use of his employees engaged in this kind of work. The respondents' public cleansing officer, Mr Boden, to whom I have already referred, a witness of wide experience, being asked, 'Have you seen in work of this kind workmen

wearing goggles to do such work?', replied 'Not in my experience. I have never seen any mechanic working in any of the repair shops that I have visited during that 37 years wearing goggles doing that repair work'. A Mr Reay, having served his time in the shops where he had neither himself worn nor seen others wearing goggles for such work, set up in business for himself. He was asked, 'When you were your own employer, did you wear goggles for such work?' and he answered 'No'. The appellant himself gave evidence, which, so far as it bears on the obviousness of the risk and corresponding duty, cannot be disregarded. I make nothing of the fact that he did not complain that goggles were not provided, for he might well hesitate to do so. But being asked, 'Have you considered as to whether it was dangerous to do this sort of job without eye protection?', he answered, 'Well, we were always working through years just doing the same thing. It became natural to get in there without protection'. Then he was asked, 'You did not think about it?' and answered, 'We had been doing it for years and never thought of it'. It is true that he added that if goggles had been provided and he had been told to use them, he would have done so. But this does not appear to carry the matter any further. For the appellant, a Captain Paterson said, in answer to the judge, that in the whole of his experience he had about a dozen times seen a man wearing goggles when he was using a hammer to knock a rusted bolt in dismantling a car, adding that would be when working under a vehicle. It is not clear whether on these occasions the man was wearing goggles for fear of a splinter of metal piercing his eye or of grit or dirt falling into it. Mr Parker, at the relevant time the mechanical superintendent of the respondents' cleansing department, while asserting that it was not normal practice to wear goggles for the work in question, said he had seen men, who were working underneath a vehicle, wearing goggles. That was 'preferably if they were laying on their backs'. Of the single instance that he could distinctly remember he assumed that the man was doing it to prevent dust getting into his eyes.

The evidence in regard to practice appears to me overwhelming. But however unlikely such an event may be in such an organised community as ours is today, it is possible that the practice, however widespread, is carried on in disregard of risks that are obvious ...

– – –

In the above case their Lordships were all of the view that the industry practice of allowing two eyed workers to undertake the work in question was an acceptable one. In the following case their Lordships were not prepared to accept the industry practice.

CAVANAGH v ULSTER WEAVING CO LTD [1960] AC 145

The appellant, who was employed by the respondents as a labourer, was seriously injured when he fell from a crawling board, which had no handrail, onto a glass roof, while carrying a bucket of cement. The trial was in Northern Ireland, before a jury. At the trial the defendants called evidence which established that the system they operated was in accordance with industry practice. It was not clear whether it was part of industry practice that, as in this case, a workman undertaking a task of this nature should wear rubber boots. In the House of Lords their Lordships had to decide whether the jury had been entitled to find the defendant employers had been negligent. The issue was whether, in the light of words of Lord Dunedin in *Morton v Wm Dixon Ltd* (1909)[5] the defendants could be said, once they showed they had complied with industry practice, to have established conclusively that they had not been negligent:

> ... the thing which [the employer] did not do was a thing which was commonly done by other persons in like circumstances or that it was a thing which was so obviously wanted that it would be folly in anyone to neglect to provide it.

Their Lordships were of the view that, in this case at least, the evidence that the employer had followed common practice was not conclusive. The point is made sufficiently in the brief judgment of Viscount Simonds at p 158:

> The evidence given by the expert called for the defence in regard to what was called 'the set up', which was not seriously or, perhaps, at all challenged, was of very great weight, but I cannot say that it was so conclusive as to require the learned trial judge to withdraw the case from the jury. There were other matters also which they were entitled to take into consideration, and it was for them to determine whether in all the circumstances the respondents had taken reasonable care. I do not think that the learned judges of the Court of Appeal were justified in concluding that reasonable men might not find the verdict which this jury found. If I may respectfully say so, I think that the error of the majority of the court lay in treating as conclusive evidence which is not conclusive, however great its weight, particularly where it has to be weighed against other evidence. But that does not mean that the familiar words of Lord Dunedin in *Morton v Wm Dixon Ltd*, which have been so often quoted, both in Scottish and English cases, are not to be regarded as of great authority in determining what is in all the circumstances reasonable care. It would, I think, be unfortunate if an employer who has adopted a practice, system or set up, call it what you will, which has been widely used without complaint, could not rely on it as at least a *prima facie* defence to an action for negligence, and I would say with the greatest respect to those who think otherwise, that it would put too great a burden on him to require him to prove that the circumstances of his own case were 'precisely' similar to those of the general practice that I have assumed. But these are not questions that arise on the present appeal and I am content to move that the appeal be allowed with costs here and below.

– – –

(d) The particular responsibilities of the employer

The status of the claimant and defendant may determine what the defendant has to do when exercising reasonable care. Case law demonstrates that the employers have the following responsibilities to their employees.

---

5   (1909) SC 807, p 809.

(i) Employer must instruct and train

If the defendant is sued as an employer by one of its own employees, rather than as an occupier by a visiting worker, it is more likely that it will be expected to have taken positive steps to safeguard the claimant. If the claimant is an employee, then what is expected from the defendant employer will depend on the skill, training and experience of the claimant.

BUX v SLOUGH METALS LTD [1974] 1 All ER 262

The claimant was a Pakistani with a limited command of English, who worked from 1968 in the defendant's die casting foundry. His work involved removing molten metal from a furnace by means of a ladle and pouring from the ladle into a die. He was trained for the work without being instructed to wear goggles. In 1969 a new works' director purchased goggles and supplied a pair to each of the 15 die casters. The claimant wore them for only a few days, because he found that they misted up. He ceased to wear them, telling the superintendent of the foundry that they were useless. In 1970 molten metal was splashed into his eyes. The claimant's action for damages included a claim that his employers had been negligent in that they had failed to instruct him to wear the goggles provided. The trial judge found that the defendant employers had been negligent, but reduced the claimant's damages by 20% to take account of his contributory negligence. The defendants appealed, claiming that as they had fulfilled their statutory duty under the Non-Ferrous Metals (Melting and Founding) Regulations 1962 to provide suitable goggles they could not be found liable for negligence. The claimant's case was that the employer owed him a common law duty that went beyond the statutory one. The following extracts are taken from the judgment of Edmund Davies LJ, beginning at p 26:

> I turn, then, to consider whether the defendants were in breach of their common law duty to the plaintiff, bearing in mind the warning of Lord Radcliffe in *Qualcast (Wolverhampton) Ltd v Haynes* (1959)[6] that:
>
> '... though, indeed, there may be cases in which an employer does not discharge his duty of care towards his workmen merely by providing an article of safety equipment, the courts should be circumspect in filling out that duty with the much vaguer obligation of encouraging, exhorting and instructing workmen, or a particular workman, to make regular use of what is provided.'
>
> ...
>
> Basing himself largely on the evidence of the defendants' own expert witness, Mr Bevan, the [trial] judge said:
>
> '... in my view [what] a reasonable and careful employer should have done was to institute a system and at least endeavour to make it a rule that goggles will be worn. I think, on the facts of this case [counsel for the defendants] was

---

6   [1959] AC 743.

entitled to say that there was, in effect, acquiescence in goggles not being worn in this department. I think that a different atmosphere should have been created and that insistence should have been shown on men wearing goggles. They should have been educated and there should have been a degree of co-operation with them about the wearing of goggles, instead of leaving the matter entirely to them, which was in fact the position.'

The non-wearing of goggles thus becoming the established and accepted practice, he concluded that negligence had been established.

Was this right? Did reasonable care for the safety of their workmen require these defendants to do more than they did? In *Haynes v Qualcast (Wolverhampton) Ltd* (1958)[7] in the Court of Appeal, where the employers were successfully sued in negligence in relation to the failure of their workmen to wear spats when dealing with molten metal, Lord Evershed MR said that the obligation of the defendants extended to more than merely having the spats available in case any experienced moulder thought he would like to ask for them. This was followed a few months later by Paull J in *Nolan v Dental Manufacturing Co Ltd* (1958).[8] *Qualcast* (1958) was, as we have seen, reversed by the House of Lords, but the *ratio decidendi* there was that the county court judge had erroneously concluded that, although no instruction or persuasion to wear spats was in his view called for, he was bound by earlier decisions to hold that it was, whereas this was in truth a pure question of fact for him.

...

The question of whether instruction or persuasion or even insistence in using protective equipment should be resorted to is, therefore, at large, the answer depending on the facts of the particular case. One of the most important of these is the nature and degree of the risk of serious harm resulting if it is not worn.

...

But, on the facts found, the plaintiff was clearly in breach of regulation 13(4) ... I have to say, with respect, that in all the circumstances I am satisfied in the present case that the 20:80 apportionment inadequately reflects the degree of blameworthiness which should be attributed to the plaintiff. For my part, I think that a 40:60 apportionment would be more just and is called for.

— — —

GENERAL CLEANING CONTRACTORS LTD v CHRISTMAS
[1952] 2 All ER 1110

The respondent was employed by the appellants to clean the windows of a club. He followed the practice of window cleaners and stood on the sill of a window to clean its outside. While he was holding on to one sash for support the other fell down on his fingers, causing him to let go, fall to the ground and suffer injury. The House of Lords took the view that the employers were

---

7   [1958] 1 All ER 441, p 444.

8   [1958] 2 All ER 449.

negligent in failing to devise a safe system for carrying out such operations on the property their employees had to visit and they ought to have instructed their employees how to avoid accidents. The occupiers of the premises were originally joined as defendants, but the Court of Appeal found that a defective sash was not an 'unusual' danger of which they ought to have warned a visiting window cleaner. The occupiers were not party to the appeal to the House of Lords. It is noteworthy that similar facts came before the Court of Appeal in *King v Smith and Another* (1995).[9] In this latter case, which is further noted below, both the employer and the occupier of the premises were held liable. The view of their Lordships as to the liability of the employers is well expressed in the judgment of Lord Oaksey, beginning at p 114:

> In my opinion, it is the duty of an employer to give such general safety instructions as a reasonably careful employer who has considered the problem presented by the work would give to his workmen. It is, I think, well known to employers, and there is evidence in this case that it was well known to the appellants, that their workpeople are very frequently, if not habitually, careless about the risks which their work may involve. It is, in my opinion, for that very reason that the common law demands that employers should take reasonable care to lay down a reasonably safe system of work. Employers are not exempted from this duty by the fact that their men are experienced and might, if they were in the position of an employer, be able to lay down a reasonably safe system of work themselves. Workmen are not in the position of employers. Their duties are not performed in the calm atmosphere of a board room with the advice of experts. They have to make their decisions on narrow window sills and other places of danger, and in circumstances in which the dangers are obscured by repetition. The risk that sashes may unexpectedly close, as the sashes in this case appear to have done, may not happen very often, but when it does, if the workman is steadying himself by a hand hold, his fall is almost certain. If the possibility is faced, the risk is obvious. If both sashes are closed, there is no longer the hand hold by which the workman steadies himself. If either sash is kept open, the hand hold is available and, on the evidence in this case, is, in my opinion, reasonably safe. But the problem is one for the employer to solve and should not, in my opinion, be left to the workman. It can be solved by general orders and the provision of appropriate appliances. The risk is undeniable and was not denied by the appellants' director, Mr Mahoney. This risk could be eliminated or lessened by orders that one sash must always be kept open where the hand hold system is adopted and suitable wedges could be provided. The appellants, knowing the risk, did nothing and have appealed to your Lordships' House, with the avowed object of having this system declared to be reasonably safe. In my opinion, the system as carried on by the appellants is not reasonably safe and the appellants did not take reasonable care to ensure that it was.

– – –

---

9   [1995] ICR 339.

(ii) Employer must operate a safe system

MCARTHUR v BRITISH RAILWAYS BOARD (1968) 6 KIR 40

British Railways Board used various classes of locomotives for distant shunting runs. The model which the deceased was driving at the time of the fatal accident provided no visibility to a driver undertaking tender-first travel, unless he put out his head and looked along the side or over the tender. The journey the deceased had to undertake included a bridge, which was generally known to provide an unusually small clearance on the controls side of a locomotive driven tender-first and there was a signal near to that bridge. Drivers had complained that tender-first running on this route with engines with poor visibility was unsafe. The depot shed master asked for better engines (Q1s), but he was told that none could be spared. The deceased suffered his fatal accident when he leant out of the cab to observe the signal and was struck when passing the bridge. The widow brought a successful action against the board for their negligence in not having re-routed her husband so that he drove engine-first, for not providing a locomotive with tender-first visibility and in not putting a notice to warn the driver against putting his head out. The following passage is from the judgment of Eveleigh J, at p 47:

> I have come to the conclusion that there was here an appreciable risk that called for something to be done. Apart from ringing Feltham and asking for a Q1, nothing was done. I do not believe that it was beyond the resources of the board to do no more than that. I think that each of the possible steps put forward by the plaintiff, namely re-routing, providing an engine or tender with visibility (and I mean by that not necessarily only from those that existed at Nine Elms; I am referring to the resources of the board) or to provide a notice, were possibilities. I think that, in failing to do more than was done, the board were negligent. I think, on the evidence before me, it was certainly reasonable to provide a different kind of tender and, if a different kind of tender had been provided, I am satisfied that there would have been no need for the deceased to put his head out and this accident would not have occurred.

– – –

(iii) Employer must protect against mental stress

WALKER v NORTHUMBERLAND COUNTY COUNCIL
[1995] IRLR 35

The plaintiff had worked for the defendants as an area social services officer for 17 years, responsible for managing four teams of social service field workers in the Blyth Valley area an area particularly productive of child care problems. In spite of the plaintiff's frequent requests to his superiors for further staff and for management guidance, neither was forthcoming.

At the end of 1986 the plaintiff suffered a nervous breakdown and, under medical advice remained off work until March 1987. He had no previous history of mental disorder and it was common ground that his illness was attributable to the impact on his personality of his work. After the plaintiff returned to work his employers did little to reduce his workload. In 1987, he suffered a second nervous breakdown; in 1988 he was dismissed from his post on the grounds of ill health.

The defendant local authority conceded that they owed the plaintiff a general duty to exercise reasonable care to provide him with a reasonably safe working system and to protect him from risks which were reasonably foreseeable, but claimed that there had been no breach of that duty. Alternatively they submitted that if the risk was reasonably foreseeable, they did not act unreasonably in failing to relieve the pressure in all the circumstances and in particular the budgetary constraints of the social services department.

Mr Justice Colman, sitting in the Queen's Bench Division, found for the plaintiff. The following extracts are from his judgment, beginning at p 41:

> There has been little judicial authority on the extent to which an employer owes to his employees a duty not to cause them psychiatric damage by the volume or character of the work which the employees are required to perform. It is clear law that an employer has a duty to provide his employee with a reasonably safe system of work and to take reasonable steps to protect him from risks which are reasonably foreseeable. Whereas the law on the extent of this duty has developed almost exclusively in cases involving physical injury to the employee as distinct from injury to his mental health, there is no logical reason why risk of psychiatric damage should be excluded from the scope of an employer's duty of care or from the co-extensive implied term in the contract of employment. That said, there can be no doubt that the circumstances in which claims based on such damage are likely to arise will often give rise to extremely difficult evidential problems of foreseeability and causation. This is particularly so in the environment of the professions where the plaintiff may be ambitious and dedicated, determined to succeed in his career in which he knows the work to be demanding, and may have a measure of discretion as to how and when and for how long he works, but where the character or volume of the work given to him eventually drives him to breaking point. Given that the professional work is intrinsically demanding and stressful, at what point is the employer's duty to take protective steps engaged? What assumption is he entitled to make about the employee's resilience, mental toughness and stability of character, given that people of clinically normal personality may have a widely differing ability to absorb stress attributable to their work?
>
> ...
>
> In the present case, the mental illness and the lasting impairment of his personality which Mr Walker sustained in consequence of the 1987 breakdown was so substantial and damaging that the magnitude of the risk to which he was exposed must be regarded as relatively large.
>
> Moreover, there can, in my judgment, be no doubt on the evidence that, by 1985 at the latest it was reasonably foreseeable to Mr Davison, given the

information which I have held that he then had, that by reason of stress of work, there was, in general *some* risk that Mr Walker might sustain a mental breakdown of some sort in consequence of his work. That said, how great was the reasonably foreseeable risk? Was the risk of incidence of illness so light as to be in all the circumstances negligible or was it a materially substantial risk? There is no evidence that the council had hitherto encountered mental illness in any other of its area officers or that area officers with heavy workloads, or others in middle management in the social services, as distinct from fieldworkers, were particularly vulnerable to stress induced mental illness. Accordingly the question is whether it ought to have been foreseen that Mr Walker was exposed to a risk of mental illness materially higher than that which would ordinarily affect a social services middle manager in his position with a really heavy workload. For if the foreseeable risk were not materially greater than that, there would not, as a matter of reasonable conduct, be any basis upon which the council's duty to act arose.

...

I find that Mr Walker was unable to cope with the work and sustained his first breakdown because, although Mr Walker's personality was normal, he was driven to the point of despair by the council's failure to provide him with what he considered to be sufficient resources to satisfy the urgent needs of the people and particularly the children of his area for social services. The stress created by his determination to provide the required services without unduly overloading his field teams and by his inability to persuade the council to support him placed him, as Professor Parsloe said, in a position where he was trapped between the two problems. Whether his inability to withstand that stress was attributable to the degree of inflexibility or frigidity in his character, which was greater than the norm is, in my judgment, beside the point. On the whole of the evidence I am not persuaded that before the first illness Mr Davison ought to have appreciated that Mr Walker was not only dissatisfied and frustrated because his area could not provide the service, but was at materially greater risk of stress-induced mental illness than an area manager with a busy area would normally be.

I therefore consider that before the 1986 illness it was not reasonably foreseeable to the council that the workload to which Mr Walker was exposed gave rise to a material risk of mental illness.

...

... I have no doubt that it ought to have been foreseen by Mr Davison that if Mr Walker was again exposed to the same workload as he had been handling at the time of his breakdown in October 1986 there was a risk that he would again succumb to mental illness and that such illness would be likely to end his career as an area manager and perhaps his career in the social services ...

Neither counsel was able to refer me to any decided case in which it had been suggested that in the context of a contract of employment between a statutory body and an employee the body could rely on considerations of policy to justify a decision which caused damage or injury to the employee to the effect that the court was, as a matter of law, precluded from evaluating the reasonableness of the statutory body's conduct.

In my judgment the policy decision/operational decision dichotomy has no more part to play in the context of the duty of care to an employee with whom a statutory body has a contract of employment than it would have in the context of any other contract made by such a body ... Since the scope of the duty of care owed to an employee to take reasonable steps to provide a safe system of work is co-extensive with the scope of the implied term as to the employee's safety in the contract of employment: (ee, for example, *Johnstone v Bloomsbury Health Authority* (1991),[10] to introduce a ring fence round policy decisions giving rise to unsafe systems of work for the purposes of claims in tort which was not available to the defendant statutory body in defences to claims in contract would be to implant into employment law a disparity which, in my judgment, would be wholly wrong in principle. Where the mutual intention to be imputed to the parties to a contract of employment with a public body could be expected to qualify the employer's duty of safety by requiring the employer to do no more than take reasonable steps to procure the employee's safety at work, it is inconceivable that such mutual intention would require the employer to take only such steps for the employee's safety as political expediency from time to time permitted if the exercise of statutory powers were involved. In the absence of authority to the contrary or of compelling common law principle, there can be no sustainable basis for subjecting the duty of care in tort to such a qualification.

– – –

(e) Particular responsibilities of occupiers to visitors

(i) THE OCCUPIER'S LIABILITY ACT 1957

Section 2

Extent of occupier's duty

...

(3) The circumstances relevant for the present purpose include the degree of care, and of want of care, which would ordinarily be looked for in such a visitor, so that (for example) in proper cases–

    (a) an occupier must be prepared for children to be less careful than adults; and

    (b) an occupier may expect that a person, in the exercise of his calling, will appreciate and guard against any special risks ordinarily incident to it, so far as the occupier leaves him free to do so.

(4) In determining whether the occupier of premises has discharged the common duty of care to a visitor, regard is to be had to all the circumstances, so that (for example)–

    (a) where damage is caused to a visitor by a danger of which he had been

---

10 [1991] IRLR 118.

warned by the occupier, the warning is not to be treated without more as absolving the occupier from liability, unless, in all the circumstances it was enough to enable the visitor to be reasonably safe; and

(b) where damage is caused to a visitor by a danger due to the faulty execution of any work of construction, maintenance or repair by an independent contractor employed by the occupier, the occupier is not to be treated without more as answerable for the danger if in all the circumstances he had acted reasonably in entrusting the work to an independent contractor and had taken such steps (if any) as he reasonably ought in order to satisfy himself that the contractor was competent and that the work had been properly done.

(5) The common duty of care does not impose on an occupier any obligation to a visitor in respect of risks willingly accepted as his by the visitor (the question whether a risk was so accepted to be decided on the same principles as in other cases in which one person owes a duty of care to another).

(6) For the purposes of this section, persons who enter premises for any purpose in the exercise of a right conferred by law are to be treated as permitted by the occupier to be there for that purpose, whether they in fact have his permission or not.

Note: s 2(1) and s 2(2) were noted in Chapter 4. This chapter is concerned with the statutory provisions spelling out what the occupier has to do to discharge the duty of reasonable care in relation to specific categories of visitors.

(ii) Case law on liability of occupier to visiting worker

There have been a number of judicial decisions on what is required of the occupier by the provisions of the Occupiers' Liability Act 1957 to discharge the duty to take reasonable care for the safety of the visiting worker, bearing in mind that the Act states that '... an occupier may expect that a person, in the exercise of his calling, will appreciate and guard against any special risks ordinarily incident to it, so far as the occupier leaves him free to do so' (s 2(3)(b)).

For many years, the leading authority was the Court of Appeal's decision in *Roles v Nathan* (1963) which appeared to take the view that the visiting workman should be able to avoid dangers attributable to the negligence of the occupier, provided those dangers relate to the task in which the visitor is skilled.

ROLES v NATHAN (TRADING AS MANCHESTER ASSEMBLY ROOMS) [1963] 1 WLR 1117

The defendants' assembly rooms were heated by an old boiler, which was difficult to light because of a poorly designed flue. Chimney sweeps were called in, but cleaning the flue did not cure the problem. A boiler expert said that the boiler room was dangerous and ordered everyone out. The sweeps did not believe him and he had to use force to get them out. The expert ordered that the inspection chamber and the sweep hole must be sealed before the boiler was lit and that the sweeps must not work by the boiler with the sweep hole open and the boiler lit. The boiler was lit while the sweeps were still working on sealing the sweep hole. The two sweeps were found dead in the boiler room. Their widows claimed damages from the defendant occupier, who, they alleged, had been negligent in lighting the boiler. The trial judge held that the defendants were in breach of their duty under s 2 of the Occupiers' Liability Act 1957, but the sweeps were contributorily negligent. On appeal the decision of the trial judge was reversed. In finding for the occupier Lord Denning MR made the following comments, beginning at p 1123:

> ... These chimney sweeps ought to have known that there might be dangerous fumes about and ought to have taken steps to guard against them. They ought to have known that they should not attempt to seal up a sweephole whilst the fire was still alight. They ought to have had the fire withdrawn before they attempted to seal it up, or at any rate they ought not to have stayed in the alcove too long when there might be dangerous fumes about. All this was known to these two sweeps; they were repeatedly warned about it and it was for them to guard against the danger. It was not for the occupier to do it, even though he was present and heard the warnings. When a householder calls in a specialist to deal with a defective installation on his premises, he can reasonably expect the specialist to appreciate and guard against the dangers arising from the defect. The householder is not bound to watch over him to see that he comes to no harm. I would hold, therefore, that the occupier here was under no duty of care to these sweeps, at any rate in regard to the dangers which caused their deaths. If it had been a different danger, as for instance if the stairs leading to the cellar gave way, the occupier might no doubt be responsible, but not for these dangers which were special risks ordinarily incidental to their calling.

\- \- \-

A possible justification for this decision is that on the particular facts the sweeps actually knew of the risk. Moreover, they were, apparently, self-employed persons, so that it was within their power to avoid the risk by refraining from working when the air was contaminated by fumes. Such a justification for the case would make it easier to reconcile with more recent cases, such as *Ogwo v Taylor* (1988)[11] which have taken the view that emergency service personnel, at least, can claim against an occupier whose negligence has created the emergency and thus led to their injury.

---

11 [1988] 1 AC 431.

It is noteworthy that the Court of Appeal's exoneration of the occupier in *General Cleaning Contractors Ltd v Christmas* (1952)[12] was not followed by the Court of Appeal in *King v Smith and Another* (1995).[13] In this latter case, it was held that a window cleaner's customer should be made responsible for ensuring that where his windows were capable of being cleaned from the inside, they were in proper working order to allow that to be done. Millett LJ remarking that, in the 40 years since *Christmas* was decided, it had become 'well appreciated' that cleaning windows from the outside sill could be a dangerous practice. Both the employer and the occupier of the premises were held liable for the cleaner's injuries, resulting from a fall from a window ledge. However, the employer was held 70% to blame and the occupier had to bear only 30% of the responsibility.

Similarly, in the following case, where the plaintiff had the status of employee rather than self-employed person the High Court so applied s 2(5) as to find for the plaintiff. It held that a visiting worker, an employee of one other than the occupier, could not be said to have accepted a risk created by the occupier simply because he attempted to carry out the task his employer had set him. Thus, the visitor was enabled, as the employee had been since *Smith v Baker & Sons* (1891),[14] to claim that there was an important difference between knowing of a risk and accepting it.

BUNKER v CHARLES BRAND & SON LTD [1969] 2 QB 480

The plaintiff was sent by his employer (a contractor) to carry out modifications on a machine which was being used in the excavation of a tunnel (part of the Victoria Underground line). To get to the place where he had to work the plaintiff had to climb over the machine which was already sited in the tunnel. He slipped on rollers on the machine and injured his knee. The following extracts are from the judgment of O'Connor J in the High Court, beginning at p 486:

> On those findings of fact, the plaintiff lays his case in two ways. He says, first, that the defendants were occupiers of this site, including the machine, and that, as occupiers, they owed him a common duty of care as laid down by the Occupiers' Liability Act, 1957 ... In the alternative, the plaintiff alleges that the defendants owed him a duty under the Construction (General Provisions) Regulations, 1961 ...
>
> I will deal with the claim under the Occupiers' Liability Act, 1957, first ...
>
> Were they in breach of that duty? It will be remembered that, until the Act of 1957 was passed, it had been held in the House of Lords that where a visitor fully knew of the danger he could not recover. That was finally decided in

---

12 [1952] 2 All ER 1110.
13 [1995] ICR 339.
14 [1891] AC 325.

London Graving Dock Co Ltd v Horton (1951).[15] In that case an experienced welder who had for a month, been carrying out work on a ship as an employee of sub-contractors engaged by ship repairers in occupation of the ship, sustained injuries, without negligence on his part, owing to the inadequacy of certain staging, constituting an unusual danger of which he had full knowledge and which, despite complaints, the ship repairers had not remedied. It was held that, the welder being an invitee, his knowledge of the unusual risk exonerated the ship repairers from liability for the damage sustained by him and that it was not essential to their defence to establish that he was *volens* in that he was not under any feeling of constraint in accepting the risk.

...

That was the position in which the law stood in 1951 and, indeed, until the Occupiers' Liability Act, 1957, came into force.

...

As far as this case is concerned, I do not hesitate to find that the plaintiff had full knowledge of the risk involved in walking over the rollers. It is to my mind quite unarguable to suggest that he did not appreciate what the danger was. The danger was that he might lose his footing and fall down. He is a perfectly sensible adult man and he knew that as well as was possible.

However, the law has been altered by the Act of 1957.

...

I read [s 2(5)] as meaning that, in order to absolve himself the occupier must show that the visitor was *volens* in the proper sense to the risk.

...

I am satisfied that the plaintiff had no alternative but to use the path which he had been shown by his own employers' superior and the method of tackling it had been confirmed during the journey which he was making at the time of his accident by a senior representative of the defendants. Therefore, I hold that the defendants were in breach of the common duty of care owed to the plaintiff under the Occupiers' Liability Act, 1957.

– – –

The courts have considered several cases in which what has been in issue has been whether firemen can be said to accept the risk of being injured when attending a fire. As the following case shows an occupier who has negligently caused a fire may be liable to a fireman who is injured while trying to put out that fire.

OGWO v TAYLOR [1988] 1 AC 431

The Court of Appeal reversed the decision of the trial judge and held that the householder was, on the facts, liable to a fireman who was injured putting out

---

15 [1951] AC 737.

a fire negligently started by the householder. The Court of Appeal considered both common law liability and liability under the Occupiers' Liability Act 1957. The House of Lords upheld the decision of the Court of Appeal; in delivering the opinion of the House, Lord Bridge referred only to common law liability. The following extracts are taken from the speech of Lord Bridge, beginning at p 443:

> My Lords, I shall refer to the parties to the appeal before your Lordships as the plaintiff and the defendant. The defendant was the occupier of a small terrace house on two floors in Hornchurch. He attempted to burn off paint from the fascia boards beneath the eaves of his house with a blow lamp and in so doing set fire to the premises. The fire brigade were called and the plaintiff, an acting leading fireman, arrived with the first fire appliance. Smoke was coming from the house, but it was impossible to locate the seat of the fire from outside. The plaintiff and a colleague entered the house wearing breathing apparatus and the usual fireman's protective clothing and armed with a hose. In due course they located the seat of the fire in the roof space. The rafters to the rear of the house were well alight from the eaves to the ridge. The two firemen were able, with the aid of a stepladder, to squeeze through a small hatch to get into the roof space and in due course to bring the fire under control by playing their hose on it. The heat within the roof space was intense until they were able to relieve it by kicking out some of the roof tiles, as they had been trained to do in such a situation. The plaintiff, although he did not realise it until after he came down from the roof, suffered serious burn injuries to his upper body and face from scalding steam which must have penetrated his protective clothing.
>
> ...
>
> Of course I accept that not everybody, whether professional fireman or layman, who is injured in a fire negligently started will necessarily recover damages from the tortfeasor. The chain of causation between the negligence and the injury must be established by the plaintiff and may be broken in a number of ways. The most obvious would be where the plaintiff's injuries were sustained by his foolhardy exposure to an unnecessary risk either of his own volition or acting under the order of a senior fire officer. But, subject to this, I can see no basis of principle which would justify denying a remedy in damages against the tortfeasor responsible for starting a fire to a professional fireman doing no more and no less than his proper duty and acting with skill and efficiency in fighting an ordinary fire who is injured by one of the risks to which the particular circumstances of the fire give rise. Fire out of control is inherently dangerous. If not brought under control, it may, in most urban situations, cause untold damage to property and possible danger to life. The duty of professional firemen is to use their best endeavours to extinguish fires and it is obvious that, even making full use of all their skills, training and specialist equipment, they will sometimes be exposed to unavoidable risks of injury, whether the fire is described as 'ordinary' or 'exceptional'. If they are not to be met by the doctrine of *volenti*, which would be utterly repugnant to our contemporary notions of justice, I can see no reason whatever why they should be held at a disadvantage as compared to the layman entitled to invoke the principle of the so called 'rescue' cases.

...

At the end of the day I am happy to find my views in full accord with those expressed in the latest authority directly in point, which is the decision at first instance of Woolf J in *Salmon v Seafarer Restaurants Ltd* (1983).[16]

...

I would particularly wish to adopt and endorse a passage in the judgment where the judge said, at p 1272:

'Where it can be foreseen that the fire which is negligently started is of the type which could, first of all, require firemen to attend to extinguish that fire, and where, because of the very nature of the fire, when they attend they will be at risk even though they exercise all the skill of their calling, there seems no reason why a fireman should be at any disadvantage when the question of compensation for his injuries arises.'

– – –

There is a strong possibility that rescuers, like firemen, may suffer post-traumatic stress disorder as a result of being engaged in assisting during, or in the aftermath of, catastrophic events. In *Hale v London Underground* (1994)[17] a fireman succeeded in a claim against the London Underground for stress disorder caused by his rescue work during the King's Cross Underground fire. It is interesting to compare these cases with *White v Chief Constable of South Yorkshire Police* (1999) (considered in the previous chapter), where the House of Lords held that no special duty was owed to rescuers in relation to psychiatric injury. *Ogwo* is reconcilable with this because the fireman suffered personal injury. The correctness of the decision in *Hale* would rest upon whether the fireman was at risk of personal injury.

THE THING SPEAKS FOR ITSELF

Normally, the burden of establishing that the defendant has broken the duty of care rests on the claimant. In some instances, the facts which the claimant establishes, concerning the circumstances in which the defendant has allegedly broken the duty, are such that 'the thing may speak for itself' (formerly known as *res ipsa loquitur*), that is to say, there is a presumption that the defendant has been negligent. The burden then shifts to the defendants to establish that the damage occurred without their negligence. In *Cassidy v Ministry of Health* (1951)[18] for example, the Court of Appeal was of the view that the very fact that the claimant emerged from treatment within the hospital with a paralysed hand raised a presumption that the defendant

---

16   [1983] 1 WLR 1264.
17   CLR March 1994.
18   [1951] 2 KB 343.

hospital had been negligent. The presumption may arise when the claimant has satisfied the court as to what has occurred but has not been able to show exactly how it occurred. For the presumption to arise, the situation must have been under the control of the defendant; thus, it is particularly likely to arise where an accident has occurred on premises under the control of the defendant. The leading case is:

SCOTT v LONDON AND ST KATHERINE DOCKS CO
(1865) 3 H & C 596

The defendants dropped a bag of sugar from a crane onto the plaintiff, causing him injury. The plaintiff having satisfied the court on this, the Court of Exchequer was prepared to find that the plaintiff had raised a presumption that the defendant had been negligent. In the judgment of Erle CJ, the rule was, at p 601:

> There must be reasonable evidence of negligence, but where the thing is shown to be under the management of the defendant or his servants, and the accident is such as, in the ordinary course of things, does not happen if those who have the management of the machinery use proper care, it affords reasonable evidence, in the absence of explanation by the defendant, that the accident arose from want of care.

This is an application of the rules of evidence. Its separate classification is something which appeals more to academics than to judges!

PROHIBITION OF EXCLUSION OF LIABILITY

A person whose negligent conduct has caused death or personal injury cannot rely on a contract term or a notice in order to escape civil liability to compensate for damage caused.

UNFAIR CONTRACT TERMS ACT 1977

Part I

Section 1

Scope of Part I

(1) For the purposes of this Part of the Act, 'negligence' means the breach:

    (a) of any obligation, arising from the express or implied terms of a contract, to take reasonable care or exercise reasonable skill in the performance of the contract;

    (b) of any common law duty to take reasonable care or exercise reasonable skill (but not any stricter duty);

(c) of the common duty of care imposed by the Occupiers' Liability Act 1957.

...

(3) In the case of both contract and tort, ss 2 to 7 apply (except where the contrary is stated in s 6(4)) only to business liability, that is liability for breach of obligations or duties arising–

(a) from things done or to be done by a person in the course of a business (whether his own business or another's); or

(b) from the occupation of premises used for business purposes of the occupier ...

Section 2

Negligence liability

(1) A person cannot by reference to any contract term or to a notice given to persons generally or to particular persons exclude or restrict his liability for death or personal injury resulting from negligence.

CHAPTER 6

LIABILITY FOR COMMON LAW NEGLIGENCE: DAMAGE

The claimant, having proved that the defendant owed a duty of care and that the defendant broke that duty, has to prove that the defendant is liable for the damage suffered.

Assuming that the claimant can prove by medical evidence that he or she was less capable, permanently or temporarily, after the defendant's wrongdoing than before it, it is still necessary to establish both that injury was caused by the defendant's conduct and the claimant's actual condition has been caused by that conduct. The issue of causation has a number of guises, some of them very complex. Normally, only damage that is the foreseeable consequence of the defendant's conduct is recoverable.

(a) Defendant must have caused claimant actionable damage

In order to succeed in an action in negligence, the claimant must satisfy the court that he or she has suffered damage. Where the allegation is that the claimant has suffered a deterioration in health as a consequence of the defendant's conduct, the court must be persuaded that the claimant has a recognised disease.

MUGHAL v REUTERS LTD [1993] IRLR 571

A journalist who worked at a VDU alleged that he suffered permanent disability as a result of his employers' failure to provide him with adequate advice and equipment to enable him to carry out his work in safety. The following extracts are from the judgment of Prosser J in the High Court, beginning at p 571:

> Three doctors gave evidence before me, one for the plaintiff and two for the defendants. Their evidence dealt specifically with the defendant's complaints, as well as the current learning on the question of upper limb disorders brought about by the use of VDUs. Whilst all recognised the existence of known pathological symptoms caused by repetitive use and over-working, such as tenosynovitis and peritendonitis crepitans and others, there were also deeply divided opinions about a condition called repetitive strain injury ('RSI'). This evidence and these diverse opinions will have to be analysed to deal with the causation of the plaintiff's alleged pain which his counsel described as being a diffuse pathological condition reflected by pain which has led to continuing disability.
>
> ...

[His Lordship referred to the various medical reports on behalf of the plaintiff.]

Before considering any of the defendant's evidence, what has struck me most forcefully in considering the plaintiff's evidence is the almost glib use made in the medical documents, be they GPs' notes or consultants' reports or letters, about terms, such as repetitive strain injury, repetitive strain syndrome, reflex sympathetic dystrophy, otherwise known to Dr Pearson as sympathetically maintained pain.

Before going any further, one must ask: what are they? Without determining what each means, it is impossible to begin to understand what the plaintiff may have had and perhaps still has. It is important to know what, if anything, the plaintiff has sustained in order to determine how and why he got it, that is, what caused whatever he had? The second question is crucial in deciding whether the causation was due to any failure of duty on the part of the employer towards him.

When the GP refers to RSI in the notes dated 12 January 1989, what symptoms was he speaking of? I do not know. He has not given evidence. Thereafter, up to February 1993, he gave six-monthly National Insurance certificates to the plaintiff on the basis that he had RSI tenosynovitis.

Tenosynovitis is a well-known condition. It is a non-infectious inflammatory condition in the tendon sheaths of the wrist. When that condition is at the musculo-tendinous junction of the muscles of the forearm, that is more properly known as peritendonitis crepitans. Both of these conditions have clear clinical signs and symptoms: in other words, each has a definite pathology and they have a cause, namely, trauma of the use of the wrist and/or forearm during repetitive operations, unaccustomed work, alterations in work tempo or persistent strain. There is abundant material in the evidence before me setting out these details of tenosynovitis and peritendonitis crepitans.

...

I have read and re-read many articles on the subject of RSI and it is quite clear that there is a wide spectrum of debate and division about RSI. I believe that the mainstream view is that there is no pathology, no clinical symptoms that can be pointed to as confirming a patient having RSI.

As to reflex sympathetic dystrophy, in April 1991, Dr Pearson said that the plaintiff had a severe repetitive strain syndrome and had tenosynovitis. He now has blood flow changes suggestive of a degree, said Dr Pearson, of reflex sympathetic dystrophy. What it means in this case, I do not know. I really do not think Dr Pearson does either.

...

For the defendants, Mr Semple told me that he had seen only one case of RSD and he thought that the diagnosis of RSD in this plaintiff was wrong. Mr Mathewson was however strong in his view that the plaintiff did not have RSD, basing his opinion on his experience and on basic pathology.

...

Returning then to that condition called RSI that has sparked off so much worldwide speculation, both Mr Semple and Mr Mathewson are clear in their own minds that RSI is in reality meaningless, in that it has no pathology. Indeed, both take the view that RSI has no place in the medical books and, from my acquaintance with it in this case, I agree with them. Its use by doctors can only serve to confuse. Bearing in mind the vast amount of study and writing on the subject, it is an expression that can lead to all kinds of speculation, not only as to what a patient really is suffering from, but as to the causation of it, thereby creating further confusion, particularly amongst employers, because of the uncertainties surrounding the condition called RSI and its apparent causation according to some people.

...

As Mr Mathewson said, one of the striking features in this case is that there is no consistent pattern or incidence to show a physical relationship between those diffuse symptoms complained of and his work. Through no fault of the plaintiff's the symptoms of complaint have manifested themselves and it makes it very difficult for an employer to deal with it.

...

Returning to the plaintiff, I feel I am bound by the evidence I have heard about his lack of competence as a sub-editor, his frequent and constant use of Temazepam long before he started to complain of his hands and arms, his feelings of being watched and even victimised. These and the reference by Dr Pearson to the need for psychiatric help all lead me to the conclusion that these factors more than anything lie at the root of the plaintiff's problems and not the allegations that he makes about his employer.

...

If I call the plaintiff's condition X, an unknown quantity, then go on to deal with causation brought about by any breach of duty by the employer, I am quite satisfied that I cannot find for the plaintiff on that score. The defendants' evidence of the care they took for their employees has led me to the conclusion that Reuters were prudent and careful employers.

– – –

This case has been cited at considerable length because of the contemporary importance of RSI. Long as the above extracts are, much of the complex medical evidence has been omitted; both as it related to strain induced physical illness in general and as it related to Mr Mughal's health. It may perhaps not be unfair to say that Prosser J considered RSI to be a rather general term, like backache, and he was concerned to identify the diseases RSI might cause. He was also not persuaded, on the evidence, that the plaintiff's distress was not caused by general concerns over his capacity to do his work, rather than stress related to ergonomic problems with his workstation. Interestingly, it was not really in issue that his work had caused his ill-health, but there was no real evidence that enabled his condition to be related to a known stress-induced disease. In any case, there was no evidence that the employer's conduct had been negligent.

The problem of RSI in a keyboard operator has now been taken before the House of Lords in the following case.

PICKFORD v IMPERIAL CHEMICAL INDUSTRIES PLC
[1998] 1 WLR 1181

In this case also, the majority of their Lordships found against the appellant typist. In the view of Lord Hope, speaking for the majority of the House, the case turned on the evidence presented to the trial judge as to whether it was a foreseeable risk that a person spending most of her working day at a keyboard would contract a recognised illness. His Lordship opined, beginning at p 1196:

> It will be clear from this summary that the issues which the judge had to decide were all issues of fact. The answers which he gave to them were the result of his assessment of all the evidence, after seeing and hearing all the witnesses. He had to resolve an acute conflict in the expert medical evidence. Another disputed question which he had to resolve was what to make of the respondent's evidence. This was important because of the account which she gave as to the development of her condition and as to the nature and amount of her typing work.
>
> ...
>
> **The medical issues**
>
> The judge described the three issues which fall under this heading in this way: first, whether PDA4, cramp of the hand due to repetitive movements, has an organic cause; secondly, whether the respondent has had PDA4; and thirdly, if she has had it, whether her PDA4 has an organic cause. I have placed them all under the heading of medical issues. But it is clear from his judgment that the judge was unable to resolve all of them without taking account of a substantial body of evidence from the lay witnesses about the work which the respondent was doing during the critical period.
>
> As to the first issue, the judge said that the most that he could find on the whole of the medical evidence was that the condition of cramp of the hand due to repetitive movements may have an organic cause or a psychogenic cause, or a combination of both causes, and that this was a matter for the court to consider on the evidence before it in each case.

– – –

(b) Damage must be a consequence of defendant's conduct

In order to succeed the claimant must establish that the injury suffered was the consequence of the defendant's conduct. The claimant will not be compensated for damage that would have occurred even if the defendant's conduct had been faultless. That is to say, it is not sufficient for the claimant to show that the defendant was negligent and the claimant has suffered damage. There must be a *causal* link between the conduct and the damage suffered. That is to say, the evidence indicates that the claimant's injury was not independent of the defendant's conduct.

MCWILLIAMS v SIR WILLIAM ARROL & CO LTD [1962] 1 WLR 295

The facts of the case appear sufficiently in these extracts from the judgment of Viscount Kilmuir LC, beginning at p 296:

On 27 May 1956, the deceased was employed by the first respondents as a steel erector in connection with the steel latticework tower of a tower crane which they were constructing for the use of the second named respondents in their Kingston shipbuilding yard, Port Glasgow. The deceased was an experienced steel erector ... While it was not established exactly what the deceased was doing at the time of the accident, it is not disputed that he fell from about the point where the staging was being erected to the ground, sustaining fatal injuries, that immediately after the accident one of the needles of the staging was observed to be markedly canted downwards towards the outer end and that there was found on the ground, close to the deceased's body, a wooden plank, which had probably prior to the accident been resting on the protruding ends of the needles and also an outrigger lashing. Safety belts, the wearing of which would have prevented the death of the deceased, had been available until two or three days before the accident but were then removed to another site.

The appellant's case against the first respondents was that the work upon which the deceased was engaged was dangerous in that he had to put his weight on battens before they were properly secured in order to secure them and had to use both hands in the work of securing; that it was the duty of the first respondents as his employers to provide and maintain a safe system of work and sufficient plant to enable the deceased safely to perform his task; that for work of this nature it was their duty to provide the deceased with a safety belt and to instruct him to wear it; that such provisions and instructions accorded with normal and proper practice for work on such steel structures and that it was particularly necessary for the work and position which I have described. The appellant in her pleadings also made a case concerned with the provision of safety nets but this was abandoned in the course of the proof and I need not mention safety nets again.

With regard to the second respondents it was averred that by their failure to provide the deceased with a safety belt they were in breach of s 26(2) of the Factories Act 1937, namely: 'Where any person is to work at a place from which he will be liable to fall a distance of more than ten feet, unless the place is one which affords secure foothold and, where necessary, secure hand hold means shall be provided, so far as is reasonably practicable, by fencing or otherwise for ensuring his safety.' The appellant averred that in the circumstances of the accident the deceased was working at a place from which he was liable to fall more than 10 feet, and which did not afford secure foothold; that the second respondents were bound to supply him with a safety belt, that it was reasonably practicable for them so to do, and that if one had been provided the accident would not have happened.

The Lord Ordinary (Lord Guest) and the learned Judges of the First Division held that the first respondents were in breach of duty at common law in failing, contrary to the proved practice of making them available, to provide a safety belt for the deceased, and that the second respondents were in breach of their statutory duty in the same respect. The Lord Ordinary and the Lord President (with whom Lord Carmont agreed) went on to hold that the appellant had failed to prove that the provision of a safety belt by the respondents would have prevented the accident, while Lord Guthrie, taking a different view of the onus of proof, held that the respondents had proved that it would not. The basis of these views was that, if safety belts had been provided, the deceased would not have been wearing one on the occasion of the accident. Lord Guest held that the question of instructions to use of safety belts was academic. The Lord President took the view that exhortation would have been useless and that if instructions had been given the deceased would have ignored them.

...

The evidence demonstrates to a high degree of probability that if safety belts had been available the deceased would, in any event, not have worn one. On this aspect the Lord Ordinary and the learned judges of the First Division found in favour of the respondents and rejected the appellant's contention. There were a number of witnesses called for the appellant and for these respondents with wide experience in structural steel operations including, in some instances, work on tower cranes such as that in which the deceased was engaged. The combined effect of evidence was that steel erectors never wear safety belts except in certain very special circumstances which do not include the erection of scaffolds for riveters on tower cranes. No witness deponed to having ever seen a safety belt worn in the course of such work and there was ample evidence from these respondents' employees and from others that safety belts were not worn when such work was being carried out. One witness spoke of having seen the deceased wearing a safety belt on one or possibly two occasions, when doing an operation of a peculiar and special nature. The Lord Ordinary did not accept his evidence on that matter, which in any event was not corroborated. There was overwhelming evidence that the deceased did not normally wear a safety belt and in particular it was proved that he had been engaged in erecting riveters' scaffolds on the crane from which he fell, at heights greater than that from which he fell, and at times when safety belts were available and that he had not on such occasions worn or asked for a safety belt. In my opinion, it was clearly open to a court to infer that the deceased would not have worn a safety belt even if it were available.

– – –

Establishing the causative link between the defendant's conduct and the claimant's injury is particularly difficult when the claimant alleges he has contracted a disease rather than suffered an accident. In these circumstances, the burden of proving the cause of the illness still rests on the claimant; however, the courts are inclined to be sympathetic to the claimant who has shown that, during the employment, there has been an exposure to circumstances which might cause the disease in question. In other words, if it is established that the defendant has negligently exposed the claimant to the risk of incurring the injury, the courts are prepared to find that the injury has followed from this exposure. This question is considered in both the following cases.

BONNINGTON CASTINGS LTD v WARDLAW [1956] 1 All ER 615

The facts are stated in the speech of Lord Reid, in the House of Lords, beginning at p 616:

My Lords, the respondent was employed by the appellants for eight years in the dressing shop of their foundry in Leith and, while employed there, he contracted the disease of pneumoconiosis by inhaling air which contained minute particles of silica. He ceased work on 12 May 1950. The Lord Ordinary (Lord Wheatley) held the appellants liable for this and awarded £2,000 damages. The First Division by a majority (Lord Carmont and Lord Russell, the Lord President (Lord Clyde) dissenting) adhered to the interlocutor of the Lord Ordinary.

The appellants produce steel castings. These are made by pouring molten metal into moulds which consist of sand with a very high silica content. When the casting has cooled, it is freed from sand so far as possible and then annealed. The annealed casting has a certain amount of the sand adhering to it, or burnt into it, and the surface of the casting is somewhat irregular. It is then necessary to remove these irregularities and smooth the surface of the casting and, in the course of doing this, any adhering sand is also removed. This is done in the dressing shop by three types of machine. In two of these machines, floor grinders and swing grinders, the means employed are grinding wheels made of carborundum, and, in the third, a hammer or chisel is driven by compressed air, so that it delivers some 1,800 blows per minute. There are several of each type of machine in the dressing shop and all of them produce dust, part of which is silica from the sand which they remove. The particles of this sand are originally sufficiently large not to be dangerous, because it is only exceedingly small particles of silica which can produce the disease – particles which are quite invisible except through a powerful microscope. But, either in the annealing process or by the working of these machines, or at both stages (the evidence on this is inconclusive), a number of the original particles are broken up and the dust produced by all of these machines contains a certain proportion of the dangerous minute particles of silica. Most of the dust from the grinders can be sucked into ducts or pipes, but, during the time when the respondent contracted his disease, there was no known means of preventing the dust from the pneumatic hammers from escaping into the air and it is now admitted that no form of mask or respirator had then been invented which was effective to protect those exposed to the dust.

Throughout his eight years in the appellants' service, the respondent operated one of these pneumatic hammers and he admits that he cannot complain in so far as his disease was caused by the dust from his own or any of the other pneumatic hammers. As there was no known means of collecting or neutralising this dust and as it is not alleged that these machines ought not to have been used, there was no breach of duty on the part of the appellants in allowing this dust to escape into the air. The respondent makes no complaint with regard to the floor grinders, because the dust-extracting plant for them was apparently effective, so far as that was possible, and it seems that any noxious dust which escaped from these grinders was of negligible amount. But the respondent alleged, and it is admitted, that a considerable quantity of dust escaped into the air of the workshop from the swing grinders, because the dust-extraction plant for these grinders was not kept free from obstruction as it should have been. It frequently became choked and ineffective.

Regulation 1 of the Grinding of Metals (Miscellaneous Industries) Regulations 1925 provides:

'No racing, dry grinding or glazing ordinarily causing the evolution of dust into the air of the room in such a manner as to be inhaled by any person employed shall be performed without the use of adequate appliances for the interception of the dust as near as possible to the point of origin thereof, and for its removal and disposal so that it shall not enter any occupied room ...'

It is admitted for the appellants that they were in breach of this regulation, in that, for considerable periods, dust from the swing grinders escaped into the shop where the respondent was working, owing to the appliances for its interception and removal being choked and, therefore, inadequate. The question is whether this breach of the regulation caused the respondent's disease. If his disease resulted from his having inhaled part of the noxious dust from the swing grinders which should have been intercepted and removed, then the appellants are liable to him in damages; but, if it did not result from that, then they are not liable.

...

I think that the position can be shortly stated in this way. It may be that, of the noxious dust in the general atmosphere of the shop, more came from the pneumatic hammers than from the swing grinders, but I think it is sufficiently proved that the dust from the grinders made a substantial contribution. The respondent, however, did not only inhale the general atmosphere of the shop; when he was working his hammer, his face was directly over it, and it must often have happened that dust from his hammer substantially increased the concentration of noxious dust in the air which he inhaled. It is, therefore, probable that much the greater proportion of the noxious dust which he inhaled over the whole period came from the hammers. But, on the other hand, some certainly came from the swing grinders, and I cannot avoid the conclusion that the proportion which came from the swing grinders was not negligible. He was inhaling the general atmosphere all the time and there is no evidence to show that his hammer gave off noxious dust so frequently or that the concentration of noxious dust above it when it was producing dust was so much greater than the concentration in the general atmosphere, that the special concentration of dust could be said to be substantially the sole cause of his disease.

The Lord President was of opinion that there was 'no evidence of any material contribution of noxious dust from the swing grinders', and I must examine his reason for taking that view. He said:

'When the evidence of noxious dust from the swing grinders is analysed it is not impressive. Much of the evidence in regard to these machines is related to dust generally, and this body of evidence has misled the Lord Ordinary into phrases such as "a fairly constant stream of silica dust in the atmosphere over a very extended period". There is no such evidence in regard to silica dust. The evidence of fellow workmen of the pursuer relates to visible dust and is not helpful on the vital issue.'

In this, I think that he was mistaken.

It is, of course, true that the only direct evidence related to harmless dust, because it alone was visible. But if the larger visible particles hung in the atmosphere for some time, then smaller, lighter and invisible particles emitted by the swing grinders must have hung there even longer. No doubt the amount of noxious dust was very much less than the amount of visible dust. But there is nothing to indicate that the castings dressed with the swing grinders had substantially less sand adhering to them than had the castings dressed with the pneumatic hammers, or that substantially less noxious dust was produced by the grinders than by the hammers. No doubt the total amount from both sources in the atmosphere was small at any one time, but the combined effect over a period of eight years was to cause the respondent's disease. The importance of the evidence of the fellow workman is that it shows that the visible dust and, therefore, also the invisible dust from the swing grinders was not immediately dispersed and, therefore, that the respondent was bound to inhale some of the invisible noxious dust from the swing grinders. On this matter, Lord Carmont said:

'Even if the majority of the pursuer's inhalations took place near the source where the silica dust was produced, ie, at his hammer, a minority of inhalations from the general atmosphere of the shop needlessly contaminated owing to the breakdown of the extracting hood, duct and fan at the swing grinders may well have contributed a quota of silica dust to the pursuer's lungs and so helped to produce the disease.'

On his view of the onus of proof, Lord Carmont did not require to go further than that. In my opinion, it is proved not only that the swing grinders may well have contributed, but that they did, in fact, contribute, a quota of silica dust which was not negligible to the respondent's lungs and, therefore, did help to produce the disease. That is sufficient to establish liability against the appellants and I am, therefore, of opinion that this appeal should be dismissed.

– – –

MCGHEE v NATIONAL COAL BOARD [1972] 3 All ER 1008

In the following case, the House of Lords again had to consider whether the defendants' wrongdoing had caused the plaintiff's injury. The full facts are set out in the judgment of Lord Reid, beginning at p 1009:

Mr Lords, the appellant was employed for many years by the respondents as a labourer at their Prestongrange brickworks. His normal work was emptying pipe kilns. On 30 March 1967 (a Thursday) he was sent to empty brick kilns. Working conditions there were much hotter and dustier than in the pipe kilns. On Sunday 2 April, he felt extensive irritation of his skin. He continued to work on the Monday and Tuesday and then went to his doctor who put him off work and later sent him to a skin specialist. He was found to be suffering from dermatitis. He sued the respondents for damages alleging breaches on their part of common law duties to him ...

...

It is now admitted that the dermatitis was attributable to the work which the appellant did in the brick kilns. The first ground of fault alleged against the respondents is that the kilns ought to have been allowed to cool 'sufficiently' before the appellant was sent to remove the bricks from them. I agree with the Scottish courts that this contention fails; the pleading lacks specification and the evidence is much too vague to prove any breach of duty. The other ground of fault alleged raises a difficult question of law. It is said in condescendence 3:

'It was their duty to take reasonable care to provide adequate washing facilities including showers, soap and towels to enable men to remove dust from their bodies. In each and all of said duties, the [respondents] failed and so caused said disease. Had the [respondents] fulfilled said duties incumbent on them the [appellant] would not have contracted said disease.'

...

The medical witnesses are in substantial agreement. Dermatitis can be caused, and this dermatitis was caused, by repeated minute abrasion of the outer horny layer of the skin followed by some injury to or change in the underlying cells, the precise nature of which has not yet been discovered by medical science. If a man sweats profusely for a considerable time the outer layer of his skin is softened and easily injured. If he is then working in a cloud of abrasive brick dust, as this man was, the particles of dust will adhere to his skin in considerable quantity and exertion will cause them to injure the horny layer and expose to injury or infection the tender cells below. Then in some way not yet understood dermatitis may result. If the skin is not thoroughly washed as soon as the man ceases work that process can continue at least for some considerable time. This man had to continue exerting himself after work by bicycling home while still caked with sweat and grime, so he would be liable to further injury until he could wash himself thoroughly. Washing is the only practicable method of removing the danger of further injury. The effect of such abrasion of the skin is cumulative in the sense that the longer a subject is exposed to injury the greater the chance of his developing dermatitis: it is for that reason that immediate washing is well recognised as a proper precaution.

I have said that the appellant began working in hot and dusty conditions on the Thursday. It appears to be accepted that his work on Thursday, Friday and Saturday, together with the fact that in these three days he had to go home unwashed, was sufficient to account for his condition on the Sunday, and that this together with what he did on the Monday and Tuesday caused the onset of dermatitis.

It was held in the Court of Session that the appellant had to prove that his additional exposure to injury caused by his having to bicycle home unwashed caused the disease in the sense that it was more probable than not that this additional exposure to injury was the cause of it. I do not think that that is the proper approach. The Court of Session may have been misled by the inadequacy of the appellant's pleadings. But I do not think that it is now too late to re-examine the whole position.

It has always been the law that a pursuer succeeds if he can show that fault of the defender caused or materially contributed to his injury. There may have been two separate causes but it is enough if one of the causes arose from fault of the defender. The pursuer does not have to prove that this cause would of itself have been enough to cause him injury. That is well illustrated by the decision of this House in *Bonnington Castings Ltd v Wardlaw* (1956).[1]

...

In the present case the evidence does not show – perhaps no one knows – just how dermatitis of this type begins. It suggests to me that there are two possible ways. It may be that an accumulation of minor abrasions of the horny layer of skin is a necessary precondition for the onset of the disease. Or it may be that the disease starts at one particular abrasion and then spreads, so that multiplication of abrasions merely increases the number of places where the disease can start and in that way increases the risk of its occurrence.

I am inclined to think that the evidence points to the former view. But in a field where so little appears to be known with certainty I could not say that that is proved. If it were then this case would be undistinguishable from *Wardlaw's* case. But I think that in cases like this we must take a broader view of causation. The medical evidence is to the effect that the fact that the man had to cycle home caked with grime and sweat added materially to the risk that this disease might develop. It does not and could not explain just why that is so. But experience shows that it is so. Plainly that must be because what happens while the man remains unwashed can have a causative effect, although just how the cause operates is uncertain. I cannot accept the view expressed in the Inner House that once the man left the brick kiln he left behind the causes which made him liable to develop dermatitis. That seems to me quite inconsistent with a proper interpretation of the medical evidence. Nor can I accept the distinction drawn by the Lord Ordinary between materially increasing the risk that the disease will occur and making a material contribution to its occurrence.

There may be some logical ground for such a distinction where our knowledge of all the material factors is complete. But it has often been said that the legal concept of causation is not based on logic or philosophy. It is based on the practical way in which the ordinary man's mind works in the everyday affairs of life. From a broad and practical viewpoint I can see no substantial difference between saying that what the respondents did materially increased the risk of injury to the appellant and saying that what the respondents did made a material contribution to his injury.

I would therefore allow this appeal.

– – –

---

1   [1956] 1 All ER 615.

(c) Defendant must compensate for all personal injuries caused

If the claimant, due to some personal characteristic, suffers greater injury than other persons might have done, the defendant must, nevertheless, compensate for the actual damage which the claimant has suffered, always providing that the circumstances are such that any person in the claimant's position would have suffered some injury. This is so, even though the actual injury was not foreseeable. This is in direct contrast to the general rule in the tort of negligence that a defendant is only liable for damage that is foreseeable. The foresight rule was first clarified in *The Wagon Mound* case, which is referred to in the following case. The following case is the most commonly cited example of the so called 'thin skull' rule. The thin skull rule is compatible with the otherwise discredited rule in the *Polemis* case; namely, that a defendant has to pay for all the direct consequences of its negligence, even though these are not foreseeable.

SMITH v LEECH BRAIN & CO LTD [1962] 2 WLR 148

The deceased employee of the defendants had, during the course of his employment, to remove galvanised articles from a tank containing molten metal. The method of protecting the deceased from being splashed by molten metal was not a good one and he had sustained a burn on his lip. The injury was treated at the time, but it ulcerated, cancer was diagnosed and in due course the man died. The case concerned a number of issues but the extracts chosen relate to causation and remoteness of damages. The judgment of Parker LCJ begins at p 151:

> On the issue of liability I am satisfied that there was a clear and known danger of molten metal flying from the tank when articles were being lowered into it. It was, in my judgment, plainly foreseeable by any reasonable employer that a workman, unless protected, would be liable to get molten metal on him, and any reasonable employer could foresee that even a fleck of molten metal lodging in the eye might well cause not trivial but serious damage. Accordingly, it seems to me that any reasonable employer must have foreseen the risks involved in a man being some three feet away from the tank at the time of lowering, and some six feet from the article being lowered, and that proper protection was necessary for such a man. The protection that was afforded has been somewhat aptly described by Mr Martin Jukes as 'Heath Robinson'.
>
> ...
>
> I have come to the conclusion that this is a case where common law negligence has been made out ...
>
> The next question is whether the cancer which the plaintiff's husband had admittedly got, and the death resulting from it, were caused in whole or in part by the burn.
>
> ...

Accordingly, I find that the burn was the promoting agency of cancer in tissues which already had a pre-malignant condition. In those circumstances, it is clear that the plaintiff's husband, but for the burn, would not necessarily ever have developed cancer. On the other hand, having regard to the number of matters which can be promoting agencies, there was a strong likelihood that at some stage in his life he would develop cancer. But that the burn did contribute to, or cause in part, at any rate, the cancer and the death, I have no doubt.

The third question is damages. Here, I am confronted with the recent decision of the Privy Council in *Overseas Tankship (UK) Limited v Morts Docks and Engineering Co Ltd (The Wagon Mound)* (1961).[2] But for that case, it seems to me perfectly clear that, assuming negligence proved, and assuming that the burn caused in whole or in part the cancer and the death, the plaintiff would be entitled to recover. It is said on the one side by Mr May that although I am not strictly bound by *The Wagon Mound* since it is a decision of the Privy Council, I should treat myself as free, using the arguments to be derived from that case, to say that other cases in these courts – other cases in the Court of Appeal – have been wrongly decided and particularly that *In Re Polemis and Furness Withy & Co* (1921)[3] was wrongly decided, and that a further ground for taking that course is to be found in the various criticisms that have, from time to time in the past been made by members of the House of Lords in regard to the *Polemis* case.

It is said, on the other hand, by Mr Martin Jukes, that I should hold that the *Polemis* case was rightly decided and, secondly, that even if that is not so I must treat myself as completely bound by it. Thirdly, he said that, in any event, whatever the true view is in regard to the *Polemis* case, *The Wagon Mound* has no relevance at all to this case.

For my part, I am quite satisfied that the Judicial Committee in *The Wagon Mound* case did not have what I may call, loosely, the thin skull cases in mind. It has always been the law of this country that a tortfeasor takes his victim as he finds him. It is unnecessary to do more than refer to the short passage in the decision of Kennedy J in *Dulieu v White & Sons* (1901), where he said:[4] 'If a man is negligently run over or otherwise negligently injured in his body, it is no answer to the sufferer's claim for damages that he would have suffered less injury, or no injury at all, if he had not had an unusually thin skull or an unusually weak heart.'

...

In those circumstances, it seems to me that this is plainly a case which comes within the old principle. The test is not whether these employers could reasonably have foreseen that a burn would cause cancer and that he would die. The question is whether these employers could reasonably foresee the type of injury he suffered, namely, the burn. What, in the particular case, is the amount of damage which he suffers as a result of that burn depends upon the characteristics and constitution of the victim.

– – –

---

2   [1961] AC 388.

3   [1921] 3 KB 560.

4   [1901] 2 KB 669, p 679.

(d) The chain of causation

The issue of causation has a number of guises, some of them very complex. Damage that is too remote a consequence of the defendant's negligence is not recoverable. Damage will be too remote either because the chain of causation has been broken or because the chain has become too long to support a claim in respect of the final consequences of the defendant's conduct. Whether damage is too remote to be recoverable is an issue relevant to the tort of negligence in whatever context liability has arisen. (This account is somewhat partial because it includes only cases following from accidents suffered and diseases incurred at the workplace.)

The following cases provide examples of how the chain of causation may be broken. Often this may be because after the incident that caused the original injury, the claimant suffers a further, and possibly different, injury. Questions then arise, as the next three cases illustrate, as to what proportion of the claimant's incapacity the defendant is liable to compensate. In some instances, some or all of the subsequent injuries may be deemed to be too remote for the defendant to incur liability for them. In these cases, it may be said that the chain of causation has been broken by the intervening events (this situation is sometimes expressed in Latin as *novus actus interveniens*).

(i) Second injury caused by claimant's own folly

MCKEW v HOLLAND & HANNEN & CUBITTS (SCOTLAND) LTD
[1969] 3 All ER 1621

The appellant sustained in the course of employment trivial injuries which were, admittedly, caused by the fault of the respondents. His back and hips were badly strained and, on several occasions, his left leg suddenly 'went away from' him. He would have recovered from his injuries in a week or two, but for a second accident in which he suffered a severe fracture of his ankle. The question was whether the respondents were liable for the damage caused by this second accident. Some days after the first accident, the appellant was offered the tenancy of a flat. He went to inspect it accompanied by his wife and child and a brother-in-law. The flat was approached by a steep stair between two walls and there was no handrail. When he left the flat, the appellant sought to descend the stair with his child in advance of his wife and brother-in-law.

The following extracts are from the speech given by Lord Reid in the House of Lords, beginning at p 1623:

> The appellant's case is that this second accident was caused by the weakness of his left leg which in turn had been caused by the first accident. The main argument for the respondents is that the second accident was not the direct or natural and probable or foreseeable result of their fault in causing the first accident.

In my view the law is clear. If a man is injured in such a way that his leg may give way at any moment he must act reasonably and carefully. It is quite possible that in spite of all reasonable care his leg may give way in circumstances such that as a result he sustains further injury. Then that second injury was caused by his disability which in turn was caused by the defender's fault. But if the injured man acts unreasonably he cannot hold the defender liable for injury caused by his own unreasonable conduct. His unreasonable conduct is *novus actus interveniens*. The chain of causation has been broken and what follows must be regarded as caused by his own conduct and not by the defender's fault or the disability caused by it. Or one may say that unreasonable conduct of the pursuer and what follows from it is not the natural and probable result of the original fault of the defender or of the ensuing disability. I do not think that foreseeability comes into this. A defender is not liable for a consequence of a kind which is not foreseeable. But it does not follow that he is liable for every consequence which a reasonable man could foresee. What can be foreseen depends almost entirely on the facts of the case and it is often easy to foresee unreasonable conduct or some other *novus actus interveniens* as being quite likely. But that does not mean that the defender must pay for damage caused by the *novus actus*. It only leads to trouble that if one tries to graft on to the concept of foreseeability some rule of law to the effect that a wrongdoer is not bound to foresee something which in fact he could readily foresee as quite likely to happen. For it is not at all unlikely or unforeseeable that an active man who has suffered such a disability will take some quite unreasonable risk. But if he does he cannot hold the defender liable for the consequences.

So in my view the question here is whether the second accident was caused by the appellant doing something unreasonable. It was argued that the wrongdoer must take his victim as he finds him and that that applies not only to a thin skull but also to his intelligence. But I shall not deal with that argument because there is nothing in the evidence to suggest that the appellant is abnormally stupid. This case can be dealt with equally well by asking whether the appellant did something which a moment's reflection would have shown him was an unreasonable thing to do.

He knew that his left leg was liable to give way suddenly and without warning. He knew that this stair was steep and that there was no handrail. He must have realised, if he had given the matter a moment's thought, that he could only safely descend the stair if he either went extremely slowly and carefully so that he could sit down if his leg gave way, or waited for the assistance of his wife and brother-in-law. But he chose to descend in such a way that when his leg gave way he could not stop himself. I agree with what the Lord Justice Clerk says at the end of his opinion and I think that this is sufficient to require this appeal to be dismissed.

– – –

(ii) Does a second accident terminate liability for the first?

BAKER v WILLOUGHBY [1970] AC 467

On appeal to the House of Lords, the principal speech was delivered by Lord Reid and contains a full statement of the facts. The following extracts from this speech begin at p 489:

> My Lords, the appellant was knocked down by the respondent's car about the middle of a straight road crossing Mitcham Common ... The car accident occurred on 12 September 1964. The trial took place on 26 February 1968. But meanwhile on 29 November 1967, the appellant had sustained a further injury and the question is whether or to what extent the damages which would otherwise have been awarded in respect of the car accident must be reduced by reason of the occurrence of this second injury.
>
> ...
>
> After the accident the appellant tried various kinds of work, finding some too heavy by reason of his partial incapacity. In November 1967 he was engaged in sorting scrap metal and while he was alone one day two men came in, demanded money, and, when they did not get it, one of them shot at him. The shot inflicted such serious injuries to his already damaged leg that it had to be amputated. Apparently he made a fairly good recovery but his disability is now rather greater than it would have been if he had not suffered this second injury. He now has an artificial limb whereas he would have had a stiff leg.
>
> The appellant argues that the loss which he suffered from the car accident has not been diminished by his second injury. He still suffers the same kind of loss of amenities of life and he still suffers from reduced capacity to earn though these may have been to some extent increased. And he will still suffer these losses for as long as he would have done because it is not said that the second injury curtailed his expectation of life.
>
> The respondent on the other hand argues that the second injury removed the very limb from which the earlier disability had stemmed,and that therefore no loss suffered thereafter can be attributed to the respondent's negligence. He says that the second injury submerged or obliterated the effect of the first and that all loss thereafter must be attributed to the second injury. The trial judge rejected this argument which he said was more ingenious than attractive. But it was accepted by the Court of Appeal.
>
> The respondent's argument was succinctly put to your Lordships by his counsel. He could not run before the second injury: he cannot run now. But the cause is now quite different. The former cause was an injured leg but now he has no leg and the former cause can no longer operate.
>
> ...
>
> If it were the case that in the eye of the law an effect could only have one cause then the respondent might be right. It is always necessary to prove that any loss for which damages can be given was caused by the defendant's negligent act. But it is a common place that the law regards many events as having two causes: that happens whenever there is contributory negligence for then the

law says that the injury was caused both by the negligence of the defendant and by the negligence of the plaintiff. And generally, it does not matter which negligence occurred first in point of time.

I see no reason why the appellant's present disability cannot be regarded as having two causes and if authority be needed for this I find it in *Harwood v Wyken Colliery Co* (1913).[5] That was a Workmen's Compensation Act case. But causation cannot be different in tort. There an accident made the man only fit for light work. And then a heart disease supervened and it also caused him only to be fit for light work. The argument for the employer was the same as in the present case. Before the disease supervened the workman's incapacity was caused by the accident. Thereafter it was caused by the disease and the previous accident became irrelevant: he would have been equally incapacitated if the accident had never happened. But Hamilton LJ said, at p 169:

'... he is not disentitled to be paid compensation by reason of the supervention of a disease of the heart. It cannot be said of him that partial incapacity for work has not resulted and is not still resulting from the injury. All that can be said is that such partial incapacity is not still resulting 'solely' from the injury.'

The respondent founded on another Workmen's Compensation Act case in this House – *Hogan v Bentick West Hartley Collieries (Owners) Ltd* (1949).[6] There the man had an accident but his condition was aggravated by an ill judged surgical operation and it was held by the majority of this House that his incapacity must be attributed solely to the operation and not to the accident. But *Harwood*'s case was not disapproved by anyone. Lord Simonds, one of the majority, quoted with approval[7] from the judgment of du Parcq LJ in *Rothwell v Caverswall Stone Co Ltd* (1944):[8]

'If, however, the existing incapacity ought fairly to be attributed to a new cause which has intervened and ought no longer to be attributed to the original injury, it may properly be held to result from the new cause and not from the original injury, even though, but for the original injury, there would have been no incapacity.'

Then having said that negligent or inefficient treatment by a doctor may amount to a new cause du Parcq LJ continued:

'In such a case, if the arbitrator is satisfied that the incapacity would have wholly ceased but for the omission, a finding of fact that the existing incapacity results from the new cause, and not from the injury, will be justified.'

This part was also quoted by Lord Simonds. I think it clear that du Parcq LJ meant that one can only attribute the disability to the new cause alone and disregard the accident if it appears that but for the new cause the man would have recovered, for then the injury by accident can no longer be operative as a cause. But this case is no authority for holding that, during the period when the

---

5   [1913] 2 KB 158.
6   [1949] 1 All ER 588.
7   *Ibid*, p 592.
8   [1944] 2 All ER 350, p 365.

injury by accident would still have incapacitated the man if he had had proper treatment, the ill judged operation could be regarded as submerging or obliterating the original accident. It therefore does not assist the respondent.

We were referred to a number of shipping cases where the question was who must pay for demurrage or loss of profit when a vessel damaged by two mishaps was in dock to have both sets of damage repaired at the same time. It would seem that much depends on which mishap rendered the vessel unseaworthy or no longer a profit-earning machine. I get no help from these cases because liability for personal injury cannot depend on which mishap renders the man 'unseaworthy' or 'not a profit-earning machine'. If any assistance is to be got, it is, I think, from *The Haversham Grange* (1905)[9] where neither collision rendered the vessel unseaworthy. The damage from the first collision took longer to repair than the damage from the second and it was held that the vessel responsible for the second collision did not have to contribute towards payment for time lost in repairs. In my view the latter would have had to pay for any time after the repairs from the first damage had been completed, because that time could not be claimed from the first wrongdoer. This first wrongdoer must pay for all damage caused by him, but no more. The second is not liable for any damage caused by the first wrongdoer but must pay for any additional damage caused by him. That was the ground of decision in *Performance Cars Ltd v Abraham* (1962).[10] There a car sustained two slight collisions: the first necessitated respraying over a wide area which included the place damaged by the second collision. So repairing the damage caused by the first collision also repaired the damage done by the second. The plaintiff was unable to recover from the person responsible for the first collision and he then sued the person responsible for the second. But his action failed. The second wrongdoer hit a car which was already damaged and his fault caused no additional loss to the plaintiff so he had nothing to pay.

These cases exemplify the general rule that a wrongdoer must take the plaintiff (or his property) as he finds him: that may be to his advantage or disadvantage. In the present case, the robber is not responsible or liable for the damage caused by the respondent: he would only have to pay for additional loss to the appellant by reason of his now having an artificial limb instead of a stiff leg.

...

If the later injury suffered before the date of the trial either reduces the disabilities from the injury for which the defendant is liable, or shortens the period during which they will be suffered by the plaintiff, then the defendant will have to pay less damages. But if the later injuries merely become a concurrent cause of the disabilities caused by the injury inflicted by the defendant, then in my view they cannot diminish the damages. Suppose that the plaintiff has to spend a month in bed before the trial because of some illness unconnected with the original injury, the defendant cannot say that he does not have to pay anything in respect of that month: during that month the

---

9   [1905] P 307.
10 [1962] 1 QB 33.

original injuries and the new illness are concurrent causes of his inability to work and that does not reduce the damages.

– – –

(iii) After the onset of an industrial disease, the plaintiff contracts another illness

In the following case the circumstances might be thought to be broadly comparable to those described in *Baker v Willoughby* (1970),[11] set out at length above and indeed some of the same authorities were considered in both cases, yet the House of Lords came to a different conclusion.

JOBLING v ASSOCIATED DAIRIES LTD [1982] AC 794

The House of Lords affirmed the decisions of the lower courts, giving an outcome unfavourable to the plaintiff. The facts of the case appear in the speech of Lord Wilberforce, which begins at p 801:

> My Lords, the question raised by this appeal is whether in assessing damages for personal injury in respect of loss of earnings, account should be taken of a condition of illness supervening after the relevant accident, but before the trial of the action, which illness gives rise to a greater degree of incapacity than that caused by the accident.
>
> The chronology is as follows. In January 1973 the appellant slipped at his place of work and sustained injury to his back. The respondents were held liable in damages in respect of this injury. In 1975 the appellant had a fall which aggravated his condition which the judge held was referable to the injury of 1973. He has not worked since this event. By 1976 his condition was such that by reason of his back injury he was only fit for sedentary work. In 1976, however, there supervened spondylitic myelopathy, which affected the appellant's neck. By the end of 1976 this had rendered him totally unfit for work.
>
> ...
>
> In an attempt to solve the present case and similar cases of successive causes of incapacity according to some legal principle, a number of arguments have been invoked:
>
> 1   Causation arguments. The unsatisfactory character of these is demonstrated by *Baker v Willoughby* (1970). I think that it can now be seen that Lord Reid's theory of concurrent causes even if workable on the particular facts of *Baker v Willoughby* (where successive injuries were sustained by the same limb) is as a general solution not supported by the authority he invokes (*Harwood v Wyken Colliery Co* (1913)) nor workable in other cases. I shall not enlarge upon this point in view of its more than sufficient treatment in other opinions.
>
> 2   The 'vicissitudes' argument. This is that since, according to accepted doctrine, allowance – and if necessary some discount – has to be made in

---

11   [1970] AC 467.

assessing loss of future earnings for the normal contingencies of life, amongst which, 'illness' is normally enumerated, so, if one of these contingencies becomes actual before the date of trial, this actuality must be taken into account. Reliance is here placed on the apophthegm 'the court should not speculate when it knows'. This argument has a good deal of attraction. But it has its difficulties: it raises at once the question whether a discount is to be made on account of all possible 'vicissitudes' or only on account of 'non-culpable' vicissitudes (ie such that if they occur there will be no cause of action against anyone, the theory being that the prospect of being injured by a tort is not a normally foreseeable vicissitude) or only on account of 'culpable' vicissitudes (such as *per contra*). And if this distinction is to be made how is the court to act when a discounted vicissitude happens before trial? Must it attempt to decide whether there was culpability or not? And how is it to do this if, as is likely, the alleged culprit is not before it?

...

In spite of these difficulties, the 'vicissitude' argument is capable in some, perhaps many cases of providing a workable and reasonably just rule and I would certainly not discountenance its use, either in the present case or in others.

The fact, however, is that to attempt a solution of these and similar problems, where there are successive causes of incapacity in some degree upon classical lines ('the object of damages for tort is to place the plaintiff in as good a position as if,' etc ... 'the defendant must compensate for the loss caused by his wrongful act – no more' – 'the defendant must take the plaintiff as he finds him,' etc) is, in many cases, no longer possible. We do not live in a world governed by the pure common law and its logical rules. We live in a mixed world, where a man is protected against injury and misfortune by a whole web of rules and dispositions, with a number of timid legislative interventions. To attempt to compensate him upon the basis of selected rules without regard to the whole must lead either to logical inconsistencies or to over- or under-compensation. As my noble and learned friend, Lord Edmund-Davies, has pointed out, no account was taken in *Baker v Willoughby* (1970) of the very real possibility that the plaintiff might obtain compensation from the Criminal Injuries Compensation Board. If he did in fact obtain this compensation he would, on the ultimate decision, be over-compensated.

In the present, and in other industrial injury cases, there seems to me no justification for disregarding the fact that the injured man's employer is insured – indeed, since 1972, compulsorily insured – against liability to his employees. The State has decided, in other words, on a spreading of risk. There seems to me no more justification for disregarding the fact that the plaintiff – presumably, we have not been told otherwise – is entitled to sickness and invalidity benefit in respect of his myelopathy the amount of which may depend on his contribution record, which in turn may have been affected by his accident. So we have no means of knowing whether the plaintiff would be over-compensated if he were, in addition, to receive the assessed damages from his employer, or whether he would be under-compensated if left to his benefit. It is not easy to accept a solution by which a partially incapacitated man becomes worse off in terms of damages and benefit through a greater degree of incapacity. Many other ingredients, of weight in either direction, may enter into individual cases. Without any satisfaction I draw from this the conclusion that no general, logical, or universally fair rules can be stated which will cover, in a manner consistent with justice, cases of supervening events whether due to tortious, partially tortious, non-culpable or wholly accidental events. The courts can only deal with each case as best they can in a manner so as to provide just and sufficient but not excessive compensation, taking all factors into account. I think that this is what *Baker v Willoughby* did – and indeed that Lord Pearson reached his decision in this way: the rationalisation of the decision as to which I at least have doubts, need and should not be applied to other cases. In the present case the Court of Appeal reached the unanswerable conclusion that to apply *Baker v Willoughby* to the facts of the present case would produce an unjust result and I am willing to accept the corollary that justice, so far as it can be perceived, lies the other way and that the supervening myelopathy should not be disregarded. If rationalisation is needed, I am willing to accept the 'vicissitudes' argument as the best available. I should be more firmly convinced of the merits of the conclusion if the whole pattern of benefits had been considered, in however general a way. The result of the present case may be lacking in precision and rational justification, but so long as we are content to live in a mansion of so many different architectures, this is inevitable.

CHAPTER 7

CIVIL LIABILITY FOR BREACH OF STATUTORY DUTY

INTRODUCTION

The matters that have to be considered in this chapter are:

(a) what is meant by civil liability for breach of statutory duty?

(b) when may an action be founded on a statutory duty?

(c) what are the criteria of liability?

The question of how much damages may be recovered if the defendant is liable is governed by the same rules as govern liability for negligence, so does not need separate treatment.

(a) The concept of civil liability for breach of regulatory legislation

The following extract provides a neat explanation of what is meant by breach of statutory duty in this context.

ROYAL COMMISSION ON CIVIL LIABILITY AND COMPENSATION FOR PERSONAL INJURY REPORT
Volume One[1]

Breach of statutory duty

65 ... Breach of statutory duty is sometimes referred to as 'statutory negligence', but more naturally regarded as a separate species of fault distinct from negligence. There can be a breach of a statutory duty without any failure to take reasonable care. For practical purposes, liability for breach of statutory duty operates as an extension of liability for negligence, because the plaintiff may allege both in the same action and, if he fails to prove negligence, may still succeed by proving a breach of statutory duty.

66 The theory of it is that, when an Act imposes a duty or provides for regulations to impose a duty for the protection of a class of persons, it may be inferred that Parliament must have intended a person of that class injured by a breach of that duty to have a civil cause of action for damages against the wrongdoer. That can be held to be the intention of Parliament even in an Act which provides a criminal penalty for the breach of duty

---

1   Cmnd 7054-1, 1978, London: HMSO.

and makes no mention of a civil remedy. The original decision to that effect was given by the courts in 1898 (*Groves v Wimborne (Lord)*).[2] It has been affirmed and applied in many subsequent cases, especially cases concerned with duties under the Factories Acts, for example, failure to fence dangerous machinery. The practical effect is that a factory worker injured by his employer's breach of some duty imposed by the Acts or regulations is entitled to succeed in his action without proving that the employer was negligent.

– – –

Groves v Wimborne (Lord) was noted in Chapter 2. In the early years of the twentieth century, judges were sympathetic to regulatory legislation being used to found an action in the civil courts, even though the primary purpose of the statutes was to impose duties enforceable in the criminal courts. The Robens Committee questioned whether it was a desirable practice to use such legislation as the basis of civil liability; though it will be seen that their arguments spilled over into general criticism of civil litigation, encompassing the common law action for negligence as well as the civil action for breach of statutory duty.

SAFETY AND HEALTH AT WORK
REPORT OF THE COMMITTEE 1970–72

Chapter 17
Compensation and prevention[3]

Damages for injuries suffered at work

431 ... Where, however, an accident is found to be the result of a breach of an employer's statutory duty (such as his duty to ensure that his machinery is securely fenced), the employer's liability is likely to be strict, and instead of proving negligence the plaintiff need only prove a factual departure from the statutory standard. In many cases the injured employee can allege both common law negligence and breach of statutory duty as alternative bases of his claim.

432 The efficiency and equity of the system as a means of providing compensation has been heavily criticised ...

433 ... Our attention has, however, been drawn very strongly to the way in which the system operates to the detriment of the accident-prevention effort. These criticisms can be summed up as follows.

434 First, the task of framing sensible and effective statutory provisions for the prevention of accidents is made much more difficult than it need be. This is because employer organisations, trade unions and others who must be consulted, inevitably and understandably tend to be concerned as much with the implications of such provisions in the compensation field as about their potential efficacy as means of preventing accidents. The general

---

2   [1898] 2 QB 402.
3   At p 144.

psychological effect is that attention is diverted from the primary objective of accident prevention to the altogether different question of compensation for injury suffered. This shows up, for example, in the constant pressure for extremely precise and detailed statutory regulations which, as we have seen in earlier chapters, leads eventually to a body of law which has serious limitations when viewed as a contribution to its primary purpose of accident prevention.

435 Secondly, another result of utilising the same body of law for two quite different purposes is that the task of those who have to maintain and enforce the statutory provisions for accident prevention is made more complicated. The accident prevention regulations are subjected to intense scrutiny and argument by contending parties in civil proceedings. In paragraph 130 we remarked that judicial interpretations in compensation cases have from time to time created (or exposed) problems in the application and scope of particular accident prevention regulations. For the most part, legal interpretation of the regulations takes place in the context of civil litigation for compensation, and there are a number of cases where these interpretations have appeared to conflict with the intentions of the authorities responsible for framing and enforcing the accident prevention provisions.

436 Thirdly, the speedy and co-operative investigation of particular accidents is impeded. Such investigations should be geared to the aim of ensuring that the same kind of accident does not happen again. However, with the possibility of litigation in the background the advisers of the parties concerned are more likely to be pre-occupied with the question of legal fault than with the broader questions of why the accident came about and how it could have been prevented ...

...

437 Fourthly, although the same body of statutory law is used both for accident prevention purposes and as a basis for actions at common law, there is no positive and constructive connection between the two systems.

...

Recommendations

...

448 ... We think that there is a very strong case for a thorough review of the present system of actions at common law for compensation for injuries sustained at work, with particular reference to the effects of the system upon accident-prevention provisions and arrangements ...

– – –

While the recommendation of the Robens Committee that the common law system of compensating persons for industrial injuries should be reviewed was one of the reasons why the Pearson Commission was set up to report on civil liability more generally, the Commission's Report did not single out liability for breach of statutory duty as an area deserving of special treatment.

(b) Will the particular statute support a civil claim?

There are two classes of statute which might be used to found a civil action for damages for personal injury:

(i) statutes which have been enacted for the sole purpose of creating civil liability to compensate victims;

(ii) statutes whose primary purpose is setting standards for the prevention of personal injury.

(i) Statutory provisions whose sole purpose is civil liability

The Occupiers' Liability Act 1957 clarified the common law; the Occupiers' Liability Act 1984 created civil liability in relation to persons other than visitors. The best example of Parliament creating civil liability is Part I of the Consumer Protection Act 1987, which created a new statutory tort, imposing strict liability on producers for the protection of consumers. This statute is considered here because 'consumer', in this context means anyone, including a worker, who suffers personal injury or significant damage to private (as opposed to commercial) property.

CONSUMER PROTECTION ACT 1987

Part I – Product liability

Section 1

Purpose and construction of Part I

(1) This Part shall have effect for the purpose of making such provision as is necessary in order to comply with the product liability Directive and shall be construed accordingly.

...

Section 2

Liability for defective products

(1) Subject to the following provisions of this Part, where any damage is caused wholly or partly by a defect in a product, every person to whom subsection (2) below applies shall be liable for the damage.

(2) This subsection applies to–

(a) the producer of the product;

(b) any person who by putting his name on the product or using a trade mark or other distinguishing mark in relation to the product, has held himself out to be the producer of the product;

(c) any person who has imported the product into a member State from a place outside the member States in order, in the course of any business of his, to supply it to another.

(3) Subject as aforesaid, where any damage is caused wholly or partly by a defect in a product, any person who supplied the product (whether to the

person who suffered the damage, to the producer of any product in which the product in question is comprised or to any other person) shall be liable for the damage if–

(a) the person who suffered the damage requests the supplier to identify one or more of the persons (whether still in existence or not) to whom subsection (2) above applies in relation to the product;

(b) that request is made within a reasonable period after the damage occurs and at a time when it is not reasonably practicable for the person making the request to identify all those persons; and

(c) the supplier fails, within a reasonable period after receiving the request, either to comply with the request or to identify the person who supplied the product to him.

...

Section 3

Meaning of 'defect'

(1) Subject to the following provisions of this section, there is a defect in a product for the purposes of this Part if the safety of the product is not such as persons generally are entitled to expect; and for those purposes 'safety', in relation to a product, shall include safety with respect to products comprised in that product and safety in the context of risks of damage to property, as well as in the context of risks of death or personal injury.

(2) In determining for the purposes of subsection (1) above what persons generally are entitled to expect in relation to a product all the circumstances shall be taken into account, including:

(a) the manner in which, and purposes for which, the product has been marketed, its get-up, the use of any mark in relation to the product and any instructions for, or warnings with respect to, doing or refraining from doing anything with or in relation to the product;

(b) what might reasonably be expected to be done with or in relation to the product; and

(c) the time when the product was supplied by its producer to another; and nothing in this section shall require a defect to be inferred from the fact alone that the safety of a product which is supplied after that time is greater than the safety of the product in question.

Section 4

Defences

(1) In any civil proceedings by virtue of this Part against any person ('the person proceeded against') in respect of a defect in a product it shall be a defence for him to show–

(a) that the defect is attributable to compliance with any requirement imposed by or under any enactment or with any Community obligation; or

(b) that the person proceeded against did not at any time supply the product to another; or

(c) that the following conditions are satisfied, that is to say–

(i) that the only supply of the product to another by the person proceeded against was otherwise than in the course of a business of that person's; and

(ii) that s 2(2) above does not apply to that person or applies to him by virtue only of things done otherwise than with a view to profit; or

(d) that the defect did not exist in the product at the relevant time; or

(e) that the state of scientific and technical knowledge at the relevant time was not such that a producer of products of the same description as the product in question might be expected to have discovered the defect if it had existed in his products while they were under his control; or

(f) that the defect:

(i) constituted a defect in a product ('the subsequent product') in which the product in question had been comprised; and

(ii) was wholly attributable to the design of the subsequent product or to compliance by the producer of the product in question with instructions given by the producer of the subsequent product.

(2) In this section, 'the relevant time', in relation to electricity, means the time at which it was generated, being a time before it was transmitted or distributed, and in relation to any other product, means–

(a) if the person proceeded against is a person to whom subsection (2) of s 2 above applies in relation to the product, the time when he supplied the product to another;

(b) if that subsection does not apply to that person in relation to the product, the time when the product was last supplied by a person to whom that subsection does apply in relation to the product.

Section 5

Damages giving rise to liability

(1) Subject to the following provisions of this section, in this Part, 'damage' means death or personal injury or any loss of or damage to any property (including land).

– – –

(ii) Statutory provisions whose primary purpose is accident prevention

In recent years, it has become customary for statutes containing provisions whose aim is to prevent personal injury to specify whether the duties they create for enforcement in the criminal courts are to confer any right to litigate in the civil courts. Both the Health and Safety at Work Act 1974 and the Consumer Protection Act 1987 (Part II of which deals with criminal liability) make such provision.

HEALTH AND SAFETY AT WORK ACT 1974

Section 47

Civil liability

(1) Nothing in this Part shall be construed–

    (a) as conferring a right of action in any civil proceedings in respect of any failure to comply with any duty imposed by ss 2–7 or any contravention of s 8; or

    (b) as affecting the extent (if any) to which breach of a duty imposed by any of the existing statutory provisions is actionable; or

    (c) as affecting the operation of s 12 of the Nuclear Installations Act 1965 (right to compensation by virtue of certain provisions of that Act).

(2) Breach of a duty imposed by health and safety regulations or agricultural health and safety regulations shall, so far as it causes damage, be actionable except in so far as the regulations provide otherwise.

(3) No provision made by virtue of s 15(6)(b) shall afford a defence in any civil proceedings, whether brought by virtue of subsection (2) above or not; but as regards any duty imposed as mentioned in subsection (2) above health and safety regulations or, as the case may be, agricultural health and safety regulations may provide for any defence specified in the regulations to be available in any action for breach of that duty.

– – –

In effect, therefore, the Health and Safety at Work Act 1974:

- preserved any existing rights to sue for breaches of the then existing safety provisions;

- prevented the Act's general duties being used in civil litigation;

- created a presumption that there would be civil liability for breach of regulations made under the Act;

- enabled regulations to carry special civil defences.

CONSUMER PROTECTION ACT 1987

Section 41

Civil proceedings

(1) An obligation imposed by safety regulations shall be a duty owed to any person who may be affected by a contravention of the obligation and, subject to any provision to the contrary in the regulations and to the defences and other incidents applying to actions for breach of statutory duty, a contravention of any such obligation shall be actionable accordingly.

– – –

Neither the Health and Safety and Work Act 1974 nor the Consumer Protection Act 1987 allow for civil actions based on the duties contained in the Act itself. Both create a presumption that Regulations made under the Act will support civil actions.

(c) Liability under Regulations

(i) *Regulations that potentially support civil liability*

Regulations made under the Health and Safety at Work Act 1974 have often replaced primary legislation whose provisions have been extensively relied on in civil litigation. Often these new Regulations have been introduced to implement EC Directives.

Thus, regulations introduced in 1992 to implement the Directive on provision and use of work equipment (89/655/EEC) repealed, and substantially re-introduced, provisions of the Factories Act 1961 relating to dangerous parts of machinery. The 1992 Regulations were themselves revoked in 1998 and replaced by similar Regulations incorporating modifications needed to comply with a further EC Directive (95/63/EC). The 1992 Regulations repealed provisions of the Factories Act 1961, including s 14(1), which provided:

Section 14

Other machinery

(1) Every dangerous part of any machinery, other than prime movers and transmission machinery, shall be securely fenced, unless it is in such a position or of such construction as to be as safe to every person employed or working on the premises as it would be if securely fenced.

— — —

Section 14(1) was very extensively relied on in civil litigation. The 1998 Regulations, being silent on the question of civil liability are governed by the presumption in s 47(2) of the 1974 Act and are therefore actionable in a civil context. There is however no evidence as yet that regulation 11 will be extensively relied on by accident victims, even though it does, unlike s 14, apply to all workplaces and situations, except on board ship.

PROVISION AND USE OF WORK EQUIPMENT REGULATIONS 1998 SI 1998/2306

Regulation 11

Dangerous parts of machinery

(1) Every employer shall ensure that measures are taken in accordance with paragraph (2) which are effective–

(a) to prevent access to any dangerous part of machinery or to any rotating stock-bar; or

(b) to stop the movement of any dangerous part of machinery or rotating stock-bar before any part of a person enters a danger zone.

(2) The measures required by paragraph (1) shall consist of–

(a) the provision of fixed guards enclosing every dangerous part or rotating stock-bar where and to the extent that it is practicable to do so, but where or to the extent that it is not, then

(b) the provision of other guards or protection devices where and to the extent that it is practicable to do so, but where or to the extent that it is not, then

(c) the provision of jigs, holders, push-sticks or similar protection appliances used in conjunction with the machinery, where and to the extent that it is practicable to do so, but where or to the extent that it is not, then

(d) the provision of information, instruction, training and supervision.

(3) All guards and protection devices provided under sub-paragraphs (a) or (b) of paragraph (2) shall–

(a) be suitable for the purpose for which they are provided;

(b) be of good construction, sound material and adequate strength;

(c) be maintained in an efficient state, in efficient working order and in good repair;

(d) not give rise to any increased risk to health or safety;

(e) not be easily bypassed or disabled;

(f) be situated at sufficient distance from the danger zone;

(g) not unduly restrict the view of the operating cycle of the machinery, where such a view is necessary;

(h) be so constructed or adapted that they allow operations necessary to fit or replace parts and for maintenance work, restricting access so that it is allowed only to the area where the work is to be carried out and, if possible, without having to dismantle the guard or protection device.

(4) All protection appliances provided under sub-paragraph (c) of paragraph (2) shall comply with sub-paragraphs (a) to (d) and (g) of paragraph (3).

(5) In this regulation:

'danger zone' means any zone in or around machinery in which a person is exposed to a risk to health or safety from contact with a dangerous part of machinery or a rotating stock-bar;

'stock-bar' means any part of a stock-bar which projects beyond the head-stock of a lathe.

– – –

(ii) Exclusion by omission

WORKPLACE (HEALTH, SAFETY AND WELFARE)
REGULATIONS 1992 SI 1992/3004

These Regulations repealed many of the provisions of the Factories Act 1961, provisions which had previously carried civil liability; particularly relevant here is s 29, which imposed duties to provide a safe means of access to a place of work in a factory.

In the Consultation Document, issued before these Regulations were made to implement the EC Directive on the Workplace (89/654/EEC), the Health and Safety Commission commented:

> 17 Among the provisions to be repealed is s 29(1) of the Factories Act 1961. This requires the provision of safe access and a safe place of work, so far as is reasonably practicable. Consideration has been given as to whether we need to include a similar general provision in the proposed Workplace Regulations. We have concluded that ss 2(2)(d) and 4(2) of the HSW Act [1974] already cover this provision adequately.

– – –

The 1992 Regulations did not include a provision comparable to that repealed. The general duties in ss 2 and 4 of the 1974 Act do not, of course, carry the right to bring a civil action.

(iii) Regulations expressly excluding civil liability

Notably, the very broad Management of Health and Safety at Work Regulations 1992, SI 1992/2051, made to implement the EC Framework Directive, did not create rights in civil proceedings. These Regulations were revoked and re-issued in 1999. It is noteworthy that the complete exclusion of liability was modified. The new provision is as follows.

MANAGEMENT OF HEALTH AND SAFETY AT WORK
REGULATIONS 1999 SI 1999/3242

Regulation 22

Exclusion of civil liability

(1) Breach of a duty imposed by these Regulations shall not confer a right of action in any civil proceedings.

(2) Paragraph (1) shall not apply to any duty imposed by these regulations on an employer:

  (a) to the extent that it relates to risk referred to in regulation 16(1) to an employee; or

  (b) which is contained in regulation 19.

Regulation 16(1) relates to risk assessment in respect of new or expectant mothers and regulation 19 relates to protection of young persons.

The Health and Safety Commission had published a Discussion Document in 1994, entitled *Rationalisation of Risk Assessment and other common provisions in health and safety legislation*. The following extract is from this Discussion Document (DD 194 C350 7/94):

Civil liability

17 The Management Regulations as presently constituted cannot be used in civil action for breach of statutory duty. People who believe that they have suffered harm because of a breach of these Regulations must, in any civil action for damages, prove that the duty holder has been negligent.

You are invited to say whether, in your view, if the regulations were expanded as suggested above, all or part of them should confer a right of action in civil proceedings for breach of statutory duty, rather than relying on the right of action for damages based on negligence.

– – –

(d) Judicial approach

Now that Parliament has taken to stipulating expressly whether civil actions are available, judges appear to be reluctant to find, if the legislation is silent, that it was, nevertheless, Parliament's intention to allow civil actions. The Court of Appeal had to consider this issue in the following case.

RICHARDSON v PITT-STANLEY AND OTHERS [1995] 2 WLR 26

The employee had suffered an accident at work; his employers had not complied with the statutory insurance requirements under the Employers' Liability (Compulsory Insurance) Act 1969 and were unable to meet the award of damages made in favour of the employee. The employee then sued the directors and secretary of the company, claiming that as, by failing to insure, they had committed criminal offences under the Act, he was entitled to claim a sum equivalent to the damage award from them personally in a civil action for breach of statutory duty. The majority of the Court of Appeal found against the employee. The following extracts are from the judgment of Russell LJ, beginning at p 30:

... Duties are owed by the employer both at common law and by statute whereby the employee is protected against the negligence or breach of statutory duty of the employer. If such a duty is breached and it causes personal injury to the employee he has the right to claim damages against the employer. The breach of statutory duty owed to the employee may also involve the employer in criminal proceedings, for example, under the Factory Acts, but the converse does not apply unless it can be shown that the particular statute creating the criminal offence, either by virtue of its express provisions or by necessary implication creates civil liability.

In the instant case, there is no express provision in the Act of 1969 creating civil liability on the part of the employers. Nor is there any such express provision relating to directors. Indeed it would be anomalous if the directors were to bear civil liability whilst the company of which they were directors was subject to no such liability.

...

In my judgment the Employers' Liability (Compulsory Insurance) Act 1969 is and was intended to be a statute within the confines of our criminal law. I say this in regard not only to employers but *a fortiori* in regard to directors. The plaintiff's remedy against the company subsisted at common law and under the Factories Act 1961. The failure to insure did not deprive the plaintiff of his remedy as such, but rather the enforcement of that remedy by way of the recovery of damages.

In the past, criminal statutes have created civil liability in the field of personal injury litigation but, generally the breach of the statute has resulted in direct physical injury to the plaintiff. Not so in this case. The breach of the Act of 1969 in this case does no more than involve the plaintiff in economic loss, namely the inability to recover damages. So far as the company is concerned the failure to insure does not provide an effective remedy to the injured workman. He can recover his damages from the assets of the company if there are any; if there are none the absence of insurance does not avail him.

All these considerations, in my judgment, tend to establish that the Act of 1969 was not intended to create civil liability ...

– – –

(e) The criteria of liability

Once it has been determined that a statutory duty may be relied on in order to found a civil action, the next question is, 'What must the claimant prove in order to establish that the defendant is in breach of a duty owed to the claimant?'. Broadly, the claimant must show:

- the defendant owed a duty to the claimant;

- the defendant broke that duty;

- breach of the duty caused the alleged damage to the claimant.

Superficially the elements of the tort resemble the elements of the common law tort of negligence. However, the resemblance is only superficial, because the claimant must establish these matters within the exact wording of the statute. This section of this chapter will address case law in relation to the first two of these elements.

Much of the case law is, inevitably, on statutes, and the regulations made under them, which pre-dated the Health and Safety at Work Act 1974, and have now, for the most part, ceased to have force. Problems arise as to whether a precedent has any continuing relevance once the statutory rule on which it turned has ceased to exist. It is therefore rather difficult to find cases which are still recognised as precedents. There have, in fact, been few cases reported for the past 20 or more years. There may be a number of reasons for this, including: litigation has already determined the meaning of the statutory wording; the decline of the heavy industries to which much of the legislation was applicable; and the common law of negligence has so developed that the statutory provisions are no longer relied on in civil courts.

Several of the cases referred to in the previous chapter (for example, *Bux v Slough Metals Ltd* (1974))[4] included claims for breach of statutory duty as well as claims for negligence, but these cases have not been relied upon in what follows, in order to give a wider selection of cases. There are situations in which the *ratio* of the case may remain of importance after the statute in question has ceased to apply, because the case discusses principles which transcend the facts and the law before the court at the time the case was heard. This account, though citing old cases, seeks to pinpoint some of the issues which are likely still to be relevant to cases for breach of statutory duty. Therefore, the cases which follow may be classified as follows:

(i) those illustrating general principles of statutory interpretation – for example, *Carroll v Andrew Barclay & Sons Ltd* (1948);[5]

(ii) those concerning criteria relevant to current legislation, though decided in relation to earlier legislation – for example, *Edwards v National Coal Board* (1949);[6]

(iii) interpretations of statutes that continue in force – for example, *Knowles v Liverpool City Council* (1993).[7]

(i) Cases illustrating general principles of statutory interpretation

Was the defendant in breach of duty to the claimant?

BOYLE v KODAK LTD [1969] 2 All ER 439

Lord Reid gave the following speech in the House of Lords, beginning at p 439:

> My Lords, the appellant sustained injury when he fell off a ladder while engaged in painting the outside of a large oil storage tank which was some 30 feet high. Other means of access had been used for the lower parts of the cylindrical wall, but the upper part had to be painted by a man standing on a ladder the top of which rested on a rail round the roof of the tank. For safety it was necessary to lash the top of the ladder to this rail to prevent it from slipping sideways, and the accident occurred while the appellant was going up

---

4   [1974] 1 All ER 262.
5   [1948] AC 477.
6   [1949] 1 KB 704.
7   [1993] IRLR 588.

the ladder in order to lash it. For some reason never discovered the ladder slipped when he was about 20 feet up and he fell with the ladder.

No negligence was proved. It was not proved that the respondents ought to have foreseen any danger involved in this method, and there is no evidence that any negligence on the part of the appellant caused or contributed to the fall of the ladder. But the appellant asserted and the respondents admitted that in the circumstances this method involved a breach of statutory duty. Regulation 29(4) of the Building (Safety Health and Welfare) Regulations 1948 provides:

'Every ladder shall so far as practicable be securely fixed so that it can move neither from its top nor from its bottom points of rest. If it cannot be so securely fixed it shall where practicable be securely fixed at the base or if such fixing at the base is impracticable a person shall be stationed at the base of the ladder to prevent slipping.'

It so happened that there was a staircase running round the outside of the tank by which it would have been possible for the appellant to reach the top of the tank, and he could then have lashed the top of the ladder to the rail, come down the staircase and then mounted the ladder. In that way he could have avoided mounting the ladder before it had been fixed in the manner which complied with the regulation. The appellant's case is that it was practicable to do this and that therefore there was a breach of the regulation when he mounted the unlashed ladder at the time of the accident. I do not have to consider whether that is right because the respondents had admitted that there was then such a breach.

It is common ground that these regulations imposed absolute duties on both the appellant and the respondents. And it is admitted that the appellant, though himself in breach, was entitled to sue the respondents relying on their absolute liability created by their breach. There is no difficulty in this case about causation: clearly this breach was the cause of the accident.

The doctrine of absolute liability, which was invented by the courts, can lead to absurd results when coupled with the employer's vicarious liability. It would be absurd if, notwithstanding the employer having done all he could reasonably be expected to do to ensure compliance, a workman, who deliberately disobeyed his employer's orders and thereby put the employer in breach of a regulation, could claim damages for injury caused to him solely by his own misdoing. So the courts have quite properly introduced a qualification of the employer's absolute liability. A principle of law has been established that, although in general the employer is under absolute liability in respect of such a breach, the employer may have a defence to an action against him by an employee who is also in breach.

...

In my opinion, these and other cases show that, once the plaintiff has established that there was a breach of an enactment which made the employer absolutely liable, and that that breach caused the accident, he need do no more. But it is then open to the employer to set up a defence that in fact he was not in any way in fault but that the plaintiff employee was alone to blame.

...

The respondents led no evidence. So, the crucial question is whether they have proved by the evidence of the appellant's witnesses that they did everything which they could reasonably be expected to do to prevent this breach.

...

It may be that neither the respondents nor their foreman knew that the work was being done in this way. But ought they to have realised, if they had given thought to the matter, that there was a substantial risk that a skilled workman would not be sufficiently familiar with the regulations to know that this method involved breach of the regulations? If they ought to have realised that, then it was plainly their duty to instruct the man as to what he ought to do in order to avoid a breach. They would be quite entitled to trust him to do what he had been told to do.

Employers are bound to know their statutory duty and take all reasonable steps to prevent their men from committing breaches. If an employer does not do that he cannot take advantage of this defence. On the respondents' admission there is a difference under this regulation between cases where there is another practicable means of access to the top of the ladder, and cases where there is none or where there is nothing to which the ladder can be lashed. In the former case the man must use the alternative means of access, here the stairway, to get to the top to lash the ladder, and then return that way before ascending the ladder; in the latter case he is permitted to ascend the ladder without lashing it. I think the evidence shows that a skilled practical man might easily fail to appreciate this and that the respondents ought to have realised that and instructed their men accordingly. So they have not proved that they did all they could reasonably be expected to do to ensure compliance and they cannot rely on this defence so as to avoid their absolute vicarious liability under the regulation.

Then it was said that the appellant would have disobeyed any order to go up the stairway to lash the ladder as soon as the foreman departed. I can find nothing in the evidence to justify this. The trial judge found that he was 'an extremely intelligent man and a nice man' and, in another passage in his judgment, 'an extremely straightforward and intelligent man'. It may be that if the foreman had merely told him about the regulation and left it to him to choose, he would have chosen to ignore the regulation. But that would not be doing his best to ensure obedience to the regulation; that implies an order, and there is nothing to show that the appellant would have disobeyed an order.

— — —

What is the scope of the duty?

Many of the duties under the pre-1974 legislation were either absolute or strict. The courts were often invited to limit the burden of them on the defendant by narrowly defining their scope. This was particularly apparent in relation to the interpretation of the employers' duty to guard dangerous parts of machinery. The frequent dispute as to the scope of the duty is reflected in the reported cases. Thus, an early appeal by way of case stated from a criminal conviction had held that the defendant employer's strict duty under the Factories Acts to fence dangerous parts of machinery applied only if the machinery was foreseeably dangerous: *Hindle and Another, Appellants v Birtwistle, Respondent* (1897).[8] However, if the machinery were dangerous, it had to be fenced, even though it was not practicable to do so because fencing would render the machine (for example, a grindstone) unusable *(John Summers & Sons Ltd v Frost* (1955)).[9] This rule did not apply when the general fencing requirement had been relaxed by special regulations in respect of the particular class of machine.

The duty to fence transmission machinery was an absolute one. In *Carroll v Andrew Barclay & Sons Ltd* (1946) it was held that the duty was only to prevent workers getting access to the dangerous parts, not to prevent them being injured by broken parts flying out from the machinery. Similarly, the strict duty to fence dangerous parts of machinery other than transmission machinery did not extend to protecting the worker from injury by work pieces being thrown out by the machinery *(Nicholls v F Austin (Leyton) Ltd* (1946)).[10] In arriving at their decision in *Carroll*, the House of Lords considered a number of other cases, including most of those mentioned in this and the preceding paragraph. The fencing provisions referred to in these cases were re-enacted in successive Factories Acts and were law for at least a century. They have ceased to apply since 1 January 1993 and it is very unlikely that there are still to be litigated cases concerning their applicability to accidents occurring before this date. It will be interesting to see whether any of these older cases will have any bearing on the interpretation of the new fencing provision in regulation 11 of the Provision and Use of Work Equipment Regulations 1998. Since the new provisions include requirements 'to prevent access to any dangerous part of machinery', it is arguable that the old authorities will remain of relevance.

Interestingly, a successful claim has now been brought against an employer for breach of regulation 6(1) of the Provision and Use of Work Equipment Regulations 1992 (now regulation 5(1) of the Regulations as re-issued in 1998). This regulation stipulates that 'every employer shall ensure that work equipment is maintained in an efficient state, in efficient working order and in good repair'.

In *Stark v The Post Office* (2000)[11] the claimant appealed against a decision of the High Court dismissing his claim for damages on the ground that the defendant employer was neither liable in negligence nor for breach of statutory duty. The claimant suffered serious personal injury when the front brake broke on the bicycle he was riding when delivering mail. The judge's unchallenged finding of fact was that the cause of the brake failure was either

---

8 [1897] 1 QB 192.
9 [1955] AC 740.
10 [1946] AC 493.
11 (2000) *The Times*, 29 March (only reported as LTL 2/3/2000).

metal fatigue or some manufacturing defect, which would not have been revealed on even the most 'perfectly rigorous' inspection. The claimant contended that, notwithstanding this finding of fact, an absolute obligation was imposed upon the Post Office by the Regulations. The Post Office contended that the contemplation of the EC Directives, which the Regulations were intended to implement, was for something less than an absolute duty. The Court of Appeal held that, in framing the regulation, the parliamentary draftsman had adopted a form of words which had long been held to impose an absolute obligation. It followed that this regulation imposed an absolute obligation. Although the Directives were to be taken as laying down minimum standards, there was nothing precluding a Member State from imposing more stringent requirements. Accordingly, the employers were liable for breach of the regulation.

CARROLL v ANDREW BARCLAY & SONS LTD [1948] AC 477

In this appeal from the Second Division of the Scottish Court of Session, the House of Lords held that the fencing of transmission machinery, as then required under s 13(1) of the Factories Act 1937, imposed on occupiers of factories a duty to erect a barricade to prevent any employees from making contact with the machinery, but did not oblige them to prevent broken machinery from flying out and injuring them. The extract is from the judgment of Lord Porter, beginning at p 483:

> My Lords, the correct solution of this problem must depend on the true construction of the terms of the Act. The provisions which deal with fencing are to be found in ss 12–16 inclusive and it is, I think, noteworthy that in the case of the first of these sections which is concerned with prime movers there is an absolute obligation to fence, without any qualification whatever except for electric generators and so forth which, by subsection 3, are subject to a less stringent rule. Apart from such generators, prime movers, which are defined in s 52 and do not include the belt in question, must be securely fenced whether they are safe or not and whatever their position or construction. If they are unfenced the occupiers of the factory are guilty of an offence. In the case of electric generators, however, and also in the case of transmission machinery (s 13) and dangerous machinery (s 14), fencing is not required if the position or construction of the machinery renders it as safe to everyone employed or working on the premises as it would be if securely fenced. The only difference between transmission and dangerous machinery is that, subject to the qualification mentioned above, the former must be fenced whether it is dangerous or not, whereas the latter must be proved to be dangerous before the duty to fence comes into existence. In either case, fencing is obligatory unless the exceptions apply. But it still remains to be determined against what dangers the fencing is to be a safeguard and what circumstances the exceptions embrace. For my own part, I find it difficult to envisage any set of circumstances in which unfenced machinery would be safe, owing to its position or indeed construction if the risk of breakage is to be taken into

consideration. In such a case no position, at any rate, could warrant that employees might not be injured or that the machinery would be as safe as if it was securely fenced. And equally if breakage is to be guarded against, the distinction between machinery which is dangerous and that which is not seems to disappear. All machinery is potentially dangerous because it may break, but the Act is not concerned with danger in that sense, it is danger in working against which it is framed to give security. Throughout the relevant sections I can find no hint that the danger of machinery breaking has been taken into account. The words 'of such construction' in s 12 subsection 3, s 13 subsection 1 and s 14 subsection 1 deal with types of construction, not with the strength of the machine; ss 22–26 provide for lifts, floors and methods of ingress and egress and have no bearing on the provision of sound machinery. Unless the matter be dealt with by regulations made under s 60, the common law obligation to use due care seems alone to be the sanction against weak or ill constructed machinery. So far indeed from suggesting that the breakage of machinery is under consideration in ss 12–16, indications to the contrary are, I think, to be found. Certainly, the provisions of s 13 subsections 3 and 4 show no tendency to keep in mind the breaking of driving belts and s 14 not only speaks of a device 'which automatically prevents the operator from coming into contact with that part' (ie, a dangerous part) in the proviso to subsection 1, but, in subsection 2(a) refers to preventing 'the exposure of a dangerous part of machinery whilst in motion', and I cannot read those phrases as intending anything more than a device to keep the workman from the dangerous part of the machine. Finally, subsection 3 talks of 'articles which are dangerous while in motion in the machine'. From all these expressions I conclude that it is risk arising from the motion of the machine which is being guarded against, whether the part concerned is the transmission or dangerous in working. Even s 15(b) contains the same suggestion when it permits certain work to be done while the machine is in motion if to stop it would seriously interfere with the carrying on of the process.

None of the cases which deal with the matter or were quoted to us seem to me to controvert this view. The latest in your Lordships' House, *Nicholls v F Austin (Leyton) Ltd* (1946) was concerned with injury caused by a piece of wood flying out from a circular saw which was said to be dangerous because of its tendency to throw out such pieces. I can imagine it being said that a circular saw is dangerous because of this tendency and that the obligation to fence dangerous machinery is to obviate its dangers, yet your Lordships held that the workman could not recover and Lord Thankerton said[12] that the obligation to fence under s 14 subsection 1 was to guard against contact with any dangerous part of a machine and not to guard against dangerous materials ejected from it. On the other hand, where there was danger, which should have been anticipated, that part of the machine (eg, a spindle) would fly out, as in *Hindle v Birtwistle* (1897),[13] it was held that the machine itself was dangerous in that respect and should have been fenced. So too where a driving shaft was

---

12   [1946] AC 493, p 499.
13   [1897] 1 QB 192.

situated 13 feet up, but it could not be assumed that the shaft would never be approached by any person employed in the factory, as in *Atkinson v L and NE Railway Co* (1926)[14] and in a case where the handle of a machine flew up and in the ordinary course of affairs danger might be contemplated from the use of the machine without protection, as in *Kinder v Camberwell Corpn* (1944),[15] the employers have been held under a duty to fence. In each case, however, it was injury, caused by the working of the machine and the danger which might reasonably be contemplated from its working. Even in the case of the flying spindle, it was not a breaking of a part of the machine, but an accident which might have been expected from its ordinary working which had to be guarded against. The machine was found to be a dangerous one because of the liability of spindles to fly out and it was that danger which was liable to occur in the course of its ordinary working, not its abnormal action in breaking, for which a fence had to be provided. *Harrison v Metropolitan Plywood Co* (1946)[16] was a decision upon the construction and effect of the Woodworking Machines Regulations 1922, regulation 17, which Hilbery J, following a decision of the Court of Appeal in *Miller v William Boothman & Sons Ltd* (1944),[17] held to supersede s 14 of the Factories Act, and not upon the wording of the Act itself, and therefore, whatever its effect, does not deal with the matter now in issue.

In my opinion, it is not necessary for your Lordships to consider in respect of any of these cases how far the facts support the decision: the principle is plain. Any risk arising from the working of a dangerous machine must be guarded against under s 14 and any danger emanating from the working of transmission machinery must likewise be guarded against under s 13. The working of transmission machinery is deemed to be dangerous; other machines need not be fenced unless they, or some part, are in fact dangerous. But in neither case does the Act aim at protection against breakage. In the present instance it was, no doubt, the duty of the respondents to fence the transmission machinery. That part, however, which a workman could enter upon was securely fenced and the belt was in such a position as to be as safe as it would be if securely fenced unless it broke. Had it been in such a position that the workman could come into contact with it, it would not have been so safe and in that case it would have been necessary to fence it. Fencing, in my opinion, means the erection of a barricade to prevent any employee from making contact with the machine, not an enclosure to prevent broken machinery from flying out. I would dismiss the appeal.

– – –

---

14 [1926] 1 KB 313.
15 [1944] 2 All ER 315; 42 LGR 317.
16 [1946] KB 255.
17 [1944] KB 337.

(ii) Concepts of continuing relevance

Reasonably practicable

The phrase 'reasonably practicable' was used quite frequently in legislation which pre-dated the Health and Safety at Work Act 1974 and it was the subject of important judicial comment in the context of civil actions for breach of statutory duty. Most of the duties in the 1974 Act and in regulations created under that Act require the duty holder to do what is reasonably practicable. The pre-1974 case law continues to influence understanding of the phrase, even in its use in the general duties under the 1974 Act, although these duties do not create any rights and obligations in civil proceedings.

What does the expression mean?

In the two following cases, the courts set out to establish a formula to determine whether all that was reasonably practicable had been done by the defendant to discharge his duty.

EDWARDS v NATIONAL COAL BOARD [1949] 1 KB 704

This was an action by the widow of a coal miner who was killed while underground by a fall of a considerable portion of the side of the roadway, along which he was walking. The Court of Appeal had to consider whether the defendants had discharged their obligations under the following sections of the Coal Mines Act 1911:

s 49   The roof and sides of every travelling road and working place shall be made secure ...

s 102(8) The owner of a mine shall not be liable to an action for damages as for breach of statutory duty in respect of any contravention of or non-compliance with any of the provisions of this Act if it is shown that it was not reasonably practicable to avoid or prevent the breach.

The Court of Appeal found for the widow, considering that the defendants had failed to establish their defence under s 102. The standard of the duty is described in the short judgment of Asquith LJ at pp 712–13:

> ... The onus was on the defendants to establish that it was not reasonably practicable in this case for them to have prevented a breach of s 49. The construction placed by Lord Atkin on the words 'Reasonably practicable' in *Coltness Iron Co v Sharp* (1938)[18] seems to me, with respect, right. 'Reasonably practicable' is a narrower term than 'physically possible' and seems to me to imply that a computation must be made by the owner, in which the quantum of risk is placed on one scale and the sacrifice involved in the measures necessary for averting the risk (whether in money, time or trouble) is placed in the other; and that, if it be shown that there is a gross disproportion between them – the risk being insignificant in relation to the sacrifice – the defendants

18 [1938] AC 90, p 94.

discharge the onus on them. Moreover, this computation falls to be made by the owner at a point of time anterior to the accident. The questions he has to answer are: (a) What measures are necessary and sufficient to prevent any breach of s 49?; (b) Are these measures reasonably practicable? In the particular type of accident caused by a 'glassy slant', it is admittedly impossible before the event to foresee at all, at what place or in what roadway or in what mine, such an accident would occur. The argument that the owners could and should have made secure the particular roadway in which, as things fell out, the glassy slant declared its presence, without having to make secure every other roadway in which it might have done so, assumes that the owners could by some process of divination, have predicted that the accident was likely to occur in the particular roadway in which it did, rather than elsewhere. But an owner who is not gifted with second sight can make no such prediction; and without it, security against this peril can only be secured by extending similar security measures to all roadways. Only so can he prevent breaches of s 49 due to glassy slants.

So far, I am inclined to agree with the learned judge. But, like my Lord, I do not think any or any sufficient evidence was adduced as to the relative quantum of risk and sacrifice involved, on the basis either that the mines as a whole, or this particular roadway, should be taken as the unit – a necessary prerequisite to any decision that the defendants have proved the necessary measures impracticable. For these reasons I think the appeal should be allowed.

— — —

In the following case the Court of Appeal had to consider s 23 of the Metalliferous Mines Regulation Act 1872 and regulation 7(3) of the Metalliferous Mines General Regulations 1938. These provisions, like those in issue in *Edwards v National Coal Board* (1949), concerned a duty to make the roof of a mine as safe as reasonably practicable. As the statutory duties were so similar, their Lordships gave careful consideration to, and cited extensively from, *Edwards*, but distinguished it. In their view, *Edwards* was concerned with what it was reasonably practicable to do to safeguard against a known risk. In *Marshall*, the question was whether there was any risk; it was accepted that there was a possibility of roof failure, but no experience of failure occurring, or indeed of the presence of the risk in the workings where the fatal accident occurred. All their Lordships explored this issue and the relevant sections of each of their judgments are set out below.

MARSHALL v GOTHAM CO LTD [1952] 2 All ER 1044

The action was brought by the widow of a man who was killed while working in a gypsum mine owned by the defendants. He was killed by a fall of marl from the roof of the working place. The fall was due to 'slickenside', a condition which was unusual anywhere and had not occurred in the defendants' mine for at least 25 years. There was no reason to suspect its presence and the probabilities were all against its occurrence there. Accordingly the roof over working places was inspected daily but no props were used. The claim had originally been for both common law negligence and breach of statutory duty: the trial judge had found there was no negligence, but there was breach of statutory duty. The defendants successfully appealed against the finding that they were in breach of their statutory duty.

Somervell LJ, having referred to *Edwards*, continued at p 1048:

The different arrangement of the provisions might possibly, at certain stages of a case, lead to different conclusions as to the onus of proof, but, for the purpose of the present case, where all the evidence is before the court, there is, in my opinion, no difference in the construction and application as between the two sets of statutory provisions. In *Edwards v National Coal Board* the death had been caused by a latent defect referred to as a 'glassy slant', which would appear to have some similarity to slickenside in that it could not be discovered by ordinary processes. In the *Edwards* case, however, there was undisputed evidence that glassy slants had been previously seen in the roadway where the accident happened although they were rare. The learned judge decided, as I gather, without evidence that the accident could have been prevented only by propping and lining throughout the roads of the defendants' mines and that this was not reasonably practicable. His decision was reversed in this court. It was held that s 49 of the Act of 1911 imposed an absolute duty to make secure and the onus rested on the defendants to satisfy the court that it was not practicable. Having called no evidence, they had failed to discharge that onus. It is suggested on behalf of the plaintiff in the present case that the unlikelihood of the 'insecurity' to be guarded against is irrelevant. If the roof turns out to be insecure, then there is an offence, however impossible it was to foresee that insecurity, provided that some reasonably practicable measure is available once its possibility is realised. If this were right, there is a good deal in the judgment of Tucker LJ which one would not have expected to find there. He said, for example,[19] that evidence to show that glassy slants were more common in some formations and areas than in others and that they were non-existent in some areas would be relevant. He also held (*ibid*), and this, I think, is not disputed by the plaintiff in the present case, that cost in relation to risk to be guarded against could properly be considered. Asquith LJ, adopted the same view, though he may have indicated (*ibid* p 747) that, in his opinion, the onus would have been more easily discharged. Singleton LJ, as I read his judgment (*ibid* p 748), placed the onus on the owners somewhat higher, but as it seems to me, insofar as there is a difference, we are bound by the views expressed by the majority ...

Per Jenkins LJ at p 1050:

An extreme form of the argument on the plaintiff's side is to the effect that, in considering what is reasonably practicable, regard should be had exclusively to what would have been possible as a matter of engineering in the way of providing support for roofs and sides without making the working of the mine physically or economically impossible, and that it is for this purpose irrelevant

---

19 [1949] 1 All ER 743, p 746.

to inquire what measures were or appeared to be necessary and sufficient to make roofs and sides secure according to the best assessment of the situation which could have been made immediately prior to the accident. This means, in other words, that what is reasonably practicable to make roofs and sides secure must be judged without reference to what appears to be necessary for that purpose. On this view a mine owner might be advised by the best mining engineers in the country that a roof in his mine was perfectly secure without artificial support, which would be wholly superfluous and a mere waste of time, labour and money, but he would, nevertheless, be obliged to put in artificial support as otherwise he would not have done all that was reasonably practicable to make the roof secure and would be liable if through some unforeseeable happening it fell and injured someone working under it. Again, if he did put in some form of artificial support of a certain design and strength, selected after careful consideration as adequate to support some particular roof, and owing to some unforeseeable happening a fall of quite exceptional size occurred, which the support provided did not suffice to prevent, it would avail him nothing in a suit by some workman injured by the fall to say with truth: 'I went into the whole matter very carefully, and I was satisfied that support of this design and strength was sufficient to prevent any fall of which there was any foreseeable risk.' He would, nevertheless, be in breach of his statutory duty on proof that support of greater strength or better design could have been provided as a matter of engineering without making the working of the mine physically or economically impossible, and would or might have prevented the fall in question. I reject this argument as stretching the mine owner's duty far beyond what is 'reasonably practicable' according to any rational construction of that expression. To my mind, that which is 'reasonably practicable' in this context is no more nor less than what is capable of being done to make roofs and sides secure within the limits of what it is reasonable to do, and it cannot be reasonable to do for this purpose anything more than that which it appears necessary and sufficient to do according to the best assessment of what is necessary and sufficient that can be made at the relevant time, that is, in the present instance a point of time immediately prior to the accident ...

Per Hodson LJ at p 1052:

The first question is: What is meant by 'reasonably practicable'? Counsel for the plaintiff argues with force that the words of qualification are directed not to the need for security, but to the means of providing the security. He says that the employer cannot say: 'I should not have provided means of security'; he can only say 'I cannot'. This, I think, is making the words 'reasonably practicable' approximate to 'physically possible', but Asquith LJ, pointed out in *Edwards v National Coal Board*[20] that there is a distinction to be drawn between these expressions. Notwithstanding that the interpretation put forward by counsel for the plaintiff in the present case is given support by the language of Singleton LJ in the *Edwards* case, I do not think it accords with the *ratio decidendi* of the judgments of the majority of the court consisting of Tucker LJ and Asquith LJ.

---

20 [1949] 1 All ER 743, p 747.

The argument of counsel for the plaintiff is substantially the same as that negatived by the majority of the court in the *Edwards* case with the modification that he recognises that, since that case was decided, the question of relative cost must be considered in arriving at a conclusion on reasonable practicability. I do not think, however, that the qualification introduced into the absolute duty by the words 'reasonably practicable' is limited to the question of cost. Tucker LJ gave an indication of the kind of evidence which might be relevant on this matter where he said (*ibid* p 746):

'Again, they might prove that, in some areas, no propping or lining was necessary for some particular reason or that different methods were required. Dealing with the particular latent defect which caused this accident – a glassy slant – it might have been possible to show that such a thing is more common in some formations and areas than it is in others or that it is non existent in some places ...'

It seems to me that the decision of the court, certainly that of the majority, turned on the absence of any sufficient evidence that the mine owners in the *Edwards* case, that is, the National Coal Board, had discharged the burden cast on them.

It is, I think, therefore, for the court to inquire whether in the circumstances of this case the defendants have proved that they did all that it was reasonably practicable for them to do to make secure the working place where the accident occurred. The knowledge which they had, or ought to have had, of the risk is, I think, relevant to the question of reasonableness ...

– – –

The statutory provision in the following House of Lords case was drafted differently from that which was before the Court of Appeal in *Edwards v National Coal Board* (1949); in that case the duty on the owner was set out in one section in absolute terms, while another section exonerated the owner in circumstances where it was not reasonably practicable to avoid the breach. In the following case, the duty itself is modified (in the same section) by the qualification of reasonable practicability. The effect seems to be that however the statutory provisions are set out, reasonable practicability is a defence and the burden of establishing that it was not reasonably practicable to achieve greater safety lies on the defendant. The following case appears to remain authoritative for civil proceedings. Section 40 of the 1974 Act clarifies beyond doubt that in the context of proceedings for a criminal offence under that Act and related legislation the burden of proving that it was not reasonably practicable to do more to achieve safety rests on the defendant. The effect, then, is, in criminal law, that the duty is an absolute one, subject to the defence.

NIMMO v ALEXANDER COWAN & SONS LTD [1968] AC 107

The case was an appeal from the First Division of the Scottish Court of Session. It concerned the interpretation of s 29(1) of the Factories Act 1961 a section since repealed. It is cited in full in the speech of Lord Guest, which is set out below, beginning at p 118:

> My Lords, in this action of damages by the appellant against the respondents,which is based on a breach by the respondents of s 29(1) of the Factories Act 1961, the respondents tabled a plea to the relevancy of the appellant's averments. The Lord Ordinary sustained the plea and dismissed the action. The First Division of the Court of Session adhered to the Lord Ordinary's interlocutor.
>
> Section 29(1) of the Factories Act 1961 is in the following terms:
>
> 'There shall, so far as is reasonably practicable, be provided and maintained safe means of access to every place at which any person has at any time to work, and every such place shall, so far as is reasonably practicable, be made and kept safe for any person working there.'
>
> The appellant avers that he had to unload two railway wagons filled with bales of pulp within the respondents' factory. He had to stand upon and make his way over the bales and, as the wagons were loosely filled, the bales formed an insecure foothold. Owing to the bale on which he was standing tipping up, he fell to the ground and was injured. After quoting the terms of s 29(1) of the Act of 1961 he avers: 'The place at which the pursuer had to work was not made and kept safe for him working there.' His ground of fault is that the respondents failed to comply with the statutory provision referred to and that this failure was the cause of the accident.
>
> Section 29(1) imposes the duty on the occupiers 'so far as is reasonably practicable' and the issue between the parties is whether, in the absence of an averment by the appellant that it was reasonably practicable for the respondents to make and keep his working place safe for him working, he has stated a relevant case. The respondents contend that as the requirement 'so far as is reasonably practicable' is an ingredient of the offence, its absence renders the appellant's pleadings irrelevant. The appellant contends that it is unnecessary for him to make such an averment and that the question of reasonable practicability is a matter of defence which, if it is to be raised, must be averred by the respondents. The record has been deliberately framed as a test case in order to raise the question in its stark form. The point as raised is one of pleading in Scotland, but the decision has wider implications, as it will inevitably affect the question of onus at the trial.
>
> Although there have been a number of cases in which expressions of opinion on this question have been made, the question is open (see *Hall v Fairfield Shipbuilding & Engineering Co Ltd* (1964),[21] *per* Lord Reid). The expression of opinion in *England* has been consistently to the effect that, in cases under sections in somewhat similar terms to s 29(1), the onus is upon the employer to establish that the precautions desiderated were not reasonably practicable. The first case was *Callaghan v Fred Kidd & Son (Engineers) Ltd*,[22] where Scott LJ said:

---

21 (1964) SC (HL) 72, pp 78–80.
22 [1944] KB 560, p 565.

'If it were necessary to decide the question of onus, the obvious fact that the difficulty or ease of doing what is necessary to maintain safety is so much more within the knowledge of the management than of their workpeople makes us disposed to hold that it is for the defence, whether in a prosecution or an action, to establish the proposition of fact involved in the words of limitation of the section.'

This was followed by *McCarthy v Coldair Ltd* (1951)[23] in which both Denning LJ (as he then was) and Hodson LJ (as he then was) expressed the view *obiter*, upon a construction of s 26(1) of the Factories Act 1937, which was in similar terms to s 29(1) of the Act of 1961, that the onus was on the employer to show what was practicable.

In *Marshall v Gotham Co Ltd* (1954)[24] the provision under consideration was regulation 7(3) of the Metalliferous Mines Regulations 1938, which provides that the regulations set out are to be in substitution for the provisions contained in the general rules in s 23 of the Metalliferous Mines Regulations Act 1872. Section 23 provides 'The following general rules shall, so far as may be reasonably practicable, be observed in every mine to which this Act applies.' Regulation 7(3) provides that the roof and sides of every travelling road shall be made secure. This House had, therefore, to construe a provision that so far as may be reasonably practicable the rule should be observed. The employers accepted the onus of establishing that the provision was not reasonably practicable. Lord Tucker, in whose speech Lord Cohen concurred, however, expressed the view that the employers rightly accepted the onus, but he said he did not think that the fact that the ease or difficulty of doing what was necessary to maintain safety was so much more within the knowledge of the management than the worker was a sufficient justification for shifting the onus. I am not sure that I can agree with this, and I prefer the opinion of Scott LJ in *Callaghan v Fred Kidd & Son (Engineers) Ltd* (1944)[25] already referred to. Lord Keith also said that it was for the mine owners to establish compliance with the regulations.

In *Trott v WE Smith (Erectors) Ltd* (1957)[26] Jenkins LJ (as he then was) expressed the view in relation to the construction of regulation 5 of the Building (Safety, Health and Welfare) Regulations 1948, that the onus of proving reasonable practicability was on the employer. The observations of Pearson LJ (as he then was) in *Braham v J Lyons & Co Ltd* (1962)[27] are, I think, helpful. He said that s 28 of the Factories Act 1961, requiring all floors, so far as is reasonably practicable, to be kept free from obstruction requires a certain result to be achieved and if that is not achieved, s 155(1) of the Act of 1961 makes the occupiers liable.

In Scotland there have been two recent Outer House cases in one of which, *Donno v British Railways Board* (1964)[28] Lord Kissen expressed the view that the

---

23 (1951) 2 TLR 1226.
24 [1954] AC 360.
25 [1944] KB 560, p 565.
26 [1957] 1 WLR 1154.
27 [1962] 1 WLR 1048.
28 1964 SLT (Notes) 108.

onus was on the pursuer which was in fact accepted by the pursuer; and, in the other, *Duncan v Smith and Phillips* (1965)[29] Lord Avonside expressed the view that the onus was on the employer, although in fact the pursuer accepted the onus.

The trend of authority in England at any rate is in favour of the appellant's contention. The question is one of the proper construction of s 29(1) and I have not found the question an easy one. The matter may be tested by asking the question as 'What is the criminal offence which is created by this section?' If there is no criminal offence, there can be no civil liability. The two must go hand in hand. The respondents say the offence created is failing to make the working place safe so far as is reasonably practicable. In this event the complaint would require to contain this qualification, and in order to establish the commission of the offence the prosecution would require to prove in what way it was reasonably practicable to comply with the terms of the section (see *Archibald v Plean Colliery Co Ltd* (1924)).[30] I am not sure, however, that this necessarily helps to the proper construction of the section.

...

I therefore return to the construction of s 29(1). Powerful reasons have been given by the Lord Ordinary and the judges of the First Division in favour of the respondents' construction. It is said that the words 'so far as is reasonably practicable' are an integral part of the offence, that they qualify the verbs 'made safe' and 'kept safe' or are, as Lord Migdale[31] graphically puts it, 'woven into the verb'. But these considerations seem to me to pay little or no regard to the purpose of the section. The object of the section was to provide for a safe working place by imposing criminal and civil liability on the occupier in the event of breach. There is doubt as to the construction of this section. The question appears to me to depend upon which construction will best achieve the result to be attained, namely, to make and keep the working place safe. On the one hand, is this result likely to be achieved by requiring the pursuer to condescend and specify the practicable measures whereby the place could be made and kept safe, or by requiring the defenders to specify and establish that it was not reasonably practicable to do this? (See the observations of Lord Justice-Clerk Cooper in *Chalmers v Speedwell Wire Co Ltd* (1942).)[32] In this connection like Scott LJ in *Callaghan v Fred Kidd & Son (Engineers) Ltd* (1944)[33] I attach some importance to the consideration that the means of achieving the end were more likely to be within the knowledge of the defenders than the pursuer. In some cases it might be comparatively simple for the pursuer to make the necessary averments, but there will be many cases where, particularly in the case of a death of a workman, it would be unreasonable to expect a widow to have to specify what steps which the defender should have taken to make the working place safe were reasonably

---

29 1965 SLT (Notes) 16.
30 (1924) SC (JC) 77.
31 1966 SLT 266, p 273.
32 (1942) SC (JC) 42, p 47.
33 [1944] KB 560.

practicable. I may instance the case of a claim by a widow under regulation 6 of the Shipbuilding and Ship Repairing Regulations 1960, for breach of the duty to provide and maintain a safe means of access where the form of access provided is inherently unsafe and cannot be made safe, but what was required is a different form of access altogether. In such a case, the widow might be faced some time after the accident with the difficult, if not impossible, task of averring what was a reasonably practicable form of access when the ship has been constructed and all the real evidence had disappeared. On the other hand, the employer would be put on inquiry immediately after the accident and would be in a position to investigate the matter timeously. To treat the onus as being on the pursuer seems to equiparate the duty under the statute to the duty under common law, namely, to take such steps as are reasonably practicable to keep the working place safe. I cannot think that the section was intended to place such a limited obligation on employers. It is said by the respondents that to impose the onus on them would mean that they would have to prove a negative. This is not so in my view. In most cases the question would be whether the provision of safety measures was reasonable, having regard to the expense involved. This would involve balancing the expense of the precautions suggested against the risks involved. That would be peculiarly within the employer's province (see *Marshall v Gotham Co Ltd* (1954)).[34]

I attach some importance to the stage at which the latter provision of s 29(1) found its way into the Statute Book. The particular part of s 29(1) relied on was first enacted by s 5 of the Factories Act 1959, and formed an addition to s 26(1) of the Factories Act 1937. This provision was enacted by Parliament in the knowledge that the current judicial opinion was in favour of the view that s 26(1) placed the onus of proving that the provisions were not reasonably practicable on the employers. Notwithstanding this state of the law the phraseology of s 26(1) was repeated. This is some indication that Parliament was content to leave the onus resting on the employers.

Upon the whole matter I would allow the appeal, recall the interlocutors of the Court of Session, repel the first plea in law for the defenders and remit to the Court of Session.[35]

--- ---

(iii) Interpretation of statutes currently in force

The following case is cited at length for a number of reasons: first, it is an interpretation of a statute which continues of importance; secondly, it demonstrates the careful analysis which judges have to make when interpreting statutes; and, thirdly, in the speech cited, his Lordship makes the important point that decisions involving the interpretation of statutes other than that before the court have to be treated with care. Most importantly,

---

34 [1954] AC 360.

35 In *Mains v Uniroyal Englebert Tyres Ltd* (1995) *The Times*, 29 September, a Scottish court held that s 29(1) imposed an absolute duty, subject only to the defence of 'reasonable practicability'. The plaintiff did not even have to show the risk was foreseeable.

perhaps, and in spite of his Lordship's warning, the House was concerned with interpreting 'equipment' and 'plant', words in common use in recent regulations.

KNOWLES v LIVERPOOL CITY COUNCIL (APPELLANTS)
[1993] IRLR 588

The House of Lords had to consider whether a flagstone was 'equipment' within the scope of the Employer's Liability (Defective Equipment) Act 1969. The following is from the speech of Lord Jauncey of Tullichettle:

> My Lords, this appeal relates to the construction of s 1 of the Employer's Liability (Defective Equipment) Act 1969. The facts are simple. The respondent was employed by the appellants as a labourer flagger repairing a pavement in a Liverpool street. While he was manhandling a flagstone into the shovel of a JCB the corner of the flagstone broke off causing the stone to drop with consequent injury to the respondent's finger. The breakage occurred because the manufacturers, who were not the appellants, had failed to cure it properly. This defect could not reasonably have been discovered before the accident.
>
> ...
>
> The respondent raised an action against the appellants claiming damages on the ground, *inter alia*, that they were liable for his injury by virtue of s 1(1) of the Act. The recorder of Liverpool upheld the respondent's statutory claim, holding that the flagstone was equipment for the purposes of the subsection and was defective. The Court of Appeal took the same view in dismissing the appellants' appeal.
>
> Before this House, Mr Braithwaite for the appellants sought to draw a distinction between 'plant' on the one hand, which comprehended such things as tools and machinery required for the performance of a particular task, and 'stock in trade' on the other, which covered articles produced by the use of plant and machinery. Equipment fell firmly on the side of plant. He argued further that material was to be distinguished from equipment and was therefore excluded from the latter. He sought to obtain support for these propositions from certain *dicta* in three cases in this House, *Davie v New Merton Board Mills Ltd* (1959),[36] *Haigh v Charles W Ireland Ltd* (1973)[37] and *Coltman v Bibby Tankers Ltd* (1988),[38] together with a consideration of certain provisions in primary and secondary legislation.
>
> It is common ground that the Act of 1969 was passed as a result of the decision in *Davie v New Merton Board Mills* ... Parliament clearly considered this to be an unsatisfactory situation and passed the Act whose purpose is set out in the long title as follows:
>
> 'An Act to make further provision with respect to the liability of an employer for injury to his employee which is attributable to any defect in equipment

---

36   [1959] AC 604.
37   [1973] 3 All ER 1137.
38   [1988] 1 AC 276.

provided by the employer for the purposes of the employer's business; and for purposes connected with the matter aforesaid.'

Mr Braithwaite argued that this House in *Davie v New Merton Board Mills Ltd* (1959) was only dealing with a tool or appliance, that the decision did not turn on the distinction which he sought to draw between tools and appliances on the one hand and stock in trade on the other and that the Act should be construed against this limited background. It is true that the article in question in *Davie* was a tool but it is quite wrong to suppose that their Lordships would have applied different principles had the cause of injury been part of an article which was being incorporated in manufacture, rather than a tool used in the manufacture thereof.

...

Given that the Act was passed to afford to the workmen a remedy which might be denied to them at common law by treating the employer as though he were vicariously liable for the defect in the tool, why should Parliament have restricted the scope of that remedy to tools and plant omitting what Mr Braithwaite described as stock in trade but what might more appropriately be described as other articles or material used by the employer in his business? To this question I have been unable to find a logical answer.

In *Haigh v Charles W Ireland Ltd* (1973) this House held that the word 'plant' in s 31(4) of the Factories Act 1961 did not cover an article which was on factory premises for the purposes of being subjected to an industrial process. Lord Diplock, in relation to the meaning to be ascribed to the word 'plant', said at p 1148C:

'It is a definition of a physical object by reference to the use to which it is being put. Where, as in the Factories Act 1961, all references to 'plant' are to plant within a factory in which an industrial process is carried on, the only relevant use, in my opinion, is that to which the physical object is being put in that factory. If it is there as part of the apparatus for use in carrying on the industrial process undertaken on those premises, it is 'plant' within the meaning of the Act even though it may be temporarily out of use or in the course of installation, repair or removal. If it is there for the purpose of being subjected to that industrial process it is an "article" as that term is used in the definition in s 175 to describe the physical objects on which are carried out those industrial processes which qualify the premises where they are undertaken as a "factory" within the meaning of the Act; it is not "plant", whatever may be the use to which it has been previously put or may be subsequently put elsewhere.'

This *dictum* of Lord Diplock, it was argued, pointed towards the narrow definition for the word 'equipment' in s 1(3) of the Act contended for by the appellant. I cannot agree. I do not find it helpful to look at the same words occurring in other statutes passed for different purposes as an aid to the construction of those words in this Act whose purpose is very clear.

Finally, in *Coltman v Bibby Tankers Ltd* (1988) it was held that a large ship which sank due to defects in construction and design was 'equipment provided by his employer for the purposes of the employer's business' within the meaning of s 1(1)(a) of the Act. Three principal arguments were advanced by the defendants in that case, namely:

(1) that the use of the word 'equipment' in juxtaposition with the word 'provided' imported the use of something such as a tool provided to the employee for use in his work;

(2) that 'equipment' was to be distinguished from the factory or workplace in which tools or machinery are provided and that a large ship was akin to a workplace; and (most importantly)

(3) that the inclusion of the words 'vehicle' and 'aircraft', without reference to ship, demonstrated a conscious intention on the part of Parliament that ships should be excluded.

Mr Braithwaite argued that in rejecting these three arguments this House did not require to address the issue in this appeal.

My Lords, in my view a number of observations of Lord Oliver of Aylmerton who delivered the leading speech in *Coltman v Bibby Tankers Ltd* are entirely apposite to this appeal. Lord Oliver, after referring, at p 269G [*sic*], to the purpose of the Act, expressed the view that if subsection (1) had stood alone and without such assistance as was provided by subsection (3) he would have had no difficulty in concluding that in the context of the Act a ship was part of the 'equipment' of the business of a ship owner. He concluded, at p 298G, that the definition in subsection (3) had been inserted not for the purpose of enlarging the word 'equipment' by including in it articles which would not otherwise fall within it in its ordinary signification but rather for clarification and avoidance of doubt. With reference to subsection (3), he said at p 299A:

'The key word in the definition is the word 'any' and it underlines, in my judgment, what I would in any event have supposed to be the case, having regard to the purpose of the Act, that is to say, that it should be widely construed so as to embrace every article of whatever kind furnished by the employer for the purposes of his business.'

The latter observation, if applicable, is undoubtedly wide enough to cover the flagstone provided by the appellants in the present case.

My Lords, there is nothing in Lord Oliver's speech to suggest that these observations were restricted to cases involving ships or any other particular article. The observations were quite general and I have no doubt that they are just as applicable to this case as they were to the ship in *Coltman v Bibby Tankers Ltd*. That being so, the flagstone which broke and injured the respondent was 'equipment' for the purposes of the Act of 1969.

Mr Braithwaite very properly drew your Lordships' attention to a case in the Outer House of the Court of Session, *Ralston v Greater Glasgow Health Board* (1987)[39] in which Lord Kincraig rejected an argument that 'equipment' did not cover materials used by cleaners in the cleaning process but applied only to instruments or appliances used in the process. He said, at p 387K:

---

39 1987 SLT 386.

'I see no reason to give a restricted construction to the word "equipment". In my judgment it includes materials provided for use in the cleaning operation. It was plainly one of the items of equipment provided to the pursuers for the necessary purpose of cleaning the mop heads.'

It does not appear that this case was cited in argument in *Coltman v Bibby Tankers Ltd* but the decision accords entirely with the reasoning of Lord Oliver. I am satisfied that the case was correctly decided. Mr Braithwaite referred to the Health and Safety at Work Act 1974 and to various regulations made under that Act and under the Factories Act in which the words 'plant or equipment', 'article', 'material' and 'appliances' were used as demonstrating that where Parliament intended to cover articles or material this was done by the use of specific words. Once again, I do not find that these provisions made for different purposes are of any assistance in construing the Act of 1969.

My Lords, I have no hesitation in concluding that the word 'equipment' in s 1(1)(a) is habile to cover the flagstone in this appeal. In the first place, the requirement of the subsection is that the equipment is provided 'for the purposes of the employer's business' and not merely for the use of the employee. Thus a piece of defective equipment which causes injury to a workman would fall within the ambit of the subsection even though the workman was neither required to use nor had in fact used it. Whatever the meaning of 'equipment' this would go further than the circumstances in *Davie* where the defective tool had been provided to the workman for the purposes of his job. In this case, the flagstone had undoubtedly been provided by the appellants for the purposes of their business of repairing and relaying the pavement. In the second place, there can be no logical reason why Parliament, having recognised the difficulties facing workmen, as demonstrated by *Davie v New Merton Board Mills* (1959), should have removed those difficulties in part rather than in whole. Indeed, partial removal, as contended for by the appellants, could produce bizarre results. To give one example which I put in argument to counsel, a pump manufacturer buys in tools required for assembling the pumps as well as some components including the bolts for holding together the two parts of the housing. Workman A is tightening a bolt which sheers and injures his eye. Workman B is tightening a similar bolt but his spanner snaps causing him a similar injury. If the appellants are right, workman B could proceed under s (1) of the Act but workman A would have no remedy thereunder. My Lords, I cannot believe that Parliament can have intended the Act to produce results such as these. In my view, the only reasonable conclusion is that Parliament intended the Act to provide a remedy in the situations where an employer had provided for the purpose of his business an article which was defective and caused injury to a workman but where he was for the reasons set out in *Davie* not in breach of a common law duty of care owed to that workman. In the third place, I consider that the conclusion which I have reached accords with the reasoning of Lord Oliver of Aylmerton in *Coltman v Bibby Tankers Ltd* (1988).

– – –

The following case has already been briefly noted as an example of an employer being liable for causing psychiatric injury.

YOUNG v CHARLES CHURCH (SOUTHERN) LTD AND ANOTHER (1997) *THE TIMES*, 1 MAY

This interesting decision of the Court of Appeal is only to be found briefly reported in *The Times*. It was held that an employee who suffered psychiatric illness after seeing a workmate electrocuted close to him could recover damages for breach of statutory duty under regulation 44(2) of the Construction (General Provisions) Regulations 1961 (SI 1961/1580).

The claimant's workmate was killed when the equipment he was carrying touched an electrically charged overhead cable. This fatal accident was undoubtedly caused by the defendant employers' breach of the regulation which provides: 'Where any electrically charged overhead cable or apparatus is liable to be a source of danger to persons employed during the course of any operations or works to which these regulations apply ... all practicable precautions shall be taken to prevent such danger ...'

The view of the court appears to have been that the defendants were in breach of duty not only to the deceased but also to the claimant who like the deceased had been put at risk by their breach of duty. Thus their liability to him was not so much for the shock of seeing his workmate killed, but for the shock of realising that he rather than the deceased might have been the victim.

The case is especially interesting because the trend of cases has been to deny redress to an employee who suffers psychiatric illness as a consequence of seeing his workmate killed.

CHAPTER 8

CIVIL LIABILITY: DEFENCES, QUANTUM AND EXTINCTION OF LIABILITY

I DEFENCES

When a claimant has made out a case by establishing that the defendant owed a duty of care, that he has broken that duty and the breach has caused actionable damage, the defendant may raise a defence to reduce – or even escape – liability. Pleading a defence must be distinguished from seeking to exclude liability by relying on a notice or a contractual term. As has been noted, exclusion of liability for death or personal injury negligently caused is prohibited by s 2(1) of the Unfair Contract Terms Act 1977. This section is concerned with pleading a defence to establish that liability has not arisen at all or is less than the claimant is alleging.

It has already been noted that, in actions founded on breach of statutory duty, there may be special defences limited to the particular statutory duty relied on; importantly, there may be the defence of reasonable practicability.

There are two general defences available in a civil action for redress for personal injury:

(a) contributory negligence;

(b) assumption of risk (*volenti non fit injuria*).

Formerly, if either of these defences was successfully pleaded, the claimant was remediless. Today, a successful plea of contributory negligence does not deprive the claimant of all remedy.

(a) Contributory negligence

If the claimant's contributory negligence is to be considered by the court, the defendant must expressly ask the court to consider it. Since the Law Reform (Contributory Negligence) Act 1945, the court will, if satisfied on the evidence that there has been contributory negligence on the part of the claimant, determine the financial value of the claimant's injury and then reduce the award of damages according to the percentage of fault on the part of the claimant. The way in which the courts operate to apportion liability where there is more than one cause for an accident has been apparent in some of the judgments already cited in this book. Those cases were concerned with causation and the defence of contributory negligence is also concerned with causation, both of the circumstances leading to the injury and also the extent of the injury – for example, a cause of the injury might be the poor working environment, but the claimant might have been largely protected from it by using the protective equipment provided. In some situations, it may be difficult to determine whether there is any fault in the defendant: there may not be if the claimant is properly informed of the risk and free to protect himself from injury. This was the situation in *Qualcast v Haynes* (1959).[1] In that case the claimant argued that there was some fault in the employer for failing to instruct him to use the protective equipment which was available for his use. The implication of the House of Lords' decision that the employer owed no duty to instruct him, an experienced worker, to use the equipment meant that he was deemed to be the sole cause of his own injury: had the employer been under a duty to instruct him, and therefore negligent in failing to do so, the claimant's damages might nevertheless have been substantially reduced to take account of his contributory negligence. A similar question as to whether the employee was the sole cause of his own fatal injury had to be considered by the House of Lords in *Stapley v Gypsum Mines Ltd*, cited below, p 194. In this latter case it will be seen that the employer was found to be in some degree responsible, possibly because of the relatively junior status of the accident victim and his fellow worker.

In former times, when contributory negligence was a complete bar to recovery of any damages, the courts were often loath to find that the victim had been contributorily negligent. Thus, it was said:

> It is not for every risky thing which a workman in a factory may do in his familiarity with the machinery that a plaintiff ought to be held guilty of contributory negligence (*per* Lawrence J, cited by the House of Lords in *Caswell v Powell Duffryn Associated Collieries Ltd* (1940)).[2]

Now that apportionment of blame is possible, there is no longer any need for judges to take such a sympathetic view of behaviour at the workplace and it is very common for awards to be reduced to take contributory negligence into account.

LAW REFORM (CONTRIBUTORY NEGLIGENCE) ACT 1945

Section 1

Apportionment or liability in case of contributory negligence

(1) Where any person suffers damage as the result partly of his own fault and partly of the fault of any other person or persons, a claim in respect of that damage shall not be defeated by reason of the fault of the person suffering the damage, but the damages recoverable in respect thereof shall be reduced to such extent as the court thinks just and equitable having regard to the plaintiff's share in the responsibility for the damage.

...

---

1   [1959] AC 743; [1959] All ER 38.
2   [1940] AC 152.

Section 4

Interpretation

The following expressions have the meanings hereby respectively assigned to them, that is to say–

'court' means, in relation to any claim, the court or arbitrator by or before whom the claim falls to be determined;

'damage' includes loss of life or personal injury;

'fault' means negligence, breach of statutory duty or other act or omission which gives rise to liability in tort or would, apart from this Act, give rise to the defence of contributory negligence.

– – –

(i) The worker was not much at fault

LASZCZYK v NATIONAL COAL BOARD [1954] 1 WLR 1426

The case came before Pearson J at Manchester Summer Assizes. His Lordship's judgment begins at p 1427:

The plaintiff, Mr Herbert Laszczyk, claims against the defendants, the National Coal Board, for damages for negligence and breach of statutory duty in respect of a shot-firing accident which occurred on March 11, 1953, at the defendant's Bickershaw colliery. The plaintiff, who is of Polish origin, came to England in 1947, having previously had some one and a half year's experience as a coal miner. He was then trained in Wales as a haulage worker, but was not trained as a coal face worker. After some work at other mines he came to Bickershaw Colliery about three years prior to the accident, which would be early in 1950, and he worked there as a haulage worker. The combined team of haulage workers would, no doubt, on some occasions be bringing the extracted coal back from the coal face along the main roads but, at other times, they would be bringing the materials required – timber and iron bars – from what may be called the underground 'tramway terminus', along the main roads to a place near the coal face, and then one or more would have to bring the materials along to the coal face to give them to the working colliers who needed such materials. The plaintiff, throughout the three years' period up to and including March 11, 1953, when the accident occurred, did in fact from time to time, execute some of this work of bringing materials along the coal face and distributing them to the persons working there.

On February 11, 1953, one Hindley, who was the Bickershaw Colliery training officer, found the plaintiff at the coal face and he told him he had no right to be there, explaining, in effect, the safety requirements under the appropriate training regulations. He then took the plaintiff to some place on the main haulage road and pointed out a particular mark or position beyond which he told the plaintiff he must not go. The plaintiff worked on certain parts of two different shifts. On part of the afternoon shift he was under a deputy or fireman whose name was Sinclair and on part of the day or morning shift he worked under another officer of the same rank, Thompson. On that same day, February 11, 1953, the colliery training officer left for the first of these deputies, Sinclair, this note: 'H Laszczyk is being used on the face. He is not face trained in any respect; please avoid using him on the face.' Sinclair received this message and I think that he probably did pass it on to the plaintiff. The attitude of the other deputy, Thompson, was quite different. He instructed the plaintiff to continue doing the same work of distributing the required materials at the coal face, but to keep out of the way of the colliery training officer if he should happen to be there. The plaintiff carried out these instructions, although he and Thompson knew that this was in breach of the mines safety requirements. Preferring the evidence of the plaintiff to that of Thompson I find that these instructions were given after the colliery training officer's conversation with the plaintiff .

On March 11, 1953, a shot-firer named Melling was about to fire a shot in the stint of a miner called Burton and in accordance with the relevant shotfiring regulations he posted himself for security at one end of the determined danger zone and he posted Burton at the other end. Burton gave the necessary warning to another miner, but he failed to give any warning to the plaintiff, who was coming along the coal face in the direction of the determined danger zone. Burton was not keeping a proper look out and not performing his duty as a shot-firer's sentry with diligence and failed to see the plaintiff at all. The plaintiff went into the danger zone and was severely injured when the shot was fired. The accident was plainly caused by the negligence on the part of the sentry, Burton, and for his negligence the defendants must be held responsible, but there is a question whether some deduction should be made from the full amount of damages by reason of the contributory negligence on the part of the plaintiff himself.

...

The next question which arises is what percentage represents the plaintiff's share of responsibility for the accident on the facts, when he had been allowed and ordered wrongfully to be working at the coal face over the whole period of three years. He had been instructed by the official – the deputy who was his 'boss' for the time being – to continue this wrongful working and to keep out of the way of the colliery training officer if he should happen to be there. I hold that the proper share must be quite small and I assess it at five per cent.

– – –

(ii) The employee was very much at fault

STAPLEY V GYPSUM MINES LTD [1953] 2 ALL ER 478

In this widow's action, the majority of the House of Lords considered that the deceased had been highly negligent, but they nevertheless considered that the defendants had to accept some responsibility, as another employee, for whom they were vicariously liable, had been in some degree at fault. Interestingly, the headnote of the report states both were in breach of their duty under regulation 15 of the Metalliferous Mines General Regulations 1938 (failing to obey orders), though, in the section cited Lord Reid leaves aside whether they were in breach of regulation 7(3) by reason of working where the roof was not secure. The following extract is from the speech of Lord Reid, beginning at p 484:

... A well recognised danger in the mine is a fall of part of the roof. The roof is not generally shored up as any weakness in it can be detected by tapping it. If it is 'drummy', giving a hollow sound, it is unsafe and must be taken down ... One morning when Stapley and Dale arrived at their stope they tested the roof and found it to be drummy. They saw the foreman, Church, about it and he ordered them to fetch it down ... They used picks, but, after half an hour had made no impression. The work was awkwardly placed as a fault ran across the mouth of the stope, and floor and roof inside being about eighteen inches higher than outside it. Probably they could not use a pinch bar, but they could easily have prepared the place for firing a shot and sent for the shot-firer. Instead, according to Dale whose evidence was accepted, they agreed that the roof was safe enough for them to resume their ordinary work and did so. There was a quantity of gypsum lying in the stope and if the roof had been safe their first task would have been to get this to the haulage way. To do that, Stapley had to enter the stope and break the gypsum into smaller pieces and Dale had to make preparations in the twitten. So they separated, and when Dale came back half an hour later he found Stapley lying dead in the stope under a large piece of the roof which had fallen on him.

...

In these circumstances it is necessary to determine what caused the death of Stapley. If it was caused solely by his own fault, then the appellant cannot succeed. But if it was caused partly by his own fault and partly by the fault of Dale, then the appellant can rely on the Law Reform (Contributory Negligence) Act 1945. To determine what caused an accident from the point of view of legal liability is a most difficult task. If there is any valid logical or scientific theory of causation, it is quite irrelevant in this connection. In a court of law, this question must be decided as a properly instructed and reasonable jury would decide it. As Lord du Parcq said in *Grant v Sun Shipping Co Ltd* (1948):[3]

'A jury would not have profited by a direction couched in the language of logicians and expounding theories of causation, with or without the aid of Latin maxims.'

The question must be determined by applying common sense to the facts of each particular case. One may find that, as a matter of history, several people have been at fault and that if any one of them had acted properly the accident would not have happened, but that does not mean that the accident must be regarded as having been caused by the faults of all of them. One must discriminate between those faults which must be discarded as being too remote and those which must not. Sometimes it is proper to discard all but one and to regard that one as the sole cause, but in other cases it is proper to regard two or more as having jointly caused the accident. I doubt whether any test can be applied generally. It may often be dangerous to apply to this kind of case tests which have been used in traffic accidents by land or sea, but, in this case I think it useful to adopt phrases from the speech of Viscount Birkenhead LC in

---

3 [1948] AC 549.

Admiralty Comrs v SS Volute (1922)[4] and to ask: Was Dale's fault 'so much mixed up with the state of things brought about' by Stapley that 'in the ordinary plain common sense of this business' it must be regarded as having contributed to the accident? I can only say that I think it was and that there was no 'sufficient separation of time, place or circumstance' between them to justify its being excluded. Dale's fault was one of omission rather than commission and it may often be impossible to say that, if a man had done what he omitted to do, the accident would certainly have been prevented. It is enough, in my judgment, if there is a sufficiently high degree of probability that the accident would have been prevented. I have already stated my view of the probabilities in this case and I think that it must lead to the conclusion that Dale's fault ought to be regarded as having contributed to the accident.

...

A court must deal broadly with the problem of apportionment and, in considering what is just and equitable, must have regard to the blameworthiness of each party, but 'the claimant's share in the responsibility for the damage' cannot, I think, be assessed without considering the relative importance of his acts in causing the damage apart from his blameworthiness. It may be that in this case Dale was not much less to blame than Stapley, but Stapley's conduct in entering the stope contributed more immediately to the accident than anything that Dale did or failed to do. I agree with your Lordships that in all the circumstances it is proper in this case to reduce the damages by eighty per cent and to award twenty per cent of the damages to the appellant. I have not dealt with the question whether at the time of the accident the respondents were in breach of regulation 7(3) of the Metalliferous Mines General Regulations 1938 because, whichever way that question was decided, it would not, in this case, affect my view as to the amount by which the damages should be reduced.

– – –

(b) Assumption of risk

In *Smith v Baker* (1891)[5] the House of Lords found that where an employee was the victim of an industrial accident caused by a risk of which he was aware, the court had to distinguish between knowledge of and consent to run risk. In *Bunker v Brand* (1969)[6] the same approach was taken where the victim was a visiting worker, required by his own employer to undertake work at the defendant's premises. The defence of *volenti non fit injuria* therefore rarely succeeds where the claimant is of the status of employee and is injured in the course of employment. An exception is the following case. The employees had acted contrary to a statutory duty under shot-firing regulations, which had to

4   [1922] 1 AC 129, pp 144, 145.
5   [1891] AC 325.
6   [1969] 2 QB 480.

be obeyed by them personally and they knew that their employers wished to enforce the observance of this duty. Nevertheless, it is, as Viscount Radcliffe's opinion recognises, difficult to distinguish this case from *Stapley*. Would their Lordships have come to a different conclusion in *Stapley* if the deceased's co-worker had also been injured? In that case, because only one worker was injured, by pitching the employer's liability at 20% of the damage caused, the cost to the employer was relatively small. Bearing in mind that the employer was personally faultless and was only sued because of vicarious liability for the fault of the deceased's co-worker, this apportionment of responsibility as between the two workers was arguably unfair to the deceased, who was probably no more to blame than his co-worker. In a case like *ICI v Shatwell*, however, where both were injured, if the court had found both workers equally to blame, the potential liability for the employer would be much greater.

IMPERIAL CHEMICAL INDUSTRIES LTD v SHATWELL
[1965] AC 656

The following extracts are from the speech of Viscount Radcliffe, beginning at p 675:

> My Lords, it sometimes helps to assess the merits of a decision, if one starts by noticing its results and only after doing that allots to it the legal principles upon which it is said to depend. Starting in that order, the present case can be summarised as follows. The Shatwell brothers have injured themselves by causing an explosion, to the danger of which they would not have been exposed if they had obeyed the shot-firing regulations, of which they knew, and their employer's instructions. This event is very unfortunate for them; but they were adults, skilled and trained men, and they went into the operation of testing the electrical circuit without taking cover in the face of their knowledge that they ought not to do it in that way. I do not suppose that, having regard to their experience, the method they adopted seemed to them to be dangerous; on the other hand, they must have been aware, in the light of the recent regulations, that it carried an element of risk and, as between the two of them, each of them must be taken to have accepted the risk of their joint operation.

> Their employer is in no way to blame. The company had done everything it could to make sure its shot-firers did not test without taking cover and it had even arranged their scale of remuneration in a way that removed any temptation to the taking of short cuts. It did not know that they were going to break its rules or were breaking its rules.

> If the decision appealed from is to stand, the respondent is nonetheless entitled to make his employer pay him damages in compensation or part compensation for his injury and, if he can get his damages, there cannot be any question that his brother is also entitled to compensation from the employer. To me this seems to be an absurd result, and I think that it so appeared to the members of the Court of Appeal. Moreover, not only can I see no consideration of public advantage that would support it, I can see only elements of public disadvantage in allowing it. For, if an employer is to be liable to pay damages

to his employee, even though he has failed in no part of his duty and has done all that vigilance can suggest to deter the employee from the action that produces the damage, the law deprives the employer of any reason to be vigilant, since that protects him no better than inertia: while, on the other hand, the employee is released by the law from a useful stimulus to prudence if he knows that not even imprudence or disobedience is going to disqualify him from looking to his employer for compensation.

...

But then there is the other way of looking at the matter, which has been taken both in the High Court and the Court of Appeal and which, I think, is an application of the method of reasoning that was used by the majority of this House in the *Stapley*[7] case. From this point of view, the actual testing of the individual detonator is not the important thing. What is looked at is the whole operation of carrying out the circuit test under the forbidden conditions, and since James made what was at any rate not a negligible contribution to this operation, it is said that he must be in some degree responsible with his partner for the damage that was the final result of the joint enterprise.

So be it. I think that there are dangers in such a line of reasoning, since it tends to equate the idea of causation with the idea of participation, and I cannot believe that in law the two conceptions are really interchangeable. But let it be that George sues James for damages on this basis, or for that matter, that James sues George. I do not see how either can succeed against the other, since, where both were joined in carrying through the whole operation and each in what he did was the agent of the other to achieve it, there was nothing that one did against the other that the other did not equally do against himself. This, in my view, is the true result of a joint unlawful enterprise, in which what is wrong is the whole enterprise and neither of the joint actors has contributed a separate wrongful act to the result. Each emerges as the author of his own injury.

...

I cannot say that I find the reasoning of the majority of this House in *Stapley* easy to follow, but the determining point seems to have been their view that once the argument was not accepted that Stapley's death was 'not in any way the result of Dale's negligence', Dale's and his employer's liability must necessarily follow. That conclusion may have been sufficient to dispose of the case before them, but I think that it would be unfortunate if it came to be regarded as authority for any general principle of causation where joint wrongdoers succeed in inflicting separate injuries on themselves. For the further question has in such cases to be met and answered, what in this context do you mean by the 'negligence' of one towards the other?

These considerations apart, there are involved in this case questions as to the application of the maxim *volenti non fit injuria* and as to the principle that in the eyes of the law a man cannot be treated as having disavowed a statutory protection enacted for his benefit in the public interest. On these points, I have

---

7   [1953] 2 All ER 478.

had the opportunity of studying in advance the opinions of your Lordships and I wish to associate myself in particular with the opinion to be delivered by my noble and learned friend, Lord Pearce. I do think it of great importance that the law should not in general allow a person to disqualify himself from the protection of a statutory duty imposed for his benefit where there is any element of public advantage in upholding the duty. But I cannot think that this is a case to which that principle applies.

– – –

II QUANTUM OF DAMAGES

The cases cited so far have focused on determining the circumstances in which the defendant may be held liable. In some cases mention has been made of the sum of money awarded and even how liability for the payment of this sum has been allocated between several defendants. In some cases the claimant may have been required to bear some of the loss himself. The person who has suffered damage claims damages. No mention has been made as to how in monetary terms the liability to pay damages has been determined. In most awards there are two elements: general and special damages.

General damages are 'unliquidated', that is to say the claimant has to leave it to the court to put a monetary value on the injury suffered: unless the claimant and defendant have agreed a figure subject to determination of liability. The principal element in the general damages is the pain and suffering and loss of facility caused by the injury; the medical evidence will be the basis for quantifying this.

Special damages are items of financial loss which can be more readily quantified, principally, in personal injury cases, loss of earned income, but including cost of replacing property and expenses, such as paying for special assistance and facilities, as a result of the injury.

The intention is to put the claimant in the position he or she would have been in had the injury not been suffered. Therefore, the claimant should not be better off financially as a result of the injury. In particular the award for loss of income should not provide the claimant with more than he or she would have received if the injury had not been suffered. Special damages should therefore be reduced to take account of income tax which would be payable on earned income and arrangements must be made to ensure that the claimant does not receive income maintenance from social security as well as a full award for loss of earned income. The matter of reducing the award to take into account the claimant's liability to income tax was addressed by the House of Lords in the following case:

BRITISH TRANSPORT COMMISSION v GOURLEY [1956] AC 185

The following extracts are from the speech of Earl Jowitt, whose speech reflects the decision of the majority. It begins at p 197:

> My Lords, the respondent, who is an eminent civil engineer, suffered severe injuries whilst travelling in a railway train, owing to the negligence of the appellants' servants, and brought his action to recover damages. The trial judge awarded him £9,000 for pain and suffering and loss of amenities, and £1,000 in respect of out of pocket expenses. No question arose in this appeal as to this part of the award. The trial judge further awarded the respondent the sum of £37,720 in respect of loss of earnings actual and prospective, and in arriving at this sum paid no regard to the fact that had the respondent been able by his activities in his profession as a civil engineer to achieve the earnings represented by the sum of £37,720 he would have had to pay a large amount in respect of income tax and surtax on the amount of such earnings. The trial judge, at the request of the appellants, made an alternative assessment of £6,695, which represented the sum he would have awarded if he ought to have taken into account in assessing damages the tax which the respondent would have had to pay if he had in fact earned by his professional activities the sums lost. It was agreed by counsel on both sides – and, I think rightly agreed – that the respondent would incur no tax liability in respect of the award of £37,720 or alternatively of £6,695.
>
> The question for determination in this appeal is whether the judge ought to have taken the tax position into account in assessing that part of the damages attributable to loss of earnings actual or prospective.
>
> The broad general principle which should govern the assessment of damages in cases such as this is that the tribunal should award the injured party such a sum of money as will put him in the same position as he would have been in if he had not sustained the injuries: see *per* Lord Blackburn in *Livingstone v Rawyards Coal Co* (1880).[8] The principle is sometimes referred to as the principle of *restitutio in integrum*; but it is manifest that no award of money can possibly compensate a man for such grievous injuries as the respondent in this case has suffered. The principle, therefore, affords little guidance in the assessment of damages for the pain and suffering undergone and for the impairment which results from the injuries, and in fixing such damages the judge can do no more than endeavour to arrive at a fair estimate, taking into account all the relevant considerations.
>
> The principle can, however, afford some guidance to the tribunal in assessing compensation for the financial loss resulting from an accident, and in such cases, it has been referred to as 'the dominant rule of law' ...
>
> ...
>
> I have now referred to all the relevant authorities bearing on the point and the question remains whether the *Billingham* case (1955),[9] which the trial judge and the Court of Appeal in this case followed, was rightly decided.

8   [1880] 5 App Cas 25, p 39.
9   *Billingham v Hughes* [1955] 2 QB 338.

My Lords, it is, I think, if I may say so with the utmost respect, fallacious to consider the problem as though a benefit were being conferred upon a wrongdoer by allowing him to abate the damages for which he would otherwise be liable. The problem is rather for what damages is he liable? and, if we apply the dominant rule, we should answer: 'He is liable for such damages as, by reason of his wrongdoing, the plaintiff has sustained.' I cannot think that the risk of confusion arising if the tax position be taken into consideration should make us hesitate to apply the rule of law if we can ascertain what that rule is. Nor should we be deterred from applying that rule by the consistent or inveterate practice of the courts in not taking the tax position into consideration in those cases in which the courts were never invited to do so.

Mr Lords, I agree with Lord Sorn in thinking that to ignore the tax element at the present day would be to act in a manner which is out of touch with reality. Nor can I regard the tax element as so remote that it should be disregarded in assessing damages. The obligation to pay tax – save for those in possession of exiguous incomes – is almost universal in its application. That obligation is ever present in the minds of those who are called upon to pay taxes and no sensible person any longer regards the net earnings from his trade or profession as the equivalent of his available income. Indeed, save for the fact that in many cases – though by no means in all cases – the tax only becomes payable after the money has been received, there is, I think, no element of remoteness or uncertainty about its incidence.

Counsel for the appellants in the course of his argument put the case of two men each enjoying a salary of £2,500 a year the one as a servant of an international body being exempted from all tax on his salary, the other having to pay income tax and surtax in the ordinary way. He pointed out that if each of these men met with an accident and each was deprived of a year's salary, for which he succeeded in recovering damages, it would be quite unreal to treat them as though they were in receipt of the same salary; for, in the absence of special and unusual circumstances, the one whose income was tax free would enjoy an income almost double the income of his fellow who had to pay taxes. My Lords, I agree with this contention. I see no reason why in this case we should depart from the dominant rule or why the respondent should not have his damages assessed upon the basis of what he has really lost, and I consider that in determining what he has really lost the judge ought to have considered the tax liability of the respondent.

It would, I think, be unfortunate if, as the result of our decision, the fixation of damages in a running-down case were to involve an elaborate assessment of tax liability. It will no doubt become necessary for the tribunal assessing damages to form an estimate of what the tax would have been if the money had been earned, but such an estimate will be none the worse if it is formed on broad lines, even though it may be described as rough and ready. It is impossible to assess with mathematical accuracy what reduction should be made by reason of the tax position, just as it is impossible to assess with mathematical accuracy the amount of damages which should be awarded for the injury itself and for the pain and suffering endured.

– – –

The following statutory provisions relate damage claims to entitlement to social security benefits. The immediately following statute originally applied to all personal injury claims; it is now (s 2(1A)) applicable only to small awards.

LAW REFORM (PERSONAL INJURIES) ACT 1948

Section 2

Measure of damages

(1) In an action for damages for personal injuries (including any such action arising out of a contract [where this section applies]), there shall in assessing those damages be taken into account, [against them], one half of the value of any rights which have accrued or probably will accrue to [the injured person] [from the injuries in respect of–

    (a) any of the relevant benefits, within the meaning of [s 81 of the Social Security Administration Act 1992]; or

    (b) any corresponding benefits payable in Northern Ireland for the five years beginning with the time when the cause of action accrued.]

(1A) This section applies in any case where the amount of the damages that would have been awarded apart from any reduction under subsection (1) above is less than the sum for the time being prescribed under s 85(1) of the Social Security Administration Act 1992 (recoupment of benefit: exception for small payments).

    ...

(3) The reference in subsection (1) of this section to assessing the damages for personal injuries shall, in cases where the damages otherwise recoverable are subject to reduction under the law relating to contributory negligence or are limited by or under any Act or by contract, be taken as referring to the total damages which would have been recoverable apart from the reduction or limitation.

(4) In an action for damages for personal injuries (including any such action arising out of a contract), there shall be disregarded, in determining the reasonableness of any expenses, the possibility of avoiding those expenses or part of them by taking advantage of facilities available under the National Health Service Act 1977 or the National Health Service (Scotland) Act 1978, or of any corresponding facilities in Northern Ireland.

Section 3

Definition of 'personal injury'

In this Act, the expression 'personal injury' includes any disease and any impairment of a person's physical or mental condition, and the expression 'injured' shall be construed accordingly.

— — —

Section 2(4) of the Law Reform (Personal Injuries) Act 1948 is in the same philosophy as the following statutory provision:

ADMINISTRATION OF JUSTICE ACT 1982

Section 5

Maintenance at public expense to be taken into account in assessment of damages

In an action under the law of England and Wales or the law of Northern Ireland for damages for personal injuries (including any such action arising out of a contract) any saving to the injured person which is attributable to his maintenance wholly or partly at public expense in a hospital, nursing home or other institution shall be set off against any income lost by him as a result of his injuries.

– – –

Provision for recovery by the State of benefits paid to a victim after incapacity and before the outcome of litigation was first provided for by the Social Security Act 1989, s 22. The relevant provision is now as follows.

SOCIAL SECURITY ADMINISTRATION ACT 1992

Section 82

Recovery of sums equivalent to benefit from compensation payments in respect of accidents, injuries and diseases

(1) A person ('the compensator') making a compensation payment, whether on behalf of himself or another in consequence of an accident, injury or disease suffered by any other person ('the victim') shall not do so until the Secretary of State has furnished him with a certificate of total benefit and shall then–

    (a) deduct from the payment an amount, determined in accordance with the certificate of total benefit, equal to the gross amount of any relevant benefits paid or likely to be paid to or for the victim during the relevant period in respect of that accident, injury or disease;

    (b) pay to the Secretary of State an amount equal to that which is required to be so deducted; and

    (c) furnish the person to whom the compensation payment is or, apart from this section, would have been made ('the intended recipient') with a certificate of deduction.

(2) Any right of the intended recipient to receive the compensation payment in question shall be regarded as satisfied to the extent of the amount certified in the certificate of deduction.

– – –

In *Hassall v Secretary of State for Social Security; Pether v Same*,[10] it was held that each applicant was unemployed at the time of his accident and in receipt of benefits. Each continued to receive approximately the same amount in benefit after the accident as before, but on a different basis, then being incapable of

---

10 [1995] 1 WLR 812.

work. Each settled his personal injury claim on the basis that no claim could be made for loss of earnings during the time of incapacity, because he would not have been able to find work even if fit. Thus, the claims were solely for general damages for pain, suffering and loss of amenity. Nevertheless, the Court of Appeal held that the Department of Social Security were entitled to recoup benefits paid. Such recoupment resulted in the applicants being under-compensated for their injuries and suggests that, as a matter of principle, a claim for loss of non-recoupable benefit should have been claimed as damages by the applicants against tortfeasors.

III EXTINCTION OF LIABILITY

(a) Limitation of actions

Statutory rules govern the time limits within which civil actions must be brought. Special rules have extended the time limits where the damage is latent and does not manifest itself until long after the injury was inflicted. Industrial diseases, such as asbestosis, often do not become apparent until many years after exposure to the toxic substance. The Limitation Acts act like a defence: that is to say the action may proceed if the defendant does not object that it is out of time, but the courts are not sympathetic to stale claims, even if they are technically within the limitation period – witnesses' memories fade with time.

LIMITATION ACT 1980

Section 11

Special time limit for actions in respect of personal injuries

(1) This section applies to any action for damages for negligence, nuisance or breach of any duty (whether the duty exists by virtue of a contract or of provision made by or under a statute or independently of any contract or any such provision) where the damages claimed by the plaintiff for the negligence, nuisance or breach of duty consist of or include damages in respect of personal injuries to the plaintiff or any other person.

...

(3) An action to which this section applies shall not be brought after the expiration of the period applicable in accordance with subsection (4) or (5) below.

(4) Except where subsection (5) below applies, the period applicable is three years from–

(a) the date on which the cause of action accrued; or

(b) the date of knowledge (if later) of the person injured.

(5) If the injured person dies before the expiration of the period mentioned in subsection (4) above, the period applicable as respects the cause of action

surviving for the benefit of his estate by virtue of s 1 of the Law Reform (Miscellaneous Provisions) Act 1934 shall be three years from–

(a) the date of death; or

(b) the date of the personal representative's knowledge, whichever is the later.

– – –

(b) Death of the victim

At common law, personal actions did not survive the person: if either claimant or defendant died the right to litigate was lost. The first inroad into this came with the Fatal Accidents Act 1846. This statute introduced the principle that the wrongdoer may be sued to obtain for the deceased victim's dependants' income maintenance at the level which the deceased had been providing. The claimant must be in one of the relationships to the deceased which is recognised in the statute and must have actually been dependent on the deceased. In order to recover, it must be established that the defendant committed a tort against the deceased and would therefore have been liable to the deceased personally if death had not intervened. Awards are related to the income provided by the deceased and take account of the age of the deceased and the number of years of working life remaining to the victim at the time of death. In the 150 years since the principle was introduced, the statutory provisions have been amended from time to time. The current law is contained in the statute cited below.

FATAL ACCIDENTS ACT 1976

Section 1

Right of action for wrongful act causing death

(1) If death is caused by any wrongful act, neglect or default which is such as would (if death had not ensued) have entitled the person injured to maintain an action and recover damages in respect thereof, the person who would have been liable if death had not ensued shall be liable to an action for damages, notwithstanding the death of the person injured.

(2) Subject to section 1A(2) below, every such action shall be for the benefit of the dependants of the person ('the deceased') whose death has been so caused.

(3) In this Act, 'dependant' means:

(a) the wife or husband or former wife or husband of the deceased;

(b) any person who–

(i) was living with the deceased in the same household immediately before the date of the death; and

(ii) had been living with the deceased in the same household for at least two years before that date; and

    (iii) was living during the whole of that period as the husband or wife of the deceased.

(c) any parent or other ascendant of the deceased;

(d) any person who was treated by the deceased as his parent;

(e) any child or other descendant of the deceased;

(f) any person (not being a child of the deceased) who, in the case of any marriage to which the deceased was at any time a party, was treated by the deceased as a child of the family in relation to that marriage;

(g) any person who is, or is the issue of, a brother, sister, uncle or aunt of the deceased.

(4) The reference to the former wife or husband of the deceased in subsection (3)(a) above includes a reference to a person whose marriage to the deceased has been annulled or declared void as well as a person whose marriage to the deceased has been dissolved.

Section 1A

Bereavement

(1) An action under this Act may consist of or include a claim for damages for bereavement.

(2) A claim for damages for bereavement shall only be for the benefit–

    (a) of the wife or husband of the deceased; and

    (b) where the deceased was a minor who was never married–

        (i) of his parents, if he was legitimate; and

        (ii) of his mother, if he was illegitimate.

(3) Subject to subsection (5) below, the sum to be awarded as damages under this section shall be £7,500.

(4) Where there is a claim for damages under this section for the benefit of both the parents of the deceased, the sum awarded shall be divided between them (subject to any deduction falling to be made in respect of costs not recovered from the defendant).

(5) The Lord Chancellor may by order made by statutory instrument, subject to annulment in pursuance of a resolution of either House of Parliament, amend the section by varying the sum for the time being specified in subsection (3) above.

Section 2

Persons entitled to bring the action

(1) The action shall be brought by and in the name of the executor or administrator of the deceased.

(2) If–

    (a) there is no executor or administrator of the deceased, or

    (b) no action is brought within six months after the death by or in the name of an executor or administrator of the deceased, the action may be brought by and in the name of all or any of the persons for whose benefit an executor or administrator could have brought it.

Section 3

Assessment of damages

(1) In the action such damages, other than damages for bereavement, may be awarded as are proportioned to the injury resulting from the death to the dependants respectively.

...

(3) In an action under this Act where there fall to be assessed damages payable to a widow in respect of the death of her husband there shall not be taken into account the re-marriage of the widow or her prospects of re-marriage.

...

Section 5

Contributory negligence

Where any person dies as the result partly of his own fault and partly of the fault of any other person or persons, and accordingly if an action were brought for the benefit of the estate under the Law Reform (Miscellaneous Provisions) Act 1934 the damages recoverable would be reduced under section 1(1) of the Law Reform (Contributory Negligence) Act 1945, any damages recoverable in an action under this Act shall be reduced to a proportionate extent.

– – –

(c) Personal representative's action

The common law principle that the right to litigate was lost if one of the parties died was radically altered by the following Act which entitled the deceased's personal representative to sue to collect any debt owing to the deceased at the time of death, and also made the personal representative liable to be sued if the deceased had died owing any debts. Claims for damages for personal injury were recognised as debts owing to the estate of the deceased.

LAW REFORM (MISCELLANEOUS PROVISIONS) ACT 1934

Section 1

Effect of death on certain causes of action

(1) Subject to the provisions of this section, on the death of any person after the commencement of this Act all causes of action subsisting against or vested in him shall survive against, or, as the case may be, for the benefit of, his estate. Provided that this subsection shall not apply to causes of action for defamation.

(1A) The right of a person to claim under section 1A of the Fatal Accidents Act 1976 (bereavement) shall not survive for the benefit of his estate on his death.

...

(5) The rights conferred by this Act for the benefit of the estates of deceased persons shall be in addition to and not in derogation of any rights conferred on the dependants of deceased persons by [the Fatal Accidents Act 1976] ... and so much of this Act as relates to causes of action against the estates of deceased persons shall apply in relation to causes of action under the said Act as it applies in relation to other causes of action not expressly excepted from the operation of subsection 1 of this section.

– – –

(d) The lost years

The victim of personal injury may have his life expectancy reduced as a result of that injury. Questions have arisen as to whether an award of damages should include sums to compensate for the amount by which the victim's life has been shortened. The dependant's action under the Fatal Accidents Act 1976 enables the widow or other dependent to obtain from the wrongdoer a sum to represent the income which the deceased victim would have provided had there been no fatal injury. A further question therefore is whether in cases where the victim on his deathbed himself sues the wrongdoer the award of damages should include a sum for the years of which the claimant has been deprived. Clearly, the claimant will not, in such cases, require this income support, but if the lost years are not accounted for in the award, then the dependants may be worse off than if the only claim against the wrongdoer was by the dependants themselves after the victim's death. The matter came before the House of Lords in the following case, where the victim initiated the action, but died during the course of the litigation.

PICKETT (ADMINISTRATRIX OF THE ESTATE OF RALPH HENRY PICKETT (DECD)) v BRITISH RAIL ENGINEERING LTD [1980] AC 136

The following extracts are taken from the speech of Lord Wilberforce whose reasoning was broadly similar to that of the majority of their Lordships. His speech begins at p 145:

> My Lords, this appeal raises three questions as to the amount of damages which ought to have been awarded to Mr Ralph Henry Pickett ('the deceased') against his employer, the respondent, for negligence and/or breach of statutory duty. From 1949 to 1974 Mr Pickett was working for the respondent in the construction of the bodies of railway coaches, which work involved contact with asbestos dust. In 1974 he developed symptoms which proved to be of mesothelioma of the lung, of which he later died. On July 14, 1975, he issued a writ against the respondent claiming damages for personal injuries or

physical harm. The respondent admitted liability but contested the issue of quantum of damages. The case came for trial before Stephen Brown J who on October 12, 1976, awarded damages under various heads. Those in issue in this appeal were three: (1) £7,000 by way of general damages in respect of pain, suffering and loss of amenities; (2) £787.50 as interest on the £7,000 at 9%, from the service of the writ; (3) £1,508.88 as a net sum in respect of loss of earnings. This sum was based on a finding that the deceased's expectation of life had been reduced to one year from the date of trial and the loss of earnings related to that period, ie the period of likely survival. The judge also awarded £500 for loss of expectation of life, and the total for which he gave judgment was £14,947.64. Mr Pickett appealed to the Court of Appeal against this judgment, but before the appeal was heard he died. An order to carry on the proceedings was made in favour of his widow as administratrix of his estate. The appeal was heard in November 1977. The Court of Appeal did not award any sum for loss of earnings beyond the survival period but increased the general damages award to £10,000 without interest. The administratrix now appeals to this House contending that a much larger amount ought to have been awarded in respect of loss of future earnings. She also claims that interest should be awarded on the general damages. The respondent appeals against the award of £10,000 general damages.

In 1974, when his symptoms became acute, the deceased was a man of 51 with an excellent physical record. He was a champion cyclist of Olympic standard, he kept himself very fit and was a non-smoker. He was leading an active life and cycled to work every day. He had a wife and two children. There was medical evidence at the trial as to his condition and prospects, which put his then expectation of life at one year; this the judge accepted. There can be no doubt that but for his exposure to asbestos dust in his employment he could have looked forward to a normal period of continued employment up to retiring age. That exposure, for which the respondent accepts liability, has resulted in this period being shortened to one year. It seems, therefore, strange and unjust that his claim for loss of earnings should be limited to that one year (the survival period) and that he should recover nothing in respect of the years of which he has been deprived (the lost years). But this is the result of authority binding on the judge and the Court of Appeal: *Oliver v Ashman* (1962).[11] The present is, in effect, an appeal against that decision.

...

The respondent, in an impressive argument, urged upon us that the real loss in such cases as the present was to the victim's dependants and that the right way in which to compensate them was to change the law (by statute, judicially it would be impossible) so as to enable the dependants to recover their loss independently of any action by the victim. There is much force in this, and no doubt the law could be changed in this way. But I think that the argument fails because it does not take account, as in an action for damages account must be taken, of the interest of the victim. Future earnings are of value to him in order that he may satisfy legitimate desires, but these may not correspond with the

---

11 [1962] 2 QB 210.

allocation which the law makes of money recovered by dependants on account of his loss. He may wish to benefit some dependants more than, or to the exclusion of, others – this (subject to family inheritance legislation) he is entitled to do. He may not have dependants, but he may have others, or causes, whom he would wish to benefit, for whom he might even regard himself as working. One cannot make a distinction, for the purposes of assessing damages, between men in different family situations.

There is another argument in the opposite sense – that which appealed to Streatfield J in *Pope v Murphy & Son Ltd* (1961)[12] Why, he asked, should the tortfeasor benefit from the fact that, as well as reducing his victim's earning capacity he has shortened his victim's life? Good advocacy but unsound principle, for damages are to compensate the victim not to reflect what the wrongdoer ought to pay:

My Lords, in the case of the adult wage earner with or without dependants who sues for damages during his lifetime, I am convinced that a rule which enables the 'lost years' to be taken account of comes closer to the ordinary man's expectation than one which limits his interest to his shortened span of life. The interest which such a man has in the earnings he might hope to make over a normal life, if not saleable in a market, has a value which can be assessed. A man who receives that assessed value would surely consider himself and be considered compensated – a man denied it would not ...

There will remain some difficulties. In cases, probably the normal, where a man's actual dependants coincide with those for whom he provides out of the damages he receives, whatever they obtain by inheritance will simply be set off against their own claim. If on the other hand this coincidence is lacking, there might be duplication of recovery. To that extent injustice may be caused to the wrongdoer. But if there is a choice between taking a view of the law which mitigates a clear and recognised injustice in cases of normal occurrence, at the cost of the possibility in fewer cases of excess payments being made, or leaving the law as it is, I think that our duty is clear. We should carry the judicial process of seeking a just principle as far as we can, confident that a wise legislator will correct resultant anomalies.

My Lords, I have reached the conclusion which I would recommend so far without reference to *Skelton v Collins* (1960),[13] in which the High Court of Australia, refusing to follow *Oliver v Ashman* (1962), achieved the same result. The value of this authority is twofold: first in recommending by reference to authority (*per* Taylor J) and in principle (*per* Windeyer J) the preferable solution, and, secondly, in demonstrating that this can properly be reached by judicial process. The judgments, further, bring out an important ingredient, which I would accept, namely, that the amount to be recovered in respect of earnings in the 'lost' years should be after deduction of an estimated sum to represent the victim's probable living expenses during those years. I think that this is right because the basis, in principle, for recovery lies in the interest which he has in making provision for dependants and others, and this he

---

12 [1961] 1 QB 222.
13 (1960) 115 CLR 94.

would do out of his surplus. There is the additional merit of bringing awards under this head into line with what could be recovered under the Fatal Accidents Acts. *Skelton v Collins* has been followed and applied recently by the High Court in *Griffiths v Kerkemeyer* (1977).[14]

I would allow the appeal on this point and remit the action to the Queen's Bench Division for damages to be assessed accordingly. We are not called upon in this appeal to lay down any rules as to the manner in which such damages should be calculated – this must be left to the courts to work out conformably with established principles.

– – –

The following statute confirmed the decision in *Pickett*'s case, insofar as it related to the award of compensation for loss of income, but abolished the right to damages for loss of expectation of life while reserving the possibility of making an award to the victim for the pain and suffering caused by knowing life expectancy had been reduced. It has the effect of preventing the administrator from claiming large sums for loss of expectation of life which, being awarded after the victim's death, would be likely to amount to a windfall to those who inherited the estate.

ADMINISTRATION OF JUSTICE ACT 1982

Section 1

Abolition of right to damages for loss of expectation of life

(1) In an action under the law of England and Wales or the law of Northern Ireland for damages for personal injuries:

    (a) no damages shall be recoverable in respect of any loss of expectation of life caused to the injured person by the injuries; but

    (b) if the injured person's expectation of life has been reduced by the injuries, the court, in assessing damages in respect of pain and suffering caused by the injuries, shall take account of any suffering caused or likely to be caused to him by awareness that his expectation of life has been so reduced.

(2) The reference in subsection (1)(a) above to damages in respect of loss of expectation of life does not include damages in respect of loss of income.

– – –

IV STRATEGIES OF LITIGATION

The claimant's advisors will have to evaluate: (a) the rules of law; (b) the evidence; and (c) the likelihood of the action resulting in sufficient damages to

---

14 [1977] 51 ALJR 792.

make litigation worthwhile. By way of summary of this section of this book, a few brief comments on each of these points may be helpful.

(a) Rules of law

Since about 1970 (*Home Office v Dorset Yacht Co Ltd*),[15] the claimant has a wide range of persons from whom to choose a defendant. It is unlikely that the courts would say that a person of the status of, for example, employer, occupier, manufacturer, worker, driver, to name but the more obvious, could not owe a duty to take reasonable care for the health and safety of the claimant. The choice of defendant is therefore less likely to depend on rules of law than on other issues.

(b) Evidence

The rationalisation of the duty issue changes the emphasis to, amongst other things, what evidence can be brought to show that there has been negligent conduct. Selection of evidence is a very strategic matter: amongst the many matters which might possibly have contributed to cause the claimant's injury, some may point to the fault of one person, whilst others may point to another person. Clearly the evidence chosen must establish the breach of duty by the defendant selected for the litigation. Collecting and presenting evidence is expensive therefore it is necessary to ensure that enough evidence is called and no more than that. Where the evidence suggests more than one person could be found at fault, another strategic decision will have to be made by the claimant as to whether to join both as defendants or whether to focus only on one. Of course if only one is chosen that person may choose to join the other wrongdoer as a co-defendant. However, the more parties that are joined in the action, the more expensive the proceedings are likely to be.

The ease with which evidence can be acquired is also a consideration. The following decision of the House of Lords is important in this respect. It concerns the availability to a claimant of a report made by an employer following an accident in which the claimant was injured.

WAUGH v BRITISH RAILWAYS BOARD [1980] AC 521

The following extracts are from the speech of Lord Wilberforce, beginning at p 529:

> My Lords, the appellant's husband was an employee of the British Railways Board. A locomotive which he was driving collided with another so that he was crushed against a tank wagon. He received injuries from which he died. The present action is brought under the Fatal Accidents Acts 1846–1959 and

---

15 [1970] AC 1004.

this appeal arises out of an interlocutory application for discovery by the board of a report called the 'joint inquiry report', made by two officers of the board two days after the accident. This was resisted by the board on the ground of legal professional privilege. The Court of Appeal, Eveleigh LJ and Sir David Cairns, Lord Denning MR dissenting, refused the application.

When an accident occurs on the board's railways, there are three reports which are made:

1   On the day of the accident a brief report of the accident is made to the Railway Inspectorate.

2   Soon afterwards a joint internal report is prepared incorporating statements of witnesses. This too is sent to the Railway Inspectorate. Preparation of this report, it appears, is a matter of practice: it is not required by statute or statutory regulation.

3   In due course a report is made by the Railway Inspectorate for the Department of the Environment.

The document now in question is that numbered 2. The circumstances in which it came to be prepared and the basis for the claim of privilege were stated in an affidavit sworn on behalf of the board by Mr GT Hustings, assistant to the general manager of the Eastern Region.

... the affidavit makes it clear that the report was prepared for a dual purpose: for what may be called railway operation and safety purposes and for the purpose of obtaining legal advice in anticipation of litigation, the first being more immediate than the second, but both being described as of equal rank or weight. So, the question arises whether this is enough to support a claim of privilege, or whether, in order to do so, the second purpose must be the sole purpose, or the dominant or main purpose. If either of the latter is correct, the claim of privilege in this case must fail.

My Lords, before I consider the authorities, I think it desirable to attempt to discern the reason why what is (inaccurately) called legal professional privilege exists. It is sometimes ascribed to the exigencies of the adversary system of litigation under which a litigant is entitled within limits to refuse to disclose the nature of his case until the trial. Thus one side may not ask to see the proofs of the other side's witnesses or the opponent's brief or even know what witnesses will be called: he must wait until the card is played and cannot try to see it in the hand. This argument cannot be denied some validity even where the defendant is a public corporation whose duty it is, so it might be thought, while taking all proper steps to protect its revenues, to place all the facts before the public and to pay proper compensation to those it has injured. A more powerful argument to my mind is that everything should be done in order to encourage anyone who knows the facts to state them fully and candidly, as Sir George Jessed MR said, to bare his breast to his lawyer: *Anderson v Bank of British Columbia* (1876).[16] This he may not do unless he knows that his communication is privileged.

But the preparation of a case for litigation is not the only interest which calls for candour. In accident cases, '... the safety of the public may well depend on

16   [1876] 2 Ch D 644, p 699.

the candour and completeness of reports made by subordinates whose duty it is to draw attention to defects': *Conway v Rimmer* (1976).[17] This however does not by itself justify a claim to privilege since, as Lord Reid continues:

'... no one has ever suggested that public safety has been endangered by the candour or completeness of such reports having been inhibited by the fact that they may have to be produced if the interests of the due administration of justice should ever require production at any time.'

So one may deduce from this the principle that while privilege may be required in order to induce candour in statements made for the purposes of litigation it is not required in relation to statements whose purpose is different – for example to enable a railway to operate safety.

It is clear that the due administration of justice strongly requires disclosure and production of this report: it was contemporary: it contained statements by witnesses on the spot; it would be not merely relevant evidence, but almost certainly the best evidence as to the cause of the accident. If one accepts that this important public interest can be overridden in order that the defendant may properly prepare his case, how close must the connection be between the preparation of the document and the anticipation of litigation? On principle I would think that the purpose of preparing for litigation ought to be either the sole purpose or at least the dominant purpose of it: to carry the protection further into cases where that purpose was secondary or equal with another purpose would seem to be excessive and unnecessary in the interest of encouraging truthful revelation. At the lowest such desirability of protection as might exist in such cases is not strong enough to outweigh the need for all relevant documents to be made available.

... It appears to me that unless the purpose of submission to the legal adviser in view of litigation is at least the dominant purpose for which the relevant document was prepared, the reasons which require privilege to be extended to it cannot apply. On the other hand to hold that the purpose, as above, must be the sole purpose would, apart from difficulties of proof, in my opinion, be too strict a requirement and would confine the privilege too narrowly: as to this I agree with Barwick CJ in *Grant v Downs* (1976),[18] and in substance with Lord Denning MR. While fully respecting the necessity for the Lord Justices to follow previous decision of their court, I find myself in the result in agreement with Lord Denning's judgment. I would allow the appeal and order disclosure of the joint report.

– – –

(c) Damages issue

Litigation is costly: even a favourable award that the other side is to pay the costs will not relieve the litigant of considerable expense in preparing and

---

17 [1968] AC 910, *per* Lord Reid, p 941.

18 (1976) 135 CLR 674.

presenting the case. The victim will therefore have to consider carefully whether the final award will be sufficiently substantial to make the outlay worthwhile, and also whether if the award is substantial the other party will have the funds with which to honour it. For example there in no reason in law why individual workers should not be liable to compensate for injuries which they unlawfully cause to their colleagues; in practice such persons are not normally sued because it is unlikely that they will be able to meet any award of damages made against them. Exceptionally the wrongdoing worker may be covered by personal insurance, for example he may have been driving his own car at the time of an accident in which the claimant was injured, but even in these circumstances, suing the driver may not be the best way forward. The rules of vicarious liability normally ensure that the employer is the defendant in actions where the actual wrongdoer was an employee.

The Employers' Liability (Compulsory Insurance) Act 1969 and the Employer's Liability (Defective Equipment) Act 1969 impose duties on the employer to carry insurance cover as specified in these Acts. For this reason alone the employer is likely to be the chosen defendant if the victim is an employee. Another reason why employees have, historically at least, tended to sue their employers, is that the employer has an onerous responsibility to provide employees with a safe system of work, including instruction and plant and equipment appropriate to the task. However, the employer may not, of course, be carrying the cover the law requires! In practice, substantial organisations are more attractive as defendants than small organisations, because they are likely to be sufficiently well managed to carry substantial insurance cover, and, if this is not so, they are nevertheless more likely than smaller organisations to have independent funds to meet their liabilities. Moreover it may be possible to bring evidence to show that a large organisation, especially if it is head contractor for the operation in which the victim was engaged, had an overriding obligation to provide a safe system of work, not dissimilar to that normally imposed upon the worker's employer.

Another factor which has to be considered is that the net sum which reaches the claimant may be relatively small, even where the injury has been a serious one. Now that the Law Reform (Contributory Negligence) Act 1945 enables courts to reduce awards to take account of the claimant's contributory negligence, the victim will need to feel confident that there is no evidence available to the defendant to show that the claimant himself was, to some extent, at fault.

Also, the defendant may make an offer of out of court settlement. If this occurs, then the claimant will need to consider carefully whether a successful hearing of his case would be likely to conclude with an award substantially higher than that being offered. If his advisers cannot feel confident of this, then he may face the delay and expense of litigation to no purpose, especially as the court becoming aware, as it will at the end of the case, that a reasonable settlement has been refused, will almost certainly require the victim to pay the other party's costs.

Finally, since recent Social Security Acts have required the compensator to reimburse the State for benefits paid to the victim, the net payable to the victim is likely in small claims to be too little to justify litigation.

PART II

CRIMINAL LIABILITY

CHAPTER 9

THE FRAMEWORK FOR PREVENTION OF WORKPLACE INJURIES

INTRODUCTION

Part I of this book was concerned with the use of the civil law to provide compensation to those who have suffered personal injury at the workplace. That part was named 'Civil Liability' and that title is not in dispute, because it is clear that, if individuals are to be entitled to claim compensation from the wrongdoers who have caused them injury, such claims must lie in the civil courts. It is not so apparent that the criminal law should be used to bring about safe workplaces to ensure that personal injury is not caused by activities at the workplace.

Broadly, the function of the criminal courts is to punish those who have failed to observe laws carrying criminal sanctions. The reasons for imposing punishment, generally in the form of a fine or imprisonment, are disputed. One reason advanced is that the fear of punishment is a deterrent: the argument is that, if the consequence of breaking the law is the imposition of a heavy penalty, then care will be taken not to break the law.

The deterrent argument is weak in situations where the wrongdoing is not intended, but is committed through failure to perceive the consequences of action or inaction. Possibly company directors and company employees may scheme to operate fraudulent systems of financial management: they are unlikely to scheme to inflict personal injury on either their employees or the general public. It is possible that they may plan to operate systems which carry an inherent risk of causing personal injury and proceed to operate according to their plans either with reckless disregard to the risks involved or negligently failing to appreciate that there is a risk. In most cases, however, injury is a result of a breakdown in a system which, on the face of it, is satisfactory: such breakdowns are likely to be caused through negligent failure in operating the system selected; as would be the case if plant and equipment is not properly maintained or workers are not trained and supervised to ensure that they operate to the system chosen.

It is questionable whether such systems failure should be classified as criminal; however, if personal injury has actually resulted from the failure, there is an emotional reaction that those who have allowed this to occur ought to be punished. The more persons who have suffered injury the more emotive the situation and the greater the demand that punishment be inflicted. Yet there is no necessary co-relation between the degree of wrongfulness of behaviour and amount of harm done. For example, one driver might travel at 150 miles an hour down a motorway without injuring anyone and another might be involved in a fatal accident while driving well within the speed limit and with due care and attention. In the first case the driver was undoubtedly, and unlawfully, creating a risk of causing injury; in the second case the driver would appear to have been faultless yet the consequences of his having engaged in the activity of driving are more serious and the relations of the victim, and, indeed the public more widely, may need persuading that he does not deserve to be punished since, however unwillingly and unwittingly, he has caused a fatality.

In recent years there has been an increased popular demand for severe criminal penalties to be imposed upon organisations and their management when commercial activity has led to catastrophic loss of life.

I PREVENTION NOT PUNISHMENT

It was noted in the first chapter of this book that Heinrich began his classic work, *Industrial Accident Prevention: A Scientific Approach*, with the statement that, 'An injury prevented is a benefaction, and injury compensated – an apology.' This statement can be directed at the legal system with particular force. While it is appropriate that societies should provide support, through litigation or otherwise, for those who suffer injury, it is preferable that effort should be focused on preventing the situations which have the potential to cause injury.

The common law has not developed the means of dealing with behaviour which puts people at risk of injury: both the civil law and the criminal law have developed only the means of dealing with those who have actually caused injury. In the criminal law the rules relating to homicide and other offences against the person cannot be invoked unless there is an actual victim; this is because these rules were originally developed through judge made case law, and such laws are responsive rather than proactive. The limitations of the general criminal law in dealing with personal injury and death of workers and the public as a consequence of industrial activity are demonstrated in the following section.

II USE OF GENERAL CRIMINAL LAW

Although the common law is not an effective tool for accident prevention there is, at first sight, no apparent reason why it should not be invoked where injury has actually been inflicted. It is in the context of fatal accidents that resort to the general criminal law may be most appropriate. There is an emotive public reaction that where a person has been killed those who have caused the death ought to be subject to the general common law of homicide.

In recent years there have been a number of well publicised catastrophes, such as the fire and explosion on the offshore installation, *Piper Alpha*, on 6 July 1988, causing 165 deaths; the capsizing of the car ferry, *Herald of Free Enterprise,* at Zeebrugge, causing 192 deaths; the sinking of the *Marchioness* pleasure boat on the Thames in 1989, killing 51 people; the rail collision at Clapham in 1987, causing 34 deaths; and the fire at King's Cross Underground station in 1987, in which 31 people lost their lives. Most recently, in October 1999, there was another catastrophic rail crash, with a death toll of 30. This time, near to Paddington station at Ladbroke Grove.

With the exception of *Piper Alpha*, all the above catastrophes involved transportation of members of the public. Possibly it is the fact that members of the general public have been killed that has caused a groundswell of public opinion that the law of homicide should be invoked against those who, while conducting their businesses for profit, operate in such a way as to lead to loss of life. In practice any criminal charge would have to be for manslaughter, because the alleged offenders would certainly lack the 'malice aforethought' which is a necessary ingredient of the offence of murder. Within the law of manslaughter, the offence would be of committing 'involuntary manslaughter', since the offenders would not have had the intention to bring about death.[1]

There are two reasons why manslaughter has not proved a useful tool to secure the sort of convictions for which there now appears to be a popular demand. The first is that the law of involuntary manslaughter is complex and far from clear; the second is that, when accidents have occurred as a result of a breakdown in the operation of a complex organisation it is usually unclear whether there is any one person to whom criminal responsibility can be attached. In the civil compensation law and under regulatory offences, liability is normally imposed upon the 'employer' but, in the general criminal law, there are difficulties in doing this because the employer is normally a corporate body, lacking a 'mind' capable of the '*mens rea*' which the common law has always considered a necessary pre-requisite of criminal liability. These problems are so profound that the Law Commission, a body set up in the 1960s for the purpose of promoting the reform of the law, has noted:

> ... The law of involuntary manslaughter is entirely a matter of common law and it has to be pieced together from decided cases. Even more than most parts of the criminal law which suffer from that handicap, involuntary manslaughter has always been notorious for its uncertainty, and its lack of any clear conceptual vocabulary.[2]

---

1   Manslaughter might be 'voluntary', that is, where the accused killed under provocation or carried out a 'mercy' killing.

2   *Criminal Law Involuntary Manslaughter*, Consultation Paper No 135, 1994, London: HMSO, para 1.22.

III COMPLEXITY OF LAW OF MANSLAUGHTER

(a) Classification of involuntary manslaughter

There are generally accepted to be two types of involuntary manslaughter: 'unlawful act manslaughter' and 'gross negligence manslaughter'. Of unlawful act manslaughter, the Commission went on to say:

> That part of it which is now described as 'unlawful act manslaughter' has been from time to time the object of complaint, not to say bewilderment, for over a century. The conceptual position has been made, if anything, worse by the efforts of courts in the last 30 years to keep the law within something like decent bounds. These efforts have had to be undertaken on an ad hoc basis, without the support of a proper framework of policy and analysis, and tainted by the doctrine of constructive liability which underpins this part of the law.

The Commission continued (para 1.23): 'The law of gross negligence manslaughter is in an even worse state.' Having thus noted the confusion in both branches of the law, they understandably continued (para 1.24): 'This unpromising background makes it inevitable that it is difficult to state the law with any certainty.'

(b) Manslaughter in the context of death caused by industrial activity

Unlawful act manslaughter?

It might be thought that 'unlawful act' manslaughter would be relied on to support charges of manslaughter when death has occurred as a result of industrial activity. For example if death were caused by an employee being caught up in a machine which, contrary to a specific statutory requirement, was unguarded, it might be argued that permitting the machine to be used without a guard was an unlawful act and the death which followed was unlawful act manslaughter. However, as has been noted, unlawful act manslaughter has not been charged in such circumstances.[3] Moreover, apart from the apparent emotional satisfaction of achieving a conviction for homicide, there is no real justification for invoking manslaughter at all in such cases, providing the regulatory offence carries a significant penalty. In the case of the Clapham rail crash, for example, British Rail was charged with, and pleaded guilty to, a regulatory offence of failing to ensure the safety of employees and passengers, and was fined £250,000.[4] It is not clear that any more appropriate penalty could have been imposed on the employer in this

3   See Wells, C, *Corporations and Criminal Responsibility*, 1993; *Criminal Law Involuntary Manslaughter*, Law Commission Paper 135 (1994).

4   (1991) *The Guardian*, 15 June.

instance; it is true that a conviction of manslaughter can result in a term of imprisonment, but this penalty could not have been imposed on a corporate employer.

Gross negligence manslaughter?

Where death has resulted from industrial activity, the charge has been of gross negligence manslaughter. The difficulty with this branch of the law, as unsuccessful prosecutions have demonstrated, is that, firstly it is not clear whether the accused conduct must be shown to have been 'grossly negligent' or 'reckless' and secondly, there is confusion as to what these expressions mean and how they should be established. So the problem is firstly of determining what conduct is wrongful and secondly of determining whether the accused did conduct himself in the proscribed manner.

Judges have struggled to determine whether the criterion of liability should be negligence or recklessness. Whichever criterion of conduct is adopted, however, there is the additional problem of identifying whether the accused was guilty of that conduct. The difficulty is that negligence and recklessness are attitudes; in other words, they are states of mind. So gross negligence manslaughter is a *mens rea* offence, rather than an offence of strict liability. The question, therefore, is how is the jury to find out the state of mind of the wrongdoer at the time when he or she caused the death? One solution is to make an objective judgment: ask, 'Does it look like reckless conduct to behave in that way?' It might be argued that any observer would regard it as reckless to drive through a built up area at 60 miles per hour and this is strong evidence that the accused, having conducted himself in this way, was reckless.[5] However, this has not been universally accepted as an appropriate approach.

This difficulty of finding an appropriate test for identifying reckless behaviour was acutely felt in road traffic law, where the two principal offences were formerly causing death by reckless driving and driving dangerously. Significantly, the Road Traffic Act 1991 (set out below, p 238) amended ss 1 and 2 of the Road Traffic Act 1988, so that reckless driving is no longer a statutory offence. The ss 1 and 2 offences are now committed by driving dangerously and s 2A defines driving dangerously in objective terms. Thus, the two principal road traffic offences have become offences of strict liability. Obtaining a conviction for one of these offences does not depend on establishing what was going on in the mind of the accused; it depends on establishing that the accused driver's conduct was not of the standard which a competent driver would have achieved. This amendment of the legislation may have clarified road traffic law and made it easier to achieve convictions for road traffic offences but, significantly, the maximum penalty under these

---

5   See *R v Lawrence* [1982] AC 510.

sections is only five years' imprisonment, whereas the maximum penalty for manslaughter is a life sentence. If manslaughter is to remain one of the most serious criminal offences, the solution may not necessarily be to apply the criteria of the statutory offence of motor manslaughter to the law of manslaughter generally.

Whatever the ultimate solution, for the time being, the problems of determining the sort of conduct which is criminal and the state of mind of the wrongdoer when so acting remain at the core of the law of reckless or gross negligence manslaughter.

IV THE CONCEPT OF CORPORATE LIABILITY

Problem of establishing corporate liability

The fact that gross negligence manslaughter is a *mens rea* offence means that it is no simple matter to fix liability to corporations for this offence.

Formerly, the common law did not allow that corporations were capable of committing any crime since, lacking a human body, they have no power to commit a crime. Slowly, this corporate immunity has been broken down. The first inroad was allowing corporate liability for failure to comply with statutory duties. For example, in the *Great North of England Railway Co* case, (1946)[6] the company were convicted of obstructing a highway when building a railway, in circumstances where they were under a statutory duty not to cause such an obstruction. The company did not escape liability by arguing that the obstruction had been caused by its agents. Thus, the civil law concept of vicarious liability crept into the criminal law.

The next major development was the principle of 'identification', which was first introduced in the 1940s,[7] explained by Lord Denning in *HL Bolton (Engineering) Co Ltd v TJ Graham & Sons Ltd* (1957)[8] and fully developed in *Tesco Supermarkets Ltd v Nattrass* (see below). The doctrine is that the corporation can be identified with and made liable for the unlawful behaviour of senior managers who are its controlling officers. Lord Denning put it thus:

> A company may in many ways be likened to a human body. It has a brain and nerve centre which controls what it does. It also has hands which hold the tools and act in accordance with directions from the centre. Some of the people in the company are mere servants and agents who are nothing more than the hands to do the work and cannot be said to represent the mind and will. Others are directors and managers who represent the directing mind and will

---

6   (1946) 9 QB 315.

7   *DPP v Kent and Sussex Contractors Ltd* [1944] KB 146; *R v ICR Haulage Ltd* (1944) KB 146, 155; *Moore v Bresler* [1944] 2 All ER 551.

8   [1957] 1 QB 159.

of the company, and control what it does. The state of mind of these managers is the state of mind of the company and is treated by the law as such.[9]

The *Tesco* case concerned an attempt to impose liability upon a corporation for a trading standard offence created by statute, but its impact on the rules of corporate liability was sufficiently important to warrant its consideration here.

TESCO SUPERMARKETS LTD v NATTRASS [1972] AC 153

The defendants were advertising within their supermarket that a particular brand of washing powder was being sold at less than its normal price. A customer selected a packet which had not been marked so as to show the reduction. The shelves had been incorrectly stacked by a shop assistant and the store manager had failed to notice this. At the checkout the purchaser was asked to pay the full price. The defendants were charged under s 11 of the Trade Descriptions Act 1968, which made it an offence to sell goods at a price higher than that at which they were advertised. The Act provided in s 24 that a person charged with an offence might raise the defence that '... the commission of the offence was due to ... the act or default of another person ...'. Tesco pleaded that the fault was that of the store manager and, within s 24, the manager should be regarded as a person other than the company which employed him. Tesco successfully appealed to the House of Lords against conviction. The principal speech was given in the House of Lords by Lord Reid. On the matter of whether the manager was a person with whom the company should be 'identified', he said, beginning at p 170:

> Where a limited company is the employer difficult questions do arise in a wide variety of circumstances in deciding which of its officers or servants is to be identified with the company so that his guilt is the guilt of the company.
>
> I must start by considering the nature of the personality which by a fiction the law attributes to a corporation. A living person has a mind which can have knowledge or intention or be negligent and he has hands to carry out his intentions. A corporation has none of these: it must act through living persons, though not always one or the same person. Then the person who acts is not speaking or acting for the company. He is acting as the company and his mind which directs his acts is the mind of the company. There is no question of the company being vicariously liable. He is not acting as a servant, representative, agent or delegate. He is an embodiment of the company or, one could say, he hears and speaks through the *persona* of the company, within his appropriate sphere, and his mind is the mind of the company.
>
> ...
>
> In some cases, the phrase '*alter ego*' has been used. I think it is misleading. When dealing with a company the word *alter* is I think, misleading. The person who speaks and acts as the company is not *alter*. He is identified with the company. And when dealing with an individual no other individual can be his

---

9   *Ibid*, p 172.

alter ego. The other individual can be a servant, agent, delegate or representative but I know of neither principle nor authority which warrants the confusion (in the literal or original sense) of two separate individuals.

...

What good purpose could be served by making an employer criminally responsible for the misdeeds of some of his servants, but not for those of others? It is sometimes argued – it was argued in the present case – that making an employer criminally responsible, even when he has done all that he could to prevent an offence, affords some additional protection to the public because this will induce him to do more. But if he has done all he can how can he do more? I think that what lies behind this argument is a suspicion that magistrates too readily accept evidence that an employer has done all he can to prevent offences. But if magistrates were to accept as sufficient a paper scheme and perfunctory efforts to enforce it they would not be doing their duty – that would not be 'due diligence' on the part of the employer.

Then it is said that this would involve discrimination in favour of a large employer like the appellants against a small shopkeeper. But that is not so ... the purpose of this Act must have been to penalise those at fault, not those who were in no way to blame.

– – –

The theories of corporate liability considered so far, namely, vicarious liability and identification have both been concerned with circumstances where the actual wrongdoing can be shown to be that of one human person. However, as the Robens Committee pointed out (para 261, quoted below, p 241) few safety offences 'can be laid without qualification at the door of a particular individual'. Catastrophic systems failures resulting in loss of life are often the result of a number of human errors, each of which, in isolation, may be a relatively minor lapse. Another question which the courts have had to answer, therefore, has been whether the faults of the individuals may be aggregated and the total be attributed to the corporate employer.

V CORPORATE LIABILITY FOR MANSLAUGHTER

Until relatively recently, it was generally believed that a corporation could not be convicted of manslaughter. Manslaughter has been considered to be a crime which, by its very nature, can only be committed by a natural person. The principle of identification, as developed, particularly in the *Tesco* case described above, opened the matter for re-consideration. In the case of *Northern Strip Mining Co Ltd* (1965),[10] a welder-burner was drowned when a railway bridge collapsed while the company was demolishing it. The company was charged with manslaughter before Glamorgan Assizes. The

10 (1965), *The Times*, 2, 4 and 5 February 1995.

company was acquitted on the facts, but the principle that the company might have been convicted of this offence was not questioned.

The principle of corporate liability came to be argued before the courts following the Zeebrugge ferry disaster. The coroner conducting the inquest held that a corporation could not be indicted. This decision was challenged by way of judicial review in *R v HM Coroner for East Kent ex p Spooner* (1989). Bingham LJ then said:[11]

> ... the question has not been fully argued and I have not found it necessary to reach a final conclusion. I am, however, tentatively of opinion that, on appropriate facts, the *mens rea* required for manslaughter can be established against a corporation. I see no reason in principle why such a charge should not be established.

Criminal proceedings were in due course brought against the company which owned the ferry and seven other defendants. At their trial, Turner J ruled that an indictment for manslaughter might properly be held to lie against the company. The citation below is confined to the reasoning of his Lordship on corporate liability.

P&O EUROPEAN FERRIES (DOVER) LTD (1991) 93 Cr App R 72

Central Criminal Court (Turner J)

... The main thrust of the argument for the company in support of the submission that the four counts of manslaughter in this indictment should be quashed was not merely that English law does not recognise the offence of corporate manslaughter but that, as a matter of positive English law, manslaughter can only be committed when one natural person kills another natural person. Hence, it was no accident that there is no record of any corporation or non-natural person having been successfully prosecuted for manslaughter in any English court. It was, however, accepted that there is no conceptual difficulty in attributing a criminal state of mind to a corporation. The broad argument advanced on behalf of the prosecution was that, there being no all embracing statutory definition of murder or manslaughter, there is, in principle, no reason why a corporation, or other non-natural person, cannot be found guilty of most offences in the criminal calendar.

...

The prosecution advanced an alternative argument to the effect that, if it were necessary that the death be, in fact, caused by a human being, then given the modern doctrine of 'identification', as to which see below, if the perpetrator of the act who was a human being which caused death could be treated as the embodiment of the corporation, then to that extent the test would be satisfied. It is obvious, however, that this alternative argument detracts from the force of the main argument.

[His Lordship reviewed the cases and continued at p 83:]

---

11 (1989) 88 Cr App R 10, p 16.

Since the 19th century there has been a huge increase in the numbers and activities of corporations whether nationalised, municipal or commercial, which enter the private lives of all or most of 'men and subjects' in a diversity of ways. A clear case can be made for imputing to such corporations social duties, including the duty not to offend all relevant parts of the criminal law. By tracing the history of the cases decided by the English courts over the period of the last 150 years, it can be seen how first tentatively and finally confidently the courts have been able to ascribe to corporations a 'mind', which is generally one of the essential ingredients of common law and statutory offences ... Once a state of mind could be effectively attributed to a corporation, all that remained was to determine the means by which that state of mind could be ascertained and imputed to a non-natural person. That done, the obstacle to the acceptance of general criminal liability of a corporation was overcome ... I find unpersuasive the argument of the company that the old definitions of homicide positively exclude the liability of a non-natural person to conviction of an offence of manslaughter. Any crime, in order to be justiciable must have been committed by or through the agency of a human being. Consequently, the inclusion in the definition of the expression 'human being' as the author of the killing was either tautologous or, as I think more probable, intended to differentiate those cases of death in which a human being played no direct part ... I am confident that the expression 'human being' in the definition of homicide was not intended to have the effect of words of limitation as might have been the case had it been found in some Act of Parliament or legal deed ... Suffice it that where a corporation, through the controlling mind of one of its agents, does an act which fulfils the prerequisites of the crime of manslaughter, it is properly indictable for the crime of manslaughter.

...

In conclusion, if my primary reason for this ruling were incorrect in law, I would be minded to follow a route close to that adopted by Henry J in *Murray Wright*'s case[12] who ruled that if it be accepted that manslaughter in English law is the unlawful killing of one human being by another human being (which must include both direct and indirect acts) and that a person who is the embodiment of a corporation and acting for the purposes of the corporation is doing the act or omission which caused the death, the corporation as well as the person may also be found guilty of manslaughter.

– – –

In the event, there were no convictions of manslaughter arising out of the Zeebrugge disaster. This was because no individual was sufficiently to blame to be liable personally and thus no person with whose wrongdoing the company could be identified. The matter is summed up thus in the Law Commission's *Consultative Document on Involuntary Manslaughter* at p 101:

---

12 [1970] NZLR 476.

The rejection of the principle of aggregation and the requirement that an individual 'controlling officer' should be guilty

431 Despite Turner J's ruling that an indictment for manslaughter could properly lie against a corporation, the prosecution against P&O European Ferries (Dover) Ltd ultimately failed. The judge directed the jury that, as a matter of law, there was no evidence upon which they could properly convict six of the eight defendants, including the company, of manslaughter. The principal ground for this decision in relation to the case against the company was that, in order to convict it of manslaughter, one of the personal defendants who could be 'identified' with the company would have himself to be guilty of manslaughter. Since there was insufficient evidence on which to convict any of those personal defendants the case against the company had to fail. In coming to this conclusion Turner J ruled against the adoption into English criminal law of the 'principle of aggregation'. This principle would have enabled the faults of a number of different individuals, none of whose faults would individually have amounted to the mental element of manslaughter to be aggregated, so that in their totality they might have amounted to such a high degree of fault that the company could have been convicted of manslaughter.

– – –

R v Great Western Trains Co (1999)[13] provides another example of an unsuccessful attempt to prosecute a corporate body for manslaughter.

This barely reported case concerns a preliminary ruling before the trial of Great Western Trains (GWT) following a crash at Southall on 19 September 1997. The Crown contended that GWT was guilty of gross negligence and sought clarification on how to put the case. It was held by the Central Criminal Court that the contention against GWT was that its system had failed and a manslaughter charge could not be brought in those circumstances. It was not accepted that manslaughter by gross negligence was an entirely objective crime. Manslaughter could only be charged where it was possible to identify fault in an individual who was the 'directing mind' of the corporation. There was no authority for any doctrine of aggregation of fault in corporate manslaughter. It was for Parliament to change the law if it were desirable that large corporations should be prosecuted for manslaughter.

In December 1994 a company known as OLL Ltd was convicted of manslaughter. The prosecution of the company followed the death of four teenagers in a canoe incident at Lyme Bay on 22 March 1993. The company ran the leisure centre in charge of the fatal expedition. Peter Kite, the company's managing director, was also charged with and convicted of manslaughter. The company was a small one and the evidence was that its managing director had been personally apprised by employees of the risks to

13 (1999) LTL 8/11/99.

which he was subjecting the children who visited the centre. The case would appear to be a clear example of the principle of identification.

The procedures followed after the Ladbroke Grove rail crash in 1999 have given rise to another controversy. In that instance, a public inquiry was rapidly set up, under the chairmanship of Lord Cullen, to take evidence to identify the causes of the crash. Shortly after this, it was suggested that the collection of evidence for this purpose, particularly the taking of evidence from witnesses, would be likely to preclude the possibility of bringing any criminal proceedings.

VI PERSONAL LIABILITY FOR COMMITTING MANSLAUGHTER

It barely needs mentioning that the statutory offence of motor manslaughter under s 1 of the Road Traffic Act 1988 will lie against those driving vehicles in the course of their employment. The focus here is upon the use of the common law crime in the context of conduct at work. There are very few examples of this and most of these examples are not well reported. The following report is of an appeal, under a now obsolete procedure before Taunton Assizes:

REX v PITTWOOD (1902) 19 TLR 37

It appeared that the prisoner occupied a hut as a gatekeeper on the Somerset and Dorset Railway near Glastonbury. His duties were to keep the gate shut whenever a train was passing along the line, which was a single line, and not many trains used to pass during the day ... On 18 July, at about 2.45 in the afternoon, White was in a hay cart crossing the line with several others, when a train came up and hit the cart, White being struck and killed. Another man was also seriously injured, while the three remaining men by jumping out of the cart saved their lives. A number of witnesses were called to show that it was really only an accommodation road and not a public road. It was shown that the train was going at a very fair rate and it was impossible to stop it, as the cart was only seen by the driver a few yards away from his train. The prisoner gave evidence before the coroner and his disposition was put in, and in it he stated that he had put the gate open about 10 minutes before to let a cart pass, and had propped it open, had forgotten to shut it again, and had gone to have some luncheon. For the defence, it was suggested that there was only mere inattention on the part of the prisoner and no criminal negligence.

Mr Justice Wright, without calling upon the prosecution, gave judgment. He said he was clearly of opinion that in this case there was gross and criminal negligence, as the man was paid to keep the gate shut and protect the public. In his opinion, there were three grounds on which the verdict could be supported:

1   There might be cases of misfeasance and cases of mere non-feasance. Here it was quite clear there was evidence of misfeasance as the prisoner directly contributed to the accident.

2   A man might incur criminal liability from a duty arising out of contract ...

3   With regard to the point that this was only an occupation road, he clearly held that it was not, as the company had assumed the liability of protecting the public whenever they crossed the road ...

- - -

The prisoner was sentenced to three weeks' imprisonment. The following points may be noted:

(a) there is no reference to any regulatory provision having been broken;

(b) the charge was for negligent manslaughter, not for unlawful act manslaughter;

(c) the judge took the view that the accused's contract of employment created a duty of care;

(d) the accused's employers had themselves a duty to protect the public, but the trial of the gatekeeper possibly was not the occasion to debate whether they had committed any offence;

(e) the actual sentence was a very light one – nowadays, if there were a conviction, it would have been likely to have resulted in a suspended sentence, possibly however for the much longer period of two years;

(f) the lightness of the sentence raises questions of the correctness of the conviction. Today, a court might be more mindful of the consequences of the conviction on reputation and employment prospects.

In *R v Morgan* (1991)[14] Mr Morgan was the driver of a passenger train. He drove the train past a warning signal without reducing speed and was unable to stop when he reached a further signal. As a result the train crashed into the rear of another train. Five people were killed and 87 were injured. He was himself injured. He could give no explanation for the accident; he had not been drinking. He pleaded guilty to a charge of manslaughter by recklessness. On conviction, he was given a sentence of 18 months' imprisonment, with six to serve and the remainder suspended. On appeal against sentence, the sentence was reduced to a term of four months' immediate imprisonment.

In the judgment, comparisons were made between the task of the engine driver and the motorist. The court considered, however, that even a 'momentary reckless error of judgment' in this case deserved punishment, for the risk of death from a disregard of signalling was very high.

Interestingly, the two cases considered so far both arose out of incidents in the operation of the railway system; neither of the accused was of senior manager status and nor was it established that they had committed offences under regulatory legislation, though, possibly, in the case of *Morgan*, ignoring a signal might have been such.

14 [1991] Crim LR 214.

The case of Mr Holt was different from the two cases just discussed in a number of respects. It aroused considerable interest amongst safety practitioners, but does not appear to have been reported, or even noted, except in the *Health and Safety Information Bulletin*.

The facts were that Norman Holt, a director of a Lancashire firm, David Holt Plastics Ltd, was charged with manslaughter following the death of an employee at the company's factory. The death occurred as a result of the employee coming into contact with the blade of an unguarded machine which was used for breaking up plastic. The case came before Preston Crown Court; the director pleaded guilty and was sentenced to 12 months' imprisonment, suspended for two years.

The case was unique for two reasons: firstly, it was the first time that a company director had been charged and convicted under the common law of manslaughter following the death of an employee; secondly, there had been a number of breaches of both the Factories Act 1961 and the Health and Safety at Work Act 1974, and proceedings were also brought in relation to these. Normally, the rule that inspectors appointed to enforce the Health and Safety at Work Act have the sole right to prosecute for offences committed under that Act prevents the prosecution of workplace offences through the Crown Prosecution Service and that, in turn, prevents consideration of whether it is appropriate to bring prosecutions within the broader spectrum of the general criminal law. For their part, health and safety inspectors are empowered only to prosecute for breaches of the duties imposed by the relevant legislation. In Mr Holt's case, the prosecution followed the inquest into the employee's death; the coroner referred the matter to the Crown Prosecution Service. The report suggests that the Director of Public Prosecutions then exercised the power given to him by s 38 of the Health and Safety at Work Act to permit the CPS to prosecute for the statutory offences as well as for manslaughter.

The final case for consideration under this section is that of Mr Holloway, an electrician who caused the death of a householder; his case came before the Court of Appeal, together with several other cases (concerning medical malpractice) raising the same issue as to the legal basis of involuntary manslaughter by breach of duty. The case is usually referred to as *R v Prentice*.

REGINA v HOLLOWAY [1993] 3 WLR 927

Before dealing with individual appeals, Lord Taylor of Gosforth remarked that all the cases were concerned with the true legal basis of involuntary manslaughter by breach of duty and proceeded to consider the precedents for guidance as to the ingredients of the offence. The extracts cited from his judgment begin at p 932:

> ... Essentially, the question is that posed in the current edition of *Archbold Criminal Pleading Evidence and Practice*, 44th edn, 1992, Vol 1, (1993), paras

19–97: 'has gross negligence manslaughter survived *R v Caldwell* (1982)[15] and *R v Lawrence (Stephen)* (1982).'[16]

In *Andrews v Director of Public Prosecutions* (1937),[17] a case of motor manslaughter, Lord Atkin ... went on:[18]

'... I do not myself find the connotations of *mens rea* helpful in distinguishing between degrees of negligence, nor do the ideas of crime and punishment in themselves carry a jury much further in deciding whether in a particular case the degree of negligence shown is a crime and deserves punishment ... simple lack of care such as will constitute civil liability is not enough: for the purposes of the criminal law there are degrees of negligence: and a very high degree of negligence is required to be proved before the felony is established. Probably of all the epithets that can be applied 'reckless' most nearly covers the case. It is difficult to visualise a case of death caused by reckless driving in the connotation of that term in ordinary speech which would not justify a conviction for manslaughter; but it is probably not all-embracing, for "reckless" suggests an indifference to risk whereas the accused may have appreciated the risk and intended to avoid it and yet shown such a high degree of negligence in the means adopted to avoid the risk as would justify a conviction.'

It is thus to be noted that the word 'reckless' was introduced by Lord Atkin to denote the degree of negligence required. Further, while he thought 'reckless' most nearly covered the case, he recognised it was not exhaustive: there was still scope for manslaughter by a high degree of negligence, even in the absence of indifference.

Lord Atkin excluded 'mere inadvertence'.[19] But he was not saying that all inadvertence falls short of creating criminal liability. On the contrary, he indicated that to establish guilt of manslaughter, the accused must be proved to have had 'criminal disregard' for the safety of others:[20] and he gave as examples 'the grossest ignorance or the most criminal inattention'. Where a duty of care is owed, the inattentive will often be negligent so as to be civilly liable even though, as a result of their inattention, they may not have adverted to the risk. But negligent inattention, characterised as 'mere inadvertence' does not create criminal liability. To do so, the inattention or inadvertence must be, in the jury's view, grossly negligent.

...

In 1981, the House of Lords decided both *R v Caldwell* (1982) and *R v Lawrence (Stephen)* (1982). Lord Diplock gave his well-known definition of recklessness in regard to the Criminal Damage Act 1971 in *R v Caldwell* and in regard to s 1

---

15 [1982] AC 341.
16 [1982] AC 510.
17 [1937] AC 576.
18 *Ibid*, p 583.
19 *Ibid*, p 582.
20 *Ibid*, p 582.

of the Road Traffic Act 1972, as amended, in *R v Lawrence*. Each definition involved two stages. The *actus reus* consisted of the defendant creating an obvious and serious risk. The *mens rea* was defined in the alternative as 'without having given any thought to the possibility of there being any such risk or, having recognised that there was some risk involved, had nevertheless gone on to take it'.

...

... in accordance with the authorities reviewed above and without purporting to give an exhaustive definition, we consider proof of any of the following states of mind in the defendant may properly lead a jury to make a finding of gross negligence:

(a) indifference to an obvious risk of injury to health;

(b) actual foresight of the risk coupled with the determination nevertheless to run it;

(c) an appreciation of the risk coupled with an intention to avoid it but also coupled with such a high degree of negligence in the attempted avoidance as the jury consider justifies conviction;

(d) inattention or failure to advert to a serious risk which goes beyond 'mere inadvertence' in respect of an obvious and important matter which the defendant's duty demanded he should address.

...

[In turning to Mr Holloway's case Lord Taylor started at p 948 by setting out the facts:]

On 30 January 1990, in the Crown Court at Maidstone before Boreham J, the appellant was convicted of manslaughter on a re-trial lasting 10 days. He was sentenced to nine months' imprisonment suspended for two years. He now appeals against conviction by leave of the single judge.

In 1987 Mrs Huskins decided to have an oil-fired central heating system installed at her home in High Halden, Kent. She engaged a firm owned by a Mr Walker to carry out the work and he in turn sub-contracted out the electrical aspects of the work to the appellant. The appellant was a qualified electrician and had done similar work on numerous occasions in the past. His task was to effect the electrical connections between various pieces of equipment which form part of the central heating system and link it up to the pre-existing electrical installation ...

Shortly after the work was completed, Mrs Huskins and other members of her family experienced a series of shocks whenever they touched radiators or 'anything metal'. The jury by their verdict found that this was because the appellant had connected terminal four of the programmer to earth, with the result that metal work in the house would be live when the programmer was running that programme. The back-up safety device, the circuit breaker, was inoperative and had been for some time. The appellant never discovered this and was criticised by the expert witnesses for not having done so.

On receipt of the complaints of the shocks, Mr Walker, the head contractor, rang the appellant who agreed to come at once, saying that 'you do not take chances with electricity'. The appellant visited the house. His evidence was that he checked his original wiring, but did not find the fault which the jury by their verdict found he had made. He went over the house with a volt stick, testing for leaks to earth, but found none. He did not believe that he had done this test on every programme – and had he done so he would have detached [*sic*] the fault. So he failed to find what was wrong, and left assuming that the shocks were due to static, even though some of the shocks had been experienced in the kitchen.

But the shocks continued ... He therefore visited again ... Again, he tested and found no specific fault. He tried some but not all of the programme, but noticed an inadequate earth stake to the tank, made a temporary replacement for this, told the householder that he would replace it, that there was no fault on her installation, but that he would replace the programmer ...

He received the parts he intended to replace at the end of April, but had not returned to the house by 2 May when the fatal accident happened. Mr French, then 23, was electrocuted in the kitchen of the house. He was touching the kitchen sink and standing in his stocking feet on a newly laid and not quite dry concrete floor ... he was killed.

...

The Crown's criticism of the appellant went beyond the creation of the lethal fault to his failure to detect that fault and to permit the fault to continue for over four months.

[Having considered the questions the judge had put to the jury, Lord Taylor concluded at p 952:]

... in our analysis of the states of mind which might properly lead a jury to make findings of [when] gross negligence may arise, this case falls squarely under (d), namely, inattention, or failure to advert to a serious risk in respect of an obvious and important matter which the defendant's duty demanded he should address. It is not an 'indifference' case. The issues are whether the prosecution has proved that the appellant was grossly negligent in not detecting the cause of the shocks and/or appreciating the risk those undiagnosed shocks reflected. The case against this appellant may have been strong, but in this summing up those issues were not addressed. For that reason we are of opinion that this appeal must be allowed and the conviction quashed.

– – –

Official statement on use of general criminal law

The following extract is taken from an article written by Richard Clifton, Head of the Policy Unit at the Health and Safety Executive (HSE). It was published in the *New Law Journal*, 28 January 2000, pp 104–05) and is a response to an article written by David Bergman and published in that Journal on 5 November 1999:

BOARDROOM GBH

When accidents at work lead to death they will normally be investigated on the basis of arrangements agreed with the HSE, CPS and the Association of Chief Police Officers. The investigation will lead to a decision as to whether it is appropriate to instigate proceedings and, if so, whether this should be a prosecution by the CPS for manslaughter, or by the authorities that enforce health and safety at work law (principally the HSE and local authorities), for breaches of health and safety legislation. Different arrangements apply in Scotland.

...

Cases that do not involve death at work are passed to the police only if the investigation leads to a conclusion that harm was really intended. Otherwise, the enforcing authorities may decide to instigate proceedings for breaches of health and safety at work law.

...

Some clarification may be helpful. The HSE has said little in public on this subject because virtually no one except David Bergman has argued that workplace accidents where someone did not actually set out to injure somebody else might lead to charges under the Offences Against the Person Act 1861.

...

Our objective is to improve compliance with health and safety at work standards required by law and if this could be best achieved by prosecuting using the Offences Against the Person Act we would take steps to achieve this. For reasons set out below, we have yet to be convinced.

David Bergman argues that it would be possible to prosecute using the Offences Against the Person Act where injury resulted from recklessness and the individual whose reckless behaviour caused the accident actually foresaw that some bodily harm might result. The requirement to prove that harm was foreseen constitutes a difficult test. But, more to the point, what would be the advantage of undertaking such a prosecution?

...

First, he [Bergman] may believe that if we pass these cases to the police with an invitation to prosecute under the 1861 Act, they will investigate the accidents, thus providing extra resources for the investigation of workplace accidents. Unfortunately the police are unlikely to allow diversion of their resources in this way.

Secondly, David Bergman appears to believe that prosecution under the Offences Against the Person Act – despite the difficulty of securing conviction – is the only way that we can convince the courts of the seriousness of the offences involved and get them to impose adequate penalties. By contrast, we have tried to convince the courts that breaches of health and safety at work law are really serious crimes. In this, we have had the support of the Lord Chancellor in a number of speeches on the subject. He said in a speech to the TUC on 1 December 1999: 'Someone injured by a breach of the Health and Safety at Work Act 1974 is no less a victim than someone who is assaulted.'

We have also sought to encourage the courts to impose more adequate penalties ...

– – –

VII ALTERNATIVES TO REGULATORY LEGISLATION

In the British system, as it will be seen, the answer has been regulatory legislation with criminal sanctions. Before considering what has actually been done in Britain, it is worthwhile considering alternative techniques that might be, and, indeed, are, to some extent, used, either within, or as an alternative to, the conventional British regulatory system.

An alternative system might be one of administrative oversight of workplace standards used in association with the general criminal law. Such a system is apparently satisfactorily employed in jurisdictions where there is a criminal code which includes a general offence of endangering life and/or makes it a general criminal offence to disregard a regulatory standard.

For example the Norwegians, who have a criminal code, were, in the early days of offshore petroleum development, able to give their Department of Labour and Petroleum Inspectorate much greater powers to introduce operational standards for application to offshore installations than either our Department of Energy or HSE enjoyed. In the British system, since regulatory standards can only be enforced in the criminal courts, they are only brought into force after lengthy consultation and with very careful scrutiny. In the Norwegian system such standards were in fact more like codes of operational practice produced and enforced in the context of provision for criminal charges under the criminal code against persons who committed 'wilful or negligent' violations of the administrative standards. In due course the early piecemeal approach was provided for, generally, under s 66 of the Petroleum Act 1985. While offshore development, both in Norway and the UK, was controlled by a licensing system, the Norwegians relied more heavily on regulation through licensing than did the British. Consequently, the special offshore regulatory system in the Norwegian sector of the North Sea was in sharp contrast to the regime in the British sector where, after the enactment of the Mineral Workings (Offshore Installations) Act 1971, control was, as onshore, through regulations (particularly the Offshore Installations (Operational Safety, Health and Welfare) Regulations 1976), which consisted of a tightly worded series of duties enforced directly through the criminal law.

The Law Commission has proposed that the criminal law in England and Wales should be codified (*Criminal Law: A Criminal Code for England and Wales*, 1989, Law Com No 177): if this proposal were adopted, then such a code might contain the kinds of offences outlined above. However, unless and, until such a time, the reliance on either the general criminal law or administrative systems is somewhat limited in Great Britain. They are only an aspect of special regulatory codes and are dependant on the enforcement system in the particular code.

VIII LEGISLATION AGAINST CAUSING DANGER

The British response to the shortcomings of the common law has been legislation. However, there have been few instances in which Parliament has legislated in broad terms to punish behaviour which endangers life. A notable exception is s 2 of the Road Traffic Act 1988, which follows a long tradition of making it an offence to drive dangerously on a road. Section 2A of that Act, as amended by the Road Traffic Act 1991, provides:

> ... a person is to be regarded as driving dangerously if ...:
>
> (a) the way he drives falls below what would be expected of a competent and careful driver, and
>
> (b) it would be obvious to a competent and careful driver that driving in that way would be dangerous.

--- --- ---

A less well known statutory provision is s 34 of the Offences Against the Person Act 1861, which relates to endangering persons on the railway. The section provides:

> Whosoever, by any unlawful act or by any wilful omission or neglect, shall endanger or cause to be endangered the safety of any person conveyed or being in or upon a railway, or shall aid or assist therein, shall be guilty of a misdemeanour and, being convicted thereof shall be liable, at the discretion of the court, to be imprisoned for any term not exceeding two years ...

--- --- ---

It appears that an offence can be committed under s 34 if a situation is created which has the potential for endangering the safety of any person. It is not necessary that any particular person should have been endangered. Interestingly, *Halsbury's Statutes*[21] comments: 'Neglect by an engine driver to keep a good lookout for signals would apparently be within the wording of this section.'

R v PEARCE [1966] 3 All ER 618

The appellant had cut copper wire linking two railway signal boxes, rendering the railway's signalling system unusable. The signalman maintained safety by stopping each train and giving personal instructions to the driver and guard. No accident occurred. The accused was convicted of an

---

21   Vol 12 (Criminal Law) 4th edn, 1997, reissue.

offence under s 34 and appealed. On appeal it was held that proof of causation of danger was not needed for a conviction: the question was whether the facts proved could properly be described as endangering the safety of any person conveyed on the railway. The conviction was therefore upheld. Giving the judgment of the court, Widgery J said at p 622:

> ... it seems to us that it cannot be entirely helpful in cases of this kind to try to analyse danger into two categories of potential and actual ... it seems to us counsel for the appellant is going too far in his submission where he seeks to persuade us that no offence is committed if the happy chance of an efficient railway servant intervening has prevented an accident. It is not causing an accident which this section contemplates, but causing a source of danger, and in our judgment the source of danger created by the accused's conduct was perfectly sufficient if the jury thought it fit to support the conviction in this case.

Even if these two statutory offences might be committed by persons, such as a lorry or train driver, in the course of their employment, they were not enacted primarily for the regulation of work or the protection of workers.

IX STATUTORY REGULATION OF WORKING CONDITIONS

In relation to occupational health and safety, from the middle of the nineteenth century, regulatory legislation imposed duties on persons, most generally employers, requiring them to conduct their operations to the standards required by the legislation or incur criminal liability. The imposition of duties, enforced through the criminal law, on employers who were, and are, normally corporate bodies, rather than human persons, had the potential for violating a fundamental principle of the common law; namely, that no person should be convicted of a criminal offence unless he had a 'guilty mind' (*mens rea*). Conflict with this general principle was avoided because these statutory offences normally imposed strict liability and, moreover, they were summary offences, triable in a magistrates' court without a jury.

The regulatory system developed in reaction to experience, rather than by careful planning. The result was piecemeal legislation, dealing with particular problems in particular work situations, principally, but not exclusively, focusing on employment in mines and quarries and factories. The matter was summed up by Sidney Webb in 1910 in his preface to *Hutchins and Harrison's A History of Factory Legislation*:

> This century of experiment in factory legislation affords a typical example of English practical empiricism. We began with no abstract theory of social justice or the rights of man. We seem always to have been incapable even of taking a general view of the subject we were legislating upon. It was in vain that objectors urged that other evils, no more defensible, existed in other trades or amongst other classes, or with persons of ages other than those to which the

particular bill applied. Neither logic nor consistency, neither the over-nice consideration of even-handed justice nor the quixotic appeal of a general humanitarianism, was permitted to stand in the way of a practical remedy for a proved wrong.[22]

Situation in 1970

The law continued to develop in a piecemeal fashion, in response to particular experiences in specific industries, for another half century. Writing of the situation in 1970, the Robens Committee said:

24 Existing safety and health legislation applying to workplaces can be divided into three broad categories. In the first category there are five major Acts, with their supporting orders and regulations, which seek to promote the health and safety of large sections of the working population. Statutory provisions for the health and safety of some 8.5 million employees in factories, shipyards, docks and construction sites are contained in the *Factories Act 1961* and its supporting orders and regulations. About eight million employees in offices, shops and railway premises are covered by the provisions of the *Offices, Shops and Railway Premises Act 1963* ... provisions for the safety and health of those employed in mines and quarries (about 345,000) are contained mainly in the *Mines and Quarries Act 1954* ... Employees in agriculture (about 340,000) are covered by the provisions of the *Agriculture (Safety, Health and Welfare Provisions) Act 1956* ...

25 The second category includes a number of Acts which provide for special regimes of control over certain specified industrial activities and substances. The Home Office and its Explosives Inspectorate are responsible for the *Explosives Act 1875*, as amended by the *Explosives Act 1923*, which control, by a system of licensing, regulations and inspection, the manufacture, storage, importation, acquisition and conveyance of conventional explosives ... The Home Office is also responsible for the *Petroleum (Consolidation) Act 1928*, which provides for controls over the storage and conveyance of petroleum spirit ... Nuclear installations (other than those operated by the United Kingdom Atomic Energy Authority and government departments) are subject to the licensing and other provisions of the *Nuclear Installations Acts 1965 and 1969*.

26 The third category comprises legislation dealing mainly with emissions and effluents from workplaces. This category lies across the borderline between occupational safety legislation and the broad area of legislation dealing with general public health and environmental pollution ... We decided to include in our initial examination two items of legislation within this category. *The Radioactive Substances Act 1960* ... [and] ... the *Alkali, etc, Works Regulation Act 1906* ...

– – –

22 3rd edn, 1966, Frank Cass & Co Ltd.

Their first criticism of the system then existing was that there was too much law! However, they also considered that the existing law was 'intrinsically unsatisfactory'.

They found that:

> The legislation is badly structured and the attempt to cover contingency after contingency has resulted in a degree of elaboration, detail and complexity that deters even the most determined reader. It is written in a language and style that renders it largely unintelligible to those whose actions it is intended to influence ... [para 29].

They also considered that the law was too fragmented, both in its content and in the system of enforcement, responsibilities for enforcement being divided between a number of government departments.

The Committee was critical not only of the then existing legal rules: they were also critical of the use of criminal prosecution as a means of achieving health and safety at the workplace. On this, they said:

> 261 The fact is – and we believe this to be widely recognised – that the traditional concepts of the criminal law are not readily applicable to the majority of infringements which arise under this type of legislation. Relatively few offences are clear-cut, few arise from reckless indifference to the possibility of causing injury, few can be laid without qualification at the door of a particular individual. The typical infringement or combination of infringements arises rather through carelessness, oversight, lack of knowledge or means, inadequate supervision or sheer inefficiency. In such circumstances the process of prosecution and punishment by the criminal courts is largely an irrelevancy.
>
> ...
>
> 263 ... We recommend that criminal proceedings should, as a matter of policy, be instituted only for infringements of a type where the imposition of exemplary punishment would be generally expected and supported by the public. We mean by this offences of a flagrant, wilful or reckless nature which either have or could have resulted in serious injury ...

– – –

Health and Safety at Work Act 1974

The Robens Report was published in 1972 and was followed a bare two years later by the Health and Safety at Work Act 1974. The 1974 Act is generally regarded as reflecting the Robens philosophy. It is a framework (or enabling) Act. It imposes broad general duties on persons at the workplace (ss 2–9) and provides for regulations to be made to make provision for more detailed control of particular situations (s 15). It set up a system for administration and law enforcement. Overall responsibility for achieving the purposes of the Act is given to the Health and Safety Commission (HSC), while responsibility for carrying out the functions of the Commission is given to the Health and Safety

Executive (HSE) (s 11). The HSE is the principal enforcing authority empowered to appoint inspectors (s 19).

In the tradition of the earlier regulatory legislation, there are criminal sanctions for breaches of the duties in the Act and regulations. However, there is a new approach in the new legislation, in that the broad general duties impose upon duty holders the responsibility for determining the way in which they will operate to achieve the objectives of the legislation. On the other hand, it gives to inspectors what were, at that time, novel powers to issue notices requiring things to be done to make particular workplaces safer. The inspectors' powers to issue improvement and prohibition notices may often be used as an effective alternative to initiating criminal proceedings.

The remaining chapters of Part II will be concerned with the system put in place under this Act, which continues in force as the framework under which the considerable number of European Directives on occupational health and safety has been, or is being, implemented.

X ADMINISTRATIVE CONTROL WITHIN THE BRITISH REGULATORY SYSTEM

The traditional British regulatory system places responsibility for selecting and operating a safe system upon the employer. If either official inspection or catastrophe causes the employer's judgment and competence to be questioned, the inquiry will take place in a criminal court. An alternative regime is to require the organisation to demonstrate its competence to a government agency prior to starting up. Under such a system, the organisation can only operate lawfully when it has been granted permission to do so. That is to say the organisation must be licensed to operate and can only operate lawfully while it keeps to the terms of the licence. Functioning without a licence, or outside the terms of the licence, is likely to be a serious criminal offence.

(a) Licensing in significant major industries

There are examples within the British system of the use of licensing to control industrial activity. Notably, the development of the hydrocarbon industry has been controlled by vesting the property in petroleum and natural gas in the Crown and then granting licences to persons to explore for and exploit petroleum resources. The legislation was originally concerned with onshore development; s 1(1) of the Petroleum (Production) Act 1934 vested the property in petroleum 'existing in its natural condition in strata in Great Britain' in the Crown and s 2(1) of that Act empowered the Board of Trade to grant licences 'to search and bore for and get petroleum'. Section 6(1)(d) of the

Act required the Board of Trade to produce, through regulations, model clauses for inclusion in licences. Section 1(1) of the Continental Shelf Act 1964 vested in the Crown the UK's rights in petroleum on the British sector of the North Sea Continental Shelf and s 1(3) provided for the licensing system established under the 1934 Act to be used in relation to offshore activity. Most significantly for present purposes, s 1(4) provided:

> Model clauses prescribed under s 6 of the Petroleum (Production) Act 1934 as applied by the preceding subsection shall include provision for the safety, health and welfare of persons employed on operations undertaken under the authority of any licence granted under that Act as so applied.

A licence granted under this legislation was in the nature of a contract between the licensee and the Government. Thus, any licensee who failed to honour the terms of the licence might have that licence revoked. However, the primary purpose was to regulate the extraction of oil and gas, and to ensure that royalties were paid to the Government. There was little likelihood that, and, indeed, no instance of, a licence being revoked for failure to honour the model clauses on safety. The capsizing of the drilling rig *Sea Gem* suggested that the model clauses were not an appropriate means of achieving safe working conditions for those employed in the offshore industry[23] and the Mineral Workings (Offshore Installations) Act 1971 provided a framework for a regulatory system not dissimilar to that used to control onshore workplaces such as factories or mines.

Nevertheless, the licensing system, or a variation of it, is still a means of controlling the provision of major public services. The Water Act 1989 (the relevant sections of which have now been largely re-enacted in the Water Industry Act 1991) introduced the framework for the 'privatisation' of the water industry; s 11 enabled the Secretary of State to appoint a company to be the water or sewerage undertaker for any area of England and Wales.[24] Section 23 empowered the Secretary of State to present a petition to the High Court that there was or was likely to be such a contravention of the company's principal duties to 'develop and maintain an efficient and economical system of water supply',[25] and to carry out its sewerage function,[26] 'as is serious enough to make it inappropriate for the company to continue to hold its appointment'. If the High Court were satisfied that the petition was justified, it might make an order appointing a person to manage the affairs of the company. In effect, the appointment of the company could be terminated for reasons of health and safety, though, in this instance, the focus is on public, rather than worker, protection.

---

23 Ministry of Power, *Inquiry into the Causes of the Accident to the Drilling Rig Sea Gem*, Cmnd 3409, 1969, London: HMSO.
24 Now the Water Industry Act 1991, s 6.
25 Now the Water Industry Act 1991, s 37.
26 Now the Water Industry Act 1991, s 94.

(b) Licensing as a normal enforcement tool?

The Robens Committee, at p 87 of its Report, considered the use of licensing as a regulatory tool:

Licensing

280 Licensing systems provide enforcing authorities with a powerful sanction. Conditions of licence can be imposed, with various penalties for non-observance. These can include withdrawal or non-renewal of the licence ... At present the licensing of occupiers of premises or sites is the main method of enforcing the safety and health requirements of the Explosives Act 1875, the Petroleum (Consolidation) Act 1928 and the Nuclear Installations Act 1965. Under the Explosives Act, licences control such matters as the layout and construction of premises used for the manufacture or storage of explosives, as well as the processes of manufacture. Under the Petroleum (Consolidation) Act all premises where petroleum spirit and certain other substances are kept must be licensed by the local authority. Under the Nuclear Installations Act, licensing powers enable the Minister to impose and supervise controls over the design, construction and operation of every nuclear installation within scope of the Act. The Mines and Quarries Act provides in effect for the licensing of particular personnel by specifying the qualifications they must possess. Managers, under-managers, surveyors and other officials and technicians must hold statutory certificates issued by the Minister on the advice of the Mining Qualifications Board.

281 Many of those submitting evidence to us suggested a considerable extension of licensing to a wide variety of premises, processes and individuals. For example some urged that all works managers should be licensed to ensure that they possess minimum qualifications of knowledge and expertise in occupational safety and health. We do not regard this as a practical proposition. In the first place there is seldom much practical value in general licensing criteria applicable to a wide variety of circumstances. If they are to have real significance, licensing criteria must be related to needs and circumstances which can be closely defined. Secondly, the administration of licensing systems is expensive in manpower and can easily become excessively bureaucratic when applied to large numbers of undertakings or individuals. Finally, too much reliance on licensing might tend to encourage the notion that the primary responsibility for exercising control lies with the licensing authorities rather than with those who create the risks.

282 Our view, then, is that, whilst licensing provides a tight means of control and a powerful sanction against abuse, licensing systems should be used very selectively. We have in mind that the licensing approach should be adopted mainly for the control of high hazard installations ...

— — —

(c) Licensing under the 1974 Act

Much of the legislation referred to in para 280 of the Robens Report has since been repealed or updated, but licensing remains a possible regulatory tool under the 1974 Act. Section 15 of the Act provides for a very wide power to make regulations under the Act and, in support of this, Schedule 3 sets out the purposes which may be the 'Subject Matter of Health and Safety Regulations'. Paragraph 4 provides:

1   Prohibiting the carrying on of any specified activity or the doing of any specified thing except under the authority and in accordance with the terms and conditions of a licence, or except with the consent or approval of a specified authority.

2   Providing for the grant, renewal, variation, transfer and revocation of licenses (including the variation and revocation of conditions attached to licences).

– – –

(d) An example of licensing regulations under the 1974 Act

ASBESTOS LICENSING REGULATIONS 1983 SI 1983/1649 (AS MODIFIED BY THE ASBESTOS (LICENSING)(AMENDMENT) REGULATIONS 1998 SI 1998/3233)

Regulation 3

Work with asbestos insulation or asbestos coating not to be carried on without a licence

(1) Subject to paragraph (2) an employer or self-employed person shall not undertake any work with asbestos insulation or asbestos coating or work with asbestos insulating board, unless he holds a licence granted under regulation 4 of these Regulations relating to such work and complies with the terms and conditions of that licence.

(2) Paragraph (1) shall not apply where–

    (a) (i) any person who carries out work with asbestos insulation or asbestos coating or work with asbestos insulating board does not spend more than a total of one hour on such work in any period of seven consecutive days, and

        (ii) the total time spent on such work by all the persons working on that work does not exceed two hours; or

    (b) the work is undertaken at premises of which the employer whose employees are carrying out the work or the self-employed person who is carrying out the work himself, as the case may be, is the occupier, and–

(i) that employer or self-employed person does not hold a valid licence to do such work granted under these Regulations, and

(ii) he has given notice of the work in accordance with regulation 5 of these Regulations; or

(c) the work consists solely of air monitoring or collecting of samples for the purposes of identification.

Regulation 4

Licences for work with asbestos insulation or asbestos coating

(1) The Health and Safety Executive may grant a licence for work with asbestos insulation or asbestos coating or work with asbestos insulating board if it considers it appropriate to do so and–

(a) the person who wishes the licence to be granted to him has made application for it on a form approved for the time being for the purposes of this Regulation by the Executive; and

(b) the application was made at least 28 days before the date from which the licence is to run, or such shorter period as the Executive may allow.

(2) A licence under this Regulation:

(a) shall come into operation on the date specified in the licence and, subject to paragraph (3) may be with or without a limit of time; and

(b) may be granted subject to such conditions as the Executive may consider appropriate.

(3) The Executive may vary the terms of a licence if it considers it appropriate to do so and, in particular, may–

(a) add further conditions and vary or omit existing ones; and

(b) impose a limit of time where none had been imposed and where a limit had been imposed may vary or remove it.

(4) The Executive may revoke a licence if considers it appropriate to do so.

(5) A licensee shall, when required by the Executive, return a licence to the Executive for any amendment or following revocation.

Regulation 5

Notification to the enforcing authority of work with asbestos insulation or asbestos coating at a person's own premises

(1) The notice to which regulation 3(2)(b) refers is a notice in writing given to the enforcing authority at least 14 days before the work is commenced ... and specifying the type of work to be carried out and the address of the premises at which it is to be carried out.

– – –

(e) Administrative control falling short of licensing

The Control of Industrial Major Accident Hazards Regulations 1984[27] introduced the concept of the 'safety case' into British safety legislation. These Regulations, which were, in part, a response to the EC 'Seveso Directive',[28] applied where hazardous or ultra hazardous activities might present a danger to employees or the public.

A National Audit Office Report[29] – *Enforcing Health and Safety Legislation in the Workplace* – made the following observations about the operation of these 1984 Regulations:

> 3.15 While the Executive are not legally required to assess the safety reports, they do carry out a detailed examination to ensure that firms have properly assessed their situation. The examination also helps the Executive to prioritise and plan inspection visits. On receiving a report, inspectors first identify whether it contains the information required by the regulations. Then, with the assistance of their specialist staff, they assess whether all relevant hazards have been included and identify any aspects of the plant and process which give cause for concern.

> 3.16 Inspectors use the reports to identify key areas for examination during preventive inspection visits and for reference in the event of an incident at the site. Although they have a good knowledge of the hazards from earlier visits, in some cases, reports have highlighted previously unidentified control deficiencies. In view of the potential danger to employees and the public from major hazard sites, the National Audit Office examined the Executive's progress in reviewing the reports.

> 3.17 Firms with major hazards sites were each required to produce a report by July 1989. In total, 331 reports were submitted. Some reports for complex sites ran to over 200 volumes. By June 1993, the Executive had completed their assessment of 199 of these reports; work on the remaining 132 was still in progress.

– – –

Following the catastrophic destruction of the offshore installation Piper Alpha, a public inquiry was conducted under the chairmanship of Lord Cullen.[30] Chapter 17 of the inquiry's report was concerned with safety assessment. The chapter includes an evaluation both of the Control of Industrial Major Accident Hazards Regulations 1984 and also of the not dissimilar safety case requirements imposed upon offshore operators in the

---

27 SI 1984/1902 (as amended).
28 Council Directive No 82/501/EEC on the major accident hazards of certain industrial activities.
29 16 February 1994, London: HMSO, p 208.
30 Department of Energy, *Public Inquiry into the Piper Alpha Disaster*, Cmnd 1310, 1990, London: HMSO.

Norwegian sector of the North Sea. Lord Cullen then continued at p 281 of Volume 2 of the report:

An offshore safety case

17.33   I am convinced by the evidence that an FSA [formal safety assessment] is an essential element in a modern safety regime for major hazard installations and that it has a crucial role to play in assuring safety offshore. Not only was there a consensus on this but also a large measure of agreement on how the matter might be taken forward. This consensus was confirmed by the parties' submissions. I consider that this FSA should take the form of a Safety Case.

        ...

17.35   Primarily the Safety Case is a matter of ensuring that every company produces an FSA to assure itself that its operations are safe and gains the benefits of the FSA already described. Only secondarily is it a matter of demonstrating this to the regulatory body. That said, such a demonstration both meets a legitimate expectation of the workforce and the public and provides a sound basis for regulatory control.

        ...

17.36   Both the evidence which I have already described and that which I will describe later make it clear that safety is crucially dependent on management and management systems. The Safety Case should show among other things that the company has a suitable safety management system.

17.37   The offshore Safety Case, like that onshore, should be a demonstration that the hazards of the installation have been identified and assessed, and are under control and that the exposure of personnel to these hazards has been minimised ...

– – –

The Offshore Installations (Safety Case) Regulations 1992 were introduced to implement Lord Cullen's recommendations. The Control of Substances Hazardous to Health Regulations 1988 (now 1999) and the Management of Health and Safety at Work Regulations 1999, (the latter originally in response to the EC's Framework Directive) have placed obligations on employers generally to assess and respond to the risks arising from their activities. However, it is only in relation to those ultra-hazardous onshore installations, which are covered by the upper tier requirements of the Control of Industrial Major Accident Hazards Regulations, and in relation to offshore installations, that it is intended that a safety case be made out and submitted to the inspectorate, before the activity commences: in the other situations, the employer's duty is to produce satisfactory evidence that there has been an assessment and an appropriate response at any time that this evidence is requested.

The Control of Industrial Major Accident Hazards Regulations 1984 have now been re-issued as the Control of Major Accident Hazards Regulations 1999. This updating was deemed necessary in order to comply with European Council Directive 96/82/EC.

The 1984 Regulation made a 'two tier' classification of hazardous installations. Where an installation was in the upper tier – that is, an installation where there was a large quantity of hazardous material – the manufacturer had to provide the HSE with a Safety Case. This had to show that the hazards had been properly identified, steps taken to control them and to limit their consequences, should emergencies occur. In relation to installations falling within the lower tier classification, manufacturers had to have available information that they had taken all measures necessary to comply with the Regulations.

The new Regulations continue this distinction between lower tier and upper tier situations, though duties are now imposed on 'the operator', rather than 'the manufacturer'. Similarly, while the old Regulations referred to 'installations', in the new Regulations, the word 'establishment' is more usually employed. Regulation 2 provides:

> ... 'establishment' means the whole area under the control of the same person where dangerous substances are present in one or more installations, and for this purpose two or more areas under the control of the same person and separated only by a road, railway or inland waterway shall be treated as one whole area.

An 'installation' in the new Regulations is 'a unit in which dangerous substances present are, or are intended to be, produced, used, handled or stored ...'.

Under the new Regulations, the operator has to supply the information as and when required by the Regulations to the 'competent authority' (in England, the Environment Agency, acting jointly with the HSE). In the case of new upper tier installations, this is prior to starting operations or, in the case of existing upper tier installations, prior to 3 February 2000.

Notably, the Regulations do not require even the most hazardous establishments to be licensed. They do not stipulate that the establishment may not be operated unless the competent authority authorises operation. Even in the case of upper tier establishments, they allow operation subject to the power of the authority to prohibit this.

CONTROL OF INDUSTRIAL MAJOR ACCIDENT HAZARDS REGULATIONS 1999 SI 1999/743

Application

3(1) These Regulations shall apply to an establishment where a dangerous substance listed in column 1 of Parts 2 or 3 of Schedule 1 is present in a quantity equal to or exceeding the quantity listed in the entry for that substance in column 2 of those Parts, except that regulations 7 to 14 shall apply only to an establishment where such a dangerous substance is present in a quantity equal to or exceeding the quantify listed in the entry for that substance in column 3 of those Parts.

...

PART 2

GENERAL

General duty

4   Every operator shall take all measures necessary to prevent major accidents and limit their consequences to persons and the environment.

Major accident prevention policy

5(1) Every operator shall prepare and keep a document setting out his policy with respect to the prevention of major accidents ...

Notifications

6(1) Within a reasonable period of time prior to the start of construction of an establishment the operator of the establishment shall send to the competent authority a notification containing the information specified in Schedule 3.

...

SAFETY REPORTS

Safety report

7(1) Within a reasonable period of time prior to the start of construction of an establishment, the operator of the establishment shall ... send to the competent authority a report containing information which is sufficient for the purposes specified in paragraph 3(a) of Part I of Schedule 4 and comprising at least such of the information specified in Part 2 of that Schedule as is relevant for that purpose.

...

PART 4

EMERGENCY PLANS

On-site emergency plan

9(1) Every operator of an establishment shall prepare an emergency plan (in these Regulations referred to as an 'on site emergency plan'), which shall be adequate for securing the objectives specified in Part 1 of Schedule 5 and shall contain the information specified in Part 2 of that Schedule.

Off-site emergency plan

10(1) The local authority, in whose area there is an establishment, shall prepare an emergency plan (in these Regulations, referred to as an 'off-site emergency plan') in respect of that establishment, and such a plan shall be adequate for securing the objectives specified in Part 1 of Schedule 5 and shall contain the information specified in Part 3 of that Schedule.

...

PART 5

PROVISION OF INFORMATION BY OPERATOR

Provision of information to the public

14(1)The operator of an establishment shall–

    (a) ensure that persons who are likely to be in an area referred to in paragraph (2) are supplied, without their having to request it, with information on safety measures at the establishment and on the requisite behaviour in the event of a major accident at the establishment;

    (b) make that information available to the public.

  (2) An area referred to in paragraph (1) is an area notified to the operator by the competent authority as being an area in which, in the opinion of the competent authority, persons are liable to be affected by a major accident occurring at the establishment.

  (3) The information referred to in paragraph (1) shall contain at least the information specified in Schedule 6.

...

Provision of information to competent authority

15(1)Every operator of an establishment shall, when requested to do so by the competent authority provide sufficient information to the authority to demonstrate that he has taken all measures necessary to comply with these Regulations, and the information shall be so provided within such period as the competent authority specifies in the request.

PART 6

FUNCTIONS OF COMPETENT AUTHORITY

Prohibition of use

18(1)The competent authority shall prohibit the operation or bringing into operation of any establishment or installation or any part thereof where the measures taken by the operator for the prevention and mitigation of major accidents are seriously deficient.

  (2) The competent authority may prohibit the operation or bringing into operation of any establishment or installation or any part thereof if the operator has failed to submit any notification, safety report or other information required by or under these Regulations within the time so required.

  (3) Where the competent authority proposes to prohibit an operation or the bringing into operation of an establishment or installation or any part thereof pursuant to this Regulation, it shall serve on the operator a notice giving reasons for the prohibition and specifying the date when it is to take effect, and any such notice may be withdrawn in writing by the competent authority.

(4) A notice served pursuant to paragraph (3) may specify measures which, if taken, would cause the competent authority to withdraw the notice.

(5) Where a notice has been served on an operator in accordance with paragraph (3) the operator shall comply with it (including any such notice as modified on appeal).

– – –

XI ACHIEVING SAFE SYSTEMS AT THE WORKPLACE

(a) Risk assessment as a normal responsibility of management

The Robens Committee stressed that the promotion of safety and health at work was a management function. Thus, they reported at p 15:

47 The promotion of safety and health is not only a function of good management, but it is, or ought to be, a normal management function – just as production or marketing is a normal function. The effective exercise of this function, as any other depends upon the application of technique. Too many firms still appear to regard accidents as matters of chance, unpredictable and therefore not susceptible to 'management'. Too few appear to have made serious efforts to assess the total problem, to identify the underlying causes or to quantify the costs. Too few make use of diagnostic and predictive techniques such as safety sampling or hazard analysis, or safety audits in which each aspect of workplace organisation and operation is subjected to a carefully planned and comprehensive safety survey; or systematic preventive procedures such as clearances for new equipment and processes, safe access permits and so on.

48 The spread within industry of a more scientific and systematic approach to accident prevention has been slow. It is many years since Heinrich began to develop his thesis that the conventional approach to prevention, by concentrating on injuries that had happened, rather than on accidental occurrences that might be predicted, looked at only a fraction of the total problem and looked at it backwards.

– – –

The preceding section on the use of administrative powers since 1974 to ensure that organisations operate safely has demonstrated some of the more noteworthy instances of the regulatory technique of imposing the duty on management to identify and operate safe systems, while empowering government enforcement agencies to bring operations to a halt when they consider management has failed to comply with its duty. The system of risk assessment and response advocated by Robens and required by these Regulations has, in fact, been widely used in health and safety regulations made since 1974, and may arguably be said to be a principal feature of contemporary regulatory control. In the occupational health and safety regime it is to be found in most of the regulations made since 1992 subsidiary to the Management of Health and Safety at Work Regulations first introduced in that year.

(b) Responsibilities and involvement of workers

Historically, regulations for particular situations have imposed personal duties on employees. An example is the Quarries (Explosives) Regulations 1959, of which regulation 27(4) was under consideration in the compensation claim of Mr Shatwell in *ICI v Shatwell* (1965)[31] which was considered in Part I of this book. This regulation stipulates that:

> No shot-firer shall fire any round of shots connected in series at a quarry by means of electric shot firing apparatus unless he has tested the circuit for continuity by means of a suitable testing device and has found it to be satisfactory. A shot-firer shall not make any such tests unless all persons in the vicinity have withdrawn to a place of safety and he himself has taken proper shelter.

– – –

Such regulations have normally only imposed duties on workers who, being properly qualified, are placed in a position of management of, or responsibility for, the operation to which the regulation applies. The Robens Committee expressly indicated that it did not have such situations in mind when referring to worker involvement.

Section 7 of the 1974 Act introduced a general duty imposed on all employees to act safely while at work. Regulations made under the Act, notably the Management of Health and Safety at Work Regulations, similarly balance worker entitlement to safety at work with worker responsibilities to act safely so far as is within their power, given their training for the task in which they are engaged and the environment in which they are placed.

On the other hand, the Robens Committee put forward the then somewhat novel proposition that workers should work with their employer to identify safe systems for their workplaces. Indeed, the Robens Committee proposed that safety at the workplace required the involvement of the workforce. On p 18 of their Report, they said:

> 59 We have stressed that the promotion of safety and health at work is first and foremost a matter of efficient management. But it is not a management prerogative. In this context more than most, real progress is impossible without the full co-operation and commitment of all employees. How can this be encouraged? We believe that if workpeople are to accept their full share of responsibility (again, we are not speaking

31 [1965] AC 656.

of legal responsibilities) they must be able to participate fully in the making and monitoring of arrangements for safety and health at their place of work.

What the Committee was proposing was to give workers the legal right to dialogue with management in the setting up and monitoring of systems at their workplaces. This right would be in the nature of a privilege, which workers might exercise if they so wished; they would not be placed under a duty to exercise these functions. The framework for a statutory system to enable this was provided for in the Act.

Section 2(4) to (7) of the 1974 Act provides that regulations may be made to give employees the right to consult with their employers on safety matters. The late 1970s was a period in which government was committed to 'corporatism'; that is to say, government both of the country and the workplace through dialogue with trade unions. Thus, the Safety Representatives and Safety Committees Regulations 1977, made to implement the Robens proposals, gave recognised trade unions the right to appoint safety representatives to consult with their employers on health and safety at their workplace. No regulations were made to make any comparable provision for workers to be consulted in situations where there was no recognised trade union. Indeed, s 2(5), providing for regulations to be made to give non-unionised workers the right to elect safety representatives, was actually repealed. Subsequently, in order to comply with the EC requirement for involvement of all workers, the Health and Safety (Consultation with Employees) Regulations 1996 had to be introduced.

The 1974 Act acknowledged the employee's 'right to know' of dangers at the workplace, both to facilitate dialogue and to encourage safe operations. By s 2(2)(c), employers are placed under a duty to provide them with such information as is necessary to ensure (so far as is reasonably practicable) their health and safety at work. This provision has now been strengthened by regulation 10 of the Management of Health and Safety at Work Regulations, which requires employers to inform their employees about the risks identified by the employers' safety assessment and the measures being taken in relation to those risks. The inspectorate are also required by the 1974 Act to provide employees with information pertinent to their health and safety (s 28(8)).

In many workplaces, the employer is now committed to empowerment of and communication with individual workers, rather than dialogue with their representatives. The Employment Rights Act 1996 gives protection to employees against dismissal (s 100) and discrimination short of dismissal (s 44) as a result of that employee's health and safety related activities, such as withdrawing from an unsafe workplace.

The Labour Government, returned to power in 1997, was committed to reviving collective representation of worker's views to their employer. Section 1 and Schedule 1 of the Employment Relations Act 1999 added a new

Schedule to the Trade Union and Labour Relations (Consolidation) Act 1992 for the purpose of facilitating collective bargaining recognition. It is too early to say whether the complex arrangements set out in the Schedule will substantially increase collective representation in general or in safety matters in particular.

The EU remains committed to worker participation and there is some justification for the assumption that the EU intends that such participation will normally be through trade unions. However, in the UK, the decline in trade unionism has resulted in many workplaces where the employer does not recognise a trade union as representing all or any of its workforce. This means that there are many more workers now than there were when Robens reported who have no trade union channel of communication with their employers on safety matters, though this is the situation that 'New Labour' took up government committed to changing.

It might possibly be argued that, 20 or so years after the publication of the Robens Report, employees have a greater entitlement to information, but less power to bring about change, than that Committee envisaged; while through 'empowerment', as granted in legislation and operated in practice, they have greater responsibilities.

SUMMARY

This chapter has indicated the background to the regulatory system operated under the Health and Safety at Work Act 1974, but touched on that system only to the extent necessary to illustrate techniques for encouraging the prevention of injury through work activities. It has focused primarily on the alternatives to the traditional system of enforcement by an inspectorate with the ultimate sanction of prosecution in the criminal courts for the offences in the regulatory legislation itself. The remaining chapters in this Part will consider in detail the regime established under the 1974 Act.

CHAPTER 10

THE REGULATORY SYSTEM IN GREAT BRITAIN

INTRODUCTION

This chapter and the two following will describe the regulatory system in Great Britain for promoting occupational health and safety. This chapter will explain the framework of the system; Chapter 11 will examine the duties within the principal Act; and Chapter 12 will consider regulations made under the principal Act.

I FRAMEWORK LEGISLATION

The Robens Committee recommended in summary that there should be a framework, or enabling Act (p 153):

469 **Chapter 5 – The form and content of new legislation –** The existing statutory provisions should be replaced by a comprehensive and orderly set of revised provisions under a new enabling Act. The new Act should contain a clear statement of the basic principles of safety responsibility ...

...

473 **Chapter 6 – The application and scope of new legislation –** The scope of the new legislation should extend to all employers and employees, except for a limited range of specific exclusions.

– – –

The Parliamentary response to the Robens Report was the Health and Safety at Work Act 1974. Since 1974 working conditions, and the hazards of the workplace, have changed at a greater rate than perhaps at any previous time in this country's history. During that period the European Community has increasingly influenced the development of the safety regime.

In 1992 the Government called for a thorough review of the law and its operation. The terms of reference included:

(a) assess whether the law is still relevant and needed;

(b) assess the compliance and enforcement burdens on business of legislation which is relevant and needed;

(c) determine whether the potential benefits still justify these burdens, and whether repeal or simplification is possible without endangering acceptable health and safety standards.

The Health and Safety Commission's (HSC) response was *Review of Health and Safety Regulation – Main Report* published in May 1994. This *Review*, though now some years old, remains a mine of valuable information about the regulatory system and its operation and will be drawn upon heavily in this and the following chapters. For immediate purposes it is useful to look to p 3, where the Commission summarised its proposals and recommendations:

The overall 'architecture' of regulation

1   The Review found widespread support for maintaining the overall architecture of regulation suggested by the Robens Committee and reflected in the Health and Safety at Work etc Act 1974 (HSW Act). Moreover:

   (a) even though the current structure had its imperfections, there was concern about the disruption and costs of further major upheaval.

   ...

2   However, it was recognised that the main force for legislative change was now the European Community, that its plans and priorities had become dominant in the area of new legislation, and that in time a new architecture might emerge to take account of the European dimension.

– – –

For the meanwhile, however, the HSC recommends that EC Directives should continue to be implemented by regulations made further to the 1974 Act:

(recommendation 1) the Commission will continue to base its revision of the law on the approach set out by Robens, involving general duties in the main (1974) Act, goal-setting legislation which applies across the board, sector – or hazard-specific legislation ...

(recommendation 2) the Commission will continue to seek to achieve the implementation of EC Directives within that structure, while recognising that over time the EC will have a decisive influence on the form of much UK health and safety law.

– – –

The response to the *Review* can be seen in the rolling Strategy Plan updated by the HSC each year. The Plan for 1999–2002 states at p 29:

Our continuing aims

• Aim 1: to modernise, simplify and support the regulatory framework, including European Union and other international work

• Aim 2: to secure compliance with the law in line with the principles of proportionality, consistency, transparency and targeting on a risk-related basis

- Aim 3: to improve the knowledge and understanding of health and safety through the provision of appropriate (and timely) information and advice
- Aim 4: to promote risk assessment and technological knowledge as the basis for setting standards and guiding enforcement activities
- Aim 5: to operate statutory schemes, including regulatory services, through, for example, the Employment Medical Advisory Service.

– – –

II THE HEALTH AND SAFETY AT WORK ETC ACT 1974

The following account will consider those provisions of Parts I and IV of the Act, and its Schedules, which set out, and interpret, the scope of the 1974 Act; describe the machinery for administering and amending the law; the system for monitoring whether, and dealing with the situations where it is found that the law has not been complied with.

The Act is in four Parts, but Part II (the Employment Medical Advisory Service) and Part III (Building Regulations, and Amendment of Building (Scotland) Act 1959) will not be referred to and Part IV (Miscellaneous and General) will be touched on only lightly.

III THE SCOPE AND PURPOSES OF THE ACT

The Act has the widest possible purposes, intended as it is to provide for all risks created by work activity. Its purposes are set out in s 1:

Section 1

Preliminary

(1) The provisions of this Part shall have effect with a view to–

    (a) securing the health, safety and welfare of persons at work;

    (b) protecting persons other than persons at work against risks to health or safety arising out of or in connection with the activities of persons at work;

    (c) controlling the keeping and use of explosive or highly flammable or otherwise dangerous substances, and generally preventing the unlawful acquisition, possession and use of such substances;

    ...

– – –

1 Application of the Act

Section 84 of the Act provides that it does not (subject to minor exceptions) apply to Northern Ireland; therefore it applies to Great Britain, that is to say England (including Wales) and Scotland. Separate provision has been made for similar rules to apply to Northern Ireland. Section 84(3) enables the Act to be extended, by Order in Council, outside of Great Britain. The most important use of this provision has been to apply it offshore to oil and gas installations on the Continental Shelf of the North Sea. The current order is the Health and Safety at Work etc Act 1974 (Application Outside Great Britain) Order 1995. Until the enquiry which followed the catastrophic fire and explosion on the *Piper Alpha* installation the 1974 Act was applied in parallel with the Mineral Workings (Offshore Installations) Act 1971 and the Department of Energy was the lead safety enforcement agency for offshore installations.

2 Scope of the Act

The Act covers not only the health and safety of employees; it covers all persons at work. That is to say it covers both the employed and the self-employed. Section 52 provides:

Section 52
Meaning of work and at work

(1) ...

    (a) 'work' means work as an employee or as a self-employed person;

    (b) an employee is at work throughout the time when he is in the course of his employment, but not otherwise; and

    (c) a self-employed person is at work throughout such time as he devotes to work as a self-employed person.

(2) Regulations made under this subsection may–

    (a) extend the meaning of 'work' and 'at work' for the purposes of this Part; ...

– – –

For the purposes of the extension of Part I of the 1974 Act to territory outside Great Britain, 'at work' was extended by regulation 16(2) of the Management of Health and Safety at Work Regulations 1992. This provision was reproduced as regulation 23(2) when the 1992 Regulations were reissued in 1999:

Regulation 23 ...

(2) For the purposes of Part I of the 1974 Act, the meaning of 'at work' shall be extended so that an employee or a self-employed person shall be treated as

being at work throughout the time that he is present at the premises to and in relation to which these Regulations apply by virtue of paragraph (1); and in that connection, these Regulations shall have effect subject to the extension effected by this paragraph.

– – –

'At work' was again extended by regulation 19 of the Control of Substances Hazardous to Health Regulations 1999 to include any activities involving the consignment, storage or use of certain biological agents.

3   Coverage of the Act

The all embracing nature of these provisions meant that over eight million workers who had not prior to 1974 been within the ambit of any statutory safety protection were brought within the regulatory system

The Act is also intended to protect persons other than persons at work from exposure to risks created by persons at work. The concept of protecting the general public from risks created by persons at work was a novel one in 1974. The general purpose in s 1(1)(b) is given effect by s 3 of the Act. This section has proved to be one of the most important provisions in the Act. It is especially relevant in that it is one way in which British occupational safety legislation goes beyond the requirements of EC Directives. However, in implementing Directives, Great Britain has, where appropriate, extended their provisions to provide, in the pattern of domestic legislation, for the protection of the public as well as the workforce. This is noticeably so in relation to the risk assessment requirement of regulation 3 of the Management of Health and Safety at Work Regulations 1999.

The very breadth of the purposes of the Act means that it has the potential for overlapping with other regulatory legislation. The Robens terms of reference excluded consideration of the regulation of transport, but the Act is not confined in this way. While the inspectorate is not likely to wish to concern itself with the regulation of road traffic on the highway (and indeed many drivers are not driving in the course of employment) it has been given express responsibility for the transport of dangerous substances by road (see Road Traffic (Carriage of Dangerous Substances in Road Tankers and Tank Containers) Regulations 1992). Following the Clapham Rail disaster in 1987 British Rail was prosecuted under the 1974 Act and subsequently rail safety was specifically brought within the scope of the 1974 Act.

When the Act was first enacted s 1(1)(d) brought the control of emissions of noxious substances into the atmosphere within the scope of the Act, but this clearly overlapped with legislation for the protection of the environment, and s 1(1)(d) was repealed by the Environmental Protection Act 1990.

4 Relevant substantive law

The system of administration and enforcement under the 1974 Act applies to the 'relevant statutory provisions'. Section 53, the interpretation section at the end of Part I of the Act, provides:

Section 53
General interpretation of Part I

'the relevant statutory provisions' means–

   (a) the provisions of this Part and of any health and safety regulations and agricultural health and safety regulations; and

   (b) the existing statutory provisions.

– – –

Thus the relevant statutory provisions are:

(i) the general duties in ss 2–9 of the 1974 Act;

(ii) legislation, and regulations subordinate to it, in existence in 1974 and, by the 1974 Act, brought within the regime established by that Act;

(iii) regulations made under, and subsequent to, the 1974 Act.

5 Review of other statutes

The enactment of the 1974 Act made no substantial repeals of legislation and regulations in force at that time: it was simply imposed as a blanket covering existing legislation and introducing regulation to work situations that had previously had no statutory protection. The statutes that were made relevant statutory provisions in 1974 comprised some 30 Acts of Parliament, or parts of them: these described as 'existing enactments which are relevant statutory provisions' were listed in Schedule 1 of the 1974 Act. Section 1(2) of the Act charged the HSC with reviewing these laws with a view to replacing them by more up to date and appropriate provisions:

– – –

Section 1
Preliminary

   ...

   (2) The provisions of this Part relating to the making of health and safety regulations and the preparation and approval of codes of practice shall in particular have effect with a view to enabling the enactments specified in the third column of Schedule 1 and the regulations, orders and other instruments in force under those enactments to be progressively replaced by a system of regulations and approved codes of practice operating in

combination with the other provisions of this Part and designed to maintain or improve the standards of health, safety and welfare established by or under those enactments.

– – –

The review process carried out over the following twenty years resulted in much of the older material being replaced. In particular the introduction, on 1 January 1993, of the Management of Health and Safety at Work Regulations 1992 and five other sets of Regulations, (known as 'The Six Pack') all to implement EC Directives, enabled very considerable pruning of older laws. The HSC noted, in its *Review of Health and Safety Regulation*, that the introduction of 'The Six Pack' enabled the following repeals and revocations:

- 43 whole sections of Acts

- 6 partial sections of Acts

- 36 whole sets of Regulations

- 19 partial sets of Regulations

In the *Review* the Commission noted the statutes which were, on 31 March 1993, in force as relevant statutory provisions under the 1974 Act. Many were older than the 1974 Act:

* the Explosives Act 1875 (except ss 30–32, 80 and 116–121)
* the Employment of Women, Young Persons and Children Act 1920
* the Celluloid and Cinematograph Film Act 1922
* the Explosives Act 1923
* the Petroleum (Consolidation) Act 1928
  the Petroleum (Production) Act 1934
* the Petroleum (Transfer of Licences) Act 1936
* the Hours of Employment (Conventions) Act 1936 (except s 5)
* the Fireworks Act 1951 (ss 4 and 7)
* the Agriculture (Poisonous Substances) Act 1952
* the Emergency Laws (Miscellaneous Provisions) Act 1953 (s 3)
* the Mines and Quarries Act 1954 (except s 151) (excluding Local Regulations)
* the Agriculture (Safety, Health and Welfare Provisions) Act 1956
* the Public Health Act 1961 (s 73)
* the Factories Act 1961 (except s 135)
* the Pipelines Act 1962 (ss 20–26, 34 and 42, Schedule 5)
* the Offices, Shops and Railway Premises Act 1963
* the Nuclear Installations Act 1965 (ss 1, 3–6, 22 and 24(a), Schedule 2)
* the Mines and Quarries (Tips) Act 1969 (ss 1–10)

* the Mines Management Act 1971

  the Mineral Workings (Offshore Installations) Act 1971

* the Employment Medical Advisory Service Act 1972 (except ss 1, 6 and Sched 1)

  the Health and Safety at Work etc Act 1974

  the Petroleum and Submarine Pipelines Act 1975

  the Employment (Continental Shelf) Act 1978

  the Petroleum Act 1987

  the Offshore Safety Act 1992

  the Offshore Safety (Protection Against Victimisation) Act 1992.

It is interesting to note how substantially this list differs from the list set out in Schedule 1 of the 1974 Act; the differences reflecting the repeals which have occurred in the interim and also the changes which have occurred as a result of Ministerial decision to bring within the regime of the 1974 Act legislation which was previously enforced by other government agencies, notably the offshore regime previously within the purview of the Department of Energy. For ease of identification the authors have placed asterisks, in the above list, against those statutes which were in the original Schedule 1, and set out below legislation in the 1974 Schedule which is not in the recent list, either because it has been repealed or because of the clearer definition of the boundary between occupational health and safety and environmental protection, following the Environmental Protection Act 1990.

IV OTHER LEGISLATION IN SCHEDULE I OF THE 1974 ACT

The Boiler Explosions Act 1882 – the whole Act.

The Boiler Explosions Act 1890 – the whole Act.

The Alkali etc Works Regulation Act 1906 – the whole Act.

The Revenue Act 1909 – s 11.

The Anthrax Prevention Act 1919 – the whole Act.

The Public Health (Smoke Abatement) Act 1926 – the whole Act.

The Hydrogen Cyanide (Fumigation) Act 1937 – the whole Act.

The Ministry of Fuel and Power Act 1945 – s 1(1).

The Coal Industry Nationalisation Act 1946 – s 42(1) and (2).

The Radioactive Substances Act 1948 – s 5(1)(a).

The Alkali etc Works Regulation (Scotland) Act 1951 – the whole Act.

The comparison is not exact because in some cases, notably the Factories Act 1961, many of the provisions of the Act have been repealed since 1974. In its *Review* the HSC proposed that the remaining sections of the Factories Act 1961 and the Offices Shops and Railway Premises Act 1963 should be repealed. Similarly they proposed to repeal the Mineral Workings (Offshore Installations) Act and were already well into the process of replacing the regulations made under that Act.

It will be clear that ongoing revision of the statutory framework means that the list of relevant provisions is constantly changing. From time to time, the HSC publish a list of provisions currently in force, but this tends to be dated even before it is available. The list provided here can therefore only be indicative!

Again, the process of review continues. Modernising, and simplifying the regulatory framework remains one of the Commission's aims.

HEALTH AND SAFETY COMMISSION
STRATEGIC PLAN FOR 1999–2002

At p 31:

To modernise, simplify and support the regulatory framework, including European Union and other international work.

Resources 1999/2000

Staff years	Staff costs £m	% staff cost
1010	32.6	27

Our work includes: working with others to develop new policy in response to new risks; negotiating on behalf of the UK at international level and in the European Union; preparing new legislation and reviewing existing legislation.

Better regulations

We will continue our work to simplify, clarify and modernise health and safety regulation to make it more effective, but without reducing health and safety standards. We are committed to helping business – small firms in particular – by:

- providing simple, clear and relevant guidance;
- ensuring the enforcement regime is consistent, proportionate, transparent and targeted; and
- cutting red tape wherever possible.

Better regulation

2.1 Our commitment to better regulation is demonstrated by a range of projects to review and evaluate legislation ...

– – –

The Annual Report for 1998–99 stated that during that year there had been an outturn of 66 sets of regulations, approved codes of practice, consultative documents and new guidance documents.

While many older regulations are amended and, in some cases, either revoked, or reissued, EC Directives necessitate the introduction of control in areas that have previously been barely regulated. An example of a situation where EC activity has required a radical new set of regulations in the UK is in the area of working time. The UK eventually responded to EC Directive 93/104 on Working Time with the Working Time Regulations 1988 (SI 1988/1833). At the same time, further Directives from the EC, in areas already addressed, necessitate the re-issuing of Regulations. For example, the Control of Substances Hazardous to Health Regulations 1994 (SI 1994/3246) has now been replaced by the Control of Substances Hazardous to Health Regulations 1999 (SI 1999/437).

6 Subordinate legislation

The HSC reported, in its *Review*, that there remained 367 sets of Regulations still in force and recommended that 100 of these should be removed because they had outlived their purpose. Of these 18 sets no longer addressed significant risks and a further 20 were duplicated by more modern provisions. They were particularly concerned that the regulatory system included some 340 different requirements or recommendations for form-filling, record-keeping and other paperwork: they suggested that, quite apart from anything else, much of this paperwork was not appropriate for an age when records might more effectively be computerised.

7 Updating or deregulation?

Section 1(2) of the 1974 Act charged the HSC with the task of removing from the regulatory system the then existing statutory provisions: it gives no remit for deregulation. It simply imposes a duty to, and provides a mechanism for, updating the regulatory system in force in 1974. So any part of a statute which is repealed, or any regulation which is revoked, has to be replaced by laws 'designed to maintain or improve the standards of health, safety and welfare established by or under those enactments'. Arguably s 1(2) might prevent the removal of a regulation which had ceased to have any value at all, for example something relating to an industrial process long since obsolete; although the total system must be considered and the effectiveness of the replacement provision must be evaluated as 'operating in combination with the other provisions of Part I'.

In practice replacement provisions have frequently substituted a systematic approach for the often narrow and generally prescriptive provisions of older laws. For example the duty holder may be required to assess the situation and make a response suitable for ensuring as far as reasonably practicable that the goal is reached. Sometimes the new provision is even more general; in which case an accompanying Approved Code of

Practice may propose what is necessary to meet the regulatory goal. Thus, s 3(2) of the Factories Act 1961 provided:

> In every workroom in which a substantial proportion of the work is done sitting and does not involve serious physical effort a temperature of less than sixty degrees shall not be deemed, after the first hour, to be a reasonable temperature while work is going on ...

With metrification, 60° F became 13° C, but the clear standard remained. The provision related only to workrooms in factories, though a similar standard applied to offices under the Offices, Shops and Railway Premises Act. Most other workplaces had no regulatory standard for the temperature of the workplace. Neither factories nor offices had any standard for maximum temperature. The legislation (the Factories Act 1961, s 3(1)) did state that 'Effective provision shall be made for securing and maintaining a reasonable temperature ...', but the significance of this for ensuring that workrooms did not get too hot was not generally appreciated in a system which related to clearly prescribed standards. Those who worked in premises which were neither factories nor offices, shops or railway premises had no comparable express statutory protection.

On 1 January 1993, the Workplace (Health Safety and Welfare) Regulations 1992, which were of very general application, were brought into force and the temperature provisions of the Factories Act and the Offices Shops and Railway Premises Act were repealed. Regulation 7 of the 1992 Regulations provides:

Regulation 7

Temperatures in indoor workplaces

(1) During working hours, the temperature in all workplaces inside buildings shall be reasonable.

– – –

The Approved Code of Practice accompanying the Regulations provides:

42 The temperature in workrooms should provide reasonable comfort without the need for special clothing ...

43 The temperature in workrooms should normally be at least 16 degrees Celsius unless much of the work involves severe physical effort ...

– – –

So generality of application and flexibility, which may facilitate accommodation to changing circumstances, has been achieved at the cost of precision. The mandatory temperature standards (which meant that a workplace had to be evacuated if the statutory minimum temperature was not achieved within an hour of starting work) have been reduced to evidence of how the regulation may be complied with.

The replacement of traditional standards by less prescriptive provisions has caused unease in some sectors of the workforce and has been challenged. In the following case one of the coal mining trade unions sought judicial review of the Secretary of State's conduct in replacing certain regulations, alleging that the new regulations, which, in the view of the unions, were less rigorous than the ones they replaced, were *ultra vires* (that is, invalid) because they did not meet the standards required by s 1(2).

R v SECRETARY OF STATE FOR EMPLOYMENT EX P NATIONAL ASSOCIATION OF COLLIERY OVERMEN, DEPUTIES AND SHOT-FIRERS[1]

The HSC, acting in accordance with s 1(2), intended to replace parts of the Mines and Quarries Act 1954 and various sets of regulations made under it which were prescriptive in nature. A formal consultation document including a draft of the regulations and code of practice was published in May 1989. There followed a series of meetings leading to revised proposals. A further consultation document was published in April 1990. Again, there were written observations followed by meetings followed by revisions of the proposals and then further meetings. A final revision of the proposals was circulated for comment in June 1992 and meetings were held in September 1992 with NACODS and other principal consultees. Except for NACODS and the National Union of Mineworkers, there was widespread general agreement with the proposals in their final form. The HSC believed that, in accordance with s 1(2), the proposals would 'maintain or improve' standards of health and safety.

The Management and Administration of Safety and Health at Mines Regulations 1993 (SI 1993/1897), which gave effect, without modification, to the HSC's proposals, were laid before Parliament and an unsuccessful motion was put down in the Commons praying for their annulment.

NACODS were not satisfied that the standards of health and safety set by the new regulations and accompanying Approved Code of Practice matched those of the measures replaced so they commenced judicial review proceedings, seeking to strike down all or part of the Regulations, contending that they were *ultra vires* the Secretary of State's regulation making power under the 1974 Act.

The leading judgment was given by Simon Brown LJ. He noted that the question was whether Parliament, on the proper construction of the 1974 Act, had entrusted to the Secretary of State's judgment whether the new regulatory regime met the requirements of s 1(2) or whether the courts had jurisdiction to

---

1   (1993) Co/2576/93. Unfortunately, the case is not otherwise reported. It was noted by Geoffrey Holgate in (1994) 23 ILJ 246. It was also noted in (1994) 222 Health and Safety Information Bulletin, June, p 15.

carry out independent fact finding so that the Secretary of State's judgment might be overruled and the regulations struck down as *ultra vires*. In his view, it was highly improbable that Parliament would have wished to leave to the courts the ultimate decision upon the respective merits of two different sets of regulations. He concluded that it was not for the court to overturn the outcome of what had been a lengthy and properly conducted consultation procedure.

His Lordship also expressed the view that the phrase 'designed to maintain or improve' health and safety standards was expressing an objective or purpose rather than describing an ascertainable result. The final limb of s 1(2) laid down a policy rather than a condition precedent. 'Designed' in that context looked to the future and embodied an expectation. It did not really matter whether, as NACODS contended, 'designed' meant 'intended' or 'suited'. Even if the word 'suited' had been used it would 'inevitably' have been construed as 'suited in the opinion of the regulation-maker'.

The HSC's *Review of Health and Safety Regulation* was placed, as it were, in the shadow of the above application for judicial review and it is not, therefore, surprising that the publication considered the role of s 1(2) at some length. However, in the light of the Divisional Court's ruling the HSC did not recommend any change to s 1(2). The following is an extract from the *Review* at p 30:

The role of s 1(2) ...

64   Its purpose is to prevent the removal – through secondary legislation made under the 1974 Act – of standards of health, safety or welfare which have been enacted by Parliament, unless the resulting system of regulations and ACoPs maintain those standards in another way. It applies only to the 'existing statutory provisions', which means primarily those standards which were in place when the 1974 Act came in.

...

68   More generally, some argue that s 1(2) might prevent the removal from the statute book of unnecessary and outdated health and safety legislation, simply because the standards – though no longer needed to safeguard health, safety or welfare at work – happened to be on the statute book in 1974.

69   The courts have recently taken the view that s 1(2) requires that the Secretary of State, having received the Commission's proposals or following consultation with the Commission, should determine whether a legislative change is designed to maintain or improve health and safety standards. The courts do not see it as their role to override the Secretary of State's assessment.

– – –

8 The burden of legislation

The debate in the 1990s about the desirability of removing longstanding regulatory provisions from the statute book through use of the powers given in the 1974 Act was undoubtedly fuelled by the then Government's desire to deregulate, so as to relieve businesses of unnecessary regulatory burdens. Indeed, the HSC's *Review of Health and Safety Regulation* was requested by the Government in this broader context. The then Conservative Government's general objectives was subsequently expressed in the following legislation:

DEREGULATION AND CONTRACTING OUT ACT 1994

Section 1

Power to remove or reduce certain statutory burdens on business, individuals, etc

(1) If, with respect to any provision made by an enactment, a Minister of the Crown is of the opinion–

    (a) that the effect of the provision is such as to impose or authorise or require the imposition of, a burden affecting any person in the carrying on of any trade, business or profession or otherwise, and

    (b) that by amending or repealing the enactment concerned and, where appropriate, by making such other provision as is referred to in subsection (4)(a) below, it would be possible, without removing any necessary protection, to remove or reduce the burden or, as the case may be, the authorisation or requirement by virtue of which the burden may be imposed, he may, subject to the following provisions of this section and ss 2 to 4 below, by order amend or repeal that enactment.

    ...

Section 37

Power to repeal certain health and safety provisions

(1) The appropriate authority may by regulations repeal, or as the case may be, revoke–

    (a) any provision which is an existing statutory provision for the purposes of Part I of the Health and Safety at Work etc Act 1974 ('the 1974 Act');

    (b) any provision of regulations under s 15 of the 1974 Act (health and safety regulations) which has effect in place of a provision which was an existing statutory provision for the purposes of that Part;

    ...

(2) Before making regulations under subsection (1) above, the appropriate authority shall consult–

    (a) in the case of regulations under paragraph (a) or (b) of that subsection, the Health and Safety Commission,

    ...

and ... such other persons as the appropriate authority considers appropriate.

(3) Instead of consulting such other persons as the appropriate authority considers it appropriate to consult under subsection (2) above, the authority may require the Health and Safety Commission ... to consult such persons as it considers appropriate for the purpose of deciding how it should respond to consultation under that subsection.

(4) Instead of consulting a person whom the appropriate authority considers it appropriate to consult under subsection (2) above, the authority may require the Health and Safety Commission ... to consult the person for the purpose of deciding how it should respond to consultation under that subsection.

(5) The appropriate authority may require consultation under subsections (3) or (4) above to be carried out in accordance with the authority's directions.

(6) Regulations under subsection (1) above may contain such transitional provisions and savings as the appropriate authority considers appropriate.

(7) Regulations under paragraph (a) or (b) of subsection (1) above shall be made by statutory instrument, and no instrument shall be made under that paragraph unless a draft of it has been laid before, and approved by a resolution of, each House of Parliament.

...

(9) In this section 'appropriate authority'–

(a) in relation to regulations under (1)(a) or (b) above, means the Secretary of State ...

— — —

Section 37 applies only to provisions pre-dating the 1974 Act or provisions which have been made under s 1(2) to replace pre-1974 laws. Section 1(2) is not repealed. Thus the HSC may still invoke that section to replace pre-1974 legislation. A careful consideration of the regulation making powers in s 15 (see below) will show that they give wide general powers to modify and repeal regulations made after 1974 under the Act. If the procedure of the 1994 Deregulation Act is used the resulting regulations will not follow the normal practice of being 'laid on the table' of the House of Commons library, so that they come into effect 40 days later unless there is a positive intervention to prevent this happening: the Regulations made under the 1994 Act will not be valid unless they have received the positive approval of both the Lords and the Commons.

It is interesting to note that the HSC's *Review of Health and Safety Regulation* did not conclude that the regulatory regime was found to be unduly burdensome to businesses. It found there was a need to ensure consistency of enforcement; to rationalise and reduce the paperwork needed from businesses and to improve understanding, particularly by small businesses; but overall the burden of regulation was not found to be generally perceived as unduly heavy as the following extract from the *Review* indicates:

How burdensome do firms perceive health and safety regulation to be?

133 Health and safety regulations have never been at the top of the list of business concerns, according to various surveys over the years. There was evidence during the *Review* – notably from the Institute of Directors' survey of April 1993 and the Forum of Private Business survey of December 1993 – that health and safety had risen in the rankings, and lay perhaps third, after concerns over PAYE and VAT. The most recent evidence, however, from a March 1994 Barclays Bank survey of new businesses, again put health and safety well down the list.

...

140 In short, there has been a rise in recent years in business concern over health and safety regulation. In part this undoubtedly reflects a broader social trend, an increasing awareness of issues such as health, safety and environmental pollution. But it can also be traced to the introduction of a small number of new pieces of legislation, mainly EC in origin. The concern seems to arise at least in part because of misunderstandings over the requirements of the legislation; but meanwhile, the great majority of health and safety regulation does not seem to be causing concern to business, and both the need for regulation and the standards it sets out are accepted by business.

– – –

V ADMINISTRATION AND MANAGEMENT OF THE SYSTEM

At the time of the Robens Report, responsibility for occupational health and safety was divided between a number of government departments each of which appointed its own inspectorates. One of the key recommendations of the Committee concerned the administration of the legislation (pp 35–36):

Unified administration – the nature of a new institution

110 We have recommended that administration of the major relevant statutes should be brought under single management, ... We believe that there should be a new administering institution, and that its form and nature should be determined by four major requirements.

111 First, it should be a separate and self contained organisation, clearly recognisable as the authoritative body responsible for safety and health at work.

112 Secondly, it should have autonomy in its day to day operations. Much of its work will be executive and technical in character, and it should be allowed to do it without unnecessary interference.

113 Thirdly, it should be organised in such a way as to provide full scope for the effective application of the principles of responsible and accountable management ...

114 Fourthly, the 'user interests' in this field – that is to say the organisations of employers and workpeople, the professional bodies, the local authorities

and so on – must be fully involved and able to play an effective part in the management of the new institution ...

Unified administration – the functions of a new institution

115 The new institution would be responsible for:

(a) The provision of advice to Ministers, government departments, local authorities, employers, trade unions, and others on safety and health at work.

(b) Management of the statutory inspection and advisory services, including their supporting scientific and technical research facilities and institutions.

(c) Administering and keeping under review the statutory and other provisions for safety and health at work. This would include formulating safety and health standards for promulgation either as codes of practice or in the form of statutory provisions ...

(d) The acquisition and provision of information, and the promotion and co-ordination of research, education and training for safety and health at work.

(e) Collaboration with the CBI and other employer-organisations, the TUC and the trade unions, the industry-level safety bodies and the voluntary safety organisations; and participation in the work of international bodies.

– – –

Sections 10–14 of the Health and Safety at Work etc Act 1974 very closely followed the recommendations of the Committee. Section 10 provides for the creation of a body corporate to be known as the Health and Safety Commission. This quango has members appointed in consultation with interested groups, namely employers, employees and local authorities. The commissioners work part time, able to retain their roles with the interest groups from which they were drawn. The Commissioners are appointed by the Secretary of State for Employment, and the Commission is responsible to Parliament through this (or occasionally another) Secretary of State. Section 10 also provided for the establishment of the Health and Safety Executive (HSE), a three person body, whose members are the senior members of the professional inspectorate. The Executive is the employer of the Health and Safety Inspectorate. In addition many local authority inspectors are engaged in enforcing, *inter alia*, occupational health and safety legislation, in the premises for which they have been given responsibility, under s 18 of the 1974 Act.

The relatively small percentage of staff actually engaged in inspection is sometimes questioned. However, the HSE is in practice concerned with carrying out the functions with which the HSC is charged, as the Commissioners themselves do not employ personnel. Thus, research, consultation with businesses and the public more generally, publication, and providing advice are all functions carried out through the HSE's staff. Indeed, by s 11(5)(b) the HSE could be called upon by a Minister to provide information going beyond the purposes of the Act; for example, the HSE might be asked to provide information concerning the incidence of an industrial disease in order to give guidance as to the provision for treatment which has to be made for it through the National Health Service, or advise concerning the safety of electric drills being marketed for 'DIY' use.

This administration system emerged as a result of the Robens Committee's perception of the need to simplify the regulatory system, not least to protect businesses from a multiplicity of inspectorates. However, 20 years later, the HSC's *Review of Health and Safety Regulation* returned to the same theme and reported:

The boundaries between health and safety regulation and other government regulation

109 Few firms are fully aware of the complexities of the Government's structure. To them, one inspector is much like another. Initial consultations suggested that there might therefore be a major problem in the 'multiple burdens' arising for business from the coexistence of separate regulatory regimes in related areas such as workplace health and safety, food safety, environmental protection, fire safety (including highly flammable liquids), lifting equipment, and product safety in the workplace and for consumers. One international company, indeed, noted that it was subject not only to such multiple burdens in the UK, but also in its many other markets such as the United States.

110 The *Review* found few specific examples of significant problems of this kind ...

111 There are inevitable regulatory overlaps in areas such as environmental protection and food safety, because the different regimes have different purposes. Thus food factories face food safety regulations designed to keep food cool, and workplace safety regulations designed to keep workers warm ...

– – –

Highlights from the Health and Safety Commission Annual Report and the Health and Safety Commission/Executive Accounts 1998–99

Of enforcement activity in the year under review, pp 9–10 states:

Securing compliance with the law ...

HSE inspectors are responsible for enforcing the law in over 600,000 establishments. Local authorities enforce the Act in around 1,250,000 establishments. In 1998–99, the HSE:

- carried out 183,000 regulatory contacts;
- investigated 32 000 incidents and complaints about working conditions;

- issued over 20% more improvement and prohibition notices;
- took 1,550 prosecutions and;
- dealt with over 750 safety cases in high hazard industries ...

– – –

That an administrative and enforcement system should engage so few of its resources in inspection may seem surprising.

VI REGULATION-MAKING POWER

When discussing the scope of the 1974 Act, it was noted that the intention in 1974 was that, in due course, the substantive law in the regulatory system should comprise the general duties in ss 2–9 of the Act and regulations made under and subsequent to the Act. While by no means all the pre-1974 legislation has yet been replaced, many areas of the law have been codified and simplified. Regulations may be made for any of the purposes of Part I of the 1974 Act: illustrations of the purposes for which they may be made are set out in Schedule 3. Section 15 of the Act enumerates what may be achieved by regulations, provided they are validly made according to the procedures set out in s 50:

Section 15

Health and safety regulations

(1) Subject to the provisions of s 50, the Secretary of State shall have power to make regulations under this section (in this part referred to as 'health and safety regulations') for any of the general purposes of this Part except as regards matters relating exclusively to agricultural operations.

(2) Without prejudice to the generality of the preceding subsection, health and safety regulation may for any of the general purposes of this Part make provision for any of the purposes mentioned in Schedule 3.

(3) Health and safety regulations–

    (a) may repeal or modify any of the existing statutory provisions;

    (b) may exclude or modify in relation to any specified class of case any of the provisions of ss 2–9 or any of the existing statutory provisions;

    (c) may make a specified authority or class of authorities responsible, to such extent as may be specified, for the enforcement of any of the relevant statutory provisions.

(4) Health and safety regulations–

    (a) may impose requirements by reference to the approval of the Commission or any other specified body or person;

(b) may provide for references in the regulations to any specified document to operate as references to that document as revised or re-issued from time to time.

(5) Health and safety regulations–

(a) may provide (either unconditionally or subject to conditions, and with or without limit of time) for exemptions from any requirement or prohibition imposed by or under any of the relevant statutory provisions;

(b) may enable exemptions from any requirement or prohibition imposed by or under any of the relevant statutory provisions to be granted (either unconditionally or subject to conditions, and with or without limit of time) by any specified person or by any person authorised in that behalf by a specified authority.

(6) Health and safety regulations–

(a) may specify the persons or classes of persons who, in the event of a contravention of a requirement or prohibition imposed by or under the regulations, are to be guilty of an offence, whether in addition to or to the exclusion of other persons or classes of persons;

(b) may provide for any specified defence to be available in proceedings for any offence under the relevant statutory provisions either generally or in specified circumstances;

(c) may exclude proceedings on indictment in relation to offences consisting of a contravention of a requirement or prohibition imposed by or under any of the existing statutory provisions, ss 2 to 9 or health and safety regulations;

(d) may restrict the punishments which can be imposed in respect of any such offence as is mentioned in paragraph (c) above.

(7) Without prejudice to s 35, health and safety regulations may make provision for enabling offences under any of the relevant statutory provisions to be treated as having been committed at any specified place for the purpose of bringing any such offence within the field of responsibility of any enforcing authority or conferring jurisdiction on any court to entertain proceedings for any such offence.

(8) Health and safety regulations may take the form of regulations applying to particular circumstances only or to a particular case only (for example, regulations applying to particular premises only).

...

Section 50

Regulations under the relevant statutory provisions

(1) Subject to subsection (5) below any power to make regulations conferred on the Secretary of State by any of the relevant statutory provisions may be exercised by him either so as to give effect (with or without modifications) to proposals for the making of regulations by him under that power submitted to him by the Commission or independently of any such proposals, but before making any regulations under any of those

provisions independently of any such proposals the Secretary of State shall consult the Commission and such other bodies as appear to him to be appropriate.

(2) Where the Secretary of State proposes to exercise any such power as is mentioned in the preceding subsection so as to give effect to any such proposals as are there mentioned with modifications, he shall, before making the regulations, consult the Commission.

(3) Where the Commission proposes to submit to the Secretary of State any such proposals as are mentioned in subsection (1) above ... it shall before so submitting them, consult–

(a) any government department or other body that appears to the Commission to be appropriate ...

(b) such government departments and other bodies, if any, as, in relation to any matter dealt with in the proposals, the Commission is required to consult under this subsection by virtue of directions given to it by the Secretary of State.

– – –

In practice, the HSC always consults very widely before making regulations, and not infrequently revises its proposals in the light of responses received to consultation. Consultation is normally through a Consultative Document which is freely available and may be responded to by any interested authority, business, or citizen, within the time stated at the time of publication. The proposals for revision of the Reporting of Injuries, Diseases and Dangerous Occurrences Regulations 1985 were a case in point: it was expected that revised regulations would be brought into force in 1995, but in order to accommodate suggestions arising from consultation it proved necessary to postpone bringing in new regulations until 1996.

VII SYSTEMS TO FACILITATE COMPLIANCE

The HSC and HSE publish information intended to assist in the interpretation and application of substantive law, particularly regulations. The 1974 Act (s 16) provides that the HSC may issue codes of practice indicating the way in which rules of law may be complied with. Provided these codes have been drawn up and published in accordance with the proper procedures they will carry the status of Approved Codes of Practice. Such codes are not mandatory; that is to say it is lawful to find other ways of complying with the legal rule in question, but an Approved Code of Practice has a special evidential value in the criminal courts.

Section 16

Approval of codes of practice by the Commission

(1) For the purpose of providing practical guidance with respect to the requirements of any provision of ss 2 to 7 or of health and safety regulations or of any of the existing statutory provisions, the Commission may, subject to the following subsection and except as regards matters relating exclusively to agricultural operations–

(a) approve and issue such codes of practice (whether prepared by it or not) as in its opinion are suitable for that purpose;

(b) approve such codes of practice issued or proposed to be issued otherwise than by the Commission as in its opinion are suitable for that purpose.

(2) The Commission shall not approve a code of practice under subsection (1) above without the consent of the Secretary of State, and shall, before seeking his consent, consult–

(a) any government department or other body that appears to the Commission to be appropriate ...

(b) such government departments and other bodies, if any, as in relation to any matter dealt with in the code, the Commission is required to consult under this section by virtue of directions given to it by the Secretary of State.

...

Section 17

Use of approved codes of practice in criminal proceedings

(1) A failure on the part of any person to observe any provision of an approved code of practice shall not of itself render him liable to any civil or criminal proceedings; but where in any criminal proceedings a party is alleged to have committed an offence by reason of a contravention of any requirement or prohibition imposed by or under any such provision as is mentioned in s 16(1) being a provision for which there was an approved code of practice at the time of the alleged contravention, the following subsection shall have effect with respect to that code in relation to those proceedings.

(2) Any provision of the code of practice which appears to the court to be relevant to the requirement or prohibition alleged to have been contravened shall be admissible in evidence in the proceedings; and if it is proved that there was at any material time a failure to observe any provision of the code which appears to the court to be relevant to any matter which it is necessary for the prosecution to prove in order to establish a contravention of that requirement or prohibition, that matter shall be taken as proved unless the court is satisfied that the requirement or prohibition was in respect of that matter complied with otherwise than by way of observance of that provision of the code.

– – –

The Robens Committee envisaged a system in which industry contributed substantially to the creation of codes of practice. As the system now operates it is HSC custom to consult widely when it has created a draft code. More controversially the HSE adopted the practice of issuing guidance suggesting how to comply with regulations. Guidance can have no evidential value in a court. In its *Review of Health and Safety Regulation*, the HSC acknowledged (at p 1) the possibilities of confusion:

> 4(a) the system of health and safety regulation includes legislation, Approved Codes of Practice, and guidance. *The respective roles of these components are not well understood.* Non-mandatory guidance is widely – but wrongly – seen as imposing obligations on business, and the limited role of Approved Codes of Practice is not generally appreciated.

– – –

Part of the confusion arose from the practice of printing in one document both the regulations and the supporting guidance. It was the practice also to print the supplementary information immediately following the regulation to which it related. In spite of the use of colour coding, it was possible to confuse whether a piece of text recorded a mandatory requirement or merely gave guidance.

It was therefore proposed that the practice of publishing guidance in this manner be discontinued. However, by the end of the twentieth century, the HSE was engaged in a major review of all its guidance titles and expected that during 2000 this would culminate in the publication of an extensive range of new material, some publications including significant modifications. Notably, the re-issue in 2000 of the Approved Code of Practice to accompany the Management of Health and Safety at Work Regulations, as revised in 1999, still follows the confusing format of the first edition. It relies largely on using different typefaces to distinguish regulations from code and code from guidance.

VIII SAFE USE OF WORK EQUIPMENT

APPROVED CODE OF PRACTICE AND GUIDANCE ON PROVISIONS AND USE OF WORK EQUIPMENT REGULATIONS 1998

What is guidance?

Guidance material describes practical means of complying with the Regulations. It does not have special status in law, but is seen as best practice. Following the guidance is not compulsory and you are free to take other action. But if you do follow the guidance you will normally be doing enough to comply with the law. Health and safety inspectors seek to secure compliance with the law and may refer to this guidance as illustrating good practice.

– – –

The case of *Walker v Wabco Automotive UK Ltd*[2] indicates judicial awareness that guidance from the HSE does not have the status of legislation. In that case, the Court of Appeal held that the trial judge was wrong to place reliance on HSE guidance about power tools leading to injuries such as carpal tunnel syndrome. In the Court of Appeal's opinion, the guidance could not be set against the fact that the employer had 20 years' experience of operating without any complaints from employees.

IX ENFORCEMENT

The 1974 Act places the responsibility for inspection of workplaces and enforcement of the law upon the HSE, while enabling arrangements to be made through regulations to transfer responsibility for some enforcement to local authorities:

Section 18

Authorities responsible for enforcement of the relevant statutory provisions

(1) It shall be the duty of the Executive to make adequate arrangements for the enforcement of the relevant statutory provisions except to the extent that some other authority or class of authorities is by any of those provisions or by regulations under subsection (2) below made responsible for their enforcement.

(2) The Secretary of State may by regulations–

    (a) make local authorities responsible for the enforcement of the relevant statutory provisions to such extent as may be prescribed;

    (b) make provision for enabling responsibility for enforcing any of the relevant statutory provisions to be, to such extent as may be determined under the regulations–

        (i) transferred from the Executive to local authorities or from local authorities to the Executive; or

        (ii) assigned to the Executive or to the local authorities for the purpose of removing any uncertainty as to what are by virtue of this subsection their respective responsibilities for the enforcement of those provisions;

    and any regulations made in pursuance of paragraph (b) above shall include provision for securing that any transfer or assignment effected under the regulations is brought to the notice of persons affected by it.

– – –

2   (1999) LTL 11/5/99.

The allocation of responsibilities between the HSE and local authorities is now governed by the following regulations:

HEALTH AND SAFETY (ENFORCING AUTHORITY) REGULATIONS 1998 (SI 1998/494)

...

Regulation 3

Local authorities to be enforcing authorities in certain cases

(1) Where the main activity carried on in non-domestic premises is specified in Schedule 1, the local authority for the area in which those premises are situated shall be the enforcing authority for them, and the Executive shall be the enforcing authority in any other case including the common parts of domestic premises.

...

Schedule 1

Main activities which determine whether local authorities will be enforcing authorities

(1) The sale or storage of goods for retail or wholesale distribution except–

    (a) at container depots where the main activity is the storage of goods in the course of transit to or from dock premises, an airport or a railway;

    (b) where the main activity is the sale or storage for wholesale distribution of any substance or preparation dangerous for supply;

    (c) where the main activity is the sale or storage of water or sewage or their by-products or natural or town gas;

    and for the purposes of this paragraph where the main activity carried on in premises is the sale and fitting of motor car tyres, exhausts, windscreens or sunroofs the main activity shall be deemed to be the sale of goods.

(2) The display or demonstration of goods at an exhibition for the purposes of offer or advertisement for sale.

(3) Office activities.

(4) Catering services.

(5) The provision of permanent or temporary residential accommodation including the provision of a site for caravans or campers.

(6) Consumer services provided in a shop except dry cleaning or radio and television repairs, and in this paragraph 'consumer services' means services of a type ordinarily supplied to persons who receive them otherwise than in the course of a trade, business or other undertaking carried on by them (whether for profit or not).

(7) Cleansing (wet or dry) in coin-operated units in launderettes and similar premises.

(8) The use of a bath, sauna or solarium, massaging, hair transplanting, skin piercing, manicuring or other cosmetic services and therapeutic treatments, except where they are carried out under the supervision or control of a registered medical practitioner, a dentist registered under the Dentists Act 1984, a physiotherapist, an osteopath or a chiropractor.

(9) The practice or presentation of the arts, sports, games, entertainment or other cultural or recreational activities except where the main activity is the exhibition of a cave to the public.

(10) The hiring out of pleasure craft for use on inland waters.

(11) The care, treatment, accommodation or exhibition of animals, birds or other creatures, except where the main activity is horse breeding or horse training at a stable, or is an agricultural activity or veterinary surgery.

(12) The activities of an undertaker, except where the main activity is embalming or the making of coffins.

(13) Church worship or religious meetings.

(14) The provision of car parking facilities within the perimeter of an airport.

(15) The provision of child care, or playgroup or nursery facilities.

– – –

The intention is that low risk activities should be within the jurisdiction of local authorities. Interestingly many of the work places are ones to which the general public is intended to have access. It may not be that the activities covered are in fact low risk. In particular sports activities frequently cause injury. A Consultative Document published by the HSC in 1994 noted that the reporting system under the then existing regulations gives insufficient information about injuries to the public.

DRAFT PROPOSALS FOR THE REPORTING OF INJURIES, DISEASES AND DANGEROUS OCCURRENCES REGULATIONS[3]

4   Injuries to members of the public

...

47 It would be impractical to extend the requirements to report over 3 day injuries to members of the public. That would require employers to follow up on the extent and outcome of every injury that came to their attention. There are practical difficulties now in that it is often not possible for employers to learn the extent of injuries to a member of the public on the grounds of medical confidentiality. We think that a simple and easily recognised reporting trigger is required and propose that every accident arising out of or in connection with work in which a member of the public is injured and is removed from the scene of the accident under medical or para-medical care should become reportable.

– – –

This proposal was adopted in the Reporting of Injuries, Diseases and Dangerous Occurrences Regulations 1995 (SI 1995/3163). The obligation to report is placed upon the occupier of the premises where the accident occurred:

---

3   CD74 C150 4/94, p 20.

Regulation 3 (1)

Subject to regulation 10, where–

...

(c) any person not at work suffers an injury as a result of an accident arising out of or in connection with work and that person is taken from the site of the accident to a hospital for treatment in respect of that injury;

(d) any person not at work suffers a major injury as a result of an accident arising out of or in connection with work at a hospital ...

– – –

In this instance the responsible person would be:

Regulation 2(1)

Interpretation

In any other case, the person for the time being having control of the premises in connection with the carrying on by him of any trade, business or other undertaking (whether for profit or not) at which, or in connection with the work at which, the accident or dangerous occurrence reportable under regulation 3 ... happened.

– – –

X APPOINTMENT AND POWERS OF INSPECTORS

The authority of both the HSE and relevant local authorities to appoint inspectors and the very extensive powers which inspectors so appointed have to enable them to inspect workplaces and take measures there with a view to enforcing the relevant statutory provisions are set out in ss 19 and 20 of the 1974 Act. It should be noted that the inspectoral powers are relevant only to the enforcement of the system under the 1974 Act and so local authority inspectors may not have similar powers when enforcing other legislation for which they have responsibilities:

Section 19

Appointment of inspectors

(1) Every enforcing authority may appoint as inspectors (under whatever title it may from time to time determine) such persons having suitable qualifications as it thinks necessary for carrying into effect the relevant statutory provisions within its field of responsibility, and may terminate any appointment made under this section.

...

Section 20

Powers of inspectors

(1) Subject to the provisions of s 19 and this section, an inspector may for the purpose of carrying into effect any of the relevant statutory provisions within the field of responsibility of the enforcing authority which appointed him, exercise the powers set out in subsection (2) below.

(2) The powers of an inspector referred to in the preceding subsection are the following, namely–

    (a) at any reasonable time (or, in a situation which in his opinion is or may be dangerous, at any time) to enter any premises which he has reason to believe it is necessary for him to enter for the purpose mentioned in subsection (1) above;

    (b) to take with him a constable if he has reasonable cause to apprehend any serious obstruction in the execution of his duty;

    (c) without prejudice to the preceding paragraph, on entering any premises by virtue of paragraph (a) above to take with him–

        (i) any other person duly authorised by his (the inspector's) enforcing authority; and

        (ii) any equipment or materials required for any purpose for which the power of entry is being exercised;

    (d) to make such examination and investigation as may in any circumstances be necessary for the purpose mentioned in subsection (1) above;

    (e) as regards any premises which he has power to enter, to direct that those premises or any part of them, or anything therein, shall be left undisturbed (whether generally or in particular respects) for so long as is reasonably necessary for the purpose of any examination or investigation under paragraph (d) above;

    (f) to take such measurements and photographs and make such recordings as he considers necessary for the purpose of any examination or investigation under paragraph (d) above;

    (g) to take samples of any articles or substances found in any premises which he has power to enter, and of the atmosphere in or in the vicinity of any such premises;

    (h) in the case of any article or substance found in any premises which he has power to enter, being an article or substance which appears to him to have caused or to be likely to cause danger to health or safety, to cause it to be dismantled or subjected to any process or test (but not so as to damage or destroy it unless this is in the circumstances necessary for the purpose mentioned in subsection (1) above);

    (i) in the case of such article or substance as is mentioned in the preceding paragraph, to take possession of it and detain it for so long as is necessary for all or any of the following purposes, namely–

        (i) to examine it and do to it anything which he has power to do under that paragraph;

(ii) to ensure that it is not tampered with before his examination of it is completed;

(iii) to ensure that it is available for use as evidence in any proceedings for an offence under any of the relevant statutory provisions or any proceedings relating to a notice under ss 21 or 22;

(j) to require any person whom he has reasonable cause to believe to be able to give any information relevant to any examination or investigation under paragraph (d) above to answer (in the absence of persons other than a person nominated by him to be present and any persons whom the inspector may allow to be present) such questions as the inspector thinks fit to ask and to sign a declaration of the truth of his answers;

(k) to require the production of, inspect, and take copies of or of any entry in–

(i) any books or documents which by virtue of any of the relevant statutory provisions are required to be kept; and

(ii) any other books or documents which it is necessary for him to see for the purposes of any examination or investigation under paragraph (d) above;

(l) to require any person to afford him such facilities and assistance with respect to any matters or things within that person's control or in relation to which that person has responsibilities as are necessary to enable the inspector to exercise any of the powers conferred on him by this section;

(m) any other power which is necessary for the purpose mentioned in subsection (l) above.

– – –

Significant information about the deployment of HSE inspectors was provided in the following Report. Although it is now some time since this Report was published (February 1994), it still provides a useful indication of the range of specialist work undertaken, and roughly shows the distribution of personnel between these areas.

REPORT OF THE NATIONAL AUDIT OFFICE, ENFORCING HEALTH AND SAFETY LEGISLATION IN THE WORKPLACE[4]

Table 2

Distribution of inspectors between inspectorates as at 1 April 1993

Inspectorate	Number of inspectors
Factory inspectorate[1]	707[2]
Agriculture inspectorate[1]	182
Nuclear inspectorate	175
Offshore inspectorate	131
Mines inspectorate	36
Railway inspectorate	34
Quarries inspectorate[1]	14
	1,279
Specialist inspectors[3]	251
Total	1,530

Notes

1   The factory, agriculture and quarries inspectorates together with scientific and medical staff, and some specialist inspectors, are grouped together in HSE's Field Operations Division. The other inspectorates operate independently.

2   109 factory inspectors cover the construction industry.

3   Specialist inspectors provide expert advice to field inspectors across a whole range of HSE's responsibilities. There are 95 specialist inspectors within the Field Operations Division.

Source: *Health and Safety Executive*

Part 2: Deployment of inspectors[5]

2.1 The Field Operations Division's 900 inspectors are responsible for enforcing health and safety law in over 600,000 workplaces – including farms, factories and building sites – in England, Scotland and Wales covering some 16 million employees and self–employed people. This part of the report examines the steps the Executive have taken to deploy inspectors between Area Offices and industrial sectors in response to health and safety risks.

Preventive inspection[6]

3.2 The Executive attach great importance to the programme of preventive inspections, under which firms are visited in a planned way in response to the likely risk. The approach allows inspectors to offer advice in good time and provides intelligence in a systematic way. In 1992–93, the factory

---

4   Cm 208, 16 February 1994, London, HMSO, p 5.
5   See p 8.
6   See p 13.

inspectorate spent over 40 per cent of their available time on preventive work, completing over 121,000 inspections.

Reactive inspection work[7]

3.23 In addition to carrying out planned programmes of preventive visits, inspectors undertake reactive investigations in response to accidents reported by employers ... and complaints ... In 1992–1993 they investigated over 24,000 accidents and complaints.

– – –

XI PROSECUTIONS AND NOTICES

The 1974 act provides that normally only an inspector can bring criminal proceedings for breach of any of the relevant statutory provisions in England and Wales. In Scotland proceedings are brought by the Procurator Fiscal. The prosecution powers of the inspectorate have, in England and Wales, survived the introduction of the Crown Prosecution Service:

Section 38

Restriction on institution of proceedings in England and Wales

Proceedings for an offence under any of the relevant statutory provisions shall not, in England and Wales, be instituted except by an inspector or by or with the consent of the Director of Public Prosecutions.

Section 39

Prosecutions by inspectors

(1) An inspector, if authorised in that behalf by the enforcing authority which appointed him, may, although not of counsel or a solicitor, prosecute before a magistrates' court proceedings for an offence under any of the relevant statutory provisions.

– – –

Since the passage of the 1974 Act inspectors have had other powers which in practice they have used more frequently than they have resorted to prosecutions. They have been authorised to issue improvement and prohibition notices, which are, in effect, orders to the individuals on whom they are served: these notices may be served independently of, and without resort to, criminal proceedings. Failure to comply with such an order is a criminal offence.

Section 21

Improvement notices

If an inspector is of the opinion that a person–

---

7   See p 19.

(a) is contravening one or more of the relevant statutory provisions; or

(b) has contravened one or more of the relevant statutory provisions in circumstances that make it likely that the contravention will continue or be repeated,

he may serve on him a notice (in this Part referred to as 'an improvement notice') stating that he is of that opinion, specifying the provision or provisions as to which he is of that opinion, giving particulars of the reasons why he is of that opinion, and requiring that person to remedy the contravention or, as the case may be, the matters occasioning it within such period (ending not earlier than the period within which an appeal against the notice can be brought under s 24) as may be specified in the notice.

Section 22
Prohibition notices

(1) This section applies to any activities which are being or are likely to be carried on by or under the control of any person, being activities to or in relation to which any of the relevant statutory provisions apply or will, if the activities are so carried on, apply.

(2) If as regards any activities to which this section applies an inspector is of the opinion that, as carried on or likely to be carried on by or under the control of the person in question, the activities involve or, as the case may be, will involve a risk of serious personal injury, the inspector may serve on that person a notice (in this Part referred to as a 'prohibition notice').

(3) A prohibition notice shall–

(a) state that the inspector is of the said opinion;

(b) specify the matters which in his opinion give or, as the case may be, will give rise to the said risk;

(c) where in his opinion any of those matters involves or, as the case may be, will involve a contravention of any of the relevant statutory provisions, state that he is of that opinion, specify the provision or provisions as to which he is of that opinion, and give particulars of the reasons why he is of that opinion; and

(d) direct that the activities to which the notice relates shall not be carried on by or under the control of the person on whom the notice is served unless the matters specified in the notice in pursuance of paragraph (b) above and any associated contraventions of paragraph (c) and any associated contraventions of provisions so specified in pursuance of paragraph (c) above have been remedied.

(4) A direction contained in a prohibition notice in pursuance of subsection (3)(d) above shall take effect–

(a) at the end of the period specified in the notice; or

(b) if the notice so declares, immediately.

...

Section 24

Appeal against improvement or prohibition notice

(1) In this section 'a notice' means an improvement notice or a prohibition notice.

(2) A person on whom a notice is served may within such period from the date of its service as may be prescribed appeal to an industrial tribunal;[8] and on such an appeal the tribunal may either cancel or affirm the notice and, if it affirms it, may do so either in its original form or with such modifications as the tribunal may in the circumstances think fit.

(3) Where an appeal under this section is brought against a notice within the period allowed under the preceding subsection, then–

(a) in the case of an improvement notice, the bringing of the appeal shall have the effect of suspending the operation of the notice until the appeal is finally disposed of or, if the appeal is withdrawn, until the withdrawal of the appeal;

(b) in the case of a prohibition notice, the bringing of the appeal shall have the like effect if, but only if, on the application of the appellant the tribunal so directs (and then only from the giving of the direction).

(4) One or more assessors may be appointed for the purposes of any proceedings brought before an industrial tribunal under this section.

– – –

The National Audit Office in its 1994 report made the following comments on the role of HSE inspectors:

Promoting compliance[9]

4.2 The Executive have a responsibility to enforce health and safety law consistently. Inspectors have discretion in deciding what action to take to protect employees or the public from risks. The choice of action ranges from oral or written advice to statutory notices requiring either immediate compliance or compliance within a specified time. In serious cases they may prosecute employers and employees for breaches of the law.

...

Advice

4.4 Most inspections result in the provision of oral or written advice ... The organisations and firms consulted by the National Audit Office thought that inspectors adopted a thorough approach to their work and that their advice was professionally and technically sound.

...

---

8 Known now as employment tribunals; see Employment Rights (Dispute Resolution) Act 1998, s 1.

9 See p 22.

Sanctions

4.7 Formal sanctions on employers and employees include statutory notices requiring specific action to improve health and safety ... and prosecution ... The Executive provide broad guidelines on enforcement criteria but rely on the judgment of individual inspectors and their line managers to decide what action is appropriate in a particular case. In view of this, they do not set targets for the use of notices or prosecution.

4.8 ... The Executive also win virtually all appeals against enforcement notices, which further supports the view that enforcement action is usually well-founded.

– – –

It will be noted that there are three kinds of notice which may be served:

(1) **Improvement notice:** served on the person allegedly in breach of duty; requiring work to be carried out;

(2) **Immediate prohibition notice:** requiring an activity to cease, or equipment to be withdrawn from use, forthwith. In *Tesco Stores Ltd v Kippax* (1990)[10] a tribunal suspended an immediate prohibition notice which had been issued in respect of revolving doors in a supermarket, because in the tribunal's view the danger was not imminent. On the other hand an undertaking by management to a tribunal, that it would take additional precautions against the risk of injury by unsafe plant was held to be insufficient for a prohibition notice to be suspended (*Grovehurst Energy Ltd v Strawson* (1990));[11]

(3) **Deferred prohibition notice**: similar to the immediate prohibition notice except that it does not come into effect immediately, thus giving the person on whom it is served time to rectify the situation and avoid having to stop the activity.

Except as regards the time at which they come into effect the two forms of prohibition are similar and differ from the improvement notice in that they do not have to be served in relation to a specific legal duty. They may be served when the inspector is of the opinion that there is a risk of personal injury.

Both improvement and prohibition notices may be appealed against. In the case of an appeal against an improvement notice, the duty to comply with the notice is suspended pending the outcome of an appeal. A prohibition notice is not suspended pending the outcome of appeal.

Once a prohibition notice has been served it remains for all time: it is not lifted by compliance. Thus should it be complied with for a while and then a lapse occur the notice remains applicable.

---

10 (1990) COIT 7605-6/90.
11 (1990) COIT 5035/90.

Appeal against a notice is initially to an employment tribunal, with further right of appeal to the High Court, with an ultimate right of appeal to the House of Lords. The rules for appeal to an employment tribunal were laid down in the Industrial Tribunals (Improvement and Prohibition Notices Appeals) Regulations 1974. These regulations were revoked by the Industrial Tribunals (Constitution and Rules of Procedure) Regulations 1993 (SI 1993/2687), The most significant rule, for present purposes, was substantially reinstated in the new Regulations and is:

Regulation 2

Time limit for bringing appeal

(1) Subject to para (2), the notice of appeal shall be sent to the Secretary within 21 days from the date of the service on the appellant of the notice appealed against.

(2) A tribunal may extend the time mentioned above where it is satisfied, on an application made in writing to the Secretary either before or after the expiration of that time, that it is not or was not reasonably practicable for an appeal to be brought within that time.

— — —

Secretary is not defined, but appears to mean Secretary to the Tribunal.

It is normally only when there is an appeal from the tribunal to the High Court, which is somewhat rare, that the proceedings are reported. Quite often, when an appeal is against an improvement notice, the issue is the interpretation of the rule of substantive law in relation to which the notice was served. In this chapter only three cases will be cited, and one other briefly mentioned. In addition, a full extract is given from a civil case in which damages were claimed from the HSE and one of its inspectors following an attempt to impose a prohibition notice where it was not appropriate to do so. First, an unreported case which put a prohibition notice in the context of the criminal law and accordingly imposed on the HSE a heavy burden of proof to establish that the notice was warranted:

READMANS LTD v LEEDS CITY COUNCIL (1992) COD 419

Readmans operated a cash and carry clothing store: the environmental health officer issued a prohibition notice in respect of the company's shopping trolleys after one had caused an 11 month old girl, who was being carried in it, to suffer injury. The notice merely required that children should not be carried in the trolleys as, in the view of the inspector, these trolleys, when fitted with child seats, involved a contravention of s 3 of the 1974 Act. The company appealed to an industrial tribunal against the notice but the tribunal dismissed their appeal saying they were not convinced by the company's evidence that the prohibition should be lifted. The company then appealed to the High

Court where Roch J upheld their appeal. He found that the tribunal had misdirected itself – the notice alleged a breach of a criminal duty and it was for the council who had issued the notice to establish the existence of the risk not for the appellant to have the burden of proving that there was no such risk. His Lordship remarked that it would be inelegant if not absurd if the burden of proof in related criminal proceedings were different from that in an appeal against a notice.

– – –

In the following case, the tribunal was not persuaded by the appellant's argument as to the cost of the remedial measures required in an improvement notice:

BELHAVEN BREWERY COMPANY LTD v A MCLEAN (HM INSPECTOR OF FACTORIES) [1975] IRLR 370

By an Improvement Notice issued on 14 June 1975 in accordance with the provisions of s 21 of the Health and Safety at Work etc Act 1974, the respondent gave notice to the appellants that he was of the opinion that they were contravening s 2(1) of the said Act, and ss 13(1) and 14(1) of the Factories Act 1961. He stated that the reasons for his said opinion were that secure fencing was not provided for the transmission machinery and various dangerous parts of machinery on the respondents' automatic kegging plant, as specified in the schedule attached to the notice; and he required them to remedy the said contraventions, or the matters occasioning them, by 11.10.75 in the manner stated in the schedule.

...

The case for the appellant was that a wire-mesh screen which incorporated a series of small gates or doors without an interlocking device would comply with the statutory requirements. In their submission an interlocking system would be too expensive; they submitted an estimate from Messrs Burnett & Rolfe Ltd showing that the cost of constructing and installing screens incorporating such a device would be over £1,900 (Production Al). A screen of the type suggested by themselves could be constructed by their own millwright for less than £200. In their submission the operators were of sufficient intelligence and integrity to see that the gates were kept in position while the plant was running; the plant was situated in a position where the managing director, the head brewer, the brewing foreman and the bottling foreman were constantly passing, about 30 times a day, and there would thus be a high level of supervision. It was accepted that an interlocking device would give a higher degree of safety than the screening suggested by the appellant, but it was submitted that it would be 'super-sophisticated', and would because of its complexity give rise to running problems.

...

The case for the respondent was that only screening of the type specified in the schedule would satisfy the statutory provisions. Any system which did not include an interlocking device meant that an operative could gain access to the machinery while it was still in motion, with all the attendant risks that that involved. In the absence of such a device, no amount of intelligence on the part of operatives, and no amount of supervision on the part of management, could establish a secure system; this was particularly the case when something (eg misalignment) had already rendered the circumstances abnormal, and recognised procedures were consequently not being followed. The fact that the appellants were presently by their own admission in breach of the statutory provisions, and the fact that they had no system whereby the machinery was switched off before adaptation of the plant for a different size of keg, raised doubts as to their ability, in the absence of an interlocking device, to operate a secure system in the future. It was accepted that cost was a relevant consideration, but the appellants' current financial position was not. There was no practical difficulty about constructing an interlocking device of the type proposed; the manufacturers had produced circuit diagrams.

...

On the whole matter, therefore, the Tribunal held on the evidence that the only method whereby the said contravention could be remedied was that of fitting an interlocking device of the type specified in the schedule. They accordingly held that the Improvement Notice should be affirmed without modification.

– – –

In the following case, the Queen's Bench Division found that the tribunal ought not to have removed a notice on the grounds that it was vague without fully considering the case:

CHRYSLER UNITED KINGDOM LTD v MCCARTHY [1978] ICR 939

The following extracts are from the judgment of Eveleigh J, beginning at p 940:

> In August 1975, there had been a fire at the appellant's company premises. In consequence of that, the premises were visited in August 1975, and, as a result of the visit and no doubt as a result of discussion at those premises, two improvement notices were served. The first recorded the visit. It alleged that the company had contravened in circumstances that made it likely that the contravention would continue or be repeated, s 2(1) of the Health and Safety at Work etc Act 1974.
>
> ...
>
> The second notice did not invoke the power under s 23 of the Act. It drew attention to a contravention in the same words as the first and referred to the same section, namely, s 2(1). The reasons given were:
>
> Effective arrangements were not made to ensure that contractors who may undertake welding or burning operations in the factory were adequately trained in the use of all types of fire fighting equipment and I hereby require you to remedy the said contraventions or, as the case may be, the matters occasioning them by 5 January 1976.
>
> The words that related to the specific method for remedy were of course crossed out, because there was no schedule to which s 23 would be related.

The company appealed to the industrial tribunal, and it is clear from what has been stated in this court that they would, if necessary, have invited the tribunal to consider other methods perhaps of conducting their operations safely and to attack proposed criticisms made of them. The details, however, of that matter are not before this court, for what happened was that the company took what I understand was put forward in effect as a preliminary point, namely, that the notices were not valid because they were imprecise and vague. In this court there have been argued as were argued before the tribunal, the details and respects in which it is alleged that the notices were vague. I do not find it necessary to go into those matters in any detail other than to give an example, and that is that the word 'effective', it is said, is so imprecise that the occupier cannot know what is required of him.

There were other points raised, but it is not necessary to have regard to those specific points, for the conclusion to which I have arrived is that the purpose of a tribunal in a case such as the present is to give effect to the requirements of safety as laid down in the Act of 1974 by, if necessary, modifying the notice in order to achieve that result.

...

The whole scheme, in my view, envisages a review of the situation, if necessary by the industrial tribunal, who, if the notice is not sufficiently precise, will be in a position to re-draft it, as it were, and make it precise.

For that reason I regard the present application to this court as out of order. What should have happened was that the matter should have been investigated as to the facts. Then, after the tribunal had exercised or failed to exercise its powers under s 24, if there had remained any cause for complaint the company would then be in a position to come to this court and argue their case. They could then argue their case thoroughly and effectively armed with information of the facts which gave rise to the issue of the improvement notice

...

— — —

The following case contained many issues. One was the cost of compliance with the notice; another the appropriateness of the system proposed for achieving safety; a third whether a general duty could support a notice. The High Court was also critical that the case had been in the nature of a test case:

WEST BROMWICH BUILDING SOCIETY LTD v TOWNSEND [1983] ICR 257

The following extracts are from the judgment of McNeill J, beginning at p 259:

This is an appeal by West Bromwich Building Society Ltd, which I shall call 'the society', from a decision of an industrial tribunal sitting at Birmingham dated August 6 1982, dismissing the society's appeal against an improvement order served upon it and dated March 22 1982, by the respondent, a principal environmental health officer of the Wolverhampton Metropolitan Borough Council. The order, expressed to be made pursuant to s 2(1) of the Health and

Safety at Work etc Act 1974, related to converted shop premises at nos 34–36, Lichfield Street, Wolverhampton, where the society carried on the business of a building society's branch office. Without at present condescending to detail, the purpose of the notice was to require the fitting by the society in the office of 'anti-bandit' screens.

By its amended notice of appeal the society challenges both the power of the respondent to issue the notice either in the form used or at all and the adequacy of the evidence before the tribunal to justify the decision; further, it contends that, if the power were there, the tribunal misdirected itself in law in propounding and in answering the questions necessary to reach its decision.

...

Section 2(1), pursuant to which it was issued, reads:

> It shall be the duty of every employer to ensure, so far as is reasonably practicable, the health, safety and welfare at work of all his employees.

...

The purpose of s 2(1) is not immediately obvious. Section 2(2) provides specifically for what might be called the traditional obligations at common law of employers towards their employees: what was described by Lord Wright, citing from earlier authority, in *Wilsons & Clyde Coal Co Ltd v English* (1938)[12] as 'the threefold obligation', namely, the provision of a competent staff of men, adequate material and a proper system and effective supervision but to which Lord Wright already in that case had to add 'a safe place of work' ...

Where the failure to discharge a duty under s 2 is charged in criminal proceedings and the duty is one set out in s 2(2) there seems to be no doubt but that the indictment should be drawn so as to specify by way of particulars the sub-paragraphs of s 2(2) imposing the duty ... It is not easy to visualise the factual situation in which a breach of s 2(1) could be charged and my impression is that it is really a parliamentary 'safety net' designed to catch any, if there be any, alleged breaches of obligations other than the obligations in s 2(2) to (7) ...

...

There is, I was told, no form of notice prescribed by the statute or by regulations ...

The notice here, so far as material, reads as follows. It is addressed to the society and continues:

I (naming the respondent) hereby give you notice that I am of the opinion that at 34–36 Lichfield Street Wolverhampton you as an employer are contravening s 2(1) of the Health and Safety at Work etc Act 1974.

The reasons for my said opinion are that staff engaged in the handling of money and in general office duties in the premises are not protected as far as is reasonably practicable from the risk of attack or personal injury from persons frequenting the area of the premises normally open to the general public and I

---

12 [1938] AC 57, p 78.

hereby require you to remedy the said contraventions or, as the case may be, the matter occasioning them by September 22 1982, in the manner stated in the schedule which forms part of the notice.

It is signed by the respondent and dated March 22 1982. Then the schedule reads:

Supply and fit suitable security screening to the customer service counter to provide a physical barrier to the vertical space formed between the counter, ceiling, and pillars or walls. The barrier should be complete with the exception of suitable cash transfer points and speech apertures which should be constructed and fitted so as to maintain the same degree of protection as set out below. The standards of materials and construction should conform to the minimum recommendations set out in BS5544: 1978 in respect of anti–bandit glazing and BS5357: 1976 in respect of supporting materials and fixing of the screens.

The industrial tribunal understood, correctly, that the respondent had served the improvement notice, which in the decision was erroneously referred to as an enforcement order or notice, as a test case. It was apparently described by a health and safety inspector at the hearing as 'a test case for all building societies'. I assume that he, or the respondent, had formed the opinion that all building societies' offices – not even just all the society's offices – should provide anti-bandit screens to protect their staff. There is no evidence, so far as I know, to indicate why the branch office at Lichfield Street was chosen. Accordingly the evidence before the tribunal proceeded with very little consideration being given to the Lichfield Street office at all. I am told that the tribunal had photographs of the office and of Lichfield Street but did not make an inspection. The tribunal was told that the estimated cost of fitting anti-bandit screens at the office would be a matter of £4,000–£5,000, though that would appear in part at least to be in the context that the total cost to this society, which has 86 branches, would come in round figures to about £0.5 million; that the branch might be holding £3,500 maximum at any one time and that on a visit to the branch three years previously staff were said to have expressed their concern about safety to the health and safety inspector. I note that the decision does not record as material either of the last two factors or that the tribunal had seen the photographs. The last sentence of this decision confirms the view that the tribunal was not applying itself to the situation of the Lichfield Street office at all ...

...

It is to my mind abundantly clear in reading the decision as a whole that the industrial tribunal itself considered the matter as one of general policy, save only, it may be, when determining that it was reasonably practicable for the screens to be erected 'physically and financially' ...

...

Further, when the tribunal came to consider the alleged contravention they were in error as to the law they should apply ...

...

The tribunal's reasons continue:

(8)   We then have to see whether it is reasonably practicable for the society to install these screens and we think it is ... But here we think it is reasonably practicable for these screens to be fitted. There is nothing physically to stop it; it is expensive but we are not dealing with a small shopkeeper on the verge of bankruptcy; the money is there, many times over.

...

The tribunal's approach seems to have been this: first it was decided that there was a risk to the society's staff which was more than minimal (that, as a proposition, was probably not challenged); finally, it was decided that it was reasonably practicable, physically and financially, to erect screens.

...

One of the problems which the form of the improvement notice here creates is that it is unclear whether the respondent is alleging an 'unsafe place of work' or an 'unsafe system' contravention: even, perhaps, some wholly new obligation of employers not comprehended by s 2(2)(a)–(e) ...

...

Although I agree with Mr Newman that s 2(1) does not of itself (as yet, if it ever could) create a new heading of employer's liability, I do not accept that the risk of injury to employees from violent criminals is outwith an employer's obligations to provide a safe system of work and, in factually appropriate cases, a safe working place, or was prior to 1974.

However, what is plain here is that this tribunal ... proceeded in the concluding words of paragraph 8 of the decision to disregard an important element in the chain: not merely weighing up the risk against available protected measures but disregarding what it was common ground before me had been the evidence before the tribunal, namely, that the society, as careful and conscientious employers, had had the question of how best to protect staff against this risk under continual consideration ...

...

Further, it seems to be insufficient to assert in an improvement notice that the inspector is of opinion that the society is contravening s 2(1) of the Act without more; I do not think that this want of particularity is cured by the giving of reasons for the opinion. A proper notice should, I believe, either identify the contravention by reference to the relevant paragraph of s 2(2), (3), (6) or (7) or, if some contravention not so identifiable is alleged, give particulars of it. This notice, as issued, suggests that the task of the tribunal is to assess the reasons given by the inspector for the works to be done instead of directing the tribunal's mind first to determining whether or not the employer in the particular circumstances has been guilty of a contravention of any provision of the Act. It may be that the use by the tribunal of the term 'enforcement order' in the first paragraph of the decision indicates an approach which may have been appropriate under public health legislation but which I think to be inappropriate under this legislation.

...

I was referred to the decision of the Divisional Court in *Chrysler United Kingdom Ltd v McCarthy* (1978)[13] where it was held inappropriate for a tribunal to decide a preliminary point on the sufficiency of the notice without first investigating the facts. I note the view of Eveleigh J.

...

In that case, the appellant apparently wished to invite the tribunal to consider methods of conducting their operations safely other than those specified in the notice but took the preliminary point that what was specified in the notice was too imprecise or vague; there is no criticism in the judgment of the proposal to invite the tribunal to consider other methods; it must follow, I think, that the tribunal must also consider whether or not the existing safety measures amount to a contravention before proceeding to other possible remedial measures.

...

In the event, therefore, and on the two bases originally postulated in this judgment, that is to say the failure of the tribunal to deal with the particular circumstances of the particular office, treating the matter as a test case, and the failure of the tribunal to apply the appropriate test ... this appeal succeeds.

– – –

The following case suggests that damages for economic loss are unlikely to be awarded to a claimant whose business has suffered as a result of the inappropriate service of a prohibition notice:

HARRIS v EVANS AND HEALTH AND SAFETY EXECUTIVE [1998] 1 WLR 1285

The plaintiff used a mobile telescopic crane for the purposes of his bungee jumping business. Mr Evans, an inspector of the HSE, gave advice to certain local authorities. As a result of his advice three local authorities each served a prohibition notice on Mr Harris preventing him from using his crane. This was although Mr Harris had, six months previously, been assured by the HSE's advisory service that he could use it. Mr Harris unsuccessfully appealed to an industrial tribunal against the notices served on him by one of the local authorities. Subsequently all three local authorities withdrew the notices. These withdrawals appeared to be the result of a letter written by the Secretary of State for Employment to a Member of Parliament. The letter stated: 'Currently there is no technical evidence available to show that there is an unacceptable level of risk in using mobile cranes for bungee jumping. It follows that the HSE does not have a policy of prohibiting the use of cranes for bungee jumping ...' Mr Harris thereupon sued Mr Evans and the HSE asserting that Mr Evans had been negligent in the advice he had given to the local authorities and this negligence had rendered the inspector himself and

---

13 [1978] ICR 939.

the HSE in breach of the duty of care that they owed to him. He claimed compensation for the economic loss he had suffered when unable to use his crane. The defendants applied to have the statement of claim struck out as disclosing no cause of action. The case reached the Court of Appeal as a result of this application. The following extracts are taken from the judgment of Sir Richard Scott VC, beginning at p 1291:

> Mr Carlisle QC for the appellant defendants, advanced two grounds for the striking out of the negligence claim. First, he submitted that, given the statutory backcloth to the advice given by Mr Evans on which the negligence claim is based, the defendants did not owe the plaintiff a common law duty of care to avoid economic loss to his business. Second, he submitted that Mr Evans, in giving his advice to the Councils, was entitled to the immunity from suit accorded to witnesses in legal proceedings. A third ground, raised in the course of the hearing, is that the negligence action represents an impermissible attempt by the plaintiff to re-litigate the issues which were decided against him by the industrial tribunal.
>
> Both the first two grounds depend upon and require a careful examination of the structure and purpose of the statutory provisions in the 1974 Act and of Mr Evans' role in giving to the Councils the advice complained of. As to the first ground, it is trite law that both the existence and the extent of a duty of care owed by A to B depend upon the particular circumstances of the case. *Hedley Byrne v Heller* [1964] AC 465 established that an action in negligence can be brought to recover economic loss caused by a negligent misstatement. It did not and could not establish that an individual whose negligent misstatement has caused economic loss to another will necessarily be liable for the loss. *White v Jones* [1995] 2 AC 207 established that a negligent discharge by a solicitor of his duty to his client that causes economic loss to a third party is capable of constituting a breach of a tortious duty of care owed by the solicitor to the third party. The case did not and could not establish that when a solicitor is discharging his duty to his client he owes a duty of care to anyone whose economic interests may be affected by what he is doing. Whether there is liability will depend in every case upon whether in the particular circumstances of the case the negligent misstatement or negligent conduct was in breach of a duty of care owed to the person who has suffered the economic loss. The question in the present case is whether Mr Evans' advice to the Councils, assumed to be incorrect and to have been negligently given, was a breach of a duty of care owed by Mr Evans to the plaintiff, Mr Harris. The circumstances of the case, on which will depend the answer to the question, include, in particular, that Mr Evans was giving the advice as an HSE inspector and that the consequences of the advice which caused the damage to the plaintiff's business were decisions taken and powers exercised by the Councils pursuant to their duties and powers under the 1974 Act.
>
> ...
>
> The effect of sections 2 and 3, for present purposes, is that Mr Harris in operating his bungee business was under a statutory duty, both to his employees working on or near to the mobile crane and to members of the public taking part in or watching the bungee jumping, to ensure so far as

practicable that they were not exposed to risks to their safety.

Having referred to the various sections of the 1974 Act that empowered the HSE and local authorities to enforce the relevant statutory provisions, he continued:

There is one other section to which I should refer because it might seem at first sight to be relevant to the question at issue in this case.

Section 26 provides as follows:

'Where an action has been brought against an inspector in respect of an act done in the execution or purported execution of any of the relevant statutory provisions and the circumstances are such that he is not legally entitled to require the enforcing authority which appointed him to indemnify him, that authority may, nevertheless, indemnify against the whole or part of any damage and costs or expenses which he may have been ordered to pay or may have incurred, if the authority is satisfied that he honestly believed that the act complained of was within his power and that his duty as an inspector required or entitled him to do it.'

Mr Jackson QC has relied on this section, as also did the judge below, as an indication that a negligent action can be brought against an inspector 'in respect of an act done in the execution or purported execution of any of the relevant statutory provisions ...'. In my judgment, the section is wholly neutral on this issue. There are a number of different types of action which might be brought against inspectors in respect of acts done by them in the exercise or purported exercise of their statutory functions or powers. Actions based on allegedly malicious acts intended to damage the owner of the business rather than to protect the public from exposure to risk caused by the business would be an example. It is possible that circumstances might arise in which actions of trespass or for breach of copyright or tortious interference with contract could be brought. No doubt other examples can be brought to mind. The language of section 26, however, neither demonstrates nor supports the viability of any particular cause of action against an inspector. I accept and agree with Mr Carlisle's submission that the section was simply intended to make clear the propriety, from a vires viewpoint, of an enforcing authority indemnifying its inspector against liabilities incurred in defending an action brought against him in respect of an act done in the exercise or purported exercise of his statutory function or powers.

...

I return to the question whether an inspector, when deciding what, if any, exercise of his powers he should make in respect of a particular business activity, owes a duty of care to the proprietor of that business.

...

The 1974 Act and the regulations made thereunder have set up a statutory system for the reduction of risks to health and safety caused by dangerous business activities. The system includes provision for appeals against acts taken by enforcing authorities in the exercise, or purported exercise, of their statutory powers. If an appeal against an Improvement Notice or a Prohibition

Notice succeeds, the error on the part of the enforcing authority is corrected. If an appeal fails, how can it then be open to the aggrieved entrepreneur to recover via a negligence action the damage caused to his business by the Notice that has been upheld by the industrial tribunal?

...

The duty of enforcing authorities, whether inspectors or local authorities, is to have regard to the health and safety of members of the public. If steps which they think should be taken to improve safety would have an adverse economic effect on the business enterprise in question, so be it. A tortious duty which rendered them potentially liable for economic damage to the business enterprise caused by the steps they were recommending to be taken would, in my judgment, be very likely to engender untoward cautiousness ...

The guidance as to approach to be found in *X (Minors) v Bedfordshire County Council* [1995] 2 AC 633 suggests, in my judgment, that the negligence action brought by the plaintiff in the present case ought not to be permitted.

...

I would decline to add the possibility of an action in negligence to the statutory remedies.

The one qualification I have in mind is this. It could be that a particular requirement imposed by an inspector, whether expressed in an Improvement Notice or Prohibition Notice or expressed in advance advice, might introduce a new risk or danger not present in the business activity as previously conducted. The new risk or danger might materialise and result in economic damage to the business itself as well a physical damage to person or to property. We do not need to decide the point but I would not be prepared to rule out the possibility that damage thus caused could be recovered by means of a negligence action.

...

Finally there is Mr Carlisle's point that, because the plaintiff appealed to the industrial tribunal against the Teignbridge District Council's Notices and lost, he cannot be allowed to re-litigate in a negligence action the question whether Mr Evans' advice was competent. The negligence action is, Mr Carlisle submitted, an impermissible collateral attack upon the decision of the industrial tribunal.

The importance, for public policy reasons, of barring 'the initiation of proceedings in a court of justice for the purpose of mounting a collateral attack upon a final decision against the intending plaintiff which has been made by another court of competent jurisdiction in previous proceedings' (*per* Lord Diplock in *Hunter v Chief Constable of the West Midlands Police*) [1982] AC 529 at p 773 was strongly affirmed by Sir Thomas Bingham MR (as he then was) in *Smith v Linskills* [1996] 1 WLR 764). But there are established exceptions to the bar, one of which is the emergence of fresh evidence. In *Walpole v Partridge and Wilson* [1994] 1 QB 106, Ralph Gibson LJ described the exception thus:

> If the plaintiff introduces fresh evidence, that is evidence which was not available, or could not by reasonable diligence have been obtained at the

first trial, which 'entirely changes the aspect of the case' (see *Hunter's Case* (1982), pp 529, 545) he may pursue his claim ... (p 115).

– – –

XII OFFENCES

Section 33

Provisions as to offences

(1) It is an offence for a person–

   (a) to fail to discharge a duty to which he is subject by virtue of ss 2 to 7;

   (b) to contravene ss 8 or 9;

   (c) to contravene any health and safety regulations ...;

   (d) to contravene any requirement imposed by or under regulations under s 14 or intentionally to obstruct any person in the exercise of his powers under that section;

   (e) to contravene any requirement imposed by an inspector under ss 20 or 25;

   (f) to prevent or attempt to prevent any other person from appearing before an inspector or from answering any question to which an inspector may by virtue of s 20(2) require an answer;

   (g) to contravene any requirement or prohibition imposed by an improvement notice or a prohibition notice (including any such notice as modified on appeal);

   (h) intentionally to obstruct an inspector in the exercise or performance of his powers or duties or to obstruct a customs officer in the exercise of his powers under s 25A;

   (i) to contravene any requirement imposed by a notice under s 27(1);

   (j) to use or disclose any information in contravention of s 27(4) or 28;

   (k) to make a statement which he knows to be false or recklessly to make a statement which is false ...;

   (l) intentionally to make a false entry in any register, book, notice or other document required by or under any of the relevant statutory provisions to be kept ...;

   (m) with intent to deceive, to use a document issued or authorised to be issued under any of the relevant statutory provisions or required for any purpose thereunder or to make or have in his possession a document so closely resembling any such document as to be calculated to deceive;

   (n) falsely to pretend to be an inspector;

   (o) to fail to comply with an order made by a court under s 42.

(1A) Subject to any provision made by virtue of s 15(6)(d), a person guilty of an offence under subsection (1)(a) above consisting of a failing to discharge a duty to which he is subject by virtue of ss 2 to 6 shall be liable–

   (a) on summary conviction, to a fine not exceeding £20,000;

(b) on conviction on indictment, to a fine.

(2) A person guilty of an offence under paragraph (d), (f), (h) or (n) of subsection (1) above, or of an offence under paragraph (e) of that subsection consisting of contravening a requirement imposed by an inspector under s 20, shall be liable on summary conviction to a fine not exceeding level 5 on the standard scale.

(2A) A person guilty of an offence under subsection (1)(g) or (o) above shall be liable–

(a) on summary conviction, to imprisonment for a term not exceeding six months, or a fine not exceeding £ 20,000, or both;

(b) on conviction, on indictment, to imprisonment for a term not exceeding two years, or a fine, or both.

(3) Subject to any provision made by virtue of s 15(6)(d) or (e) or by virtue of paragraph 2(2) of Schedule 3, a person guilty of an offence under subsection (1) above not falling within subsections (1A), (2) or (2A) above, or of an offence under any of the existing statutory provisions, being an offence for which no other penalty is specified, shall be liable–

(a) on summary conviction, to a fine not exceeding the prescribed sum;

(b) on conviction on indictment–

(i) if the offence is one to which this sub-paragraph applies, to imprisonment for a term not exceeding two years, or a fine, or both;

(ii) if the offence is not one to which the preceding sub-paragraph applies, to a fine.

(4) Subsection (3)(b)(i) above applies to the following offences–

(a) an offence consisting of contravening any of the relevant statutory provisions by doing otherwise than under the authority of a licence issued by the Executive something for the doing of which such a licence is necessary under the relevant statutory provisions;

(b) an offence consisting of contravening a term of or a condition or restriction attached to any such licence as is mentioned in the preceding paragraph;

(c) an offence consisting of acquiring or attempting to acquire, possessing or using an explosive article or substance (within the meaning of any of the relevant statutory provisions) in contravention of any of the relevant statutory provisions;

...

(e) an offence under subsection (1)(j) above.

– – –

XIII SENTENCING POLICY

There had been some concern that courts might not be imposing fines of sufficient severity for the magnitude of health and safety offences. The following case was, therefore, of considerable importance:

R v HOWE & SON (ENGINEERS) LTD [1999] 2 All ER 249

The case came to the Court of Appeal, Criminal Division, because the appellant employer contended that the fine, amounting to £48,000 (with a further £7,500 costs) imposed by the trial judge in the Crown Court at Bristol, was excessive. The appellant had been convicted on a number of counts under the 1974 Act, the Electricity at Work Regulations 1989 and the Management of Health and Safety at Work Regulations 1992. The prosecution came about as a result of the death by electrocution of an employee of the appellant. At the time of the fatal accident, the employee was cleaning the appellant's factory. The cleaning operation caused a lot of water to accumulate on the floor. A vacuum machine (a Freddy) was used to remove the water. The appellant had purchased the cleaner second hand. It became live while the employee was holding it. The employee was certified dead on arrival at hospital. The inspector who visited the premises after the accident found that the immediate cause of the accident was that the cable to the machine was damaged. This damage would have been visible on inspection prior to the accident. In addition the wall-mounted socket into which the 13 amp cable was plugged was fitted with 32 amp fuses which had been bridged by fuse wire! It was evident that the circuit breaker (RDC) had been deliberately interfered with to render it inoperable. A fitter, employed by electrical contractors, who had done work at the premises on a number of occasions, had advised the appellant that the supply was overloaded. There was a dispute between the appellant and the fitter as to who had disabled the RDC. At the trial the prosecution accepted the appellant's plea of not guilty of interfering with the RDC and sentencing was on that basis. However, in giving judgment in the appeal, Scott Baker J noted that the appellant had failed to check whether the system was working. He also noted that the company was a small one, making a net profit of approximately £27,000 pa. It paid no dividends and neither of the working directors received more than £20,000 pa salary, though they, like the employees, received a Christmas bonus. There was no pension scheme and no company car. Following the accident, the appellant had spent £15,000 on a complete overhaul of its electrical system. Scott Baker J continued at p 263:

> We are not persuaded that the size of the company and its lack of ability to provide its own specialist safety and electrical personnel mitigates these offences. The means of the company is, on the other hand a very material factor to the amount of the fine. As to the level of fines imposed generally for

offences of this nature, it is the view of each member of this court that they are too low and therefore not an appropriate yardstick for determining the level of fine in the present case.

...

We accept that this is not a case where safety regulations have been deliberately flouted for reasons of economy. Had they been this would have been a seriously aggravating feature.

...

In the early 1990s Parliament introduced the exemplary maximum fine of £20,000 for breach of the general duties under ss 2 to 6 of the Act where the offence is dealt with summarily. Following this the average fine in the magistrates' courts per offence prosecuted for breaches of the general duties increased from £844 to £2,110 in 1992/93 and has since risen to £6,223 but is still less than one-third of the maximum. And almost half the fines in magistrates' courts for the offences in 1997/98 was below one-quarter of the maximum of £20,000. In the Crown Court, where the level of fine is unlimited, the 1997/98 average fine per offence was £17,768.

Disquiet has been expressed in several quarters that the level of fine for health and safety offences is too low. We think there is force in this and that the figures with which we have been supplied support the concern. There has been increasing recognition in recent years of the seriousness of health and safety offences. The circumstances of individual cases will, of course, vary almost infinitely and very few cases have reached this court. Accordingly it is difficult for judges and magistrates, who only rarely deal with these cases, to have an instinctive feel for the appropriate level of penalty.

We shall endeavour to outline some of the relevant factors that should be taken into account. In doing so we emphasise that it is impossible to lay down any tariff or to say that the fine should bear any specific relationship to the turnover or net profit of the defendant. Each case must be dealt with according to its own particular circumstances.

In assessing the gravity of the breach it is often helpful to look at how far short of the appropriate standard the defendant fell in failing to meet the reasonably practicable test.

Next, it is often a matter of chance whether death or serious injury results from even a serious breach. Generally where death is the consequence of a criminal act it is regarded as an aggravating feature of the offence. The penalty should reflect public disquiet at the unnecessary loss of life.

Financial profit can often be made at the expense of proper action to protect employees and the public. Cost cutting is a crucial tool in achieving a competitive edge. A deliberate breach of the health and safety legislation with a view to profit seriously aggravates the offence.

There is some evidence that safety standards in small organisations may generally be lower than in larger ones and that proportionately more accidents occur in companies with less than 50 employees than those with a large staff. We wish to emphasise that the standard of care imposed by the legislation is the same regardless of the size of the company. A man who, for example, works with a circular saw should be no less safe if he works for company A than for company B. The size of a company and its financial strength or weakness cannot affect the degree of care that is required in matters of safety. Otherwise the employee of a small concern would be liable to find himself at greater risk than the employee of a large one. How an individual company discharges its health and safety obligations will depend on the particular circumstances. A large organisation with a health and safety department will approach matters differently from a smaller one with perhaps one safety officer or none at all. Those organisations who do not have their own expertise in-house can obtain it, if necessary by seeking assistance from the HSE.

Other matters that may be relevant to sentence are the degree of risk and extent of the danger created by the offence, the extent of the breach or breaches, for example, whether it was an isolated incident or continued over a period and importantly, the defendant's resources and the effect of the fine on its business.

Particular aggravating features will include (1) a failure to heed warnings and (2) where the defendant has deliberately profited financially from a failure to take necessary health and safety steps or specifically run a risk to save money.

Particular mitigating features will include (1) prompt admission of responsibility and a timely plea of guilty, (2) steps to remedy deficiencies after they are drawn to the defendant's attention and (3) a good safety record.

Any fine should reflect not only the gravity of the offence but also the means of the offender, and this applies just as much to corporate defendants as to any other (see s 18(3) of the Criminal Justice Act 1991). Difficulty is sometimes found in obtaining timely and accurate information about a corporate defendant's means. The starting point is its annual accounts. If a defendant company wishes to make any submission to the court about its ability to pay a fine it should supply copies of its accounts and any other financial information on which it intends to rely in good time before the hearing both to the court and to the prosecution ...

The objective of prosecutions for health and safety offences in the workplace is to achieve a safe environment for those who work there and for other members of the public who may be affected. A fine needs to be large enough to bring that message home where the defendant is a company not only to those who manage it but also to its shareholders.

Mr Dixey argues that in the present case the fine should not be so large as to imperil the earnings of employees or create a risk of bankruptcy. Whilst in general we accept that submission, as Rose LJ observed in argument there may be cases were the offences are so serious that the defendant ought not to be in business. That, however, is not this case.

....

In our judgment, the learned judge in the present case gave inadequate weight to the financial position of the appellant. It may well be that he did so because such financial information as he had was not supplied until the very last moment. This is a small company with limited resources ... In our judgment, an appropriate fine was, in the circumstances, one totalling £15,000 ...

– – –

This decision has been commented on favourably by the HSC:

REVITALISING HEALTH AND SAFETY, CONSULTATIVE DOCUMENT, JULY 1999

At p 21:

53 The 1998 *'Howe'* judgment of the Court of Appeal which expressed disquiet over the low level of health and safety fines and set out observations on how the courts should reach more realistic sentencing decisions, was encouraging. This judgement has contributed to some landmark fines: a construction company was fined £1.2 million and their tunnelling sub-contractors were fined £500,000 when an underground tunnel collapsed at Heathrow in the UK's worst ever civil engineering disaster, though miraculously no one was killed. Earlier this year, during the case of R *v Rollco Screw and Rivet Co Ltd and Others, The Times*, 29 April (1999)), the Lord Chief Justice gave unqualified support to the observations of the *Howe* judgment, concluding that courts should ensure that the financial penalties imposed on those convicted under the Health and Safety at Work etc Act 1974 were appropriate to mark the gravity of the case.

54 More needs to be done to encourage unscrupulous employers to take their health and safety responsibility seriously. The Government is considering whether to make imprisonment available to the courts for all health and safety offences, and whether the maximum fine for breaches on summary conviction should be increased from the present level of £20,000 for offences under the 1974 Act.

– – –

In December 1999, a Private Member's Bill was introduced to make new provision about the prosecution and punishment of offences under the Health and Safety at Work Act 1974. It is the intention of the Bill to amend the 1974 Act by substituting for the present s 33(1)–(4) set out above the penalties provided for in Schedule 1 of the Bill. This Schedule is intended to be Schedule 6(A) of the 1974 Act:

HEALTH AND SAFETY AT WORK (OFFENCES) BILL

SCHEDULE 1

New Schedule 6A to the Health and Safety at Work etc Act 1974

Schedule 6A

Prosecution and punishment of offences

Item	Offence	Mode of trial	Penalty on summary conviction	Penalty on conviction on indictment
1	An offence under s 33(1)(a) consisting of the failure of a person to discharge a duty to which he is subject by virtue of ss 2–6	Either way	Imprisonment for a term not exceeding six months, a fine not exceeding £20,000, or both	Imprisonment for a term not exceeding two years, a fine, or both
2	An offence under s 33(1)(a) consisting of the failure of a person to discharge a duty to which he is subject by virtue of s 7	Either way	Imprisonment for a term not exceeding six months, a fine not exceeding the statutory maximum, or both	Imprisonment for a term not exceeding two years, a fine, or both
3	An offence under s 33(1)(b) consisting of a contravention of s 8	Either way	Imprisonment for a term not exceeding six months, a fine not exceeding £20,000, or both	Imprisonment for a term not exceeding two years, a fine, or both
4	An offence under s 33(1)(b) consisting of a contravention of s 9	Either way	A fine not exceeding £20,000	A fine
5	An offence under s 33(1)(c)	Either way	Imprisonment for a term not exceeding six months, a fine not exceeding £20,000, or both	Imprisonment for a term not exceeding two years, a fine, or both
6	An offence under s 33(1)(d)	Summary only	A fine not exceeding level 5 on the standard scale	
7	An offence under s 33(1)(e), (f) or (g)	Either way	Imprisonment for a term not exceeding six months, a fine not exceeding £20,000, or both	Imprisonment for a term not exceeding two years, a fine, or both
8	An offence under s 33(1)(h)	Summary only	Imprisonment for a term not exceeding six months, a fine not exceeding level 5 on the standard scale, or both	

9	An offence under s 33(1)(i)	Either way	A fine not exceeding the statutory maximum	A fine
10	An offence under s 33(1)(j)	Either way	Imprisonment for a term not exceeding six months, a fine not exceeding the statutory maximum, or both	Imprisonment for a term not exceeding two years, a fine, or both
11	An offence under s 33(1)(k), (l) or (m)	Either way	Imprisonment for a term not exceeding six months, a fine not exceeding £20,000, or both	Imprisonment for a term not exceeding two years, a fine, or both
12	An offence under s 33(1)(n)	Summary only	A fine not exceeding level 5 on the standard scale	
13	An offence under s 33(1)(o)	Either way	Imprisonment for a term not exceeding six months, a fine not exceeding £20,000, or both	Imprisonment for a term not exceeding two years, a fine, or both
14	An offence under any of the existing statutory provisions, being an offence for which no other penalty is specified	Either way	Imprisonment for a term not exceeding six months, a fine not exceeding £20,000, or both	Imprisonment for a term not exceeding two years, a fine, or both

POSTSCRIPT

At the time of writing, the Government is undertaking a strategic appraisal of the health and safety system, to mark the 25th anniversary of the implementation of the Health and Safety at Work Act 1974. It is too early to say what the outcome of this review will be. However, a recent consultative document (referred to below in Chapter 13) indicates that steps may be taken to increase the role of the worker, either by strengthening the existing safety representative system, or by other means.

CHAPTER 11

THE GENERAL DUTIES

INTRODUCTION

This chapter will consider the general duties in ss 2–9 of the Health and Safety at Work Act 1974, the case law on these duties and other sections of the Act which impose liability on or restrict the liability of particular categories of person.

I DUTIES ON THE EMPLOYER

Section 2(1) of the Act imposes a broad general duty on the employer for the protection of that organisation's own employees and subsections 2–7 spell out the employer's obligations in further detail. Section 3 is concerned with the obligations imposed on the employer (and the self-employed businessman) to ensure the safety of persons not in their employment. These two sections are arguably the most important of the general duties. Section 2 reflects the concern which the law has always had for the safety of persons while in employment; s 3 reflects the novel, but important, purpose of the 1974 Act of protecting the whole workforce and the public from the risks created by the activities of an organisation. The important case of *R v Swan Hunter Shipbuilders Ltd and Telemeter Installations Ltd* (1981)[1] shows the relationship between ss 2 and 3:

Section 2

General duties of employers to their employees

(1) It shall be the duty of every employer to ensure, so far as is reasonably practicable, the health, safety and welfare at work of all his employees.

(2) Without prejudice to the generality of an employer's duty under the preceding subsection, the matters to which that duty extends include in particular–

　　(a) the provision and maintenance of plant and systems of work that are, so far as is reasonably practicable, safe and without risks to health;

　　(b) arrangements for ensuring, so far as is reasonably practicable, safety and absence of risks to health in connection with the use, handling, storage and transport of articles and substances;

1　[1981] IRLR 403.

(c) the provision of such information, instruction, training and supervision as is necessary to ensure, so far as is reasonably practicable, the health and safety at work of his employees;

(d) so far as is reasonably practicable as regards any place of work under the employer's control, the maintenance of it in a condition that is safe and without risks to health and the provision and maintenance of means of access to and egress from it that are safe and without such risks;

(e) the provision and maintenance of a working environment for his employees that is, so far as is reasonably practicable, safe, without risks to health, and adequate as regards facilities and arrangements for their welfare at work.

(3) Except in such cases as may be prescribed, it shall be the duty of every employer to prepare and as often as may be appropriate revise a written statement of his general policy with respect to the health and safety at work of his employees and the organisation and arrangements for the time being in force for carrying out that policy, and to bring the statement and any revision of it to the notice of all of his employees.

Section 3

General duties of employers and self-employed to persons other than their employees

(1) It shall be the duty of every employer to conduct his undertaking in such a way as to ensure, so far as is reasonably practicable, that persons not in his employment who may be affected thereby are not thereby exposed to risks to their health or safety.

(2) It shall be the duty of every self-employed person to conduct his undertaking in such a way as to ensure, so far as is reasonably practicable, that he and other persons (not being his employees) who may be affected thereby are not thereby exposed to risks to their health or safety.

(3) In such cases as may be prescribed, it shall be the duty of every employer and every self-employed person, in the prescribed circumstances and in the prescribed manner, to give to persons (not being his employees) who may be affected by the way in which he conducts his undertaking the prescribed information about such aspects of the way in which he conducts his undertaking as might affect their health or safety.

– – –

Relationship between s 2 and s 3 duties

In the following case, the Court of Appeal held that an employer needed to provide instructions to visiting workers not only to ensure their safety, but also to ensure the safety of its own employees.

R v SWAN HUNTER SHIPBUILDERS LTD AND
TELEMETER INSTALLATIONS LTD [1981] IRLR 403

The facts are set out in the judgment of Dunn LJ, given in the Court of Appeal, beginning at p 404:

> During 1976 *HMS Glasgow* was under construction by Swan Hunter Shipbuilders Ltd at their Neptune Yard on the River Tyne. By September she had reached the stage of being fitted out and moored alongside the jetty.
>
> At 7.50 on the morning of Thursday 25.9.76, a welder in G4 – a small compartment on the lowest deck forward of the bridge – without any negligence on his part struck his arc with his welding torch and, instantly a fierce fire started. Of some 11 men down below deck only three got out.
>
> The reason for this intense fire and the rapidity with which it spread was that the atmosphere had become oxygen enriched to the extent of 45%, which was more than double the normal. It was accepted that the enrichment came from the escape of oxygen from a hose left overnight in Deck G3 by a Mr Burton.
> ...
>
> In relation to this enrichment of the atmosphere in G4, it was accepted firstly that the hose which caused the trouble on the Thursday morning must have been connected to a manifold and that the relevant tap must have been turned on or left on, and everyone was agreed that that ought not have been the case. Secondly, the working end was in G3, a place where all are agreed it ought not to have been for the purpose of the work which was being carried out there ...
> ...
>
> On the day shift there were about 1,000 workmen, most of them ex-employees of Swan Hunter. Many of them were employed by persons other than Swan Hunter: contractors such as Marriott and subcontractors of Marriott's such as Telemeter. In the circumstances, it was inevitable that Swan Hunter employees were working side by side with workers from other companies, contractors and subcontractors. The appellants knew this and there was no dispute as to the position.
> ...
>
> The charges laid against Swan Hunter and Telemeter (who pleaded guilty) were under ss 2 and 3 of the Health and Safety at Work Act 1974. We were told that this was the first occasion when charges under the Act had been tried in the Crown Court before a jury, and this is the first case in which this court has had to consider the provisions of the Act.
> ...
>
> The principal question of law raised by the appeal is whether the duty imposed on Swan Hunter under these sections includes the duty to provide the employees of Telemeter, firstly, with information as to the danger of an oxygen enriched atmosphere, and secondly, with such instructions as might be necessary to ensure the safety of the workers on board *HMS Glasgow*, including the employees of Swan Hunter and Telemeter.
>
> The dangers of oxygen-enriched atmosphere were well known to Swan Hunter, especially to Mr Douglas, who was the Chief Safety Officer, a Director of Swan Hunter and the Chief Executive Officer of a subsidiary of Swan

Hunter, Swan Hunter Training and Safety Company Ltd. Two fatal fires caused by oxygen enrichment, one in 1969 and the other in 1970, had convinced Mr Douglas that people were not really aware of the insidious nature of the dangers of an oxygen enriched atmosphere. There was no smell, no noise, no discomfort. So, he embarked upon a programme of disseminating knowledge of oxygen and the risks involved in its use. With this in mind, he caused to be compiled a 'Blue Book' of instructions for all users of fuel and oxygen. The user group aimed at was some 2,500 employees of Swan Hunter, though originally 14,000 copies of the book were made. Copies of the book were also issued to supervisors and managers. Another set of instructions, which contained all that was in the blue book and even more was sent to the management. The book was re-issued from time to time, finally in November 1975, so far as this case is concerned. Apart from that it was left to the shipyards to requisition such copies as they might require.

...

The essence of the case for the Crown was that the distribution or mailing list of the blue book was not wide enough and did not include Telemeter employees. This was the principal matter in dispute, because it was admitted that the blue book was not distributed to subcontractors working on board the vessel. There was also introduced by Swan Hunter a system of checks carried out by night patrolmen which was designed to ensure that the instructions in the blue book were carried out.

At the conclusion of the case for the Crown a submission was made on behalf of Swan Hunter that on a true construction of ss 2 and 3, no duty lay upon them to provide information or instruction to the employees of Telemeter, or indeed to any employees other than their own. The judge ruled against this submission and the main ground of the appeal is that as a matter of law the judge was wrong.

Mr Lawton, for Swan Hunter, submitted that, in relation to s 2(2)(a), the concept of a safe system of work is brought into the statutory field for the first time. He submits that this is a penal statute and should be construed strictly, and that *prima facie*, a safe system of work involves only the employees of the particular employer and does not extend to the instruction of persons other than employees. It was submitted that the subcontractors were not only under a duty to their own employees under the Act of 1974, but also under a duty, by reason of regulation 58(3) of the Shipbuilding Regulations 1960. That regulation, so far as is material, provides that 'Moveable pipes or hoses used for conveying oxygen or inflammable gas or vapour shall, in the case of a *vessel* undergoing construction, be brought to the topmost completed deck or, in the case of a *vessel* undergoing repair, to a weather deck or in either case, to some other place of safety which is adequately ventilated to prevent any dangerous concentration of gas or fumes'.

So it was submitted that Telemeter being under that duty, it would be wrong to hold that Swan Hunter were under a duty to Telemeter employees by reason of the provision of s 2(2)(a). It was said that to hold that the duty under s 2(2)(a) extended to persons other than the employees of Swan Hunter would place an intolerable burden on all contractors and subcontractors working in shipyards where there are many tradesmen working who are employed by different employers.

So far as subsection (2)(c) is concerned, it was submitted that an employer had no right to instruct other employees and that therefore the duty under (c) to provide information, instruction and training could not extend to employees of other undertakings. Those arguments were repeated in relation to s 3(1).

A further argument was deployed which depended on the specific duty in subsection (3) of that section, namely, to give information in prescribed cases. It was submitted that if the general duty under subsection (1) was wide enough to include the giving of information, then subsection (3) was unnecessary. Subsection (3) it was said limited the giving of information to prescribed cases. If subsection (1) included the giving of information in the words 'to conduct his undertaking in such a way', then one would have expected subsection (3) to start with the words 'Without prejudice to the foregoing', or some such phraseology. It was submitted that, in the absence of such words, the duty to give information under s 3 was confined to the prescribed cases.

Reliance was placed in support of this submission on *Aitchison v Howard Doris Ltd* (1979).[2] That was a case which went to the High Court on a case stated from a Sheriff. It was a prosecution under s 3(1). The High Court in giving its opinion, at p 23, said:

'This is a penal statute which must be strictly construed; and s 4 very clearly defines not only the class of persons to whom the duty is owed, but also the matters to which the duties relate, one of which is access. If the legislature had intended that the main contractor should be under a duty to take care that means of access to or from premises controlled by another party should be guilty of an offence for which the controller was primarily responsible, we think that it would have been more clearly spelled out. We find it significant that the duty imposed by s 2(2)(d) on employers *quoad* safe means of access for their own employees is restricted to "any place of work under the employer's control". We see grave difficulties in the conductor of an undertaking exercising powers over another party who controls premises upon which the undertaking is going on. In this complaint, it is not libelled that the accused, the main contractor, did have control of the ships where the means of access is libelled as defective. In our opinion, the liability for defective access is primarily upon the party who directly controls that access as defined in s 4. If, therefore, it had been libelled that the main contractor was in control of the vessels between which the access existed, in our opinion the proper charging section would have been s 4. It is not so libelled, and we add, *obiter*, that, even if it had been libelled that the main contractor was not in control of the vessels between which this alleged defective access existed, we are of opinion that s 3 was not intended to impose upon the main contractor a duty to control, not in respect of his own employees but in respect of other persons not in his employment, the safety of an access which was under the direct control of a third party.'

2   (1979) Scots Law Times 22.

It was submitted that by analogy in this case, this being a penal statute a strict and narrow construction should be put on s 3. As Mr Justice Lincoln commented in the course of argument, in paragraph (d) of subsection (2) of s 2, reasonable practicability is limited to a place of work under the employer's control. There is no such limitation in the other paragraphs of subsection (2) and, in any event, in this case *HMS Glasgow* was under the control of Swan Hunter.

...

So far as s 3 was concerned, Mr Potts [counsel] submitted that subsection (1) simply lays down in statutory form the situation which existed prior to the passing of the Act in a general way. Subsection (3), he submitted, was limited to dealing with certain situations, and, in those situations only prescribed information was to be given to persons outside the employment of the contractors conducting the undertaking. Subsection (3) envisages regulation and, in Mr Potts' submission, there was no inconsistency between the judge's interpretation of subsection (1) and subsection (3), which, in his submission, was quite separate from it. He points out that the words in subsection (1), 'It shall be the duty of every employer to conduct his undertaking in such a way as to ensure ... ' were very wide in terms and quite apt to cover the provision of information and instruction.

We accept the submission of Mr Potts so far as the construction of the sections is concerned. In our view the duties are all covered by the general duty in subsection (1) of s 2: 'It shall be the duty of every employer to ensure, so far as is reasonably practicable, the health, safety and welfare at work of all his employees.' As the judge said, that is a strict duty. If the provision of a safe system of work for the benefit of his own employees involves information and instruction as to potential dangers being given to persons other than the employer's own employees, then the employer is under a duty to provide such information and instruction. His protection is contained in the words 'so far as is reasonably practicable' which appear in all the relevant provisions. The onus is on the defendants to prove on a balance of probabilities that it was not reasonably practicable in the particular circumstances of the case.

As the judge pointed out in relation to paragraph (c) of subsection (2), if another employer obstructs the giving of the necessary information or instruction, then that employer would himself be guilty of an offence under s 36 of the Act ...

– – –

Does s 2 apply when no one is at work?

In the following case, the Divisional Court found that s 2 required an employer to ensure that the workplace, and plant and equipment there, was safe at all times. It was not sufficient for it to be safe during the period that employees were at work.

BOLTON METROPOLITAN BOROUGH COUNCIL
v MALROD INSULATIONS LTD [1993] IRLR 274

The facts are sufficiently stated in the following extracts from the judgment of Tudor Evans J in the Divisional Court of the Queen's Bench Division, beginning at p 274:

> This is a prosecutor's appeal by case stated from the decision of Mr Recorder Clifton sitting at the Crown Court at Bolton on 25 May 1991. The Recorder allowed the appeal of the respondent against a conviction on 4 December 1990 by justices sitting at the Bolton Magistrates' Court. The information was laid down on 24 May 1990 by the appellant alleging that the respondent, at the premises of Ingersoll Rand Ltd in Bolton, failed on 21 November 1989 to discharge a duty to which it was subject by s 2(1) and s 2(2) of the Health and Safety at Work Act 1974.
>
> ...
>
> The respondent was a contractor engaged to strip asbestos insulation from the premises of Ingersoll Rand Ltd. The decontamination unit, which was a necessary safety measure for the work of removing asbestos, was operated by electrical current. Another safety feature of the plant was the provision of an enclosure involving an airlock for the use of the men in the work. The undisputed evidence before the Recorder was that on 21 November 1989, the decontamination unit was inspected by Mr Shaw who was employed as a technical assistant by the Environmental Health Services of the Bolton Metropolitan Borough Council. It was his evidence that there were four defects in the electrical equipment supplying current to the unit. At the time of the inspection, the work of stripping the asbestos had not yet begun. If the unit had passed the inspection, smoke tests on the enclosure to which I have already referred would have been carried out on 22 November in order to prevent any contamination and to make sure that the enclosure was not leaking. If these tests were found to have been successful, the work of stripping the asbestos would have begun on that day.
>
> ...
>
> The appellant called a substantial body of evidence. I shall refer to parts of it later. At the end of the case for the prosecution, the Recorder upheld a submission that there was no case to answer. The essence of the submission was that upon a proper construction of the statute, before the respondent could be found guilty of the offence charged, their employees had in fact to be at work in the removal of the asbestos, whereas on the evidence at the time of the alleged offence, no one was at work. It was submitted that the statutory duty only arose when the respondent's employees were at work. The appellant contended that the statutory duty arose when the plant was provided. The Recorder summarised the contention of the appellant in paragraph 60 of the case which encapsulates the appellant's argument before us:
>
> ... 'It is not the fact of men being at work while in the course of employment which creates the offence. The Act must protect the employee who comes to work tomorrow.'
>
> ...

On behalf of the respondent, Mr King QC repeated the submission that, as a matter of construction of the statutory language, the duty can arise only when men are at work. Mr King pointed to s 22 of the Act as indicating that there is a statutory power to prohibit the use of unsafe plant when men are not at work and submitted that this power suggests that the narrow construction of the relevant sections for which he contended is the proper construction. It is not necessary for me to repeat the language of s 22. It confers upon inspectors who have been appointed under s 19 of the Act to secure the enforcement of the statutory provisions a power to serve a notice prohibiting, if it is deemed necessary with immediate effect, activities which are or are likely to be carried on and which involve or may involve a risk of serious personal injury. Counsel submitted that the fact that an inspector may act in advance to stop an activity being carried out, supports his contention that a breach of s 2(1) and s 2(2) can exist only when employees are at work.

...

In my opinion, the duty within s 2 is not confined to employees who are engaged in a specific process. The duty applies to 'all employees' of an employer.

...

With respect to the duty arising under s 2(2), it seems to me that the subsection creates a duty to provide plant which is safe, subject to the question of reasonable practicability. 'To provide', in the relevant code of legislation including the Factories Act 1961, means 'to supply or to make available'. There is a long standing authority to this effect: see, for example, *Norris v Syndic Manufacturing Co* (1952),[3] a case concerned with s 119 of the Factories Act 1937, where Romer LJ said at p 144:

> The primary meaning of the word 'provide' is to 'furnish' or 'supply' ...

Thus, in cases where there is a statutory duty to provide, if an employer makes available plant which is not safe there will be a breach of duty and that result follows even though the unsafe plant in question has not been used or is not being used. If, for example, an employer had a statutory duty to provide goggles and he made them available on a site, but before they could be used a safety inspector found that they were defective, he would be able to institute proceedings even though the goggles had not been used. The question for decision is whether there is anything in the language of s 2(2)(a) which leads to a different result. I agree that the duty in s 2(1) is imported in subsection (2) by the words in the subsection: 'Without prejudice to the generality of a employer's duty under the preceding subsection, the matters to which that duty extends ...' But in my view the use of the words 'at work' cannot on any common sense basis mean that the duty to provide safe plant arises only when the men are actually at work. Such a construction would lead to the conclusion that the duty would come to life when the employees reported for work in the morning, that it would exist through the working day but that it would then fall into limbo at the end of the day only to be revived next morning. In this state of affairs, if a safety inspector were to come onto a site after the end of the working day and find a

3   [1952] 2 QB 135.

defect in the plant, he would be powerless to institute proceedings for breach of duty, because employees were not actually at work.

In my opinion, if it had been intended to produce a result so out of keeping with the general interpretation of the safety provisions of the code of legislation, Parliament would have said so in plain language. In my opinion, s 2 creates a duty to ensure that there is safety when the employees come to work and, specifically in relation to the alleged facts of this case, that the plant (the decontamination unit) will be safe for use when the employees come to use it. In my opinion, the appellant's argument that the Act is designed to ensure that the plant is safe so that it protects, as counsel for the appellant put it, the employee who comes to work tomorrow is well founded. I may add that, in my opinion the powers existing under s 22 do nothing to detract from this conclusion.

– – –

Relevance of s 2(2)

Both the cases cited have involved one or more of the paragraphs of s 2(2), as well, in the *Swan Hunter* case, as s 2(1). Indeed, as was noted in the previous chapter, it has been questioned in an appeal against an improvement notice whether a criminal case can be founded on s 2(1) alone *(West Bromwich Building Society v Townsend)* (1983);[4] this view is difficult to maintain, however, because, as will be seen below, there have been several successful prosecutions which rested on the similar very general duty in s 3(1). Moreover, s 2(2) opens with the words 'Without prejudice to the generality of an employer's duty under the preceding subsection', indicating that the matters set out in s 2(2) provide examples of the duty under s 2(1), but do not exhaust that section. The paragraphs within s 2(2) cover a wide range of matters, some of which are novel and some well tried within earlier legislation:

- *Paragraph (a)*, covering provision and maintenance of plant carries forward protective provisions, which featured largely in earlier legislation, particularly the Factories Acts, but is novel, in that it extends the protection to *systems of work*;

- *Paragraph (b)*, relating to handling, storage and transport of articles and substances was not only novel; it carried the Act beyond the framework envisaged by the Robens Committee, whose brief did not extend to matters relating to transport;

- *Paragraph (c)*, which featured so importantly in the *Swan Hunter* case, is at the core of the Act, concerned not primarily with the working environment, but with human behaviour in the working environment,

---

4   [1983] ICR 257.

requiring the employer to inform, instruct, train and supervise both his own employees and other workers who might, by their behaviour endanger his employees;

- *Paragraph (d),* dealing with safe means of access to and egress from the place of work, reflects s 29(1) of the Factories Act 1961, but extends to all workplaces and, unlike s 29(1) (now repealed), cannot found a civil action;

- *Paragraph (e),* the provision and maintenance of a safe working environment: the limits of this 'mopping up' provision are not entirely clear, but it is possible that it might, as it includes welfare arrangements, include coverage of protection against mental stress, such as might be caused by overwork, or harassment by fellow workers.

Section 2(3): the safety policy

The absolute requirement that organisations prepare a safety policy and publish it to their employees was one of the novel duties imposed by the 1974 Act. The subsection is somewhat opaque, but there are, in fact three requirements:

(a) a safety policy – a statement of the employer's philosophy and commitment to safety;

(b) a statement of the organisation and arrangements for carrying out that policy – in the hierarchical management structures of the 1970s, employers tended to comply with this provision by providing a 'family tree', showing the line management chain from the shop floor to the board of directors. Such structures are probably rare today, now that the norm is for 'flatter' management structures, with devolved budgets;

(c) the arrangements for carrying out the policy.

In the 1970s, the expectation was that the original policy would be drawn up by management in consultation with employees. The section also required employers to revise the policy as necessary and bring revisions to the notice of their employees.

The requirement to set out safety arrangements can, with hindsight, be seen to be the most significant requirement of the subsection: it is the prototype for the later 'safety case' regulations, though none of the subsequent regulations, including the risk assessment Regulation in the Management of Health and Safety at Work Regulations 1992, refers to this subsection.

The Employers' Health and Safety Policy Statements (Exceptions) Regulations 1975 exempt small organisations from the requirement to write a safety policy. These regulations were interpreted in the following case.

OSBORNE v BILL TAYLOR OF HUYTON LTD [1982] ICR 168

The report is of the hearing before the Divisional Court of the Queen's Bench Division. The judgment cited is that of Ormrod LJ and the extracts quoted begin at p 172:

> This is an appeal by way of case stated by the prosecutor from a decision of the justices sitting at St Helens on 5 March 1981, whereby they dismissed a summons under s 33(1)(g) of the Health and Safety at Work Act 1974, the allegation being that the defendant employers failed to comply with a so called improvement notice under s 21 of the Health and Safety at Work Act 1974, which required the employers to remedy a contravention of s 2(3) of the Act of 1974 by 1 December 1980.

> The contravention relied upon was a failure to prepare an adequate written statement of the employers' general policy with respect to the health and safety at work of employees and the organisation and arrangements for the time being in force for carrying out that policy.

> The justices decided that the employers were entitled to take advantage of an exception to that obligation created by regulation 2 of the Employers' Health and Safety Policy Statements (Exceptions) Regulations 1975. That Regulation, in a sentence, exempts employers who carry on an undertaking in which, for the time being, less than five employees are employed.
> ...

> Two questions arise in this appeal. The first is as to the construction to be given to the word 'undertaking' in the Regulations and, secondly, to the phrase 'for the time being, he employs less than five employees'.

> The justices, having heard the evidence, came to the conclusion that the employers in this case were not carrying on an undertaking in which more than five employees were employed for the time being. The employers carry on the business of betting shops. It was contended by the employers that they carry on 31 separate betting offices connected by a central: (a) accounting system, (b) advisory service on security, (c) management training programme and (d) grading of premises and staff to determine levels of responsibility and salary. They argued that each individual betting shop was, for the purposes of the Regulations, an 'undertaking', whereas the prosecutor contended that the 'undertaking' was the running of all 31 betting shops combined.

> That is the first and most difficult point that we have to consider on this appeal. Speaking for myself, I find it a very difficult task to decide what the word 'undertaking' means in the Regulations. One can look at it this way. It is a little difficult to imagine a general statement of policy in the terms obviously envisaged by subsection (3) which could be applied in a sensible way to a series of separate betting shops scattered over, presumably the whole country. But the question still remains as to which of these contentions as to the meaning of 'undertaking' is correct.

> There is no definition of 'undertaking' in the Act of 1974 or in the Regulations of 1975, and the only two places in which the word occurs in the Act of 1974, as far as I know, are s 3, which relates to the duty of employers in relation to other persons not in his employment ... and in s 1(3).
> ...

The justices obviously gave great care to considering this extremely difficult question of construction, and in the case they say that they were of the opinion that the wording of regulation 2 is ambiguous and could support either view. They comment that the same difficulty would have arisen had the word 'premises' been used instead of 'undertaking', although I am bound to say I think it would have been much easier myself.

...

The view which I have formed is that in relation to that last expression of opinion the justices asked themselves the wrong question. It is not a question as to whether this particular betting shop was a distinct place of work. The question is whether that betting shop was being carried on as a separate undertaking from the others or, putting it in a different way, whether the employers were in effect carrying on 31 separate businesses in separate betting shops or whether they were carrying on a single undertaking in 31 separate places. That is a matter ultimately of fact for the justices, although I recognise for myself that it is a very difficult question of fact for them to determine. However, it does seem clear from the way in which the case is stated that they have not actually asked themselves that precise question and it is upon the answer to that question that the outcome of this prosecution depends.

In those circumstances I think that we are obliged, though with great reluctance, to send the case back to the justices to consider whether, looking at the evidence as a whole, it is right to conclude that each of these betting shops is a separate undertaking so far as the Regulations are concerned or whether they are merely part of a single overall undertaking. That must be, in the last resort, a matter of fact and degree, requiring the exercise of judgment, and no doubt in the process of deciding that the justices will have regard to the overall purpose of the Act of 1974 itself.

On the second part of the case the question is whether the justices were right in holding that the employers are entitled to exemption from the obligations of s 2(3) by reason of the fact that for the time being they employ less than five persons in the business.

As to that, the justices' findings was that there was a total of five people employed on these premises, of whom only three were there at any one time, ie the manageress and a cashier, who were regular employees, together with a man who is referred to as 'Jock', who worked as and when he wished and was paid out of the betting office cash. But in addition to the manageress and cashier, two people were employed by the employers as itinerant relief personnel, who would stand in respectively for Mrs Knowles and for Mrs Jackson when they were away or off duty.

There are two points here: first of all, whether the man 'Jock' was to be treated as an employee for the purposes of the Act of 1974 or the Regulations of 1975. The justices found, so far as he was concerned, that there was a contract between him and the employers, although it was not a contract which one would normally regard, I think, as the contract of employment. They state in the case: '... there was an oral and implied contract of employment between [the employers] and the person known as "Jock"', and consequently they counted him in the head count of five.

But the real issue upon which they determined the case was as to whether the two stand in people were to be counted in the total of the number of employees employed. The answer to that question depends on the meaning to be given to the words 'for the time being'. It seems to me that there are only two possible meanings for that phrase. One is that it means the time at which the written statement of general policy is prepared or revised, and the alternative is 'at any one time'. For my part, I would favour the second of those alternative meanings and read regulation 2 as meaning 'any employer who carries on an undertaking in which, at any one time, he employs less than five employees'. That reading of it seems to me to be more in accordance with the general tenor of the Act of 1974 itself, which is clearly related to regulating the conditions of work and providing for the safety and health of employees in organisations where there are a reasonable number of employees whose health and safety have to be considered in so far as general arrangements are concerned. It would make more sense, to my mind, if the exception was read as being directed to a situation where at any one time there were less than five employees employed on the premises. That being so, for my part, I would agree with the justices' conclusion that the two stand in people should not be counted for the purposes of this regulation.

– – –

Worker involvement

Section 2(4)–(7) laid the foundation for employee involvement in the maintenance of health and safety at their workplace. These provisions will be considered in Chapter 13.

The ambit of s 3

Interpreting the general duty in s 3(1) has given rise to a number of important cases, seven of which are included here. Section 3(2), the duty of self-employed persons to themselves and others has not been litigated in the appeal courts. Nor has s 3(3) been relied on for the making of regulations concerning provision of information by an employer to persons not in their employment.

Several of the cases which have been appealed have concerned the meaning of the phrase 'conduct his undertaking' – querying whether an employer can be conducting the undertaking if his own workforce is not at work; questioning the extent to which the employer has to accept responsibility for the activities of the workforce of another. Two cases concerned whether an employer should be liable for the wrongdoing of an employee and another touched on whether the employer should be liable for the wrongdoing of a visiting worker. One case concerned the risks from which an employer ought to protect the public.

Conduct his undertaking

In the next case, the Court of Appeal found that an employer could be conducting its undertaking even at times when its own employees were not at work. This case was cited by the House of Lords with approval in *R v Associated Octel Ltd* (1996),[5] discussed below.

R v MARA [1987] IRLR 154

The following extracts are from the judgment of Parker LJ, given in the Court of Appeal, beginning at p 154:

> In December 1983 CMS entered into a contract with International Stores plc (IS) to clean their premises at High Street, Solihull, for a consideration of £94 a week plus VAT. The work to be done by CMS was carried out on weekday mornings before the store opened.
>
> ...
>
> Originally the contracted work involved the cleaning of the loading bay for the store, but the cleaning of such bay in the mornings was inconvenient because it was frequently interrupted by the arrival of delivery lorries. It was therefore agreed that cleaning of the loading bay should be removed from the ambit of the contract and the weekly charge reduced from £94 per week to £81.74 per week. At the time CMS agreed, at the request of IS, that their cleaning machines could be used by IS employees for the cleaning of the loading bay and perhaps also other cleaning and to the knowledge of the appellant they were so used.
>
> On Saturday afternoon, 10 .11.84, one Diarmid Cusack, an employee of IS, was using a CMS polisher/scrubber for cleaning the loading bay, when he was electrocuted due to the defective condition of the machine's cable.
>
> ...
>
> The particulars of the sole offence charged against the appellant were as follows:
>
> 'On the 10th day of November 1984 being a director of CMS Cleaning and Maintenance Services Limited, consented to or connived at the breach by the said company of its duty as an employer under s 3(1) of the Health and Safety at Work Act 1974, to conduct its undertaking in such a way as to ensure that persons not in its employment, namely employees of International Stores plc at High Street, Solihull, were not thereby exposed to risks to their health or safety or the said breach of duty by the company was due to his neglect.'
>
> The appellant pleaded not guilty, but was, on 27.2.86 convicted of that offence after a two-day trial before His Honour Judge Harrison-Hall and jury. He was fined £200.
>
> He now appeals against conviction.
>
> ...

---

5   [1996] 1 WLR 1543.

It was first submitted, somewhat tentatively, that the subsection had no application to undertakings consisting in the provision of services. There is no indication anywhere that the undertakings referred to were intended to be restricted in any way and we have no hesitation in rejecting this submission.

Next it was submitted that CMS were not, on Saturday morning, conducting their undertaking at all and that the only undertaking then being conducted was the undertaking of IS. Accordingly it was submitted that CMS were not in breach of the duty imposed by s 3(1) and the appellant could not therefore have consented to or connived at any such breach or caused any such breach by his neglect.

This submission has more force but, in our judgment, it is not permissible to treat the section as being applicable only when an undertaking is in the process of actively being carried on. A factory, for example, may shut down on Saturdays or Sundays for manufacturing purposes, but the employer may have the premises cleaned by a contractor over the weekend. If the contractor's employees are exposed to risks to health or safety because machinery is left insecure, or vats containing noxious substances are left unfenced, it is, in our judgment, clear that the factory owner is in breach of his duty under s 3(1). The way in which he conducts his undertaking is to close his factory for manufacturing purposes over the weekend and to have it cleaned during the shut down period. It would clearly be reasonably practicable to secure machinery and noxious vats, and on the plain wording of the section, he would be in breach of his duty if he failed to do so.

The undertaking of CMS was the provision of cleaning services. So far as IS is concerned, the way in which CMS conducted its undertaking was to do the cleaning on weekday mornings and leave its machines and other equipment on the premises in the intervals with permission for IS employees to use the same and knowledge that they would use the same.

That equipment included an unsafe cable. The failure to remove or replace cable was clearly a breach by CMS of its duty to its own employees imposed by s 2(2)(a) and (b) of the Act. The manner in which it carried out its undertaking was such that it had not provided and maintained plant which was, so far as reasonably practicable, safe, nor had it made arrangements for ensuring, so far as reasonably practicable, safety in connection with the use and handling of articles. Since the cable would or might be used by IS employees it follows that IS employees might be affected by, and exposed to, risks by the way in which CMS carried out its undertaking.

...

In our judgment, there was a clear case for the appellant to answer and he was rightly convicted.

– – –

The correctness of the following decision of the Court of Appeal was doubted by the House of Lords in *R v Associated Octel Ltd* (1996). Lord Hoffmann there took the view that whether an employer was conducting its undertaking in particular circumstances was a matter of fact for the court of first instance.

RMC ROADSTONE PRODUCTS LTD v JESTER [1994] IRLR 330

The following extracts are taken from the judgment in the Divisional Court of Mrs Justice Smith, beginning at p 331:

> The information laid by one of Her Majesty's Inspectors of Factories alleged that on 18 March 1992, at the premises of British Gypsum Ltd, Church Manorway, Erith, Kent, the appellant, being an employer within the meaning of the 1974 Act did fail to discharge a duty to which it was subject by virtue of s 3(1) of the Health and Safety at Work Act 1974, in that it failed to conduct its undertaking so as to ensure the safety of persons not in its employment, including Mr Hans Derhun (now deceased), who were removing roof sheets from an asbestos cement roof, whereby the appellant was guilty of an offence as provided by s 33(1) of the said Act and liable to a penalty as provided by s 33(3).

> At the hearing the magistrates convicted the appellant, but have stated a case for the consideration of this court. The magistrates made the following findings of fact.

> In 1991 Messrs Derhun and Poulter started a business called 'Iron Age' in which they did welding, metalwork and general repair work. Mr Poulter had never before been in such employment, although he had done his own household repairs. Mr Derhun was a skilled man and had some experience of working with heights, although always under supervision. He had always worn a safety harness. He had no previous experience of roof work.

> ... Mr Sibley, on behalf of the appellant, invited Iron Age to tender for various contracts, which they successfully did. One item of work was to replace some broken asbestos sheets in the side of a transfer tower. Originally it was intended that the appellant should obtain some new sheets, but Mr Derhun suggested that use might be made of some old sheets which formed part of the roof of the disused factory of British Gypsum adjacent to the appellant's premises. Mr Sibley obtained permission from British Gypsum for eight sheets to be removed from the roof of a loading bay. They were about 16 feet above ground.
> ...

> On 18 March 1992, Messrs Derhun and Poulter returned to the site, bringing a single scaffold board from the appellant's premises. They also brought the front-loading shovel, which they climbed upon and used as a means of access to the roof. The work began of cropping the securing bolts and releasing the sheets. Initially both men were working on the roof itself. Mr Poulter worked on the part of the roof where the purlin bolts protruded. Mr Derhun did likewise, but he also used the scaffold board. Mr Poulter then climbed into the bucket of the shovel to receive the sheets and lower them to the ground. Mr Derhun stayed on the roof. As they were putting the last sheet into the bucket Mr Derhun fell through the skylight to the ground below and suffered fatal injuries. Precisely what had happened to lead to the accident was not known.

> The magistrates found that asbestos sheets are a cheap form of weather protection and are not designed to bear any weight. Walking along the purlin bolts is not a safe method of moving about on such a roof. The minimum safety precaution should have entailed the provision of two crawling boards of at least 17 inches wide.

They also found that the asbestos sheets could have been removed without Messrs Derhun and Poulter climbing on to or walking on the roof. A scaffold tower could have been erected below the roof and the bolts cropped from below. Such a scaffold tower could have been hired locally, quite easily and cheaply. This method, said the magistrates, 'should have been obvious both to Mr Sibley and to Mr Derhun and Mr Poulter'. It would have greatly reduced the risk to safety.

...

Accordingly they convicted the appellant.

...

In order to establish *prima facie* liability under s 3(1) the Crown must, in my judgment, prove three elements. First, they must show that the defendant was an employer. Second, they must prove that the activity or the state of affairs which gave rise to the complaint fell within the ambit of the defendant's conduct of his undertaking. Third, they must show that there was a risk to the health or safety of persons, other than his employees, who were affected by that aspect of his conduct of his undertaking. If these three are proved, the conviction will follow unless the defendant is able to satisfy the court on the balance of probabilities that it has done all that was reasonably practicable to comply with the duty imposed (see s 40 of the Act).

The word 'employer' is not in itself defined in the Act. In s 53(1) (the definition section) 'employee' is defined as an individual who works under a contract of employment. It is said that related expressions are to be construed accordingly. Thus 'employer' must mean one who employs one or more individuals to work for him under a contract of employment. Here the magistrates found that the appellant was an employer. It plainly did employ employees in its business of manufacturing road-making parts.

Next the Crown had to show that the removal of asbestos sheets from the premises of British Gypsum was within the ambit of the appellant's conduct of its undertaking. If it was, then the third element was plainly made out, as the justices found that the system of work for the removal of the sheets was dangerous. Messrs Derhun and Poulter, who were not the appellant's employees but who were affected by the removal of the asbestos sheets, were indeed exposed to risks to their safety.

The question which falls to be decided is whether the magistrates were right, as a matter of law, when they expressed the opinion that the removal of the asbestos sheets from the British Gypsum roof fell within the ambit of the appellant's conduct of its undertaking. They so found on the basis that the appellant was able to exercise complete control of the way in which the contractors carried out their work, in that they were in a position to give specific directions as to how the work was to be done.

The term 'undertaking' is not defined in the Act, but the dictionary definitions include the expression 'enterprise'. A defendant's undertaking is its business or enterprise.

Counsel accepted that the appellant's business of manufacturing road-making materials carried out at its premises at Erith, Kent, included, as part of the undertaking, the maintenance and repair of the premises ... If the appellant had sent its own employees to remove and collect the asbestos sheets, there could be no doubt that the activity of the removal of the sheets would have been an activity of the appellant in the conduct of its undertaking.

However, the appellant did not remove the sheets by its own employees. Mr Sibley arranged for them to be removed by independent contractors ... The question which falls to be determined was whether by acting through contractors instead of using their own employees, the appellant can still be said to have been conducting its undertaking. If it was conducting its undertaking through contractors, it owed a duty to ensure the safety of Mr Derhun and it was properly convicted. There is no criticism made of the justices' approach to the issue of whether or not the appellant did all that was reasonably practicable.

...

I am unable to accept that the mere capacity or opportunity to exercise control over an activity is enough to bring that activity within the ambit of the employers' conduct of his undertaking. Before he can say that an activity is within the conduct of his undertaking, the employer must, in my judgment, either exercise some actual control over it or be under a duty to do so. If the principal chooses to leave the independent contractor to do the work in the way he thinks fit, I consider that the work is not within the ambit of the principal's conduct of his undertaking. It is wholly the contractor's undertaking. If the principal does involve himself, albeit voluntarily – as, for example, by instructing the contractors to adopt a certain method of work or by lending a piece of equipment – then it may be that his involvement would be within the ambit of his undertaking. If the system of work proved to be unsafe or the equipment proved to be defective and gave rise to a risk to the safety of the contractors, then it may be that the principal would be guilty of an offence under s 3.

Here the appellant appointed a subcontractor to do the work of removing the asbestos sheets. The justices found that the only equipment asked for by the contractors and lent by the appellant was the front-loading shovel. No stipulations were made about when the work was to be done.

It seems to me that it could properly have been said that the appellant's act of appointing contractors to do work for it would fall within the ambit of its conduct of its undertaking. However, once the contractors are appointed and have accepted responsibility for what is to be done, the actual work is not within the ambit of the appellant's undertaking. Here the case was put on the basis that it was the actual work of removing the sheets which was within the ambit of the appellant's undertaking, and not the appointment of the contractors. I have already concluded that the actual work of the contractors could not fall within the ambit of the appellant's undertaking.

...

I turn then to answer the justices' second and third questions. The second question – were we correct in our opinion that the work being carried out by Mr Hans Derhun at the British Gypsum works formed part of the appellant's undertaking? – must be answered in the negative.

– – –

This case has been cited at some length to provide her Ladyship's reasoning, although the authority of the decision (and the reasoning) is doubtful, following the House of Lord's decision in the *Octel* case, cited immediately below. It may, however, be significant that the Octel premises where the accident occurred was a major hazard installation, so that Octel had particular responsibilities to ensure that work undertaken there was carried out safely.

R v ASSOCIATED OCTEL LTD [1996] 1 WLR 1543

The following is taken from the speech of Lord Hoffmann, beginning at p 1545:

> The appellants, Associated Octel Co Ltd ('Octel'), operate a large chemical plant at Ellesmere Port. On 25 June 1990 there was an accident at the chlorine works. The plant was shut down for its annual maintenance and a small firm of specialist contractors called Resin Glass Products ('RGP') were engaged in repairing the lining of a tank. Mr Cuthbert, an employee of RGP, was working in the tank by the light of an electric light bulb attached to a lead. After grinding the damaged area of the lining he had to clean it down with acetone before applying a fibreglass matting patch with resin. He had his supply of acetone in an old paint bucket which he had found in a refuse bin. While he was applying the acetone with a brush, the light bulb broke. Some of the liquid had probably dripped onto it. Acetone is volatile and gives off highly inflammable vapour. As Mr Cuthbert was using an open bucket, there was a good deal of vapour in the tank. The broken bulb caused a flash fire in which Mr Cuthbert was badly burned.

> Octel was prosecuted for breach of sections 3(1) and 33(1)(a) of the Health and Safety at Work Act 1974.

> ...

> In voluntary particulars of the indictment, the Crown said that the conduct of Octel's undertaking upon which they relied was the manner and method by which works of maintenance and repair were carried out. The failure of duty was a failure to control the works so as to ensure that persons not in Octel's employment – Mr Cuthbert was, of course, employed by RGP and not by Octel – were not exposed to risks to their health and safety.

> At the trial, the prosecution led evidence of the way in which the work had been arranged. Octel had been using RGP for a number of years. Its eight employees spent virtually all their time on the site. Like all other such contractors on Octel's site, they operated under what was called a 'permit to work' system. This meant that for every job they had to fill in a form, saying what they were going to do and obtain authorisation from Octel's engineers, who would consider what safety precautions were needed. Authorisation would be accompanied by a 'safety certificate' imposing conditions under which the work was to be done. The whole plant was designated by the Health and Safety Executive as a 'major hazard site' and the 'permit to work' system was part of a statement of safety procedures which Octel was obliged to draw up and submit to the Executive.

> ...

In the present case the Crown adduced evidence by way of advance rebuttal of a defence that prevention of the accident had not been 'reasonably practicable'. It showed that the permit to work system had been operated in a perfunctory manner. The RGP specification said that grinding would take place and so Octel supplied Mr Cuthbert with protective clothing and a face mask. But nothing was said about the use of acetone. Octel did not supply a special air lamp (which could have been specified on the standard form) or a closed container for the acetone or forced air extraction for the tank.

At the close of the prosecution's case, Mr Walker QC submitted on behalf of Octel that there was no case to answer. He said that on the evidence the injury to Mr Cuthbert was not caused by the way in which Octel had conducted its undertaking within the meaning of section 3(1). RGP were independent contractors and the cleaning of the tank was part of the conduct of their undertaking. Control was essential to liability under section 3(1) and Octel had no right to control the way in which its independent contractors did their work.

His Honour Judge Prosser rejected the submission.

...

Octel's main ground of appeal to the Court of Appeal was that the judge had been wrong to reject its submission of no case to answer. The Court of Appeal rejected this argument and so would I. It is based on what seems to me a confusion between two quite different concepts: an employer's vicarious liability for the tortious act of another and a duty imposed upon the employer himself. Vicarious liability depends (with some exceptions) on the nature of the contractual relationship between the employer and the tortfeasor. There is liability if the tortfeasor was acting within the scope of his duties under a contract of employment. Otherwise, generally speaking, the employer is not vicariously liable. But section 3 is not concerned with vicarious liability. It imposes a duty upon the employer himself. That duty is defined by reference to a certain kind of activity, namely, the conduct by the employer of his undertaking. It is indifferent to the nature of the contractual relationships by which the employer chooses to conduct it.

...

Mr Walker says that the absence of a right to control the way in which the work is done is traditionally the badge of an employer's relationship with an independent contractor. So, as RGP were independent contractors, it must follow that Octel were not in a position to exercise that complete control which is the basis of liability under section 3.

This, again, seems to me a confusion of thought ...

The concept of control as one of the tests for vicarious liability serves an altogether different purpose. An employee is free to engage either employees or independent contractors. If he engages employees, he will be vicariously liable for torts committed in the course of their employment. If he engages independent contractors, he will not. The law takes the contractual relationship as given and in some cases the control test helps to decide the category to which it belongs. But for the purposes of section 3, the category is not decisive.

The question, as it seems to me, is simply whether the activity in question can be described as part of the employer's undertaking. In most cases, the answer will be obvious. Octel's undertaking was running a chemical plant at Ellemere Port. Anything which constituted running the plant was part of the conduct of its undertaking. But there will also be ancillary activities such as obtaining supplies, making deliveries, cleaning, maintenance and repairs which give rise to more difficulty.

[His Lordship then cited with approval the words of Parker LJ in *R v Mara* (1987).]

...

It is part of the conduct of the undertaking, not merely to clean the factory, but also to 'have the factory cleaned' by contractors. The employer must take reasonably practical steps to avoid risk to the contractors' servants which arise, not merely from the physical state of the premises (there are separate provisions for safety of premises in section 4), but also from the inadequacy of the arrangements which the employer makes with the contractors for how they will do the work.

Likewise in the present case I think that it was part of the conduct of Octel's undertaking at Ellesmere Port to have the chlorine tank repaired. But I would not accept the extreme position of Mr Carlisle QC for the Crown, who submitted that 'works of cleaning, repair and maintenance which are necessary for the conduct of the employer's business' attract the duty under section 3(1). That would suggest that any repairs, cleaning or maintenance, wherever and by whomsoever they may be done, form part of the conduct by the employer of his undertaking. The cleaning of the office curtains at the dry cleaners; the repair of the sales manager's car in the garage, maintenance work on machinery returned to the manufacturer's factory: all would in principle impose upon the employer a duty under section 3(1) to ensure that they did not create risks to the health and safety of workers and others at the dry cleaners, garage and factory respectively. Mr Carlisle said that the employer could always rely on the defence that it was not reasonably practicable to take steps to prevent risks arising from what other people did on their own premises. But I do not think that such a defence needs to be invoked. In the context of the Act, such activities cannot fairly be described as the conduct by the employer of his undertaking. If he has a repair shop as part of his plant, that is an ancillary part of his undertaking. Likewise, as in this case, if he has independent contractors to do cleaning or repairs on his own premises, as an activity integrated with the general conduct of his business. But not in the case of activities carried on by another person entirely separately from his own.

It seems to me wrong to try to find some formula such as that of Mr Carlisle to take the place of the simple words of the statute. Whether the activity which has caused the risk amounts to part of the conduct by the employer of his undertaking must in each case be a question of fact. The place where the activity takes place will in the normal case be very important; possibly decisive. But one cannot lay down rigid rules. A difficult borderline case was *RMC Roadstone Products Ltd v Jester* (1994) ...

[Considering that case, his Lordship said that he could not accept the reasoning of Smith J.]

The employer is under a duty under section 3(1) to exercise control over an activity if it forms part of the conduct of his undertaking. The existence of such a duty cannot therefore be the test for deciding whether the activity is part of the undertaking or not. Likewise, the question of whether an employer may leave an independent contractor to do the work as he thinks fit depends upon whether having the work done forms part of the employer's conduct of his undertaking. If it does, he owes a duty under section 3(1) to ensure that it is done without risk – subject, of course, to reasonable practicability, which may limit the extent to which the employer can supervise the activities of a specialist independent contractor. Although the case was very much on the borderline, I think that there was evidence upon which the justices were entitled to find in the particular circumstances of the case that having the asbestos sheets removed was part of the employer's undertaking. The facts were a matter for them and their decision should not have been disturbed.

The question of whether having the tank repaired was part of the conduct of Octel's undertaking was also one of fact, it should properly have been left to the jury. Even if, as I think, the only rational answer was yes, it should properly still have been left to the jury ...

... the question of fact which should have been left to the jury is simply whether having the tank repaired was part of the conduct of Octel's chemical undertaking at Ellesmere Port, I cannot imagine what evidence could have been called by the appellant which would have led a properly instructed jury to return a negative answer. The tank was part of Octel's plant. The work formed part of a maintenance programme planned by Octel. The men who did the work, although employed by an independent contractor, were almost permanently integrated into Octel's larger operation. They worked under the permit to work system. Octel provided their safety equipment and lighting. None of these facts was disputed. In these circumstances, a properly instructed jury would undoubtedly have convicted. I would therefore apply the proviso, dismiss the appeal and affirm the conviction.

– – –

Liability for acts of employees

In the *Octel* case, Lord Hoffmann opined that the doctrine of vicarious liability had no place in the regulatory system of the Health and Safety at Work Act 1974. Nevertheless, in the two following cases, the Court of Appeal was concerned with the circumstances in which an employer might be criminally liable for the actions of its employees. In the first (*R v British Steel*), the Court of Appeal refused to apply, in the context of the 1974 Act, the argument adopted by the House of Lords in *Tesco Supermarkets Ltd v Nattrass* (1972)[6] to enable the employer to avoid liability for the acts of its employee. In the second (*R v*

---

6   [1972] AC 153.

Nelson), where the employer appeared faultless, while the employee was in breach of regulations imposing duties on him personally, the employer did escape liability. It may be that the argument made in these cases – that an employer should not be liable for the casual negligence of an employee where it is not reasonably practicable to prevent such lapses – will not be persuasive in the light of regulation 22 of the Management of Health and Safety at Work Regulations 1999 (see Chapter 12).

R v BRITISH STEEL PLC [1995] IRLR 310

British Steel wanted to re-position part of a steel platform at one of its plants. The task was given to subcontractors on a labour-only basis and the work was to be supervised by British Steel's own employee. The engineer told the subcontractor's two men not to remove the supporting columns of the platform until the crane had taken its weight. In the event, the platform was cut free of nearly all its supports without being secured to the crane. The platform collapsed, fell onto and killed one of the visiting workmen. British Steel was charged and convicted in the Crown Court under s 3(1). On appeal, British Steel reiterated the argument it had presented to the trial court, namely, that their engineer had carried out his supervisory duty properly. The accident had occurred because the two men had disobeyed instructions. It was further argued that, even if their employee were at fault, the company had, at the level of its 'directing mind', taken reasonable care to delegate supervision of the operation and, accordingly, the company was not responsible under s 3(1) for their engineer's actions. The judgment of the Court of Appeal was delivered by Steyn LJ. The following extracts begin at p 313:

> Counsel for British Steel submitted that properly construed s 3(1) permits a corporate employer to escape criminal liability if at 'directing mind' level the company has taken reasonable care. He asked us to read the words 'it shall be the duty of every employer to conduct his undertaking in such a way as to ensure' in s 3(1) as if the words 'through senior management' appear immediately after the word 'employer'. We are conscious that there are perhaps some ambiguities in the way in which we have summarised counsel's submission. But that is inherent in the submission. When pressed to explain the foundation of the submission in the language of s 3(1) or its contextual setting, counsel said it derived from the very concept of a corporate employer, who can only act through directors and senior management or from the words 'conduct his undertaking' which have similar overtones. He relied strongly on the decision of the House of Lords in *Tesco Supermarkets Ltd v Nattrass* ... That case involved a charge against a supermarket chain under the Trade Descriptions Act 1968. Section 20(1) of the 1968 Act provides that if an offence has been committed with the connivance of a director, manager, secretary or other similar officer of the company, he as well as the company will be guilty of the offence. Section 24(1) provides as follows:
>
> > In any proceedings for an offence under this Act, it shall ... be a defence for the person charged to prove (a) that the commission of the offence was due

to ... the act or default of another person; ... and (b) that he took all reasonable precautions and exercised all due diligence to avoid the commission of such an offence ...

The company's defence was that the commission of the offence was due to an act of another person, namely, the manager of the store at which it was committed, and that the company had taken all reasonable precautions and exercised all due diligence to avoid the commission of such an offence. The question arose whether the acts of the shop managers were the acts of the company itself. Lord Reid concluded, at p 175-A:

> The [the board of directors] set up a chain of command through regional and district supervisors, but they remained in control. The shop managers had to obey their general directions and also take orders from their superiors. The acts or omissions of shop managers were not acts of the company itself.

There were five speeches. Lord Reid's observations reflected the ratio decidendi of the case. Once that decision was reached, the company was able to establish a defence that the commission of the offence was due to a mistake or to the act or default of another person, namely the store manager, himself an employee. The presence of such a 'due diligence' provision was a powerful indication that the purpose of the Trade Descriptions Act 1968 must indeed 'have been to penalise those at fault, not those who were in no way to blame'. Significantly there is no due diligence defence in the 1974 Act. It is worth noting that s 161 of the Factories Act 1961, which did provide such a defence, has been repealed with effect from 1 January 1977 and has no part in the new regime. Thus quite apart from the fact that *Tesco* involves consumer protection, the legislative techniques of the two statutes are quite different, as is apparent from a comparison of ss 20(1) and 24(1) of the Trade Descriptions Act 1968 and s 3(1) of the Health and Safety at Work Act 1974. Subject to the qualifying words 'so far as is reasonably practicable', which have been taken from s 29(1) of the Factories Act 1961, s 3(1) of the 1974 Act is prima facie cast in absolute terms. The words 'so far as is reasonably practicable' are simply referable to measures necessary to avert the risk (see *Taylor v Coalite Oil and Chemicals Ltd* [1967] Knights Ind Reports 315 and Redgrave, Fife and Machin, 'Introductory Notes', in *Health and Safety*, 2nd edn, p lxxxii). In our judgment the decision in *Tesco* does not provide the answer to the problem of construction before us. The answer must be found in the words of s 3(1) of the 1974 Act read in its contextual setting. It is on the 1974 Act and in particular s 3(1) that our construction of s 3(1) must have relevance to the interpretation of s 2(1) which provides for the employer's duty to his own employees.

We have observed that prima facie, and subject to the stated qualification, s 3(1) created an absolute prohibition. The point is, in fact, covered by the direct authority of two decisions in this Court. In *R v Board of Trustees of the Science Museum* [1994] IRLR 25, this court considered the provenance of s 3(1) as well as the assistance to be gained from a consideration of other provisions of the Act. Subject to repeating that it is right to consider the interpretation of s 3(1) against the spectrum of risks contemplated by s 3(1) we do not propose to cover that ground again.

...

In *R v Associated Octel Co Ltd*, another division of this court considered and followed the *Science Museum* case.[7]

...

We are, of course, bound by these two decisions. But we have had the benefit of argument calling them into question. If we had to consider the matter de novo we would have still concluded that the words of s 3(1) are in the context capable of one interpretation only, namely that subject to the defence of reasonable practicability, s 3(1) creates an absolute prohibition. The defence is a narrow one, analogous to the defence under s 29(1) of the Factories Act 1961, which simply comprehends the idea of measures necessary to avert the risks to health and safety.

Given the interpretation which prevailed in *Science Museum* and *Octel*, and which we have adopted, counsel for British Steel concedes that it is not easy to fit the idea of corporate criminal liability only for acts of the 'directing mind' of the company into the language of s 3(1). We would go further. If it be accepted that Parliament considered it necessary for the protection of public health and safety to impose, subject to the defence of reasonable practicability, absolute criminal liability, it would drive a juggernaut through the legislative scheme if corporate employers could avoid criminal liability where the potentially harmful event is committed by someone who is not the directing mind of the company. After all, as Stuart-Smith LJ observed in *Octel*, s 3(1) is framed to achieve a result, namely, that persons not employed are not exposed to risks to their health and safety by the conduct of the undertaking. If we accept British Steel's submission, it would be particularly easy for large industrial companies, engaged in multifarious hazardous operations, to escape liability on the basis that the company, through its 'directing mind' or senior management was not involved. That would emasculate the legislation.

That brings us to a point raised by counsel for British Steel which has proved troublesome. He argued that the interpretation which we have preferred would lead to manifestly absurd consequences. Postulate, he said, the employee who drops a spanner or an employee who drives without due care and attention. Both could be within the scope of s 3(1). He submitted that in neither case would the corporate employer have a defence of reasonable practicability. But we think that the suggested absurdities are unlikely to arise in practice. An action such as the dropping of a spanner will only be relevant if it exposes a person not in the employer's employment to a risk to his health or safety. That will only occur if he is, as it were, in the danger zone. Thus he will only be exposed to the risk if the system (if any) designed to ensure his safety has broken down and it does not matter for the purposes of s 3(1) at what level in the hierarchy of employees that breakdown has taken place. Similarly, the driver's carelessness may have resulted from something for which his employer is to be regarded as responsible, such as trying to meet excessively tight delivery schedules or tiredness due to over long hours of work. We do recognise that there may be circumstances in which it might be regarded as absurd that an employer should even be technically guilty of a criminal

---

7   This case was heard before the House of Lords had heard the appeal in *Octel*.

offence. An example might perhaps be the driver who is guilty of an error of judgment when driving his employer's lorry on his employer's business. But, in any event, so called absurdities are not peculiar to this corner of the law: at the extremities of the field of application of many rules surprising results are often to be found. That circumstance is inherent in the adoption of general rules to govern an infinity of particular circumstances. Fortunately, the cases to which counsel referred will in practice cause no real difficulty in relation to s 3(1) of the 1974 Act. Nobody has suggested that there has ever been a prosecution in such a case and it is most unlikely that there would in future be a prosecution in such cases. Moreover, if such prosecutions are brought, they are not likely to be viewed sympathetically by a judge and jury or by magistrates.

– – –

R v NELSON GROUP SERVICES LTD (MAINTENANCE)
[1998] 4 All ER 331

The appellant, Nelson Group Services (Maintenance) Ltd, was a national company involved in the installation, servicing and maintenance of gas appliances. It employed between 800 and 900 fitters, in addition to supervisory staff and office and management personnel. It had its own centre for training employees. Between June 1997 and January 1998 it faced six indictments for offences under the Health and Safety at Work Act 1974 and was acquitted on three. It was convicted of one or more offences on the other three indictments. It had no convictions prior to these. The main issue in two of the appeals was the extent of the duty placed upon an employer by s 3(1) of the 1974 Act. The question was whether, if the company's fitters had not performed their duties properly, the company should be liable for any risk the fitters thus created. It was accepted that the fitters concerned were properly trained, properly certificated, received proper instructions and supplied with equipment which would have allowed them to discharge their work as fitters satisfactorily and safely. The appellant made two submissions. The first was that a negligent act by its fitter was not 'the employer conducting his undertaking'. The second was that the employer was not prevented, by the fitter's negligent act or omission, from showing that it had, so far as is reasonably practicable, conducted its undertaking in such a way as to ensure that persons not in its employment who might be affected thereby were not thereby exposed to risk to their health or safety. In addition to the charges under the 1974 Act, the fitters and the company were charged and convicted under the Gas Safety (Installation and Use) Regulations 1994. These Regulations placed duties on the employer and also on the fitters personally. The charges arose out of the fitters having left private dwellings with gas installations that were unsafe.

Roch LJ delivered the judgment of the Court of Appeal. In relation to one of the counts on which the appellant had been charged, his Lordship addressed the question of whether, since members of the public had been put at risk by the activities of the company's employees, a *prima facie* case of breach of s 3(1) had been established. After citing from the judgments in *R v Associated Octel Ltd* and *R v British Steel plc,* he continued at p 350:

> ... there can be no doubt that the activities of the appellant's fitters are part of the conduct by the appellant of their undertaking. Moreover it is clear that such acts and omissions of the fitters exposed the householders to risks to their health or safety.

The remaining issue is whether the appellants were unable to establish a defence of reasonable practicability by the simple fact that an act or omission of one of their employees had exposed the householder to danger?

We have found the decision of this court in *R v Gateway Food Markets Ltd* [1997] 3 All ER 78 of assistance. In this case the court was concerned with the construction of s 2(1) of the 1974 Act. In the court's judgment, at page 83B the court said:

> 'However, the same wording appears in s 3(1) and, in our judgment, the general considerations referred to in the authorities, including the purpose and object of the legislation, make it overwhelmingly clear that s 2(1), like s 3(1), should be interpreted so as to impose liability on the employer wherever the relevant event occurs, namely a failure to ensure the health, etc, of an employee.'

The court went on to consider the passage from the judgment of Steyn in the *British Steel* case dealing with so called absurdities and suggested that a principled answer could be found. The court then said:

> 'We agree that it is a somewhat extreme contention that the employer should be held criminally liable even for an isolated act of negligence by a junior employee, affecting the health, safety or welfare either of a fellow employee (s 2(1)), or of some other person (s 3(1)) ...
>
> The answer lies, we suggest, in the application of a qualification or caveat contained in the statute itself. The duty under each section is broken if the specified consequences occur, but only if "so far as is reasonably practicable", they have not been guarded against. So the company is in breach of duty unless all reasonable precautions have been taken, and we would interpret this as meaning 'taken by the company or on its behalf'. In other words, the breach of duty and liability under the section do not depend upon any failure by the company itself, meaning those persons who embody the company, to take all reasonable precautions. Rather, the company is liable in the event that there is a failure to ensure the safety etc, of any employee, unless all reasonable precautions have been taken – as we would add, by the company or on its behalf.'

In that case this court concluded that a failure at store management level was certainly attributable to the employer, whilst leaving open the question whether the employer is liable in circumstances where the only negligence or failure to take reasonable precautions has taken place at some more junior level.

We derive considerable assistance from the judgment of this court in the *Gateway* case. We would summarise the law in this way: first, if persons not in the employment of the employer are exposed to risks to their health or safety by the conduct of the employer's undertaking, the employer will be in breach of s 3(1) and guilty of an offence under s 33(1)(a) of the Act unless the employer can prove on the balance of probability that all that was reasonably practicable had been done by the employer or on the employer's behalf to ensure that such persons were not exposed to such risks. It will be a question of fact for the jury in each case whether it was the conduct of the employer's undertaking which exposed the third persons to risks to their health or safety. The question what was reasonably practicable is also a question of fact for the jury depending on the circumstances of each case. The fact that the employee who was carrying out the work, in this case, the fitter installing the appliance, has done the work carelessly or omitted to take a precaution he should have taken does not of itself preclude the employer from establishing that everything that was reasonably practicable in the conduct of the employer's undertaking to ensure that third persons affected by the employer's undertaking were not exposed to risks to their health and safety had been done.

In our view this analysis is consistent with the distinction which appears in the Regulations between the duties of employers of persons and the duties of persons performing the work. It is not necessary for the adequate protection of the public that the employer should be held criminally liable even for an isolated act of negligence by the employee performing the work. Such persons are themselves liable to criminal sanctions under the Act and under the Regulations. Moreover it is a sufficient obligation to place on the employer in order to protect the public to require the employer to show that everything reasonably practicable has been done to see that a person doing the work has the appropriate skill and instruction, has had laid down for him safe systems of doing the work, has been subject to adequate supervision, and has been provided with safe plant and equipment for the proper performance of the work.

That being our view of the correct interpretation of s 3(1) it remains to consider the conviction of the appellants of the first count in the first indictment and their conviction on the first count in the third indictment.

As no criticism is made of the direction of HHJ Shawcross on count 1 in the first indictment, and as the two issues of fact which we have identified were left fairly to the jury, there can be no complaint of the appellant's conviction on this count. In our judgment that conviction is not unsafe and the appeal against that conviction will be dismissed.

With regard to the conviction of the appellants on the first count in the third indictment, the direction of HHJ Darwall-Smith that the disconnecting of the gas fire at Mrs West's home by Mr Brennan was part of the conduct of the appellant's undertaking, although removing from the jury a question of fact which strictly should have been left to them, was a question which the jury could only have answered in one way. The further factual question whether Mr Brennan had failed to cap the pipe was left to the jury, who by their verdict, ere clearly satisfied that he had failed to cap the pipe. The essential issue in the appeal on this ground is whether the judge left the defence of reasonable practicability to the jury. The direction the judge gave on this defence was:

> 'Well, you may ask why there is strict liability against an employer with such a limited statutory defence? Members of the jury, it is to ensure that when the public are exposed to danger the responsibility has to fall on the employer of the person who actually created the danger. In law the defendants cannot delegate their duty to some fitter or supervisor and wash their hands of it if something goes wrong. The basic duty is upon the defendant company to make sure their business is operated in such a way that other people are not exposed to risk. It doesn't matter at what level in the hierarchy of the company that that breakdown occurs. It could be the fault of the lowliest employee at the most basic level. It doesn't matter that the management or directing mind of the company took no active part themselves in the act or omission that created that danger.
>
> It comes to this: if the defendants have satisfied you that the probability is that everything reasonably practicable had been done that could be done to avoid an unsealed gas pipe being left in Mrs West's house then they are entitled to be acquitted. If you think that the probability is that they have not done everything practicable to prevent that happening then your verdict will be one of guilty.'

Just before the jury retired, the judge returned to this issue, saying:

> 'If you are driven to the conclusion that the open gas pipe must have been down to Brennan then you will have to consider whether the defendant company has satisfied you that everything reasonably practicable had been done in Count 1, and all reasonable steps had been taken in Count 2.'

The effect of these directions was that if the jury found Mr Brennan had not capped the gas pipe then they could not find that the appellants had done all that was reasonably practicable to ensure that Mrs West was not exposed to risk to her health or safety. That in our judgment was a misdirection which rends that conviction unsafe ...

– – –

Risk to the public

The following case, while happening to concern public safety, is principally about the circumstances in which there will be deemed to be an unlawful risk of personal injury.

REGINA v BOARD OF TRUSTEES OF THE SCIENCE MUSEUM
[1993] 1 WLR 1171

Steyn LJ gave the judgment of the Court of the Appeal. The following extracts start at p 1172:

The conviction

In October 1990 the appellants were tried in the Crown Court at Knightsbridge on a charge of failing to discharge the duty imposed upon them by s 3(1) of the Health and Safety at Work Act 1974.

...

The focus of the prosecution case was not a risk to the health and safety of employees of the Science Museum. The prosecution alleged that, by reason of the appellants' inadequate system of maintenance, treatment and monitoring, members of the public outside the Science Museum were exposed to risks to their health from LP. It was common ground that the escape of LP from the cooling tower of the Science Museum could expose members of the public within a cordon of 500 yards to risks to their health and safety.

...

The judge's rulings and summing up

The judge had to resolve an important issue as to the interpretation of the words 'thereby exposed to risks to their health and safety'. The prosecution contended that they did not have to prove that the members of the public actually inhaled LP or that LP was actually there to be inhaled. It was sufficient if there was a risk of it being there. The defence argued that this interpretation was wrong and submitted that the prosecution had to go further because a possible danger, or a potential danger, cannot impair the health and safety of the public. That can only come about when the danger ceases to be potential and becomes real.

The construction put forward by the defence formed the basis of a submission at the end of the prosecution case, which was repeated after the defence called their expert witness, that there was no case for the defence to answer. The judge ruled against the defence on both occasions.

In a careful and lucid summing up the judge adopted the interpretation put forward by the prosecution.

...

The critical question of interpretation is as follows: Was it enough for the prosecution to prove that there was a risk that LP might emerge, or did the prosecution have to go further and show that LP did in fact emerge into the atmosphere and was available to be inhaled? Mr Carlisle, leading counsel for the prosecution, illustrated the problem with a simple example. Imagine, he said, a loose object on a roof near a pavement. In case A, the loose object is in a position in which it might fall off and hit a pedestrian. In that case, there is a mere risk. In case B, the object in fact falls off and exposes pedestrians to actual danger. In case C, the object falls and causes actual injury to a pedestrian. The prosecution submits that exposure to risk in case A constitutes a *prima facie* case under s 3(1). The defence submits that s 3(1) only covers cases B and C.

The starting point must be the ordinary meaning of the language of s 3(1). In our judgment the interpretation of the prosecution fits in best with the language of s 3(1). In the context the word 'risks' conveys the idea of a possibility of danger. Indeed, a degree of verbal manipulation is needed to introduce the idea of actual danger which the defendants put forward. The ordinary meaning of the word 'risks' therefore supports the prosecution's interpretation and there is nothing in the language of s 3 or, indeed in the context of the Act which supports a narrowing down of the ordinary meaning. On the contrary, the preventive aim of ss 3, 20, 21 and 22 reinforces the construction put forward by the prosecution and adopted by the judge. The adoption of the restrictive interpretation argued for by the defence would make enforcement of s 3(1), and to some extent also of ss 20, 21 and 22 more difficult and would in our judgment result in a substantial emasculation of a central part of the Act of 1974. The interpretation which renders those statutory provisions effective in their role of protecting public health and safety is to be preferred.

We have not lost sight of the defence submission that we ought to concentrate on the word 'exposed' rather than 'risks' in s 3(1). If the word 'risks' has the meaning which we consider it has the point disappears. In that event exposure to a possibility of danger is sufficient. The word 'exposed' simply makes clear that the section is concerned with persons potentially affected by the risk. In this case that refers to members of the public within range of the infill building. But the word 'exposed' cannot change the meaning of 'risks' from a possibility of danger to actual danger. On the principal point in this case the argument of the defence is really a red herring.

The defence also argued that if the prosecution's submission is accepted the result may be that, subject to the defence of reasonable practicability, all cooling towers in urban areas are *prima facie* within the scope of the prohibition contained in s 3(1). On the evidence led in the present case that may be correct. Almost certainly such a result would be true of a number of extra hazardous industrial activities. Subject only to the defence of reasonable practicability, s 3(1) is intended to be an absolute prohibition. Bearing in mind the imperative of protecting public health and safety, so far as it is reasonably practicable to do so, the result can be faced with equanimity.

...

It is now necessary to consider the merits of the appellants' arguments on the state of the evidence. This aspect must be considered on the basis of the interpretation which we have given to s 3(1). This consideration on its own serves to filter out a number of arguments of the appellants' which were linked with their now rejected submission. Bearing in mind that there are no material misdirections, the question is simply whether there was a case to be answered.

The prosecution case revealed an ever present risk of LP escaping from the appellants' cooling towers. From 7 August 1988 to 10 January 1989 the appellants were not pumping fresh water into the towers. Instead water was irregularly pumped via the first water supply. That water contained stagnant dead-ends. The jury was entitled to infer on the expert evidence led in this case that any cooling tower which is in operation, poses a risk to persons in the vicinity of it. They were entitled to infer that in the present case that risk was increased by the appellants' failure to maintain an efficient water treatment regime from August 1988 to January 1989.

– – –

Duties of controllers of premises

Section 4 imposes duties on persons who are controllers of premises for the protection of those who are not their employees. This section (unlike s 3) expressly acknowledges that persons may share control of particular premises and in rather convoluted language s 4(2) requires each controller to do what it is reasonable for someone in his position to do to ensure (so far as is reasonably practicable) the safety of the premises:

Section 4
General duties of persons concerned with premises to persons other than their employees

(1) This section has effect for imposing on persons duties in relation to those who–

   (a) are not their employees; but

   (b) use non-domestic premises made available to them as a place of work or as a place where they may use plant or substances provided for their use there,

   and applies to premises so made available and other non-domestic premises used in connection with them.

(2) It shall be the duty of each person who has, to any extent, control of premises to which this section applies or of the means of access thereto or egress therefrom or of any plant or substance in such premises to take such measures as it is reasonable for a person in his position to take to ensure, so far as is reasonably practicable, that the premises, all means of access thereto or egress therefrom available for use by persons using the premises, and any plant or substance in the premises or, as the case may be, provided for use there, is or are safe and without risks to health.

(3) Where a person has, by virtue of any contract or tenancy, an obligation of any extent in relation to–

   (a) the maintenance or repair of any premises to which this section applies or any means of access thereto or egress therefrom; or

   (b) the safety of or the absence of risks to health arising from plant or substances in any such premises;

   that person shall be treated, for the purpose of su-section (2) above, as being a person who has control of the matters to which his obligations extends.

(4) Any reference in this section to a person having control of any premises or matter is a reference to a person having control of the premises or matter in connection with the carrying on by him of a trade, business or other undertaking (whether for profit or not).

– – –

Two cases are of special interest: one extended the duty to the lift of a block of flats; the other, a House of Lords' decision, concerned the relationship between employer and subcontractor and is not easily reconciled with the cases which, on similar facts have, more recently, been heard on s 3.

Non-domestic premises

In the following case the court had to decide whether 'the common parts', for example, the entrance hall, of a block of flats should be deemed 'domestic premises' and, therefore, beyond the jurisdiction of the 1974 Act.

WESTMINSTER CITY COUNCIL v SELECT MANAGEMENTS LTD
[1985] 1 ALL ER 897

The following extracts are taken from the judgment of Parker LJ in the Court of Appeal, beginning at p 898:

> The appellants manage a block of flats at 6 Hall Road, London NW8. They are in control of the common parts of the block in connection with the carrying on by them of the business or undertaking of managing the block. The common parts include two lifts, staircases, landings and a ground floor hall or foyer.
>
> Three questions arise for determination on this appeal:
>
> (1) Are the common parts 'non-domestic premises' within the meaning of s 4(1) of the Health and Safety at Work Act 1974?
>
> ...
>
> (2) If so, are such common parts made available to persons not in the appellants' employment as a place of work and so used by them?;
>
> (3) Are such common parts made available to such persons as a place where they may use plant and substances provided for their use there and so used by them?
>
> Owing to the manner in which the matter has reached this court, very little is known of the persons who are not employed by the appellants but who use the common parts of the block. There is a resident caretaker but it is not known by whom he is employed or what his duties are. Persons not employed by the appellants attend at the block from time to time for the purpose of inspecting, maintaining and repairing the lifts and the electrical installations in the common parts. No more was established by evidence. It may be inferred, however, that the common parts are regularly cleaned and from time to time decorated. The persons who do the cleaning and decorating, however, may or may not be the appellants' employees. It may also be inferred that the lifts, landings, staircases and hall are used both by the tenants of the flats and those visiting them. Such visitors will, no doubt, include some who visit in the course of their employment such as delivery men or doctors.
>
> With this preliminary, I turn to the three questions.

(1) Are the common parts 'non-domestic premises'?

Part I of the 1974 Act contains in s 53 its own definition section. For the purposes of the present question two of the definitions only are relevant. I set them out:

... 'domestic premises' means premises occupied as a private dwelling (including any garden, yard, garage, outhouse or other appurtenance of such premises which is not used in common by the occupants of more than one such dwelling), and 'non-domestic premises' shall be construed accordingly ...

... 'premises' includes any place and, in particular, includes – (a) any vehicle, vessel, aircraft or hovercraft, (b) any installation on land (including the foreshore and other land intermittently covered by water), any offshore installation, and any other installation (whether floating, or resting on the seabed or the subsoil thereof, or resting on other land covered with water or the subsoil thereof), and (c) any tent or movable structure ...

It is clear that each flat is a place and is occupied as a private dwelling. Each of the flats is therefore within the definition of 'domestic premises'. It is equally clear that the lifts and other common parts are not within the definition for, since they are used in common by the occupants of more than one private dwelling, they are, even if appurtenances of each of the flats, excluded from being domestic premises. If the common parts are not domestic premises then, by the concluding words of the definition, they are, if premises at all, non-domestic premises.

Counsel for the appellants submitted that the common parts were not premises at all. This submission might have had substance were it not for the fact that the definition of 'premises' is so wide as to include things which one would not ordinarily consider to be within the meaning of the word. When, however, the definition brings within that meaning any 'place' and then particularises as being within that meaning vehicles, vessels, aircraft and hovercraft, installations on land and offshore, tents and movable structures, there can, in my view, be no doubt that the hall, landing and staircases of a block of flats are places and thus within the definition of 'premises'. As to the lifts (in which I include the lift cages, shafts, gates, wells and motor rooms) they are also, in my view, within the definition either specifically as being installations on land or generally as being places. The judge held that the electrical installation for the common parts was in a like position. For myself, albeit it makes no difference to the end result, I cannot accept this. The electrical installation is merely a collection of wires, fittings, switches, plug sockets etc for lighting the common parts and enabling such things as vacuum cleaners and floor polishers to take electric power from the sockets. To describe such a collection or any part of it as a 'place' is, in my view, quite unreal. It can, no doubt, be described as an installation as can anything which has been installed, such as an entry phone, intercommunication system or television line system. 'Installations' within the definition of 'premises' do not, however, in my view, cover such systems. If an electrician is working on a switch or length of wire in the hall of a block, the 'place' where he is working is, in my view, the hall and not the switch.

Before turning to the second of the three questions, I should refer to a further argument of counsel for the appellants, namely that the block of flats should be considered as a whole and that, so considered, it fell within the definition of 'domestic premises'. This argument I reject. The block consists of a number of places occupied as separate dwellings and thus of a number of domestic premises and of certain common parts which, by reason of their common use, are excluded from the definition. Counsel for the appellants was constrained to accept that, if, on the ground floor, there was a movable stall for selling goods, this would be a movable structure and thus premises within the definition, but non-domestic premises. It is, in my view, wholly artificial to construe the definition so that the entire block would be domestic premises if there was no such stall, but not domestic premises if there were such a stall.

(2) Are the common parts made available to persons not employed by the appellants as a place of work?

'Place of work' is not defined in the Act but there are definitions of 'work' and 'at work' in s 52 (1).

...

When lift engineers or electricians attend at the block to inspect, maintain or repair the lifts or electrical installations they are, when carrying out inspection, maintenance or repair, plainly 'at work' within the definition. If the lift engineers spend three weeks working on the lifts or electricians spend three weeks working in or on the hall, landings and staircases, it appears to me that the common parts are made available to them as a place of work. Such parts are for the duration of the three weeks, as a matter of plain language, their place of work and are made available to them by the appellants, who might, for example, give notice to all tenants that no 1 lift was out of use for the period in order that the work might be carried out. In the same way, if the common parts are redecorated by a firm of contractors, such parts are made available to the contractor's employees as their place of work.

It was submitted that the common parts were not made available as a place of work to maintenance men. I cannot see why not. Electricians and lift engineers are, it seems to me, within the ambit of this section just as much as the employees of a cleaning contractor who attend daily to clean the common parts. It may be that, in the case of maintenance men, the duty imposed by s 4(2) will, in some cases, afford them less protection, but that is a separate matter.

(3) Are the common parts made available to persons not employed by the appellants as a place where they may use plant or substances provided for their use there?

By s 53, 'plant' includes any machinery, equipment or appliance. The lifts and electrical installation are, in my judgment, within the definition of 'plant' and are provided for the use of all persons lawfully using the common parts, be they tenants, visitors in the course of their employment and thus 'at work', maintenance men, cleaners, decorators and so on. Such plant is made available for the use of all such persons and, in so far as such persons are not employees of the appellants, s 4 will apply. If they are such employees, the appellants will have similar duties under s 2.

In reaching the above conclusions I have not found it necessary to rely on the provisions of s 1 of the Act, for I have felt no doubt about the meaning of the particular provisions which fall to be construed. Had I felt any such doubt, it would, however, have been set at rest by those provisions. The objects of the Act are, so far as immediately material, to secure the health, safety and welfare of persons at work and to protect persons not at work against risks to health and safety arising in connection with the activities of persons at work, which risks are to be treated as including risks attributable to the manner of conducting an undertaking (see s 1(1)(a) and (b) and s 1(3)). The lift engineers and electricians are persons at work. If the appellants' manner of conducting their undertaking is to allow the lifts and electrical installations to become dangerous, all persons, whether or not at work, will be exposed to risks and the object of the Act will be defeated if a narrow construction is given to the succeeding sections.

– – –

II OTHER GENERAL DUTIES

Controller's relationships with contractors

The following case deals with the allocation of responsibilities where two or more persons share control of premises. Section 4(2) of the Act states in a somewhat convoluted way that it is the responsibility of each controller to do what is reasonable (for a person in his position) to ensure, so far as is reasonably practicable that the premises are safe.

MAILER v AUSTIN ROVER GROUP PLC [1989] 2 ALL ER 1087

The following extracts are taken from the speech of Lord Jauncey, given in the House of Lords, beginning at p 1094:

> The circumstances giving rise to the prosecution, as found by the justices, may be summarised as follows. Austin Rover had in their Cowley works a number of paint spray booths, including no 2 sealer booth ('the booth'). The floor of the booth sloped downwards towards centrally positioned downpipes, which led into a sump beneath. The floor was covered with a metal grid and excess paint and solvents from the spraying operation together with water used in connection therewith found their way into the sump by way of the downpipe. In one of the walls of the booth was a projecting pipe which supplied thinners under pressure from a ring main for use during painting. There was on this projecting pipe a lever operated valve which controlled the flow of thinners. There was a further valve on the pipe outside the booth which could also shut off the flow. When the ring main was not under pressure, thinners would flow by gravity at a reduced rate from the pipe in the booth if both values were open. The thinners were highly inflammable. The booth was equipped with a mechanical ventilation system which, when operating, effected rapid changes of air in the sump. Space in the sump was restricted and it had neither light nor a ventilation system independent of that of the booth.

> The booth and sump required to be regularly cleaned and this was normally done at weekends when the plant was shut down and the ventilation system switched off. Until 1982 this cleaning was carried out by Austin Rover employees, but in that year Austin Rover entered into a contract with

Wesleyshire Industrial Services Ltd who thereafter carried out the work. On 30 August 1986 one of Wesleyshire's employees, Brian Eldridge, went into the sump to clean it, while a fellow employee, James Mackie, was working in the booth above. Some time afterwards a sudden flash fire erupted in the sump as a result of which Brian Eldridge died. The ventilation system was switched off at the time. Wesleyshire were prosecuted under s 2 of the 1974 Act, pleaded guilty and were fined £2,000.

In terms of the current contract between Austin Rover and Wesleyshire, the latter were required to and did provide their own thinners for cleaning purposes. Furthermore, Wesleyshire's employees were instructed (1) not to use Austin Rover's thinners from the projecting pipe, (2) not to enter the sump when other cleaning operations were taking place in the booth above, and (3) only to enter the sump with an approved safety lamp. After the accident it was discovered (1) that thinners were flowing from the projecting pipe by way of an attached rubber hose into a drum belonging to Wesleyshire. The valve inside the booth was partially open and thinners were running slowly over the top of the drum. Mackie had rigged up this arrangement some hours earlier; (2) that there were thinners in the sump which had either come from the overflowing drum or had been tipped by Mackie contrary to instructions; (3) that the lamp used by the deceased in the sump was not an approved safety lamp. Samples from the thinners found in the sump were found to flash at two degrees centigrade.

...

Counsel for the inspector submitted that at the time of the fire the premises were unsafe in two respects, namely (1) that the thinners had not been isolated, and (2) that the sump was not being mechanically ventilated while the deceased was working therein. Austin Rover had total control of the premises and modest measures were available to them to make the premises and the thinners far safer. Having failed to take those measures, they were in breach of their statutory duty under s 4, and it mattered not that they could not foresee the particular circumstances of the accident which occurred. Counsel for the respondents contended that so far as Austin Rover were concerned, the premises were at the material time safe and that, in any event, it would not have been reasonable for them to have taken any further steps to that end. It was not contended that if it were reasonable for Austin Rover to take steps to ensure the safety of the sump and the thinners, it would not have been reasonably practicable for them to have done so.

...

Sections 2 and 3 impose duties in relation to safety on a single person, whether an individual or a corporation, who is in a position to exercise complete control over the matters to which the duties extend. An employer can control the conditions of work of his employees and the manner in which he conducts his undertaking. However, s 4, which imposes duties in relation to the safety of premises and plant and substances therein, recognises that more than one person may have a degree of control of those premises at any one time and hence be under a duty in relation thereto. The words 'to any extent' and 'to take such measures as it is reasonable for a person in his position to take' ('the middle words') point to the distinction between the unified control contemplated in ss 2 and 3 and the possible divided control contemplated in s 4.

Two main questions of construction were involved in the arguments before your Lordships, namely: (1) what is meant by the words 'safe and without risks to health' in the context of the premises and substances to which s 4 refers, and (2) what factors may be taken into account in determining what measures it is reasonable for an accused to take to ensure safety.

In relation to the first question, counsel for the inspector submitted that regard must be had to the use to which the premises were being put at the relevant time. If it was reasonably foreseeable that such use involved risks to health the premises were then unsafe. Counsel for the respondents on the other hand argued that 'premises' were safe when they were in such a condition as to be unlikely to be the cause of injury, harm or risk to health to persons using premises for which they were made available. The difference between these submissions lay in the fact that counsel for the inspector looked at safety at the time when the risk to health arose which, in the present case was immediately prior to the fire, whereas counsel for the respondents looked at it when the premises were first made available for non-employees to work in.

Safety of premises is not an abstract concept. It must be related to the purposes for which the premises are being used at any one time. Some premises may be unsafe for any normal use, for example because of large unguarded holes in the floor or unstable walls. Other premises may be completely safe for the purpose for which they were designed but completely unsafe for other purposes. For example an upper floor warehouse designed to a loading capacity of x lbs per square foot is safe when used within the capacity but would become unsafe if loaded to 2x lbs per square foot. If A makes available a warehouse to B who uses it within the designed loading capacity it could not be said that the warehouse was unsafe and a risk to health for the purposes of s 4(2) because B might at some future date exceed the designed loading capacity contrary to A's instructions. If, however, B in fact overloaded the floor the premises would thereby become unsafe for the purposes of the subsection.

In my view the submission of counsel for the inspector on this matter is correct. It would be not only to place too narrow a construction on s 4(2) to consider the safety of premises only at the time of their being made available but would be to ignore reality when a danger arose because of supervening events.

I turn now to consider the second main question. Counsel for the inspector argued that in determining what measures it was 'reasonable for a person in his position to take to ensure' safety regard should be had only to the extent of his control. Total control meant total measures. Counsel for the respondents on the other hand maintained that not only control but other considerations such as knowledge and foresight should be taken into account. Counsel for the inspector argued with some force that if more general factors had to be considered in determining what measures were reasonable, little content would be left for the succeeding words 'so far as is reasonably practicable', since it was difficult to envisage a situation in which it would be reasonable for a person to take measures, but not reasonably practicable for him so to do. I was initially attracted by this argument, but have come to the conclusion that it is unsound.

The ambit of s 4 is far wider than that of ss 2 and 3. It applies to anyone who is in occupation of non domestic premises and who calls in tradesmen to carry out repairs, it applies to those tradesmen in relation to the employees of others, and it applies to anyone who makes the premises available on a temporary basis for others to carry out work in. Thus organisations varying from multinational corporations to the village shop are brought under the umbrella of the section. In the example of the warehouse to which I have already referred, it would be contrary to common sense and justice that A should be prosecuted if B had acted contrary to his instruction and without his knowledge. Indeed, if A were to be guilty of an offence in such circumstances, criminal liability would arise solely *ex dominio*. I do not consider that such a result was intended by Parliament, particularly in a provision capable of such broad application. In my view, it was to deal with such a situation as I have exemplified that the middle words were included in s 4(2). These words require consideration to be given not only to the extent to which the individual in question has control of the premises, but also to his knowledge and reasonable foresight at all material times. Thus when a person makes available premises for use by another, the reasonableness of the measures which he requires to take to ensure the safety of those premises must be determined in the light of his knowledge of the anticipated use for which the premises have been made available and of the extent of his control and knowledge, if any, of the actual use thereafter. If premises are not a reasonably foreseeable cause of danger to anyone acting in a way in which a human being may be reasonably expected to act in circumstances which may reasonably be expected to occur during the carrying out of the work or the use of the plant or substance for the purpose of which the premises were made available, I think that it would not be reasonable to require an individual to take further measures against unknown and unexpected events towards their safety. Applying this test to the warehouse example, A would escape liability under s 4(2) because it would not be reasonable for him to take further measures against B's unauthorised use, whereas B would incur liability because he must have foreseen the consequences of his overloading.

I would stress that in the middle words, 'reasonable' relates to the person and not to the measures. The question is not whether there are measures, which themselves are reasonable, which could be taken to ensure safety and the absence of risk to health but whether it is reasonable for a person in the position of the accused to take measures with these aims. The emphasis is on the position of the accused. Thus while only one yardstick determines whether premises are safe at any one time the measures to ensure the safety required of each person having a degree of control may vary. Approaching the matter in this way, content may be given to the words 'so far as reasonably practicable'. It could, having regard to his degree of control and knowledge of likely use, be reasonable for an individual to take a measure to ensure the safety of premises, but it might not be reasonably practicable for him to do so having regard to the very low degree of risk involved and the very high cost of taking the measure.

My Lords, I shall summarise the approach as I see it to a successful prosecution under s 4. The prosecutor must first prove that the premises are unsafe and constitute risks to health. If he so proves he must then go on to prove what persons have at that time any degree of control of those premises. Thereafter he must prove that it would be reasonable for one or more of the persons having a degree of control to take measures which would ensure safety. If he proves these three matters the onus shifts to the accused to prove that it was not reasonably practicable to take the measures in question.

My Lords, prior to the outbreak of fire in the sump, a number of events took place which should not have taken place if Wesleyshire or their servants had acted as they should have done in accordance with the contract or their instructions. In the first place, Mackie drew off thinners into the drum from the projecting pipe in the booth. In the second place, he tipped thinners from time to time into the sump. In the third place, the deceased went into the sump when Mackie was working in the booth above. In the fourth place, he went into the sump with a lamp which was not an approved safety lamp. The justices made no findings that any of these four events should have been foreseen by Austin Rover. In the absence of any such findings, I do not see how it could be said that it was reasonable for Austin Rover to have taken measures to make the premises safe against this unanticipated misuse thereof.

— — —

Emissions into the atmosphere

Section 5 imposes on persons in control of certain prescribed premises a general duty to control emissions into the atmosphere. The Environmental Protection Act 1990 made provision for this section to be repealed, so that the control of such emissions could become the responsibility of HM Inspectors of Pollution, rather than the HSE.

Duty in relation to articles and substances

Section 6, imposing duties on manufacturers and others to ensure that articles and substances supplied for use at work should be as safe as reasonably practicable, was, in 1974, a novel duty, which then caused some concern to industry. Similar provisions for the protection of the general public have now been made under the Consumer Protection Act 1987. That Act also amended s 6 of the 1974 Act, both to make special provision for fairground equipment, and also to make minor amendments to certain phrases of the original which had proved difficult to interpret. One particular point of concern was subsection (8), which enabled the supplier of an article expressly to transfer some responsibility for the safety of an article to the person to whom that article was being supplied. This provision is, however, intended to be the exception to the general rule, relating only to special contracts for the provision of articles for a particular purpose, for example, as components.

It is possible that the general duty in s 6 has less significance now that product harmonisation in the EC has led to the identification of standards for many commodities and regulatory provisions, some EC inspired, have been introduced to deal with specific hazards. See the Control of Substances Hazardous to Health Regulations 1999 and the Chemicals (Hazard Information and Packaging) Regulations 1993:

Section 6

General duties of manufacturers, etc, as regards articles and substances for use at work

(1) It shall be the duty of any person who designs, manufactures, imports or supplies any article for use at work or any article of fairground equipment–

   (a) to ensure, so far as is reasonably practicable, that the article is so designed and constructed as to be safe and without risks to health when it is being set, used, cleaned or maintained by a person at work;

   (b) to carry out or arrange for the carrying out of such testing and examination as may be necessary for the performance of the duty imposed on him by the preceding paragraph;

   (c) to take such steps as are necessary to secure that persons supplied by that person with the article are provided with adequate information about the use for which the article is designed or has been tested and about any conditions necessary to ensure that it will be safe and without risks to health at all such times as are mentioned in paragraph (a) above and when it is being dismantled or disposed of;

   (d) to take such steps as are necessary to secure, so far as is reasonably practicable, that persons so supplied are provided with all such revisions of information provided to them by virtue of the preceding paragraph as are necessary by reason of its becoming known that anything gives rise to a serious risk to health or safety.

(1A) It shall be the duty of any person who designs, manufactures, imports or supplies any article of fairground equipment ...

   ...

(2) It shall be the duty of any person who undertakes the design or manufacture of any article for use at work or any article of fairground equipment to carry out or arrange for the carrying out of any necessary research with a view to the discovery and, so far as is reasonably practicable, the elimination or minimisation of any risks to health or safety to which the design or article may give rise.

(3) It shall be the duty of any person who erects or installs any article for use at work in any premises where that article is to be used by persons at work or who erects or installs any article of fairground equipment, to ensure, so far as is reasonably practicable, that nothing about the way in which it is erected or installed makes it unsafe or a risk to health at any such time as is mentioned in paragraph (a) of subsection (1) or, as the case may be, in paragraph (a) of subsections (1) or 1(A) above.

(4) It shall be the duty of any person who manufactures, imports or supplies any substance for use at work–

   (a) to ensure, so far as is reasonably practicable, that the substance will be safe and without risks to health when it is being used, handled, processed, stored or transported by a person at work or in premises to which s 4 above applies;

   (b) to carry out or arrange for the carrying out of such testing and examination as may be necessary for the performance of the duty imposed on him by the preceding paragraph;

   (c) to take such steps as are necessary to secure that persons supplied by that person with the substance are provided with adequate information about any risks to health or safety to which the inherent properties of the substance may give rise, about the results of any relevant tests which have been carried out on or in connection with the substance and about any conditions necessary to ensure that the substance will be safe and without risks to health at all such times as mentioned in paragraph (a) above and when the substance is being disposed of; and

   (d) to take such steps as are necessary to secure, so far as is reasonably practicable, that persons so supplied are provided with all such revisions of information provided to them by virtue of the preceding paragraph as are necessary by reason of its becoming known that anything gives rise to a serious risk to health or safety.

(5) It shall be the duty of any person who undertakes the manufacture of any substance to carry out or arrange for the carrying out of any necessary research with a view to the discovery and, so far as is reasonably practicable, the elimination or minimisation of any risks to health or safety to which the substance may give rise at all such times as mentioned in paragraph (a) of subsection (4) above.

(6) Nothing in the preceding provisions of this section shall be taken to require a person to repeat any testing, examination or research which has been carried out otherwise than by him or at his instance, in so far as it is reasonable for him to rely on the results thereof for the purposes of those provisions.

(7) Any duty imposed on any person by any of the preceding provisions of this section shall extend only to things done in the course of a trade, business or other undertaking carried on by him (whether for profit or not) and to matters within his control.

(8) Where a person designs, manufactures, imports or supplies an article for use at work or an article of fairground equipment and does so for or to another on the basis of a written undertaking by that other to take specified steps sufficient to ensure, so far as is reasonably practicable, that the article will be safe and without risks to health at all such times as are mentioned in paragraph (a) or, as the case may be, in paragraph (a) of subsections (1) or (1A) above, the undertaking shall have the effect of relieving the first mentioned person from the duty imposed by virtue of

that paragraph to such extent as is reasonable, having regard to the terms of the undertaking.

(8A) Nothing in subsections (7) or (8) above shall relieve any person who imports any article or substance from any duty in respect of anything which–

(a) in the case of an article designed outside the United Kingdom, was done by and in the course of any trade, profession or other undertaking carried on by, or was within the control of, the person who designed the article; or

(b) in the case of an article designed outside the United Kingdom, was done by and in the course of any trade, profession or other undertaking carried on by, or was within the control of, the person who manufactured the article or substance.

(9) Where a person ('the ostensible supplier') supplies any article for use at work or substance for use at work to another ('the customer') under a hire purchase agreement, conditional sale agreement or credit sale agreement, and the ostensible supplier–

(a) carries on the business of financing the acquisition of goods by others by means of such agreements; and

(b) in the course of that business, acquired his interest in the article or substance supplied to the customer as a means of financing its acquisition by the customer from a third person ('the effective supplier'),

the effective supplier and not the ostensible supplier shall be treated, for the purposes of this section as supplying the article or substance to the customer, and any duty imposed by the preceding provisions of this section on suppliers shall accordingly fall on the effective supplier and not on the ostensible supplier.

(10) For the purposes of this section an absence of safety or a risk to health shall be disregarded in so far as the case in or in relation to which it would arise is shown to be one the occurrence of which could not reasonably be foreseen; and in determining whether any duty imposed by virtue of paragraph (a) of subsections (1), (1A) or (4) above has been performed, regard shall be had to any information or advice which has been provided to any person by the person by whom the article has been designed, manufactured, imported or supplied.

Section 7

Duties of the employee

[Section 7 will be considered in Chapter 13.]

– – –

III DUTIES OF OTHER PERSONS

Section 8

Duty not to interfere with or misuse things provided pursuant to certain provisions

No person shall intentionally or recklessly interfere with or misuse anything provided in the interests of health, safety or welfare in pursuance of any of the relevant statutory provisions.

While this duty is imposed on the world at large, it creates a *mens rea* offence, in that the persons on whom it is imposed are not liable, unless they have acted recklessly or intentionally. The difficulty of identifying what is meant by 'reckless' has already been discussed in Chapter 9. It is not clear whether a person could be liable for intentionally interfering if the interference was well intentioned, but ill-informed, for example, switching off a machine which appeared to be unnecessarily in operation.

Duty to supply equipment, etc

Section 9

Duty not to charge employees for things done or provided pursuant to certain specific requirements

No employer shall levy or permit to be levied on any employee of his any charge in respect of anything done or provided in pursuance of any specific requirement of the relevant statutory provisions.

This section might possibly be difficult to interpret if an employer chose to charge for safety equipment (for example, safety boots) which, in his view, it was desirable to supply in the interests of health or safety, but was not actually prescribed by legislation. Arguably, to make a charge would be contrary to this section, since the employer had formed the view that the equipment was needed in order to perform the general duty of doing what is reasonably practicable to ensure health and safety.

The real wrongdoer

Section 36

Offences due to fault of other person

(1) Where the commission by any person of an offence under any of the relevant statutory provisions is due to the act or default of some other person, that other person shall be guilty of the offence and a person may be charged with and convicted of the offence by virtue of this subsection, whether or not proceedings are taken against the first mentioned person.

(2) Where there would be or have been the commission of an offence under s 33 by the Crown but for the circumstance that that section does not bind the Crown, and that fact is due to the act or default of a person other than the Crown, that person shall be guilty of the offence which, but for that circumstance, the Crown would be committing or would have committed, and may be charged with and convicted of that offence accordingly.

...

Thus, a person might be charged with an offence under s 2, although not an employer (indeed, the employer might be a corporation), if the offence is at least in part the wrongdoing of the person charged. In such a case, it is for the prosecution to decide whether to bring proceedings against the person (in the example, the employer) on whom the duty is imposed.

The Crown immunity to which the section refers is set out in s 48 of the Act. The fact that the Crown may not itself be prosecuted does not prevent an inspector from going on to premises occupied by the Crown.

Director's liability

Section 37
Offences by bodies corporate

(1) Where an offence under any of the relevant statutory provisions committed by a body corporate is proved to have been committed with the consent or connivance of, or to have been attributable to any neglect on the part of, any director, manager, secretary or other similar officer of the body corporate or a person who was purporting to act in any such capacity, he, as well as the body corporate shall be guilty of that offence and shall be liable to be proceeded against and punished accordingly.

(2) Where the affairs of a body corporate are managed by its members, the preceding subsection shall apply in relation to the acts and defaults of a member in connection with his functions of management as if he were a director of the body corporate.

– – –

The following two cases are concerned with whether the defendant had sufficient status to have responsibility for ensuring the statutory duty was observed.

J ARMOUR v J SKEEN (PROCURATOR FISCAL, GLASGOW) [1977] IRLR 310

The following extracts are from a report of the proceedings in the Scottish High Court of Justiciary:

The appellant is the Director of Roads of the Strathclyde Regional Council. He was charged on summary complaint with six offences, each libelling a contravention of s 37(1) of the Health and Safety at Work Act 1974, linked with a contravention of an appropriate section of the Factories Act 1961 and/or relevant Regulations. In the result, the appellant was acquitted of Charge Two and convicted of the other five charges.

...

The Regional Council is a body corporate – s 2 of the Local Government (Scotland) Act 1973. It was established that the council had been in breach of the statutory provisions of the Factories Act 1961 and/or the relevant Regulations libelled in the respective charges, and these were relevant statutory provisions within s 37(1). The Crown had to prove in each charge that the statutory breach was attributable to neglect on the part of the appellant and that he was a person who fell within the categories set out in s 37(1).

If Finding No 16 is justified, and this involved consideration of whether the appellant was a person who came within s 37(1), then the other findings establish that in relation to each of these five charges there was neglect on his part and the contravention was attributable to that neglect.

It was submitted on his behalf that he had no direct duty to carry out the particular duties libelled in the charges, and in particular he had no duty to prepare a general statement of policy in relation to his department which would have led to the statutory requirements being carried out. As a rider to that it was said that no such duty was libelled. So far as that last point is concerned, the libelling of s 37(1) in each charge is sufficient to meet it. So far as the other propositions are concerned, it was argued that, since s 2(1) of the 1974 Act imposed on the employers, ie, the council, the duty to ensure *inter alia* the safety at work of the employees, so far as reasonably practicable, the members of the council, who were the policy makers, were alone responsible for the safety policy and the function of the employees was simply to carry out that policy. There was accordingly no duty on the appellant to carry out the policy, and if there was no duty, there was no neglect.

This argument proceeds on the basis that the neglect on the part of the person in one of the categories mentioned in s 37(1) must be a neglect in relation to a duty which the legislation has placed on that person. In my opinion that is a misconception. Section 37(1) refers to any neglect and that seems to me to relate to any neglect in duty, however constituted, to which the contravention of the safety provisions was attributable. That being so, I am satisfied that the 'Statement of Safety Policy' and, in particular, paragraph 3 thereof (cf Finding 14), and the circular of 18.6.75 (cf Finding 15), both of which were issued by the Council to *inter alia* directors in departments, imposed on the appellant the duty to prepare, on the bones of these documents, a general safety policy in relation to the work of his department. Attention is drawn in the circular to the fact that existing legislation in respect of safety and welfare will continue to be effective.

One of the statutory provisions which he should have had in contemplation was s 127(6) of the Factories Act 1961 which provided for the service of a notice on the inspector within seven days of the work being started, stating the location and nature of the operations. This was a duty imposed on him by the council by virtue of their common law powers as employers and was not based on s 2(1). On the other hand the circular states that the general safety policy which had to be revised (in this case by the appellant) had to be in accordance with the 1974 Act. This included the requirement for a written statement of general policy (s 2(3)) and *inter alia* this should have had in contemplation what might be required to meet the provisions of s 127(6) of the Factories Act. This is reflected in Finding 18 which is not challenged by way of a question as Finding 16 is.

It was then argued that the appellant was not a person within the purview of s 37. There is no question of equiparating a Director of Roads with the term 'director' as used in that section. It was said, however, that the appellant did not fall within the class of 'manager, secretary or other similar officer of the body corporate, or a person who was purporting to act in any such capacity'. Reference was made to *Tesco (Supermarkets) Ltd v Nattrass* (1972).[8] It was held in that case that the manager of one of many stores within a large organisation was not a 'manager' within a similar provision to s 37(1) in the Trades Description Act 1968. Each case will depend on its particular facts, and on this issue will turn on the actual part played in the organisation. Having regard to the position of the appellant in the organisation of the council and the duty which was imposed on him in connection with the provision of a general safety policy in respect of the work of his department I have no difficulty in holding that he came within the ambit of the class of persons referred to in s 37(1).

It was further submitted that the sheriff in making his Findings in Fact, had proceeded on inferences and not on hard evidence. Apart from the fact that the only finding challenged is Finding 16, to which this criticism is not directed, I am of the opinion that any inferences drawn by the sheriff were justifiable inferences from the facts which he had found admitted or proved.

– – –

In proceedings brought under the Fire Precautions Act 1971 against the manager of a shop, it was doubted that he was of sufficient seniority to have to carry 'director's' liability.

REGINA v BOAL [1992] 2 WLR 980

Simon Brown J read the following judgment of the Court of Appeal:

The appellant is employed by W&G Foyle Ltd ('Foyles'), the well known booksellers in Charing Cross Road. He has worked for them now for some 10 years in all. In about November 1988 he was promoted from being senior sales assistant in their technical department to assistant general manager.

On 15 February 1989 the appellant was in charge of the shop: the general manager, Mr Cruickshank, had gone away on a week's holiday. That day officers of the London Fire and Civil Defence Authority inspected the shop following a complaint by a member of the public. They found a number of serious breaches of the premises' fire certificate. To instance but a few, various

---

8   [1972] AC 153.

lighting was defective, certain fire escape routes were narrowed or blocked by an accumulation of boxes and books, a number of doors were bolted and, most serious of all, two sets of double entrance doors were padlocked shut.

On 10 January 1990 both the appellant and Foyles were arraigned before Middlesex Crown Court upon an indictment containing 11 pairs of counts, 22 counts in all. Each even numbered count charged against the appellant an offence contrary to s 7(4) of the Fire Precautions Act 1971, criminal liability on his part being alleged to arise by virtue of s 23 of the Act.

Section 23(1), in its material parts, provides:

> Where an offence under this Act committed by a body corporate is proved ... to be attributable to any neglect on the part of, any director, manager, secretary or other similar officer of the body corporate ... he, as well as the body corporate shall be guilty of that offence ...

The 11 counts directed against the appellant charged that he was 'a manager' of Foyles when the relevant offences were committed by them and that such offences were attributable to his neglect.

On 17 January 1990, following a trial, the jury found him guilty of seven additional counts: he was acquitted of one. That same day he was sentenced by Judge Lowe to three months' imprisonment suspended for 12 months. That was the sentence passed concurrently on each of the two counts involving padlocked double doors. Concurrent sentences of one month's imprisonment suspended for 12 months were imposed upon each of the other eight counts for which he fell to be sentenced.

...

The appellant initially sought leave to appeal solely against sentence, contending that a term of imprisonment, albeit suspended, was wholly inappropriate for a first time offender in his position. Upon leave being refused by the single judge, his application was renewed to the full court. On 2 October 1990, this court, presided over by Lord Lane CJ, of its own motion expressed doubt whether the appellant was in fact a 'manager of the body corporate' within s 23, and in the upshot granted leave to appeal not merely against sentence but also, out of time, against conviction. Thereupon counsel originally instructed settled grounds of appeal against conviction in which he asserted that the appellant was at no material time a 'manager or other similar officer' of Foyles within s 23 and that his pleas of guilt had been made 'under the misapprehension that he was'.

...

It follows from all this that the appellant was only properly to be regarded as imperilled by s 23 if, as the assistant general manager of the shop, he had 'the management of the whole affairs of the company', 'was intrusted with power to transact the whole of the affairs of the company', and was 'managing in a governing role the affairs of the company itself'. The intended scope of s 23 is, we accept, to fix with criminal liability only those who are in a position of real authority, the decision-makers within the company who have both the power and responsibility to decide corporate policy and strategy. It is to catch those responsible for putting proper procedures in place; it is not meant to strike at underlings.

What, then, was the appellant's real position in the company? The fact is that because this whole question went by default, there is scant evidence about this in the documents before us. We are told that the only directors of the company are Miss Christina Foyle and her husband, and that the only other person senior to the appellant was Mr Cruickshank the general manager. In evidence, the appellant described his duties thus:

'My primary duty was to be the chief buyer, checking the orders generated by our assistants and presented to me by the representatives. The rest of my work was in the cash office counting the money sent up from the shopfloor, making sure that it was sent down to the bank in its correct fashion, and generally anything else required of management. I had to maybe ensure that staff were in when they were supposed to be in. I had to assist them in anything that they required. There were all other managerial functions.'

That said, it certainly appears that the appellant was given no management training by the company, least of all in matters of health and safety at work or fire precautions. When, however, asked at trial, 'Who is generally responsible on the premises within your organisation for fire safety?' he answered in the broadest terms that he and the general manager 'both have responsibility for the whole thing really', and accepted that he was aware of the general responsibilities imposed by the fire certificate.

Were these admissions sufficient to indicate that, even on the correct, narrow, approach to s 23, the appellant was properly to be regarded as a manager of the company?

...

We disagree. Whilst declining to accept the full width of Mr de Haan's submissions – which include the proposition that not even Mr Cruickshank as the general manager could properly be said to fall within s 23 – we are certainly disposed to agree that this appellant could well have been regarded as responsible only for the day to day running of the bookshop rather than enjoying any sort of governing role in respect of the affairs of the company itself. Whether or not such a defence, had it been advanced at the trial, must inevitably have prospered, it is frankly not possible to say. The issue would clearly have needed to be explored a good deal further than it was. But we do conclude not merely that such defence would have had a realistic prospect of success but that in all likelihood it would have prevailed.

The director of a company registered under the Companies Acts may be disqualified from holding office as a director under s 2(1) of the Company Directors Disqualification Act 1986, should he be found guilty of an indictable offence. Some health and safety offences are indictable and there has been at least one occasion on which a director has been so disqualified.[9]

---

9   See 200 Health and Safety Information Bulletin (August 1992) at p 12.

CHAPTER 12

REGULATIONS RELEVANT TO OCCUPATIONAL HEALTH AND SAFETY

INTRODUCTION

In this account so far, reference has been made, as appropriate, to certain regulations. In this chapter, it is only possible to treat in any detail the Control of Substances Hazardous to Health Regulations 1999 (COSHH) and the so called 'Six Pack' as updated – that it is to say the Management of Health and Safety at Work Regulations 1999, made to implement most of the provisions of the EC's Framework Directive – and the five sets of Regulations which, like the Management Regulations, were first brought into force in the UK on 1 January 1993 to implement the first five of the Directives which the EC has made subordinate to the Framework Directive. All seven sets of Regulations have in common that they apply to most workplaces and they impose upon employers the duty to assess and respond to risks. They also stress the need to train and inform workers.

To put the matter into perspective, it may be recalled that, at the time that the HSC published its *Review of Health and Safety Regulation* in 1994, there were 367 sets of Regulations in force. However, part of the work which the Review identified as being necessary was the revocation of many of the Regulations, especially those pre-dating the 1974 Act, which no longer serve a useful purpose. The first proposals to be published in the wake of the *Review* were to streamline the requirements for the display of health and safety information in the workplace. It was expected that it would be possible to remove, without replacement, 51 of the 78 statutory instruments concerning the display of information. This was to be done mainly by repealing s 139 of the Factories Act 1961 and measures made under that Act. This objective was addressed by the Health and Safety Information for Employees (Modifications and Repeals) Regulations 1995 (SI 1995/2923). It is also noteworthy that the Lifting Operations and Lifting Equipment Regulations 1998 (SI 1998/2307) came into force on 5 December 1998. These Regulations, though made in partial response to EC Directive 89/655 on minimum health and safety standards for the use of work equipment, provided an opportunity to replace a number of statutory codes governing lifting operations in particular industries and operations.

The Working Time Regulations 1998 (SI 1998/1833), also made in response to an EC Directive, are sufficiently significant and sufficiently unrelated to the mainstream health and safety regulations for them to be treated separately in the next chapter.

THE MANAGEMENT OF HEALTH AND SAFETY AT WORK REGULATIONS

The Management of Health and Safety at Work Regulations 1992 (SI 1992/2051) were made under the 1974 Act as the principal vehicle for implementing the EC's Framework Directive. These Regulations were subject to amendment on more than one occasion, in order to incorporate further EC Directives. They were re-issued in the form set out below in 1999. The principal requirement of these Regulations (though many other requirements are important) is the assessment of the risks of the workplace. The original risk assessment requirement in the 1992 Regulations was subsequently expanded (to meet EC Directives) to spell out the special need to assess whenever young persons or pregnant women are employed. An important addition to the 1999 Regulations is regulation 4 and Schedule 1, setting out the general principles of prevention as specified in the EC Framework Directive. The new Regulations also expressly refer to compliance with the Fire Precautions (Workplace) Regulations 1997. This is necessary, since these Regulations are not otherwise relevant statutory provisions, although they were made further to implement Article 8(1) and (2) of the Framework Directive.

MANAGEMENT OF HEALTH AND SAFETY AT WORK REGULATIONS 1999 SI 1999/3242

Extracts from the Approved Code of Practice, which was published with these Regulations, are set out in italics following the regulation to which the extract relates; the full Code is not reproduced. The extracts from the Code are only indicative of the content of the full Code.

Regulation 3
Risk assessment

(1) Every employer shall make a suitable and sufficient assessment of–

    (a) the risks to the health and safety of his employees to which they are exposed whilst they are at work; and

    (b) the risks to the health and safety of persons not in his employment arising out of or in connection with the conduct by him of his undertaking,

for the purpose of identifying the measures he needs to take to comply with the requirements and prohibitions imposed upon him by or under the relevant statutory provisions and by Part II of the Fire Precautions (Workplace) Regulations 1997.

(2) Every self-employed person shall make a suitable and sufficient assessment of–

    (a) the risks to his own health and safety to which he is exposed whilst he is at work; and

(b) the risks to the health and safety of persons not in his employment arising out of or in connection with the conduct by him of his undertaking,

for the purpose of identifying the measures he needs to take to comply with the requirements and prohibitions imposed upon him by or under the relevant statutory provisions.

(3) Any assessment, such as is referred to in paragraph (1) or (2), shall be reviewed by the employer or self-employed person who made it if–

(a) there is reason to suspect that it is no longer valid; or

(b) there has been a significant change in the matters to which it relates; and where as a result of any such review changes to an assessment are required, the employer or self-employed person concerned shall make them.

(4) An employer shall not employ a young person unless he has, in relation to risks to the health and safety of young persons, made or reviewed an assessment in accordance with paragraphs (1) and (5).

(5) In making or reviewing the assessment, an employer who employs or is to employ a young person shall take particular account of–

(a) the inexperience, lack of awareness of risks and immaturity of young persons;

(b) the fitting out and layout of the workplace and the workstation;

(c) the nature, degree and duration of exposure to physical, biological and chemical agents;

(d) the form, range, and use of work equipment and the way in which it is handled;

(e) the organisation of processes and activities;

(f) the extent of the health and safety training provided or to be provided to young persons; and

(g) risks from agents, processes and work listed in the Annex to Council Directive 94/33/EC on the protection of young people at work.

(6) Where the employer employs five or more employees, he shall record–

(a) the significant finds of the assessment; and

(b) any group of his employees identified by it as being especially at risk.

A risk assessment should usually involve identifying the hazards present in any working environment or arising out of commercial activities and work activities, and evaluating the extent of the risks involved, taking into account existing precautions and their effectiveness. In this Approved Code:

(a) a hazard is something with the potential to cause harm (this can include substances, plant or machines, methods of work, the working environment and other aspects of work organisation);

(b) a risk is the likelihood of potential harm from that hazard being realised. The extent of the risk will depend on:

(i) the likelihood of that harm occurring;

(ii) the potential severity of that harm, ie of any resultant injury or adverse health effect; and

(iii) the population which might be affected by the hazard, ie the number of people who might be exposed.

The purpose of the risk assessment is to help the employer or self-employed person to determine what measures should be taken to comply with the employer's or self-employed person's duties under the 'relevant statutory provisions' and Part II of the Fire Regulations.

...

Regulation 4

Principles of prevention to be applied

Where an employer implements any preventive and protective measures, he shall do so on the basis of the principles specified in Schedule 1 to these Regulations.

Regulation 5

Health and safety arrangements

(1) Every employer shall make and give effect to such arrangements as are appropriate, having regard to the nature of his activities and the size of his undertaking, for the effective planning, organisation, control, monitoring and review of the preventive and protective measures.

(2) Where the employer employs five or more employees, he shall record the arrangements referred to in paragraph (1).

This regulation requires employers to have arrangements in place to cover health and safety. Effective management of health and safety will depend, amongst other things, on a suitable and sufficient risk assessment being carried out and the findings being used effectively. The health and safety arrangements can be integrated into the management system for all other aspects of the organisation's activities. The management system adopted will need to reflect the complexity of the organisation's activities and working environment. Where the work process is straightforward and the risks generated are relatively simple to control, then very straightforward management systems may be appropriate. For large complicated organisations more complex systems may be appropriate. Although the principles of the management arrangements are the same irrespective of the size of an organisation ...

[The Code continues with paragraphs spelling out the need for employers to plan, organise, control, monitor and review.]

Regulation 6

Health surveillance

Every employer shall ensure that his employees are provided with such health surveillance as is appropriate having regard to the risks to their health and safety which are identified by the assessment.

The risk assessment will identify circumstances in which health surveillance is required by specific health and safety regulations (eg COSHH). Health surveillance should also be introduced where the assessment shows the following criteria to apply:

(a) *there is an identifiable disease or adverse health condition related to the work concerned; and*

(b) *valid techniques are available to detect indications of the disease or condition; and*

(c) *there is a reasonable likelihood that the disease or condition may occur under the particular conditions of work; and*

(d) *surveillance is likely to further the protection of the health of the employees to be covered.*

Regulation 7

Health and safety assistance

(1) Every employer shall, subject to paragraphs (6) and (7), appoint one or more competent persons to assist him in undertaking the measures he needs to take to comply with the requirements and prohibitions imposed upon him by or under the relevant statutory provisions and by Part II of the Fire Precautions (Workplace) Regulations 1997.

(2) Where an employer appoints persons in accordance with paragraph (1), he shall make arrangements for ensuring adequate co-operation between them.

(3) The employer shall ensure that the number of persons appointed under paragraph (1), the time available for them to fulfil their functions and the means at their disposal are adequate having regard to the size of his undertaking, the risks to which his employees are exposed and the distribution of those risks throughout the undertaking.

(4) The employer shall ensure that–

    (a) any person appointed by him in accordance with paragraph (1) who is not in his employment–

        (i) is informed of the factors known by him to affect, or suspected by him of affecting, the health and safety of any other person who may be affected by the conduct of his undertaking, and

        (ii) has access to the information referred to in regulation 10; and

    (b) any person appointed by him in accordance with paragraph (1) is given such information about any person working in his undertaking who is–

        (i) employed by him under a fixed-term contract of employment, or

        (ii) employed in an employment business,

    as is necessary to enable that person properly to carry out the function specified in that paragraph.

(5) A person shall be regarded as competent for the purposes of paragraphs (1) and (8) where he has sufficient training and experience or knowledge and other qualities to enable him properly to assist in undertaking the measures referred to in paragraph (1).

(6) Paragraph (1) shall not apply to a self-employed employer who is not in partnership with any other person where he has sufficient training and

experience or knowledge and other qualities properly to undertake the measures referred to in that paragraph himself.

(7) Paragraph (1) shall not apply to individuals who are employers and who are together carrying on business in partnership where at least one of the individuals concerned has sufficient training and experience or knowledge and other qualities–

    (a) properly to undertake the measures he needs to take to comply with the requirements and prohibitions imposed upon him by or under the relevant statutory provisions; and

    (b) properly to assist his fellow partners in undertaking the measures they need to take to comply with the requirements and prohibitions imposed upon them by or under the relevant statutory provisions.

(8) Where there is a competent person in the employer's employment, that person shall be appointed for the purposes of paragraph (1) in preference to a competent person not in his employment.

Employers are solely responsible for ensuring that those they appoint to assist them with health and safety measures are competent to carry out the tasks they are assigned and are given adequate information and support. In making decisions on who to appoint, employers themselves need to know and understand the work involved, the principles of risk assessment and prevention, and current legislation and health and safety standards. Employers should ensure that anyone they appoint is capable of applying the above to whatever task they are assigned.

Regulation 8
Procedures for serious and imminent danger and for danger areas

(1) Every employer shall–

    (a) establish and where necessary give effect to appropriate procedures to be followed in the event of serious and imminent danger to persons at work in his undertaking;

    (b) nominate a sufficient number of competent persons to implement those procedures in so far as they relate to the evacuation from premises of persons at work in his undertaking; and

    (c) ensure that none of his employees has access to any area occupied by him to which it is necessary to restrict access on grounds of health and safety unless the employee concerned has received adequate health and safety protection.

(2) Without prejudice to the generality of paragraph (1)(a), the procedures referred to in that sub-paragraph shall–

    (a) so far as is practicable, require any persons at work who are exposed to serious and imminent danger to be informed of the nature of the hazard and of the steps taken or to be taken to protect them from it;

    (b) enable the persons concerned (if necessary by taking appropriate steps in the absence of guidance or instruction and in the light of their knowledge and the technical means at their disposal) to stop work and immediately proceed to a place of safety in the event of their being exposed to serious, imminent and unavoidable danger; and

(c) save in exceptional cases for reasons duly substantiated (which cases and reasons shall be specified in those procedures), require the persons concerned to be prevented from resuming work in any situation where there is still a serious and imminent danger.

(3) A person shall be regarded as competent for the purposes of paragraph (1)(b) where he has sufficient training and experience or knowledge and other qualities to enable him properly to implement the evacuation procedures referred to in that sub-paragraph.

Regulation 9

Contact with external services

Every employer shall ensure that any necessary contacts with external services are arranged, particularly as regards first aid, emergency medical care and rescue work.

Employers should establish procedures for any worker to follow if situations presenting serious and imminent danger were to arise, eg a fire or for the police and emergency services an outbreak of public disorder. The procedures should set out:

(a) *the nature of the risk ...*

(b) *additional procedures needed to cover risks beyond those posed by fire and bombs ...*

(c) *the additional responsibilities of any employees, or groups of employees, who may have specific tasks to perform in the event of emergencies ...*

(d) *the role, responsibilities and authority of the competent people nominated to implement the detailed actions ...*

(e) *any requirements laid on employers by health and safety regulations which cover some specific emergency situations;*

(f) *details of when and how the procedures are to be activated ...*

Regulation 10

Information for employees

Every employer shall provide his employees with comprehensible and relevant information on–

(a) the risks to their health and safety identified by the assessment;

(b) the preventive and protective measures;

(c) the procedures referred to in regulation 8(1)(a) and the measure referred to in regulation 4(2)(a) of the Fire Precautions (Workplace) Regulations 1997;

(d) the identity of those persons nominated by him in accordance with regulation 8(1)(b) and regulation 4(2)(b) of the Fire Precautions (Workplace) Regulations 1997; and

(e) the risks notified to him in accordance with regulation 11(1)(c).

(2) Every employer shall, before employing a child, provide a parent of the child with comprehensible and relevant information on–

(a) the risks to his health and safety identified by the assessment;

(b) the preventive and protective measure; and

(c) the risks notified to him in accordance with regulation 11(1)(c).

(3) The reference in para (2) to a parent of the child includes–

    (a) in England and Wales, a person who has parental responsibility, within the meaning of section 3 of the Children Act 1989 for him; and

    (b) in Scotland, a person who has parental rights, within the meaning of section 8 of the Law Reform (Parent and Child) (Scotland) Act 1986 for him.

Regulation 11

Co-operation and co-ordination

(1) Where two or more employers share a workplace (whether on a temporary or a permanent basis) each such employer shall:

    (a) co-operate with the other employers concerned so far as is necessary to enable them to comply with the requirements and prohibitions imposed upon them by or under the relevant statutory provisions and by Part II of the Fire Precautions (Workplace) Regulations 1997;

    (b) (taking into account the nature of his activities) take all reasonable steps to co-ordinate the measures he takes to comply with the requirements and prohibitions imposed upon him by or under the relevant statutory provisions and by Part II of the Fire Precautions (Workplace) Regulations 1997 with the measures the other employers concerned are taking to comply with the requirements and prohibitions imposed upon them by that legislation; and

    (c) take all reasonable steps to inform the other employers concerned of the risks to their employees' health and safety arising out of or in connection with the conduct by him of his undertaking.

(2) Paragraph (1) (except in so far as it refers to Part II of the Fire Precautions (Workplace) Regulations 1997) shall apply to employers sharing a workplace with self-employed persons and to self-employed persons sharing a workplace with other self-employed persons as it applies to employers sharing a workplace with other employers; and the references in that paragraph to employers and the reference in the said paragraph to their employees shall be construed accordingly.

Where a particular employer controls the workplace, others should assist the controlling employer in assessing the shared risks and co-ordinating any necessary measures. In many situations providing information may be sufficient. A controlling employer who has established site-wide arrangements will have to inform new employers or self-employed people of those arrangements so that they can integrate themselves into the co-operation and co-ordination procedures.

Regulation 12

Persons working in host employers' or self-employed undertakings

(1) Every employer and every self-employed person shall ensure that the employer of any employees from an outside undertaking who are working in his undertaking is provided with comprehensive information on–

(a) the risks to those employees' health and safety arising out of or in connection with the conduct by that first mentioned employer or by that self-employed person of his undertaking; and

(b) the measures taken by that first mentioned employer or by that self-employed person in compliance with the requirements and prohibitions imposed upon him by or under the relevant statutory provisions and by Part II of the Fire Precautions (Workplace) Regulations 1997, in so far as the said requirements and prohibitions relate to those employees.

(2) Paragraph (1) (except in so far as it refers to Part II of the Fire Precautions (Workplace) Regulations 1997) shall apply to a self-employed person who is working in the undertaking of an employer or a self-employed person as it applies to employees from an outside undertaking who are working therein; and the reference in that paragraph to the employer of any employees from an outside undertaking who are working in the undertaking of an employer or a self-employed person and the references in the said paragraph to employees from an outside undertaking who are working in the undertaking of an employer or a self-employed person shall be construed accordingly.

(3) Every employer shall ensure that any person working in his undertaking who is not his employee and every self-employed person (not being an employer) shall ensure that any person working in his undertaking is provided with appropriate instructions and comprehensible information regarding any risks to that person's health and safety which arise out of the conduct by that employer or self-employed person of his undertaking.

(4) Every employer shall–

(a) ensure that the employer of any employees from an outside undertaking who are working in his undertaking is provided with sufficient information to enable that second-mentioned employer to identify any person nominated by that first mentioned employer in accordance with regulation 8(1)(b) to implement evacuation procedures as far as those employees are concerned; and

(b) take all reasonable steps to ensure that any employees from an outside undertaking who are working in his undertaking receive sufficient information to enable them to identify any person nominated by him in accordance with regulation 8(1)(b) to implement evacuation procedures as far as they are concerned.

(5) Paragraph (4) shall apply to a self-employed person who is working in an employer's undertaking as it applies to employees from an outside undertaking who are working therein; and the reference in that paragraph to the employer of any employees from an outside undertaking who are working in an employer's undertaking and the references in the said paragraph to employees from an outside undertaking who are working in an employer's undertaking shall be construed accordingly.

The risk assessment carried out under regulation 3 will identify risks to people other than the host employers' employees. This will include other employers' employees and self-employed people working in that business. Employers and self-employed people need to ensure that comprehensive information on those risks, and the measures taken to control them is given to other employers and self-employed people ...

Regulation 13

Capabilities and training

(1) Every employer shall, in entrusting tasks to his employees, take into account their capabilities as regards health and safety.

(2) Every employer shall ensure that his employees are provided with adequate health and safety training–

    (a) on their being recruited into the employer's undertaking; and

    (b) on their being exposed to new or increased risks because of–

        (i) their being transferred or given a change of responsibilities within the employer's undertaking;

        (ii) the introduction of new work equipment into or a change respecting work equipment already in use within the employer's undertaking;

        (iii) the introduction of new technology into the employer's undertaking; or

        (iv) the introduction of a new system of work into or a change respecting a system of work already in use within the employer's undertaking.

(3) The training referred to in paragraph (2) shall–

    (a) be repeated periodically where appropriate;

    (b) be adapted to take account of any new or changed risks to health and safety of the employees concerned; and

    (c) take place during working hours.

When allocating work to employees, employers should ensure that the demands of the job do not exceed the employees' ability to carry out the work without risk to themselves or others. Employers should take account of the employees' capabilities and the level of their training, knowledge and experience ...

Regulation 14

Employees' duties

(1) Every employee shall use any machinery, equipment, dangerous substance, transport equipment, means of production or safety device provided to him by his employer in accordance both with any training in the use of the equipment concerned which has been received by him and the instructions respecting that use which have been provided to him by the said employer in compliance with the requirements and prohibitions imposed upon that employer by or under the relevant statutory provisions.

(2) Every employee shall inform his employer or any other employee of that employer with specific responsibility for the health and safety of his fellow employees–

(a) of any work situation which a person with the first mentioned employee's training and instruction would reasonably consider represented a serious and immediate danger to health and safety; and

(b) of any matter which a person with the first mentioned employee's training and instruction would reasonably consider represented a shortcoming in the employer's protection arrangements for health and safety,

in so far as that situation or matter either affects the health and safety of that first mentioned employee or arises out of or in connection with his own activities at work, and has not previously been reported to his employer or to any other employee of that employer in accordance with this paragraph.

Employees' duties under section 7 of the Health and Safety at Work Act 1974 include co-operating with their employer to enable the employer to comply with statutory duties for health and safety. Under these Regulations, employers or those they appoint (eg under regulation 7) to assist them with health and safety matters therefore need to be informed without delay of any work situation which might present a serious and imminent danger. Employees should also notify any shortcomings in the health and safety arrangements even when no immediate danger exists ...

Regulation 15

Temporary workers

(1) Every employer shall provide any person whom he has employed under a fixed-term contract of employment with comprehensible information on–

(a) any special occupational qualifications or skills required to be held by that employee if he is to carry out his work safely; and

(b) any health surveillance required to be provided to that employee by or under any of the relevant statutory provisions,

and shall provide the said information before the employee concerned commences his duties.

(2) Every employer and every self-employed person shall provide any person employed in an employment business who is to carry out work in his undertaking with comprehensible information on–

(a) any special occupational qualifications or skills required to be held by that employee if he is to carry out his work safely; and

(b) any health surveillance required to be provided to that employee by or under any of the relevant statutory provisions.

(3) Every employer and every self-employed person shall ensure that every person carrying on an employment business whose employees are to carry out work in his undertaking is provided with comprehensible information on–

(a) any special occupational qualifications or skills required to be held by those employees if they are to carry out their work safely; and

(b) the specific features of the jobs to be filled by those employees (in so far as those features are likely to affect their health and safety);

and the person carrying on the employment business concerned shall ensure that the information so provided is given to the said employees.

Regulation 16

Risks to new or expectant mothers

(1) Where–

(a) the persons working in an undertaking include women of childbearing age; and

(b) the work is of a kind which could involve risk, by reason of her condition, to the health and safety of a new or expectant mother, or that of her baby, from any processes or working conditions, or physical, biological or chemical agents, including those specified in Annexes I and II of Council Directive 92/85/EEC on the introduction of measures to encourage improvements in the safety and health at work of pregnant workers and workers who have recently given birth or are breastfeeding,

the assessment required by regulation 3(1) shall include an assessment of such risk.

(2) Where, in the case of an individual employee, the taking of any other action the employer is required to take under the relevant statutory provisions would not avoid the risk referred to in paragraph (1) the employer shall, if it is reasonable to do so, and would avoid such risks, alter her working conditions or hours of work.

(3) If it is not reasonable to alter the working conditions or hours of work, or if it would not avoid such risk, the employer shall, subject to s 67 of the 1996 Act[1] suspend the employee from work for so long as is necessary to avoid such risk.

(4) In paragraphs (1) to (3) references to risk, in relation to risk from any infectious or contagious disease, are references to a level or risk at work which is in addition to the level to which a new or expectant mother may be expected to be exposed outside the workplace.

Regulation 17

Certificate from registered medical practitioner in respect of new or expectant mothers

Where–

(a) a new or expectant mother works at night; and

---

1   Employment Rights Act 1996.

(b) a certificate from a registered medical practitioner or a registered midwife shows that it is necessary for her health or safety that she should not be at work for any period of such work identified in the certificate,

the employer shall, subject to section 67 of the 1996 Act, suspend her from work for so long as is necessary for her health or safety

Regulation 18

Notification by new or expectant mothers

(1) Nothing in paragraphs (2) or (3) of regulation 16 shall require the employer to take any action in relation to an employee until she has notified the employer in writing that she is pregnant, has given birth within the previous six months or is breastfeeding.

(2) Nothing in paragraphs (2) or (3) of regulation 16 or in regulation 17 shall require the employer to maintain action taken in relation to an employee:

(a) in a case –

(i) to which regulation 16(2) or (3) relates; and

(ii) where the employee has notified her employer that she is pregnant, where she has failed, within a reasonable time of being requested to do so in writing by her employer, to produce for the employer's inspection a certificate from a registered medical practitioner or a registered midwife showing that she is pregnant;

(b) once the employer knows that she is no longer a new or expectant mother; or

(c) if the employer cannot establish whether she remains a new or expectant mother.

Where the risk assessment identifies risks to new and expectant mothers and these risks cannot avoided by the preventive and protective measures taken by an employer, the employer will need to:

(a) *alter her working conditions or hours of work if it is reasonable to do so and would avoid the risks or, if these conditions cannot be met;*

(b) *identify and offer her suitable alternative work that is available and, if that is not feasible;*

(c) *suspend her from work ...*

Regulation 19

Protection of young persons

(1) Every employer shall ensure that young persons employed by him are protected at work from any risks to their health or safety which are a consequence of their lack of experience, or absence of awareness of existing or potential risks or the fact that young persons have not yet fully matured.

(2) Subject to paragraph (3), no employer shall employ a young person for work–

(a) which is beyond his physical or psychological capacity;

(b) involving harmful exposure to agents which are toxic or carcinogenic, cause heritable genetic damage or harm to the unborn child or which, in any other way, chronically affect human health;

(c) involving harmful exposure to radiation;

(d) involving the risk of accident which, it may reasonably be assumed, cannot be recognised or avoided by young persons, owing to their insufficient attention to safety or lack of experience or training; or

(e) in which there is a risk to health from–

   (i) extreme cold or heat;

   (ii) noise; or

   (iii) vibration,

and in determining whether work will involve harm or risks for the purposes of this paragraph, regard shall be had to the results of the assessment.

(3) Nothing in paragraph (2) shall prevent the employment of a young person who is no longer a child for work–

(a) where it is necessary for his training;

(b) where the young person will be supervised by a competent person; and

(c) where any risk will be reduced to the lowest level that is reasonably practicable.

(4) The provisions contained in this regulation are without prejudice to–

(a) the provisions contained elsewhere in these Regulations; and

(b) any prohibition or restriction, arising otherwise than by this regulation, on the employment of any person.

...

Regulation 21

Provisions as to liability

Nothing in the relevant statutory provisions shall operate so as to afford an employer a defence in any criminal proceedings for a contravention of those provisions by reason of any act or default of–

(a) an employee of his, or

(b) a person appointed by him under regulation 7.

Regulation 22

Exclusion of civil liability

(1) Breach of a duty imposed by these Regulations shall not confer a right of action in any civil proceedings.

(2) Paragraph (1) shall not apply to any duty imposed by these Regulations on an employer–

(a) to the extent that it relates to risk referred to in regulation 16(1) to an employee; or

(b) which is contained in regulation 19.

...

Schedule 1

Regulation 4

General principles of prevention

(This Schedule specifies the general principles of prevention set out in Article 6(2) of Council Directive 89/391/EEC:)

(a) avoiding risks;

(b) evaluating the risks which cannot be avoided;

(c) combating risks at source;

(d) adapting the work to the individual, especially as regards the design of workplaces, the choice of work equipment and the choice of working and production methods, with a view, in particular, to alleviating monotonous work and work at a predetermined work rate and to reducing their effect on health;

(e) adapting to technical progress;

(f) replacing the dangerous by the non-dangerous or the less dangerous;

(g) developing a coherent overall prevention policy which covers technology, organisation of work, working conditions, social relationships and the influence of factors relating to the working environment;

(h) giving collective protective measures priority over individual protective measures; and

(i) giving appropriate instructions to employees.

– – –

Comment

The Management of Health and Safety at Work Regulations are almost certainly the most important regulations made since the 1974 Act. Like the Act, they apply to all workplaces (apart from the disapplication in regulation 2 to ships and the provision in regulation 20 for the exemption of defence establishments). They spell out that risk assessment and control form the basis of all occupational health and safety. They impose duties on employers, self-employed, and employees. They require organisations to work together to ensure safe systems and they require employers to train their employees to operate safely; employees themselves are required to inform their employers if they become aware of unsafe situations. The risk assessment and training requirements are largely repeated in other regulations in relation to specific hazards.

While the Regulations are primarily concerned with the implementation of the Framework Directive, they also, in regulation 15, seek to implement the

Temporary Workers Directive 91/383/EEC. Regulations 17, 18 and 19 were introduced in order to implement provisions of the EC Directive on Pregnant Workers (92/85/EC); other parts of this latter Directive are covered in the Employment Rights Act 1996. Regulation 19 is in partial implementation of the Directive on the Protection of Young People at Work (94/33/EC).

It has been suggested that, since the Regulations are made under and are, therefore, subordinate to the 1974 Act, they may fall short of compliance with the Directive. In particular, it has been suggested that the qualification of the general duties in the 1974 Act by 'reasonable practicability' ill matches the EC requirement for absolute safety. While risk assessment has to be carried out to ensure compliance with the general duties and other statutory duties, it is true that the duties in ss 2–9 of the 1974 Act, though described by judges as absolute duties, are, in most cases, qualified by the defence of reasonable practicability. However, the duty in regulation 3 to assess risks is an absolute one and so also are certain other of the duties in these Regulations, for example, that in regulation 19, relating to the protection of young persons. Significantly, the 1999 Regulations introduce regulation 19, providing that an employer may not plead the act or omission of either an employee or a competent person appointed under these Regulations by way of defence where he is charged with a breach of any of the relevant statutory provisions. The significance of this new regulation cannot be overstated. It would appear to mean that the debate, noted in the previous chapter, about whether an employer can escape criminal liability by pleading that it was not reasonably practicable to prevent the casual negligence of a properly trained and appointed employee, cannot be pursued in future.

WORKPLACE (HEALTH, SAFETY AND WELFARE) REGULATIONS 1992 SI 1992/3004

Extracts from the Approved Code of Practice are printed in italics following the regulation to which the extract applies. The extracts given are only indicative of the nature of the Code; readers should not be confused into believing that the whole Code is produced here.

Regulation 4
Requirements under these Regulations

(1) Every employer shall ensure that every workplace, modification, extension or conversion which is under his control and where any of his employees work complies with any requirement of these Regulations which–

    (a) applies to that workplace or, as the case may be, to the workplace which contains that modification, extension or conversion; and

    (b) is in force in respect of the workplace, modification, extension or conversion.

...

Regulation 5

Maintenance of workplace, and of equipment, devices and systems

(1) The workplace and the equipment, devices and systems to which this regulation applies shall be maintained (including cleaned as appropriate) in an efficient state, in efficient working order and in good repair.

(2) Where appropriate, the equipment, devices and systems to which this regulation applies shall be subject to a suitable system of maintenance.

(3) The equipment, devices and systems to which this regulation applies are–

(a) equipment and devices a fault in which is liable to result in a failure to comply with any of these Regulations; and

(b) mechanical ventilation systems provided pursuant to regulation 6 (whether or not they include equipment or devices within sub-paragraph (a) of this paragraph).

The workplace, and the equipment and devices mentioned in these Regulations, should be maintained in an efficient state, in efficient working order and in good repair. 'Efficient' in this context means efficient from the view of health, safety and welfare (not productivity or economy). If a potentially dangerous defect is discovered, the defect should be rectified immediately or steps should be taken to protect anyone who might be put at risk, for example by preventing access until the work can be carried out or the equipment replaced. Where the defect does not pose a danger but makes the equipment unsuitable for use, for example a sanitary convenience with a defective flushing mechanism, it may be taken out of service until it is repaired or replaced but, if this would result in the number of facilities being less than that required by the Regulations, the defect should be rectified without delay.

Steps should be taken to ensure that repair and maintenance work is carried out properly.

Regulation 5(2) requires a system of maintenance where appropriate, for certain equipment and devices and for ventilation systems. A suitable system of maintenance involves ensuring that:

(a) regular maintenance (including, as necessary, inspection, testing, adjustment, lubrication and cleaning) is carried out at suitable intervals;

(b) any potentially dangerous defects are remedied, and that access to defective equipment is prevented in the meantime;

(c) regular maintenance and remedial work is carried out properly; and

(d) a suitable record is kept to ensure that the system is properly implemented and to assist in validating maintenance programmes.

Regulation 6

Ventilation

(1) Effective and suitable provision shall be made to ensure that every enclosed workplace is ventilated by a sufficient quantity of fresh or purified air.

(2) Any plant used for the purpose of complying with paragraph (1) shall include an effective device to give visible or audible warning of any failure of the plant where necessary for reasons of health or safety.

...

In many cases, windows and other openings will provide sufficient ventilation in some or all parts of the workplace. Where necessary, mechanical ventilation systems should be provided for parts or all of the workplace, as appropriate.

Workers should not be subject to uncomfortable draughts. In the case of mechanical ventilation systems it may be necessary to control the direction or velocity of air flow. Workstations should be re-sited or screened if necessary.

In the case of mechanical ventilation systems which recirculate air, including air conditioning systems, recirculated air should be adequately filtered to remove impurities. To avoid air becoming unhealthy, purified air should have some fresh air added to it before being recirculated. Systems should therefore be designed with fresh air inlets which should be kept open.

Regulation 7

Temperature in indoor workplaces

(1) During working hours, the temperature in all workplaces inside buildings shall be reasonable.

(2) A method of heating or cooling shall not be used which results in the escape into a workplace of fumes, gas or vapour of such character and to such extent that they are likely to be injurious or offensive to any person.

(3) A sufficient number of thermometers shall be provided to enable persons at work to determine the temperature in any workplace inside a building.

Regulation 8

Lighting

(1) Every workplace shall have suitable and sufficient lighting.

(2) The lighting mentioned in paragraph (1) shall, so far as is reasonably practicable, be by natural light.

(3) Without prejudice to the generality of paragraph (1) suitable and sufficient emergency lighting shall be provided in any room in circumstances in which persons at work are specially exposed to danger in the event of failure of artificial lighting.

Lighting should be sufficient to enable people to work, use facilities and move from place to place safely and without experiencing eye strain. Stairs should be well lit in such a way that shadows are not cast over the main part of the treads. Where necessary, local lighting should be provided at individual workstations, and at places of particular risk such as pedestrian crossing points on vehicular traffic routes. Outdoor traffic routes used by pedestrians should be adequately lit after dark.

Dazzling lights and annoying glare should be avoided ...

Lights should not be allowed to become obscured, for example by stacked goods, in such a way that the level of light becomes insufficient. Lights should be replaced, repaired, or cleaned, as necessary, before the level of lighting becomes insufficient. Fittings or lights should be replaced immediately if they become dangerous, electrically or otherwise.

...

Emergency lighting should, however, be provided in workrooms where sudden loss of light would present a serious risk, for example if process plant needs to be shut down under manual control or a potentially hazardous process needs to be made safe, and this cannot be done safely without lighting.

Regulation 9

Cleanliness and waste materials

(1) Every workplace and the furniture, furnishing and fittings therein shall be kept sufficiently clean.

(2) The surfaces of the floor, wall and ceiling of all workplaces inside buildings shall be capable of being kept sufficiently clean.

(3) So far as is reasonably practicable, waste materials shall not be allowed to accumulate in a workplace, except in suitable receptacles.

Floors and indoor traffic routes should be cleaned at least once a week. In factories and other workplaces of a type where dirt and refuse accumulates, any dirt and refuse which is not in suitable receptacles should be removed at least daily ...

Interior walls, ceilings and work surfaces should be cleaned at suitable intervals. Except in parts which are normally visited only for short periods, or where any soiling is likely to be light, ceilings and interior walls should be painted, tiled or otherwise treated so that they can be kept clean, and the surface treatment should be renewed when it can no longer be cleaned properly ...

Regulation 10

Room dimensions and space

(1) Every room where persons work shall have sufficient floor area, height and unoccupied space for purposes of health, safety and welfare. ...

The total volume of the room, when empty, divided by the number of people normally working in it should be at least 11 cubic metres. In making this calculation a room or part of a room which is more than 3.0 metres high should be counted as 3.0 metres high. The figure of 11 cubic metres per person is a minimum and may be insufficient if, for example, much of the room is taken up by furniture, etc ...

Regulation 11

Workstations and seating

(1) Every workstation shall be so arranged that it is suitable both for any person at work in the workplace who is likely to work at that workstation and for any work of the undertaking which is likely to be done there.

(2) Without prejudice to the generality of paragraph (1), every workstation outdoors shall be so arranged that–

(a) so far as is reasonably practicable, it provides protection from adverse weather;

(b) it enables any person at the workstation to leave it swiftly or, as appropriate, to be assisted in the event of an emergency; and

(c) it ensures that any person at the workstation is not likely to slip or fall.

(3) A suitable seat shall be provided for each person at work in the workplace whose work includes operations of a kind that the work (or a substantial part of it) can or must be done sitting.

(4) A seat shall not be suitable for the purposes of paragraph (3) unless–

    (a) it is suitable for the person for whom it is provided as well as for the operations to be performed; and

    (b) a suitable foot rest is also provided where necessary.

Workstations should be arranged so that each task can be carried out safely and comfortably. The worker should be at a suitable height in relation to the work surface. Work materials and frequently used equipment or controls should be within easy reach, without undue bending or stretching.

Workstations including seating, and access to workstations, should be suitable for any special needs of the individual worker, including workers with disabilities.

Each workstation should allow any person who is likely to work there adequate freedom of movement and the ability to stand upright. Spells of work which unavoidably have to be carried out in cramped conditions should be kept as short as possible and there should be sufficient space nearby to relieve discomfort.

Regulation 12

Condition of floors and traffic routes

(1) Every floor in a workplace and the surface of every traffic route in a workplace shall be of a construction such that the floor or surface of the traffic route is suitable for the purpose for which it is used.

(2) Without prejudice to the generality of paragraph (1), the requirements in that paragraph shall include requirements that–

    (a) the floor, or surface of the traffic route, shall have no hole or slope, or be uneven or slippery so as, in each case, to expose any person to a risk to his health or safety;

    (b) every such floor shall have effective means of drainage where necessary.

(3) So far as is reasonably practicable, every floor in a workplace and the surface of every traffic route in a workplace shall be kept free from obstructions and from any article or substance which may cause a person to slip, trip or fall.

(4) In considering whether, for the purposes of paragraph (2)(a), a hole or slope exposes any person to a risk to his health or safety–

    (a) no account shall be taken of a hole where adequate measures have been taken to prevent a person falling;

    (b) account shall be taken of any handrail provided in connection with any slope.

(5) Suitable and sufficient handrails and, if appropriate, guards shall be provided on all traffic routes which are staircases except in circumstances in which a handrail cannot be provided without obstructing the traffic route.

Floors and traffic routes should be of sound construction and should have adequate strength and stability taking account of the loads placed on them and the traffic passing over them. Floors should not be overloaded.

...

Floors and traffic routes should be kept free of obstructions which may present a hazard or impede access. This is particularly important on or near stairs, steps, escalators and moving walkways, on emergency routes, in or near doorways or gangways, and in any place where an obstruction is likely to cause an accident, for example near a corner or junction. Where a temporary obstruction is unavoidable and is likely to be a hazard, access should be prevented or steps should be taken to warn people or the drivers of vehicles of the obstruction by, for example, the use of hazard cones. Where furniture or equipment is being moved within a workplace, it should, if possible be moved in a single operation and should not be left in a place where it is likely to be a hazard ... Materials which fall onto traffic routes should be cleared as soon a possible.

...

Every open side of a staircase should be securely fenced ...

Regulation 13

Falls or falling objects

(1) So far as is reasonably practicable, suitable and effective measures shall be taken to prevent any event specified in paragraph (3).

(2) So far as is reasonably practicable, the measures required by paragraph (1) shall be measures other than the provision of personal protective equipment, information, instruction, training or supervision.

(3) The events mentioned in this paragraph are–

    (a) any person falling a distance likely to cause personal injury;

    (b) any person being struck by a falling object likely to cause personal injury.

(4) Any area where there is a risk to health or safety from any event mentioned in paragraph (3) shall be clearly indicated where appropriate.

...

Secure fencing should be provided wherever possible at any place where a person might fall 2 metres or more. Secure fencing should also be provided where a person might fall less than 2 metres, where there are factors which increase the likelihood of a fall or the risk of serious injury; for example where a traffic route passes close to an edge, where large numbers of people are present, or where a person might fall onto a sharp or dangerous surface or into the path of a vehicle. Tanks, pits or similar structures may be securely covered instead of being fenced.

...

Materials and objects should be sorted and stacked in such a way that they are not likely to fall and cause injury. Racking should be of adequate strength ...

...

The need for people to climb on top of vehicles or their loads should be avoided as far as possible ...

...

Where loaded lorries have to be sheeted before leaving a workplace, suitable precautions should be taken against falls ...

...

People should not be allowed into an area where, despite safeguards, they would be in danger, for example, from work going on overhead.

Regulation 14

Windows, and transparent or translucent doors, gates and walls

(1) Every window or other transparent or translucent surface in a wall or partition and every transparent or translucent surface in a door or gate shall, where necessary for reasons of health or safety–

  (a) be of safety material or be protected against breakage of the transparent or translucent material; and

  (b) be appropriately marked or incorporate features so as, in either case, to make it apparent.

Transparent or translucent surfaces in doors, gates, walls and partitions should be of a safety material or be adequately protected against breakage in the following cases:

  (a) in doors and gates, and door and gate side panels, where any part of the transparent or translucent surface is at shoulder level or below;

  (b) in windows, walls and partitions, where any part of the transparent or translucent surface is as waist level or below, except in glasshouses where people there will be likely to be aware of the presence of glazing and avoid contact.

This paragraph does not apply to narrow panes up to 250 mm wide, measured between glazing beads.

Regulation 15

Windows, skylights and ventilators

(1) No window, skylight or ventilator which is capable of being opened shall be likely to be opened, closed or adjusted in a manner which exposes any person performing such operation to a risk to his health or safety.

(2) No window, skylight or ventilator shall be in a position when open which is likely to expose any person in the workplace to a risk to his health or safety.

It should be possible to reach and operate the control of openable windows, skylights and ventilators in a safe manner ...

Open windows, skylights or ventilators should not project into an area where persons are likely to collide with them. The bottom edge of opening windows should normally be at least 800 mm above floor level, unless there is a barrier to prevent falls.

Regulation 16

Ability to clean windows etc safely

(1) All windows and skylights in a workplace shall be of a design or be so constructed that they may be cleaned safely.

(2) In considering whether a window or skylight is of a design or so constructed as to comply with paragraph (1), account may be taken of equipment used in conjunction with the window or skylight or of devices fitted to the building.

Suitable provision should be made so that windows and skylights can be cleaned safely if they cannot be cleaned from the ground or other suitable surface.

Suitable provision includes:

(a) *fitting windows which can be cleaned safely from the inside, for example windows which pivot so that the outer surface is turned inwards;*

(b) *fitting access equipment such as suspended cradles, or travelling ladders with an attachment for a safety harness;*

(c) *providing suitable conditions for the future use of mobile access equipment, including ladders up to 9 metres long. Suitable conditions are adequate access for the equipment, and a firm level surface in a safe place on which to stand it. Where a ladder over 6 metres long will be needed, suitable points for tying or fixing the ladder should be provided.*

(d) *suitable and suitably placed anchorage points for safety harness.*

Regulation 17
Organisation etc of traffic routes

(1) Every workplace shall be organised in such a way that pedestrians and vehicles can circulate in a safe manner.

(2) Traffic routes in a workplace shall be suitable for the persons or vehicles using them, sufficient in number, in suitable positions and of sufficient size.

(3) Without prejudice to the generality of paragraph (2), traffic routes shall not satisfy the requirements of that paragraph unless suitable measures are taken to ensure that –

(a) pedestrians or, as the case may be, vehicles may use a traffic route without causing danger to the health or safety of persons at work near it; and

(b) there is sufficient separation of any traffic route for vehicles from doors or gates or from traffic routes for pedestrians which lead onto it;

(c) where vehicles and pedestrians use the same traffic route, there is sufficient separation between them.

(4) All traffic routes shall be suitably indicated where necessary for reasons of health or safety.

There should be sufficient traffic routes, of sufficient width and headroom, to allow people on foot or in vehicles to circulate safely and without difficulty ...

In some situations people in wheelchairs may be at greater risk than people on foot, and special consideration should be given to their safety ...

Access between floors should not normally be by way of ladders or steep stairs ...

Routes should not be used by vehicles for which they are inadequate or unsuitable ...

Uneven or soft ground should be made smooth and firm if vehicles might otherwise overturn or shed their loads. Sharp or blind bends on vehicle routes should be avoided as far as possible ...

Regulation 18

Doors and gates

(1) Doors and gates shall be suitably constructed (including being fitted with any necessary safety devices).

(2) Without prejudice to the generality of paragraph (1), doors and gates shall not comply with that paragraph unless–

    (a) any sliding door or gate has a device to prevent it coming off its track during use;

    (b) any upward opening door or gate has a device to prevent it falling back;

    (c) any powered door or gate has suitable and effective features to prevent it causing injury by trapping any person;

    (d) where necessary for reasons of health or safety, any powered door or gate can be operated manually unless it opens automatically if the power fails; and

    (e) any door or gate which is capable of opening by being pushed from either side is of such a construction as to provide, when closed, a clear view of the space close to both sides.

Doors and gates which swing in both directions should have a transparent panel ...

Sliding doors should have a stop ... to prevent the door coming off the end of the track ...

Upward opening doors should be fitted with an effective device ... to prevent them falling back in a manner likely to cause injury.

Power operated doors and gates should have safety features to prevent people being injured as a result of being struck or trapped ...

Regulation 19

Escalators and moving walkways

(1) Escalators and moving walkways shall–

    (a) function safely;

    (b) be equipped with any necessary safety devices;

    (c) be fitted with one or more emergency stop control which is easily identifiable and readily accessible.

Regulation 20

Sanitary conveniences

(1) Suitable and sufficient sanitary conveniences shall be provided at readily accessible places.

(2) Without prejudice to the generality of paragraph (1), sanitary conveniences shall not be suitable unless–

    (a) the rooms containing them are adequately ventilated and lit;

(b) they and the rooms containing them are kept in a clean and orderly condition; and

(c) separate rooms containing conveniences are provided for men and women, except where and so far as each convenience is in a separate room the door of which is capable of being secured from inside.

...

Regulation 21

Washing facilities

(1) Suitable and sufficient washing facilities, including showers if required by the nature of the work or for health reasons, shall be provided at readily accessible places.

(2) Without prejudice to the generality of paragraph (1), washing facilities shall not be suitable unless–

(a) they are provided in the immediate vicinity of every sanitary convenience, whether or not provided elsewhere as well;

(b) they are provided in the vicinity of any changing rooms required by these Regulations, whether or not provided elsewhere as well;

(c) they include a supply of clean hot and cold, or warm, water (which shall be running water so far as is practicable);

(d) they include soap or other suitable means of cleaning;

(e) they include towels or other suitable means of drying;

(f) the rooms containing them are sufficiently ventilated and lit;

(g) they and the rooms containing them are kept in a clean and orderly condition; and

(h) separate facilities are provided for men and women, except where and so far as they are provided in a room the door of which is capable of being secured from inside and the facilities in each such room are intended to be used by only one person at a time.

(3) Paragraph (2)(h) shall not apply to facilities which are provided for washing the hands, forearms and face only.

Sufficient facilities should be provided to enable everyone at work to use them without undue delay.

...

Facilities should provide adequate protection from the weather.

Water closets should be connected to a suitable drainage system and be provided with an effective means for flushing with water. Toilet paper in a holder or dispenser and a coat hook should be provided. In the case of water closets used by women, suitable means should be provided for the disposal of sanitary dressings.

Washing stations should have running hot and cold, or warm water, and be large enough to enable effective washing of face, hands and forearms. Showers or baths should also be provided where the work is:

(a) particularly strenuous;

(b) *dirty; or*

(c) *results in contamination of the skin by harmful or offensive materials.*

This includes, for example, work with molten metal in foundries and the manufacture of oil cake.

Regulation 22

Drinking water

(1) An adequate supply of wholesome drinking water shall be provided for all persons at work in the workplace.

(2) Every supply of drinking water required by paragraph (1) shall–

    (a) be readily accessible at suitable places; and

    (b) be conspicuously marked by an appropriate sign where necessary for reasons of health or safety.

(3) Where a supply of drinking water is required by paragraph (1), there shall also be provided a sufficient number of suitable cups or other drinking vessels unless the supply of drinking water is in a jet from which persons can drink easily.

Drinking water should normally be obtained from a public or private water supply by means of a tap on a pipe connected directly to the water main.

...

Drinking water taps should not be installed in places where contamination is likely, for example in a workshop where lead is handled or processed. As far as is reasonably practicable they should also not be installed in sanitary accommodation.

...

Drinking cups or beakers should be provided unless the supply is by means of a drinking fountain ...

Drinking water supplies should be marked as such if people may otherwise drink from supplies which are not meant for drinking ...

Regulation 23

Accommodation for clothing

(1) Suitable and sufficient accommodation shall be provided–

    (a) for any person at work's own clothing which is not worn during working hours; and

    (b) for special clothing which is worn by any person at work but which is not taken home.

(2) Without prejudice to the generality of paragraph (1) the accommodation mentioned in that paragraph shall not be suitable unless–

    (a) where facilities to change clothing are required by regulation 24, it provides suitable security for the clothing mentioned in paragraph (1)(a);

    (b) where necessary to avoid risks to health or damage to the clothing, it includes separate accommodation for clothing worn at work and for other clothing;

(c) so far as is reasonably practicable, it allows or includes facilities for drying clothes; and

(d) it is in a suitable location.

Accommodation for work clothing and workers' own personal clothing should enable it to hang in a clean, warm, dry, well-ventilated place where it can dry out during the course of a working day if necessary ...

Where work clothing (including personal protective equipment) which is not taken home becomes dirty, damp or contaminated due to the work it should be accommodated separately from the worker's own clothing. Where work clothing becomes wet, the facilities should enable it to be dried by the beginning of the following work period unless other dry clothing is provided.

Regulation 24

Facilities for changing clothing

(1) Suitable and sufficient facilities shall be provided for any person at work in the workplace to change clothing in all cases where–

    (a) the person has to wear special clothing for the purpose of work; and

    (b) the person can not, for reasons of health or propriety, be expected to change in another room.

Without prejudice to the generality of paragraph (1), the facilities mentioned in that paragraph shall not be suitable unless they include separate facilities for, or separate use of facilities by, men and women where necessary for reasons of propriety.

Changing facilities should be readily accessible from workrooms and eating facilities, if provided. They should be provided with adequate seating and should contain, or communicate directly with, clothing accommodation and showers or baths if provided. They should be constructed and arranged to ensure the privacy of the user.

Regulation 25

Facilities for rest and to eat meals

(1) Suitable and sufficient rest facilities shall be provided at readily accessible places.

(2) Rest facilities provided by virtue of paragraph (1) shall–

    (a) where necessary for reasons of health or safety include, in the case of a new workplace, extension or conversion, rest facilities provided in one or more rest rooms, or, in other cases, in rest rooms or rest areas;

    (b) include suitable facilities to eat meals where food eaten in the workplace would otherwise be likely to become contaminated.

(3) Rest rooms and rest areas shall include suitable arrangements to protect non-smokers from discomfort caused by tobacco smoke.

(4) Suitable facilities shall be provided for any person at work who is a pregnant woman or nursing mother to rest.

(5) Suitable and sufficient facilities shall be provided for persons at work to eat meals where meals are regularly eaten in the workplace.

...

Where workers regularly eat meals at work suitable and sufficient facilities should be provided for the purpose. Such facilities should also be provided where food would otherwise be likely to be contaminated, including by dust or water ...

... Workers who work during hours or at places where hot food cannot be obtained in, or reasonably near to, the workplace should be provided with the means for heating their own food.

Eating facilities should be kept clean to a suitable hygiene standard ...

– – –

Comment

These Regulations are to implement the EC Directive on the Workplace.[2] When they were brought into force a number of provisions in earlier legislation were repealed; namely, ss 1–7, 18, 28, 29, 57–60 and 68 of the Factories Act 1961, ss 4–16 of the Offices, Shops and Railway Premises Act 1963 and ss 3 and 5 and s 25(3) and (6) of the Agriculture (Safety, Health and Welfare Provisions) Act 1956 and part or all of some 36 sets of Regulations. They apply to almost all workplaces; indeed regulation 3 starts with the proposition that they apply to every workplace and then lists the exceptions, which are primarily building sites, mines, quarries and oil rigs. As with other sets of Regulations in the Six Pack, the Secretary of State for Defence, may, in the interests of national security, claim exemption from the application of these regulations to military forces.

These Regulations are accompanied by both an Approved Code of Practice and guidance from the Health and Safety Executive and, in the HSE publication, the paragraph numbering does not clearly distinguish one from the other. The standards provided in the Approved Code of Practice are in many instances those which were built into the earlier legislation, particularly the Factories Act 1961 and regulations made under that Act. However, the Code applies to many workplaces which were not within the ambit of the 1961 Act: on the other hand the Code does not have the same mandatory status as the old laws had. The guidance frequently refers to other publications which give more detailed information about particular matters dealt with in the Code or guidance.

PROVISION AND USE OF WORK EQUIPMENT REGULATIONS 1998
SI 1998/2306

Regulation 2

Interpretation

(1)   In these Regulations, unless the context otherwise requires–

...

2   89/654/EEC.

'inspection' in relation to an inspection under paragraph (1) or (2) of regulation 6–

(a) means such visual or more rigorous inspection by a competent persons as is appropriate for the purpose described in the paragraph;

(b) where it is appropriate to carry out testing for the purpose, includes testing the nature and extent of which are appropriate for the purpose;

'power press' means a press or press brake for the working of metal by means of tools, or for die proving, which is power driven and which embodies a flywheel and clutch;

...

'use' in relation to work equipment means any activity involving work equipment and includes starting, stopping, programming, setting, transporting, repairing, modifying, maintaining, servicing and cleaning, and related expressions shall be construed accordingly;

'work equipment' means any machinery, appliance, apparatus or tool and any assembly of components which, in order to achieve a common end, are arranged and controlled so that they function as a whole.

...

PART II GENERAL

Regulation 4

Suitability of work equipment

(1) Every employer shall ensure that work equipment is so constructed or adapted as to be suitable for the purpose for which it is used or provided.

(2) In selecting work equipment, every employer shall have regard to the working conditions and to the risks to the health and safety of persons which exist in the premises or undertaking in which that work equipment is to be used and any additional risk posed by the use of that work equipment.

(3) Every employer shall ensure that work equipment is used only for operations for which, and under conditions for which, it is suitable.

(4) In this regulation 'suitable' means suitable in any respect which it is reasonably foreseeable will affect the health or safety of any person.

Regulation 5

Maintenance

(1) Every employer shall ensure that work equipment is maintained in an efficient state, in efficient working order and in good repair.

(2) Every employer shall ensure that where any machinery has a maintenance log, the log is kept up to date.

Regulation 6

Inspection

(1) Every employer shall ensure that, where the safety of work equipment depends on the installation conditions, it is inspected–

(a) after installation and before being put into service for the first time; or

(b) after assembly at a new site or in a new location,

to ensure that it has been installed correctly and is safe to operate.

(2) Every employer shall ensure that work equipment exposed to conditions causing deterioration which is liable to result in dangerous situations is inspected–

(a) at suitable intervals; and

(b) each time that exceptional circumstances which are liable to jeopardise the safety of the work equipment have occurred,

to ensure that health and safety conditions are maintained and that any deterioration can be detected and remedied in good time.

(3) Every employer shall ensure that the result of an inspection made under this regulation is recorded and kept until the next inspection under this regulation is recorded.

(4) Every employer shall ensure that no work equipment–

(a) leaves his undertaking; or

(b) if obtained from the undertaking of another person, is used in his undertaking,

unless it is accompanied by physical evidence that the last inspection required to be carried out under this regulation has been carried out.

...

Regulation 7

Specific risks

(1) Where the use of work equipment is likely to involve a specific risk to health or safety, every employer shall ensure that–

(a) the use of that work equipment is restricted to those persons given the task of using it; and

(b) repairs, modifications, maintenance or servicing of that work equipment is restricted to those persons who have been specifically designated to perform operations of that description (whether or not also authorised to perform other operations).

(2) The employee shall ensure that the persons designated for the purposes of sub-paragraph (b) of paragraph (1) have received adequate training related to any operations in respect of which they have been so designated.

Regulation 8

Information and instructions

(1) Every employer shall ensure that all persons who use work equipment have available to them adequate health and safety information and, where appropriate, written instructions pertaining to the use of the work equipment.

(2) Every employer shall ensure that any of his employees who supervises or manages the use of work equipment has available to him adequate health and safety information and, where appropriate, written instructions pertaining to the use of the work equipment.

(3) Without prejudice to the generality of paragraphs (1) or (2), the information and instructions required by either of those paragraphs shall include information and, where appropriate, written instructions on –

(a) the conditions in which and the methods by which the work equipment may be used;

(b) foreseeable abnormal situations and the action to be taken if such a situation were to occur; and

(c) any conclusions to be drawn from experience in using the work equipment.

(4) Information and instructions required by this regulation shall be readily comprehensible to those concerned.

Regulation 9

Training

(1) Every employer shall ensure that all persons who use work equipment have received adequate training for purposes of health and safety, including training in the methods which may be adopted when using the work equipment, any risks which such use may entail and precautions to be taken.

(2) Every employer shall ensure that any of his employees who supervises or manages the use of work equipment has received adequate training for purposes of health and safety, including training in the methods which may be adopted when using the work equipment, any risks which such use may entail and precautions to be taken.

Regulation 10

Conformity with Community requirements

(1) Every employer shall ensure that an item of work equipment has been designed and constructed in compliance with any essential requirements, that is to say requirements relating to its design or construction in any of the instruments listed in Schedule 1 (being instruments which give effect to Community directives concerning the safety of products).

(2) Where an essential requirement is applied to the design or construction of an item of work equipment, the requirements of regulations 11 to 19 and 22 to 29 shall apply in respect of that item only to the extent that the essential requirement did not apply to it.

Regulation 11

Dangerous parts of machinery

[This regulation was set out in full in Chapter 7 (see pp 164–65).]

Regulation 12

Protection against specified hazards

(1) Every employer shall take measures to ensure that the exposure of a person using work equipment to any risk to his health or safety from any hazard specified in paragraph (3) is either prevented, or, where that is not reasonably practicable, adequately controlled.

(2) The measures required by paragraph (1) shall

    (a) be measures other than the provision of personal protective equipment or of information, instruction, training and supervision, so far as is reasonably practicable; and

    (b) include, where appropriate, measures to minimise the effects of the hazard as well as to reduce the likelihood of the hazard occurring.

(3) The hazards referred to in paragraph (1) are–

    (a) any article or substance falling or being ejected from work equipment;

    (b) rupture or disintegration of parts of work equipment;

    (c) work equipment catching fire or overheating;

    (d) the unintended or premature discharge of any article or of any gas, dust, liquid, vapour or other substance which, in each case, is produced, used or stored in the work equipment;

    (e) the unintended or premature explosion of the work equipment or any article or substance produced, used or stored in it.

(4) For the purposes of this regulation 'adequately' means adequately having regard only to the nature of the hazard and the nature and degree of exposure to the risk.

(5) This regulation shall not apply where any of the following Regulations apply in respect of any risk to a person's health or safety for which such Regulations require measures to be taken to prevent or control such risk, namely–

    (a) the Ionising Radiations Regulations 1985;

    (b) the Control of Asbestos at Work Regulations 1987;

    (c) the Control of Substances Hazardous to Health Regulations 1994;[3]

    (d) the Noise at Work Regulations 1989;

    (e) the Construction (Head Protection) Regulations 1989;

    (f) the Control of Lead at Work Regulations 1998.

Regulation 13

High or very low temperature

Every employer shall ensure that work equipment, parts of work equipment and any article or substance produced, used or stored in work equipment

---

3   Now SI 1999/437.

which, in each case, is at a high or very low temperature shall have protection where appropriate so as to prevent injury to any person by burn, scald or sear.

Regulation 14

Controls for starting or making a significant change in operating conditions

(1) Every employer shall ensure that, where appropriate, work equipment is provided with one or more controls for the purposes of–

    (a) starting the work equipment (including restarting after a stoppage for any reason); or

    (b) controlling any change in the speed, pressure or other operating conditions of the work equipment where such conditions after the change result in risk to health and safety which is greater than or of a different nature from such risks before the change.

(2) Subject to paragraph (3), every employer shall ensure that where a control is required by paragraph (1), it shall not be possible to perform any operation mentioned in sub-paragraph (a) or (b) of that paragraph except by a deliberate action on such control.

(3) Paragraph (1) shall not apply to restarting or changing operating conditions as a result of the normal operating cycle of an automatic device.

Regulation 15

Stop controls

(1) Every employer shall ensure that, where appropriate, work equipment is provided with one or more readily accessible controls the operation of which will bring the work equipment to a safe condition in a safe manner.

(2) Any control required by paragraph (1) shall bring the work equipment to a complete stop where necessary for reasons of health and safety.

(3) Any control required by paragraph (1) shall, if necessary for reasons of health and safety, switch off all sources of energy after stopping the functioning of the work equipment.

(4) Any control required by paragraph (1) shall operate in priority to any control which starts or changes the operating conditions of the work equipment.

Regulation 16

Emergency stop controls

(1) Every employer shall ensure that, where appropriate, work equipment is provided with one or more readily accessible emergency stop controls unless it is not necessary by reason of the nature of the hazards and the time taken for the work equipment to come to a complete stop as a result of the action of any control provided by virtue of regulation 15(1).

(2) Any control required by paragraph (1) shall operate in priority to any control required by regulation 15(1).

Regulation 17

Controls

(1) Every employer shall ensure that all controls for work equipment shall be clearly visible and identifiable, including by appropriate marking where necessary.

(2) Except where necessary, the employer shall ensure that no control for work equipment is in a position where any person operating the control is exposed to a risk to his health or safety.

(3) Every employer shall ensure where appropriate–

   (a) that, so far as is reasonably practicable, the operator of any control is able to ensure from the position of that control that no person is in a place where he would be exposed to any risk to his health or safety as a result of the operation of that control, but where or to the extent that it is not reasonably practicable;

   (b) that, so far as is reasonably practicable, systems of work are effective to ensure that, when work equipment is about to start, no person is in a place where he would be exposed to a risk to his health or safety as a result of the work equipment starting, but where neither of these is reasonably practicable;

   (c) that an audible, visible or other suitable warning is given by virtue of regulation 24 whenever work equipment is about to start.

(4) Every employer shall take appropriate measures to ensure that any person who is in a place where he would be exposed to a risk to his health or safety as a result of the starting or stopping of work equipment has sufficient time and suitable means to avoid that risk.

Regulation 18

Control systems

(1) Every employer shall–

   (a) ensure, so far as is reasonably practicable, that all control systems of work equipment are safe; and

   (b) are chosen making due allowance for the failures, faults and constraints to be expected in the planned circumstances of use.

(2) Without prejudice to the generality of paragraph (1), a control system shall not be safe unless–

   (a) its operation does not create any increased risk to health or safety;

   (b) it ensures, so far as is reasonably practicable, that any fault in or damage to any part of the control system or the loss of supply of any source of energy used by the work equipment cannot result in additional or increased risk to health or safety;

   (c) it does not impede the operation of any control required by regulations 15 or 16.

Regulation 19

Isolation from sources of energy

(1) Every employer shall ensure that where appropriate work equipment is provided there are suitable means to isolate it from all its sources of energy.

(2) Without prejudice to the generality of paragraph (1), the means mentioned in that paragraph shall not be suitable unless they are clearly identifiable and readily accessible.

(3) Every employer shall take appropriate measures to ensure that re-connection of any energy source to work equipment does not expose any person using the work equipment to any risk to his health or safety.

Regulation 20

Stability

Every employer shall ensure that work equipment or any part of work equipment is stabilised by clamping or otherwise where necessary for purposes of health or safety.

Regulation 21

Lighting

Every employer shall ensure that suitable and sufficient lighting, which takes account of the operations to be carried out, is provided at any place where a person uses work equipment.

Regulation 22

Maintenance operations

Every employer shall take appropriate measures to ensure that work equipment is so constructed or adapted that, so far as is reasonably practicable, maintenance operations which involve a risk to health or safety can be carried out while the work equipment is shut down or, in other cases–

(a) maintenance operations can be carried out without exposing the person carrying them out to a risk to his health or safety; or

(b) appropriate measures can be taken for the protection of any person carrying out maintenance operations which involve a risk to his health or safety.

Regulation 23

Markings

Every employer shall ensure that work equipment is marked in a clearly visible manner with any marking appropriate for reasons of health and safety.

Regulation 24

Warnings

(1) Every employer shall ensure that work equipment incorporates any warnings or warning devices which are appropriate for reasons of health and safety.

(2) Without prejudice to the generality of paragraph (1), warnings given by warning devices on work equipment shall not be appropriate unless they are unambiguous, easily perceived and easily understood.

– – –

Comment

These Regulations were introduced in 1992 to implement EC Directive 89/655/EEC. They did not have an Approved Code of Practice, but they were published by the HSE with extensive guidance. Introducing them provided the opportunity to repeal sections of older legislation, including ss 12–16 and 17–19 of the Factories Act 1961, and the whole or parts of 17 sets of Regulations. Unlike the laws which they replaced, they are intended to apply right across the workforce. Like others Regulations in the Six Pack, these regulations built on the 1974 Act but also incorporated the basic concepts of the Management of Health and Safety at Work Regulations regarding risk assessment and response; they also imposed duties on employers to provide equipment suitable for the task and to train employees to use the equipment. The Regulations also apply to the self-employed. The 1992 Regulations were revised in 1998 and republished in the form cited here. With the exception of regulation 6, which is new, there are few changes in the extracts given here. However, the 1998 Regulations have been much extended and contain two new Parts. Part III is concerned with mobile work equipment. The employer is required to ensure that such equipment is stable and constructed so as to minimise the likelihood or effect of roll over. Regulation 27 is specifically concerned with fork lift trucks. Part IV is concerned with the safety of power presses, particularly their guards and other protection devices. An approved Code of Practice has now been issued.

By reference back to the obligations under the Management Regulations, employees are under a duty to use properly the equipment which has been supplied to them in accordance with training they have received, and report any dangers to their employers.

PERSONAL PROTECTIVE EQUIPMENT AT WORK REGULATIONS 1992 SI 1992/2966

Regulation 2

Interpretation

(1) In these Regulations, unless the context otherwise requires, 'personal protective equipment' means all equipment (including clothes affording

protection against the weather) which is intended to be worn or held by a person at work and which protects him against one or more risks to his health or safety, and any addition or accessory designed to meet that objective;

...

Regulation 3
Disapplication of these Regulations

(1) ...

(2) Regulations 4 to 12 shall not apply in respect of personal protective equipment which is–

    (a) ordinary working clothes and uniforms which do not specifically protect the health and safety of the wearer;

    ...

    (e) equipment used during the playing of competitive sports.

    ...

Regulation 4
Provision of personal protective equipment

(1) Every employer shall ensure that suitable personal protective equipment is provided to his employees who may be exposed to a risk to their health or safety while at work except where and to the extent that such risk has been adequately controlled by other means which are equally or more effective.

(2) Every self-employed person shall ensure that he is provided with suitable personal protective equipment where he may be exposed to a risk to his health or safety while at work except where and to the extent that such risk has been adequately controlled by other means which are equally or more effective.

(3) Without prejudice to the generality of paragraphs (1) and (2), personal protective equipment shall not be suitable unless–

    (a) it is appropriate for the risk or risks involved and the conditions at the place where exposure to the risk may occur;

    (b) it takes account of ergonomic requirements and the state of health of the person or persons who may wear it;

    (c) it is capable of fitting the wearer correctly, if necessary, after adjustments within the range for which it is designed;

    (d) so far as is practicable, it is effective to prevent or adequately control the risk or risks involved without increasing overall risk;

    (e) it complies with any enactment (whether in an Act or instrument) which implements in Great Britain any provision on design or manufacture with respect to health or safety in any relevant Community Directives listed in Schedule 1 which is applicable to that item of personal protective equipment.

Regulation 5

Compatibility of personal protective equipment

(1) Every employer shall ensure that where the presence of more than one risk to health or safety makes it necessary for his employee to wear or use simultaneously more than one item of personal protective equipment, such equipment is compatible and continues to be effective against the risk or risks in question.

(2) Every self-employed person shall ensure that where the presence of more than one risk to health or safety makes it necessary for him to wear or use simultaneously more than one item of personal protective equipment, such equipment is compatible and continues to be effective against the risk or risks in question.

Regulation 6

Assessment of personal protective equipment

(1) Before choosing any personal protective equipment which by virtue of regulation 4 he is required to ensure is provided, an employer or self-employed person shall ensure that an assessment is made to determine whether the personal protective equipment he intends will be provided is suitable.

(2) The assessment required by paragraph (1) shall include;

    (a) an assessment of any risk or risks to health or safety which have not been avoided by other means;

    (b) the definition of the characteristics which personal protective equipment must have in order to be effective against the risks referred to in sub-paragraph (a) of this paragraph, taking into account any risks which the equipment itself may create;

    (c) comparison of the characteristics of the personal protective equipment available with the characteristics referred to in sub-paragraph (b) of this paragraph.

(3) Every employer or self-employed person who is required by paragraph (1) to ensure that any assessment is made shall ensure that any such assessment is reviewed if–

    (a) there is reason to suspect that it is no longer valid; or

    (b) there has been a significant change in the matters to which it relates;

and where as a result of any such review changes in the assessment are required, the relevant employer or self-employed person shall ensure that they are made.

Regulation 7

Maintenance and replacement of personal protective equipment

(1) Every employer shall ensure that any personal protective equipment provided to his employees is maintained (including replaced or cleaned as appropriate) in an efficient state, in efficient working order and in good repair.

(2) Every self-employed person shall ensure that any personal protective equipment provided to him is maintained (including replaced or cleaned as appropriate) in an efficient state, in efficient working order and in good repair.

Regulation 8

Accommodation for personal protective equipment

Where an employer or self-employed person is required, by virtue of regulation 4, to ensure personal protective equipment is provided, he shall also ensure that appropriate accommodation is provided for that personal protective equipment when it is not being used.

Regulation 9

Information, instruction and training

(1) Where an employer is required to ensure that personal protective equipment is provided to an employee, the employer shall also ensure that the employee is provided with such information, instruction and training as is adequate and appropriate to enable the employee to know –

    (a) the risk or risks which the personal protective equipment will avoid or limit;

    (b) the purpose of which and the manner in which personal protective equipment is to be used; and

    (c) any action to be taken by the employee to ensure that the personal protective equipment remains in an efficient state, in efficient working order and in good repair as required by regulation 7(1).

(2) Without prejudice to the generality of paragraph (1), the information and instruction provided by virtue of that paragraph shall not be adequate and appropriate unless it is comprehensible to the persons to whom it is provided.

Regulation 10

Use of personal protective equipment

(1) Every employer shall take all reasonable steps to ensure that any personal protective equipment provided to his employees by virtue of regulation 4(1) is properly used.

(2) Every employee shall use any personal protective equipment provided to him by virtue of these Regulations in accordance both with any training in the use of the personal protective equipment concerned which has been received by him and the instructions respecting that use which have been provided to him by virtue of regulation 9.

(3) Every self-employed person shall make full and proper use of any personal protective equipment provided to him by virtue of regulation 4(2).

(4) Every employee and self-employed person who has been provided with personal protective equipment by virtue of regulation 4 shall take all reasonable steps to ensure that it is returned to the accommodation provided for it after use.

Regulation 11

Reporting loss or defect

Every employee who has been provided with personal protective equipment by virtue of regulation 4(1) shall forthwith report to his employer any loss of or obvious defect in that personal protective equipment.

– – –

Comment

These Regulations were made to implement an EC Directive.[4] They are published by the HSE with accompanying guidance, both as to the interpretation of the Regulations and as to the different types of personal protective equipment (PPE) available and the activities which may require PPE to be worn. A number of work situations are covered by other Regulations and so these do not apply. Work situations falling within certain specific sets of Regulations, for example, the Control of Substances Hazardous to Health, are specifically excluded from these Regulations by regulation 3(3). Standards for particular items of PPE are in many cases European standards arrived at further to Article 95 of the Treaty establishing the European Community (EC Treaty)[5] (harmonisation of products). The duties are imposed on employers (for the protection of employees) and on the self-employed. The guidance points out that where other persons who may be at risk (for example, school children or voluntary workers), the employer may well be obliged to consider their safety under the general duties of the 1974 Act, and, where this is so, by implication observing the standards and systems in these Regulations will be the most effective means of discharging the general duties. The guidance points out that providing PPE as a protection against risk should be a last resort:

> ... There is in effect a hierarchy of control measures, and PPE should always be regarded as the 'last resort' to protect against risks to safety and health; engineering controls and safe systems of work should always be considered first. It may be possible to do the job by another method which will not require the use of PPE ...

Thus, while the Regulations themselves require an assessment and response, both as regards to the need for PPE at all and the suitability of the PPE for the particular person and the particular tasks, these Regulations have to be seen in the wider context of the general duty to assess and respond to risks as set out in regulation 3 of the Management of Health and Safety at Work Regulations 1992.

---

4   89/656/EEC.
5   Formerly, EC Treaty, Art 100A.

HEALTH AND SAFETY (DISPLAY SCREEN EQUIPMENT) REGULATIONS 1992 SI 1992/2792

Regulation 1

Citation, commencement, interpretation and application

(1) ...

(2) In these Regulations–

    (a) 'display screen equipment' means any alphanumeric or graphic display screen, regardless of the display process involved;

    (b) 'operator' means a self-employed person who habitually uses display screen equipment as a significant part of his normal work;

    (c) 'use' means for or in connection with work;

    (d) 'user' means an employee who habitually uses display screen equipment as a significant part of his normal work; and

    (e) 'workstation' means an assembly comprising–

        (i) display screen equipment (whether provided with software determining the interface between the equipment and its operator or user, a keyboard or any other input device),

        (ii) any optional accessories to the display screen equipment,

        (iii) any disk drive, telephone, modem, printer, document holder, work chair, work desk, work surface or other item peripheral to the display screen equipment, and

        (iv) the immediate work environment around the display screen equipment.

(3) ...

(4) Nothing in these Regulations shall apply to or in relation to–

    (a) drivers' cabs or control cabs for vehicles or machinery;

    (b) display screen equipment on board a means of transport;

    (c) display screen equipment mainly intended for public operation;

    (d) portable systems not in prolonged use;

    (e) calculators, cash registers or any equipment having a small data or measurement display required for direct use of the equipment; or

    (f) window typewriters.

Regulation 2

Analysis of workstations to assess and reduce risks

(1) Every employer shall perform a suitable and sufficient analysis of those workstations which–

    (a) (regardless of who has provided them) are used for the purposes of his undertaking by users; or

    (b) have been provided by him and are used for the purposes of his undertaking by operators, for the purpose of assessing the health and safety risks to which those persons are exposed in consequence of that use.

(2) Any assessment made by an employer in pursuance of paragraph (1) shall be reviewed by him if–

    (a) there is reason to suspect that it is no longer valid; or

    (b) there has been a significant change in the matters to which it relates;

and where as a result of any such review changes to an assessment are required, the employer concerned shall make them.

(3) The employer shall reduce the risks identified in consequence of an assessment to the lowest extent reasonably practicable.

(4) The reference in paragraph (3) to 'an assessment' is a reference to an assessment made by the employer concerned in pursuance of paragraph (1) and changed by him where necessary in pursuance of paragraph (2).

Regulation 3

Requirements for workstations

(1) Every employer shall ensure that any workstation first put into service on or after 1 January 1993 which–

    (a) (regardless of who has provided it) may be used for the purposes of his undertaking by users; or

    (b) has been provided by him and may be used for the purposes of his undertaking by operators,

meets the requirements laid down in the Schedule to these Regulations to the extent specified in paragraph 1 thereof.

(2) Every employer shall ensure that any workstation first put into service on or before 31 December 1992 which–

    (a) (regardless of who provided it) may be used for the purposes of his undertaking by users; or

    (b) was provided by him and may be used for the purposes of his undertaking by operators,

meets the requirements laid down in the Schedule to these Regulations to the extent specified in paragraph 1 thereof not later than 31 December 1996.

Regulation 4

Daily work routine of users

Every employer shall so plan the activities of users at work in his undertaking that their daily work on display screen equipment is periodically interrupted by such breaks or changes of activity as reduce their workload at that equipment.

Regulation 5

Eyes and eyesight

(1) Where a person–

(a) is already a user on the date of coming into force of these Regulations; or

(b) is an employee who does not habitually use display screen equipment as a significant part of his normal work but is to become a user in the undertaking in which he is already employed,

his employer shall ensure that he is provided at his request with an appropriate eye and eyesight test, any such test to be carried out by a competent person.

(2) Any eye and eyesight test provided in accordance with paragraph (1) shall–

(a) in any case to which sub-paragraph (a) of that paragraph applies, be carried out as soon as practicable after being requested by the user concerned; and

(b) in any case to which sub-paragraph (b) applies, be carried out before the employee concerned becomes a user.

(3) At regular intervals after an employee has been provided with an eye and eyesight test in accordance with paragraphs (1) and (2), his employer shall, subject to paragraph (6), ensure that he is provided with a further eye and eyesight test of an appropriate nature, any such test to be carried out by a competent person.

(4) Where a user experiences visual difficulties which may reasonably be considered to be caused by work on display screen equipment, his employer shall ensure that he is provided at his request with an appropriate eye and eyesight test, any such test to be carried out by a competent person as soon a practicable after being requested as aforesaid.

(5) Every employer shall ensure that each user employed by him is provided with special corrective appliances appropriate for the work being done by the user concerned where–

(a) normal corrective appliances cannot be used; and

(b) the result of any eye and eyesight test which the user has been given in accordance with this regulation shows such provision to be necessary.

(6) Nothing in paragraph (3) shall require an employer to provide any employee with an eye and eyesight test against that employee's will.

Regulation 6

Provision of training

(1) Where a person–

(a) is already a user on the date of coming into force of these Regulations; or

(b) is an employee who does not habitually use display screen equipment as a significant part of his normal work but is to become a user in the undertaking in which he is already employed

his employer shall ensure that he is provided with adequate health and safety training in the use of any workstation upon which he may be required to work.

(2) Every employer shall ensure that each user at work in his undertaking is provided with adequate health and safety training whenever the organisation of any workstation in that undertaking upon which he may be required to work is substantially modified.

Regulation 7

Provision of information

(1) Every employer shall ensure that operators and users at work in his undertaking are provided with adequate information about–

(a) all aspects of health and safety relating to their workstations; and

(b) such measures taken by him in compliance with his duties under regulations 2 and 3 as relate to them and their work.

(2) Every employer shall ensure that users at work in his undertaking are provided with adequate information about such measures taken by him in compliance with his duties under regulations 4 and 6(2) as relate to them and their work.

(3) Every employer shall ensure that users employed by him are provided with adequate information about such measures taken by him in compliance with his duties under regulations 5 and 6(1) as relate to them and their work.

– – –

Comment

The Regulations are intended to implement Directive 90/270/EEC. The Schedule to them sets out the minimum requirements in the Annex to the Directive for workstations for work with display screen equipment. It deals with the display screen equipment itself (the screen, the keyboard) and the workstation (the desk and the chair). It also deals with the working environment (the space requirements; lighting; reflections and glare, noise, heat, radiation and humidity). Additionally, it requires that the software be suitable for the task.

The application of the Regulations is somewhat uncertain in that 'user' is not clearly defined. Employers were concerned at the possible expense of providing eye sight tests, though in fact the employers' obligation, beyond testing itself, is fairly narrow since they have to provide spectacles only in situations where the user requires something specially for use at the display screen: also the onus is on the user to request the eye test.

The Regulations are accompanied by extensive HSE guidance. The guidance states:

- *display screen equipment not covered by the Regulations will still be within the general duties of the 1974 Act if used at work;*

- *the onus is on the employer to decide which of their employees are display screen users and whether they also make use of other users (employed by other employers) or self-employed persons (whom the regulations describe as 'operators');*

- *there are risks of musculoskeletal problems, visual fatigue and mental stress;*

- *the risk assessment should be systematic, including investigation of non-obvious causes of problems, such as poor posture which could be a response to screen reflections or glare, rather than poor furniture. Information provided by the user is an essential part of an assessment, but workers should be trained before being asked to make an assessment. If a worker is working at home, that worker should complete a checklist on the workstation being used. Assessments should normally be recorded;*

- *regulation 4, on the daily routine of the worker is very important. Breaks need to be taken before the onset of fatigue and short, frequent breaks are more satisfactory than occasional, longer breaks. A five to 10 minute break after 50–60 minutes continuous screen and/or keyboard work is likely to be better than a 15 minute break every 2 hours.*

MANUAL HANDLING OPERATIONS REGULATIONS 1992
SI 1992/2793

Regulation 2
Interpretation

(1) In these Regulations, unless the context otherwise requires–

'injury' does not include injury caused by any toxic or corrosive substance which–

    (a) has leaked or spilled from a load;

    (b) is present on the surface of a load but has not leaked or spilled from it; or

    (c) is a constituent part of a load;

    and 'injured' shall be construed accordingly;

'load' includes any person and any animal;

'manual handling operations' means any transporting or supporting of a load (including the lifting, putting down, pushing, pulling, carrying or moving thereof) by hand or by bodily force.

(2) Any duty imposed by these Regulations on an employer in respect of his employees shall also be imposed on a self-employed person in respect of himself.

Regulation 4
Duties of employers

(1) Each employer shall–

    (a) so far as is reasonably practicable, avoid the need for his employees to undertake any manual handling operations at work which involve a risk of their being injured;

(b) where it is not reasonably practicable to avoid the need for his employees to undertake any manual handling operations at work which involve a risk of their being injured–

(i) make a suitable and sufficient assessment of all such manual handling operations to be undertaken by them ...

(ii) take appropriate steps to reduce the risk of injury to those employees arising out of their undertaking any such manual handling operations to the lowest level reasonably practicable.

(iii) take appropriate steps to provide any of those employees who are undertaking any such manual handling operations with general indications and, where it is reasonably practicable to do so, precise information on–

(aa) the weight of each load, and

(bb) the heaviest side of any load whose centre of gravity is not positioned centrally.

(2) Any assessment such as is referred to in para (1)(b)(i) of this regulation shall be reviewed by the employer who made it if–

(a) there is reason to suspect that it is no longer valid; or

(b) there has been a significant change in the manual handling operations to which it relates,

and where as a result of any such review changes to an assessment are required, the relevant employer shall make them.

Regulation 5

Duty of employees

Each employee while at work shall make full and proper use of any system of work provided for his use by his employer in compliance with regulation 4(1)(b)(ii) of these Regulations.

– – –

Comment

These Regulations were introduced to implement EC Directive 90/269/EEC. They are a relatively short set of Regulations but the HSE has provided very extensive guidance on handling of loads. They like all the other Regulations in the Six Pack stress the need to assess and respond to risks. The importance of the Regulations should not be judged by their length; the HSE guidance points out that more than a quarter of the accidents reported each year are associated with manual handling and the most common form of injury is sprain or strain to the back. In view of the stress laid upon avoiding manual handling operations wherever possible, either by avoiding moving the articles at all, or, if moving them, doing so by mechanical means, these Regulations should now be read in conjunction with the Lifting Operations and Lifting Equipment Regulations 1998 (SI 1998/2307). The Lifting Regulations replaced a number of earlier piecemeal regulations and were made in partial compliance with EC Directive 98/655/EEC on minimum health and safety standards for use of work equipment. These Regulations impose duties on employers, self-employed persons, and certain persons having control of equipment. They contain detailed provisions on the safe use of such equipment, including regulations relating to strength, stability, installation, marking and examination of lifting equipment, and the keeping of records of testing and examination of such equipment.

CONTROL OF SUBSTANCES HAZARDOUS TO HEALTH REGULATIONS 1999 SI 1999/437

Regulation 3

Duties under these Regulations

(1) Where any duty is placed by these Regulations on an employer in respect of his employees, he shall, so far as is reasonably practicable, be under a like duty in respect of any other person, whether at work or not, who may be affected by the work carried on by the employer except that the duties of the employer–

   (a) under regulation 11 (health surveillance) shall not extend to persons who are not his employees; and

   (b) under regulations 10 and 12(1) and (2) (which related respectively to monitoring and information, training, etc) shall not extend to persons who are not his employees, unless those persons are on the premises where the work is being carried on.

(2) These Regulations shall apply to a self-employed person as they apply to an employer and an employee and as if that self-employed person were both an employer and employee, except that regulations 10 and 11 shall not apply to a self-employed person.

...

Regulation 5

Application of regulations 6 to 12

(1) Regulations 6 to 12 shall have effect with a view to protecting persons against risks to their health, whether immediate or delayed, arising from exposure to substances hazardous to health except–

   (a) where and to the extent that the following Regulations apply, namely–

   (i) the Control of Lead at Work Regulations 1998,

   (ii) the Control of Asbestos at Work Regulations 1987;

   (b) where the substance is hazardous to health solely by virtue of its radioactive, explosive or flammable properties, or solely because it is at a high or low temperature or a high pressure;

   (c) where the risk to health is a risk to the health of a person to whom the substance is administered in the course of his medical treatment;

(d) where the substance hazardous to health is total inhalable dust which is below ground in any mine of coal.

(2) In paragraph (1)(c) 'medical treatment' means medical or dental examination or treatment which is conducted by, or under the direction of a registered medical practitioner ...

Regulation 6

Assessment of health risks created by work involving substances hazardous to health

(1) An employer shall not carry on any work which is liable to expose any employees to any substance hazardous to health unless he has made a suitable and sufficient assessment of the risks created by that work to the health of those employees and of the steps that need to be taken to meet the requirements of these Regulations.

(2) The assessment required by paragraph (1) shall be reviewed regularly, and forthwith if–

(a) there is reason to suspect that the assessment is no longer valid; or

(b) there has been a significant change in the work to which the assessment relates,

and where, as a result of the review, changes in the assessment are required, those changes shall be made.

Regulation 7

Prevention or control of exposure to substances hazardous to health

(1) Every employer shall ensure that the exposure of his employees to substances hazardous to health is either prevented or, where this is not reasonably practicable, adequately controlled.

(2) So far as is reasonably practicable, the prevention or adequate control of exposure of employees to a substance hazardous to health, except to a carcinogen or a biological agent, shall be secured by measures other than the provision of personal protective equipment.

(3) Without prejudice to the generality of paragraph (1), where the assessment made under regulation 6 shows that it is not reasonably practicable to prevent exposure to a carcinogen by using an alternative substance or process, the employer shall apply all the following measures, namely–

(a) the total enclosure of the process and handling systems unless this is not reasonably practicable;

(b) the use of plant, processes and systems of work which minimise the generation of, or suppress and contain, spills, leaks, dust, fumes and vapours of carcinogens;

(c) the limitation of the quantities of a carcinogen at the place of work;

(d) the keeping of the number of persons who might be exposed to a carcinogen to a minimum;

(e) the prohibition of eating, drinking and smoking in areas that may be contaminated by carcinogens;

(f) the provision of hygiene measures including adequate washing facilities and regular cleaning of walls and surfaces;

(g) the designation of those areas and installations which may be contaminated by carcinogens, and the use of suitable and sufficient warning signs; and

(h) the safe storage, handling and disposal of carcinogens and use of closed and clearly labelled containers.

(4) Where the measures taken in accordance with paragraph (2) or (3), as the case may be, do not prevent, or provide adequate control of, exposure to substances hazardous to health to which those paragraphs apply, then, in addition to taking those measures, the employer shall provide those employees with such suitable personal protective equipment as will adequately control their exposure to those substances.

(5) Any personal protective equipment provided by an employer in pursuance of this regulation shall comply with any provision in the (EC Directive) Personal Protective Equipment Regulations 1992 which is applicable to that item of personal protective equipment.

(6) Where there is exposure to a substance for which a maximum exposure limit has been approved, the control of exposure shall, so far as the inhalation of that substance is concerned, only be treated as being adequate if the level of exposure is reduced so far as is reasonably practicable and in any case below the maximum exposure limit.

(7) Without prejudice to the generality of paragraph (1), where there is exposure to a substance for which an occupational exposure standard has been approved, the control of exposure shall, so far as the inhalation of that substance is concerned, be treated as being adequate if–

(a) that occupational exposure is not exceeded; or

(b) where that occupational exposure standard is exceeded, the employer identifies the reasons for the standard being exceeded and takes appropriate action to remedy the situation as soon as is reasonably practicable.

(8) Where respiratory protective equipment is provided in pursuance of this regulation, then it shall–

(a) be suitable for the purpose; and

(b) comply with paragraph (5) or, where no requirement is imposed by virtue of that paragraph, be of a type approved or shall conform to a standard approved, in either case, by the Executive.

(9) In the event of the failure of a control measure which might result in the escape of carcinogens into the workplace, the employer shall ensure that –

(a) only those persons who are responsible for the carrying out of repairs and other necessary work are permitted in the affected area and they are provided with suitable respiratory protective equipment and protective clothing; and

(b) employees and other persons who may be affected are informed of the failure forthwith.

(10) Schedule 3 of these Regulations shall have effect in relation to biological agents.

(11) In this regulation, 'adequate' means adequate having regard only to the nature of the substance and the nature and degree of exposure to substances hazardous to health and 'adequately' shall be construed accordingly.

Regulation 8

Use of control measures etc

(1) Every employer who provides any control measure, personal protective equipment or other thing or facility pursuant to these Regulations shall take all reasonable steps to ensure that it is properly used or applied as the case may be.

(2) Every employee shall make full and proper use of any control measure, personal protective equipment or other thing or facility provided pursuant to these Regulations and shall take all reasonable steps to ensure it is returned after use to any accommodation provided for it and, if he discovers any defect therein, shall report it forthwith to his employer.

Regulation 9

Maintenance, examination and test of control measures etc

(1) Every employer who provides any control measure to meet the requirements of regulation 7 shall ensure that it is maintained in an efficient state, in efficient working order and in good repair and, in the case of personal protective equipment, in a clean condition.

(2) Where engineering controls are provided to meet the requirements of regulation 7, the employer shall ensure that thorough examinations and tests of those engineering controls are carried out–

  (a) in the case of local exhaust ventilation plant, at least once very 14 months, or for local exhaust ventilation plant used in conjunction with a process specified in Column 1 of Schedule 4, at not more than the interval specified in the corresponding entry in Column 2 of that Schedule;

  (b) in any other case, at suitable intervals.

(3) Where respiratory protective equipment (other than disposable respiratory protective equipment) is provided to meet the requirements of regulation 7, the employer shall ensure that at suitable intervals thorough examinations and, where appropriate, tests of that equipment are carried out.

(4) Every employer shall keep a suitable record of the examinations and tests carried out in pursuance of paragraphs (2) and (3) and of any repairs carried out as a result of those examinations and tests, and that record or a suitable summary thereof shall be kept available for at least 5 years from the date on which it was made.

Regulation 10

Monitoring exposure at the workplace

(1) In any case in which–

    (a) it is requisite for ensuring the maintenance of adequate control of the exposure of employees to substances hazardous to health; or

    (b) it is otherwise requisite for protecting the health of employees,

the employer shall ensure that the exposure of employees to substances hazardous to health is monitored in accordance with a suitable procedure.

(2) Where a substance or process is specified in Column 1 of Schedule 5, monitoring shall be carried out at least at the frequency specified in the corresponding entry in Column 2 of that Schedule.

(3) The employer shall keep a suitable record of any monitoring carried out for the purpose of this regulation and that record or a suitable summary thereof shall be kept available–

    (a) where the record is representative of the personal exposures of identifiable employees, for at least 40 years;

    (b) in any other case, for at least five years.

Regulation 11

Health surveillance

(1) Where it is appropriate for the protection of the health of his employees who are, or are liable to be, exposed to a substance hazardous to health, the employer shall ensure that such employees are under suitable health surveillance.

(2) Health surveillance shall be treated as being appropriate where–

    (a) the employee is exposed to one of the substances specified in Column 1 of Schedule 6 and is engaged in a process specified in Column 2 of that Schedule, unless that exposure is not significant; or

    (b) the exposure of the employee to a substance hazardous to health is such that an identifiable disease or adverse health effect may be related to the exposure, there is a reasonable likelihood that the disease or effect may occur under the particular conditions of his work and there are valid techniques for detecting indications of the disease or the effect.

(3) The employer shall ensure that a health record, containing particulars approved by the Executive, in respect of each of his employees to whom paragraph (1) relates is made and maintained and that that record or a copy thereof is kept in a suitable form for at least 40 years from the date of the last entry made in it.

(4) Where an employer who holds records in accordance with paragraph (3) ceases to trade, he shall forthwith notify the Executive thereof in writing and offer those records to the Executive.

(5) If an employee is exposed to a substance specified in Schedule 6 and is engaged in a process specified therein, the health surveillance required

under paragraph (1) shall include medical surveillance under the supervision of an employment medical adviser or appointed doctor at intervals of not more than 12 months or at such shorter intervals as the employment medical adviser or appointed doctor may require.

(6) Where an employee is subject to medical surveillance in accordance with paragraph (5) and an employment medical adviser or appointed doctor has certified by an entry in the health record of that employee that in his professional opinion that employee should not be engaged in work which exposes him to that substance or that he should only be so engaged under conditions specified in the record, the employer shall not permit the employee to be engaged in such work except in accordance with the conditions, if any, specified in the health record, unless that entry has been cancelled by an employment medical adviser or appointed doctor.

(7) Where an employee is subject to medical surveillance in accordance with paragraph (5) and an employment medical adviser or appointed doctor has certified by an entry in his health record that medical surveillance should be continued after his exposure to that substance has ceased, the employer shall ensure that the medical surveillance of that employee is continued in accordance with that entry while he is employed by the employer, unless that entry has been cancelled by an employment medical adviser or appointed doctor.

(8) On reasonable notice being given, the employer shall allow any of his employees access to the health record which relates to him.

(9) An employee to whom this regulation applies shall, when required by his employer and at the cost of the employer, present himself during his working hours for such health surveillance procedures as may be required for the purposes of paragraph (1) and, in the case of an employee who is subject to medical surveillance in accordance with paragraph (5), shall furnish the employment medical adviser or appointed doctor with such information concerning his health as the employment medical adviser or appointed doctor may reasonably require.

(10) Where, for the purpose of carrying out his functions under these Regulations, an employment medical adviser or appointed doctor requires to inspect any workplace or any record kept for the purposes of these Regulations, the employer shall permit him to do so.

(11) Where an employee or an employer is aggrieved by a decision recorded in the health record by an employment medical adviser or appointed doctor to suspend an employee from work which exposes him to a substance hazardous to health (or to impose conditions on such work), he may, by an application in writing to the Executive within 28 days of the date on which he was notified of the decision, apply for that decision to be reviewed in accordance with a procedure approved for the purposes of this paragraph by the Health and Safety Commission, and the result of that review shall be notified to the employee and employer and entered in the health record in accordance with the approved procedure.

(12) In this regulation–

'appointed doctor' means a fully registered medical practitioner who is appointed for the time being in writing by the Executive for the purposes of this regulation;

'employment medical adviser' means an employment medical adviser appointed under s 56 of the 1974 Act;

'health surveillance' includes biological monitoring.

Regulation 12

Information, instruction and training for persons who may be exposed to substances hazardous to health

(1) An employer who undertakes work which may expose any of his employees to substances hazardous to health shall provide that employee with such information, instruction and training as is suitable and sufficient for him to know–

(a) the risks to health created by such exposure; and

(b) the precautions which should be taken.

(2) Without prejudice to the generality of paragraph (1), the information provided under that paragraph shall include–

(a) information on the results of any monitoring of exposure at the workplace in accordance with regulation 10 and, in particular, in the case of any substance hazardous to health for which a maximum exposure limit has been approved, the employee or his representatives shall be informed forthwith, if the results of such monitoring show that the maximum exposure limit has been exceeded; and

(b) information on the collective results of any health surveillance undertaken in accordance with regulation 11 in a form calculated to prevent it from being identified as relating to any particular person.

(3) Every employer shall ensure that any person (whether or not his employee) who carries out any work in connection with the employer's duties under these Regulations has the necessary information, instruction and training.

...

Regulation 16

Defence in proceedings for contravention of these Regulations

In any proceedings for an offence consisting of a contravention of these Regulations it shall be a defence for any person to prove that he took all reasonable precautions and exercised all due diligence to avoid the commission of that offence.

– – –

Comment

Prior to the Management of Health and Safety at Work Regulations these Regulations (first introduced in 1988) were possibly the most important made under the 1974 Act: they were the first to impose an express duty on employers to assess for and respond to risks. To a large extent they now overlap with the Management Regulations, but the health surveillance provisions with the requirement for the keeping of long term records go beyond anything in earlier Regulations; similarly, the Management Regulations do not spell out, as do these Regulations, the substances and processes which are dangerous; nor do they impose detailed requirements, for example, to notify the HSE of the first use in the workplace of biological agents.

Much of the system is contained in Schedules which specify substances in regard to which the employer has to take particular precautions and the precautions, etc, which must be taken.

The Regulations are cross-referenced to the Chemicals (Hazard Information and Packaging) Regulations 1993 for further identification of substances which are hazardous to health and which themselves classify carcinogenic substances and preparations for the purposes of packaging and labelling.

These Regulations are the medium through which Britain has implemented a number of EC Directives on toxic substances, including Directives on carcinogens and biological agents.

The Regulations are accompanied by several Approved Codes of Practice (that is, a general one and risk-specific ones). There is also HSE guidance.

CHAPTER 13

THE ROLE OF THE WORKER

INTRODUCTION

It was noted in Part I that English law has traditionally focused on the relationship between employers and their own employees and distinguished those from other categories of workers; that is workers who have the status of employee but work for another employer or those who are self-employed. Thus in *Lane v Shire Roofing Co (Oxford) Ltd* (1995)[1] (concerning injury of a roofing worker who was purporting to be self-employed) Henry LJ, in the Court of Appeal, noted that whatever the parties might intend there was in health and safety matters a public interest in recognising the employer and employee relationship because statutory rights and duties were based upon that framework of employment.

Most of the statutory provisions discussed in this Chapter had their origins in the 1970s when the norm was for the worker to be an employee, so the worker referred to here will normally be the employee. However other Member States in the EU do not necessarily make the same distinction between employee and other workers as is the case in the UK; thus EC Directives which now have such an influence on our law are very often concerned with the position of the worker rather than that of the employee. Relating employment protection to the contract of employment is questionable even in England as work is increasingly casualised and organisations sub-contract more and more of their work to other organisations or to individual workers who purport to be self-employed.

I WORKER INVOLVEMENT

It was part of the Robens philosophy that safety awareness at the workplace would only be achieved by consultation between management and workers for the identification of safety issues and the selection of means for controlling them, though the Committee was clear that safety was not a matter for negotiation and in the last instance responsibility rested with management for ensuring that workplaces were safe. The Report put the matter thus at p 18:

---

1   [1995] IRLR 493.

The involvement of workpeople

59 We have stressed that the promotion of safety and health at work is first and foremost a matter of efficient management. But it is not a management prerogative. In this context more than most, real progress is impossible without the full co-operation and commitment of all employees. How can this be encouraged? We believe that if workpeople are to accept their full share of responsibility (again we are not speaking of legal responsibilities) they must be able to participate fully in the making and monitoring of arrangements for safety and health at their place of work .

– – –

Accepting the Robens philosophy, the 1974 Act made more provision for the role of the workforce in achieving health and safety than previous legislation, which had focused on the employer's duty to provide a healthy and safe working environment with safe equipment.

The Act made provision for communication with individual members of the workforce and for consultation with representatives of workers collectively. It also placed responsibilities on workers individually; these responsibilities, however, were of a somewhat negative nature, the emphasis being more on obeying orders than on taking initiatives.

II INSPECTOR'S DUTY TO INFORM WORKERS

The 1974 Act introduced a novel duty for inspectors who had hitherto been obliged to observe confidentiality as to their findings in the course of an inspection of a workplace. By s 28(8) of the 1974 Act they became required, notwithstanding the obligation not to disclose information, which continued to be imposed upon them by s 28(7), to give information to workers:

Section 28

Restrictions on disclosure of information

(8) Notwithstanding anything in the preceding subsection an inspector shall, in circumstances in which it is necessary to do so for the purpose of assisting in keeping persons (or the representatives of persons) employed at any premises adequately informed about matters affecting their health, safety and welfare, give to such persons or their representatives the following descriptions of information, that is to say–

  (a) factual information obtained by him as mentioned in that subsection which relates to those premises or anything which was or is therein or was or is being done therein; and

  (b) information with respect to any action which he has taken or proposes to take in or in connection with those premises in the performance of his functions;

and where an inspector does as aforesaid, he shall give the like information to the employer of the first–mentioned persons.

III EMPLOYERS' DUTIES TO INFORM AND CONSULT

(a) Employers' duties to involve employees

In the 1970s the norm was for workers to be employed to work full time under a contract of employment as employees of a single employer; the prevailing philosophy of worker involvement assumed that worker involvement would be in the form of a dialogue between the employees and their own employer. The employer's duties in this matter are therefore spelt out in s 2, that is in the section concerned with the employer's responsibilities to their own employees:

(i) Duty to provide information

Section 2(2)(c) and s 2(3) both include an obligation on the employer to provide information to employees, individually.

Section 2(2)(c) also requires that the employer provide instruction, training and supervision. This paragraph is very significant. It imposes on the employer an obligation to manage people to ensure (so far as is reasonably practicable) the health and safety of his employees. To ensure safety he has not only to give them information, he has to require them to act safely, training them to do this and monitoring them to ensure that they carry out their duties in accordance with their training. These broad requirements have been reiterated in regulations made subsequently to the Act, as was apparent in the Regulations considered in the previous chapter. If employers perform their duty and the worker behaves in an unsafe manner contrary to the system the employers have sought to enforce, then the employers are likely to be entitled to dismiss the disobedient worker, for misconduct, possibly for breach of contract.

While s 2(2)(c) is central to the relationship between the employer and employee, and must relate to the way in which the employee performs at the workplace, it has a much wider significance as the *Swan Hunter* case[2] established. To discharge their duties to protect their own employees employers may have to provide information, instruction, training and supervision to persons other than their employees, to ensure that the behaviour of these other persons does not put their own employees at risk.

---

2   [1981] IRLR 403.

Section 2(3) requires the employer to bring the organisation's safety policy to the notice of all their employees. In the 1970s employers were urged to draw up their safety policies, and any revisions of them in consultation with their employees. In those days however the focus was on the statement of policy and the management organisation for achieving safety. Increasingly the emphasis has shifted to the safety arrangements which form part of the policy. In a sophisticated organisation nowadays individual employees will be informed, instructed, trained and supervised in the arrangements made further to the general policy statement for carrying out the particular roles they individually are expected to perform at the workplace. The employers' arrangements may be governed by Regulations made under the Act; for example, the arrangements which have to be made for manual handling of loads are indicated by the Manual Handling Operations Regulations 1992 and guidance published with those Regulations. Interestingly, recent Regulations like the Six Pack, which require employers to have systems for dealing with assessment and response to risk do not expressly refer to s 2(3) of the 1974 Act.

(ii) Duty to consult

Section 2(4) to (7) sets out a framework for the appointment of safety representatives and imposed on the employer a duty to consult with such appointees:

HEALTH AND SAFETY AT WORK ETC ACT 1974

Section 2

Duty of employers to employees

(4) Regulations made by the Secretary of State may provide for the appointment in prescribed cases by recognised trade unions (within the meaning of the regulations) of safety representatives from amongst the employees, and those representatives shall represent the employees in consultations with the employers under subsection (6) below and may have such other functions as may be prescribed.

...

(6) It shall be the duty of every employer to consult any such representatives with a view to the making and maintenance of arrangements which will enable him and his employees to co-operate effectively in promoting and developing measures to ensure the health and safety at work of the employees, and in checking the effectiveness of such measures.

(7) In such cases as may be prescribed it shall be the duty of every employer, if requested to do so by the safety representatives mentioned in subsection (4) ... above, to establish, in accordance with regulations made by the Secretary of State, a safety committee having the function of keeping under review the measures taken to ensure the health and safety at work of his employees and such other functions as may be prescribed.

Section 2(4) and (7) had no immediate impact; they merely enabled the making of Regulations to introduce a system of safety representation. Section 2(5) provided that Regulations might be made to enable a system whereby those who worked at workplaces which were not unionised might elect safety representatives. However, this subsection was repealed almost immediately, by a Labour government committed to encouraging collective bargaining. Section 2(4) was implemented by Regulations brought into effect in 1978:

SAFETY REPRESENTATIVES AND SAFETY COMMITTEES REGULATIONS SI 1977/500

Regulation 3

Appointment of safety representatives

(1) For the purposes of s 2(4) of the 1974 Act, a recognised trade union may appoint safety representatives from amongst the employees in all cases where one or more employees are employed by an employer by whom it is recognised, except in the case of employees employed in a mine within the meaning of s 180 of the Mines and Quarries Act 1954 which is a coal mine.

(2) Where the employer has been notified in writing by or on behalf of a trade union of the names of the persons appointed as safety representatives under this Regulation and the group or groups of employees they represent, each such safety representative shall have the functions set out in regulation 4 below.

(3) A person shall cease to be a safety representative for the purposes of these Regulations when–

(a) the trade union which appointed him notifies the employer in writing that his appointment has been terminated; or

(b) he ceases to be employed at the workplace but if he was appointed to represent employees at more than one workplace he shall not cease by virtue of this sub-paragraph to be a safety representative so long as he continues to be employed at any one of them; or

(c) he resigns.

(4) A person appointed under paragraph (1) above as a safety representative shall so far as is reasonably practicable either have been employed by his employer throughout the preceding two years or have had at least two years experience in similar employment.

Regulation 4

Functions of safety representatives

(1) In addition to his function under s 2(4) of the 1974 Act to represent the employees in consultations with the employer under s 2(6) of the 1974 Act (which requires every employer to consult safety representatives with a view to the making and maintenance of arrangements which will enable him and his employees to co-operate effectively in promoting and developing measures to ensure the health and safety at work of the

employees and in checking the effectiveness of such measures), each safety representative shall have the following functions–

(a) to investigate potential hazards and dangerous occurrences at the workplace (whether or not they are drawn to his attention by the employees he represents) and to examine the causes of accidents at the workplace;

(b) to investigate complaints by any employee he represents relating to that employee's health, safety or welfare at work;

(c) to make representations to the employer on matters arising out of sub-paragraphs (a) and (b) above;

(d) to make representations to the employer on general matters affecting the health, safety or welfare at work of the employees at the workplace;

(e) to carry out inspections in accordance with regulations 5, 6 and 7 below;

(f) to represent the employees he was appointed to represent in consultations at the workplace with inspectors of the Health and Safety Executive and of any other enforcing authority;

(g) to receive information from inspectors in accordance with s 28(8) of the 1974 Act; and

(h) to attend meetings of safety committees where he attends in his capacity as a safety representative in connection with any of the above functions;

but without prejudice to ss 7 and 8 of the 1974 Act, no function given to a safety representative by this paragraph shall be construed as imposing any duty on him.

(2) An employer shall permit a safety representative to take such time off with pay during the employee's working hours as shall be necessary for the purposes of–

(a) performing his functions under s 2(4) of the 1974 Act and paragraph (1)(a) to (h) above;

(b) undergoing such training in aspects of those functions as may be reasonable in all the circumstances having regard to any relevant provisions of a code of practice relating to time off for training approved for the time being by the Health and Safety Commission under s 16 of the 1974 Act.

...

In this paragraph 'with pay' means with pay in accordance with the Schedule to these Regulations.

Regulation 4(A)

Employer's duty to consult and provide facilities and assistance

(1) Without prejudice to the generality of s 2(6) of the Health and Safety at Work etc Act 1974, every employer shall consult safety representatives in good time with regard to–

(a) the introduction of any measure at the workplace which may substantially affect the health and safety of the employees the safety representatives concerned represent;

(b) his arrangements for appointing or, as the case may be, nominating persons in accordance with regulations 6(1) and 7(1)(b) of the Management of Health and Safety at Work Regulations 1992;[3]

(c) any health and safety information he is required to provide to the employees the safety representatives concerned represent by or under the relevant statutory provisions;

(d) the planning and organisation of any health and safety training he is required to provide to the employees the safety representatives concerned represent by or under the relevant statutory provisions; and

(e) the health and safety consequences for the employees the safety representatives concerned represent of the introduction (including the planning thereof) of new technologies into the workplace.

(2) Without prejudice to regulations 5 and 6 of these Regulations, every employer shall provide such facilities and assistance as safety representatives may reasonably require for the purpose of carrying out their functions under s 2(4) of the 1974 Act and under these Regulations.

Regulation 5

Inspections of the workplace

(1) Safety representatives shall be entitled to inspect the workplace or a part of it if they have given the employer or his representative reasonable notice in writing of their intention to do so and have not inspected it, or that part of it, as the case may be, in the previous three months; and may carry out more frequent inspections by agreement with the employer.

(2) Where there has been a substantial change in the conditions of work (whether because of the introduction of new machinery or otherwise) or new information has been published by the Health and Safety Commission or the Health and Safety Executive relevant to the hazards of the workplace since the last inspection under this Regulation, the safety representatives after consultation with the employer shall be entitled to carry out a further inspection of the part of the workplace concerned notwithstanding that three months have not elapsed since the last inspection.

(3) The employer shall provide such facilities and assistance as the safety representatives may reasonably require (including facilities for independent investigation by them and private discussion with the employees) for the purpose of carrying out an inspection under this Regulation, but nothing in this paragraph shall preclude the employer or his representative from being present in the workplace during the inspection.

---

3   Now re-issued as SI 1999/3242.

(4) An inspection carried out under s 123 of the Mines and Quarries Act 1954 shall count as an inspection under this Regulation.

Regulation 6

Inspections following notifiable accidents, occurrences and diseases

(1) Where there has been a notifiable accident or dangerous occurrence in a workplace or a notifiable disease has been contracted there and–

   (a) it is safe for an inspection to be carried out; and

   (b) the interests of employees in the group or groups which safety representatives are appointed to represent might be involved,

   those safety representatives may carry out an inspection of the part of the workplace concerned and so far as is necessary for the purpose of determining the cause they may inspect any other part of the workplace; where it is reasonably practicable to do so they shall notify the employer or his representative of their intention to carry out the inspection.

(2) The employer shall provide such facilities and assistance as the safety representatives may reasonably require (including facilities for independent investigation by them and private discussion with the employees) for the purpose of carrying out an inspection under this Regulation; but nothing in this paragraph shall preclude the employer or his representative from being present in the workplace during the inspection.

(3) In this Regulation 'notifiable accident' or 'dangerous occurrence' and 'notifiable disease' mean any accident, dangerous occurrence or disease, as the case may be, notice of which is required to be given by virtue of any of the relevant statutory provisions within the meaning of s 53(1) of the 1974 Act.

Regulation 7

Inspection of documents and provision of information

(1) Safety representatives shall for the performance of their functions under s 2(4) of the 1974 Act and under these Regulations, if they have given the employer reasonable notice, be entitled to inspect and take copies of any document relevant to the workplace or to the employees the safety representatives represent which the employer is required to keep by virtue of any relevant statutory provision within the meaning of s 53(1) of the 1974 Act except a document consisting of or relating to any health record of an identifiable individual.

(2) An employer shall make available to safety representatives the information, within the employer's knowledge, necessary to enable them to fulfil their functions except–

   (a) any information the disclosure of which would be against the interests of national security; or

   (b) any information which he could not disclose without contravening a prohibition imposed by or under an enactment; or

(c) any information relating specifically to an individual, unless he has consented to its being disclosed; or

(d) any information the disclosure of which would, for reasons other than its effect on health, safety or welfare at work, cause substantial injury to the employer's undertaking or, where the information was supplied to him by some other person, to the undertaking of that other person; or

(e) any information obtained by the employer for the purpose of bringing, prosecuting or defending any legal proceedings.

(3) Paragraph (2) above does not require an employer to produce or allow inspection of any document or part of a document which is not related to health, safety or welfare.

Regulation 8

Cases where safety representatives need not be employees

(1) In the cases mentioned in paragraph (2) below safety representatives appointed under regulation 3(1) of these Regulations need not be employees of the employer concerned; and s 2(4) of the 1974 Act shall be modified accordingly.

(2) The said cases are those in which the employees in the group or groups the safety representatives are appointed to represent are members of the British Actors' Equity Association or of the Musicians' Union.

(3) Regulations 3(3)(b) and (4) and 4(2) of these Regulations shall not apply to safety representatives appointed by virtue of this Regulation and in the case of safety representatives to be so appointed regulation 3(1) shall have effect as if the words 'from amongst the employees' were omitted.

Regulation 9

Safety committees

(1) For the purpose of s 2(7) of the 1974 Act (which requires an employer in prescribed cases to establish a safety committee if requested to do so by safety representatives) the prescribed cases shall be any cases in which at least two safety representatives request the employer in writing to establish a safety committee.

(2) Where an employer is requested to establish a safety committee in a case prescribed in paragraph (1) above, he shall establish it in accordance with the following provisions–

(a) he shall consult with the safety representatives who made the request and with the representatives of recognised trade unions whose members work in any workplace in respect of which he proposes that the committee should function;

(b) the employer shall post a notice stating the composition of the committee and the workplace or workplaces to be covered by it in a place where it may be easily read by the employees;

(c) the committee shall be established not later than three months after the request for it.

...

Regulation 11

Provisions as to industrial tribunals[4]

(1) A safety representative may, in accordance with the jurisdiction conferred on industrial tribunals ... present a complaint to an industrial tribunal that–

    (a) the employer has failed to permit him to take time off in accordance with regulation 4(2) of these Regulations; or

    (b) the employer has failed to pay him in accordance with regulation 4(2) of and the Schedule to these Regulations.

(2) An industrial tribunal shall not consider a complaint under paragraph (1) above unless it is presented within three months of the date when the failure occurred or within such further period as the tribunal considers reasonable in a case where it is satisfied that it was not reasonably practicable for the complaint to be presented within the period of three months.

(3) Where an industrial tribunal finds a complaint under paragraph (1)(a) above well-founded the tribunal shall make a declaration to that effect and may make an award of compensation to be paid by the employer to the employee which shall be of such amount as the tribunal considers just and equitable in all the circumstances having regard to the employer's default in failing to permit time off to be taken by the employee and to any loss sustained by the employee which is attributable to the matters complained of.

(4) Where on a complaint under paragraph (1)(b) above an industrial tribunal finds that the employer has failed to pay the employee the whole or part of the amount required to be paid under paragraph (1)(b), the tribunal shall order the employer to pay the employee the amount which it finds due to him.

– – –

Comment

The Regulations were somewhat unusual in that they created a floor of rights which recognised trade unions could invoke if they wished to have a system of safety representatives and their employer was not sympathetic to this wish. They imposed no duty on an employer to introduce a system if the unions were uninterested; they also left much to negotiation. The employer and union(s) may negotiate a system which bears little similarity to that provided in the Regulations: even if they propose to operate the statutory system it is still necessary to negotiate the constituencies and the detail of the operation of the safety representative's functions. There is no mechanism for bringing together the various sectors of a workforce where several unions may be involved or some sectors may not be unionised.

---

4   Now called employment tribunals.

Regulation 4A was inserted through the Management of Health and Safety at Work Regulations to give safety representatives the right to be consulted when safety related changes to working conditions are proposed. This addition was made to the Regulations to comply with EC law.

The implementation of these Regulations gave to trade union appointed safety representatives much more status than had been officially accorded to shop stewards. In the late 1970s the TUC and individual unions were heavily engaged in training safety representatives and for a time it appeared that there was more expertise in the safety representatives than in first line management. The number of safety representatives at a workplace is for the trade union to decide: the employer's only protection is to put an upper limit on the time and salary allowances available for safety representatives' activities. Thus while appointed safety representatives are entitled to paid time off for training and performance of their duties the employer could indicate displeasure at the number of representatives appointed by giving very small allowances to individual representatives, or by making it difficult for them to attend training courses. The representative has legal protection against an unfair exercise of such power in that he/she can complain to an Employment Tribunal. This occurred in the following case:

WHITE v PRESSED STEEL FISHER [1980] IRLR 176

The following extracts are taken from the judgment of Slynn J in the Employment Appeal Tribunal:

> Regulation 11 provides that ... an Industrial Tribunal [shall have] jurisdiction to determine complaints relating to time off with pay for safety representatives appointed under Regulations made under the Health and Safety at Work Act. A safety representative may apply to an Industrial Tribunal, complaining that an employer has failed to permit him to take time off in accordance with regulation 4(2) to which we have referred. If such complaint is well founded, the Industrial Tribunal has power to make a declaration and may also award compensation.

> Mr White is employed by Pressed Steel Fisher. He made a complaint that he had been appointed a safety representative but he had been refused paid leave to attend a health and safety course in Swindon. The Industrial Tribunal heard his complaint and rejected it. He now appeals to this Tribunal.

> ...

> The Code of Practice on time off for the training of safety representatives recites in its preamble that it is to set out a Code of Practice relating to time off for the purpose of undergoing training – 'approved by the Trades Union Congress or independent unions'. That states that employers should also make arrangements for training in the technical hazards of the workplace and relevant precautions on safe methods of work and other matters which – 'are to complement the training approved by the TUC or by independent unions for safety representatives'. It is not necessary to set out the whole of this Code in this judgment, but we should draw attention to paragraphs 3 and 4 in particular.

Paragraph 3 provides that, as soon as possible after their appointment, safety representatives should be permitted time off with pay to attend basic training facilities approved by the TUC or by the independent union or unions which appointed their safety representatives. Further training should be given for special responsibilities. The length of the training, it is said, cannot be rigidly prescribed but it should take account of the role of safety representatives and safety committees, and of trade union practices in relation to, firstly, the legal requirements relating to the health and safety of persons at work; the nature and extent of workplace hazards and, if necessary, measures to eliminate them; and the health and safety policy of employers. The Code provides that if the trade union wishes safety representatives to receive training, then it should so inform management and provide a copy of the syllabus. It goes on to say that unions and management should endeavour to reach agreement on the appropriate numbers and arrangements, and refer any problems which may arise to the relevant agreed procedures.

The Industrial Tribunal, having set that document out fully, and having said that they should have regard to it, found that in the present case Mr White was employed at a factory at Swindon which employed 5,000 people. The company is a part of the British Leyland group. Mr White wanted to go to the course at Swindon. The company sought to negotiate with Mr White's union with a view to providing a health and safety course on its own premises, staffed by its own safety officer. The Tribunal find that the union declined to negotiate on this matter. The Tribunal appear to have been satisfied that Mr Anderson, the training officer employed by the company, was fully aware of the need to train safety representatives; he was very experienced. He drew up a course which dealt with the various aspects of training which were required. It was a course which would involve each safety representative spending eight days undergoing training in the course of 1979. The Swindon course, on the other hand, was a 10-day course on one day in each of 10 consecutive weeks. Mr Anderson had very much in mind that these courses should have a trade union aspect to them; so, the Tribunal find, he got in touch with the education officer of the TUC in Bristol to ask if he would help with the 'In Plant' course. The Tribunal find that that TUC education officer declined to give assistance on the ground that there was no trade union aspect in the course. The Tribunal took the view that the man's own trade union – the Transport and General Workers' Union – had refused to consider the training course set up by the company – the union simply took the line that they wanted Mr White to go to Swindon. The Tribunal say that the union:

'do not attempt to show why the respondents' own course is unsatisfactory except it does not contain a trade union aspect in it. We therefore approached this case on the basis that the respondents' course is as adequate as that at the Swindon Technical College except that it does not contain the trade union aspect in it. That is not the respondents' fault. They have tried to involve the TUC training officer. He refuses to contribute to the course. We feel that the applicant should have come before us with evidence to show that his union had considered the course offered by the respondents' and the aspects with which they disagreed or found inadequate. They have not done so. They have refused to consider whether or not to approve the respondents' course. We also feel that if the applicant's trade union had felt that the respondents' course was inadequate and could not reach agreement upon it, that they should have invoked the procedure agreement in order to endeavour to reach agreement and iron out any problems.'

So they found that Mr White had not shown that the course offered by the company lacked any of the aspects of the functions as might be reasonable in all the circumstances, having regard to the provisions of the Code of Practice.

...

Accordingly we consider, in this case, that the Industrial Tribunal was entitled to have regard to the course available to the man at the plant where he worked. We do not accept the submission that the Industrial Tribunal gave no weight to the Code. They refer to it, they say they took into account, but they find on the facts that it was not necessary for Mr White to go to the course at Swindon. To that extent, it seems to us that their general approach to this matter was justified.

However, when one looks at paragraph 7 of the reasons for the decision of the Industrial Tribunal, it seems to us that they considered that the course arranged by the company was adequate save that it did not contain a trade union aspect to it. That paragraph seems to us to be saying that on the technical aspect of training concerned with safety at the workplace the course was adequate and that it was not necessary for the man to take time off, because it was not reasonable in all the circumstances for him to go to Swindon to deal with this particular aspect of the matter. This, it seems to us, the Tribunal was entitled to decide. It is not suggested that there was no material on which they could reach that conclusion other than in connection with the prior approval of the TUC for the employer's own course.

But, the Tribunal seems to be saying equally that the trade union aspect was not covered, or not adequately covered, in the course provided by the company. It seems to us that this side of the training – the trade union or representational side – is clearly of importance, as s 2(4) and regulation 4 of the 1977 Regulations make clear. It seems to us that the Industrial Tribunal rejected the application here because the union will not co-operate. Even if that were right – and Mr Tabachnik says there was no evidence for the broad way in which it was put – this is not, in our view, an answer to the claim. The important thing is that the safety representative should be given the necessary time off for such training as is reasonable in all the circumstances in regard to his functions. In our view, if the union thinks it right, the union is entitled to take the line that it prefers aspects of trade union or representational training to be taught on courses other than those under the aegis of the employers, and not to take part in those courses. Under the legislation they are entitled to take that line, but it is to be hoped – despite Mr Tabachnik's argument that there is no duty of co-operation – that there will in most cases be a proper degree of discussion and co-operation between the union and management, as the Code of Practice itself in its final sentence indicates. The fact that the union does not take part in the training of the representational side may not mean automatically that the course is necessarily defective; what it does mean, in our view, is that the failure of the union to participate, or the man to invoke the agreed procedures to deal with the matter, is not automatically an answer to his claim.

So, at the end of the day, we read the Industrial Tribunal's decision as saying that there was this gap in the course provided by the respondents. It is a gap in respect of a very important part of the functions defined by the section and by regulation 4. We do not have enough information to know whether the employer's course is adequate in this respect; whether in the circumstances it is necessary to allow time off; whether it would be reasonable for Mr White to undergo training in this aspect of the matter. Accordingly we propose to allow the appeal and remit the case to the Industrial Tribunal for them to consider whether, under regulation 11(5), it was here necessary for Mr White to have had time off to undergo training in the representational side of his functions as was reasonable in the circumstances, having regard to the relevant provisions of the Code.

If the Tribunal consider that is was necessary, and would have been reasonable, for him to go to Swindon for this aspect of the training, and if the course could have been severed so that this aspect of the training could be dealt with separately, then no doubt they will so declare. If, on the other hand, they come to the view that, in the light of the content of the employer's course, it was not necessary for him to go, and not reasonable in all the circumstances; or if the Swindon course could not have been divided up so as to allow him to go only for this trade union or representational side of his functions, then they will so declare and the application will fail.

In this case no question of compensation arises; all that is sought is a declaration.

— — —

The decline in trade union power in the 1990s, accompanied by very substantial restructuring of work units, has led to a comparable reduction in the number of recognised trade unions and thus fewer safety representatives, and less power for those who remain. The nature of the offshore workforce (which is very largely sub-contracted labour), as well as the relative weakness of the trade union movement in the offshore industry made it an obvious candidate for alternative Regulations. Special Regulations were made to enable workers on offshore installations to elect safety representatives. The intention of the Offshore Installation (Safety Representatives and Safety Committee) Regulations 1989 (SI 1989/971) is to allow representation of workers regardless of whether or not they are either in the direct employment of the installation owner or members of trade unions. However, there is no indication that the offshore Regulations are proving particularly successful: labour which is not unionised is not likely to discover a 'corporate' identity in the cause of safety.

IV WORKER INVOLVEMENT IN THE 1990s AND BEYOND

EC Directives on matters of employment tend to provide for worker involvement, through consultation or other means of participation. By the 1990s it had become apparent that the British 1970s system of giving rights to recognised trade unions did not meet the European criteria for worker involvement. Certainly the implementation, through the Employment Protection Act 1975 (now Trade Union and Labour Relations (Consolidation) Act 1992, ss 188–198) of consultation with recognised trade unions in the event of redundancy, was found by the European Court of Justice not to comply with the Directive on collective redundancies.[5]

The Framework Directive on health and safety (which it has been seen was largely implemented in Britain through the Management of Health and Safety at Work Regulations 1992) is couched throughout in terms which presuppose worker consultation, information and training.

Article 6 of the Directive, imposing general obligations on employers requires employers to provide workers with information and training in relation to risks. The same Article requires the employer to ensure that the planning and introduction of new technologies are the subject of consultation with the workers and/or their representatives. Article 10 requires the employer to provide workers and/or their representatives with all the necessary information concerning the safety and health risks. Article 11 requires employers to consult workers and/or their representatives and allow them to take part in discussions on all questions relating to safety and health at work. Article 12 imposes obligations on employers to train workers.

The Directive thus imposes obligations on employers towards workers both collectively and individually.

The British system of consultation, so long as it was provided only by the 1977 Regulations, was clearly flawed because these Regulations grant a floor of rights only where there is a recognised trade union. With the decline in trade union representation this meant that for the majority of workplaces onshore there was no effective safety representative system.

It was argued that the culture in Britain in the 1990s made further extension of safety representation pointless. At that time employers were preferring to communicate with employees individually rather than collectively through worker representatives. Nevertheless it was doubtful whether the regulatory situation was a compliance with the requirement in Article 11 of the Directive for 'balanced participation in accordance with national laws and/or practices.' Therefore the following Regulations were

---

5   See now the Collective Redundancies and Transfer of Undertakings (Protection of Employment) (Amendment) Regulations 1995, SI 1995/2587 and SI 1999/1925.

made under s 2(2) of the European Communities Act 1972 to provide for safety representatives in workplaces where there was no trade union:

HEALTH AND SAFETY (CONSULTATION WITH EMPLOYEES) REGULATIONS 1996 SI 1996/1513

Regulation 3

Duty of employer to consult

Where there are employees who are not represented by safety representatives under the 1977 Regulations, the employer shall consult those employees in good time on matters relating to their health and safety at work and, in particular, with regard to–

(a) the introduction of any measure at the workplace which may substantially affect the health and safety of those employees;

(b) his arrangements for appointing or, as the case may be, nominating persons in accordance with regulations 6(1) and 7(1)(b) if the Management of Health and Safety at Work Regulations 1992;[6]

(c) any health and safety information he is required to provide to those employees by or under the relevant statutory provisions;

(d) the planning and organisation of any health and safety training he is required to provide to those employees by or under the relevant statutory provisions; and

(e) the health and safety consequences for those employees of the introduction (including the planning thereof) of new technologies into the workplace.

Regulation 4

Persons to be consulted

(1) The consultation required by regulation 3 is consultation with either–

(a) the employees directly; or

(b) in respect of any group of employees, one or more persons in that group who were elected, by the employees in that group at the time of the election, to represent that group for the purposes of such consultation (and any such persons are in these Regulations referred to as 'representatives of employee safety').

(2) Where an employer consults representatives of employee safety he shall inform the employees represented by those representatives of–

(a) the names of those representatives; and

(b) the group of employees represented by those representatives.

(3) An employer shall not consult a person as a representative of employee safety if–

---

6   Now regulations 7(1) and 7(1)(b) of the revised regulations.

(a) that person has notified the employer that he does not intend to represent the group of employees for the purposes of such consultation;

(b) that person has ceased to be employed in the group of employees which he represents;

(c) the period for which that person was elected has expired without that person being re-elected; or

(d) that person has become incapacitated from carrying out his functions under these regulations;

and where pursuant to this paragraph an employer discontinues consultation with that person he shall inform the employees in the group concerned of that fact.

(4) Where an employer who has been consulting representatives of employee safety decides to consult employees directly he shall inform the employees and the representatives of that fact.

Regulation 5

Duty of employer to provide information

(1) Where an employer consults employees directly he shall, subject to paragraph (3) make available to those employees such information, within the employer's knowledge, as is necessary to enable them to participate fully and effectively in the consultation.

(2) Where an employer consults representatives of employee safety he shall, subject to paragraph (3) make available to those representatives such information, within the employer's knowledge, as is–

(a) necessary to enable them to participate fully and effectively in the consultation and in the carrying out of their functions under these Regulations;

(b) contained in any record which he is required to keep by regulation 7 of the Reporting of Injuries, Diseases and Dangerous Occurrences Regulations 1995 and which relates to the workplace or the group of employees represented by those representatives.

(3) Nothing in paragraph (1) or (2) shall require an employer to make available any information–

(a) the disclosure of which would be against the interests of national security;

(b) which he could not disclose without contravening a prohibition imposed by or under any enactment;

(c) relating specifically to an individual, unless he has consented to its being disclosed;

(d) the disclosure of which would, for reasons other than it effect on health or safety, cause substantial injury to the employer's undertaking or, where the information was supplied to him by some other person, to the undertaking of that other person; or

(e) obtained by the employer for the purpose of bringing, prosecuting or defending any legal proceedings;

or to provide or allow the inspection of any document or part of a document which is not related to health or safety.

Regulation 6

Functions of representatives of employee safety

Where an employer consults representatives of employee safety each of those representatives shall, for the period for which that representative is so consulted, have the following functions–

(a) to make representations to the employer on potential hazards and dangerous occurrences at the workplace which affect, or could affect, the groups of employees he represents;

(b) to make representations to the employer on general matters affecting the health and safety at work of the group of employees he represents and, in particular, on such matters as he is consulted about by the employer under regulation 3; and

(c) to represent the group of employees he represents in consultations at the workplace with inspectors appointed under section 19(1) of the 1974 Act.

Regulation 7

Training, time off and facilities for representatives of employee safety and time off for candidates

(1) Where an employer consults representatives of employee safety, he shall–

(a) ensure that each of those representatives is provided with such training in respect of that representative's functions under these Regulations as is reasonable in all the circumstances and the employer shall meet any reasonable costs associated with such training including travel and subsistence costs; and

(b) permit each of those representatives to take such time off with pay during that representative's working hours as shall be necessary for the purpose of that representative performing his functions under these Regulations or undergoing any training pursuant to paragraph (1)(a).

(2) An employer shall permit a candidate standing for election as a representative of employee safety reasonable time off with pay during that person's working hours in order to perform his function as such a candidate.

(3) Schedule 1 (pay for time off) and Schedule 2 (provisions as to industrial tribunals) shall have effect.

(4) An employer shall provide such other facilities and assistance as a representative of employee safety may reasonably require for the purpose of carrying out his functions under these Regulations.

– – –

Comment

While it can be seen that the 1996 Regulations follow broadly the same pattern as those of 1977 in detail the more recent Regulations are less sympathetic to the system of collective representation. Regulation 4 empowers the employer to consult with workers directly rather than through their representatives. The functions of the representatives under the 1996 Regulations are considerably more limited than those representing a unionised workforce. In the former case they are not entitled to investigate nor do they have the right to carry out inspections of the workplace. Likewise they do not have the right to receive information from inspectors, under s 28(8) of the Act: however this apparent omission from the list of their functions may not be significant since s 28 requires the inspector to communicate with the workforce or their representatives, so arguably it is not necessary to make special reference to this in the regulations as being a function of the representatives.

V TERMS AND CONDITIONS OF EMPLOYMENT

In Part I of this book it was noted that in recent years there has been an increased awareness of health problems created by subjecting persons to stressful working conditions. The civil courts, in cases such as *Walker v Northumberland County Council* (1995) have established that it may be negligence for an employer to expose employees to conditions where they are so stressed as to be caused psychiatric injury. In this section are set out some of the legislative provisions aimed to protect workers, particularly employees, from the risks to their health to which they may be exposed by over long working hours, or by discrimination or loss of their employment as a result of asserting their rights in relation to health and safety issues.

(a) Hours of employment

The following Regulations were made by the British Government under the European Communities Act 1972, s 2(2) to comply with EC Directive 93/104 concerning organisation of working time and provisions concerning working time in EC Directive 94/33 on the protection of young people at work. Interestingly the Factories Act 1961 had contained provisions limiting the hours that women and young persons could be employed in factories. The provisions protecting women were first introduced a hundred years ago in the belief that women were less able than men to bargain for their own protection. In the *laissez-faire* spirit of those days it was accepted that men were able to bargain for the working hours they wanted. The Factories Act provisions protecting women were enforced by the Factory Inspectorate, but they were repealed following the enactment of the Sex Discrimination Act 1975.

The EC Directive on working time was adopted under Article 118A of the Treaty of Rome, relying on the qualified majority voting procedure available under that Article in spite of the opposition of the UK Government. The UK Government then unsuccessfully challenged the validity of the Directive, alleging that Article 118A was not an appropriate basis for it. The UK contention was that working hours are not a matter of health and safety. It was only after this challenge had proved unsuccessful (see *UK v EU Council* [1996] All ER (EC) 877) that the provisions of the Directive were brought into force in October 1998 although the final date set by the EC for implementing the Directive had been November 1996.

It was speculated that any person who was deprived of the entitlements granted by the Directive, during the period between 1996 and 1998 when the UK was in default of its EC obligations, might claim compensation. In at least one reported case the Employment Appeal Tribunal appeared to have accepted this argument. In *Gibson v East Riding of Yorkshire District Council* (1999) *The Times*, 12 February a swimming instructor employed by a local authority successfully relied on the directive to obtain an entitlement to four weeks paid annual leave. The EAT found that the Directive had direct effect even though it had not been implemented. However the Court of Appeal subsequently held Article 7 was insufficiently precise to have direct effect against Yorkshire District Council.[7] It is unlikely that a person employed in the private sector would have been able to claim compensation from the employer: however, such a person might possibly have relied on *Francovich v Italian Republic* (1992) and claimed damages from the UK government.

The reluctance of the UK to implement the Directive was demonstrated by using the 1972, rather than the 1974 legislation, as a basis for the Regulations. Nevertheless the Health and Safety Executive is the principal enforcement agency, but some of the regulations are also linked to the Employment Rights Act 1996 to give workers rights to seek compensation in an employment tribunal.

WORKING TIME REGULATIONS1998 SI 1998/1833

PART II

RIGHTS AND OBLIGATIONS CONCERNING WORKING TIME

...

Regulation 4

Maximum weekly working time

(1) Subject to regulation 5, a worker's working time, including overtime, in any reference period which is applicable in his case shall not exceed an average of 48 hours for each seven days.

---

7   June 21st 2000 – LTL 26/7/98.

(2) An employer shall take all reasonable steps, in keeping with the need to protect the health and safety of workers, to ensure that the limit specified in paragraph (1) is complied with in the case of each worker employed by him in relation to whom it applies.

(3) Subject to paragraphs (4) and (5) and any agreement under regulation 23(b), the reference periods which apply in the case of a worker are

    (a) where a relevant agreement provides for the application of this regulation in relation to successive periods of 17 weeks, each such period, or

    (b) in any other case, any period of 17 weeks in the course of his employment.

(4) Where a worker has worked for his employer for less than 17 weeks, the reference period applicable in his case is the period that has elapsed since he started work for his employer.

(5) Paragraphs (3) and (4) shall apply to a worker who is excluded from the scope of certain provisions of these Regulations by regulation 21 as if for each reference to 17 weeks there were substituted a reference to 26 weeks.

(6) For the purposes of this regulation, a worker's average working time for each seven days during a reference period shall be determined according to the formula–

$$\frac{A + B}{C}$$

Where–

A is the aggregate number of hours comprised in the worker's working time during the course of the reference period;

B is the aggregate number of hours comprised in his working time during the course of the period beginning immediately after the end of the reference period and ending when the number of days in that subsequent period on which he has worked equals the number of excluded days during the reference period; and

C is the number of weeks in the reference period.

(7) In paragraph (6) 'excluded days' means days comprised in–

    (a) any period of annual leave taken by the worker in exercise of this entitlement under regulation 13.

    (b) any period of sick leave taken by the worker;

    (c) any period of maternity leave taken by the worker; and

    (d) any period in respect of which the limit specified in paragraph (1) did not apply in relation to the worker by virtue of regulation 5.

Regulation 5

Agreement to exclude the maximum

(1) The limit specified in regulation 4(1) shall not apply in relation to a worker who has agreed with his employer in writing that it should not apply in his

case, provided that the employer complies with the requirements of paragraph (4).

(2) An agreement for the purposes of paragraph (1)–

    (a) may either relate to a specified period or apply indefinitely; and

    (b) subject to any provision in the agreement for a different period of notice, shall be terminable by the worker by giving not less than seven days notice to his employer in writing.

(3) Where an agreement for the purposes of paragraph (1) makes provision for the termination of the agreement after a period of notice, the notice period provided for shall not exceed three months.

(4) The requirements referred to in paragraph (1) are that the employer–

    (a) maintains up-to-date records which–

        (i) identify each of the workers whom he employs who has agreed that the limit specified in regulation 4(1) should not apply in his case.

        (ii) set out any terms on which the worker agreed that the limit should not apply; and

        (iii) specify the number of hours worked by him for the employer during each reference period since the agreement came into effect (excluding any period which ended more than two years before the most recent entry in the records);

    (b) permits any inspector appointed by the Health and Safety Executive or any other authority which is responsible under regulation 28 for the enforcement of these Regulations to inspect those records on request; and

    (c) provides any such inspector with such information as he may request regarding any case in which a worker has agreed that the limit specified in regulation 4(1) should not apply in his case.

Regulation 6

Length of night work

(1) A night worker's normal hours of work in any reference period which is applicable in his case shall not exceed an average of eight hours for each 24 hours.

(2) An employer shall take all reasonable steps, in keeping with the need to protect the health and safety of workers, to ensure that the limit specified in paragraph (1) is complied with in the case of each night worker employed by him.

...

Regulation 7

Health assessment and transfer of night workers to day work

(1) An employer–

    (a) shall not assign an adult worker to work which is to be undertaken during periods such that the worker will become a night worker unless–

> (i) the employer has ensured that the worker will have the opportunity of a free health assessment before he takes up the assignment; or
>
> (ii) the worker had a health assessment before being assigned to work to be undertaken during such periods on an earlier occasion, and the employer has no reason to believe that that assessment is no longer valid, and

(b) shall ensure that each night worker employed by him has the opportunity of a free health assessment at regular intervals of whatever duration may be appropriate in his case.

(2) Subject to paragraph (4), an employer–

(a) shall not assign a young worker to work during the period between 10 pm and 6 am ('the restricted period') unless–

[young worker to have same opportunity for health assessment as in (1)(a)(i) and (ii) except assessment to also cover his 'capacities]

...

(4) The requirements in paragraph (2) do not apply in a case where the work a young worker is assigned is of an exceptional nature

...

Regulation 8

Pattern of work

Where the pattern according to which an employer organises work is such as to put the health and safety of a worker employed by him at risk, in particular because the work is monotonous or the work-rate is predetermined, the employer shall ensure that the worker is given adequate rest breaks.

Regulation 9

Records

An employer shall–

(a) keep records which are adequate to show whether the limits specified in regulations 4(1) and 6(1) and (7) and the requirements in regulations 7(1) and (2) are being complied with in the case of each worker employed by him in relation to whom they apply; and

(b) retain such records for two years from the date on which they were made.

Regulation 10

Daily rest

(1) An adult worker is entitled to a rest period of not less than 11 consecutive hours in each 24-hour period during which he works for his employer.

(2) Subject to paragraph (3) a young worker is entitled to a rest period of not less than twelve consecutive hours in each 24-hour period during which he works for his employer.

(3) The minimum rest period provided for in paragraph (2) may be interrupted in the case of activities involving periods of work that are split up over the day or of short duration.

Regulation 11

Weekly rest period

(1) Subject to paragraph (2), an adult worker is entitled to an uninterrupted rest period of not less than 24 hours in each 7-day period during which he works for his employer.

...

(3) Subject to para (8) a young worker is entitled to a rest period of not less than 48 hours in each 7-day period ...

...

Regulation 12

Rest breaks

(1) Where an adult worker's daily working time is more than 6 hours, he is entitled to a rest break.

...

Regulation 13

Entitlement to annual leave

(1) Subject to paragraphs (5) and (7), a worker is entitled in each leave year to a period of leave determined in accordance with paragraph (2)

...

– – –

Comment

The above selected extracts indicate the complexity of the Regulations: it will be evident that in the case of many of the Regulations referred to only the broad rule has been given. It will have been noticed that these Regulations, contrary to the normal practice in British employment law, apply in relation to 'workers' rather than employees. Regulation 2 (interpretations) provides:

'worker' means an individual who has entered into or works under (or where the employment has ceased, worked under)–

(a) a contract of employment; or

(b) any other contract, whether express or implied and (if it is express) whether oral or in writing, whereby the individual undertakes to do or perform personally any work or services for another party to the contract whose status is not by virtue of the contract that of a client or customer of any profession or business undertaking carried on by the individual ...

The same regulation provides:

'young worker' means a worker who has attained the age of 15 but not the age of 18 and who, as respects England and Wales, is over compulsory school age

...

Workers who have not received their proper entitlements under Regulations 10, 11, 12, or 13, may by virtue of Regulation 30 make a claim to an employment tribunal which can in appropriate cases award compensation.

All the above extracts have been taken from Part II of the Regulations. Part III is entitled 'Exceptions'. Regulation 18 lists a number of excluded sectors, including various categories of transport works and doctors in training. Regulation 20 provides that the majority of the regulations do not apply to those who have 'unmeasured working time'. Significantly this regulation applies to 'managing executives or other persons with autonomous decision-taking powers'. In addition to this Regulation 21 identifies 'other special cases' who are not subject to the full impact of the Regulations. This excepted list includes various categories of workers 'Where the worker's activities involve the need for continuity of service or production', or 'where there is a foreseeable surge of activity'. The activities in respect of which these exemptions may apply include those who work in communications (press, radio, television cinematographic production, postal and telecommunications services), those who work in public utilities (such as refuse collection) and agriculture.

It may be doubted that these Regulations will make any real impact on the work culture of the UK. Individual workers may contract out of the 48 hour maximum working week, and employers may make this contracting out a term of the initial contract of employment. In other cases the work force may collectively agree that the 48 hour maximum will not apply to them. When this entitlement to 'opt out' of the Regulations is taken in conjunction with the exclusions and exemptions it appears that the Regulations have little force. It is especially significant that the professions will not be affected. Trainee doctors are expressly excluded and other professional people are likely to be exempted as being employed on contracts where their working time is unmeasured. This is ironical in that it is professional workers who appear to be most subject to stress at work at the present time.

Use of employment tribunal in working time cases

EMPLOYMENT RIGHTS ACT 1996

Rights not to suffer detriment

Section 45A

Working time cases

(1) A worker has the right not to be subjected to any detriment by any act, or any deliberate failure to act, by his employer done on the ground that the worker–

  (a) refused (or proposed to refuse) to comply with a requirement which the employer imposed (or proposed to impose) in contravention of the Working Time Regulations, 1998, or

    (b) refused (or proposed to refuse) to forgo a right conferred on him by those Regulations,

    (c) failed to sign a workforce agreement for the purposes of those Regulations, or to enter into, or agree to vary or extend, any other agreement with his employer which is provided for in those Regulations.

    (d) being–

        (i) a representative of members of the workforce for the purposes of Schedule 1 to those Regulations, or

        (ii) a candidate in an election in which any person elected will, on being elected, be such a representative,

    performed (or proposed to perform) any function or activities as such a representative or candidate,

    (e) brought proceedings against the employer to enforce a right conferred on him by those Regulations, or

    (f) alleged that the employer had infringed such a right.

(2) It is immaterial for the purposes of subsection (1)(e) or (f)–

    (a) whether or not the worker has the right, or

    (b) whether or not the right has been infringed,

    but, for those provisions to apply, the claim to the right and that it has been infringed must be made in good faith.

(3) it is sufficient for subsection (1)(f) to apply that the worker, without specifying the right, made it reasonably clear to the employer what the right claimed to have been infringed was.

(4) This section does not apply where a worker is an employee and the detriment in question amounts to dismissal within the meaning of Part X.

Rights not to be unfairly dismissed

Section 101A

Working time cases

An employee who is dismissed shall be regarded for the purposes of this Part as unfairly dismissed if the reason (or, if more than one) the principal reason for the dismissal is that the employee–

    (a) refused (or proposed to refuse) to comply with a requirement which the employer imposed (or proposed to impose) in contravention of the Working Time Regulations 1998,

    (b) refused (or proposed to refuse) to forego a right conferred on him by those Regulations.

    (c) refused to sign a workforce agreement for the purposes of those Regulations, or to enter into, or agree to vary or extend, any other agreement with his employer which is provided for in those Regulations, or

    (d) being–

    (i)   a representative of members of the workforce for the purposes of Schedule 1 to those Regulations, or

    (ii) a candidate in an election in which any person elected will, on being elected, be such a representative,

performed (or proposed to perform) any functions or activities as such a representative or candidate.

Section 120

Basic award: minimum in certain cases

(1)   the amount of the basic award ... shall not be less than £2,900 where the reason (or if more than one, the principal reason)–

    ...

is one of those specified in section 100(1)(a) and (b), 101A(d) ...

– – –

Comment

These rights are enforced by complaint to an employment tribunal which has its normal powers to make a declaration or award compensation. In the case of discrimination short of dismissal the compensatory award shall be the sum that is just and equitable. In the case of dismissal contrary to s 101A(d) (a worker representative) the basic award must not be less than the minimum set out in s 120, cited above. In other cases the basic award will be calculated by reference to the worker's age, weekly pay and length of service, subject to the limits set in the Act. It will be noted that the safety representative (s 100(1)(a)) and the representative for the purposes of the Working Time Regulations are treated in the same way.

HEALTH AND SAFETY COMMISSION'S PROPOSALS FOR FURTHER CHANGE

In a Consultative Document published early in 2000 the Health and Safety Commission expressed its commitment to further increasing worker involvement. It sought to promote public debate on arrangements for employee consultation and for greater involvement in workplace health and safety. Having reviewed the present position it suggested:

HEALTH AND SAFETY COMMISSION DISCUSSION DOCUMENT
EMPLOYEE CONSULTATION AND INVOLVEMENT IN HEALTH AND SAFETY

    ...

Options

48 We believe that worker consultation and involvement helps improve workplace health and safety. Existing systems can work well but do not operate in a significant proportion of workplaces.

49 The challenge is to find ways to:

- secure effective consultation in workplaces (particularly small firms) where no (or inadequate) consultation takes place now;

- ensure that workers in more complex employment relationships (ie those employed via agencies, those on short-term contracts, and those working for contractors in other employers' workplaces) are properly consulted;

- ensure that effective consultation takes place irrespective of the gender, ethnicity or language of the worker; and

- enhance the effectiveness of the contribution which workers or their representatives make.

50 Taking account of the developments, trends and pressures for change outlined earlier we see a number of options.

— — —

It did not consider that retaining the status quo was a valid option. It went on to consider a range of 'non-legislative options', including the use of publicity to increase employers' awareness of the value of employee consultation, the encouragement of a framework of best practice initiatives between employer and employee organisations, provision of training for safety representatives and improved enforcement systems. It also suggested legislative options, such as harmonisation of the existing regulations, and the granting of increased powers to safety representatives. The Consultative Document invited response. The arguments put forward by HSC indicate that legislation is likely.

(b) Employment rights

The Employment Rights Act 1996 s 108 protects employees who have one year's service with their employer from being unfairly dismissed. The Trade Union and Labour Relations (Consolidation) Act 1992 protects employees who suffer either dismissal (s 152) or discrimination short of dismissal (s 146) for reasons related to trade union membership and activities. The importance of these provisions of the 1992 Act is that employees may complain to an industrial tribunal in relation to matters covered by these sections even though they have not the one year's employment which is the normal pre-requisite to protection against unfair dismissal. There was room for doubt whether the 1992 Act protected trade union safety representatives from discrimination: and very unlikely that persons other than properly appointed trade union representatives would be protected against discrimination or dismissal if they protested, even justifiably, about the safety of their workplaces; though if an employee had more than two years service the burden would be on the employer to justify a dismissal. The Employment

Protection (Consolidation) Act 1978 provisions have now been amended, in the Employment Rights Act 1996, expressly to give coverage to safety representatives, and to some extent other employees, (either those with special safety responsibilities, or employees who have no safety representative or no available representative) against dismissal and discrimination short of dismissal for matters related to safety. These provisions specifically cover an employee who leaves what is, or he reasonably believes to be, an unsafe workplace.

EMPLOYMENT RIGHTS ACT 1996

PART V

PROTECTION FROM SUFFERING DETRIMENT IN EMPLOYMENT

Rights not to suffer detriment

Section 44

Health and safety cases

(1) An employee has the right not to be subjected to any detriment by any act, or any deliberate failure to act, by his employer done on the ground that–

(a) having been designated by the employer to carry out activities in connection with preventing or reducing risks to health and safety at work, the employee carried out, or proposed to carry out, any such activities;

(b) being a representative of workers on matters of health and safety at work, or a member of a safety committee–

    (i) in accordance with arrangements established under or by virtue of any enactment, or

    (ii) by reason of being acknowledged as such by the employer, the employee performed (or proposed to perform) any functions as such a representative or a member of such a committee,

(ba) the employee took part (or proposed to take part) in consultation with the employer pursuant to the Health and Safety (Consultation with Employees) Regulations 1996 or in an election of representatives of employee safety within the meaning of those Regulations (whether as a candidate or otherwise),

(c) being an employee at a place where–

    (i) there was no such representative or safety committee, or

    (ii) there was such a representative or safety committee but it was not reasonably practicable for the employee to raise the matter by those means,

the employee brought to his employer's attention, by reasonable means, circumstances connected with his work which he reasonably believed were harmful or potentially harmful to health or safety,

(d) in circumstances of danger which the employee reasonably believed to be serious and imminent and which he could not reasonably have been expected to avert, he left (or proposed to leave) or (while the danger persisted) refused to return to his place of work or any dangerous part of his place of work, or

(e) in circumstances of danger which the employee reasonably believed to be serious and imminent, he took (or proposed to take) appropriate steps to protect himself or other persons from the danger.

(2) For the purposes of subsection (1)(e) whether steps which an employee took (or proposed to take) were appropriate is to be judged by reference to all the circumstances including, in particular, his knowledge and the facilities and advice available to him at the time.

(3) An employee shall not be regarded as having been subjected to any detriment on the ground specified in subsection (1)(e) if the employer shows that it was (or would have been) so negligent for the employee to take the steps which he took (or proposed to take) that a reasonable employer might have treated him as the employer did.

(4) This section does no apply where the detriment in question amounts to dismissal.

...

Right not to be unfairly dismissed

...

Fairness

...

Section 100

Health and safety cases

(1) An employee who is dismissed shall be regarded for purposes of this Part as having been unfairly dismissed if the reason (or, if more than one, the principal reason) for the dismissal is that–

(a) having been designated by the employer to carry out activities in connection with preventing or reducing risks to health and safety at work, the employee carried out (or proposed to carry out) any such activities;

(b) being a representative of workers on matters of health and safety at work or a member of a safety committee–

(i) in accordance with arrangements established under or by virtue of any enactment, or

(ii) by reason of being acknowledged as such by the employer,

the employee performed (or proposed to perform) any functions as such a representative or a member of such a committee,

(ba)the employee took part (or proposed to take part) in consultation with the employer pursuant to the Health and Safety (Consultation with Employees) Regulations 1996 or in an election of representatives of employee safety within the meaning of those Regulations (whether as a candidate or otherwise),

(c) being an employee at a place where–

    (i) there was no such representative or safety committee, or

    (ii) there was such a representative or safety committee but it was not reasonably practicable for the employee to raise the matter by those means,

he brought to his employer's attention, by reasonable means, circumstances connected with his work which he reasonably believed were harmful or potentially harmful to health or safety,

(d) in circumstances of danger which he reasonably believed to be serious and imminent and which he could not reasonably have been expected to avert, left (or proposed to leave) or (while the danger persisted) refused to return to his place of work or any dangerous part of his place of work, or

(e) in circumstances of danger which he reasonably believed to be serious and imminent he took (or proposed to take) appropriate steps to protect himself or other persons from the danger.

(2) For the purpose of subsection (1)(e) whether steps which an employee took (or proposed to take) were appropriate is to be judged by reference to all the circumstances including, in particular, his knowledge and the facilities and advice available to him at the time.

(3) Where the reason (or, if more than one, the principal reason) for the dismissal of an employee was that specified in subsection (1)(e), he shall not be regarded as unfairly dismissed if the employer shows that it was (or would have been) so negligent for the employee to take the steps which he took (or proposed to take) that a reasonable employer might have dismissed him for taking (or proposing to take) them.

– – –

Comment

The above provisions protect employees only in their relationship with their employer: thus they do not appear to protect disclosure of information to a third party, even an inspector, much less the media. Such disclosure might in appropriate circumstances be protected by the Public Interest Disclosure Act 1998. This Act adds 'Part IVA Protected Disclosures' to the Employment Rights Act. The new s 43B provides:

Section 43B

Disclosures qualifying for protection

(1) In this Part a 'qualifying disclosure means any disclosure of information which, in the reasonable belief of the worker making the disclosure, tends to show one or more of the following–

    (a) that a criminal offence has been committed, is being committed or is likely to be committed,

   (b) that a person has failed, is failing or is likely to fail to comply with any legal obligation to which he is subject ...

However the worker is expected to make the disclosure to the employer or other persons (including inspectors) specified in the Act. Only in default of being able to get the situation rectified through these channels is he protected if he makes a disclosure to another person and then only if he does so in good faith, believing the facts and without seeking personal gain. Sections 47B and 103A of the 1996 Act protect the worker who makes a protected disclosure from suffering, respectively, detriment and dismissal.

A likely problem, even in relationships with the employer, is establishing that the issue was in fact safety related. This was an aspect of *Harris v Select Timber Frame Ltd* (1994)[8] an unreported industrial tribunal case. Mr Harris had been employed by his father's company. Mr Harris complained to an industrial tribunal after his dismissal. He had previously complained to his employer (his father) about workplace safety; his complaint was followed by a visit from an HSE inspector; shortly afterwards he was dismissed just before he was due to be examined by an HSE doctor. At the hearing the father had stated that 'health and safety did come into it,' although he claimed that this was not the reason for the dismissal. The fact that there was no evidence of any other shortcoming on the part of the employee, and there had been no previous warning as to his conduct, caused the tribunal to conclude that the dismissal was contrary to what is now s 100 and unfair.

Among other (many of them unreported) recent cases of interest is *Smiths Industries Aerospace and Defence Systems v Rawling* [1996] IRLR 656 in which the EAT ruled that safety representatives had no special protection against redundancy, although they must not be disadvantaged.

VI DUTIES OF THE EMPLOYEE

The Health and Safety at Work Act 1974, s 7, imposes a general duty on the employee:

Section 7

Duties of employees at work

It shall be the duty of every employee while at work–

   (a) to take reasonable care for the health and safety of himself and of other persons who may be affected by his acts or omissions at work; and

   (b) as regards any duty or requirement imposed on his employer or any other person by or under any of the relevant statutory provisions, to

---

8   Case No 59214/93, 222 Health and Safety Information Bulletin 16 .

> co-operate with him so far as is necessary to enable that duty or
> requirement to be performed or complied with.

– – –

This duty bears a criminal sanction and therefore an employee who fails to comply with it may be prosecuted by an inspector. This general provision is now given some content by regulation 14 of the Management of Health and Safety Regulations 1999. In practice there are relatively few prosecutions brought against individual employees. The responsibility for ensuring that the employee operates safely lies primarily on the employer. The general duty under s 2(2)c) requires the employer to provide instruction, training, and supervision to ensure the safety of employees. The Management Regulations and other Regulations in the Six Pack and elsewhere impose more specific requirements on the employer to instruct and train.

If an employer has set up a safe system of work and done all that is reasonable to maintain it then any employee who through misconduct or incompetence, violates that system, to the endangerment of himself or others, should at least be disciplined, or in the case of very seriously unsafe conduct, or persistent disregard of requirements, be dismissed. The employers will need, in their own protection, to enforce observance of safe systems: if they neglect to do so then they are at risk of being prosecuted for failing to conduct their business safely, and, should anyone suffer personal injury they may well be sued for damages.

The employee who has not continuous employment has little protection under the Employment Rights Act 1996 (except as described above) against the arbitrary termination of the contract of employment: common law remedies are weak. However the employer is entitled to dismiss, even an employee who has continuous employment, if that employee has been guilty of misconduct or lacks competence the job requires, and the employer has conducted a proper enquiry to establish the facts, (hearing the employee's side of the story as well). In matters of conduct and capability (the two can be closely related) it will be important to ascertain whether the employee has been asked to undertake tasks beyond those he was employed and trained to do. An employee who wishes to contest dismissal must complain to an employment tribunal; the burden lies on the employee to establish the dismissal. Where an employee is shown to have been dismissed the burden shifts to the employer to show the dismissal was for one of the reasons allowed by the legislation. The dismissal, even if for a reason allowed by the Act, will still be unfair if the employer's behaviour was not reasonable: the employer will normally have been unreasonable if the offence was trivial or the employer had not gone through proper procedures, such as giving the employee warnings, and/or conducting a proper enquiry to establish the facts.

EMPLOYMENT RIGHTS ACT 1996

PART X

UNFAIR DISMISSAL

Chapter I

Right not to be unfairly dismissed

Section 94

The right

(1) An employee has the right not to be unfairly dismissed by his employer.

...

Section 95

Circumstances in which an employee is dismissed

(1) For the purposes of this Part an employee is dismissed by his employer if–

 ...

 (a) the contract under which he is employed is terminated by the employer (whether with or without notice)

 (b) ...

 (c) the employee terminates the contract under which he is employed (with or without notice) in circumstances in which he is entitled to terminate it without notice by reason of the employer's conduct.

 ...

Section 98

General

(1) In determining for the purposes of this Part whether the dismissal of an employee was fair or unfair, it shall be for the employer to show–

 (a) what was the reason (or, if more than one, the principal reason) for the dismissal, and

 (b) that it was either a reason falling within subsection (2) or some other substantial reason of a kind such as to justify the dismissal of an employee holding the position which that employee held.

(2) A reason falls within this subsection if it–

 (a) relates to the capability or qualifications of the employee for performing work of the kind which he was employed by the employer to do,

 (b) relates to the conduct of the employee,

 (c) is that the employee was redundant, or

 (d) is that the employee could not continue to work in the position which he held without contravention (either on his part or on that of his employer) of a duty or restriction imposed by or under an enactment.

(3) In subsection (2)(a)–

   (a) 'capability', in relation to an employee, means his capability assessed by reference to skill, aptitude, health or any other physical or mental quality, and

   (b) 'qualifications', in relation to an employee, means any degree, diploma or other academic, technical or professional qualification relevant to the position which he held.

(4) Where the employer has fulfilled the requirements of subsection (1), the determination of the question whether the dismissal is fair or unfair (having regard to the reason shown by the employer)–

   (a) depends on whether in the circumstance (including the size and administrative resources of the employer's undertaking) the employer acted reasonably or unreasonably in treating it as a sufficient reason for dismissing the employee; and

   (b) shall be determined in accordance with equity and the substantial merits of the case.

– – –

Cases in which the employment tribunal's decision is not appealed are not normally reported in the law reports, so it is not easy to ascertain how many dismissals on safety issues are contested, and even less clear how many actually occur. Appeals on a point of law lie from the employment tribunal to the Employment Appeal Tribunal and from there to the Court of Appeal, and are more likely to be reported. The following cases nevertheless show the operation of the rules of unfair dismissal in safety cases. They fall into three categories:

(a) the employer was justified in dismissing;

(b) the employee was justified in terminating the employment on safety grounds (constructive dismissal);

(c) the employer unfairly dismissed employees for their reaction to unsafe work.

(a) Employee's conduct made dismissal fair

TAYLOR v ALIDAIR LTD [1978] IRLR 82

The case was appealed to the Court of Appeal and the following extracts are taken from the judgment of Lord Denning:

A Vickers Viscount was coming in to land at the airport at Guernsey. It was a fine day in September 1975 with some wind, but nothing out of the ordinary. The aircraft came down much too sharply. It hit the ground with a big bump. So hard was the landing, that it immediately bounced back into the air. It bounced up about 10 feet. Then it hurtled forward and came down heavily again further down the runway. In this second bump the front nose wheel came down hard: so hard that the structure above it collapsed; and the nose of the aircraft came down on the tarmac. Emergency procedures were put into action. The passengers got out very quickly. Fortunately there was no fire and no one was seriously hurt; but the damage to the aircraft, its engines and airframe, was very considerable.

The company at once suspended the pilot Captain Taylor. They held an enquiry; and that inquiry found that it was the pilot's fault. So the company dismissed him. He then brought a claim for unfair dismissal. The Industrial Tribunal held that he was unfairly dismissed and he must either be re-engaged or awarded compensation. If he was awarded compensation, it was to be reduced by 25% because of this accident. The Employment Appeal Tribunal set that decision aside. They held that he was fairly dismissed. He now appeals to this Court.

...

As the Employment Appeal Tribunal said: 'There are some occupations – such as the pilot of an aircraft – where the public safety is entrusted to a single individual. It is of the first importance that a person so engaged should be competent and capable. If it appears that he is no longer competent or capable, then the employer can very properly say: 'I'm afraid we cannot entrust you with these serious duties any longer and we must dismiss you.' It is not necessary that he should be given a further chance or further training or the like before he is dismissed. We have been referred to the Code of Practice on the proceedings in disciplinary matters, especially No 132 which says: 'The procedure should be in writing and should ... give the employee the opportunity to state his case and the right to be accompanied by his employee representative.' That may be desirable in many cases: but it should not be regarded as of universal application. Captain Taylor here was given at the inquiry full opportunity to hear what was said against him and to state his case. But, as I put in the course of the argument, suppose there had been no Board of Inquiry at all but the managing director of the company had called Captain Taylor in and said: 'I was there on that aircraft that day with my wife and my child: and, in view of this heavy landing, I have lost confidence in your ability to continue flying on behalf of the company. Have you anything to say why you should no longer be employed by the company?' Then having listened to what he has to say, he can say, 'I'm afraid that there it is; we have no option; we have the safety of the public to consider; we must dismiss you.' I should have thought that that was entirely reasonable and the dismissal could not be said to be unfair. It would not be necessary for any inquiry[9] to be held as to whether the managing director was correct in his belief ... Whenever a man is dismissed for incapacity or incompetence it is sufficient that the employer honestly believes on reasonable grounds that the man is incapable or incompetent. It is not necessary for the employer to prove that he is in fact incapable or incompetent.

So I find myself in agreement with the Employment Appeal Tribunal in saying that the Industrial Tribunal did err in point of law. The plain fact was that this company honestly believed on reasonable grounds that it was no longer right to have Captain Taylor as a pilot, and they properly and fairly dismissed him...

– – –

---

9   Tribunals would nowadays need to be reassured that the procedure was fair.

(b) Constructive dismissal under s 95(1)(c)

P PAGANO v HGS [1976] IRLR 11

These extracts are from the report of a case brought before a Scottish Industrial Tribunal, in which it was held that the employee had been constructively dismissed by his employer although the employee wrote the final letter purporting to terminate the contract:

> The applicant was employed as a gas converter by the respondents from 1.2.74 until 9.6.75. The applicant claims that he was unfairly dismissed ... The respondents deny that the applicant was dismissed. They claim that he resigned from his employment with the respondents in circumstances that did not entitle him to terminate the contract without notice by reason of their conduct. Putting the matter more shortly, the question at issue was whether the applicant had been constructively dismissed by the respondents.

> The respondents have been engaged in contracts throughout Central Scotland in connection with the conversion from coal gas to North Sea gas. The applicant worked for them as a conversion fitter ... He said that, throughout his period of employment, he had driven about 15 different vans, and he had made numerous complaints regarding the state of the vehicles. On occasion, he had refused to drive vehicles because he did not regard them as being in a safe condition. His complaints included rusty bodywork, loose doors, bald tyres, loose seats, faulty steering and inefficient, or even dangerous, brakes.

> ...

> On 26 May, the applicant was driving a van, registration number FLT 276J. Mr Davies told the Tribunal, in his opening statement, that this van was some four years old and had covered about 95,000 miles. He also said that the respondents' records showed that it had been serviced on 13 March and various repairs had been carried out. On 26 May, while the applicant was using the van, the gear lever came off and this was repaired by a mechanic. No other repairs were carried out on that day. On 30 May, the applicant reported that this van had the following defects: loose doors and seats, faulty steering and a bald tyre. He refused to drive the van and Mr Davies, again in his opening statement, accepted that the faults described by the applicant were present with the result that the van was not in a safe condition to be driven on the road.

> On 2 June, the applicant was issued with a replacement van to drive: its registration number was GVX 278H: it was some five years old. The Tribunal were not told the mileage which this van had covered, but Mr Foster's evidence was that the average annual mileage covered by the vans was about 20,000. On that basis, this van is likely to have been run for about 100,000 miles. Almost as soon as the applicant had driven this van out of the depot, he claims to have discovered that the brakes were in a dangerous condition. He said that he had to put his foot right down to make the foot brake work at all and the handbrake was also defective. In view of his many previous complaints, which rightly or wrongly the applicant thought had not received proper attention, he decided that there was no point in returning the van to the depot. As far as the

applicant was concerned he had had enough of being given faulty vans to drive and he was determined to do something about this situation. He drove to a site where Mr Mooney, a shop steward, was working. The applicant stated that he had been instructed to go to this site, in any event, to deliver some conversion kits. He consulted Mr Mooney regarding the state of his van. Mr Mooney also had a van, which he regarded as faulty, and both employees decided to take the vans to the police for inspection. They drove to Govan Road Police Station and asked the police to inspect the vans. The police warned the applicant and Mr Mooney that, if as a result of an inspection by them, the vans were found to be defective both employees were liable to be charged with an offence for driving the vehicles on the road. Wisely, as matters turned out, the applicant and Mr Mooney did not insist that the police should inspect the vans, but took them instead to the Vehicle Testing Station at the Department of Environment Building in Helen Street, Glasgow. Both vehicles were tested and prohibition orders were issued as a result of the faults which were found ...

It was discovered by Mr Campbell that Mr Mooney and the applicant were absent from their places of work ... Some time after this, Mr Campbell encountered the applicant and Mr Mooney and he was handed the prohibition orders, which had been issued ... Mr Campbell reported the matter to Mr Brown, who in turn reported it to his superior ... The next day ... Mr Campbell instructed the applicant and Mr Mooney that they were to attend at Coatbridge for a meeting with management. The respondents' witnesses accepted that this was to be a meeting to investigate the complaint that the applicant and Mr Mooney had been absent from their place of work ... The accounts of this meeting... were not completely at one ... What did become plain was, that it was a meeting to investigate the complaint that the applicant and Mr Mooney had been absent from their place of work as a result of taking the two vans to the Department of Environment Testing Station. At an early stage, Mr Mooney appears to have enquired whether it was a disciplinary meeting ... At this stage Mr Mooney submitted his resignation from the respondents' employment, which he appears to have brought with him to the meeting, already typed out. Mr Mooney then left the meeting ... The meeting continued and appears to have been concerned mainly with complaints which the applicant was making regarding the state of the respondents' vehicles. The meeting seems to have concluded on the note that further investigation of these complaints would be made before a decision was made as to what disciplinary action, if any, should be taken against the applicant.

...

Between the meeting on 4 June and the applicant leaving the respondents' employment on 9 June, the applicant did not drive a company van again and he claims he was given no work to do ...

... [the applicant] came to the conclusion that the respondents were going to take disciplinary action against him and that, one way or another, they would find an excuse to dismiss him. He claimed that as he had not been given any work to do, or a van to drive, he was justified in thinking that the respondents were about to get rid of him. For this reason, and also because he was not reassured that the respondents would take proper and adequate steps to replace and maintain faulty vehicles, he decided to end his employment with the respondents. He wrote a letter ...

'Dear Sir,

As a result of the meeting which took place on 4.6.75 and your subsequent letter of 4.6.75 I feel you are about to take disciplinary action against me. In view of this and of incidents concerning vans I have no alternative but to terminate the contract of employment due to your misconduct. This is effective, without notice, from Monday 9.6.75.

Please forward all monies due to me to the above address.

Yours faithfully

PM Pagano'

As a result of the above letter being written, the applicant's employment with the respondents came to an end ...

— — —

BRITISH AIRCRAFT CORPORATION LTD v AUSTIN [1978] IRLR 332

This was an employer's appeal to the Employment Appeal Tribunal against the decision of an Industrial Tribunal that an employee who had terminated her contract had in fact been constructively dismissed because it was her employer's conduct which had driven her to leave the employment. The extracts below are from the judgment of Phillips J in the EAT:

This is an appeal by the British Aircraft Corporation Ltd from the decision of an Industrial Tribunal sitting in Cambridge which found that the complainant before them, Mrs Austin had been unfairly dismissed, and awarded her compensation.

...

... it is necessary to note, only in outline, the nature of Mrs Austin's case. By August 1976 it was obvious that it was necessary for her and fellow employees to have suitable eye protection. She wore spectacles and, initially to protect her eyes she wore goggles. She did not find this satisfactory, and matters went on until November 1976 when, because she found that she could not make satisfactory use of the protection, she was not, and wrongly on her part, using any sort of protection at all, That led to discussions. What she really wanted was safety glasses, or goggles, or protection of one kind or another, but incorporating the prescription peculiar to her own spectacles. Up to this stage, in some respects at all events, matters were not unsatisfactorily dealt with and it was arranged for the safety officer (this was all in November) to investigate matters. He did so, he inspected the work, he discovered what the problem was and he decided the correct answer to the problem was to see whether or not the employers would accept the expenditure of money; it is put in the document at p 28 in this way:

'... after an inspection of the job decided that there was still a requirement to wear protective eye pieces and that he would approach management with regards to paying for prescription lenses fitted to frames.'

That led to nothing. The evidence called for the employers did not disclose what, if anything was ever done, and the Industrial Tribunal record in paragraph 7:

'There was no evidence as to whether he (that is the safety officer) took such action or its outcome and certainly the applicant heard no more about it.'

For present purposes it is not necessary to recount the rest of the story, but the end of it was that she gave in her own notice and left on 17.5.77. As we have already indicated, the Industrial Tribunal found that in this respect the employers had acted otherwise than in accordance with good industrial practice. Her reason for leaving was really that the employers, from November onwards, had done nothing at all, or anyhow very little, to clarify the position and she felt that the time had come when she could not carry on as things were, and so she left.

...

Well, as a first step, we have all of us, individually and collectively, considered this case in the light of the findings of the Industrial Tribunal and it is the opinion of each of us, and in particular that of the lay members of the Appeal Tribunal, that in *this* case – and we stress in this particular case *(BAC v Mrs Austin)* – the procedure followed was, to use a short, not particularly terse but polite expression, thoroughly bad and that, in those circumstances, the employer – and again we stress in *this* particular instance – was one of whom this employee was entitled without notice to rid herself. We hasten to say that this, of course, is not a general condemnation of the employers in this case. It may well be that in other cases and other circumstances they have behaved impeccably. We are only concerned with the case of Mrs Austin and that is the limit of our remarks; but it has to be said, and said absolutely clearly, that we consider, as indeed did the Industrial Tribunal, that for one reason or another their behaviour as far as she was concerned in respect of this matter was bad.

If it is necessary to fit those conclusions along the lines of the judgment of the Master of the Rolls into the formal terms of the contract of employment and the contractual obligations of the employer, we are prepared to do so. There is no doubt, and it has been the law for more than 100 years now, that employers are under a duty to take reasonable care for the safety of their employees. It is possible, but not necessary, to elaborate that, to break the proposition down into a number of subordinate obligations. It seems to us that it is also plainly the case that employers, as part and parcel of that general obligation, are also under an obligation under the terms of the contract of employment to act reasonably in dealing with matters of safety, or complaints of lack of safety, which are drawn to their attention by employees, because, unless the matter drawn to their attention or the complaint is obviously not bona fide or is frivolous, it is only by investigating promptly and sensibly individual complaints that they can discharge their general obligation to take reasonable care for the safety of their employees.

We are satisfied that in this case, for the reasons given by the Industrial Tribunal, the employers were in breach of that obligation, and that it was for that reason that Mrs Austin left. We think that in those circumstances the contractual test, as summarised in *Western Excavating (ECC) Ltd v Sharp* (1978),[10] is fully satisfied. It was a breach going to the root of the contract of employment, or one which showed that the employers no longer intended to be bound by an essential term of the contract because – as has already been pointed out – it put Mrs Austin in a wholly unfair dilemma: either she must go, and without being dismissed; without a remedy, and perhaps without another job; or she must swallow her complaint, although it had never been considered or attended to, and risk the results which might follow if indeed her complaint was well-founded. It is in our judgment not material for present purposes whether it was well-founded or not, because it is quite impossible to suggest on the evidence that she was other than genuine and bona fide in raising the matter; off and on over a long period of time.

For these reasons, the appeal will be dismissed.

– – –

(c) Employer's response to employee's refusal to do allegedly unsafe work

PIGGOTT BROS & CO LTD v JACKSON AND OTHERS
[1991] IRLR 309

This case was appealed to the Court of Appeal: set out below are extracts from the judgment of Lord Donaldson, Master of the Rolls:

> The three appellants were employed by Piggott Brothers & Co Ltd as machinists on their caravan-awning floor. They were employees of relatively long standing. Mrs Jackson joined the company in September 1976, Mrs Wood in September 1978 and Mrs Mortlock in March 1974.
>
> In January 1988 the company received a supply of PVC-coated material from a Belgian company called Sioen. The material gave off unusual fumes and those working on the factory floor were seriously affected. Most of them experienced symptoms of dry throat and mouth, sore eyes, sore gums, irritation of the nose and dizziness. The company had been dealing with Sioen since 1982 without cause for complaint and the only apparent difference in the new material was that it was grey in colour rather than beige as had originally, or brown as had later been supplied.
>
> The employers took various measures designed to find out what was the cause of the problem and to minimise its effects by increasing the ventilation in the workplace. They also consulted the Health and Safety Executive. In April 1988 the employment medical adviser to the Executive visited the factory and, taking a more serious view of the situation than an inspector, who had previously attended, advised some of the workers, including the appellants, to consult their family doctors. They did so and were all off sick for some weeks. In early May they returned to work, but refused to continue to work on materials from Sioen. Temporarily they were given work in other areas.

10   [1978] 1 All ER 713.

Meanwhile there were further visits from inspectors from the Health and Safety Executive and new and improved ventilation was brought into operation. The inspectors were unable to identify what had been the cause of the trouble, but expressed themselves as satisfied that the problem no longer existed. It had been a one off incident.

The appellants were not reassured and when in July they were asked to resume work on the caravan-awning floor, they refused to do so if they were expected to work with grey or brown materials supplied by Sioen. The employers urged them to reconsider their attitude and gave them time for reflection but, when they persisted, gave them notice of dismissal.

The appellants then applied to the London (North) Industrial Tribunal claiming that they had been unfairly dismissed. That they had been dismissed was not in doubt. Nor was there any serious dispute as to the reason for that dismissal: it was the employees' conduct in refusing to resume work on Sioen materials. Whether the appellants were or were not unfairly dismissed turns solely upon the Industrial Tribunal's answer to the question posed by s 57(3)[11] of the Employment Protection (Consolidation) Act 1978, namely:

'Whether in the circumstances (including the size and administrative resources of the employer's undertaking) the employer acted reasonably or unreasonably in treating [that refusal by the appellants] as a sufficient reason for dismissing the employee; and that question shall be determined in accordance with equity and the substantial merits of the case.'

...

In giving its reasons, which were succinctly but wholly adequately stated, the Tribunal found the facts in more detail than I have found it necessary to set them out and concluded:

'18 It is clear that the applicants were dismissed. We find that the reason for the dismissals was the refusal of the applicants to continue to work in the space-maker department as long as grey or brown PVC materials from Sioen were used. This is a reason relating to conduct and as such it is a potentially justifiable reason.

19 We say 'potentially justifiable', because we have next to consider whether the employer acted reasonably in accordance with s 57(3) of the Employment Protection (Consolidation) Act 1978. We think that in the context of this case what we have to decide is whether the employer took reasonable steps to deal with the problem created by the materials, and whether the applicants were acting reasonably in refusing to work with those materials. The employer certainly took a number of steps to deal with the matter as set out in the previous paragraphs of this decision, but they never got a definitive answer from Oakwood or from the Health and Safety Executive or from anyone as to what was the cause of the symptoms. We think that that was a failure on the part of the employer to

---

11 Now s 98(4); here and throughout this case the Act would now be the Employment Rights Act 1996.

take a reasonable step. We further think that in the absence of the discovery of the cause of the symptoms the applicants were reasonable in declining to work with grey or brown materials from Sioen, since so long as the cause was unknown it could not be known that no harmful, secret, long–term adverse effects on their health were inherent in the use of the materials. We find that the dismissals were unfair.'

The employers appealed to the Employment Appeal Tribunal. It is similarly constituted to an Industrial Tribunal in the sense that it consists of two lay members with experience of both sides of industry and a legally qualified chairman or presider who, in the case of the EAT, is a judge of the High Court or of the Court of Session. Its official title incorporating the word 'Tribunal' could mislead in two respects. First, unlike an Industrial Tribunal, it is a superior court of record (see paragraph 12 of Schedule 11 to the 1978 Act). Second, again unlike an Industrial Tribunal, it has no jurisdiction to decide any issues of fact.

The EAT, in unanimously allowing the employer's appeal, reminded itself of the limitations upon its own jurisdiction in the following passage in the judgment delivered by Knox J:

'We were very properly reminded by Miss Warren that the jurisdiction of this tribunal is limited to questions of law by s 136 of the Act, that it is not right that questions of fact should be dressed up as points of law so as to encourage appeals or to go through the reasoning of Industrial Tribunals with a fine-tooth comb to see if some error can be found here or there.'

In my judgment the Industrial Tribunal were holding that the employers could reasonably have been expected to do more with a view to obtaining a definite answer than they did and that, in the light of the employees' reasonable fears for their own health, until more had been done and either an answer had emerged or it had become clear that nothing further could be done, it was not reasonable to dismiss the employees. What the EAT was doing was to decide that no reasonable employer could be expected to do more than rely upon the Health and Safety Executive. That was not a decision for it.

I have no idea whether I would have reached the same conclusion as the Industrial Tribunal, particularly as I do not know what evidence was given by the employees as to the extent and basis of their fears, but that is in any event irrelevant. I can see no possible grounds for holding that no reasonable Industrial Tribunal, properly directing itself, could have reached such a conclusion and accordingly cannot and would not hold its decision to be perverse.

...

I would allow the appeal and restore the decision of the Industrial Tribunal.

— — —

Comment

Most of the above cases, if they occurred today, might be founded on s 100 of the Employment Rights Act 1996, which, it has been noted, protects an employee from dismissal in safety cases. However, it seems likely that even now, as when these cases were heard, there would be dispute as to whether on the facts there was a problem of unsafe working conditions. An actual example is *Kerr v Nathan's Wastesavers Ltd*,[12] where the EAT upheld a tribunal finding that the employee's dismissal was not within this section. He had honestly believed his working conditions were potentially unsafe, but he had no reasonable grounds for that belief. In none of these cases was there any question of the employee having insufficient length of service, by the rules then currently in force, to qualify to lodge a claim in an Industrial Tribunal.

VII SUSPENSION ON MEDICAL GROUNDS

Under the Employment Right Act 1996, s 64, an employer may justify a dismissal on the grounds that it would have been a contravention of a statutory duty for the employee to have continued to work. However, there are some safety provisions which prohibit the employment of persons in circumstances in which they might be exposed to substances which endanger their health. Broadly there are two circumstances which may occur: either the persons concerned may have already reached an exposure which is the maximum their bodies are likely to tolerate or their workplace has been contaminated so that it would be dangerous for them to work there.

In the situations to which these Regulations apply the employer must not dismiss the employees concerned but must suspend them for up to six months:

EMPLOYMENT RIGHTS ACT 1996

Section 64

Right to remuneration on suspension on medical grounds

(1) An employee who is suspended from work by his employer on medical grounds is entitled to be paid by his employer remuneration while he is so suspended for a period not exceeding twenty-six weeks.

(2) For the purposes of this Part an employee is suspended from work on medical grounds if he is suspended from work in consequence of–

   (a) a requirement imposed by or under a provision of an enactment or of an instrument made under an enactment, or

   (b) a recommendation in a provision of a code of practice issued or approved under section 16 of the Health and Safety at Work etc Act 1974, and the provision is for the time being specified in subsection (3).

---

12 [1995] IRLIB 530.

(3) The provisions referred to in subsection (2) are

Regulation 16 of the Control of Lead at Work Regulations 1980

Regulation 16 of the Ionising Radiations Regulations 1985, and

Regulation 11 of the Control of Substances Hazardous to Health Regulations 1988

(4) The Secretary of State may by order add provisions to or remove provisions from the list of provisions specified in subsection (3).[13]

(5) For the purposes of this Part an employee shall be regarded as suspended from work on medical grounds only if and for so long as he–

(a) continues to be employed by his employer, but

(b) is not provided with work or does not perform the work he normally performed before the suspension.

Section 65

Exclusion from right to remuneration

(1) An employee is not entitled to remuneration under section 64 unless he has been continuously employed for a period of not less than one month ending with the day before that on which the suspension begins.

(2) An employee who is employed–

(a) under a contract for a fixed term of three months or less, or

(b) under a contract made in contemplation of the performance of a specific task which is not expected to last for more than three months,

is not entitled to remuneration under section 64 unless he has been continuously employed for a period of more than three months ending with the day before that on which the suspension begins.

(3) An employee is not entitled to remuneration under s 64 in respect of any period during which he is incapable of work by reason of disease or bodily or mental disablement.

(4) An employee is not entitled to remuneration under s 64 in respect of any period if–

(a) his employer has offered to provide him with suitable alternative work during the period (whether or not it is work which the employee is under his contract, or was under the contract in force before the suspension, employed to perform) and the employee has unreasonably refused to perform that work, or

(b) he does not comply with reasonable requirements imposed by his employer with a view to ensuring that his services are available.

– – –

---

13 Regulations given in sub-s (3) have already been reissued.

Comment

The right to suspension with pay only applies to employees who are fit to work (s 64): those who are ill, including those who are ill as a result of exposure to one of the toxic substances covered by the Regulations listed in the Schedule to the Act, are entitled to claim sick pay as laid down in the Social Security and Housing Benefits Act 1982, as subsequently amended. This anomaly was highlighted in *Stallite Batteries Co Ltd v Appleton and Hopkinson* (1988).[14] In this unreported case, the EAT had to consider the case of two men who, working for a lead-acid battery manufacturer, suffered over-exposure to lead such as to require them to be treated in hospital. The EAT found that they were nevertheless entitled only to state sickness benefit during their time off work. In the case of Mr Appleton he had, after a few weeks of working with the company actually fallen into a skip containing lead paste; after this his blood-lead level was very high and his doctor did not consider him fit for work for many months; by which time he had been dismissed by his employer. Mr Hopkinson did not suffer an accident, but he received his P45, indicating his dismissal, after a period of absence due to exposure to lead. The EAT confirmed that the men being unfit for work were unable to claim remuneration under s 19. However the EAT, pointing out that the general law of unfair dismissal, under the provision which is now s 108(2) of the Employment Rights Act 1996 the normal period of continuous employment needed to claim for unfair dismissal is reduced to one month, so that both men appeared to be eligible for compensation for unfair dismissal.

---

14   (1988) 147 Health and Safety Information Bulletin.

ADDENDUM

CHAPTER 14

THE ROLE OF THE EUROPEAN UNION

INTRODUCTION

In Part II of this book, considerable emphasis has been placed on the impact of the European Community upon the British regulatory system. This chapter traces the development of the authority which was vested in the European Economic Community, now known as the European Union, to direct the development of the laws of the Member States, with particular reference to the United Kingdom.

I THE TREATY OF ROME

This Treaty established the European Economic Community. It was signed by the founder members in 1957. It was amended from time to time, most importantly, for present purposes, by the Single European Act in 1987. It was this latter Act which introduced into the Treaty the Articles which have had most relevance to occupational health and safety; namely Article 100A (concerned with harmonisation of product standards) and Article 118A (concerned with improvement of working conditions).

Article 118A was within Title III of the Treaty; the Title concerned with Social Policy. The Treaty on European Union signed by the Member States of the EC in February 1992 (the so called Maastricht Treaty) included a Protocol on Social Policy and an agreement, annexed to the Protocol, signed by 11 Member States: the UK did not sign the Protocol. The Protocol recorded that the 11 wished to continue on the path laid down in the 1989 Social Charter and they were adopting an Agreement for that purpose. All 12 Member States agreed that the 11 might proceed to implement their agreement, but that the UK would not take part in the deliberations and the adoption of proposals made on the basis of the Protocol and Agreement. While this situation prevailed, on issues of social policy the EU could elect to bring proposals under the Treaty itself, or, should the UK protest the matter, they could proceed with the other Member States (since 1 January 1995, there have been additional Member States joining the Union) acting under the Protocol rather than the Treaty. The Council Directive 94/45/EEC of 22 September 1994 on the establishment of a European Works Council was adopted on the legal basis of the Maastricht Treaty Social Protocol Agreement.

The Directive on Adaptation of Working Time (93/104/EEC) was adopted under Article 118A on 23 November 1993 but the UK challenged the

Directive's legal basis in Article 118A as it did not accept that the working time regulations (primarily a maximum 48 hour average week) were justifiable on health and safety grounds.

As an outcome of a meeting at Maastricht, a revised founding Treaty was signed on 7 February 1992. This, the Treaty of European Union, recorded the renewed commitment of the Member States to the Union, 'resolved to mark a new stage in the process of European integration undertaken with the establishment of the European Communities ...'. But, at this stage, the UK did not commit itself to the Social Chapter (based on the 1989 Community Charter of the Fundamental Social Rights of Workers) agreed by the other Member States.

Following the election of a new UK Government in 1997, the UK committed itself fully to the Social Chapter, which had been adopted by the other Members States at Maastricht. After a meeting held at Amsterdam in October 1997, a Consolidated Version of the Treaty Establishing the European Community was published. This Treaty to some extent amended, but largely reproduced, the substantive provisions of the Treaty of Rome as it had evolved since 1957. There is, however, considerable re-numbering of these Articles. The former Article 100A is now Article 95 and the former Article 118 is now Articles 137–40, representing the changes introduced by the Social Chapter adopted at Maastricht. The renumbering relates to the period after Maastricht rather than to the original Treaty of Rome. There is no longer an Article exclusively concerned with occupational health and safety. Thus, the transformation of Article 118A is sufficient to warrant both the old Article and the new ones being set out below.

The former Article 118A was placed in the social policy area of the Treaty but directives founded on it could be adopted by a qualified majority vote. This procedure gives each Member State a number of votes according to its size in relation to the Community as a whole. Nevertheless, no single State, even a large one like the UK, has sufficient votes to prevent the adoption of a measure. This may have been one reason why Article 118A was heavily relied on during the period when the UK was not fully committed to the Community's social policy. The Working Time Directive was one such directive.

THE TREATY OF ROME

...

Article 118A

1   Member States shall pay particular attention to encouraging improvements, especially in the working environment, as regards the health and safety of workers, and shall set as their objective the harmonisation of conditions in this area, while maintaining the improvements made.

2   In order to help achieve the objective laid down in the first paragraph, the Council, acting by a qualified majority on a proposal from the Commission, in co-operation with the European Parliament and after consulting the Economic and Social Committee, shall adopt, by means of directives, minimum requirements for gradual implementation, having regard to the conditions and technical rules obtaining in each of the Member States.

Such directives shall avoid imposing administrative, financial and legal constraints in a way which would hold back the creation and development of small and medium-sized undertakings.

3   The provisions adopted pursuant to this Article shall not prevent any Member State from maintaining or introducing more stringent measures for the protection of working conditions compatible with this Treaty.

– – –

II TREATY ESTABLISHING THE EUROPEAN COMMUNITY

Chapter 3
Approximation of laws

Article 94 (ex Article 100)

The Council shall, acting unanimously on a proposal from the Commission and after consulting the European Parliament and Social Committee, issue directives for the approximation of such laws, regulations or administrative provisions of the Member States as directly affect the establishment or functioning of the common market.

Article 95 (ex Article 100A)

1   By way of derogation from Article 94 and save where otherwise provided in this Treaty, the following provisions shall apply for the achievement of the objectives set out in Article 14. The Council shall, acting in accordance with the procedure referred to in Article 251 and after consulting the Economic and Social Committee, adopt the measures for the approximation of the provisions laid down by law, regulation or administrative action in Member States which have as their object the establishment and functioning of the internal market.

2   Paragraph 1 shall not apply to fiscal provisions, to those relating to the free movement of persons nor to those relating to the rights and interests of employed persons.

3   The Commission, in its proposals envisaged in paragraph 1 concerning health, safety, environmental protection and consumer protection, will take as a base a high level of protection, taking account in particular of any new development based on scientific facts. Within their respective powers, the European Parliament and the Council will also seek to achieve this objective.

4   If, after the adoption by the Council or by the Commission of a harmonisation measure, a Member State deems it necessary to maintain national provisions on grounds of major needs referred to in Article 30, or relating to the protection of the environment or the working environment,

it shall notify the Commission of these provisions as well as the grounds for maintaining them.

5 Moreover, without prejudice to paragraph 4, if, after the adoption by the Council or by the Commission of a harmonisation measure, a Member State deems it necessary to introduce national provisions based on new scientific evidence relating to the protection of the environment or the working environment on grounds of a problem specific to that Member State arising after the adoption of the harmonisation measure, it shall notify the Commission of the envisaged provisions as well as the grounds for introducing them.

6 The Commission shall, within six months of the notifications as referred to in paragraphs 4 and 5, approve or reject the national provisions involved after having verified whether or not they are a means of arbitrary discrimination or a disguised restriction on trade between Member States and whether or not they shall constitute an obstacle to the functioning of the internal market.

In the absence of a decision by the Commission within this period the national provisions referred to in paragraphs 4 and 5 shall be deemed to have been approved.

When justified by the complexity of the matter and in the absence of danger for human health, the Commission may notify the Member State concerned that the period referred to in the paragraph may be extended for a further period of up to six months.

7 When, pursuant to paragraph 6, a Member State is authorised to maintain or introduce national provisions derogating from a harmonisation measure, the Commission shall immediately examine whether to propose an adaptation to that measure.

8 When a Member State raises a specific problem on public health in a field which has been the subject of proper harmonisation measures, it shall bring it to the attention of the Commission which shall immediately examine whether to propose appropriate measures to the Council.

9 By way of derogation from the procedure laid down in Articles 226 and 227, the Commission and any Member State may bring the matter directly before the Court of Justice if it considers that another Member State is making improper use of the powers provided for in this Article.

10 The harmonisation measures referred to above shall, in appropriate cases, include a safeguard clause authorising the Member States to take, for one or more of the non-economic reasons referred to in Article 30, provisional measures subject to a Community control procedure.

Article 96 (ex Article 101)

Where the Commission finds that a difference between the provisions laid down by law, regulation or administrative action in Member States is distorting the conditions of competition in the common market and that the resultant distortion needs to be eliminated, it shall consult the Member States concerned.

If such consultation does not result in an agreement eliminating the distortion in question, the Council shall, on a proposal from the Commission, acting by a qualified majority, issue the necessary directives. The Commission and the Council may take any other appropriate measures provided for in this Treaty.

TITLE XI

SOCIAL POLICY, EDUCATION, VOCATIONAL TRAINING AND YOUTH

Chapter 1

Social provisions

Article 136 (ex Article 117)

The Community and the Member States, having in mind fundamental social rights such as those set out in the European Social Charter signed at Turin on 18 October 1961 and in the 1989 Community Charter of the Fundamental Social Rights of Workers, shall have as their objectives the promotion of employment, improved living and working conditions, so as to make possible their harmonisation while the improvement is being maintained, proper social protection, dialogue between management and labour, the development of human resources with a view to lasting high employment and the combating of exclusion.

To this end the Community and the Member States shall implement measures which take account of the diverse forms of national practices, in particular in the field of contractual relations, and the need to maintain the competitiveness of the Community economy.

They believe that such a development will ensue not only from the functioning of the common market, which will favour the harmonisation of social systems, but also from the procedures provided for in this Treaty, and from the approximation of provisions laid down by law, regulation or administrative action.

Article 137 (ex Article 118)

1   With a view to achieving the objectives of Article 136, the Community shall support and complement the activities of the Member States in the following fields:

  – improvement in particular of the working environment to protect workers' health and safety:

  – working conditions;

  – the information and consultation of workers;

  – the integration of persons excluded from the labour market, without prejudice to Article 150;

  – equality between men and women with regard to labour market opportunities and treatment at work.

2   To this end, the Council may adopt, by means of directives, minimum requirements for gradual implementation, having regard to the conditions and technical rules obtaining in each of the Member States. Such directives shall avoid imposing administrative, financial and legal constraints in a

way which would hold back the creation and development of small and medium-sized undertakings.

The Council shall act in accordance with the procedure referred to in Article 251 after consulting the Economic and Social Committee and the Committee of the Regions.

The Council, acting in accordance with the same procedure, may adopt measures designed to encourage co-operation between Member States through initiatives aimed at improving knowledge, developing exchanges of information and best practices, promoting innovative approaches and evaluating experiences in order to combat social exclusion.

3   However, the Council shall act unanimously on a proposal from the Commission, after consulting the European Parliament, the Economic and Social Committee and the Committee of the Regions in the following areas:

  –   social security and social protection of workers;

  –   protection of workers where their employment contract is terminated;

  –   representation and collective defence of the interests of workers and employers, including co-determination, subject to paragraph 6;

  –   conditions of employment for third country nationals legally residing in Community territory;

  –   financial contributions for promotion of employment and job creation, without prejudice to the provisions relating to the social fund.

4   A Member State may entrust management and labour, at their joint request, with the implementation of directives adopted pursuant to paragraphs 2 and 3.

In this case, it shall ensure that, no later than the date on which a directive must be transposed in accordance with Article 249, management and labour have introduced the necessary measures by agreement, the Member State concerned being required to take any necessary measure enabling it at any time to be in a position to guarantee the results imposed by that directive.

5   The provisions adopted pursuant to this Article shall not prevent any Member State from maintaining or introducing more stringent protective measures compatible with this Treaty.

6   The provisions of this Article shall not apply to pay, the right of association, the right to strike or the right to impose lock-outs.

Article 138 (ex Article 118a)

1   The Commission shall have the task of promoting the consultation of management and labour at Community level and shall take any relevant measure to facilitate their dialogue by ensuring balanced support for the parties.

2   To this end, before submitting proposals in the social policy field, the Commission shall consult management and labour on the possible direction of Community action.

3   If, after such consultation, the Commission considers Community action advisable, it shall consult management and labour on the content of the envisaged proposal. Management and labour shall forward to the Commission an opinion or, where appropriate, a recommendation.

4   On the occasion of such consultation, management and labour may inform the Commission of their wish to initiate the process provided for in Article 139. The duration of the procedure shall not exceed nine months, unless the management and labour concerned and the Commission decide jointly to extend it.

Article 139 (ex Article 118b)

1   Should management and labour so desire, the dialogue between them at Community level may lead to contractual relations, including agreements.

2   Agreements concluded at Community level shall be implemented either in accordance with the procedures and practices specific to management and labour and the Member States or, in matters covered by Article 137, at the joint request of the signatory parties, by a Council decision on a proposal from the Commission.

The Council shall act by qualified majority, except where the agreement in question contains one or more provisions relating to one of the areas referred to in Article 137(3), in which case it shall act unanimously.

Article 140 (ex Article 118c)

With a view to achieving the objectives of Article 136 and without prejudice to the other provisions of this Treaty, the Commission shall encourage co-operation between the Member States and facilitate the co-ordination of their action in all social policy fields under this chapter, particularly in matters relating to:

– employment;
– labour law and working conditions;
– basic and advanced vocational training;
– social security;
– prevention of occupational accidents and diseases;
– occupational hygiene;
– the right of association and collective bargaining between employers and workers.

To this end, the Commission shall act in close contact with Member States by making studies, delivering opinions and arranging consultations both on problems arising at national level and on those of concern to international organisations.

Before delivering the opinions provided for in this Article, the commission shall consult the Economic and Social Committee.

– – –

III LEGISLATIVE PROCEDURES

Article 100A (now Article 95) was intended to play an important role in harmonising throughout the EU product standards, including workplace equipment and personal protective equipment.

On 7 May 1985, the European Commission adopted a resolution setting out a 'New Approach to Technical Harmonisation and Standards'. Under this, a series of Article 100A trading directives were to set 'essential requirements', mainly relating to safety and written in general terms, which products must satisfy before they were placed on the market anywhere in the Community. Under this procedure, European standards harmonised under a particular directive will fill in the detail. Compliance with such standards is likely to be the main way by which manufacturers, importers and suppliers will demonstrate that the essential requirements of the directive have been satisfied. Claims of conformity with the requirements of a directive are demonstrated by the affixing of a CE mark. Any product displaying the CE mark is entitled to unrestricted movement and sale throughout the EU. In the UK, the Department of Trade and Industry has been, and is, the lead body.

The procedure for adopting and implementing directives where the qualified majority voting procedure is used is that the European Commission makes a proposal based on the Article; and then the proposal goes to the Council of Ministers of the EU, the European Parliament, the Economic and Social Committee and the social partners for comment. The social partners are ETUC (the European Trades Union Council) and UNICE (the European Association of National Employers' Associations). The Commission then revises the proposal and forwards it to the Council of the EU which negotiates and adopts a common position by qualified majority vote. The proposal is then forwarded to the European Parliament which comments on the common position: the European Commission revises the common position and forwards it to the Council of Ministers of the EU, which adopts the revised common position by qualified majority vote, or by unanimous vote if it wishes to overrule revisions.

The adopted Directive has to be implemented by each Member State, in accordance with its legal system, by the deadline named in the Directive. Britain has implemented directives made under Article 118A by Regulations made under the Health and Safety at Work Act 1974. The Directives which resulted in the British Six Pack all had to be implemented by 31 December 1992. The British Regulations, made in 1992 all came into effect on 1 January 1993. The Six Pack represents the first six Directives to be adopted by the above procedure under Article 118A. The burden of negotiating such directives falls on the HSE.

The Council of Ministers of the EU is the decision making body which negotiates and adopts all European legislation and policy. It comprises one representative from each Member State's government: this will be the Prime Minister, or a Minister or government official, depending on the subject and level of meeting.

Since the expansion of the EU in January 1995 qualified majority vote means that 62 of the available 87 votes must be in favour of the proposal. Member States have block votes according to their population size. The UK, France, Germany and Italy each have 10 votes. Thus, no one, not even the larger States, can alone prevent the adoption of a directive. The exact distribution of voting rights is subject to review with the development and expansion of the EU.

It will be noted that, under the revised Treaty, improvement of health and safety is no longer given separate treatment. It is now one of five items covered by Article 137. However, directives to impose minimum standards may, as formerly, be adopted by qualified majority vote, that is, according to the procedures now set out in Article 251. This is in contrast with the matters itemised in Article 137.3 (including social security and social protection of workers) where the Council has to act unanimously for a directive to be adopted. Health and safety matters do not appear to be exempt from the new procedures which these Articles introduce for the involvement of management and labour in the formulation of directives (Article 138). Surprisingly, Article 139 apparently allows occupational health and safety standards to be determined through collective agreement at Community level. There appears to be no provision for governmental enforcement at Member State level for standards arrived at through the procedure set out in Article 139. Arguably, however, standards so arrived at could, in the UK, be enforced by reliance on the general duties in the 1974 Act.

Procedure for adopting a directive under Article 251

Article 251

1   Where reference is made in this Treaty to this Article for the adoption of an act, the following procedure shall apply.

2   The Commission shall submit a proposal to the European Parliament and the Council.

   The Council, acting by a qualified majority after obtaining the opinion of the European Parliament,

   –   if it approves all the amendments contained in the European Parliament's opinion, may adopt the proposed act thus amended;

   –   if the European Parliament does not propose any amendments, may adopt the proposed act;

   –   shall otherwise adopt a common position and communicate it to the European Parliament. The Council shall inform the European Parliament fully of the reasons which led it to adopt its common position. The Commission shall inform the European Parliament fully of its position.

If, within three months of such communication, the European Parliament:

(a) approves the common position or has not taken a decision, the act in question shall be deemed to have been adopted in accordance with that common position;

(b) rejects, by an absolute majority of its component members, the common position, the proposed act shall be deemed not to have been adopted;

(c) proposes amendments to the common position by an absolute majority of its component members, the amended text shall be forwarded to the Council and to the Commission, which shall deliver an opinion on those amendments.

3   If, within three months of the matter being referred to it, the Council, acting by a qualified majority, approves all the amendments of the European Parliament, the act in question shall be deemed to have been adopted in the form of the common position thus amended; however, the Council shall act unanimously on the amendments on which the Commission has delivered a negative opinion. If the Council does not approve all the amendments, the President of the Council, in agreement with the President of the European Parliament, shall within six weeks convene a meeting of the Conciliation Committee.

4   The Conciliation Committee, which shall be composed of the members of the Council or their representatives and an equal number of representatives of the European Parliament, shall have the task of reaching agreement on a joint text, by a qualified majority of the members of the Council or their representatives and by a majority of the representatives of the European Parliament. The Commission shall take part in the Conciliation Committee's proceedings and shall take all the necessary initiatives with a view to reconciling the positions of the European Parliament, and the Council. In fulfilling this task, the Conciliation Committee shall address the common position on the basis of the amendments proposed by the European Parliament.

5   If, within six weeks of its being convened, the Conciliation Committee approves a joint text, the European Parliament, acting by an absolute majority of the votes cast, and the Council, acting by a qualified majority, shall each have a period of six weeks from that approval in which to adopt the act in question in accordance with the joint text. If either of the two institutions fails to approve the proposed act within that period, it shall be deemed not to have been adopted.

6   When the Conciliation Committee does not approve a joint text, the proposed act shall be deemed not to have been adopted.

7   The periods of three months and six weeks referred to in this Article shall be extended by a maximum of one month and two weeks respectively at the initiative of the European Parliament or the Council.

– – –

Example of a directive

Parts of the Framework Directive on Health and Safety were referred to in the previous chapter in relation to worker involvement: the whole of that directive is now set out to illustrate the form a directive takes. It will be noted that the language is not easily reconciled with the language normally used in UK legislation. In particular, the European practice of imposing broad general duties 'to ensure' is somewhat alien to the common law approach.

The Management of Health and Safety at Work Regulations follow the requirement of the directive in respect of specific regulations, for example, regulation 6 requires an employer to ensure that his employees are provided with such health surveillance as is appropriate.

Of particular significance is that it is questionable whether the directive's modification, in Article 5, of the employer's absolute duty to ensure the health and safety of workers is comparable to the modification of the general duties contained in ss 2–9 of the British Health and Safety at Work Act 1974. The directive relaxes the duty 'where occurrences are due to unusual and unforeseeable circumstances'. The British legislation qualifies its absolute duties by the phrase 'reasonably practicable'. Arguably, risks may be foreseeable but not removable on the cost/benefit criteria that is the essence of the British qualification.

COUNCIL DIRECTIVE 89/391/EEC OF 12 JUNE 1989

On the Introduction of Measures to Encourage Improvements in the Safety and Health of Workers at Work (OJ 1989 L183/1)

The Council of the European Communities,

- Having regard to the Treaty establishing the European Economic Community, and in particular Article 118A thereof;

- Having regard to the proposal from the Commission, drawn up after consultation with the Advisory Committee on Safety, Hygiene and Health Protection at Work;

- In co-operation with the European Parliament;

- Having regard to the opinion of the Economic and Social Committee;

- Whereas Article 118A of the Treaty provides that the Council shall adopt, by means of Directives, minimum requirements for encouraging improvements, especially in the working environment, to guarantee a better level of protection of the safety and health of workers;

- Whereas this Directive does not justify any reduction in levels of protection already achieved in individual Member States, the Member State being committed, under the Treaty, to encourage improvements in conditions in this area and to harmonising conditions while maintaining the improvements made;

- Whereas it is known that workers can be exposed to the effects of dangerous environmental factors at the workplace during the course of their working life;

- Whereas, pursuant to Article 118A of the Treaty, such Directives must avoid imposing administrative, financial and legal constraints which would hold back the creation and development of small and medium-sized undertakings;

- Whereas the communication from the Commission on its programme concerning safety, hygiene and health at work provides for the adoption of directives designed to guarantee the safety and health of workers;

- Whereas the Council, in its resolution of 21 December 1987 on safety, hygiene and health at work, took note of the Commission's intention to submit to the Council in the near future a Directive on the organisation of the safety and health of workers at the workplace;

- Whereas in February 1988 the European Parliament adopted four resolutions following the debate on the internal market and worker protection; whereas these resolutions specifically invited the Commission to draw up a framework Directive to serve as a basis for more specific Directives covering all the risks connected with safety and health at the workplace;

- Whereas Member States have a responsibility to encourage improvements in the safety and health of workers on their territory; whereas taking measures to protect the health and safety of workers at work also helps, in certain cases, to preserve the health and possibly the safety of persons residing with them;

- Whereas Member States' legislative systems covering safety and health at the workplace differ widely and need to be improved; whereas national provisions on the subject, which often include technical specifications and/or self-regulatory standards, may result in different levels of safety and health protection and allow competition at the expense of safety and health;

- Whereas the incidence of accidents at work and occupational diseases is still too high; whereas preventive measures must be introduced or improved without delay in order to safeguard the safety and health of workers and ensure a higher degree of protection;

- Whereas, in order to ensure an improved degree of protection, workers and/or their representatives must be informed of the risks to their safety and health and of the measures required to reduce or eliminate these risks; whereas they must also be in a position to contribute, by means of balanced participation in accordance with national laws and/or practices, to seeing that the necessary protective measures are taken;

- Whereas information, dialogue and balanced participation on safety and health at work must be developed between employers and workers and/or their representatives by means of appropriate procedures and instruments, in accordance with national laws and/or practices;

- Whereas the improvement of workers' safety, hygiene and health at work is an objective which should not be subordinated to purely economic considerations;

- Whereas employers shall be obliged to keep themselves informed of the latest advances in technology and scientific findings concerning work-place design, account being taken of the inherent dangers in their undertaking, and to inform accordingly the workers' representatives exercising participation rights under this Directive, so as to be able to guarantee a better level of protection of workers' health and safety;

- Whereas the provisions of this Directive apply, without prejudice to more stringent present or future Community provisions, to all risks, and in particular to those arising from the use at work of chemical, physical and biological agents covered by Directive 80/1107 (OJ 1980 L327/8), as last amended by Directive 88/642 (OJ 1988 L356/74);

- Whereas pursuant to Decision 74/325 (OJ 1974 L185/15), the Advisory Committee on Safety, Hygiene and Health Protection at Work is consulted by the Commission on the drafting of proposals in this field;

- Whereas a Committee composed of members nominated by the Member States needs to be set up to assist the Commission in making the technical adaptation to the individual Directives, provided for in this Directive;

- Has adopted this Directive.

SECTION I: GENERAL PROVISIONS

Article 1

Objective

1   The object of the Directive is to introduce measures to encourage improvements in the safety and health of workers at work.

2   To that end it contains general principles concerning the prevention of occupational risks, the protection of safety and health, the elimination of risk and accident factors, the informing, consultation, balanced participation in accordance with national laws and/or practices and training of workers and their representatives, as well as general guidelines for the implementation of the said principles.

3   This Directive shall be without prejudice to existing or future national and Community provisions which are more favourable to protection of the safety and health of workers at work.

Article 2

Scope

1   This Directive shall apply to all sectors of activity, both public and private (industrial, agricultural, commercial, administrative, service, educational, cultural, leisure, etc).

2   This Directive shall not be applicable where characteristics peculiar to certain specific public service activities, such as the armed forces or the police, or to certain specific activities in the civil protection services inevitably conflict with it.

In that event, the safety and health of workers must be ensured as far as possible in the light of the objectives of this Directive.

Article 3

Definitions

For the purpose of this Directive, the following terms shall have the following meanings:

(a)   worker: any person employed by an employer, including trainees and apprentices but excluding domestic servants;

(b)   employer: any natural or legal person who has an employment relationship with the worker and has responsibility for the undertaking and/or establishment;

(c)   workers' representative with specific responsibility for the safety and health of workers: any person elected, chosen or designated in accordance with national laws and/or practices to represent workers where problems arise relating to the safety and health protection of workers at work;

(d)   prevention: all the steps or measures taken or planned at all stages of work in the undertaking to prevent or reduce occupational risks.

Article 4

1   Member States shall take the necessary steps to ensure that employers, workers and workers' representatives are subject to the legal provisions necessary for the implementation of this Directive.

2   In particular, Member States shall ensure adequate controls and supervision.

SECTION II: EMPLOYERS' OBLIGATIONS

Article 5

General provision

1   The employer shall have a duty to ensure the safety and health of workers in every aspect related to the work.

2   Where, pursuant to Article 7(3), an employer enlists competent external services or persons, this shall not discharge him from his responsibilities in this area.

3   The workers' obligations in the field of safety and health at work shall not affect the principle of the responsibility of the employer.

4   This Directive shall not restrict the option of Member States to provide for the exclusion or the limitation of employers' responsibility where occurrences are due to unusual and unforeseeable circumstances, beyond the employers' control, or to exceptional events, the consequences of which could not have been avoided despite the exercise of all due care.

Member states need not exercise the option referred to in the first sub-paragraph.

Article 6

General obligations on employers

1   Within the context of his responsibilities, the employer shall take the measures necessary for the safety and health protection of workers, including prevention of occupational risks and provision of information and training, as well as provision of the necessary organisation and means.

The employer shall be alert to the need to adjust these measures to take account of changing circumstances and aim to improve existing situations.

2   The employer shall implement the measures referred to in the first sub-paragraph of paragraph 1 on the basis of the following general principles of prevention:

(a) avoiding risks;

(b) evaluating the risks which cannot be avoided;

(c) combating the risk at source;

(d) adapting the work to the individual, especially as regards the design of workplaces, the choice of work equipment and the choice of working and production methods, with a view, in particular, to alleviating monotonous work and work at a predetermined work-rate and to reducing their effect on health;

(e) adapting to technical progress;

(f) replacing the dangerous by the non-dangerous or the less dangerous;

(g) developing a coherent overall prevention policy which covers technology, organisation of work, working conditions, social relationships and the influence of factors related to the working environment;

(h) giving collective protective measures priority over individual protective measures;

(i) giving appropriate instructions to the workers.

3   Without prejudice to the other provisions of this Directive, the employers shall, taking into account the nature of the activities of the enterprise and/or establishment:

(a) evaluate the risks to the safety and health of workers, inter alia in the choice of work equipment, the chemical substances or preparations used, and the fitting out of workplaces.

Subsequent to this evaluation and as necessary, the preventive measures and the working and production methods implemented by the employer must:

- assure an improvement in the level of protection afforded to workers with regard to safety and health,

- be integrated into all the activities of the undertaking and/or establishment and at all hierarchical levels;

(b) where he entrusts tasks to a worker, take into consideration the worker's capabilities as regards health and safety;

(c) ensure that the planning and introduction of new technologies are the subject of consultation with the workers and/or their representatives, as regards the consequences of the choice of equipment, the working conditions and the working environment for the safety and health of workers;

(d) take appropriate steps to ensure that only workers who have received adequate instructions may have access to areas where there is serious and specific danger.

4 Without prejudice to the other provisions of this Directive, where several undertakings share a workplace, the employers shall co-operate in implementing the safety, health and occupational hygiene provisions and, taking into account the nature of the activities, shall co-ordinate their actions in matters of the protection and prevention of occupational risks, and shall inform one another and their respective workers and/or workers' representatives of these risks.

5 Measures related to safety, hygiene and health at work may in no circumstances involve the workers in financial cost.

Article 7

Protective and preventive services

1 Without prejudice to the obligations referred to in Articles 5 and 6, the employer shall designate one or more workers to carry out activities related to the protection and prevention of occupational risks for the undertaking and/or establishment.

2 Designated workers may not be placed at any disadvantage because of their activities related to the protection and prevention of occupational risks.

Designated workers shall be allowed adequate time to enable them to fulfil their obligations arising from this Directive.

3 If such protective and preventive measures cannot be organised for lack of competent personnel in the undertaking and/or establishment, the employer shall enlist competent external services or persons.

4 Where the employer enlists such services or persons, he shall inform them of the factors known to affect, or suspected of affecting the safety and health of the workers and they must have access to the information referred to in Article 10(2).

5   In all cases:

- the workers designated must have the necessary capabilities and the necessary means,
- the external services or persons consulted must have the necessary aptitudes and the necessary personal and professional means; and
- the workers designated and the external services or persons consulted must be sufficient in number

to deal with the organisation of protective and preventive measures, taking into account the size of the undertaking and/or establishment and/or the hazards to which the workers are exposed and their distribution throughout the entire undertaking and/or establishment.

6   The protection from, and prevention of, the health and safety risks which form the subject of this Article shall be the responsibility of one or more workers, of one service or of separate services whether from inside or outside the undertaking and/or establishment.

The worker(s) and/or agency(ies) must work together whenever necessary.

7   Member States may define, in the light of the nature of the activities and size of the undertakings, the categories or undertakings in which the employer, provided he is competent, may himself take responsibility for the measures referred to in paragraph 1.

8   Member States shall define the necessary capabilities and aptitudes referred to in paragraph 5.

They may determine the sufficient number referred to in paragraph 5.

Article 8
First aid, fire-fighting and evacuation of workers, serious and imminent danger

1   The employer shall:

- take the necessary measures for first aid, fire-fighting and evacuation of workers, adapted to the nature of the activities and the size of the undertaking and/or establishment and taking into account other persons present;
- arrange any necessary contacts with external services, particularly as regards first aid, emergency medical care, rescue work and fire-fighting.

2   Pursuant to paragraph 1, the employer shall, inter alia, for first aid, fire-fighting and the evacuation of workers, designate the workers required to implement such measures.

The number of such workers, their training and the equipment available to them shall be adequate, taking account of the size and/or specific hazards of the undertaking and/or establishment.

3   The employer shall:

(a) as soon as possible, inform all workers who are, or may be, exposed to serious and imminent danger of the risk involved and of the steps taken or to be taken as regards protection;

(b) take action and give instructions to enable workers in the event of serious, imminent and unavoidable danger to stop work and/or immediately to leave the workplace and proceed to a place of safety;

(c) save in exceptional cases for reasons duly substantiated, refrain from asking workers to resume work in a working situation where there is still a serious and imminent danger.

4 Workers who, in the event of serious, imminent and unavoidable danger, leave their workstation and/or a dangerous area may not be placed at any disadvantage because of their action and must be protected against any harmful and unjustified consequences, in accordance with national laws and/or practices.

5 The employer shall ensure that all workers are able, in the event of serious and imminent danger to their own safety and/or that of other persons, and where the immediate superior responsible cannot be contacted, to take the appropriate steps in the light of their knowledge and the technical means at their disposal, to avoid the consequences of such danger.

Their actions shall not place them at any disadvantage, unless they acted carelessly or there was negligence on their part.

Article 9

Various obligations on employers

1 The employer shall:

(a) be in possession of an assessment of the risks to safety and health at work, including those facing groups of workers exposed to particular risks;

(b) decide on the protective measures to be taken and, if necessary, the protective equipment to be used;

(c) keep a list of occupational accidents resulting in a worker being unfit for work for more than three working days;

(d) draw up, for the responsible authorities and in accordance with national laws and/or practices, reports on occupational accidents suffered by his workers.

2 Member States shall define, in the light of the nature of the activities and size of the undertakings, the obligations to be met by the different categories of undertakings in respect of the drawing up of the documents provided for in paragraph 1(a) and (b) and when preparing the documents provided for in paragraph 1(c) and (d).

Article 10

Worker information

1 The employer shall take appropriate measures so that workers and/or their representatives in the undertaking and/or establishment, receive, in accordance with national laws and/or practices which may take account, *inter alia*, of the size of the undertaking and/or establishment, all the necessary information concerning:

(a) the safety and health risks and protective and preventive measures and activities in respect of both the undertaking and/or establishment in general and each type of workstation and/or job;

(b) the measures taken pursuant to Article 8(2).

2   The employer shall take appropriate measures so that employers of workers from any outside undertakings and/or establishments engaged in work in his undertaking and/or establishment receive, in accordance with national laws and/or practices, adequate information concerning the points referred to in paragraph 1(a) and (b) which is to be provided to the workers in question.

3.   The employer shall take appropriate measures so that workers with specific functions in protecting the safety and health of workers, or workers' representatives with specific responsibility for the safety and health of workers shall have access, to carry out their functions and in accordance with national laws and/or practices, to:

(a) the risk assessment and protective measures referred to in Article 9(1)(a) and (b);

(b) the list and reports referred to in Article 9(1)(c) and (d);

(c) the information yielded by protective and preventive measures, inspection agencies and bodies responsible for safety and health.

Article 11

Consultation and participation of workers

1   Employers shall consult workers and/or their representatives and allow them to take part in discussions on all questions relating to safety and health at work.

This presupposes:

- the consultation of workers;
- the right of workers and/or their representatives to make proposals;
- balanced participation in accordance with national laws and/or practices.

2   Workers or workers' representatives with specific responsibility for the safety and health of workers shall take part in a balanced way, in accordance with national laws and/or practices, or shall be consulted in advance and in good time by the employer with regard to:

(a) any measure which may substantially affect safety and health;

(b) the designation of workers referred to in Articles 7(1) and 8(2) and the activities referred to in Article 7(1);

(c) the information referred to in Articles 9(1) and 10;

(d) the enlistment, where appropriate, of the competent services or persons outside the undertaking and/or establishment, as referred to in Article 7(3);

(e) the planning and organisation of the training referred to in Article 12.

3 Workers' representatives with specific responsibility for the safety and health of workers shall have the right to ask the employer to take appropriate measures and to submit proposals to him to that end to mitigate hazards for workers and/or to remove sources of danger.

4 The workers referred to in paragraph 2 and the workers' representatives referred to in paragraphs 2 and 3 may not be placed at a disadvantage because of their respective activities referred to in paragraphs 2 and 3.

5 Employers must allow workers' representatives with specific responsibility for the safety and health of workers adequate time off work, without loss of pay, and provide them with the necessary means to enable such representatives to exercise their rights and functions deriving from this Directive.

6 Workers and/or their representatives are entitled to appeal, in accordance with national law and/or practice, to the authority responsible for safety and health protection at work if they consider that the measures taken and the means employed by the employer are inadequate for the purposes of ensuring safety and health at work.

Workers' representatives must be given the opportunity to submit their observations during inspection visits by the competent authority.

Article 12
Training of workers

1 The employer shall ensure that each worker receives adequate safety and health training, in particular in the form of information and instructions specific to his workstation or job:

- on recruitment;
- in the event of a transfer or a change of job;
- in the event of the introduction of new work equipment or a change in equipment;
- in the event of the introduction of any new technology.

The training shall be:

- adapted to take account of new or changed risks; and
- repeated periodically if necessary.

2 The employer shall ensure that workers from outside undertakings and/or establishments engaged in work in his undertaking and/or establishment have in fact received appropriate instructions regarding health and safety risks during their activities in his undertaking and/or establishment.

3 Workers' representatives with a specific role in protecting the safety and health of workers shall be entitled to appropriate training.

4   The training referred to in paragraphs 1 and 3 may not be at the workers' expense or at that of the workers' representative.

The training referred to in paragraph 1 must take place during working hours.

The training referred to in paragraph 3 must take place during working hours or in accordance with national practice either within or outside the undertaking and/or the establishment.

SECTION III: WORKERS' OBLIGATIONS

Article 13

1   It shall be the responsibility of each worker to take care as far as possible of his own safety and health and that of other persons affected by his acts or omissions at work in accordance with his training and the instructions given by his employer.

2   To this end, workers must in particular, in accordance with their training and the instructions given by their employer:

(a) make correct use of machinery, apparatus, tools, dangerous substances, transport equipment and other means of production;

(b) make correct use of the personal protective equipment supplied to them and, after use, return it to its proper place;

(c) refrain from disconnecting changing or removing arbitrarily safety devices fitted, eg to machinery, apparatus, tools, plant and buildings, and use such safety devices correctly;

(d) immediately inform the employer and/or the workers with specific responsibility for the safety and health of workers of any work situation they have reasonable grounds for considering represents a serious and immediate danger to safety and health and of any shortcomings in the protection arrangements;

(e) co-operate, in accordance with national practice, with the employer and/or workers with specific responsibility for the safety and health of workers, for as long as may be necessary to enable any tasks or requirements imposed by the competent authority to protect the safety and health of workers at work to be carried out;

(f) co-operate, in accordance with national practice, with the employer and/or workers with specific responsibility for the safety and health of workers, for as long as may be necessary to enable the employer to ensure that the working environment and working conditions are safe and pose no risk to safety and health within their field of activity.

SECTION IV: MISCELLANEOUS PROVISIONS

Article 14

Health surveillance

1   To ensure that workers receive health surveillance appropriate to the health and safety risks they incur at work, measures shall be introduced in accordance with national law and/or practices.

2   The measures referred to in paragraph 1 shall be such that each worker, if he so wishes, may receive health surveillance at regular intervals.

3   Health surveillance may be provided as part of a national health system.

Article 15

Risk groups

Particularly sensitive risk groups must be protected against the dangers which specifically affect them.

– – –

Failure to implement directives

Member States do not always implement directives by the deadline set by the EU. The UK record for implementation is good compared with other Member States. The failure of the Member State may be complete or partial. For example, the UK, in common with other Member States, was late to implement the Construction Sites Directive:[1] this should have been implemented by 1 January 1994. Implementation in the UK took place at the end of March 1995 through the Construction (Design and Management) Regulations 1994 (SI 1994/3140).

Where European legislation is not implemented, enforcement proceedings may be brought to the European Court of Justice. Such proceedings may be brought by the Commission, or through the courts by an individual who is being disadvantaged by the failure to implement the law. In *Commission v United Kingdom (Safeguarding of Employees' Rights in the Event of Transfers of Undertakings); Commission v United Kingdom (Collective Redundancies)*,[2] the UK Government was subject to infraction proceedings for failure to implement key aspects (concerning consultation with workers) of the Acquired Rights Directive[3] and the Collective Redundancies Directive,[4] as implemented in the Transfer of Undertaking (Protection of Employment) Regulations 1981 (SI

---

1   92/57/EEC.
2   [1994] IRLR 412.
3   77/187/EEC.
4   75/129/EEC.

1981/1794) and ss 99–107 of the Employment Protection Act 1975 (subsequently ss 188–98 of the Trade Union and Labour Relations (Consolidation) Act 1992).

State employees may seek to enforce EU law directly against their employers should the UK have failed to implement a directive; the courts have interpreted 'State' broadly to include the now privatised public utilities (see *Foster v British Gas* (1991)[5] and *Griffen and Others v South West Water Services Ltd* (1995).[6] However, the requirement of the directive must be very precise and unconditional for direct enforcement: in *Griffen* it was held that the Collective Redundancy Directive could not be so enforced because Article 2 of it did not sufficiently indicate how a worker representative should be identified for consultation for the purposes of that directive.

Aligning national law and EU laws

Under the European Communities Act 1972, enacted by the UK Parliament at the time of the UK's accession to the EC, provision is made for EU laws to be incorporated into UK law and for reference to be made from a UK court to the European Court of Justice in the event of it being necessary to clarify the meaning of EC legislation.

The relevant provisions of the Act are set out below as amended by the European Communities (Amendment) Act 1986.

EUROPEAN COMMUNITIES ACT 1972

Section 2

General implementation of Treaties

(1) All such rights, powers, liabilities, obligations and restrictions from time to time created or arising by or under the Treaties, and all such remedies and procedures from time to time provided for by or under the Treaties, as in accordance with the Treaties, are without further enactment to be given legal effect or used in the United Kingdom shall be recognised and available in law, and be enforced, allowed and followed accordingly; and the expression 'enforceable Community right' and similar expressions shall be read as referring to one to which this subsection applies.

(2) Subject to Schedule 2 to this Act, at any time after its passing Her Majesty may by Order in Council, and any designated Minister or department may by regulations, make provision–

    (a) for the purpose of implementing any Community obligation of the United Kingdom, or enabling any such obligation to be implemented, or of enabling any rights enjoyed or to be enjoyed by the United Kingdom under or by virtue of the Treaties to be exercised;

---

5 [1991] IRLR 268.
6 [1995] IRLR 15.

(b) for the purpose of dealing with matters arising out of or related to any such obligation or rights or the coming into force, or the operation from time to time, of subsection (1) above;

and in the exercise of any statutory power or duty, including any power to give directions or to legislate by means or orders, rules, regulations or other subordinate instrument, the person entrusted with the power or duty may have regard to the objects of the Communities and to any such obligation or rights as aforesaid.

In this subsection 'designated Minister or department' means such Minister of the Crown or Government department as may from time to time be designated by Order in Council in relation to any matter or for any purpose, but subject to such restrictions or conditions (if any) as may be specified by the Order in Council.

Section 3

Decisions on, and proof of, Treaties and Community instruments etc

(1) For the purposes of all legal proceedings any questions as to the meaning or effect or any of the Treaties, or as to the validity, meaning or effect of any Community Instrument, shall be treated as a question of law (and, if not referred to the European Court, be for determination as such in accordance with the principles laid down by and any relevant decision of the European Court or any court attached thereto).

(2) Judicial notice shall be taken of the Treaties, of the Official Journal of the Communities and of any decision of, or expression of opinion by, the European Court or any court attached thereto on any such question as aforesaid; and the Official Journal shall be admissible as evidence of any instrument or other act thereby communicated of any of the Communities or of any Community institution.

– – –

Challenging British safety laws

There has, as yet, been no occasion on which the Health and Safety at Work Act 1974 and Regulations made under it have been measured against European legislation in either the British courts or the European Court of Justice. This is in contrast to the Product Liability Directive 85/373/EEC. The Consumer Protection Act 1987 expressly states that it is intended to implement the EC Directive. Nevertheless the Commission, in the event unsuccessfully, challenged the UK, alleging it had failed properly to implement the Directive (see *European Commission v UK*).[7]

---

7   [1997] All ER (EC) 481.

Record of implementation

The Government has, in the main, been sympathetic to EC safety directives and has attempted to bring them into British law.

Possible weaknesses

The following comments can be made in respect of British occupational health and safety legislation:

(a) consultation with workers: this area is the one in which there has been the biggest question about UK compliance. As a result of the Health and Safety (Consultation with Employees) Regulations 1996, it is no longer the position that only unionised workplaces have the opportunity to legal right to safety representatives. However, the culture of employment in the UK, now that the power of the trade unions is so much reduced, does not encourage the appointment of safety representatives. In the alternative, the supposed commitment of British management to personal rather than collective relationships between employer and the workforce does not easily accommodate meaningful consultation on intended changes in the workplace safety arrangements. It therefore remains doubtful whether, in practice, there is compliance with Article 11 of the Framework Directive's requirement for consultation and participation of workers. National practice may well fall short of the 'balanced participation' referred to in that Article. The British regulatory system appears to make adequate provision for the provision of information and training to individual workers. The British system of commitment to personal rather than collective relationships between employer and the workforce does not easily accommodate meaningful consultation on intended changes in the workplace safety arrangements;

(b) reasonable practicability: the particular nature of the British regulatory tradition with its emphasis on tightly drawn duties, does not entirely fit happily with the broader European approach. The official UK position is that in practice is it not possible to 'ensure' safety at the workplace and therefore the British statutory formula is a sensible pragmatic response to the wording of the Directives which place an apparently stricter duty.

Directives impose minimum standards

The European directives are enforced through the criminal courts in Britain. It is not obvious that aggrieved individuals would challenge standards which imposed a lower standard than directives required: should British standards in fact be higher, there would be no right to challenge them because the directives purport only to stipulate minimum standards. It is, however, just possible, but rather unlikely, that the Commission might challenge the concept of 'reasonable practicability'.

European laws invalidate earlier national laws

In *R v Secretary of State ex p Factortame*,[8] the House of Lords referred to the European Court the question of whether or not Community law provides interim protection of rights under Community law in the event of the existence of inconsistent national legislation. The European Court held that Community law required a national court to set aside a rule of national law when that court, considering a question of Community law, believed that the sole obstacle precluding it from granting interim relief was the rule of national law.

In the light of this, it might possibly occur that the 1974 Act or regulations made under it or earlier British legislation might have to concede to later European law. However, the 1974 Act is so broad that it seems unlikely that it would conflict with European laws.

Damages against the State

The European Court of Justice held in *Francovich v Italian Republic* (1992)[9] that an individual who has suffered loss as a result of the failure of a Member State to take all the necessary steps to achieve the result required by a directive may sue the state for damages under Community law, It can only be a matter of speculation whether persons might invoke this decision if they suffered injury at the workplace as a result of a failure of British regulations to impose the standards required under European directives. It seems highly improbable that, given the generality of the 1974 Act, such a situation could be claimed to have occurred. Even if that matter could be established, it is even more unlikely that the rule in *Francovich* would be applied in such circumstances, given the difficulty of establishing causation of personal injuries and of quantifying the damages.

In any case, UK personal injury compensation law is now so firmly based on the tort of negligence that it is hard to envisage circumstances in which a claimant would ignore that and prefer to sue the State. The only situation in which this would be at all likely to occur would be if the claimant saw no prospect of obtaining compensation in the normal way because the defendant organisation was uninsured and without funds.

---

8   [1990] 3 CMLR 867.
9   [1992] IRLR 84.

INDEX